CONTENTS

Fifth Edition

TERRORISM TODAY

THE PAST, THE PLAYERS, THE FUTURE

Jeremy R. Spindlove

Clifford E. Simonsen

Boston Columbus Indianapolis New York San Francisco Upper Saddle River Amsterdam
Cape Town Dubai London Madrid Milan Munich Paris Montreal Toronto Delhi
Mexico City São Paulo Sydney Hong Kong Seoul Singapore Taipei Tokyo

—This edition is dedicated to Esther, Tim, Peter, Laura, and Ashley

Editorial Director: Vernon R. Anthony
Executive Editor: Gary Bauer
Assistant Editor: Tiffany Bitzel
Editorial Assistant: Lynda Cramer
Director of Marketing: David Gesell
Senior Marketing Manager: Mary Salzman
Senior Marketing Coordinator: Alicia Wozniak
Senior Marketing Assistant: Les Roberts
Production Manager: Holly Shufeldt
Art Director: Jayne Conte
Cover Designer: Karen Noferi
Cover Image: Shutterstock
Full-Service Project Management and Composition: Integra Software Services, Ltd.
Text Printer/Binder and Cover Printer: Courier

Credits and acknowledgments borrowed from other sources and reproduced, with permission, in this textbook appear on the appropriate page within text.

Library of Congress Cataloging-in-Publication Data
Spindlove, Jeremy R.
  Terrorism today : the past, the players, the future / Jeremy R. Spindlove, Clifford E. Simonsen.—5th ed.
    p. cm.
  ISBN-13: 978-0-13-268311-1 (alk. paper)
  ISBN-10: 0-13-268311-3 (alk. paper)
  1. Terrorism. 2. Terrorism—History. 3. Terrorism—Prevention. I. Simonsen, Clifford E. II. Title.
  HV6431.S53 2013
  363.325—dc23

                                                                    2012012509

4 5 6 7 8 9 10 V092 16 15 14

ISBN 10:   0-13-268311-3
ISBN 13: 978-0-13-268311-1

LIST OF MAPS

FIGURES

PREFACE

When we first contemplated a text that discusses terrorism in its very broad scope, very little of that focus was on the United States. Texts on terrorism are not new, and prior to 9-11 they focused quite naturally on left- and right-wing groups and paramilitaries in Europe, Asia, and South America. The concept of terrorism includes such a wide range of activities that the most difficult task was how to make a text short enough to be effective for instructors, casual readers, and students, but long enough that it adequately covers an acceptable depth into this discipline. The rapidly changing world we now inhabit has become preoccupied with terrorism and the threats posed to our daily lives, and we admit that, at times, it seemed like we were trying to paint a moving bus—the players, organizations, and operations often changed faster than the speed at which we could write the words, and this continues to be the case!

This edition picks up where the fourth left off and is also written in an admittedly broad-brush manner. We reexamine where terrorism came from, where it is today, and where it seems to be going as we reel from the effects of global terrorism, the War on Terror, and the arrangement of new pieces on the world chessboard of terror.

"What is terrorism?" As you read this book, it will become apparent that most terrorism actions are committed by groups of fanatics or dissidents, often with conflicting goals and little interface; but that has changed with the use of the Internet to spread global jihad. Many of these groups are continuing their plans to upset security and safety in Western democracies primarily. We hope that the knowledge we have assembled in this book will stimulate students and others to seek out ways to offer better safety and security to all persons worldwide.

Your authors have attempted to provide a clear overview of many of the sectors and operations that comprise the broad terms *terrorism* and *counterterrorism*. We explore some specific subjects and locations in greater depth than others, reduce redundancy, and cover as many differences and similarities as possible. We present this edition with the belief that any learning experience should be enjoyable as well as educational. We offer instructors a text that we have organized and written with the goal of making teaching and the learning experience as interesting and effective as possible. We cover the essentials of the subject and include a large array of pedagogical tools in each chapter.

Security is an ancient need for humans—a basic rung on the ladder of Maslow's hierarchy of needs. The twenty-first century dawned and we awoke to a decade of unspeakable terrorist atrocities—attacks in New York, London, Washington, Madrid, Stockholm, and Bali, to name but a few. How our world will unfold in the next decade and what atrocities will be meted out and what successes our counterterror operations will have is anyone's guess!

THE TRADITION CONTINUES

The methodology for textbook development, which we have used successfully in the past, continues to be the foundation and cornerstone for this edition of *Terrorism Today*. We have built on the comments of readers, instructors, and students to the book's previous editions:

- An engaging writing style, resulting in a book that is highly readable and effective as an informational, teaching, and learning tool.

- A balanced treatment of practical examples, technology, history, and data from available documents and academic research.
- A systems approach to exploring the varied elements of terrorism, terrorists, and the various motives for terrorist groups as a potentially integrated and interrelated series of subsystems.
- An unbiased presentation of a wide range of topics, making for a text suitable for instructors and students from many disciplines and points of view.
- In-chapter and end-of-chapter materials that augment the textual materials with examples of events, persons, stories, terms to remember, maps, and websites for further research.

ORGANIZATION OF THE TEXT

This edition has again been divided into three major parts and fifteen chapters that build from historical backgrounds to predictions about terrorism in the twenty-first century. Each chapter begins with a set of Learning Objectives, which should be accomplished after completion of the text. Information on specific terror events of note is included in the body of the text to illustrate and frame each chapter. Extensive endnotes, placed at the end of each chapter, provide helpful content and applicability to the subject matter. These should be considered as important as the textual materials themselves for presentation and study. The materials we have selected come from the best and most currently available sources in the field. We presented them in their original form, or blended them into our own writing to minimize confusion.

Part One: The Definitions and History of Terrorism

Part One offers a historical look at terrorism's origins. Learning about the types of terror and their history will provide the student/reader with the background necessary to understand the evolution of terrorism in the present and into the future.

CHAPTER 1: IN SEARCH OF A DEFINITION FOR TERRORISM   Chapter 1 presents some basic definitions for terminology used throughout the following chapters. The information will allow the student to understand and differentiate between terrorist acts and ordinary criminal acts. The chapter presents defining issues, operational terms, useful typologies, as well as forms and tactics of terrorism in today's troubled world. Terrorism as criminal behavior and its use as a method for change are detailed. Such acts as ambush, assassination, arson, bombing, hijacking, hostage taking, kidnapping, blackmail, and protection are included. The initiation and development of the Department of Homeland Security are covered in detail.

CHAPTER 2: A BRIEF HISTORY OF TERRORISM   Chapter 2 describes an act of violence as a logical progression, but one that can take place in microseconds within a single individual. Violence perpetrated for ideological reasons and for a systematically organized cause or complaint is shown to be much different. Chapter 2 also explores the motives and methods employed by individual terrorists or groups and state sponsors with some perceived agenda as compared to the motives of a state for suppressing dissent and revolution. The student/reader is introduced to the concept of state-sponsored terrorism, a concept that supports terrorist groups and individual terrorists with weapons, money, and supplies to achieve a government's goals. Discussions range from the Crusades to the continuing frictions between major religions around the world today. Islam, jihad, and a media involvement in terrorism are broadly reviewed.

Part Two: Terrorism Around the World

Part Two brings the reader to terrorist events—both left and right wing—of the twentieth and early twenty-first centuries. We examine the right-wing factions in various countries and regions, their similarities and differences, and their goals and objectives. We also look at the left-wing factions in various countries and regions, using a similar methodology, and we contrast the two. Part Two covers regions and nations in the investigation of terrorism, its many different forms and factions, and their interrelationships.

CHAPTER 3: THE UNITED STATES OF AMERICA   We examine the events leading up to 9-11 and the so-called intelligence "dots" that were never connected to prevent that cataclysmic event. We examine what has happened since 9-11 in the U.S. War on Terror. We examine and analyze "homegrown" terrorism in the United States to see how it compares with terrorism in other parts of the world. The United States is no longer free from the violent terrorist actions that have been plaguing the rest of the world. Defending the Homeland, the Patriot Act coupled with rendition tactics and how Americans are being radicalized will also be discussed.

CHAPTER 4: CANADA AND THE CARIBBEAN   We now examine the problems of immigration, illegal aliens and refugees, and the threat posed not just to Canada but also to the United States. Canada has for several decades expounded on its program of "multiculturalism," and this chapter reviews how Canada has become a haven for fund-raising activities for terror groups including the Tamil Tigers and Sikh extremists. Canada suffered one of the worst terrorist attacks prior to 9-11, namely the downing of Air India Flight 182 in the Irish Sea, and this chapter examines that case in detail.

CHAPTER 5: GREAT BRITAIN AND NORTHERN IRELAND   Sectarian violence and terrorism associated with a long-enduring fight typifies Northern Ireland for much of the last century, and we examine the background to the "Irish Problem" and bring the reader up to date with examples of friction and terrorism on both sides of the issues; "the Troubles," as they have been termed, lasted for more than forty years and have only now reached the final, almost peaceful chapter. This chapter provides a model for examining other terror spots of the world. It shows similarities and differences in the use of terrorism in meeting political or religious goals. Ireland and mainland Britain have been embroiled in terrorism for more than four decades. Here, we examine the current political processes and the methods employed to reach a solution to the violence. We discuss the concerns of security forces and the export of terror knowledge to other international terror groups. The rise of Islamic extremism and suicide attacks by young British-born men on the London transport system are also discussed.

CHAPTER 6: WESTERN EUROPE   Chapter 6 examines terrorism, past and present, in Western Europe. The rise and fall of the ETA movement is tracked and draws comparisons with Ireland's Republican terrorist movement. We look at the turbulent history of Spain—from the inquisition to the fascist reign of terror under Franco, to the many terrorist activities in Spain, especially those involving the Basque separatists and Islamic extremists. In the twenty-first century, Europe is the target for international terror cells plotting and planning mayhem in other regions as well as their adopted homelands.

CHAPTER 7: EASTERN EUROPE AND THE BALKANS   Chapter 7 recounts the sad history of the multiracial, multireligious region formerly known as Yugoslavia, from the partisan terrorism and German terrorism in World War II to the divided state that has seen constant interracial and interreligious fighting since its breakup. Terrorism and even genocide will be the main weapons in these battles for ethnic purity. We discuss the tensions between Uzbeks and Kyrgyz and the presence of Islamic radicals that will try and dictate outcome following decades of cultural repression under the Soviet boot. We examine the Russians and their long history of national terrorism to keep the populace under control, from the Czars, to the Soviet Union, and Stalin's murder of 50 million of his countrymen. The role of the ICTY in bringing war criminals who have committed crimes against humanity to justice is also reviewed.

CHAPTER 8: NORTH AFRICA AND THE MIDDLE EAST   Chapter 8 examines this most complex region of the world, where terrorism is a way of life in both local and international conflicts. We realize that all of the conflicts are similar in this region and terror is the primary weapon used by all sides. From the Ottoman Empire to the creation of the State of Israel, the region has been subjected to wars, internal battles involving nationhood, religion and ethnic divides that have seen methods of terrorism, and the creation of terror groups that have spread throughout the world.

CHAPTER 9: THE PERSIAN GULF   Chapter 9 explores the Persian Gulf states, an area rich with oil and gas deposits and also the presence of diverging religious beliefs of Islam. We discuss the persecution of the Kurds in Iraq, the use of oil revenue to sponsor worldwide terrorism, and the threat of the use of nuclear, biological, and chemical weapons stirring the pot of terrorism in this area. The second Gulf War, the fall of Saddam Hussein, the U.S. military presence, and the rise of Islamic fighter groups have had a destabilizing effect on the entire region. The rise and presence of al Qaeda in Yemen and its effects on the region are also reviewed.

CHAPTER 10: NORTHEAST, CENTRAL, AND SOUTHERN AFRICA   Chapter 10 examines the Dark Continent, from the long struggle for freedom from apartheid in South Africa to a quite different struggle in Robert Mugabe's dictatorship in Zimbabwe. We explore the genocide in the Congo, Uganda, and Rwanda and tribalism that divides most of these regions. We examine the presence of al Qaeda and its affiliates and Islamic groups in Nigeria and the threats from piracy along the Horn of Africa.

CHAPTER 11: SOUTHERN AND SOUTHEAST ASIA   Chapter 11 looks at past and present terrorism in southern and southeast Asia. India has a long history of terrorism; also, it possesses nuclear weapons. Following independence, India has had to combat attacks from religious factions and rebel causes. Pakistan and India maintain a tense relationship, with sporadic border violence bringing both countries to the brink of all-out war. The 2008 attacks by extremists in Mumbai is also reviewed as having relevance for destabilizing the region. We re-examine Afghanistan, the first battlefield of the post-9-11 War on Terror. This chapter covers a long, ongoing war suffered by Sri Lanka (formerly Ceylon) with the Tamil Tigers and their eventual surrender. From the Khmer Rouge in Cambodia to the guerrilla fighters in the jungles of Malaysia and Indonesia, terrorism has seemed to find a long-term home in Southeast Asia.

CHAPTER 12: THE PACIFIC RIM   Chapter 12 explores the countries of the Pacific Rim. We examine China, which has moved past its terror-filled period following the ascension of Communism. Terror as a philosophy can be traced back through Chinese history as a viable means to control that vast nation. From the fighters against the government at the turn of the twentieth century to World War II and the Japanese occupation and to the terrorist tactics of the Marcos regime, the history of the Philippines has also shown that terror can be a useful tool in controlling a large, scattered, and very poor country. We explore the "successful" deployment of a WMD by a Japanese cult/terror group, which stands as an example of the threat such weapons pose to the West in the twenty-first century. Indonesia with its vast Muslim population has encountered Islamic extremism with links to al Qaeda.

CHAPTER 13: LATIN AMERICA AND SOUTH AMERICA   Chapter 13 discusses Latin America's struggles with terrorism. The so-called banana republics have long suffered from dictators who used terrorism against their people as well as rebels who used terrorism against governments. We examine major conflicts in terms of past history and present status and the roles of Mexico and Cuba in these struggles. Mexico has a long history of terrorism and revolution. The "other America" has been rife with terrorist activities for a long time, from The Shining Path of Peru to the "disappeared" in Brazil and Argentina. We discuss the drug cartels in Colombia that have led to political upheavals. The violence and danger of this region, as well as suppressive Latin American governments, invite terrorist organizations to emerge.

Part Three: The War on Terror

Part Three discusses the varying efforts of nations around the world to detect or defeat terrorism, to find other ways to deal with it, and to manage the threats of terrorism in the post 9-11 era. We will examine what the future of terrorism might be.

CHAPTER 14: COUNTERING TERRORISM   Chapter 14 examines the world of counterterrorism—both politically and operationally. We determine which methods are effective and which have failed. These range from national paramilitary groups to local activities by regular citizens. We study in detail the importance of intelligence gathering, the cycle of intelligence, and the proper uses of intelligence against terrorism. The threats to aviation from acts of terror, along with maritime piracy, are discussed. The chapter examines worldwide counterterrorist groups and strategies, from the Delta Force in the United States, Delta 88 in Indonesia and to the Mossad in Israel, to the Special Air Service in the United Kingdom, and many other highly organized and effective groups both police and military. We discuss the strategies of the United Nations and regional governments and their successes and failures. The threats posed by chemical and biological agents have to be considered as the world prepares for the unexpected and the possibility of attack with weapons of mass destruction (WMD).

CHAPTER 15: THE FUTURE—WHAT NEXT FOR TERRORISM?   Chapter 15, as in the words of Pogo Possum, *"predicting stuff is difficult, especially if it's in the future"*. In looking forward we have to look back, and looking back at the last twenty-plus years we can possibly get a better understanding of terrorism and the future trends in terrorist activity. We will also look at the methods that we will need to employ to deter future terror actions wherever they might spring from.

SUPPLEMENTS

The following supplements accompany this textbook:

- Instructor's Manual and Test Bank
- PowerPoint Presentations
- MyTest

To access supplementary materials online, instructors need to request an instructor access code. Go to www.pearsonhighered.com/irc to register for an instructor access code. Within 48 hours of registering, you will receive a confirming e-mail including an instructor access code. Once you have received your code, go to the site and log on for full instructions on downloading the materials you wish to use.

ACKNOWLEDGMENTS

Trying to acknowledge all those who have provided help and advice will make a long list, and here I must start with our families who have provided endless support together with our close personal friends, then our colleagues and international friends in academia, as well as professionals and practitioners in terrorism at the international, federal, state, and local levels. To each of them we extend our deepest appreciation and gratitude for encouraging and assisting us in putting together a text about this important topic that seems to work. We would, however, like to thank the special people at Pearson Education in particular Lynda Cramer and Holly Shufeldt who helped the authors turn their prose, ideas, and concepts for a book about terrorism into a textbook that will greatly assist students, readers, and instructors alike.

Special thanks to Mike Mcguire and Dave Roberts in Edmonton and to Gary Wilson, a good friend and colleague and former Royal Ulster Constabulary Police officer; to Tony Forward, former chief superintendent, Surrey Constabulary, and Sian Evans of London UK Sian Evans for their photography skills; and to Arik Garber, who arrived in Lebanon with the IDF as Jeremy evacuated to Syria! Last, but by no means least, thanks to our wonderful families, especially Fran and Esther, Tim and Laura, and Peter and Ashley. We have found that writing can be a lonely task, especially when it involves such a specific and rapidly changing field. It is not easy to discuss the book with anyone else, while we are in the frantic throes of creation and revision. We deeply appreciate the understanding and support we have received over the past periods of hard work, and love you all for understanding and caring.

ABOUT THE AUTHORS

Jeremy R. Spindlove Presently, Jeremy R. Spindlove holds the position of Director of Safety and Risk Management for DHL/EXEL Supply Chain., a global leader in supply chain management. Based in Vancouver, Canada, his responsibilities extend throughout Canada and the United States. He is also a principal in LLA Technologies Inc a company developing state of the art mesh networked security and life safety systems deployable in almost any environment. He has had firsthand experience in terrorism—first, through his service in the Surrey Constabulary (the United Kingdom) as a first responder on the scene in 1974 when a Provisional Irish Republican Army cell detonated two bombs, one in the Horse and Groom and the second in the 7 Stars pub in Guildford, which killed six and wounded more than sixty. Jeremy went on to be recruited by British Airways as an overseas security officer to supervise air terminal security operations for the airline in Baghdad, Iraq, for two years; in Amman, Jordan, for three months; and in Beirut, Lebanon, for six months. He traveled globally throughout the network conducting airport risk assessments for BA. On his return to the UK, Jeremy set up a fraud investigation unit, tracking and intercepting illegal immigrants transiting the UK en route to North America on forged passports and travel documents. He has been assigned to security duties escorting H.M. Queen Elizabeth to the Far East in 1987 and to Rome in 1988. Jeremy immigrated to Canada in 1988 and holds dual Canadian/British citizenship. He has held critical security leadership positions as Manager of Security and then Director of Airport Security at Vancouver International Airport. He is a qualified Passenger Screening Instructor and, during his airport tenure in 1994, served on a Canadian Advisory Board reviewing airport and aviation security regulations. In 1996, he moved to the Tibbett and Britten Group North America as Manager and, later, Director of Loss Prevention, Health and Safety for Western Canada and the United States, advancing to his present position with broader responsibilities. Jeremy Spindlove was presented the Royal Humane Society Award by Britain's Queen Elizabeth in 1976 for his courage in saving a woman's life. He is a longtime member of the International Society for Industrial Security and the Academy of Criminal Justice Sciences and the coauthor of the four successful previous editions of *Terrorism Today: The Past, the Players, The Future*. He is a frequent guest commentator on airport security and terrorism for Canada's Global News Network. He has also authored a contributory text on victims of terrorism entitled *Victimology—A Study of Crime Victims and Their Roles*, edited by Judith M. Scarzi and Jack McDevitt.

Clifford E. Simonsen, Ph.D. Formerly President of Criminology Consultants Inc., Clifford E. Simonsen has an extensive background and education related to the topics of terrorism, crime, and criminal behavior. His extensive education includes B.S., University of Nebraska at Omaha, Law Enforcement and Corrections; M.S., Florida State University, Criminology and Corrections; MPA, the Ohio State University, Correctional

Administration; and Ph.D., the Ohio State University, Administration of Criminal Justice and Deviant Behavior. Cliff retired after 32½ years as a Military Police Colonel. His extensive education in the military includes the Military Police Officer Basic Course; the Military Police Officer Advanced Course; the Advanced Police Administration Course; the U.S. Army Command and General Staff College; the OR/SA Executive Course; the Industrial College of the Armed Forces; and the U.S. Army War College.

Cliff has been an active member and supporter of many prestigious professional associations, including American Correctional Association (ACA) International Committee, Washington State Correctional Association (WCA), American Society for Industrial Security (ASIS) (lifetime award), Certified Protection Professional CPP (lifetime award), The International Association of Professional Security Consultants (IAPSC), International Academy of Criminology (IAC), Academy of Criminal Justice Sciences (ACJS), and The Retired Officers Association (TROA).

His honors and awards include two Meritorious Service Awards, U.S. Army; Legion of Merit, U.S. Army; Korean National Police Medal of Merit, Korean government; Outstanding Service International Association of Halfway Houses; Outstanding Achievement as a Scholar, Washington State Council on Crime and Delinquency; Fellow of the International Institute for Security and Safety Management, IISSM, New Delhi, India.

He has authored *Corrections in America: An Introduction*, 11th ed., Prentice Hall Publishing Co., NJ (2006); *Juvenile Justice Today*, 4th ed., Prentice Hall Publishing Co., NJ (2003); *Terrorism Today: The Past, the Players, the Future*, 4th ed., Prentice Hall Publishing Co., NJ (2006).

The Definitions and History of Terrorism

In Search of a Definition for Terrorism

Terror is nothing other than justice, prompt, severe, inflexible.

—Maximilien Robespierre

LEARNING OBJECTIVES

After studying this chapter, the student should be able to:

1. Understand and appreciate the difficulties in designing a globally accepted definition for terrorism.
2. Identify how and why the changes in definition over the past thirty years have taken place to accommodate varying trends in terrorist behavior.
3. State the necessity for arriving at a common definition for terrorism.
4. Differentiate an international definition of terrorism as opposed to a definition of international terrorism.
5. Describe the rationale for the creation of the U.S. Department of Homeland Security.

KEY WORDS TO NOTE

Assassination—The targeted killing of an important person for political or ideological reasons

Hague Conventions—International treaties first negotiated at The Hague in the Netherlands pronouncing formal statements on the laws of war

Islamic Sharia—Islamic law that influences legal process and codes in most Muslim countries

Jihad—Islamic term used to describe a holy war against religious or political oppression

Prescribed—To establish rules, laws, and direction

Proscribed—To outlaw and ban terror organizations

Reign of Terror—In France, Robespierre masterminded a Reign of Terror after the death of King Louis XVI in 1763

OVERVIEW

Terrorism constitutes one of the most serious threats to global security. Universal acceptance of a definition that fits every terrorist event and meets every country's political need, as well as that of the United Nations, has not been achieved. Terrorism has been around for centuries. Since 2001, when hijackers flew commercial airliners into New York's World Trade Center Towers and the Pentagon in Washington, DC, and the subsequent attacks in London, Madrid, and Mumbai, the fear of terrorism has spawned a global response led primarily by the United States and strongly supported by Great Britain. This became the now-familiar "War on Terror," a phrase coined by then U.S. president George W. Bush in the aftermath of 9-11. With the prospect of the next attack taking place in Chicago, Delhi, Singapore, or Melbourne, the specter of a feared but unknown doom has required the expenditure of huge sums of money to protect us from the threat of dangerous, threatening fanatics we call, for lack of a better title, "terrorists." The prospect of more attacks has become an everyday reality to Western nations. This threat has forced airlines and the aviation industry to make drastic changes in their methods for securing thousands of flights each day as well as the hardening of terminal facilities and operations. The Internet and other media streams respond and immediately inform and frighten the public about terrorist acts from around the globe. We also need to realize that there is no globally accepted definition of terrorism.

This chapter examines and asks several key questions: Just who is this larger-than-life monster that we call a "terrorist?" What are terrorist acts? Can we protect ourselves against them? How do we define "terrorism"? Combs, discussing this problem, says, "Terrorism is a political as well as a legal and military issue; its precise definition in modern terms has been slow to evolve. Not that there are not numerous definitions available—there are hundreds! But few of them are of sufficient legal scholarship to be useful in international law, and most of those which are legally useful lack the necessary ambiguity for any political acceptance."[1] The 9-11 attacks provided a wake-up call for the U.S. government, which quickly passed the USA Patriot Act of 2001. This legislation provides funding and oversight on a massive scale.

We now begin the exercise of trying to define "terrorism" and/or "terrorist behavior." The terms must be carefully constructed so that they project the precise meanings intended. A terrorist incident is any violent act that can become a broader threat as the purpose and intention for such action becomes clearly known, and the act is clearly of a criminal nature. What it is (and is not) called hinges on finding a commonly understood meaning for the term "terrorism." This chapter will lay a foundation for the reader/student to use throughout the rest of this text.

To better understand these concepts, we must explore some historical context and the specific rules that society has developed over time to define the use of criminal and antisocial acts to meet political or social goals. Behavior in social groups, whether they are for primitive tribes or complex modern nation-states, can be regarded as points on a simple continuum.

TERRORISM: SEARCHING FOR A DEFINITION

It is perhaps too easy to use terms such as "terror," "terrorism," and "terrorist" for acts and persons that shock the senses of most reasonable people. The **Reign of Terror**, which took place in France from 1792 to 1794, is generally accepted by most as the first event to be commonly called "terrorism." During the French Revolution, those who resisted the dictums of the revolutionaries faced arrest, imprisonment, and death by the guillotine. Most convictions were made without the benefit of trials or legal due process. The revolutionary groups went to extreme lengths to eliminate every possible threat, eventually seeking out those with even moderate-to-mild opposition to their cause. Those who considered themselves to be possible targets of the revolutionaries finally decided to adopt countermeasures for their self-preservation. On July 27, 1794, members of the Jacobin dissenters murdered Robespierre and his council of supporters. The Reign of Terror, in which over 400,000 "suspects" (including children and women) had been imprisoned, hanged, or beheaded, finally came to an end. But the seminal concepts of terror tactics as a part of a political strategy grew directly out of this bloody episode. From a devastating beginning, terrorism and terrorist acts became defined as, "the systematic application of violence to establish and maintain a new political or religious system." Such a definition may be difficult to use today, primarily because it fails to separate terrorism from other acts of aggression that use terror as only a small component, not the primary objective, of such behavior. For example, terror in conventional warfare between nation-states is a natural by-product of the violence and confusion of combat. Military objectives and tactics are usually chosen in order to effect the quickest elimination of an enemy's force, its morale, and will to fight through the destruction or disruption of its command, control, communication, and support and supply networks. Victory is decided by force of numbers, skill at arms, weapon superiority, or strategy and tactics, or a combination thereof. Terror is not intended to be a primary factor or function in such military actions.

Trained soldiers or citizens frightened into surrender or compliance but not physically injured are the most logical and realistic targets of terrorism; other casualties are easily classified according to the way they were injured or killed. Rosie offers a tentative definition of terrorism for our consideration: "The use and/or threat of repeated violence in support of, or in opposition to, some authority, where violence is employed to induce the fear of similar attack in as many non-immediate victims as possible so that those so threatened accept and comply with the demands of the terrorists."[2]

Within this awkward definition, we can perhaps work out a methodology for describing the variety of behaviors springing from terrorists acting from a wide range of motives. This definition remains neutral with regard to the great variety of traits that characterize particular groups. It can be applied to political terrorism, revolutionary terrorism, state terrorism, religious terrorism, insurgencies, and all the many other variations. It eliminates the need for suggesting a particular type of motivation as part of the definition of terrorism and creates a temptation to infer that terrorism has to be politically motivated.

Is the twenty-first-century assassin the quintessential suicide bomber? The suicide bomber regardless of gender calculates his or her acts to induce extreme fear in a wider populous, hoping to have a major impact on a far larger population than those likely to be injured by the acts themselves. The perpetrators would most likely believe that these drastic means could and would coerce a wider group into abandoning a political or military agenda that lies at the root of the terrorists' actions. This definition also excludes acts of violence in which the terror component is incidental, or secondary, to a primary objective. The death of the owner operator of a major oil company may be the primary goal of environmental extremists who wish to silence him or his leadership. Or, more likely, the owner could be about to influence legislation that is clearly in opposition to the environmental extremist group's goals. In this situation, the fear generated by the killing is of secondary importance to the actual silencing of that individual. This act should probably be more accurately labeled as "murder" or "assassination," rather than as "terrorism." If the extremist group that killed this leader were also to issue a statement of demands, however, and threaten that more such industrialists and even private citizens would be attacked if the group's demands were not met, then it would be more accurate to refer to the group's actions as "terrorism."

Labeling persons or groups as terrorists does not preclude also categorizing those same persons or groups as "guerrillas," "ideologues," or "revolutionaries." An example could go as follows: "A grocery store owner, who plays baseball on weekends, might be sometimes referred to as a 'baseball player.' But he has not, however, stopped being a grocer." Members of the IRA (Irish Republican Army), PLO (Palestine Liberation Organization), or ETA (Euzkadi Ta Azkatasuna) may be revered as freedom fighters by their subgroups of the local political system. But, to others they clearly continue to be seen as "terrorists." Without some recourse to established definitional parameters, these kinds of labels are just a matter of value judgment. If the person making the judgment does not agree with the objectives of the group using such methods to gain some goal, they will be called (with very few exceptions) terrorists. The group thus categorized immediately denies this, of course, and calls itself a National Liberation Army, or a "Workers Army," or some similar identifying term. The conclusion is that a terrorist group invariably has no legitimacy and therefore its goals have no validity. The label of "terrorist" then becomes a catchall term of derision and, thus, obscures whatever legitimate complaints the group may have had. In order to understand the phenomenon of terrorism, one must always assess the divergent views of what precisely constitutes terrorism and then ask, "What is the current definition in use?" Reaching a general consensus on a universal definition of terrorism has generated many debates in the social sciences. No single definition seems to satisfy every terrorist or act of terrorism, and there is no "one-size-fits-all" for terrorist/terrorism situations.

Terrorism is clearly a very special type of violence. It is a tactic used in many situations—peace, conflict, and even war. The threat of terrorism can be ever-present, and an attack, such as the one on the World Trade Center in 2001, can occur when least expected. The 9-11 attacks were the kind of events that almost always forces a transition from peaceful coexistence to conflict—or war. As an example of a terrorist act, the assassination of Archduke Franz Ferdinand in 1914 led to the outbreak of World War I in Europe.

Combating terrorism is a factor that must be considered in all military plans and operations. Combating terrorism requires a continuous state of intelligence gathering and awareness, and should be a constant practice, rather than a particular type of military operation. Terrorism is also a criminal offense under nearly every national and international legal code. With few exceptions, acts of terrorism are forbidden in war—just as they are in times of peace.[3]

SOME APPROACHES TO DEFINING TERRORISM

The following diverse definitions are also used to describe terrorism:

Simple: Violence or threatened violence intended to produce fear or cause change.

Legal: Criminal violence violating legal codes and punishable by the state.

Analytical: A specific political and/or social factor behind individual violent acts.

State sponsored: National or other groups used to attack Western or other vested interests.

State: Power of the government used to repress its people to the point of submission.[4]

In his book *Political Terrorism* (1983), Alex Schmid surveyed 100 scholars and experts in the field and asked for their definition of terrorism. This analysis found two constant characteristics:

1. An individual being threatened.
2. The terrorist act's meaning is derived from the choice of target and victims. Schmid's analysis concluded that the following elements are common throughout the 100 definitions surveyed:
   - Terrorism is an abstract concept with no real essence.
   - A single definition cannot account for all the possible uses of the term.

- Many different definitions often share common elements.
- The meaning of terrorism derives from the victims or targets.[5]

Schmid also provided the following from his research of those 100 definitions:

Terrorism is an anxiety inspiring method of repeated violent action, employed by (semi-) clandestine individual, group or state actors, for idiosyncratic, criminal or political reason, whereby—in contrast to assassination—the direct targets of violence are not the main target.

The perpetrators of terrorism may truly believe that their cause is altruistic and that it serves for the betterment of society. In Bruce Hoffman's (1998) *Inside Terrorism*, he states that the terrorist is fundamentally a violent intellectual who is prepared to use and, indeed, is committed to using, force in the attainment of perceived goals.

Hoffman also adds that by distinguishing terrorists from other types, such as thugs or common criminals, we come to appreciate that terrorism is

- Primarily political in aims and motives;
- Violent or—equally important—threatens violence;
- Designed to have far-reaching psychological repercussions, beyond the immediate victim or target;
- Conducted by an organization with an identifiable chain of command or conspiratorial cell structures (whose members wear no uniform or identifying insignia); and
- Perpetrated by a subnational group or nonstate entity.[6]

Can we accept that "terrorism" is simply a means to an end—nothing more and nothing less? Can we apply the term to an event without the inclusion of moral beliefs and sociological-political mumbo jumbo? The operatives of the PLO are clearly terrorists. But that fact alone does not mean that their aims and objectives are not without some validity. Provisional IRA members might be described as "freedom fighters"; even if they do not accept the label of terrorist, they would almost always be labeled so by those whom their actions affect, be they the general public, government, or specific individuals. Militant groups, particularly those like the Irish terror groups and Spain's ETA, whose *modus operandi* includes bombings in public places and targeted assassinations, are universally condemned and labeled terrorists.

It is often easier for one to perceive a long-established, freely elected (even dictatorial, religious, or royalist) regime as "legitimate" than it is to accept that a handful of individuals with views significantly different from the majority might deserve the same classification. This holds true if the individuals use methods that provoke moral indignation against a sanctioned, "legitimate" target, such as the government. When an indiscriminate "enemy" label is applied to those not actually supportive of a dissenting aggressor's objective, the situation becomes far more disturbing, even more so because the aggressors frequently use violence as a means to their ends. Wearing no uniforms, they employ weapons that may not need to be personally fired or activated (e.g., letter bombs, improvised explosive devices (IEDs), vehicle-borne explosive devices (VBIEDs), and time bombs). Likewise, unknown aggressors kill unknown victims for reasons that are seldom made clear until after the attack.

There will always be "bottom-line" considerations, of course, even when the targets are considered "acceptable enemies" in the eyes of many. Violence against the former Soviet-backed regimes, for example, finds more favor among Western observers, even when such strikes could be clearly defined as terrorist actions. But if the nature of the assault transgresses certain unwritten, but widely accepted, boundaries of decency or fair play, then condemnation is more likely to be applied. The downing of a Russian helicopter gunship by Chechen rebels is more likely to be interpreted (except by supporters of the Russians) as acceptable, than would be the downing of a civilian airliner by the PLO. The deliberate slaughter of armed soldiers in an ambush is more easily accepted than is the slaughter of small children. In descending order, "fair game" for terrorists or dissenters might be depicted as follows:

- Military personnel
- Government officials
- Civilians unconnected in any way with the continuance of the policy against which the terrorist is fighting

This same attenuated sample list might constitute the basis of a target selection for almost any military offensive. However, a terrorist group would consider the following order to be more appropriate for maximum impact:

- Civilians unconnected in any way with the continuance of the policy against which the group is fighting
- Government officials
- Military personnel

This second, seemingly illogical, order is the one that is very logical for terrorists because maximum fear can be generated by attacks against noncombatants. This prioritizing demonstrates to the populace as a whole that the targeted regime is clearly unable to protect them. Such actions are generally a far safer technique—for the terrorist group—than trying to prove that the regime cannot protect itself. Terror groups will choose to cause outrage and revulsion in their target audience in order to maintain the required level of terror, fear, and anger against government agencies. You should now have a clearer basis for understanding that while strategies incorporating acts of terrorism in the past centuries have changed in delivery and methods, the primary aims of terrorist acts have always remained generally constant:

- To bring attention to perceived grievances or causes by some act or acts;
- To use media coverage of such acts in order to get the widest possible dissemination of their message;
- To contain reaction by the public at large through fear and intimidation; and
- To coerce change and destabilize opponents through the threat of further and continued use of such acts until the grievances or causes are recognized and acted upon.

Over a quarter of a century ago, Jenkins argued that "terrorism is theatre; therefore terrorists do not want a lot of people dead ... they want a lot of people watching and listening."[7] In recent years, that rationale has significantly diminished with the advent of Islamist terror attacks. This watching and listening has been used over the centuries—from a few villagers who stood by while terrorists acted out or gave their speeches, up to today's instant and live worldwide television coverage by all of the major networks of the most vile acts, piped directly into millions of homes. It is seldom that one hears much about the barbarous acts committed in Third World countries, such as Rwanda, Congo, Zimbabwe, Burma, and Sudan, on the evening news in other than a quick sound bite. But let a few armed attackers take over a commercial airliner from a developed country, with 150–300 or so paying passengers, and the media flocks to stand by and listen to the demands of the terrorists and broadcast them around the globe.

Following the London subway suicide attacks, the British government sought to define terrorism as it might apply to the current threat and attack scenarios. At the time, the existing legislation, the Prevention of Terrorism Act of 1989, which had been formulated to deal with Irish nationalist terrorism, defined terrorism as "the use of violence for political ends, and includes any use of violence for the purpose of putting the public or any section of the public in fear." As it is written, this is obviously a very broad definition of terrorism and excludes violence for religious ends or for a nonpolitical ideological end. Subsequently, the Terrorism Act, 2000, was developed to remedy the defects of the 1989 definition. In the United States, the Homeland Security Act of 2002 defines terrorism as "any activity that involves an act that is dangerous to human life or potentially destructive of critical infrastructure or key resources; and is a violation of the criminal laws of the United States or of any State or other subdivision of the United States and appears to be intended to intimidate or coerce a civilian population; to influence the policy of a government by intimidation or coercion or to affect the conduct of a government by mass destruction, assassination, or kidnapping."

Another current U.K. definition for terrorism can be found in The Reinsurance (Acts of Terrorism) Act, 1993, section 2(2), which states: "In this section 'acts of terrorism' means acts of persons acting on behalf of, or in conjunction with any organization which carries out activities directed towards the overthrowing or influencing, by force or violence, of Her Majesty's government in the United Kingdom or any other government de jure or de facto."

This chapter just begins our study of the topic "terrorism" and examines the difficulty in deciding just what that term really means. Author George Rosie further highlights this difficulty as follows:

> Terrorism is a complex, multifaceted, and often baffling subject. The organizations involved have a way of emerging, splintering, disappearing and then reappearing, which makes it very difficult for the average person to follow. Individuals come and go, are jailed, die, go underground, or apparently vanish. Counter terror bureaucracies are formed then reformed, names are changed, and leaders are shuffled around, like deck chairs on the Titanic, as they are promoted, demoted, forced to resign, or put out to pasture. Incidents proliferate across the world, some of which can trigger a chain of events that will destabilize a whole region and bring nations and governments to the edge of ruin. At the same time, major terrorist actions can shock for a short while, and then be quickly forgotten (except by those who were directly affected by the inevitable tragedy). Treaties are written, theories propounded, grievances aired, tactics discussed, occasionally to some effect, but usually not. Causes are picked up by the world's media, examined, probed, and then all too soon often overlooked, until the next explosion occurs, or the next airliner is hijacked.[8]

We now continue our examination of what terrorism is (and what it is not) with a few more commonly used definitions. Acts of terrorism conjure emotional responses in the victims (those hurt by the violence and affected by the fear) as well as in the practitioners. Even the U.S. government cannot agree on one, single definition. Following are a few more common definitions of terrorism:

- Terrorism is the use or threatened use of force designed to bring about political change—Brian Jenkins.
- Terrorism constitutes the illegitimate use of force to achieve a political objective when innocent people are targeted—Walter Laqueur.

- Terrorism is the premeditated, deliberate, systematic murder, mayhem, and threatening of the innocent to create fear and intimidation in order to gain a political or tactical advantage, usually to influence an audience—James M. Poland.
- Terrorism is the unlawful use or threat of violence against persons or property to further political or social objectives. It is usually intended to intimidate or coerce a government, individuals, or groups, or to modify their behavior or politics—U.S. vice president's Task Force, 1986.
- Terrorism is the unlawful use of force or violence against persons or property to intimidate or coerce a government, the civilian population, or any segment thereof, in furtherance of political or social objectives—FBI definition.
- Terrorism is the calculated use of violence or the threat of violence to inculcate fear; intended to coerce or to intimidate governments or societies in the pursuit of goals that are generally political, religious, or ideological—Department of Defense definition.[9]

THE FBI CONSTRUCT

The FBI seems to have developed a very useful construct of what is to be considered terrorism in the United States. This issue concerns foreign power–sponsored or foreign power–coordinated activities that

a. Involve violent acts that are dangerous to human life and a violation of the criminal laws of the United States or any state, or that would be a criminal violation if committed within the jurisdiction of the United States, or any state.
b. Appear to be intended to
   - Intimidate or coerce a civilian population;
   - Influence the policy of a government by intimidation or coercion; and
   - Affect the conduct of a government by assassination or kidnapping.
c. Occur totally outside of the United States, or transcend national boundaries in terms of the means by which they are accomplished, the persons they appear intended to coerce or intimidate, or the locale in which their perpetrators operate or seek to find asylum.

Investigating acts of terrorism overseas includes interviewing victims, collecting forensic evidence, and apprehending terrorist fugitives. The FBI coordinates all overseas investigations with the U.S. Department of State and the host foreign government.[10]

THE U.S. DEPARTMENT OF DEFENSE (DOD) CONSTRUCTS

Christopher G. Essig stated at the United Nations, quoting from his paper *Terrorism: Is It a Criminal Act or an Act of War?*:

> This is discussed in depth at the Army War College at Carlisle Barracks, Pennsylvania, and its implications for National Security in the 21st century, but there is no single determination for classifying all acts of terrorism, neither as acts of war, nor criminal acts. In light of a predicted terrorist threat significant enough to threaten the survival of the nation (catastrophic terror), this determination is less a legal or academic exercise and more practically one based on how such a determination governs this situation (law enforcement or national security?) to respond to the threat. More important is how that response protects our

nation's interests and our status in the world community. Catastrophic terror makes relying solely on a law enforcement response a dangerous option. Yet, reflecting on the changing strategic environment, an act of war determination, in a classical legal sense, is equally impractical. A new determination, carrying the same weight as an act of war must be developed and accepted, domestically and internationally, to provide legal response options offering greater latitude to law enforcement and national security forces. This latitude will provide the means to better meet threats to national security in the 21st century.

Terrorism, as further defined by the DOD, is usually considered to be calculated, and the selection of a target preplanned and rational. The perpetrators know the effect they seek. Terrorist violence is considered to be neither spontaneous nor random. Terrorism is intended to produce fear in someone other than the victim. In a layperson's terms, "Terrorism is a psychological act conducted primarily for its impact on a specific audience." It is abundantly clear that the attack on 9-11 was calculated and that the terrorists knew what they were doing, but the impact caused exactly the opposite to what they had expected—it awakened a sleeping giant! Or in awakening this sleeping giant, maybe, the expectations of the Islamist terrorists were in fact realized. In the decade since 9-11, the Islamist threat has hardened against Western democracies as well as secular Middle East regimes. Many believe that the 9-11 attacks and the subsequent invasions of both Iraq and Afghanistan were exactly what the Islamists hoped to achieve. For the Islamists, the presence of foreign troops in the Middle East gives them the excuse they so dearly need to extend, prolong, and widen their **jihad** to global proportions.

The DOD definition also addresses goals. Terrorism may be motivated by political, religious, or ideological objectives. In one sense, terrorist goals are invariably political—extremists are driven by religious or ideological beliefs and usually seek political power to compel the general society to conform to their views. The objectives of terrorism distinguish it from other violent acts aimed at personal gain, such as criminal violence. However, the definition permits including violence by organized crime when it also seeks to influence government policy. Some drug cartels and other international criminal organizations engage in political action when their activities influence governmental functioning. As noted previously, the essence of terrorism is the intent to inculcate fear into persons other than its direct victims in order to make a government or other audience finally changes its political behavior.

Terrorism is common practice in insurgencies, but insurgents are not necessarily terrorists; especially if they comply with the rules of war and do not engage in forms of violence that could be clearly identified as terrorist acts, then they should probably not be termed as "terrorists." Insurgents can be defined as those who rebel against leadership and authority and could well be termed as "rebels" or "rebellious." Insurgents may resort to tactics that are by their very act considered acts of terrorism. The terms "terrorist" and "terrorism" are so widely used by politicians and commentators alike that being able to discern who is a terrorist and how to define the term becomes markedly complex. Terrorists are rarely inhibited with their attacks and actions, convincing themselves their actions are justified by an even higher law or principle. Their single-minded dedication to a goal, however poorly it may be articulated, renders legal sanctions ineffective. By contrast, war is subject to the rules of international law and of course the terrorists recognize no rules. No person, place, or object of value is immune from terrorist attack; there are no innocents.

The U.S. Department of State

Office of the coordinator for Counter Terrorism—Section 2656f(a) of Title 22 of the U.S. Code states as follows:

1. The term "international terrorism" means terrorism involving citizens of the territory of more than one country;
    a. The term "terrorism" means premeditated, politically motivated violence perpetrated against non-combatant targets by sub national groups or clandestine agents; and
    b. The term "terrorist group" means any group practicing, or which has significant subgroups which practice, international terrorism.

INTERPRETATION AND APPLICATION OF KEY TERMS: The terms "international terrorism," "terrorism," and "terrorist group" have the definitions assigned to them in 22USC 2656f(d) (see above). The term "non-combatant," which is referred to but not defined in 22 USC 2656f(d) (2), is interpreted to mean, in addition to civilians, military personnel (whether or not armed or on duty) who are not deployed in a war zone or a warlike setting.

The definition allows for military targets or personnel to be included in the definition of terrorism, thus the U.S. State Department considers attacks against noncombatants as terrorism, and this not only encompasses the general public but also military personnel who are unarmed or off duty. This would apply to attacks in which military personnel have been targets in civilian locations such as the Berlin Disco bombing in 1986, which resulted in the deaths of two U.S. servicemen. Also, the bombing of the USS *Cole* in the port of Aden in 2000 is an event that by definition is considered by the United States as a terrorist attack. This suicide attack resulted in the death of seventeen U.S. servicemen. The above-mentioned U.S. definition considers it to be terrorism when acts of terror target military installations or personnel when a state of military hostilities does not exist at a specific site or location.

THE UNITED NATIONS—ACTIONS TO COUNTER TERRORISM

The League of Nations, the forerunner organization to the United Nations and formed after the Great War of 1914–1918, in its attempt to bring a measure of world stability defined terrorism as follows:

> All criminal acts directed against a State either intended or calculated to create a state of terror in the minds of particular persons or a group of persons or the general public.

The United Nations General Assembly continues to struggle defining terrorism and between 1963 and 1999 has come up with thirteen international conventions aimed at terrorist actions and, in particular, outlawing airline hijackings and diplomatic hostage taking. The UN came up with a draft, which still remains contentious to many member states—however, the General Assembly has resolved to fight "terrorism," even if it has failed to adequately define the term. The UN General Assembly's Ad Hoc Committee (AHC) on Measures to Eliminate International Terrorism concluded its Fourteenth Session on April 16, 2010, without reaching agreement on the draft Comprehensive Convention on International Terrorism (CCIT).

The United Nation's Global Counterterrorism Strategy was adopted by member states on September 8, 2006. The strategy—in the form of a resolution and an annexed plan of action—is a unique global instrument that enhances national, regional, and international efforts to counter terrorism. This was the first time that all member states agreed to a common strategic approach to fight terrorism, even if they couldn't agree to a definition, not only sending a clear message that terrorism is unacceptable in all its forms and manifestation but also resolving to take practical steps individually and collectively to prevent and combat it. These steps include a wide array of measures ranging from strengthening state capacity to counter terrorist threats to better coordinating United Nation's counterterrorism activities. The adoption of the strategy fulfilled the commitment made by world leaders at the 2005 September Summit, and the strategy built on many of the elements proposed by the secretary-general in his May 2, 2006, report entitled *Uniting Against Terrorism: Recommendations for a Global Counterterrorism Strategy.*[11]

The Arab Convention for the Suppression of Terrorism

Unofficial translation from Arabic by the United Nations English translation service

Preamble

The Arab states signatory hereto,

Desiring to promote mutual cooperation in the suppression of terrorist offences, which pose a threat to the security and stability of the Arab Nation and endanger its vital interests, being committed to the highest moral and religious principles and, in particular, to the tenets of the **Islamic Sharia**, as well as to the humanitarian heritage of an Arab Nation that rejects all forms of violence and terrorism and advocates the protection of human rights, with which precepts the principles of international law conform, based as they are on cooperation among peoples in the promotion of peace, being further committed to the Pact of the League of Arab States, the Charter of the United Nations and all the other international convents and instruments to which the Contracting States to this Convention are parties.

Affirming the right of peoples to combat foreign occupation and aggression by whatever means, including armed struggle, in order to liberate their territories and secure their right to self-determination, and independence and to do so in such a manner as to preserve the territorial integrity of each Arab country, of the foregoing being in accordance with the purposes and principles of the Charter of the United Nations and with the Organization's resolutions.

The Arab States have agreed to conclude this convention and to invite any Arab State that did not participate in its conclusion to accede hereto.

Part One: Definitions and General Provisions

Article 1

Each of the following terms shall be understood in the light of the definition give;

1. **Contracting State**
   Any member State of the League of Arab States that has ratified this Convention and that has deposited its instruments of ratification with the General Secretariat of the League.
2. **Terrorism**
   Any act or threat of violence, whatever its motives or purposes, that occurs in the advancement of an individual or collective criminal agenda and seeking to sow panic among people, causing fear by harming them, or placing their lives, liberty or security in danger, or seeking to cause damage to the environment or to public or private

installations or property or to occupying or seizing them, or seeking to jeopardize a national resources.

3. **Terrorist offence**

   Any offence or attempted offence committed in furtherance of a terrorist objective in any of the Contracting States, or against their nationals, property or interests, that is punishable by their domestic law. The offences stipulated in the following conventions, except where conventions have not been ratified by Contracting States or where offences have been excluded by their legislation, shall also be regarded as terrorist offences:

   (a) The Tokyo Convention on offences and Certain Other Acts Committed on Board Aircraft, of 14 September 1963;

   (b) The **Hague Convention** for the Suppression of Unlawful Seizure of Aircraft, of 16 December 1970;

   (c) The Montreal Convention for the Suppression of Unlawful Acts against the Safety of Civil Aviation, of 23 September 1971, and the Protocol thereto of 10 May 1984;

   (d) The Convention on the Prevention and Punishment of Crimes against Internationally Protected Persons, including Diplomatic Agents, of 14 December 1973;

   (e) The International Convention against the Taking of Hostages, of 17 December 1979;

   (f) The provisions of the United Nations Convention on the Law of the Sea, of 1982, relating to piracy on the high seas.

The League has twenty-two current members and includes the following states:

Egypt, Sudan, Algeria

Morocco, Iraq, Saudi Arabia

Yemen, Syria, Tunisia

Somalia, Libya, Jordan

United Arab Emirates, Lebanon, Palestine

Mauritania, Kuwait, Oman

Qatar, Djibouti, Bahrain, and Comoros

STRUCTURES OF TERRORIST GROUPS

Terrorists tend to organize themselves all over the world in ways that enable them to function well in the specific environment in which they are located and then be able to carry out the acts of terrorism. We shall now discuss some general organizational principles for terrorists that shed insight into how a terrorist thinks. Above all else, the most important thing to a terrorist is tight security. Why? Because they are always operating in a hostile environment!

It does not matter if the terrorists are in Europe, Asia, or the Americas, as wherever they are is a hostile environment. Their safety and security is best provided by what is called a "cellular structure." This is primarily most important because the structure ensures that not one of them can identify any more terrorists than those in their specific cell of operation. It is like a safety net for them. Terrorist groups—those that are not supported by a specific government or are not state sponsored—always create what is called a tight support structure of "sympathizers" or many other people who may have been coerced into supporting or helping them for various reasons. Such a support system can be either active or passive. By that we mean intelligence collection, recruiting, monetary support, logistics, dissemination of propaganda, or, worse, a young person strapped up with explosives and sent to a specific target for self-destruction. This is clearly despicable, but it is a reality in terrorism just as is the use of women and children as human shields for covert operations. It is a fact in the lifestyle of terrorism and terrorists, wherever they are to be found.

COMMON TERRORIST QUALITIES

What qualities does a terrorist leader look for when selecting his followers for an operation? It is difficult to give a categorical or simple answer to this question. However, certain qualities separate terrorists who form the "hard core" of terrorist organizations from those who comprise the peripheral elements, whose activities are mostly seen in a supportive role.

First, they must believe passionately in the justness of their cause! This is a most important quality, because this is also the motivating factor for all their subsequent actions. The obvious example of this is the radicalization of young Muslim men and women over the last decade being drawn by calls for global Jihad either from Jihadist websites or from actually immersing themselves in self-styled training camps.

Second, they must possess a "killer instinct," in other words, a predilection to kill, not in anger, not in the heat of the moment, not during a fight or a battle, but kill at anytime, anywhere, in absolute coldblood, and without any pangs of conscience or feelings of pity and remorse for the targeted victims.

Third, they must possess an ability to act effectively as loners, if circumstances so warrant, even though in their private lives they may not be loners. Members of conventional armies, and insurgent and guerrilla organizations, train, live, and move together. They normally operate in groups, although there may be circumstances when individual members may have to operate totally alone. On the contrary, in the case of terrorist organizations, they may train and occasionally live together, but more often their members operate as loners unless they are tasked for specific operations, such as the hijacking of an aircraft, a kidnapping, a coordinated series of suicide attacks as took place in London in 2005 and the 2008 attacks on hotels and train stations in Mumbai, India.

About 60 percent of the terrorist incidents reported every year are operations in which the terrorists acted as loners for assassinations, sniper missions, throwing of hand grenades, planting of explosives, improvised explosive device or vehicle-borne improvised devices, suicide bombings, and so on. Thus, operating as a loner requires greater physical and mental courage and individual determination and even greater dedication and loyalty than operating in groups. Independent groups that have been inspired by al Qaeda and the Islamist extremist preaching of Osama bin Laden have seen a level of "religious" violence and considerable bravery on behalf of the autonomous cell members, unmatched by the likes of European groups such as ETA and the Irish terrorist groups.

Fourth, they must have a very high degree of physical courage, because a terrorist risks not only death but even worse than death—capture, physical torture, and long imprisonment—if caught.

The development of bureaucratic states led to a profound change in terrorism. Modern democratic governments have continuity that older, charismatic, royal, religious-based, or inherited governments do not. Terrorists soon found that the death of a single individual, even a monarch, did not necessarily make a great enough impact to produce the policy changes they had sought. Terrorists reacted by turning to an indirect method of attack. By the early twentieth century, terrorists began to attack people who were previously considered "innocents" to generate political pressure from and by the public. These indirect attacks managed to create a public atmosphere of anxiety, fear, and an undermining of confidence in government. Their very unpredictability, and apparent randomness, makes it virtually impossible for governments to protect all potential victims. The public then cries out for safety and protection that the state cannot give. Frustrated and fearful, the people then demand that the government make concessions to the terrorists in order to stop the attacks.

Modern terrorism behavior and philosophy offers its practitioners many advantages. First, by not recognizing innocents, terrorists can acquire and attack an infinite number of targets. They can select their target and then determine when, where, and how to attack. This range of choices gives terrorists a high probability of success with minimum risk. If the attack goes wrong, or fails to produce the intended results, they can simply deny responsibility.

Ironically, as democratic governments become more common, it may be getting even easier for terrorists to operate. The first terrorist bombing of the World Trade Center in New York City, the Oklahoma City Federal Building truck bombing, the bombing of the two U.S. embassies in Kenya and Tanzania, and the suicide attack on the USS *Cole* in Yemen—all were **dots** that were never connected, culminating in the hijacked aircraft attacks on the World Trade Center on 9-11! Such "follow-the-dots roadmaps" proved how easy it could be for terrorists to operate in a free or democratic society. Authoritarian governments, whose populace may have even better reasons to revolt, may also be less constrained by requirements for due process and impartial justice when combating terrorists. As national leaders and politicians address terrorism, they must consider several relevant characteristics:

1. Anyone can be a victim. Some terrorists may still operate under certain cultural restraints, such as a desire to avoid harming women; but essentially, there are no more innocents these days.
2. Attacks that may appear to be senseless and random may not be senseless or random to the perpetrators/terrorist. Their attacks have made perfect sense. Acts such as suicide bombings in public places of assembly or shooting into crowded restaurants are guaranteed to heighten public anxiety. This is always the terrorists' immediate objective.
3. The terrorist or terrorist group needs to publicize the attack. If no one knows about it, it will not generate the desired fear and pressure on government. The need for publicity often drives target selection—the greater the symbolic value of the target, the more publicity the attack brings to the terrorists and the more fear it generates. The media often provide the notoriety, intentionally or inadvertently, that the terrorists desire, simply by just covering the terrorist event.
4. Any leader planning for effective ways to combat terrorism must understand that nothing can protect every possible target all the time. It must be seen clearly that terrorists would most likely just change their attack tactics from more-protected targets to less-protected ones. This is the key to defensive measures.[12]

Motivations for Terrorists

Terrorists are inspired by many and diverse motives. One can even classify them into three distinct categories: *rational, psychological,* and *cultural.* Many combinations and variations of these factors may shape a terrorist. Rational terrorists will think through their goals and options, often conducting a sort of "cost/benefit analysis" of expected results. They seek information to determine whether there are less costly or more effective ways with which to achieve their individual or group objectives. To assess the risk, they weigh the target's defensive capabilities against their own offensive abilities to accomplish an attack. They analyze the terrorist group's capabilities to sustain the effort. The essential question is whether terrorism will probably work and accomplish the desired goals, given societal conditions at the time. The terrorist's rational analysis is similar to that of a military commander or a business entrepreneur considering available resources and courses of action. Groups considering terrorism as an option always ask a crucial question: "Can terrorism induce enough anxiety to attain their goals without causing a backlash that will destroy the cause and perhaps even the terrorists themselves?" To misjudge the answer to that question is to court disaster. After 9-11, the backlash was the "War on Terror." Psychological motivations for resorting to terrorism usually derive from the terrorist organizations' or individuals' personal depth of dissatisfaction with their life and accomplishments. Individuals find a reason to be involved in a dedicated terrorist action. Although no clear psychopathy can always be found among terrorists, there is a nearly universal element in them that can be described as the "true believer." Terrorists seldom even attempt to consider that they may be wrong or that other views might have some merit. Terrorists tend to project their own antisocial attitudes and motivations onto others, creating a polarized "us-versus-them" outlook. They attribute evil motives to anyone outside their own group. This enables the terrorists to dehumanize their victims and removes any sense of ambiguity from their minds. The resulting clarity of purpose appeals to those who crave and need a use of violence to relieve their constant anger.

Another common characteristic of the psychologically motivated terrorist is the desperate need to belong to a like-minded group. With some terrorists, group acceptance is a stronger motivator than the stated political objectives of the organization. Such individuals define their social status by group acceptance.

Terrorist groups with strong internal motivations find it necessary to justify the group's existence continuously. A terrorist group must, as a minimum, commit some violent acts to maintain group self-esteem and legitimacy. Another result of psychological motivation is the intensity of the group dynamics among terrorists. They tend to demand unanimity and are intolerant of any dissent or different opinions. With the enemy clearly identified and determined to be unequivocally evil, pressure to escalate the frequency and intensity of operations is ever present. The need to belong to the group discourages any possible resignations, and the fear of compromise disallows their acceptance; compromise is also usually rejected. Terrorist groups lean toward inflexible positions. Having placed themselves "beyond the pale" (forever unacceptable to ordinary society), they cannot consider any compromise. They can then expect any negotiation to be dishonorable, even treasonous. Such dynamics also make any announced group goal nearly impossible to achieve. By definition, a group that has achieved its stated purpose is no longer necessary. As a result, success threatens the psychological well-being of its members. Therefore, when a terrorist group approaches its stated goal, it is inclined to pause and redefine it. The group may reject the achievement as false or inadequate, or the result of the duplicity of the unknown, unnamed "them." Terrorist groups also often suffer from a nagging fear of success. One effective psychological defense against success is to define goals so broadly that they are impossible to achieve. Even if the world proclaims the success of a political movement, the terrorists can deny it and fight on. Cultural concepts also shape values and motivate people to actions that seem unreasonable to outside observers. For example, Americans are often generally reluctant to appreciate the intense impact that cultural factors have on behavior. They too often easily accept the myth that rational behavior guides all human actions. It is easy to reject as unbelievable such things as vendettas, martyrdom, suicide bombers, and self-destructive group behavior when Americans observe them in others. There is disbelief that such things as the destruction of a viable state can be done just for the sake of ethnic purity, especially when the resulting state becomes economically or politically unstable.

The treatment of life, in general, and individual life, in particular, is a cultural characteristic that has a tremendous impact on terrorism. In societies in which people identify themselves in terms of group memberships (family, clan, or tribe), there may be a willingness to accept levels of self-sacrifice seldom seen elsewhere. At times, terrorists seem to be eager to give their lives for their organization or cause. The lives of "others," even strangers, whom they perceive as being totally evil by their terrorist value system, can therefore be snuffed out without any sense of remorse. Other factors include the manner in which aggression is channeled and the concepts of social organization. In many political systems, there are effective, nonviolent means for succession to power. A culture may have a high tolerance for nonpolitical violence, such as banditry or ethnic turf battles, and remain relatively free of political violence. The United States, for example, is one of the most violent societies in the world; yet political violence remains a rare aberration. By contrast, both France and Germany, with low tolerance for violent crime, have had long histories of political violence.

A major cultural determinant of terrorism is the perception of "outsiders" and anticipation of their threat to long-held ethnic values or to a terrorist group's survival. Fear of cultural dilution or extermination leads to violence that, to someone who has not experienced it, seems irrational. All human beings are sensitive to threats to their personal values and beliefs, those with which they identify themselves. These include language; religion; tribal, racial, or group membership; and a sense of homeland territory. The possibility of losing any of these can trigger defensive, even xenophobic, reactions.

Religion may be the most volatile of cultural identifiers because it encompasses values and beliefs deeply rooted in a long-standing and ancient cultural paradigm. A threat to one's religion puts not only the present at risk but also one's entire cultural past, present, and future. Many religions, including Christianity and Islam, are so confident they are right that they have often used force to make converts or to eliminate nonbelievers. Terrorism in the name of religion can be especially violent, and will be discussed in detail in Chapter 2. Like all terrorists, those who are religiously motivated view their acts with moral certainty and even divine sanctions. What would otherwise be extraordinary acts of desperation becomes a religious duty in the mind of the religiously motivated terrorist. This helps explain the high level of commitment among religious extremist groups and suicide bombers and their willingness to risk their own deaths.

TERRORISM AS CRIMINAL BEHAVIOR

The broad range of violent activities that are often labeled as "terrorism" can now be seen as difficult, even impossible, to define in a simplistic and universal way. There are some specific acts that seem to straddle the behavioral continuum in such a way so as to cloud the effort to somehow distinguish between criminal acts and terrorist acts. Some so-called terrorist acts are as specific and localized as to be outside the scope of the broader definitions. We shall now examine a few of those that seem especially relevant as we examine crime and terror in the twenty-first century.

HOSTAGE TAKING

Taking hostages, whether for political reasons or for extortion of funds to support terrorist groups, is an often-used tactic. The policy of the United States is to make no concessions to terrorists who hold official or private U.S. citizens as hostages. The United States will not pay ransom, release prisoners, change its policies, or agree to other acts that might encourage terrorism. At the same time, the United States will use every available and appropriate resource to gain the safe return of American citizens who are being held hostage by terrorists. Hostage taking is defined under international law (the International Convention Against the Taking of Hostages, adopted December 17, 1979) as "the seizing or detaining, threatening to kill, injure, or continue to detain a person in order to compel a third party to do, or abstain from doing, any act as an explicit or implicit condition for the release of the seized or detained person. Such activity is also considered a criminal act in most countries around the world, as a part of extortion or kidnapping for profit." It is generally accepted in the international community that local governments are responsible for the safety and welfare of persons within the borders of their nations. Terrorist threats and public safety shortcomings in many parts of the world have caused the United States to develop enhanced physical and personal security programs for U.S. citizens and to establish cooperative arrangements with the U.S. private sector to help warn and protect business travelers. The United States has established bilateral counterterrorism assistance programs and close intelligence and law enforcement relationships with many nations to help prevent terrorist incidents, or to resolve them in a manner that will deny the terrorists political or financial benefits from their actions. The United States also seeks to employ adequate and effective judicial prosecution and punishment for terrorists who seek to victimize the U.S. government, or its citizens, and will use all appropriate legal methods toward these ends, including extradition alone and/or, hopefully, with appropriate cooperation from the other governments. After many serious incidents, the United States has finally concluded that paying ransom or making other concessions to terrorists in exchange for the release of hostages only increases the probability and danger that others will then be taken hostage—*ad infinitum*. A good example of hostage taking and ransom and the overall ineptitude of international response is well documented in relation to acts of piracy (see Chapter 14). In some very poor nations, kidnapping and ransom are considered growth industries. The Horn of Africa and Nigeria are good examples of Third World countries where hostage taking and piracy are growth industries. U.S. policy strongly encourages U.S. companies and private citizens not to respond to terrorist ransom demands. It believes that good security practice, relatively modest security training and expenditures, and continual close cooperation with embassy and local authorities will lower the risk to Americans abroad who are living and working in such high-threat environments.

Although the United States is concerned for the welfare of its citizens, it cannot support requests from private companies that host governments should violate their own laws or abdicate their normal law enforcement responsibilities. On the other hand, if the employing organization or company of a hostage works closely with local authorities and follows U.S. policy, U.S. foreign service posts can be involved actively in efforts to bring such stressful incidents to a successful conclusion. This includes providing reasonable administrative services and, if desired by the local authorities and the American organization, full participation in strategy sessions. Requests for U.S. technical assistance or expertise are considered on a case-by-case basis. The full extent of U.S. government participation must await an analysis of each specific set of circumstances. This again demonstrates the problems involved with making precise definitions of who can do what in a situation that may or may not be terrorism.

LEGAL ISSUES IN HOSTAGE TAKING

Under current U.S. law (18 USC 1203, Act for the Prevention and Punishment of the Crime of Hostage-Taking, enacted in October, 1984, on implementation of the UN convention on hostage taking), seizure of a U.S. national as a hostage anywhere in the world is a crime, as is any hostage taking in which the U.S. government is a target or the hostage taker is a U.S. national. Such acts are, therefore, subject to investigation by the FBI and to prosecution by U.S. authorities.

ASSASSINATION

On September 11, 2001, Osama bin Laden and his al Qaeda cohorts struck a blow against Western social values and have, by these acts, created a lingering and justifiable fear that they will attempt to strike at the United States again. This fear increased pressure on U.S. officials, and around the talk-show circuit, to perhaps reconsider **assassination** as a method of solving problems with world leaders whom we consider to be dangerous. The old argument still remains, "How many lives would we have saved if Hitler had been assassinated in 1938?" This argument is strong, and for a long time, many countries have ordered and approved using "extreme sanction" against leaders of unfriendly countries or against leaders of criminal or terrorist organizations. "Cut the head off the snake" was considered a good response to perceived danger. But, ordering an assassination today would mean moving away from long-established policy and practice.

Time will tell whether or not the United States can ever accumulate the needed backing of the international community to head into "a sure-to-spiral upward" path of assassinations adopted to meet perceived solutions to growing problems. The problem is similar to that of euthanasia—"Who decides when a person is so evil, or in such bad health, that their elimination is the only alternative?" This issue will have a long discussion period, in times when cooler emotions may eventually prevail. The situation in Iraq showed what methods had to be used to oust Saddam Hussein—and his trial and execution will help to clarify whether such actions were justifiable or considered too extreme. Bin Laden's killing or assassination by U.S. Navy SEALs in May 2011 did not raise the ire or angst of many countries, and the U.S. military action authorized by President Obama was supported by both the UN and NATO. The fact that bin Laden was possibly unarmed at the time of his death was raised as an issue by groups such as Amnesty International.

Examples of Past Hostage Crises

Lebanese Hostage Crisis—1982–1992   Lebanon was in complete turmoil by 1981, and the kidnapping most effectively conducted by organizations fronting for Hezbollah saw some ninety-six foreign hostages being kidnapped mostly from Western countries and primarily journalists, diplomats, or teachers from the American University in Beirut. The majority of those kidnapped were from the United States, France, West Germany, Great Britain, and Switzerland. Captive Terry Waite, a special envoy of Britain's Archbishop of Canterbury, was in Beirut negotiating independently for the release of other kidnap victims when he was seized and remained in almost solitary confinement from the time of his capture in January 1987 until his ultimate release in November 1991. The longest-held hostage was U.S. citizen and the senior Middle East correspondent for the Associated Press, Terry Anderson, who was kidnapped by elements of Hezbollah in March 1985 and was not released until December 1991.

Black September—Munich Olympic Games, September 1972   A group of eight Palestinian terrorists entered the Athlete Village and took eleven Israeli athletes and some of their trainers hostage. Their demands were simple; the release of some 200 Palestinians held by the Israeli government. The standoff with West German Police lasted around eighteen hours, and on the evening of September 5, 1972, the hostages and their kidnappers were ferried by helicopter to Fusrtenfeldbruk Airport. West German Police attempted a rescue mission that resulted in all eleven hostages being killed. This single event prompted the West German Police to develop a counterterror force to combat terrorist events, and ultimately the crack force **GSG-9** came into being.

Japanese Ambassador's Residence, Lima, Peru—December 1996   Members of Peru's Tupac Amaru Revolutionary Movement seized the ambassador's residence during a

Christmas reception and took Peruvian government officials, foreign diplomats, and Japanese businessmen hostage while demanding the release of Tupac Amaru members in Peruvian prisons. A majority of the foreign diplomats were released, but the hostage crisis continued for nearly four months and ended only when Peruvian "special forces" tunneled into the compound and successfully rescued the remaining eighty hostages.

Taliban Kidnappings—Afghanistan July 2007   The Taliban kidnapped twenty-three South Koreans, who were working as Christian aid volunteers, on a highway in central Afghanistan in July 2007. The pastor leading the team and another man were shot dead soon after the abduction. All the remaining hostages were released on August 11, 2007, after protracted negotiations with South Korea. Under the agreement, South Korea reaffirmed a pledge to withdraw its 200 troops from Afghanistan by the end of the year, as previously planned, and agreed to prevent any evangelical activities by South Korean churches in Afghanistan. The Taliban, for its part, dropped a demand that eight senior Taliban prisoners be released in exchange for the South Koreans.[13]

There were some obvious concerns with the Korean incident, as it seemed highly probable that the Korean government capitulated to Taliban demands and surrendered millions of dollars for the return of their citizens. At the same time, a German hostage, also held by the Taliban, had not been released. In light of the exposure and arrest of Islamist networks uncovered in Germany during the summer of 2007, that government had stood firm in its resolve not to negotiate with the Taliban. Paying a ransom was not unusual; however, the agreement to end all missionary work in the country would have likely sent the wrong message to other Islamist groups who had witnessed that South Korea had the ability and willingness to not only pay a ransom but also restrict or prohibit missionary work in a foreign country. This may mean that in countries where there had been violent opposition to Christians and missionaries but where incidents of kidnapping had rarely occurred, such as India, Pakistan, and Indonesia, this incident may be seen as an opportunity to embrace the same style of attack to force out foreign Christians.

Boko Haram—Nigeria—May 2011   Islamic militants seized two construction workers, a Briton and an Italian, and held them captive for ten months. The captors were believed to be a faction of Boko Haram calling itself "Al Qaeda in the land beyond Sahil." They produced videos of their captors, but no clear demands were ever made. The British government had gathered intelligence that suggested they might be either traded to an even more dangerous group or killed, and in early March 2012, the British Special Boat Squadron (SBS), a group of highly trained Special Forces, and the Nigerian military stormed the kidnappers compound in an effort to release the hostages. During the attempt, both hostages were killed by their captors, and the captors were also killed.

Kidnapping for ransom or political gain remains a global issue. Some of the most significant countries and the elements most likely to engage in kidnapping of Westerners are primarily as follows:

- Mexico—drug cartels and associated gangs
- Lebanon—elements sponsored by Hezbollah
- Yemen—a favorite past time of tribes in the region and now al Qaeda in the Arabian Peninsula (AQAP)
- Algeria and Niger—al Qaeda-inspired al Qaeda in the Islamic Maghreb (AQIM)
- Nigeria—Boko Haram—al Qaeda inspired and possibly sponsored by affiliated al Qaeda groups

CONSTITUTIONAL RIGHTS

Finally, we raise the question of subversion of constitutionally guaranteed federal rights. The Fourteenth Amendment of the U.S. Constitution defines "residents" as being citizens of both the federal government and the state in which they reside. It expressly forbids states from making any ordinance, law, or regulation that abridges the federal rights of citizens. If there is a constitutional right to abortion, and the effects (whether by "color" or "usage") of local, county, or state government clearly abridge that right, is that right an issue that might be considered by federal courts? If one defines antiabortion terrorism as an effort to impose a set of religious beliefs on others, is there a colorable question of separation of church and state? Students of constitutional history may later consider these early years of this millennium as an odious period of challenge to and denial of their liberties.

Clearly, terrorism is a complex, multifaceted, and often baffling subject to define. The players involved have a way of rising to prominence, splintering, disappearing for years, and then suddenly reappearing. Counterterrorism bureaucracies are formed and then reformed, names are changed, and leaders are shuffled around as they are promoted, demoted, killed, or forced to resign. Incidents proliferate across the world, some of which can trigger off a chain of events that will destabilize a whole region and bring nations to the edge of ruin. At the same time, major terrorist actions can shock for a short while and then be eventually forgotten by all except those seriously impacted by the tragedy. Treatises are written, theories propounded, grievances aired, and tactics discussed, occasionally, to some effect, but more often, not. Causes are picked up by the world media, examined, probed, and then all too often overlooked in the rush to cover some new breaking story—until the next bomb explodes, or the next airliner is hijacked or downed, like those in Russia in 2004; or another cataclysmic event, like the 9-11 attacks, happens in some major city, as London experienced in July 2005, the bungled attacks on Glasgow Airport, Scotland, in July 2007, and the Mumbai attacks in 2008.

With the various definitions of terrorism and their application to specific events, you should have a good foundation for the study of terrorism and terrorist acts. Terrorism drastically shocks the senses and promotes fear and concern around the world. In the next chapter, we shall review state-sponsored and religious terrorism from several viewpoints. Terrorist causes are often looked upon as bizarre or weird in the context of the present. But most issues (political, religious, racial, or ethnic) have a long, historic pattern that always needs to be discovered and examined in a particular context. We believe that those who understand the historic foundations of these issues that have shaped the free world, since the attacks of 9-11, will never again be able to view the evening news in the same way ever again.

You can now appreciate that there is neither a universally accepted nor a simple definition of terrorism. According to acknowledged terrorism expert Walter Laqueur, "the only characteristic generally agreed upon, is that terrorism involves violence and the threat of violence." This criterion alone does not produce a useful definition as it includes many acts not usually considered terrorism, such as war, organized crime, revolution, or even a simple riot. *Asymmetric warfare* and *low-intensity operations* are military terms for tactics that sometimes include terrorism. At its core, the definition of terrorism is not so much a description of a particular kind of violence, like bombing or assassination, but a way to characterize an act of violence relative to terrorists and their point of view.

"Terrorism," then, is a term that attempts to define, as a separate phenomenon, a philosophy of coordinated violence that tends to have a high degree of social impact on a targeted society. Rebels in opposition to an established social order may perpetrate terrorist violence, or a state may inflict it upon its own citizens or those of another state. One study by the U.S. Army discovered over 100 definitions that have been used. A few more of such examples will highlight and emphasize the problem of settling upon any precise definition:

U.S. Code of Federal Regulations   "The unlawful use of force and violence against persons or property to intimidate or coerce a government, the civilian population, or any segment thereof, in furtherance of political or social objectives" (28 C.F.R. Section 0.85).

Current U.S. National Security Strategy   "Premeditated, politically motivated violence against innocents."

U.S. Department of Defense   The "calculated use of unlawful violence to inculcate fear; intended to coerce or intimidate governments or societies in pursuit of goals that are generally political, religious, or ideological."

The U.S. Department of Justice   "The unlawful use of force or violence committed by a group or individual against persons or property to intimidate or coerce a Government, the Civilian population or any segment thereof in furtherance of political or social objectives."

A 1984 U.S. Army Training Manual   "Terrorism is the calculated use of violence, or the threat of violence, to produce goals that are political or ideological in nature."

Brian Jenkins   "Terrorism is the use or threatened use of force designed to bring about political change."

James M. Poland   "Terrorism is the premeditated, deliberate, systematic murder, mayhem, and threatening of the innocent to create fear and intimidation in order to gain a political or tactical advantage, usually to influence an audience."

As is so often the case, a planned series of attacks by any disparate group will cause governments to establish emergency and often far-reaching legislation aimed at protecting the nation. After the 9-11 suicide attacks, the U.S. government moved quickly to pass the Patriot Act, which addressed and formalized into law a U.S. response to how terrorism would be combated from within.

THE U.S. CODE, TITLE 18 PART I CHAPTER 113B SEC 2331

Sec 2331—Definitions:

(1) "International terrorism" means activities that -
   (a) involve violent acts or acts dangerous to human life that are a violation of the criminal laws of the United States or of any State, or that would be a criminal violation if committed within the jurisdiction of the United States or of any State;
   (b) appear to be intended -
      (i) to coerce or intimidate a civilian population
      (ii) to influence the policy of a government by intimidation or coercion; or to affect the conduct of a government by mass destruction, assassination, or kidnapping; and
      (iii) to affect the conduct of a government by mass destruction, assassination, or kidnapping;
   (c) occur primarily outside the territorial jurisdiction of the United States, or transcend national boundaries in terms of the means by which they are accomplished, the persons they appear intended to intimidate or coerce, or the locale in which their perpetrators operate or seek asylum;

(2) the term "national of the United States" has the meaning given such term in section 101(a)(22) of the Immigration and Nationality Act;

(3) the term "person" means any individual or entity capable of holding a legal or beneficial interest in property;

(4) the term "act of war" means any act occurring in the course of -

    (a) declared war;

    (b) armed conflict, whether or not war has been declared, between two or more nations; or

    (c) armed conflict between military forces of any origin; and

(5) the term "domestic terrorism" means activities that -

    (a) involve acts dangerous to human life that are a violation of the criminal laws of the United States or of any State;

    (b) appear to be intended -

        (i) to intimidate or coerce a civilian population;

        (ii) to influence the policy of a government by intimidation or coercion; or to affect the conduct of a government by mass destruction, assassination, or kidnapping; and

    (c) occur primarily within the territorial jurisdiction of the United States.[14]

THE USA PATRIOT ACT 2001

An Act H. R. 3162 in the Senate of the United States

The USA Patriot Act came into law on October 26, 2001, and aimed at expanding police powers to investigate terrorism in the homeland. The act is broken into ten titles as listed below:

Title I—Enhancing Domestic Security against Terrorism

Title II—Enhanced Surveillance Procedures

Title III—International Money Laundering Abatement and Antiterrorist Financing Act 2001

Title IV—Protecting the Border

Title V—Removing Obstacles to Investigating Terrorism

Title VI—Providing for Victims of Terrorism, Public Safety Officers, and Their Families

Title VII—Increased Information Sharing for Critical Infrastructure Protection

Title VIII—Strengthening Criminal Laws against Terrorism

Title IX—Improved Intelligence

Title X—Miscellaneous[15]

Civil libertarians were less than happy about the sweeping powers of the Patriot Act, particularly sections that authorized roving wiretaps, which effectively allowed police to obtain a wiretap warrant on *any* phone used by a *suspected* terrorist. Prior to the Patriot Act, police would have to seek judicial approval/authorization for each individual phone. Lawmakers sought to minimize the effect on civil liberties by including a sunset clause, which would cause the act to expire at the end of four years. In even the most primitive societies, certain acts or groups of acts have been universally forbidden or discouraged, or **proscribed**. Such acts include murder, rape, incest, kidnapping, and treason (or some form of rebellion affecting the entire social group's safety and the leadership's authority). In contrast, most societies have encouraged or sponsored, or **prescribed**, behaviors such as marrying, having children, hunting, growing food, and other actions that clearly benefit the group's, or tribe's, common social welfare and survival. Terrorism often falls into the range of behaviors that are not only a violation of laws but also a violation of the politics and practices (mores) of a social group or tribal organization. Often the violation of codified law requires that a person must call a public safety officer to make an investigation or an arrest. All of these behaviors are related to the ways that social groups or subcultures choose to respond to transgressions that violate their mutually agreed-to standards of conduct. In 2001, shortly after 9-11, the U.S. Department of Homeland Security was born out of public outrage and the aftereffects of the attacks. Terrorism from abroad had struck at the United States and awakened a "sleeping giant," one that realized that the world had changed. Something had to be done quickly to assure Americans that the government was going to respond strongly and would not allow something terrible like this to happen again at the hands of foreign terrorists. As the horrific attacks of September 11, 2001, recede into time, only the lasting effects of security are clear to us all. The world certainly has not become a safer place, particularly for citizens from Western countries and in particular those from the United States and Great Britain traveling abroad; the United States is engaged in a conventional war against insurgents in both Iraq and Afghanistan and is still a target for the hatred and ire of Islamist terror cells, be they foreign or home grown. However, since 2001, the U.S. government has

- Created the Department of Homeland Security (DHS) by merging twenty-two separate agencies into a cohesive department with a primary mission of protecting the U.S. homeland;
- Provided billions of U.S. dollars to DHS to support federal, state, and local preparedness through 2011;
- Leveraged detection technology and deployed additional personnel to enhance border and transportation security, increasing spending by nearly $9 billion;
- Protected the nation's aviation system by deploying a well-trained screener workforce and state-of-the-art screening equipment; and
- Secured $5.6 billion as part of President Bush's Project BioShield to buy cutting edge drugs, vaccines, and other medical supplies for bio-defense.

THE DEPARTMENT OF HOMELAND SECURITY

The President proposes to create a new Department of Homeland Security, the most significant transformation of the U.S. government in over half century, by largely transforming and realigning the current confusing patchwork of government activities into a single department, whose primary mission is to protect our homeland. The creation of a Department of Homeland Security is one more key step in the President's national strategy for homeland security.

—From the Department of Homeland Security,
*June 2002—*GEORGE W. BUSH

Department subcomponents and agencies are as follows:

- Department Components
- Office of the Secretary
- Advisory Panels and Committees

Homeland security leverages resources within federal, state, and local governments, coordinating the transition of multiple agencies and programs into a single, integrated agency, focused on protecting the American people and their homeland. More than 87,000 different governmental jurisdictions at the federal, state, and local levels have homeland security responsibilities. The comprehensive national strategy seeks to develop a complementary system connecting all levels of government, without duplicating effort. Homeland security is truly a "national mission."

The following list contains the major components that currently make up the Department of Homeland Security.

Department Components

The Directorate for National Protection and Programs works to advance the department's risk-reduction mission. Reducing risk requires an integrated approach that encompasses both physical and virtual threats and their associated human elements.

The Directorate for Science and Technology is the primary research and development arm of the department. It provides federal, state, and local officials with the technology and capabilities to protect the homeland.

The Directorate for Management is responsible for department budgets and appropriations, expenditure of funds, accounting and finance, procurement; human resources, information technology systems, facilities and equipment, and the identification and tracking of performance measurements.

The Office of Policy is the primary policy formulation and coordination component for the Department of Homeland Security. It provides a centralized, coordinated focus to the development of departmentwide, long-range planning to protect the United States.

The Office of Health Affairs coordinates all medical activities of the Department of Homeland Security to ensure appropriate preparation for and response to incidents having medical significance.

The Office of Intelligence and Analysis is responsible for using information and intelligence from multiple sources to identify and assess current and future threats to the United States.

The Office of Operations Coordination is responsible for monitoring the security of the United States on a daily basis and coordinating activities within the department and with governors, Homeland Security Advisors, law enforcement partners, and critical infrastructure operators in all fifty states and in more than fifty major urban areas nationwide.

The Federal Law Enforcement Training Center provides career-long training to law enforcement professionals to help them fulfill their responsibilities safely and proficiently.

The Domestic Nuclear Detection Office works to enhance the nuclear detection efforts of federal, state, territorial, tribal, and local governments and the private sector and to ensure a coordinated response to such threats.

The Transportation Security Administration (TSA) protects the nation's transportation systems to ensure freedom of movement for people and commerce.

United States Customs and Border Protection (CBP) is responsible for protecting our nation's borders in order to prevent terrorists and terrorist weapons from entering the United States, while facilitating the flow of legitimate trade and travel.

United States Citizenship and Immigration Services is responsible for the administration of immigration and naturalization adjudication functions and establishing immigration services policies and priorities.

United States Immigration and Customs Enforcement (ICE), the largest investigative arm of the Department of Homeland Security, is responsible for identifying and shutting down vulnerabilities in the nation's border and for economic, transportation, and infrastructure security.

The United States Coast Guard protects the public, the environment, and U.S. economic interests in the nation's ports and waterways, along the coast, on international waters, or in any maritime region, as required to support national security.

The Federal Emergency Management (FEMA) prepares the nation for hazards, manages federal response and recovery efforts following any national incident, and administers the National Flood Insurance Program.

The United States Secret Service protects the president and other high-level officials, and investigates counterfeiting and other financial crimes, including financial institution fraud, identity theft, computer fraud, and computer-based attacks on our nation's financial, banking, and telecommunications infrastructure.

Office of the Secretary

The Office of the Secretary oversees activities with other federal, state, local, and private entities as part of a collaborative effort to strengthen borders, provide for intelligence analysis and infrastructure protection, improve the use of science and technology to counter weapons of mass destruction and to create a comprehensive response and recovery system. The Office of the Secretary includes multiple offices that contribute to the overall homeland security mission.

The Privacy Office works to minimize the impact on the individual's privacy, particularly the individual's personal information and dignity, while achieving the mission of the Department of Homeland Security.

The office for Civil Rights and Civil Liberties provides legal and policy advice to department leadership on civil rights and civil liberties issues, investigates and resolves complaints, and provides leadership to Equal Employment Opportunity programs.

The Office of Inspector General is responsible for conducting and supervising audits, investigations, and inspections relating to the programs and operations of the department and recommending ways for the department to carry out its responsibilities in the most effective, efficient, and economical manner possible.

The Citizenship and Immigration Services Ombudsman provides recommendations for resolving individual and employer problems with the U.S. Citizenship and Immigration Services in order to ensure national security and the integrity of the legal immigration system, increase efficiencies in administering citizenship and immigration services, and improve customer service.

The Office of Legislative Affairs serves as primary liaison to members of Congress and their staffs, the White House, and Executive Branch, and to other federal agencies and governmental entities that have roles in assuring national security.

The Office of the General Counsel integrates approximately 1,700 lawyers from throughout the department into an effective, client-oriented, full-service legal team comprising a headquarters office with subsidiary divisions.

The necessity to create a government department that would address protection for the homeland came as a direct result of the attacks on the United States on September 11, 2001. DHS established five key components with five directorates: Border and Transportation Security, Emergency Preparedness and Response, Information Analysis and Infrastructure Protection, Science and Technology, and Management. There are also three mission agencies: Coast Guard, U.S. Citizenship and Immigration Services, and U.S. Secret Service.[16]

FIGURE 1-1 Structure of the U.S. Department of Homeland Security (*Source*: U.S. Department of Homeland Security).

In the years since 9-11 a warning system has been developed to immediately advise the public of the threat status in the United States. Many observers do not find, given the passage of time and the frequency of output of these "advisories," that they actually have any real effect on the public at large.

Summary

Finding a complete, all encompassing, and generally accepted definition for terrorism continues to elude us all; definitions exist, and more will be forthcoming over the years. Terrorism is used daily to describe all manner of atrocities, many related to global events and others totally unconnected to conventional terrorism. This chapter has taken a broad approach to looking at the many and various definitions that are currently favored by government, academia, and the judiciary, and though each of the definitions listed has some descriptive bearing on the word "terror" as we observe it today; definitions will ultimately change with the types of terror events we become exposed to. The world is changing, and the definition for terror will also change. After 9-11, there is a stark realization in the United States that terrorists have successfully targeted the nation and that they continue to threaten, quite possibly, from within the nation itself. In these intervening years, many attempts have been made, which were thwarted by vigilance and intelligence gathering. Homeland Security was developed to protect the homeland; so far it has been successful, whether by luck or not, but as they always say, terrorists have to get lucky only once, but law enforcement has to be lucky all the time. The use of the term "War on Terror" may only have context for the United States in general, and the former Bush administration in particular, but with the passing of time, it is referred to in many countries where terrorism is prevalent. We will see in the next chapter that although al Qaeda and their affiliates persist in having designs on a global jihad, global terrorism has been fought by a large number of nations on a global scale for decades, and in this we will consider the European, Middle East, as well as Central American terrorist organizations. Although this chapter will give the student pause for thought on how best to create a definition for terrorism, it will, we believe, continue to be elusive as the nature of terrorism constantly changes.

Review Questions

1. Discuss the geopolitical conditions that make the task of defining terrorism complicated for the UN General Assembly.
2. Describe from which period of European history the word "terrorism" is derived.
3. Discuss how and why the United Nations has been unable to define terrorism.
4. Discuss hostage taking as a criminal incident as opposed to a terrorist event and what elelments may complicate the determination.
5. Determine the similarities between the U.S. definitions of terrorism and those of the Arab League.

Websites

1. Constitutional Rights Foundation—*http://www.crf-usa.org/terror/What_Is_Terrorism_rev.htm*
2. George Mason University' History News Network—*http://hnn.us/articles/299.html*
3. The Peace Encyclopedia—*http://www.yahoodi.com/peace/terrorism.html*
4. International Assessment and Strategy Center—*http://www.strategycenter.net*
5. The National Academic Press—*http://www.nap.edu/openbook.php?record_id=10301&page=25*

End Notes

1. Cindy C. Combs. *Terrorism in the Twenty-First Century* (Upper Saddle River, NJ: Prentice Hall, 1997).
2. George Rosie. *International Terrorism: A New Mode of Conflict* (Los Angeles: Crescent, 1975, p. 4).
3. The Hague Regulation of 1907 and the Geneva Conventions of 1949.
4. George Rosie. *The Directory of International Terrorism* (New York: Paragon House, 1987).
5. *U.S. Army Field Manual 100-20*, "Combating Terrorism." Stability and Support Operations (Washington, DC: Department of Defense, U.S. Government Printing Office, 1993), Chapter 8.
6. Editors: "FBI Counterterrorism Responsibilities." *FBI Website*, see Internet index (Washington, DC: Department U.S. Government Printing Office, Department of Justice, 1996).
7. *U.S. Army Field Manual.* "Combating Terrorism."
8. Ibid.
9. Jonathan R. White. *Terrorism: An Introduction* (Pacific Grove, CA: Brooks/Cole Publishing, 1991, p. 13).
10. Alex P. Schmidt. *Political Terrorism* (Cincinnati, OH: Transaction Books, Anderson Press, 1983, p. 107).
11. United Nations General Assembly Adopts Global Counterterrorism Strategy (September 8, 2006), www.UN.org.
12. Bruce Hoffman. "Defining Terrorism." *Inside Terrorism* (New York: Columbia University Press, 1998, p. 19).
13. New York Times online. www.nytimes.com/2007/08/31/world/asia/31afghan.html.
14. Cornell University Law School: Legal Information Institute, http://www.law.cornell.edu/uscode/text/18/2331, Retrieved March 2011.
15. An Act: H. R. 3162 in the Senate of the United States of America.
16. Department of Homeland Security. http://www.dhs.gov/index.shtm.

2

A Brief History of Terrorism

The terrible thing about terrorism is that ultimately it destroys those who practice it. Slowly but surely, as they try to extinguish life in others, the light within them dies.

—TERRY WAITE (BRITISH ENVOY KIDNAPPED IN BEIRUT)

LEARNING OBJECTIVES

After studying this chapter, the student should be able to:

1. Describe how terrorism has evolved in its application in the last fifty years.

2. Discuss the multiple viewpoints of historical terrorism.

3. Discuss the effects that suicide terrorism has on Western democracies in particular.

4. Discuss Islamic extremism and why "jihad" is a popular term when discussing terrorism in the twenty-first century.

KEY WORDS TO NOTE

Ayatollah Khomeini—Iranian Grand Ayatollah, leader of the revolution against the Shah of Iran in 1979

Ethnic cleansing—Depopulation or deporting (war crime) often during wartime and associated with genocide (crime against humanity)

Hashish Eater—Origin of the word "assassin" in ancient times

Improvised Explosive Device (IED)—An explosive device or homemade bomb sometimes using military munitions—also referred to as roadside bombs

Muslim Council of Britain—Established in 1997 with membership from more than 250 Muslim organizations in Great Britain and primarily to promote cooperation, consensus, and unity on Muslim affairs in the United Kingdom

Rogue States—Term applied to countries or states deemed as a threat to global security and/or supporters or sponsors of terrorism

Troubles—Generally describes the period of conflict (Catholic vs. Protestant) in Northern Ireland between 1968 and the Belfast Agreement of 1998

State-Sponsored Terrorism—Term to describe governments that support terrorist groups either by ideology or through material support and training

OVERVIEW

The term "terrorism" was coined during the French Revolution and the Jacobean reign of terror. However, that does not mean that individual and group acts—what we might classify as today's terrorism—cannot be traced back to the earliest activities of humankind. This chapter will briefly examine human violence and how it evolved into the label of "terrorism" in the twenty-first century. We shall examine the evolution of human behavior into what we have attempted to define (with considerable difficulty) in Chapter 1. This viewpoint will provide the reader with a different perspective on the behavioral aspects of violence.

VIOLENCE AND TERRORISM

What conditions generate violence? What are the justifications for using violence as a stepping-stone to terrorism? What allows a person or a group to apply violence to a specific situation, complaint, or event and believe it to be a logical, or natural, response? Violence is the application of destructive and harmful power that results in measurable damage caused by a conscious decision by an individual, or individuals, to apply it. Violence in this sense has had broad usage throughout history, demonstrated by the application of great force to achieve specific short-term goals by persons acting alone, or in mobs, or even as part of an organized group of like-minded individuals.

If we think about the paradigm of violence as seen in the fury of a wounded or humiliated animal, we can readily see that violence, or something very much like it, is not even a uniquely *human* behavior. Animals also release their energies in violent and destructive ways. In fact, it is the very similarity of such behavior by brutes that makes violence so distasteful to a rational human mind.[1]

In the earliest social groups, or tribes, violence could be identified, controlled, or quickly dealt with by either individual or group retaliation. Violent people were considered to be behaving like animals and banished to the wilds; they were forced to live as "outlaws," those who chose to operate outside the rules/laws of the group. Probably the earliest examples of what might be called terrorist behaviors were those actions intended to frighten another group into running away or surrendering by threat of violence. Individuals took actions such as painting themselves in bright patterns and colors, brandishing weapons and shouting threats, killing enemies and placing their heads on poles, and perhaps wearing the skins, teeth, and claws of violent animals. The goal was to shock or frighten the "enemy" so badly that it would either run away in fear or finally submit and surrender to the will of its adversaries.

Modern societies are composed of diverse religious, ethnic, and racial groupings that often seem out of context or not in sync with the ruling structures. Use of one-on-one violence as a way to draw attention to an individual (or group) and grievance becomes more difficult. When public officials seem to be inaccessible, a natural temptation for a frustrated constituent is to burst into their office, pound on the desk, or perhaps even wave a weapon or stalk the officials and then attack them verbally or physically at an open-air market or other public place. At the extreme, some may even attempt to seriously injure or even kill. When a bureaucracy refuses to respond to a perceived grievance, it can result in spectacular and destructive behavior. Shooting a politician or destroying public property is not always a rational choice for the aggrieved person's situation. The motivation is often to not just stand there but also "do something" out of anger, frustration, fear, and a deep sense of hopelessness. The self-perceived hapless "victim(s)" begins to see all of society as a monstrous machine, out to get him or her or them! It is against this background that the distraught and frustrated person begins to believe that some kind of a serious "payback" blow must be struck. In today's global societies, there is a definite tendency to consider violence as an attractive, attention-getting solution, as most actions are social in nature. There are very few constructive, autonomous, and well-thought-out actions open to those who are not writers, doctors, or self-employed professionals. The doing of virtually anything worthwhile usually requires cooperation with, and actions of, others. Violence and destruction, however, are among a small number of things that are easily available to a single individual. The aggrieved needs no assistance to shoot at drivers from a freeway overpass or to drive a car into a group of pedestrians. But this "natural" desire to "do something" can often easily be channeled into a "violent" something. The fast-moving pace of modern society may make one feel that it is critical to do something—anything—whether it is bad or good! The catchy phrase is relevant here: "Don't just stand there...do something!" Violence, precisely because it is usually structured as an individual decision, leaves an individual with a feeling of actually having active involvement.

An act of violence can be described as a logical three-step progression:

1. Formation of intent
2. Execution
3. Immediate consequences.

All can take place in microseconds. The feeling that whatever we do is not caused by something of our own design has been verified and replaced by thoughts that are all unique and individually formed in regard to one's own action(s).

Violence perpetrated for ideological reasons, and for a systematically promoted cause or complaint, is significantly different. Organizations in the business of doing such things frequently suffer from too much thinking and discussion and very little action. In the mind of an individual person, being told to do something does not nearly match the satisfaction of an act both conceived and performed by that specific person. Individuals who take violent action on their own, on the other hand, can take satisfaction in the self-empowered nature of their individually conceived act. They then can both claim and accept responsibility for their acts: "I did that, and I'm proud of it." Acts of violence planned and executed by a group, on the other hand, always have to share diluted credit. As a result, the blame or credit is spread so broadly it fails to satisfy anyone.

For example, Lachs presents a thoughtfully surprising positive side of the horrors of war: "Many people report that great danger leads to an exhilaration that renders an experience vibrant. Some say they can never recapture the keen sense of being totally alive that they felt in battle, or even when they merely supported the war effort."[2] The often dull and predictable regularity of most individuals' daily lives seems to validate such claims as just believable and natural. Living in a boring routine, in a cocoonlike, safe society, eventually makes life dull. War makes one begin to contemplate one's death and life—up close and personal—feeling and living the moment with crystal clarity. Something akin to this effect happens in connection with violence. In these outbursts, the adrenaline flows in great quantities, the eyes focus tightly into "tunnel vision," and blood rushes to the brain and other vital organs. Any soldier in combat, or police officer who has been involved in a street shootout, can describe that effect absolutely clearly. This is a drug that is not available on the street or in a pharmacy but, once experienced, can be just as addictive.

WHEN DID VIOLENCE BECOME TERRORISM?

By definition, the assassination of Julius Caesar, in 44 B.C., was an act of terrorism. This holds true as well when a modern political assassination is defined as terrorism.[3] Most modern political scientists generally treat assassination as a terrorist act, whether by an individual acting alone (as John Hinckley did when he shot President Ronald Reagan) or in concert with a group (as with Charles Manson's "groupies" in the attempted shooting of President Ford).

Group terrorism became common in as early as the Middle Ages. In fact, the word "assassin" comes from the Arabic term *hashashin*, which literally means **hashish eater**. It was used to describe a sectarian group of Muslims who were employed by their spiritual and political leader (the local Caliph) to spread terror in the form of murder and destruction among their religious enemies, with the promise of instant acceptance, of being directly transported to paradise, if they were killed themselves.[4] This promise is similar to the incentives claimed for suicide bombers in the Israel-Palestinian ongoing cycle of violence throughout the 1990s and the current suicide bombings that have been occurring with groups and individuals in Iraq and Afghanistan and of course the highjackers of the four civilian aircraft used in the 9-11 attacks. Marco Polo's travel journals included lurid tales of murder committed by these assassins. These early terrorists were motivated not only by promises of eternal reward in the "afterlife" but also by unlimited access to sex, hashish, and other drugs. Even the Crusaders made mention of this group of fanatics and the terror they inspired.[5]

The region from which the original assassins emerged was then known as Persia (the present-day Iran). In recent times, the **Ayatollah Khomeini** became the religious leader of the Shi'ites in Iran during its religious revolution in the late 1970s. It is widely believed and accepted that the young men in the Iran-Iraq War had been told that they would go directly to paradise if they fought bravely and died fighting for Allah. Reports from that war claimed that fifteen- and sixteen-year-olds were walked into the guns of their enemies, the Iraqis, in waves, unarmed and unafraid. Islam, Christianity, Judaism, and Hinduism are not, by doctrine, violent religions; neither are most of the other religions. It is the mixture of religion and politics that has often resulted in violence, frequently against innocent victims, which clearly makes it, according to the definition we suggested in Chapter 1, "terrorism." The Middle East, as the home of three major world religions, has been plagued by a variety of violent sects and religions. The creation of violent sects, and the blending of religion and politics, are similar to the Brotherhood of Assassins, and continue to fan the flames of violence. Religion is a special kind of "narcotic" that can both motivate terrorist actions in its name and deaden consciences to the slaughter inflicted on innocent people.

If terrorist acts were perceived as the proper way to "right the wrongs" committed by government, then the use of political assassins would not always be looked upon with disfavor. Vidal, a leading French legal scholar, has noted that, whereas formerly the political offender was treated as a public enemy, he or she is today considered a friend of the public good—a person of progress, desirous of bettering the political institutions of his country, having laudable intentions, hastening the onward march of humanity. His only fault is that he wishes to go much too fast and then employs, attempting to realize the progress that he desires, irregular, illegal, and violent means.[6]

Not until the middle of the twentieth century was the murder of a head of state, or any member of his family, formally designated as terrorism. Even today, those who commit the "political" crime of murdering a head of state can often enjoy a type of special protection in the form of political asylum.[7]

More than 2,000 years ago, the first known acts of what we now call terrorism were perpetrated by a radical offshoot of the Zealots, a Jewish sect active in Judea during the first century A.D. The Zealots resisted the Roman Empire's rule of what is today Israel through a determined campaign primarily involving assassinations. Most of the violence perpetrated occurred in broad daylight with the intent to inculcate fear into the local as well as the wider community. They acted like our twentieth- and twenty-first century terrorists, sending their open message to the Romans and any of the local population that may have considered siding with the Roman occupation.

We have seen many instances of suicide attacks used by Islamic extremists in the twenty-first century, and this was also evident in early history when an Islamic movement called the Assassins used the same type of tactic. Between the tenth and twelfth centuries, the Assassins waged numerous suicide attacks against the Christian Crusaders who had invaded parts of the area we now refer to as the Middle East. The Assassins embraced the same notions of self-sacrifice and suicidal martyrdom evident in Islamic extremist ideology today. The Assassins, 800 years ago, believed that violence was a divine act that assured their ascendancy to heaven, should they perish during the task.

STATE-SPONSORED AND RELIGIOUS TERRORISM

State terrorism, whether internal (against its own people or dissenters) or external (using or funding outside terrorist groups or individuals), offers a real threat to international stability and security. Internal terrorism can often inspire the formation of resistance movements, which then may resort to revolutionary or terror tactics. This cycle of terror and violence can result in a whirlwind that can suck in all sanity within its reach—innocent or guilty. Exportation of the support for external terror, sponsored by **rogue states**, has resulted in a proliferation of terrorist attacks worldwide. Even nations whose official policy specifically rejects the use of terror have been guilty of providing financial and operational aid, often clandestinely, to those who would promote and perform their terrorism. Early attacks on Jews in what is now Israel were sponsored and supported by religious leaders such as Haj Muhammed Amin Al-Husseini (1893–1974), the Grand Mufti of Jerusalem who dedicated his entire life to forcibly removing Jews from Arab land. After his death in 1974, his dedication to the Arab cause was carried on by his nephew Yasser Arafat.

State-Sponsored Terrorism as Warfare in the Twenty-First Century

There is no global consensus as to a definition of **state-sponsored terrorism**. During the second half of the twentieth century, various countries began to use terrorist organizations to promote state interests in the international domain. In some cases, states have established "puppet" terrorist organizations, whose purpose is to act on behalf of the sponsoring state, to further the interests of the state, and to represent its positions in domestic or regional fronts. The patron state provides its beneficiary terrorist organization with political support, financial assistance, and the sponsorship necessary to maintain and expand its struggle. The patron uses the beneficiary to perpetrate acts of terrorism as a means of spreading its ideology throughout the world or, in some cases, the patron ultimately expects the beneficiary to gain control of a state or impart its ideology to the general public. The following list details countries designated by the United States as sponsors of terrorism. (See Figure 2-1.) Iran, besides sponsoring insurgent acts in Iraq, has ongoing association with and provides support to Hezbollah, Hamas, Palestinian Islamic *Jihad*,

Country	Designation Date
Cuba	March 1, 1982
Iran	January 19, 1984
Sudan	August 12, 1993
Syria	December 29, 1979

Countries determined by the secretary of state to have repeatedly provided support for acts of international terrorism are designated pursuant to three laws: section 6(j) of the Export Administration Act, section 40 of the Arms Export Control Act, and section 620A of the Foreign Assistance Act. Taken together, the four main categories of sanctions resulting from designation under these authorities include restrictions on U.S. foreign assistance; a ban on defense exports and sales; certain controls over exports of dual-use items; and miscellaneous financial and other restrictions.

Designation under the above-referenced authorities also implicates other sanctions laws that penalize persons and countries engaging in certain trade with state sponsors. Currently, there are four countries designated under these authorities: Cuba, Iran, Sudan, and Syria.

FIGURE 2-1   List of State sponsors of terrorism.   *Source*: U.S. Department of State.

and al Qaeda. Hezbollah the Lebanese-based terrorist organization formed in 1982 by Iranian Revolutionary Guards Corps is closely allied to the Syrian Ba'ath Party regime. With Iran and Syrian support, it is accountable for the 1983 suicide bombing of the U.S. Marine Corps barracks in Beirut, the 1982 Israeli embassy bombing in Argentina, the bombing of the Jewish Cultural Center in Buenos Aires, and the 1996 Khober Towers bombing in Saudi Arabia. Hamas, based in the Palestinian territories, also sponsored by Iran, and its terror wing, the Izz al Din al Qassam Brigades, are involved in suicide attacks primarily against Israeli targets. Hamas was formed in 1987 and since 2000 has conducted over 425 attacks, with 377 killed and 2,070 injured. Hamas is also responsible for the 2002 suicide bombing at Natanya, which killed twenty-three people.

State Sponsor: Implications

Designating countries that repeatedly provide support for acts of international terrorism (i.e., placing a country on the terrorism list) imposes four main sets of U.S. Government sanctions:

1. A ban on arms-related exports and sales.
2. Controls over exports of dual-use items, requiring a thirty-day congressional notification for goods or services that could significantly enhance the terrorist-list country's military capability or ability to support terrorism.
3. Prohibitions on economic assistance.
4. Imposition of miscellaneous financial and other restrictions, including

   - Requiring the United States to oppose loans by the World Bank and other international financial institutions;
   - Lifting diplomatic immunity to allow families of terrorist victims to file civil lawsuits in U.S. courts;
   - Denying companies and individuals tax credits for income earned in terrorist-listed countries;
   - Denial of duty-free treatment for goods exported to the United States;

- Authority to prohibit any U.S. citizen from engaging in a financial transaction with a terrorist-list government without a Treasury Department license; and
- Prohibition of Defense Department contracts above $100,000 with companies controlled by terrorist-list states.[8]

State-sponsored terrorism can achieve strategic ends where the use of conventional armed forces is neither practical nor effective. The high costs of modern warfare and concern about nonconventional escalation have turned terrorism into an efficient, convenient, and generally discrete weapon for attaining sponsor state interests in the international realm. Some specific advantages are as follows:

- **Low cost—financially:** Terrorism offers a relatively inexpensive method of making a point for insurgent groups who lack the finances, personnel, or armaments to win against a nation's army on a conventional battlefield. Terrorist tactics also can provide small non-"superpower" nations a low-cost way to wage war, whether overtly or clandestinely, on a hostile state whose resources provide a serious obstacle to waging a full-scale war.
- **Low cost—politically:** For states, particularly those that can successfully provide and hide clandestine support for terrorist groups, the political cost can be quite low as long as such support remains secret. On the other hand, profit in arms sales might become temptingly high.
- **High yields—financially:** States that are arms dealers to terrorists can usually profit quite handsomely, with little or no political, military, or economic impact. Sometimes being caught results in the recall of a couple of ambassadors, but seldom is there any impact on diplomatic or trade relations.
- **High yields—politically:** For dissenters who decide to use terrorism as a political weapon, the political currency can be very large in value. This is especially true when the targeted government's reactions are not supported by citizens in the middle and could lead to a regime being ousted from power. Major concessions can then be "bought" when a successful terrorist incident shocks the populace too much.
- **Low risk—politically and financially:** The costs of financing terrorist operations can be much less than those of maintaining a fully equipped and trained army. And the individuals carrying out these operations are not subjected to as much risk as there would be in conventional warfare. In a successful terrorist operation, the rewards are often very big. For a failed operation, the losses are generally small, unless the failure can be traced back to a state sponsor. The finding of these linkages has become very costly in financial and, more importantly, political terms.[9]

Iran under the leadership of President Mahmoud Ahmadinejad is a prime example of a state sponsor of terrorism. Ahmadinejad joined the Revolutionary Guards in 1986, and there have been reports, denied by Iran, that he was one of the student leaders who held Americans hostage in the U.S. embassy in Tehran. He is virulently anti-Semitic, denies that the Holocaust took place, and wants to see Israel wiped off the face of the earth. His involvement in supporting the insurgency in Iraq is well documented, and much of the weaponry being used and the fighters involved have been both trained and funded by his regime.

In May 2002, Colin Powell, the then U.S. secretary of state, clearly designated the governments that are supporting terrorism. Those named were Cuba, Iran, Iraq, Libya, North Korea, Sudan, and Syria. Since the U.S.-led invasion, Iraq is no longer on that list, and Libya is making moves to be fully accepted back into the "international community." By and large these governments have continued to provide support to international terrorism, either by engaging in terrorist activity themselves or by providing arms, training, safe havens, diplomatic facilities, financial backing, logistics, and/or other support to terrorists. The U.S. policy of bringing maximum pressure to bear on state sponsors of terrorism and encouraging other countries to do likewise has paid dividends. There has been a clear decline in state-sponsored terrorism in recent years. A range of bilateral and multilateral sanctions serves to discourage state sponsors of terrorism from continuing their support for international acts of terrorism, but continued pressure is essential. In January 1991, President George Herbert Bush informed Congress that he was continuing sanctions against Libya as the "Libyan government continues to employ international terrorism and to support it, in violation of international law and international rules of conduct." Currently, Libya has become cooperative with both the United Kingdom and United States in extraditing terrorist suspects, and in 2006 signed a treaty to that effect with the UK government. The United States continues to designate Cuba, Iran, Syria, Sudan, and North Korea as states sponsoring terrorism.

THE TURKS AND THE FIRST CRUSADE

The Turks were not originally from Turkey as most people think—they were a nomadic people from Central Asia, known today as Turkmenistan ("Land of the Turks"). One Turkish tribe, the Seljuks, began moving into the Anatolian peninsula, or the area we now call Turkey. These Turks were Muslims, but a Christian emperor, Michael VIII, controlled the peninsula. The emperor appealed to Pope Urban II to help him rid Anatolia of "unbelievers." The Pope received Michael's call for assistance but decided to use the situation to advance a more ambitious plan. Jerusalem was considered Holy Land to Christians, Jews, and Muslims, but in 1095, Muslims controlled the city. The message from Emperor Michael VIII presented Pope Urban II with an opportunity to justify and wage a "War of the Cross," or Crusade, retake the Holy Lands, and eradicate the unbelievers.

Pope Urban II persuaded the knights of Europe to join in the Crusade, by appealing to their religious convictions. They were told that Muslim Turks were robbing, raping, and killing Christian pilgrims journeying to Jerusalem. The Pope suggested that the knights fight Muslims instead of continuing to fight one another. Crusaders left their homes and families for a long journey into the unknown. While they did not succeed in ridding the Holy Lands of nonbelievers, the Crusaders found other, more worldly benefits:

- An increase in trade with Europe
- Travels to new lands and learning about new and interesting cultures
- Spices that allowed food to last longer and taste better
- Fine cloths manufactured in the Middle East

The Christians had recaptured the Holy Lands by the end of the Second Crusade, but a Muslim general named Saladin launched a jihad (an Islamic holy war) and recaptured Jerusalem. Saladin was neither an Arab nor a Turk—he was Kurdish. The Kurds lived between the Turks and Arabs in the mountainous lands of northern Iraq and eastern Turkey, even as they do to this day. When Saladin recaptured Jerusalem in 1187, the Christians launched a Third Crusade, perhaps the most famous, led by "King Richard the Lion-Hearted" of England. The Christians fought hard in the Third Crusade, but Saladin was able to hold Jerusalem for the Muslims. The two warriors agreed to a truce that left the Muslims controlling the Holy Lands, but with Christians free to visit their shrines. Although many other so-called Holy Wars have taken place over countless centuries, the Crusades are considered to be the eight campaigns into the Holy Lands that occurred from 1095 to 1291 A.D. The following is a listing of those eight major campaigns:

- The First Crusade, 1095–1099
- The Second Crusade, 1147–1149
- The Third Crusade, 1189–1192
- The Fourth Crusade, 1202–1204
- The Fifth Crusade, 1218–1221
- The Sixth Crusade, 1228–1229
- The Seventh Crusade, 1248–1254
- The Last Crusade, 1270–1291

Hundreds of wars and attempts at extermination of certain groups of people have stemmed from religious, ethnic, racial, and tribal differences since the Crusades, and even before—Catholics against Protestants, Jews against Arabs, Sikhs against Hindus, Hindus against Muslims, Tutsis against Hutus, Communists against Democracies, Kosovo against Serbia, Khmer Rouge against Republicans, Shiites against Sunnis. The endless list goes on and on, all with the same religious fervor. The main weapon in these latter-day attempts at **ethnic cleansing** has been terrorism, using the greatest terror of all—genocide. From the inquisition to ethnic cleansing, the resulting terror has created deep splits among religions, tribes, and ideologies throughout the world.

RELIGIOUS TERRORISM   Were the Crusades simply a form of terrorism in the name of religion? One definition of "genocide" is as follows: "A conspiracy aimed at the total destruction of a group and thus requires a concerted plan of action. The instigators and initiators of a genocide are cool-minded theorists first, and barbarians only second. The specificity of genocide does not arise from the extent of the killings, nor their savagery or resulting infamy, but solely from the intention: the destruction of a group."[10]

Terrorist acts in the name of religion have been more frequent in the latter part of the twentieth century. Many groups like to link their grievances to religion when in fact they are in reality concealing a political agenda or motivation. There are many books and reports covering the topic of suicide and terrorism but little empirical research on the people who carry out these attacks and why. After the event takes place, there is in-depth coverage of the individual participant but no real understanding of the motivation. Families often report they had no prior knowledge that their family member was intent on blowing himself or herself to kingdom come in the name of religion! Obviously those recruiting for the suicide mission remain as instructors and would never consider the act for themselves. So the recruiter must target those who may already be susceptible to the idea of suicide. Research being conducted with failed suicide bombers has indicated that the young men in at least half of the cases were already depressed and "defeated" and may have considered suicide even if they had not been recruited to a suicide mission. Prior to the 1980s, there are no recorded cases of Islamic suicide bombers, and the first is most likely the truck bomb attack on the U.S. Marine Base in Beirut in 1983. In nearly all cases, the suicide bomber has no criminal record and is therefore difficult at best to track—but in general they do not act alone and require a network to train them acquire materials and target selection. Of the more that 3,000 suicide bombers of the last thirty years, only four are believed to have been unaided. If we study the most recent attacks in UK and Sweden and failed attempts in the United States, we see that those individuals were most likely lacking self-esteem, were inhibited loners but keen to please, and invariably did not belong to any terrorism group or organization until they were recruited for the act or suicide mission. Suicide terrorism or martyrdom is efficient, inexpensive, easily organized, and extremely difficult to counter, delivering maximum damage for little cost. The shocking nature of a suicide attack also attracts public attention. Glorifying the culture of martyrdom benefits the terrorist organization and inspires more people to join the group or even consider independent action.

ISLAM

Twenty-first-century terrorism centers on fanatical elements preaching a firebrand and extreme version of Islam. Considered one of the oldest of religions, it refers to the doctrines of the Prophet Mohammed dating back to the sixth century. Mohammed was born in Mecca and is revered as God's representative, and in Islam, God is referred to as Allah. Muslim adherents can be found in vast numbers throughout the globe and number around one-fifth of the global population. At the dawn of the tenth century, Islam and the Caliphs held control over a vast section of the globe, stretching from India in the east to Spain in the west. Jerusalem was considered the Holiest of places not just by Christians but also by Muslims and Jews, and this brings us to the Crusades. During the Middle Ages, religion was at the forefront when it came to territorial conquest, and the kings of European countries, including France and England, mounted a series of campaigns, in fact, a total of eight between 1096 and 1270—the aim being not only the conquest of rich lands but also to establish their religious claim to Jerusalem. Control of Jerusalem changed numerous times during the Crusades. Islam itself has been consumed with internal battles over the centuries on the rightful succession of Caliphs (rulers). A split within the religion created two separate groups of adherents within the Muslim faith, Shia and Sunni; the Sunni Muslims have the larger following and dominate countries of the Middle East. Osama bin Laden's al Qaeda adherents are followers of the Sunni version of Islam who believe in and follow the teachings of the Prophet Mohammed. The Shiite sect believes that the rightful Prophet of Islam is Ali, a cousin of Mohammed. The Middle East conflict is currently drawn along religious lines in Iraq and Iran; both countries have Shia Muslims as the dominant sect within their respective nations. The former president of Iraq, Saddam Hussein, held power with a Sunni minority government and inflicted his awesome power not just against the Kurds but also against any and all Shia opponents of his totalitarian regime for over a quarter of a century. Since the attacks against the United States on 9-11, the Madrid trains bombings in Spain, the London tube train and bus bombings of 2005, and the global wave of Islamic violence some months after a Danish newspaper Jyllands-Posten produced cartoons linking the Prophet Mohammed to violent acts, many in both the media and general discussion have linked Islam with extreme violence and fanaticism. Politicians have even referred to Islamist fascism as having declared war on the West.

Islamism

Islamism is an ideology that demands an individual's complete adherence to the sacred law of Islam and rejects as much as possible outside influence. It is imbued with a deep antagonism toward non-Muslims and has a particular hostility toward the West. It amounts to an effort to turn Islam, a religion and civilization, into an ideology.

Islamism is yet another twentieth-century radical utopian scheme. Like Marxism-Leninism or fascism, it offers a way to control the state, run society, and remake the human being. It is an Islamic-flavored version of totalitarianism. Islamism is also a total transformation of traditional Islam. Islamism is not a medieval program but one that responds to the stress and strains of the twentieth century.

Islamism is a huge change from traditional Islam. One illustration: Whereas traditional Islam's sacred law is a personal law, a law a Muslim must follow wherever he is; Islamism tries to apply a Western-style geographic law that depends on where one lives. Take the case of Sudan, where traditionally a Christian was perfectly entitled to drink alcohol, for he is a Christian, and Islamic law applies only to Muslims. But the current regime has banned alcohol for every Sudanese. It assumes Islamic law is territorial, because that is the way a Western society is run.

Islamism has few connections to wealth or poverty; it is not a response to deprivation. There is no discernible connection between income and Islamism. The ideology appeals primarily to modern people; I am always fascinated to note how many Islamist leaders (e.g., in Turkey and Jordan) are engineers.

Islamism is a powerful force. It runs governments in Iran, Sudan, and under the Taliban, Afghanistan. It is an important force of opposition in Algeria, Egypt, Turkey, Lebanon, and the Palestinian authority. Islamists are also present in the United States and, to a stunning extent, dominate the discourse of American Islam.

The Islamists' success in Iran, Sudan, and Afghanistan show that were they to come to power elsewhere, they would create enormous problems for the people they rule, for the region, and for the United States. Their reaching power would lead to economic contraction, the oppression of women, terrible human rights abuses, the proliferation of arms, terrorism, and the spread of a viciously anti-American ideology. These are, in short, rogue states, dangerous first to their own people and then to the outside world.[11]

JIHAD

"Jihad" is a term that the West has come to know and fear. It dates back to the Middle Ages. In the linguistic sense, the Arabic word "jihad" means struggling or striving and applies to any effort exerted by anyone. In this sense, a student struggles and strives to get an education and pass course work; an employee strives to fulfill his or her job and maintain good relations with his or her employer; a politician strives to maintain or increase his or her popularity with his or her constituents and, so on. The terms "strive" and "struggle" may be used for/by Muslims as well as non-Muslims; for example, Allah, the One and Only True God, says in the Qur'an:

> We have enjoined on people kindness to parents; but if they strive (Jahadaka) to make you ascribe partners with Me that of which you have no knowledge, then obey them not ...
>
> (The Holy Quran, 29:8; also see 31:15)

In the above verse of the Qur'an, it is non-Muslim parents who strive (*jahadaka*) to convert their Muslim child back to their religion. In the West, jihad is generally translated as "holy war," a usage the media have popularized. According to Islamic teachings, it is unholy to instigate or start war; however, some wars are inevitable and justifiable.

If we translate the words "holy war" back into Arabic, we find *harbun muqaddasatu*, or for "the holy war," *al-harbu al-muqaddasatu*. We challenge any researcher or scholar to find the meaning of jihad as holy war in the Qur'an or authentic Hadith collections or in early Islamic literature. Unfortunately, some Muslim writers and translators of the Qur'an, the Hadith, and other Islamic literature translate the term "jihad" as "holy war" because of the influence of centuries-old Western propaganda.

This could be a reflection of the Christian use of the term "Holy War" to refer to the Crusades of a thousand years ago. However, the Arabic words for "war" are *harb* or *qital*, which are found in the Qur'an and Hadith.

For Muslims, the term "Jihad" is applied to all forms of striving and has developed some special meanings over time. In its defense of Islam, Allah declares in the Qur'an:

> To those against whom war is made, permission is given (to defend themselves), because they are wronged—and verily, Allah is Most Powerful to give them victory—(they are) those who have been expelled from their homes in defiance of right—(for no cause) except that they say, 'Our Lord is Allah'...
>
> (THE HOLY QURAN, 22:39–40)

> Fight in the cause of Allah against those who fight against you, but do not transgress limits. Lo! Allah loves not aggressors.... And fight them until persecution is no more, and religion is for Allah. But if they desist, then let there be no hostility except against transgressors.
>
> (THE HOLY QURAN, 2:190, 193)[12]

In trying to understand the modern-day applications of jihad, the following from the Ontario Consultants on Religious Tolerance is perhaps easier to comprehend:

A small percentage of Muslims who are from the extreme, radical, and violent wing of Islamic Fundamentalism, and who are "passionate, [deeply] religious and anti-Western"[13] might dwell on passages or verses dealing with conflict, war, and resistance to oppression. Many conclude that the Qur'an expects them to engage in acts of terrorism, assassinations, suicide bombings, armed aggression against persons of other religions, oppression of women, executing innocent persons, and so on.

Those Muslim fundamentalists who are not extreme, violent, and radical, and those Muslims from mainline or liberal wings of the religion, might concentrate on passages and themes of spirituality, justice, personal struggle, peace, freedom, and so on.

They are consulting the same book with a different emphasis and achieve very different results. We see the same split among Christians as they study Islam and the Qur'an.

Some emphasize the earlier passages in the Qur'an, which stress on cooperation with the Jews and Christians—the *People of the Book*. They tend to interpret Jihad in terms of personal struggle toward purity.

Others emphasize later passages of the Qur'an, which were received during a time of conflict. They tend to interpret Jihad as holy war.

They come to opposite conclusions about whether Islam is a religion of peace or war.[14] Jihad came to us in the twenty-first century from Osama bin Laden, who claimed that God not men make laws, understanding and interpreting God's laws is the role of religious scholars, while not believing in legislators, all law is eternal. He had no possible need of legislators. His view was that Sharia law is absolute, and this vision underpinned his hatred of secular regimes in the Muslim world, whether democratic or dictatorial. He at best took a cynical view of the United Nations, or any world body that would support not only the presence but the original creation of Israel in 1947 on Palestinian territory. Bin Laden's position maintained that when Islam is threatened, the correct course taken is to struggle in its defence and it is the duty of Muslims everywhere to defend Islam; this struggle is termed "Jihad."

In February 1998, bin Laden, together with Muslim fundamentalists from Pakistan, Bangladesh, and Egypt, declared jihad on the United States, benefactor of Israel and of the tyrants who rule the Islamic birthplace in Saudi Arabia. The four fundamentalists pronounced the following:

> To kill the Americans and their allies—civilians and military—is an individual duty incumbent upon every Muslim in all countries, in order to liberate the al-Aqsa Mosque and the Holy Mosque from their grip, so that their armies leave all the territory of Islam, defeated, broken and unable to threaten any Muslim. This is in accordance with the words of God Almighty: 'Fight the idolaters at any time, if they first fight you.

Since September 11, 2001, the global jihad and, probably in more particular terms, the war against the United States, can be easily witnessed in the hatred we see in the media. The media is a strong communicator, particularly in the Middle East, with a diet of hate being spewed forth by religious leaders calling for death to Americans, Jews, Israelis, and Britons. Not only is the insidious nature of their broadcasts abhorrent, but they are also educating their children on a diet of jihad to become suicide bombers and murderers.

Following the attacks in London in July 2005, there was considerable revulsion at the fact that young British Muslims were responsible for the attacks. The original thought was that these were marginalized youth who had some axe to grind, but the truth here is that all came from good backgrounds and were well educated and part of mainstream society. However, the Muslim Councils in Great Britain, far from denouncing the perpetrators, claimed that it was the Muslim community that was under attack and that the young men were not Muslims. This was a claim voiced by Mohammed Naseem, chairman of the Birmingham Center Mosque. Blaming the attacks squarely on Tony Blair (former Labor Party prime minister) for his government's support of the U.S.-led war in Iraq, Dr. Azzam Tammimmi from the Muslim Association of Britain stated in the *London Evening Standard*: "and God knows what will happen afterwards, our lives are in real danger and it would seem, so long as we are in Iraq and so long as we are contributing to injustices around the world, we will continue to be in real danger. Tony Blair has to come out of his state of denial and listen to what the experts have been saying that our involvement in Iraq is stupid." Among those experts would have to be included the leader of the **Muslim Council of Britain**, Sir Iqbal Sacranie, who has labeled Israel a "Nazi state" responsible for the "ethnic cleansing" of Palestine.[15]

The defensive nature of Islam's religious leaders became more evident when Sir Iqbal's comments during a televised BBC Panorama program in August 2005 colorfully compared suicide bombers from Hamas with Mahatma Gandhi and Nelson Mandela. He went on to state that those fighting oppression and occupation were in fact freedom fighters, not terrorists. He referred to Sheikh Yassin, the former leader of Hamas, as a "renowned Islamic scholar."

JIHADIZATION

This is the phase in which the group members accept their individual duty to participate in jihad and self-designate themselves as holy warriors, or *mujahedeen*. Ultimately, the group will begin operational planning for a terrorist attack. These activities include planning, reconnaissance, preparation, and execution. While the previous phases can take months or even years to reach "Jihadization," this final phase can be a very rapid process taking only a few months or weeks to run its course.[16]

The far-reaching inspiration of Osama bin Laden and his al Qaeda terrorist organization has resulted in attempts by self-styled jihadists to attack U.S. targets (see Figure 2-2 for Global

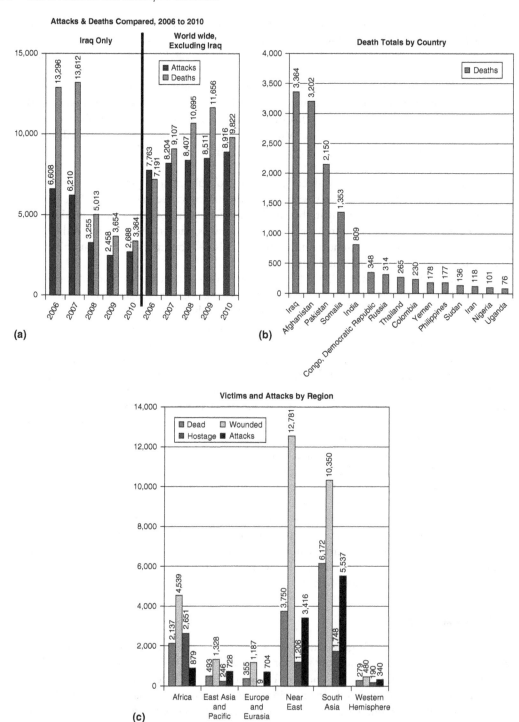

FIGURE 2-2   Terrorist incidents worldwide (*2010 Report on Terrorism. Office of the Director of National Intelligence, National Counter Terrorism Center, Washington, DC, April 30, 2011*).

Terrorist attacks and comparisons by year). One such attack that was disrupted by the FBI in early 2007 was that of a group of Islamists who planned to attack the Fort Dix Army camp. Six men began practicing with semiautomatic weapons in rural Pennsylvania, and in January 2006, a video tape of their activities that they had taken to a local store to have it transferred into a DVD format raised the clerk's suspicion, who contacted the FBI. During the ensuing investigation, the FBI successfully infiltrated the group. All the members of the group held down normal jobs throughout the planning phases. The six conspirators, four ethnic Albanians from the former Yugoslavia, a Turkish immigrant, and a U.S. citizen from Jordan, planned to buy M16's AK-47s as well as rocket-propelled grenades and mount an attack on the New Jersey Army Base at Fort Dix and kill as many service personnel as they could. The far-reaching tenets of Osama bin Laden's jihadist ideology come from the belief that

- This is a clash of civilizations. Militant jihad is a religious duty before God. The clash is necessary for the salvation of one's soul and to defend the Muslim nation.
- Only two camps exist, and there can be no middle ground in an apocalyptic showdown with both the West and the Muslims that do not agree with al Qaeda's vision of "true Islam."
- Violence is the only solution, peace is an illusion.
- Many of the theological and legal restrictions on the use of violence by Muslims do not apply to this war.
- The United States' power is based on its economy and, thus, large-scale mass-casualty attacks, especially focused on the United States and Western economic targets, are a major goal.
- Muslim governments that are religiously unacceptable and cooperate with the West must be violently overthrown.[17] The U.S. government has been steadfast on its position relative to enemy combatants that now reside at Guantanamo Bay. The United States has also adopted tactics that have been broadly criticized by such groups as Amnesty International for its actions.

THE MEDIA AND TERRORISM

Prior to 9-11, the media in North America would not be concentrating that much on terrorism as a daily topic, but since that date, terrorism has become the number one topic for every news media outlet. Although we could consider the 9-11 attack as a single and one-off event, the speculation about what will come next consume the media. Although the number of terrorist attacks is at their lowest for twenty years, media reporting on terrorism is at its most sustained. Everything that has the possibility of being terrorist related now gets ample and even excessive media coverage. The media is sometimes at fault for glamorizing a terrorist event, and one such event is the hijacking of an Israeli airliner over Europe in 1970 by a Palestinian group led by a vivaciously portrayed Leila Khaled. The media created an impression the she was an adventurer to be admired, while at the same time ignoring her criminal acts. Scant coverage was provided to the Israeli security officer who shot and killed her colleague. Terrorists need publicity if they are to inspire fear and respect, and secure favorable understanding of their cause, if not their act of itself. The first airliner attack on the World Trade Center was not caught on news media film, but the second airliner hitting the Twin Towers most certainly was—whether the terrorists intended this or not, the coverage they received and the fear, panic, and attention they got has created a frenzy of news coverage ever since. Margaret Thatcher's metaphor that publicity is the oxygen of terrorism underlines the point that public perception is a major terrorist target, and the media are central in shaping and moving it. For terrorism, the role of the media is critical.[18]

Terrorists' Needs and the Media

- Terrorists are not in the market to go out and buy media space; so publicity, free publicity that a group can generate is a definite asset. From the terrorist perspective, an unedited interview with Osama bin Laden by CNN in May 1997 was an enormous coup for al Qaeda. For news networks, access to a terrorist will always be a coup and a hot story and is treated as such.
- The sympathetic ear of the media and a modicum of editorial spin may turn a media event to the terrorists' advantage. One may not agree with terrorist acts, but this does not preclude being sympathetic to their plight and cause. Terrorists believe that the public needs to be educated and that their cause is just and terrorist violence is the only course of action available to them.
- Terrorist organizations may also seek to court or place sympathetic personnel in press positions—particularly in wire services. The Al-Jazeera news network in the Middle East continues to be a particular favorite news wire service of terrorists as its avenue to disseminate information.
- Legitimacy. Terrorist causes want the press to give legitimacy to what is often portrayed as ideological or personality feuds, or divisions between armed groups and political wings. For the military tactician, war is the continuation of politics by other means; for the sophisticated terrorist, politics is the continuation of terror by other means. IRA and Hamas are examples of groups having "political" and "military" components. Musa Abu Marzuq, for example, who was in charge of the political wing of Hamas, is believed to have approved specific bombings and assassinations.[19] Likewise, the "dual hat" relationship of Gerry Adams of Sinn Féin—the political wing of the IRA—to other IRA activities is subject to speculation. Distinctions are often designed to help people join the ranks or financially contribute to the terrorist organization.

They also need the press to provide a level of legitimacy to the findings and viewpoints of specially created nongovernmental organizations (NGOs) and study centers that may serve as covers for terrorist fund-raising, recruitment, and travel by terrorists into the target country. The World and Islam Studies Enterprise funded and controlled by the Palestinian Islamic Jihad is but one known example.[20] In hostage situations, terrorists need to have details on identity, number, and value of hostages, as well as details about pending rescue attempts and details on the public exposure of their operation. Particularly where state sponsors are involved, they want details about any plans for military retaliation.

- Terrorist organizations seek media coverage that causes damage to their enemy. This is particularly noticeable when the perpetrators of the act and the rationale for their act remain unclear. Terrorists need the media to spread and magnify the panic and fear on their behalf, to facilitate economic loss (like scaring away investment and tourism); one example of this comprised the threats proclaiming that a summer bombing campaign of tourist locations along the Spanish coast by ETA would take place. The local populous and the visiting populations would then lose faith in their governments' ability to protect them, and to trigger government and popular overreaction to specific incidents and the overall threat of terrorism.

Internet use to spread the message of Jihad is not particularly new and has been available since the mid-1990s to globally reach and radicalize impressionable minds. Internet accessible magazines such as *Inspire* are produced by al-Malahim Media, the branch of al-Qaeda in the Arabian Peninsula in July 2010. The U.S. government believes that *Inspire*, which is in English, was produced by a Saudi-born U.S. citizen, Samir Khan, who left the United States for Yemen in 2009. Khan has a history of producing Jihadist publications so it seems likely that he is involved in this venture. The magazine editor also clearly states that *Inspire* is an effort by al-Malahim Media to reach out to, radicalize, and train the millions of English-speaking Muslims in the West, Africa, South Asia, and Southeast Asia. *Inspire* follows the trend of AQAP publications and leaders in praising Fort Hood shooter Maj. Nidal Hasan and failed Christmas Day bomber Umar Farouk Abdulmutallab and lifting them up as examples for all jihadists to follow. "We call on every Muslim who feels any jealousy for their religious beliefs to expel the polytheists from the Arabian Peninsula, by killing all of the crusaders working in embassies or otherwise, and to declare war against the crusaders in the land of the Prophet Muhammad—peace be upon him—on the ground, sea and air."

In addition to the recycled content from al Qaeda's core leadership, *Inspire* also contains interesting content from AQAP's military and theological leaders. An interview with AQAP leader Nasir al-Wahayshi provided al-Wahayshi the opportunity to reinforce several points he has been making for months now regarding his call for jihadists to conduct simple attacks using readily available weapons. "My advice to my Muslim brothers in the West is to acquire weapons and learn methods of war. They are living in a place where they can cause great harm to the enemy and where they can support the Messenger of Allah." Al-Wahayshi continued "…a man with his knife, a man with his gun, a man with his rifle, a man with his bomb, by learning how to design explosive devices, by burning down forests and buildings, or by running over them with your cars and trucks. The means of harming them are many so seek assistance from Allah and do not be weak and you will find a way."

What Government Leaders Want from the Media

Governments seek understanding, cooperation, restraint, and loyalty from the media in efforts to limit terrorist harm to society. In the West, where there is freedom of the press to a great extent, governments need cooperation from the press to push their agenda in efforts to punish or apprehend those responsible for terrorist acts, specifically the following:[21]

- Both governments and terrorists want to advance their agendas but, of course, from completely different perspectives. From their perspective, the media should support government courses of action when operations are under way and disseminate government-provided information when requested. This includes understanding of policy objectives, or at least a balanced presentation (e.g., why governments may seek to mediate, yet not give in to terrorist demands).
- An important goal is to separate the terrorist from the media to deny the terrorist a platform, unless doing so is likely to contribute to his or her imminent defeat.[22]
- Another goal is to have the media present terrorists as criminals and avoid glamorizing them; to foster the viewpoint that kidnapping a prominent person, blowing up a building, or hijacking an airplane is a criminal act regardless of the terrorists' cause.
- In hostage situations, governments often prefer to exclude the media and others from the immediate area, but they want the news organizations to provide information to authorities when reporters have access to the hostage site.
- They seek publicity to help diffuse the tension of a situation, not contribute to it. Keeping the public reasonably calm is an important policy objective.

- It is generally advantageous if the media, especially television, avoids "weeping mother" emotional stories on relatives of victims; as such coverage builds public pressure on governments to make concessions.
- During incidents, they wish to control terrorist access to outside data to restrict information on hostages that may result in their selection for harm; government strongly desires the media not to reveal planned or current antiterrorist actions or provide the terrorists with data that help them.
- After incidents, they want the media not to reveal government secrets or detail techniques on how successful operations were performed and not to publicize successful or thwarted terrorist technological achievements and operational methods so that copycat terrorists do not emulate or adapt them.[23]
- They want the media to be careful about disinformation from terrorist allies, sympathizers, or others who gain from its broadcast and publication. Many groups have many motives for disseminating inaccurate or false data, including, for example, speculation as to how a plane may have been blown up or who may be responsible.
- They want the media to boost the image of government agencies. Agencies may carefully control leaks to the press, giving scoops to newsmen who depict the agency favorably and avoid criticism of its actions.
- They would like journalists to inform them when presented with well-grounded reasons to believe a terrorist act may be in the making or that particular individuals may be involved in terrorist activity.
- In extreme cases, where circumstances permit, vital national security interests may be at stake, and chances of success high, they may seek cooperation of the media in disseminating a ruse that would contribute to neutralizing the immediate threat posed by terrorists. In common criminal investigations involving heinous crimes, such media cooperation is not uncommon, when media members may hold back on publication of evidence found at a crime scene, or assist law enforcement officials by publishing misleading information or a non-promising lead to assist authorities in apprehending a suspect by, for example, lulling him or her into a false sense of security.

Evolving technology has played an immense role in allowing terrorists to publicize and expand their reach into any home that has access to the Internet; with programs such as You Tube and live video streaming, terrorists have successfully been able to disseminate whatever acts they want shown. From Iraq we have had examples of beheadings of kidnapped Westerners, roadside detonations of **Improvised Explosive Devices (IEDs)**, items of news that mainstream media would not normally show in television news reports. This ability on the part of the terrorist groups has allowed media, more particularly in the Middle East, to inspire attacks against the West. Although the media has a duty to report responsibly and track down the next biggest news scoop, the reporters themselves have become targets for terrorists in the modern era; the case of Daniel Pearl from the Wall Street Journal in 2002 is a case in point. Many, if not all, journalists view getting to the story a primary objective over their own personal safety. Pearl, aged thirty eight, the *Wall Street Journal*'s South Asia bureau chief, was taken hostage in Pakistan in January 2002. At the time, he was attempting to track down and interview the leader of Jamaat al-Fuqra; after meeting a go-between at a Karachi restaurant, he was taken to a house, where two weeks later his execution was videotaped and broadcast for the world to see. Al Qaeda's Number 3 man, Khaled Sheikh Mohammed, claimed responsibility for Pearl's death. With their ability to manipulate their audience through the medium of the Internet, is there necessity to set any specific code of conduct on mainstream news coverage while attempting to preserve the independence of the media's role? This is a hotly debated topic, and although there may be voluntary guidelines, there are four other policy decisions that may help preserve that independence and overcome some objections to their treatment of terrorism:

1. To consider matters relating to the timing of news. Temporary withholding of news may be legitimate in some instances such as a kidnapping.
2. To make deliberate attempts to balance coverage (an extremely difficult goal to attain) may counteract some of the negative effects of terrorism.
3. To acknowledge that news tailoring is a fact of everyday news production and focus on reporting that might be expected to lessen tensions and aid the negotiating process.
4. To accept that the media have an important role to play in public education and, at times other than during terrorist incidents, to feature items regarding the ethics of using violence for political ends, the legitimate needs of law enforcement in a democratic society, the nonromantic side of terrorism, and the existence of avenues of dissent. Part of this role must also encompass a vigorous determination to investigate and report on the injustices and inequalities in society that, if left to fester, may be the cause of acts of terrorism.[24]

STATE TERROR AND GENOCIDE

State-approved use of power and resources to terrorize and attempt to liquidate a specific group of citizens, immigrants, and religious or ethnic groups has created some ambivalence about what to label as a proper designator. Raphael Lemkin, in his 1944 book, *Axis Rule in Occupied Europe*, coined the word "genocide." He constructed this term from the Greek word *genos* (race or tribe) and the Latin suffix *cide* (to kill). At the end of World War II, the War Crimes Tribunal in Nuremberg was at a loss as to what this crime should be called. History was of little use in finding a proper word to fit the nature of the crimes that Nazi Germany had engaged in at its extermination and concentration camps. "Ethnic cleansing" has been used in recent years to soften the term for eradication of specific groups of people. But hard or soft, the word "genocide" better describes "the destruction of a nation or an ethnic group." It implies the existence of a coordinated plan, aimed at total extermination, to be put into effect against individuals selected as victims purely, simply, and exclusively because they are members of some target group.[25]

"Mass murder," the term that was often used at the time, is an inadequate description of the atrocities committed in Nazi-occupied territories. It could not account for the motives, which arose solely from "racial, national, homosexual, gypsy, or religious" considerations, not the conduct of the war. Genocide required a separate definition, as it was clearly not just against the rules of war, but also a crime against humanity. Raphael Lemkin was the first person to put forward the theory that genocide is not a war crime and that the immorality of genocide should not be confused with the amorality of war.[26]

Terrorist acts have too often created a vicious "cycle of violence," with those against whom the terror violence is first carried out becoming so angered that they themselves resort to terrorism in response. This is clear in the present situation in the Israel-Palestine disputes in the Middle East and the Northern Ireland **troubles**, which have resulted in the deaths of thousands of innocent people by countering "their" violence with "our" violence in an endless cycle of "tit-for-tat" attacks. Each violent action calls for an equal or greater violent reaction—*ad infinitum*. When the violence is nonselective, and innocent people are killed by car bombs and purely random acts of violence, the reaction of the victims is likely to "break all the rules" in their selection of targets and become terrorist violence itself. "Round and round it goes and where it stops nobody knows" becomes the theme song of terrorism. In the same way as in a case of homicide, the natural right of the individual to exist is implied, so in the case of genocide as a crime, the principle that any national, racial, or religious group has an equal right to exist is then clearly evident. Attempts to eliminate such groups violate this right to exist and to develop within the international human community. Lemkin's efforts and his single-minded perseverance brought about the Convention for the Prevention and the Punishment of the Crime of Genocide, which was voted into existence by the Convention of the General Assembly of the United Nations in 1948. After stating in Article I that genocide is a crime under International Law, the convention laid down the following definition:

Any of the following acts committed with intent to destroy, in whole or in part, a national, ethnical, racial, or religious group, as such:

- Killing members of the group;
- Causing serious bodily or mental harm to members of the group;
- Deliberately inflicting on the group conditions of life calculated to bring about its physical destruction in whole or in part;
- Imposing measures intended to prevent births within the group;
- Forcibly transferring children of the group to another group;
- A criminal act…with the intention of destroying…an ethnic, national, or religious group… targeted as such.[27]

The controversial thousand-plane carpet bombings that took place over Germany; incendiary and nuclear bombs over Japan during World War II; and, in more recent times, Napalm and Agent Orange over Vietnam; the poison gas attacks on the Kurds in Iraq; and the killing of over 500,000 Tutsis by the Hutus in Rwanda, all claimed their victims in a totally haphazard manner. Intrinsic meaning is lost when words like "genocide" or "holocaust" are used loosely to describe any human disaster with a large number of victims, regardless of the cause. It would be hard to deny that some form of evil has always existed in the world. But if such evil is seen in general, impersonal terms such as "barbarism," human's inhumanity to human, chance circumstance, or plain hatred, then there are no individual culprits toward whom an accusing finger can be pointed. So-called collective blame is just another way of denying the facts.

CYCLICAL NATURE OF TERRORISM

Perhaps the most prominent proponents of individual and collective violence as a means of destroying governments and social institutions were the Russian anarchists. These were revolutionaries within Russia who sought an end to the Czarist state of the late nineteenth century. "Force only yields to force," and terror would provide the mechanism of change, according to the Russian radical theorist Alexander Serno-Solovevich.[28]

In the writings of two of the most prominent spokesmen for revolutionary anarchism, Mikhail Bakunin and Sergei Nechaev, one finds philosophies often echoed by modern terrorists. Bakunin, for example, advocated in his *National Catechism* (1866) the use of "selective, discriminate terror." Nechaev, in his work *Revolutionary Catechism*, went further in advocating both the theory and practice of pervasive terror violence. He asserted of the revolutionary: "Day and night he must have one single thought, one single purpose: merciless destruction. With this aim in view, tirelessly and in cold blood, he must always be prepared to kill with his own hands anyone who stands in the way of achieving his goals."[29]

This is surely a very large step in the evolution of a terrorist from the use of a lone political assassin in earlier centuries. Even the religious fanatics of the Assassins were arguably less willing to kill "anyone" to achieve a political objective. But this difference may well have existed more on paper than it did in practice. In spite of this written willingness to "kill anyone" who stood in the way, even the Socialist Revolutionary Party resorted primarily to selective terror violence and took special pains to avoid endangering innocent bystanders. The Union of Russian Men, which formed to combat the growing revolutionary movement "by all means," was not only sanctioned by the Tsar but also granted special protection by him. This reactionary group engaged in a variety of terrorist activities, including, but not limited to, political murders, torture, and bombing. The Okrana (the Czarist secret police) used vicious counterterror against the militant revolutionaries in an unabated attack until World War I began. John Thompson, commenting on the rising tide of "terrorism" in Russia during the last half of the nineteenth century, explained the relationship of state and revolutionary terrorism in this way: "Wrong a man…deny him all redress, exile him if he complains, gag him if he cries out, strike him in the face if he struggles, and at the last he will stab and throw bombs."[30]

During the struggle to gain a homeland free of Nazi terror, the Jewish Irgun had also committed terrorist acts against the indigenous population. Israel finally declared itself to be an independent state in 1948. Then, some of the dispossessed people within its borders and those who fled to surrounding states began a terrorism campaign against the new nation of Israel, whose terror violence against the Palestinian people sparked a conflict, which today continues to rend the fragile fabric of peace in the Middle East. Born in bloodshed, violence, and desperation, Israel continues to struggle against the terrorist violence that its very creation evoked.[31]

CONTEMPORARY EVENTS: HISTORICAL ROOTS

If contemporary terrorism is somehow different from historical terrorism, how is it different? One reason for briefly reviewing the historical pattern and roots of terrorism is to be able to discover whether that pattern still remains accurate in the contemporary world. If terrorism today is just like the terrorism of previous centuries, but with better weapons, then we can use historical patterns to more accurately predict behavior. Then we can construct responses based on successful attempts that were used to combat this phenomenon in the past. If terrorism today is actually different, however, historical patterns are less useful in designing responses, although such patterns may still be of use in understanding the dynamics of such a phenomenon. Terrorism has clearly existed for centuries. What we need to know, as we move ahead in the twenty-first century, is whether these new forms of terrorism are actually that much different from their historical counterparts.

Related to the differences between historical and modern terrorism are important developments in the contemporary world. Modern methods of travel, for example, make it possible to carry out an assassination in the morning in country "X" and be halfway around the world from that nation within a matter of hours. Modern communications, too, have created a "smaller world." Events in places like Nigeria, Cape Town, or Sri Lanka, for instance, are immediately transmitted in a dozen ways around the world. Such rapid communications, too, have served to expand the theater and enlarge the audience to which the terrorist plays out the drama of death and violence. To catch the attention of America, the Third World terrorists need not hijack airliners, fly to New York City and Washington DC, and crash them into the World Trade Center Towers and the Pentagon.

The dramatic increase in the arsenal of weapons available to modern terrorists is also worthy of consideration. The would-be assassin need not rely on a rifle or a handgun to eliminate his victim. A letter bomb, an envelope containing anthrax, or explosives can do the job without endangering the perpetrator, as the Unabomber in the United States has demonstrated. The potential for destruction through chemical and biological weapons has not yet been fully field-tested either (see Chapter 14), although the Sarin toxin attacks in subways in Japan in 1995 gave ample evidence of the potential for such biochemical weapons when used on the vulnerable mass transit system of a modern city. Perhaps, until recently, the consequences of using such weapons were too dramatic for most groups to contemplate. But modern technology has certainly put at the terrorist's disposal a vast array of lethal and largely indiscriminate weapons, of which the Sarin toxin apparently used in Japan represents only a very simple example. With this arsenal, the selection of victims has become devastatingly indiscriminate.

We hope the student can now see that, as historical precedents for terrorism grow, it becomes very hard to distinguish between legitimate and illegitimate violence. As nations born out of a climate of violence, such as Ireland and Israel, become themselves illegitimate, it is increasingly difficult to condemn the terrorist for using such methods, also employed in the struggles for independence and survival. The longer the history of terrorism, the harder it is to make the label of "terrorism" stick to the actions of any group or nation.

Summary

If violence begets terrorism, then terrorism must be as old as society and must have begun with the first peoples of the earth. This chapter was not especially long. It was deliberately written that way to tweak the curiosity of the reader/student and, hopefully, make them want to learn more. Understanding terrorism without learning something about the history of a terrorist group, individual terrorists, and the conditions that spawned them is much like eating soup without salt. It feeds the body but is pretty bland and tasteless. Following chapters will involve places, cultures, and issues that have strange names and exotic locations, as well as many well-known names and places that have been touched by terrorism. Some will be covered in more depth than others. All of them will reveal something about the social, religious, or economic conditions that allowed the cancer of violence to grow into terrorism, whether by the state or by groups of people—those that have gone beyond the pale. Part Two will take the reader on an exciting and interesting trip around the world, examining the most significant terrorist locations, starting with the problems before and after the attacks of 9-11 in North America, and a tour of the major regions of the world. Throughout history, from the time of the ancient Egyptians, who always took time to kill every member of a defeated army, to the "Killing Fields" of Cambodia, Rwanda, and the Sudan, ethnic cleansing and genocide continue as either a state form of terror or conducted by individual terror groups for whatever social, religious, or political gain or goal. State-sponsored terrorism in the twentieth century alone resulted in untold millions of deaths. Human rights movements, such as Amnesty International and others, have begun to shine bright light on the depredations committed by nations against their own people. Power and religious fanaticism have driven the kinds of terrorism that resulted in Hitler's Holocaust and the conflicts between the Irish Catholics and Protestants, the Jews and Arabs, Shia and Sunni Muslims, and dozens of other conflicts around the globe. Instantaneous television coverage of these atrocities has finally begun to make the world aware that the most pernicious forms of terrorism are not those used by a single fanatic throwing bombs. In Part Two, we will explore in detail the causes of terrorism around the world.

Review Questions

1. Discuss how Islam has been able to spread jihad and the radicalization of impressionable Muslims and converts.
2. Why is suicide such an effective tool of the terrorist arsenal?
3. Review why financially low-cost terrorist operations may be easier to bring to conclusion rather than high-cost operations.
4. Analyze a recent terrorist incident in the West and discuss whether these perpetrators were radicalized homegrown terrorists and how they might have been prevented from taking such action.

Websites

1. **Center for the Study of Terrorism and Political Violence**—*www.st-andrews.ac.uk*
2. **Human Rights Watch**—*www.hrw.org*
3. **Center for Defense Information**—*www.cdi.org*
4. **United Nations**—*http://www.un.org/terrorism/*
5. **The Constitutional Rights Foundation**—*http://www. crf-usa.org/terror/terrorism_links.htm*
6. **U.S. Department of State**—*http://www.state.gov/s/ct/ rls/crt/2009/140901.htm*

End Notes

1. John Lachs. "Violence as Response to Alienation." *Alienation and Violence* (Middlesex, UK: Science Reviews Ltd., 1988, pp. 147–160).
2. Ibid., p. 15.
3. Cindy C. Combs. *Terrorism in the Twenty-First Century* (Upper Saddle River NJ: Prentice Hall, 1997).
4. Ibid., p. 21.
5. See Marshall G.S. Hodgson. *The Order of the Assassins* (London, UK: The Institute of Ismaili Studies, 1960); Bernard Lewis. *The Assassins: A Radical Sect in Islam* (London, UK: The Institute of Ismaili Studies, 1968).
6. B. Harwood. *Society of the Assassin: A Background Book on Political Murder* (London, UK: International Institute for Strategic Studies, 1996).
7. Carl Sandburg. *Abraham Lincoln: The War Years.* Vol. 4 (Cambridge, MA: MIT Press, 1939, p. 482).
8. *Country Reports on Terrorism: —Released by the Office of the Coordinator for Counter Terrorism* (April 28, 2006), http:///wwwstate.gov.
9. Political asylum is sanctuary or refuge for a person who has committed a crime such as assassination of a political figure. It is granted by one government against requests by another government for the extradition of that person to be prosecuted for this "political" crime. *Funk and Wagnall's Standard Dictionary*, Comprehensive International Ed., vol. 1, p. 86, col. 3.
10. U.S. State Department of State. *Patterns of Global Terror Report* (2002–2003).
11. Distinguishing between Islam and Islamism—Center for Strategic Studies (June 30, 1998).
12. Jihad Explained. The Institute of Islamic Information and Education Brochure No. 18 Chicago.
13. Craig Branch, *Act of War—Jihad, Apologetics Resource Center.* http://www.apologeticsresctr.org/ act_of_war.htm.
14. B.A. Robinson. Ontario Consultants on Religious Tolerance Originally written (March 28, 2003), http://www.religioustolerance.org/isl_jihad.htm.
15. Jewish Chronicle, May 27, 2005.
16. Mitchell D. Silber and Avril Blatt. *NYPD Radicalization in the West: Senior Intelligence Analysts* (New York Police Department: NYPD Intelligence Division).
17. Raphael F. Perl. *CRS Issue Brief*, Specialist in International Affairs Foreign Affairs and National Defense Division, Congressional Research Service (October 22, 1997).
18. *Islamic Terrorism from Midwest to Mideast* by Steven Emerson, Christzan Science Monitor (August 28, 1996).
19. *Terrorism and the Middle East Peace Process: The Origins and Activities of Hamas in the United States,*

testimony by international terrorism consultant, Steven Emerson, before the Senate Subcommittee on the Near East and South Asia (March 19, 1996, p. 11).

20. *Impact of Television on U.S. Foreign Policy*, 1994, U.S. Congress, House Committee on Foreign Affairs, 103rd Congress, 2nd Session, GPO, Washington (April 26, 1994, p. 53).

21. In the case of the anonymous "Unabomber," it was publication of a manifesto in the New York Times and Washington Post that triggered the leads and actions by the suspect's family, which resulted in an arrest.

22. John F. Burns. "Spiriting Off of Fugitive by U.S. Irks Pakistanis." *New York Times* (June 23, 1997, p. A9).

23. Grant Wardlaw. *Political Terrorism, Theory, Tactics and Counter Measures* (Melbourne, Australia: Cambridge University Press, 1989, p. 85).

24. The U.S. Central Intelligence Agency, *World Fact Book.*

25. Ibid.

26. Ibid.

27. Ibid.

28. U.S. Department of State, *Country Reports on Human Rights Practices*, 1998.

29. Ralph Lemkin. *Axis Rule in Occupied Europe* (Warsaw, Poland: University of Stockholm, 1944).

30. Convention for the Prevention and Punishment for the Crime of Genocide; General Assembly of the United Nations, 1948.

PART TWO

Global Terrorism

3

The United States of America

While nothing is easier than to denounce the evildoer, nothing is more difficult than to understand him.

—Fyodor Mikhailovich Dostoevsky

LEARNING OBJECTIVES

After studying this chapter, the student should be able to:

1. Discuss the threat that exists from Islamic extremism in the United States.
2. Discuss the trail of events that led to the intelligence failures that resulted in the attacks on the United States on September 11, 2001.
3. Explain the stages to radicalization.
4. Discuss why the War on Terror will likely continue for decades to come.
5. Discuss why the threat from right-wing extremists can be just as potent as from radical Islamists.

KEY WORDS TO NOTE

Extraordinary rendition—The extrajudicial transfer of a person from one country to another—a practice of the U.S. government to transfer suspected terrorists to countries known to practice torture

Fatwa—An Islamic pronouncement or ruling—considered a scholarly opinion on Islamic law

Hizb ut-Tahir—A global Islamic political party whose goal is to unite all Muslim countries to unify as an Islamic Caliphate

JTTF—Joint Terrorism Task Force established in July 2002 to serve as a coordinating mechanism with the FBI's partners. Some forty agencies are now represented in the National JTTF, a focal point for information sharing

Jamaat al-Fuqra—Terrorist group established in Pakistan and with operations inside the United States—considered a probable al Qaeda affiliate

Lynch Law—The process of condemning and punishing a person by mob rule without any trial—dates back to the eighteenth century, when William Lynch self-instituted tribunals

Patriot Act—The USA Patriot Act was signed into law by President George Bush immediately after the 9-11 terror attacks

OVERVIEW

Unable to achieve their unrealistic goals by conventional means, international terrorists attempt to send an ideological or religious message by terrorizing the general public. Through the choice of their targets, which are often symbolic or representative of the targeted nation, terrorists attempt to create a high-profile impact on the public of their targeted enemy or enemies with their act of violence, despite the limited material resources that are usually at their disposal.[1]

"Jihad," "radicalization," "Islamaphobia," and "homegrown terrorists" are terms or words unheard of in the United States before the attacks on the World Trade Center in New York on September 11, 2001, but now form part of daily discussions on protecting the homeland. In the decade since 9-11, the threat from terror attacks from both external and internal forces has not diminished. Al Qaeda and all its varying affiliate followers, be they in the Arabian Peninsula or regions of Africa, the Indian subcontinent, or in the United States, continue to pose threats to the safety of U.S. citizens and businesses around the world. During the last thirty years of the twentieth century, most terror groups and subgroups operating throughout the world had their specific stated agenda; al Qaeda and its inspired followers appear to have no political agenda in mind but simply death and destruction of Western democracies. In attacking the West, their prime agenda is to set up Islamic Caliphates and overthrow Western

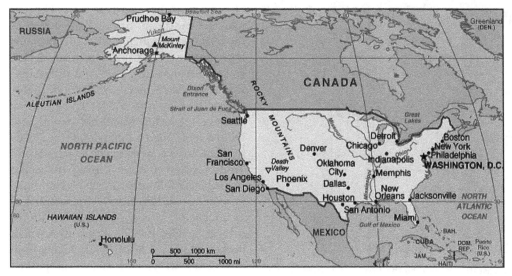

FIGURE 3-1 Map of the United States (Central Intelligence Agency, *The World Factbook, 2008*).

democracies and secular states, and the challenge now is to determine how to undermine as well as understand what it is that is driving impressionable and somewhat unremarkable young men and women to turn against their adopted homelands. In Britain, the attacks in 2005 were the work of "homegrown terrorists," so make no mistake, the same threat exists in the United States. In this chapter, we will review the events of the last two decades with obvious emphasis on jihad in America. The following "Failure to connect the Dots" indicates that although the indications were all there, connecting the so-called dots either was beyond the intelligence community's ability or the unspeakable events coming were too unfathomable to be credible.

CONNECTING THE DOTS

Dot No. 1—1993: World Trade Center Bombing in New York City

A car bomb exploded underneath the World Trade Center in New York, killing six people and injuring more than a thousand others. The bombing shocked the United States, which had not suffered from the terrorist acts that had plagued other parts of the world. Mario Cuomo, then New York State governor, said: "No foreign people or force has ever done this to us. Until now, we felt invulnerable." At approximately 12:18 P.M. February 26, 1993, an improvised explosive device in the back of a rental vehicle detonated on the second level of the parking basement. The resulting blast produced a crater approximately 150 feet in diameter and five floors deep in the parking basement. That structure consisted mainly of steel-reinforced concrete, twelve to fourteen inches thick. The epicenter of the blast was approximately 8 feet from the south wall of World Trade Center Tower One, near a support column. The device had been placed in the rear-cargo portion of a 1-ton Ford F350 Econoline van, which had been rented from a Ryder Rental agency in Jersey City. Approximately 6,800 tons of concrete and steel were displaced by the massive blast. The main explosive charge consisted primarily of approximately 1,200–1,500 pounds of homemade (nitrogen fertilizer–based) explosive and urea nitrate. The fusing system

was made from twenty 220-minute lengths of nonelectric, burning-type fuses. The fuse material ended up in lead azide acting as the terminator/initiator. Also, incorporated into this thrown-together homemade device, and placed under the main explosive charge, were three large metal cylinders of highly compressed hydrogen gas. The resulting massive explosion killed six people and injured more than a thousand. Over 50,000 people were evacuated from the huge World Trade Center complex during the hours immediately following the blast. The initial inspection, on February 27, was described as a scene of "massive devastation, almost surreal in appearance." There were small pockets of fire, electrical sparks arcing from damaged wiring, and dozens of parked automobile alarms whistling, howling, and

FIGURE 3-2 Devastation caused by the first World Trade Center bombing 1993 (Federal Bureau of Investigation).

honking. The explosion ruptured two of the main sewage-removal lines from both of the World Trade Center towers and the Vista Hotel, plus several water mains from the air-conditioning system. In all, more than 2 million gallons of water and sewage drained into the tower and was then pumped out of the crime scene.

Dot No. 2—1995: The Oklahoma City Bombing

According to a classified Pentagon study, the Oklahoma City bombing was caused by more than one bomb. Two independent Pentagon experts concluded that five separate bombs caused the destruction of the Oklahoma City Federal Building in April 1995. A huge truck bomb destroyed most of that building, leaving 168 people dead and

FIGURE 3-3 Devastation caused by the first World Trade Center bombing 1993 (Federal Bureau of Investigation).

more than 500 others injured. Preliminary reports indicated that the bomber might have been from the Middle East. After many more unconfirmed rumors, prejudice and public anger rose to a fever pitch. The arrest of Timothy McVeigh and his subsequent trial, conviction, and execution, as well as the arrest and conviction of his friend and accomplice, Terry Nichols, grated on the already-raw nerves of an entire nation. When it was revealed that both were members of local right-wing militias, it became clear that American, and not foreign, domestic terrorists had planned and committed this terrible act. Those two events and many others since have caused officials and security and law enforcement agencies in the United States to rethink and reorganize their perceptions of where serious terrorist threats might really lie. But the dots still had not yet been connected, and the general public soon slipped back into their everyday lives.

Dot No. 3—1998: U.S. Embassies Targeted in Africa

On August 7, 1998, very powerful, almost simultaneous, explosions rocked two U.S. embassies in East Africa. The blasts took place at almost the exact same time, 10:30 a.m. in Kenya and Tanzania. Embassy officials confirmed that the explosions were the result of car bombs detonated near the two embassies, one in the capital of Kenya, Nairobi, and the other in Dar es Salaam, the capital of Tanzania. In Kenya, the explosion toppled the tall Ufundi Cooperative Bank building over onto the U.S. Embassy. The blast occurred shortly after the U.S. ambassador, Prudence Bushnell, had met with the Kenyan Trade Minister at the nearby bank. She was taken from the site on a stretcher, feared to be badly injured, but later found to have sustained only minor wounds from flying glass and debris. The bank building, located between the trade center and the embassy, was leveled almost to the ground. Apparently the bomb had been placed there, rather than at the embassy itself, because of the embassy's bombproof construction. In Tanzania, another massive explosion left a large crater outside of the U.S. embassy. An eyewitness stated: "The people at the front of the building didn't stand a chance." The blast occurred near the spot where a gasoline tanker truck had been observed parked in the embassy parking lot. The attack took the lives of 224 people including 12 Americans. Ahmed Khalfan Ghailani who was sentenced to life in prison on January 25, 2011 was an al Qaeda operative and Tanzanian national who conspired with Osama bin Laden to attack both embassies. Each embassy was attacked by a suicide bomber driving large truck bombs packed with approximately 1,000 pounds of TNT. Ghailani purchased the truck as well as tanks of oxygen and acetylene gas that were used in the bombing of the U.S. embassy in Tanzania. He also stored detonators that were used in the bomb at his residence.[2]

Dot No. 4—2000: The Suicide Bombing of the USS *Cole*

A gaping hole in the hull of the USS *Cole* testified to the force of the suicide terrorist bombing that killed seventeen sailors as the U.S. Navy vessel was docked in Yemen in October 2000. The ship was attacked in a suicide mission by a small inflatable packed with explosives that rammed into the port side of the ship just above the waterline. This was not the first such attempt to attack a U.S. naval vessel—a similar attack planned to coincide with the new millennium on January 3, 2000, also in the port of Aden, on the USS *The Sullivans* had failed as the heavily laden boat carrying the explosives capsized.

Dot No. 5—December 25, 2009: The Underwear Bomber—Detroit

The attempt to blow up an airliner over Detroit on Christmas Day by Umar Farouk Abdulmutallab with a hidden explosive device in his underpants was a significant blow to the American psyche, a blow to the international traveler, and not least to the intelligence community. There has been much discourse from both the United States and Great Britain as to where exactly he had received his radical indoctrination. Although the British contend it was not until he was out of the country and in Yemen, there are, of course, telltale snippets that indicate that he had already been a target of Britain's security service M-15 for his radical activities at University College London (UCL). Abdulmutallab had attended this institution from 2005 to 2008 and was president of the UCL Islamic Society (ISOC) and during the academic year 2006–2007 organized a controversial War on Terror week. Extremist speakers have regularly spoken at UCL, including supporters of the terrorist group Hamas and members of **Hizb ut-Tahir**, and those who have spoken in support of the Taliban warned Muslims not to integrate into Western societies, argued in favor of domestic violence, and advocated the destruction of Israel.

There is an accepted perception in government and particularly in the United Kingdom that Islamic extremism deserves special consideration, which again hinges on a false belief that the experience of poverty and exclusion can create specific grievances, which may then lead to radicalization. Further study of recent and well-publicized attacks, for instance the 9-11 attacks, the London tube train bombings, and the Glasgow airport attacks, quickly dispels any rational belief that poverty plays any part on the perpetrators' side.

Timothy McVeigh—Oklahoma City Bombing 1995

In 1995, homegrown terrorism surfaced in the United States when McVeigh bombed the Alfred P Murrah Federal Building in Oklahoma City, killing 150 people. This was notably the most vicious attack by an American citizen on fellow Americans. McVeigh was a member of the Patriot movement that developed in the early 1990s, a group that believed in the true American ideals of individualism, armed citizens, and minimum interference from governments. McVeigh used a rented Ryder truck packed with ammonium nitrate, fuel oil, and Tovex high explosive. Most counterterrorism experts were candid in stating that they had not predicted the sort of attack that was carried out in Oklahoma. In 1995, there were a considerable number of right-wing "militia" groups, rabidly antiestablishment and antigovernment, stemming not from social injustices but more likely from proposed gun control legislation. After the ATF raid on the Waco compound of the Branch Davideons, there was notable unrest and disillusionment from "patriot," "militia," and "constitutionalist" groups who believed that the attack at Waco was a massacre by the authorities. The early 1990s were not a time when U.S. terrorism experts were paying much, if any, attention to Islamic In the mid-1990s, international terrorism within the United States was generally not considered a major threat. Nevertheless, there were indications that if some foreign terrorist group became disgruntled enough at the United States, and was determined to act out that anger, it could create major problems to U.S. commerce, infrastructure, and population, given leadership and financing.

The levels of terrorism experienced in places like Beirut, Belfast, Paris, London, Madrid, Kabul, Islamabad, and Palestine did not carry much impact in the United States except as a news item; nor did terrorism create major nervousness or any impact on the American lifestyle. Public credibility about threats from foreign terrorism in the United States is not enhanced when a violent act occurs. Even then, media "talking heads" merely issue a brief sound bite and then quickly move on to another story. Later, the media reveal that the act was not foreign terrorism after all! Such reporting creates confusion and mistakes. Three especially relevant examples of this syndrome are as follows:

1. The bombing of a van belonging to Naval Captain Will Rogers III, the former captain of the USS *Vincennes*;
2. The Aegis missile-equipped U.S. Navy warship that mistakenly shot down an Iranian civilian airliner during the Iran-Iraq War; and
3. The mysterious "Middle Eastern man" who was brought back to the United States for questioning in regard to the bombing of Alfred P. Murrah Federal Building in Oklahoma City.

In all three cases, the media jumped to the conclusion that these had been foreign terrorist attacks, planned and executed by someone other than U.S. domestic terrorists. When contrary facts surfaced, the public reached a different conclusion and put less credence in media reports and ignored any comments presented by the media in regard to reports of terrorism for a long time.

The United States, after all, had never been subjected to as much political violence or international terrorism as the likes of Europe, the Balkans, the Middle East, Northern Ireland, the Persian Gulf, Africa, or South and Southeast Asia. A few exceptions come to mind—the Symbionese Liberation Army (SLA), the Black Panthers, the Weathermen, the Unabomber, and even single issue groups such as Animal Liberation Front (ALF)—but such domestic terrorist acts have been few and far between. On the other hand, the IRA's ongoing slaughter in Northern Ireland with car bombs (as the reader will learn about in Chapter 5) continued to be frequent and unremitting. But, after August 7, 1998, the United States was slowly awakening to the fact that it was no longer immune to larger-scale attacks, clearly identifiable as foreign terrorist acts. The first World Trade Center explosion became (perhaps) a significant marker of the first salvo by foreign terrorists using politically motivated actions that attack random victims. The bombing was intended to incite fear as well as add a determined and well-planned external terrorist signature to an act of violence.

But terrorism in the United States was not to be limited to those with external agendas from foreign sources, as demonstrated by the attack on the Federal Building in Oklahoma City, Oklahoma. The terrorists in this case were Americans, members of a paramilitary survivalist militia from Michigan. They had responded to a long-festering anger over the U.S. government's bungling of the "Waco Massacre" of the Branch Davideons, a fringe religious group headed by David Koresh.

DOMESTIC TERRORISM AND EXTREMISM

The face of domestic terrorism continues to change. The FBI has defined *domestic terrorism* "as groups of individuals who are based and operate entirely in the United States and Puerto Rico without foreign direction and whose acts are directed at elements of the U.S. government or population." This definition is suitably wide enough to class terror events from both the ideological left and right. If we study traditional attacks in the United States, we can see that domestic issue terror can then be categorized accordingly as

- Revolutionary nationalist groups
- Extreme right-wing ideological groups (Ku Klux Klan)
- Extreme left-wing ideological groups (Weather Underground)
- Foreign groups operating in the United States
- Religious extremist groups.

The FBI identified a further decline in traditional left-wing domestic extremism and an increase in activities among extremists associated with right-wing groups and special-interest, radical organizations. Since 2001 and with an African American president in the White House, there has been a significant increase in the growth of right-wing groups. Currently, there are estimated to be 926 "hate groups" active in the United States and fall into the following groupings:

- Ku Klux Klan—186
- Neo-Nazi—196
- White Nationalist—111
- Racist Skinhead—98
- Christian Identity—39
- Neo-Confederate—93
- Black Separatist—113
- General Hate—90

The above groups to a great extent espouse violence as a means to fulfill their hate-filled mandates. The definition used to determine a hate crime comes close enough to be almost indistinguishable with terrorism: "A hate crime, also known as a bias crime, is a criminal offence committed against a person, property, or society that is motivated, in whole or in part, by the offender's bias against a race, religion, disability, sexual orientation or ethnicity/national origin." The Southern Poverty Law Center that monitors civil rights noted an increase of 300 percent in the number of known militia groups between 2008 and 2009 (from 42 to 127). Militia groups have been a part of U.S. history since the revolutionary wars against the British, and they make a resurgence particularly at times like the present, with a severely depressed economy, a total collapse, and loss of faith in the financial system and the first African American president in power. Militia groups are not alone in fermenting violent response to social or political problems. Militias tend to attract those whose focus is political, whereas hate groups such as the racial purists of the Supreme White Alliance or the Christian fundamentalist Army of God are similarly frequent advocates of violence. Where is the line drawn between hateful speech and inciting violence and between a militia group and a terrorist organization? Was the act of the shooter at Fort Hood the work of a "Lone Wolf" or because he was of Muslim faith and possibly radicalized over the Internet he would therefore be classified as a terrorist? **The Patriot Act** allows U.S. law enforcement significant leeway in dealing with terrorist investigations and rarely if ever has the term "terrorism" been applied to militia or extremist groups. The arrest in March 2010 of nine Hutaree Militia members for "conspiracy to levy war" against the U.S. government and "being an anti-government organization which advocates violence against local, state, and federal law enforcement questions whether the charges should have been for terrorist panning and activity. They were charged with seditious conspiracy and attempts to use weapons of mass destruction, but there was no mention of terrorism in the charges."[3]

The Weather Underground

The 1960s was a decade of change around the world. In the United States, the war in Vietnam was beginning and so too were movements and activists challenging the respected norms and values particularly in areas of human rights. The Weather Underground is one activist group worthy of mention. Formed originally as a splinter group that believed that peaceful protests were ineffective, they began advocating violence as a means to social and political change. In early March 1970, one of its mainstream leaders, Bernardine Dohrn, proclaimed a declaration of war, and days later three Weathermen were killed by one of their own bombs that accidentally detonated in their basement apartment in Manhattan. The bomb had been intended for a dance at a military base. Reaching the point where violence takes the place of peaceful protest may have been brought about by actions of the Chicago Police Department in a shootout with members of the Black Panther movement that saw Mark Clark and Fred Hampton shot to death. Many believed this to be a government-sanctioned hit to wipe out militant groups such as the Panthers, making this a pivotal moment in the Weather Underground's history. Most of the members found themselves on the FBI's Ten Most Wanted list for at least the next decade. Their activities continued until the late 1970s, at which time the leaders had come out of hiding and begun serving terms of imprisonment. The movement came to an unofficial end in 1981 when Kathy Boudin from the Weathermen resurfaced to participate in an armed robbery in New York, which resulted in the shooting deaths of three men. Boudin was sentenced to twenty-two years in prison and released in 2003[4].

Left-Wing Terrorism

Over several decades, left-wing-oriented extremist groups posed the predominant domestic terrorist threat in the United States. In the 1980s, however, the FBI neutralized many of these groups by arresting key members who were conducting criminal activity. The failure of Communism and the fall of the former Soviet Union in 1989 deprived many leftist groups of a coherent ideology or tangible support. As a result, membership and belief in the "cause" in these groups have waned.

The United States still faces a threat from some left-wing extremists, including a few Puerto Rican terrorist groups and a Cuban group. Although Puerto Rico voted to remain within the U.S. Commonwealth in 1993, some extremists still plan and conduct minor terrorist acts to draw attention to their support for independence.

Right-Wing Terrorism

Right-wing extremist groups, located at the opposite end of the political spectrum, generally adhere to an antigovernment or racist ideology. These groups still continue to attract some followers. Many of these recruits feel disenfranchised by rapid changes in the U.S. culture and economy or are seeking some form of personal affirmation. As American social structures continue to change, the potential for escalating hate crimes by extremist right-wing groups is an increasingly valid concern. Of particular note, many state and local law enforcement organizations consider a broader range of activities and acts as terrorist, or potentially terrorist, than does the FBI. The official FBI statistics do not count many threatening acts by organizations such as the skinheads, street gangs, and drug dealers as terrorist acts. States and municipalities are equally adamant in identifying right-wing (neo-Nazi, the Ku Klux Klan, anti-Semitic, anti-federalist, and militias) and issue-specific (antiabortion, animal rights, environmentalist) organizations as major potential sources for supporters of terrorism in the United States.

The burgeoning militia movement in the United States was placed under the spotlight on the admissions by Timothy McVeigh and Terry Nichols. Such paramilitary, rabid, antigovernment groups will continue to attract supporters. Several factors have contributed to the increase of this generally antigovernment mood. In a changing political and economic environment, issues such as gun control legislation, the United Nations' involvement in international affairs, U.S. efforts around the world seemingly unsupported by our former allies, and clashes between dissidents and law enforcement are cornerstones of militia ideology. When tied into neo-Nazi zeal and radical philosophies, you have an explosive situation. Some militia members firmly believe that the U.S. government is deeply involved in a conspiracy to create a "New World Order." According to their adherents and radical believers, international boundaries will be dissolved and the United Nations will be allowed to become the ruling power in the world. Other militia advocates believe that the federal government has gotten either too powerful or simply illegal and out of control. Many of these militants continue to conduct paramilitary training and stockpile illegal weapons in preparation for an armed Armageddon-type of confrontation with the government. A few of these extreme militia members could pose a serious terrorist threat.

Special-Interest Extremists

Special-interest extremists continue to conduct acts of politically oriented crime and terrorism. Violent antiabortion advocates are responsible for many of these activities. The Department of Justice's Task Force on Violence against Abortion Providers (TFVAAP) decreased the number of abortion-related crimes from the high 1994 levels. Although the number of incidents has declined, the TFVAAP has still investigated more than 100 violations of the Freedom of Access to Clinic Entrances (FACE) Act. Two of the most prominent abortion-related events in the 1990s included the following:

- On February 22, 1995, Dr. Elizabeth Karlin, a physician in Madison, Wisconsin, received two letters with death threats. Vincent Whitaker, an inmate at a local county jail, who was serving a sixty-seven-year sentence for reckless injury with a motor vehicle, later admitted writing the letters. On September 12, 1995, Whitaker was tried and convicted of two counts of the FACE Act and sending threats through the U.S. mail. On November 21, 1995, Whitaker was sentenced to an additional sixty-three months of imprisonment.
- In August 1995, John Salvi, the suspected murderer of two receptionists during a December 30, 1994, shooting spree at an abortion clinic in Brookline, Massachusetts, was declared

competent to stand trial. Salvi was charged under Massachusetts law with the murders of Shannon Lowney and Lee Ann Nichols and five other counts of aggravated assault. He received a life sentence in March 1996 and died, of possible suicide, in November the same year. The Civil Rights Division of the Department of Justice, through the TFVAAP, investigates any instance in which customers or providers of reproductive health services are criminally threatened, obstructed, or injured while seeking or providing services.

Revolutionary Nationalist Groups

The U.S. government's experience with the Puerto Rican nationalist group, Los Macheteros, dates back to an armed robbery on September 12, 1983, at an armored car depot in West Hartford, Connecticut. After the day's pickups were done, a guard named Victor M. Gerena suddenly turned on his two comrades. He then restrained them at gunpoint, injected both with an unknown substance, and began packing blocks of currency into his rented car.

Authorities eventually determined that Gerena's robbery had been planned by Los Macheteros, a group founded in the 1970s by Ojeda Rios, a musician who had turned communist and Puerto Rican revolutionary. Using bombings and attacks on police officers and U.S. government personnel, the group pushed for an end to U.S. control of the island.

The FBI caught up with the leader of this group in Puerto Rico in September 2005; Filiberto Ojeda Rios was tracked to a farmhouse, which was then surrounded by agents, and during the ensuing shootout Rios died of a single gunshot wound.[5]

Left-Wing Aggression

The radical student movements, civil rights marches, and anti-Vietnam war demonstrations of the 1960s galvanized a large number of student organizations to frame their struggles around an antiestablishment theme. As the Vietnam War intensified, so too did the attitudes and activities of the growing student movements. One such group that supported the use of terrorism and violence was the Weather Underground Organization (Weathermen), which had its roots within the Students for Democratic Society and aimed at a revolutionary overthrow of the United States government. The group engaged mainly in sporadic bomb attacks at police stations and at the Pentagon. However, when the Vietnam War ended in 1973, the Weather Underground began to dissolve.

THE BLACK PANTHERS AND NATION OF ISLAM

The New Black Panther Party for Self-Defense takes its name from the original Black Panther Party, formed by Huey Newton and Bobby Seale in Oakland, California, in 1966. The original Panthers combined militant Black Nationalism with Marxism and advocated black empowerment and self-defense, often through violent confrontation. By 1969, the group had an estimated 5,000 members spread through twenty chapters around the country. In the early 1970s, however, the group lost momentum and most of its support due to internal disputes, violent clashes with police, and infiltration by law enforcement agencies. Despite the collapse, the group's mystique continued to influence radicals, and by the early 1990s a new generation of militant activists began to model themselves after the original Panthers. Essentially a black supremacist movement but with anti-Semitic undertones, the Nation of Islam has been around since the 1930s and became more prominent with notorious speeches from NOI national spokesman Malcolm X until his assassination in 1965.

THE KU KLUX KLAN

Ku Klux Klan (KKK) has its beginnings in small-town America and was born out of boredom and small-town life by six Confederate veterans, in December 1885. The Klan began life as a social club in Pulaski, Tennessee, not far from the Alabama border. As a means of distraction, the members began to ride around town at night wearing white sheets, and then extended this to pointed hats; they adopted this bizarre costume as their official regalia. They formed up like a college fraternity and began to hold elaborate initiation ceremonies for new members, with a form of hazing rituals. The KKK would likely have faded away as quietly as they had been formed, but in 1886 the membership expanded to other towns, and activities became more sinister and violent toward the black communities. As the KKK expanded and developed, it engaged in some of the most brutal terror attacks over the early decades of the twentieth century. It was well known for decades as the major advocate for white supremacy and power, and segregation of the races is foremost among its agenda. KKK members allege there was a conspiracy between Jewish people, white liberals, blacks, and other minorities to take over the United States.

Since 1865, KKK has provided a vehicle for racial hatred in America, and its members have been responsible for atrocities that are difficult for most people to even imagine. Although the membership and actions of the traditional and historical KKK declined in the last half of the twentieth century, there are too many other groups that go by a variety of names and symbols that have been at least as dangerous as the KKK ever was.

Some of these comprise teenagers who shave their heads and wear storm trooper jackboots, display swastika tattoos, and call themselves "skinheads" or "neo-Nazis." Some of them are young men who wear camouflage fatigues and practice guerrilla warfare tactics at secret locations for training in weaponry and violence. Some of them are conservatively dressed professionals who publish materials filled with their bizarre beliefs—ideas that range from denying that the Nazi Holocaust against the Jews in World War II had ever happened, to those with the conviction that the federal government is an illegal body and that all governing power should rest with county sheriffs or militias. Despite their peculiarities, they all share the deep-seated hatred and resentment that had given life to the Klan and terrorized racial minorities, the weak, and Jews in this country for almost a century and a half.

The Klan itself has had three periods of significant strength in American history: first, in the latter half of the nineteenth century, then again in the 1920s, and, more recently, during the 1950s and early 1960s, when the Civil Rights Movement was at its height. The Klan finally experienced a small resurgence in the 1970s, but it never again approached its past level of influence. Since then, with open and universal access to the Internet, the Klan has become just one element in a much broader spectrum of white supremacist and hatred activity. It is important for the student/reader to understand, however, that violent prejudice is not limited to the KKK or any other white supremacist organization. People who have no ties to any organized group, but who share their virulent hatred, commit bombings, assaults, murders, and arsons every year.

Historical research explains the roots of racism and prejudice, which sustains the Ku Klux Klan beliefs even into the twenty-first century. As for current events, that is an even easier lesson for most minorities who grew up in the racially torn years of the 1950s. Young civil rights activists, working alongside John Lewis, Andrew Young, the late Dr. Martin Luther King, Jr., Julian Bond, and many others, saw the KKK as an all-too-visible power in many of the places they went to organize voter registration and protest segregation. They knew what the Klan was and often had a pretty good idea of who its members were. They also knew what Klan members would happily do to them if they thought they could get away with it.

You can read in almost any news media stories about crosses being burned in the yards of minorities or mixed-race couples, and it seems as if we are suddenly thrust back into the 1960s. Some claim the Klan today should just be ignored and it will fade away. Past history, however, will not let us ignore current events. Those who would use violence to deny others their rights cannot be ignored. The background of the KKK and its battles with the law illustrate why hate groups cannot be ignored. It is unattractive part of American history—some of the things you read here will make you angry or ashamed; some will turn your stomach and make you sick at heart. But it is important that we try to understand the villains as well as the heroes in our past if we are to continue building a nation where equality, freedom, and democracy are preserved.

Victims of the Klan

The image of a black man hanging lifeless by a rope from a tree limb has become a symbol for the worst of Klan violence. Between 1889 and 1941, 3,811 black people were lynched for "crimes" such as threatening to sue a white man, attempting to register to vote, joining labor unions, being "disrespectful" to a white man, even looking at a white woman, or just for no reason at all. During the American Revolution, the term **Lynch Law** described an informal court run by Colonel Charles Lynch of Bedford County, Virginia, who tried Tories and criminals in an effort to restore law and order to the frontier. Lynch's punishments consisted generally of fines or an occasional whipping. In the 1850s, the KKK used "Lynch Law." Later, the term was used to commonly describe a quick finding of guilty and the hanging of one of a group's objects of hate.

Today, there is a trend to spread hate and racism by forming so-called militias that freely use the Internet through social media to spread their twisted messages of hatred and intolerance. In the late 1920s, during the years of prohibition, gangs and mobsters preyed on society and each other with deadly violence. Mobsters gunned down those who opposed or interfered with their bootlegging and traumatized all those who witnessed or heard of such carnage. Terror strikes at the public's basic need for safety. Serial killers are unwitting terrorists when their deeds are publicized, and street gangs in American cities today use drive-by shootings as a tactic for creating fear and terror in their "hoods." These demonstrations keep their rivals in check and neighborhood citizens afraid to report these and other crimes against their own communities to the police. The same kinds of fear-inducing methods have long been the favorite tactics of the Mafia, or "Cosa Nostra" ("Our Thing"). From killings in schools and fast-food places to motorcycle gangs terrorizing an entire town, all forms of violence can be utilized as a means to incite terror.

With a population rapidly approaching over 300 million, the United States remains a "nation of immigrants," people who came to a great and prosperous land, legally and illegally, from the four corners of the earth. As far as terrorism is concerned, many of these immigrants escaped from various forms of it, leaving their home countries to come to a place where such actions were unthinkable. As we have now seen, the history of the United States does not support that premise, and many forms of terror have scarred its brief but bloody past—and even now sometimes mar its present.

The United States has the most powerful, diverse, and technologically advanced economy in the world. It boasts a per capita annual income that is the highest among all major industrial nations. In this market-oriented economy, private individuals and business firms make most of the decisions, and the government buys needed goods and services predominantly in the private marketplace. American business firms enjoy considerably greater flexibility than their counterparts in Western Europe and Asia in their decisions to expand capital plant, lay off surplus workers, and develop new products.

A growing terrorism threat in the United States is not only from foreign sources but also from dissatisfied, domestic purveyors of violence, hate, and terror.

OSAMA BIN LADEN AND AL QAEDA THREAT TO AMERICA

Osama bin Laden, the master planner behind the 9-11 attacks and prior attacks on the USS *Cole* in Yemen and the embassy bombings in Nairobi and Dar es Salaam, announced a **fatwa**, an interpretation of an Islamic law, in a London Arabic newspaper in 1998. In this proclamation, he stated that the United States had declared war against God and His messenger. Bin Laden called for the killing of Americans anywhere as being a sacred duty of all Muslims. In a television interview with ABC in Afghanistan, bin Laden expounded even further on this theme by stating the importance for Muslims to kill Americans more so than other infidels.

Bin Laden was one of the many sons of a Saudi construction magnate—a wealthy son who went to Afghanistan to fight against the Soviet invasion in 1980. Arabs from the Middle East, Africa, and Asia headed to Afghanistan to wage jihad against the Soviets. Bin Laden's actual involvement in the fighting has never been established. However, his role became that of a financier for the movement in Afghanistan. When bin Laden was in Afghanistan, the United States and Saudi Arabia supplied him with hundreds of millions of U.S. dollars in secret aid and support to the jihad against the Soviet invasion. The ultimate defeat and the full pullout of the Soviet forces in 1988 left bin Laden with an interesting dilemma—what to do next? Bin Laden and his Islamic fighters had managed to defeat the Soviet Army and, in doing so, had set up a base for their operations in Afghanistan. A literal translation of "al Qaeda" is "the base," or "the foundation." The al Qaeda of the 1980s was a far cry from what it is today. In those post-Soviet months, the group developed and organized along corporate structures, complete with departments that dealt with arms procurement, media relations, and propaganda and intelligence. In Afghanistan, bin Laden worked closely with a Palestinian cleric, Abdullah Yusuf Azzam, who was nicknamed the "Godfather of Jihad." During the 1980s, Azzam was the central figure in the global development of the militant Islamist movement. He built a scholarly, ideological, and practical paramilitary infrastructure for the globalization of Islamist movements, which, until then, had been focused on separate national, revolutionary, and liberation struggles. Azzam envisioned a pan-Islamic transnational movement that would transcend the political map of the Middle East drawn by non-Islamic colonial powers.[6] Azzam traveled throughout Europe, the Middle East, and North America, where he visited more than fifty cities to raise money and preach jihad. His belief was that Afghanistan was a model for future struggles with the objective of establishing an Islamic Caliphate across all Muslim lands under foreign occupation. Azzam's radical ideology, combined with his skill at organizing paramilitary training for more than 20,000 Muslim recruits from about twenty countries around the world, created an international cadre of highly motivated and experienced militants, intent on perpetuating his vision of global Islamic revolution. In his book *Join the Caravan*, Sheik Azzam implored Muslims to rally in defense of Muslim victims of aggression, restore Muslim lands from foreign domination, and uphold the Muslim faith.[7]

Azzam's success, and that of his fighters in Afghanistan, was solidified with the support of the CIA and Saudi Arabia. When the CIA began supplying Azzam's fighters with FIM-92 Stinger

---

Terrorist Group: "Lone Wolf" attack

Case Facts: On the morning of January 25, a Pakistani named Mir Aimal Kansi approached the CIA headquarters in a pickup truck. At a stoplight he exited his truck with an AK 47 and fired 11 shots into five vehicles that had stopped at the stoplight. He killed two CIA employees and wounded three others. He then left the scene and flew to Pakistan.

Investigation: The FBI investigation and overseas with the assistance of the CIA in Pakistan and Afghanistan tracked the assailant to the border region between Afghanistan and Pakistan four years after the attack in 1993. He was subsequently extradited and returned to the United States and tried for capital murder. He pleads guilty to the charges against him claiming his anger at U.S. policy in the Middle East. The investigation determined that he had acted alone and was not part of a terrorist group or conspiracy. He was convicted of murder in November 1997 and executed by lethal injection on November 14, 2002.

FIGURE 3-4 Terrorist attack brief: Headquarters Central Intelligence Agency, Langley Virginia—January 25, 1993. *Source*: http://www.clarkprosecutor.org/html/death/US/kasi807.htm.

man-portable, surface-to-air missiles, the conventional military superiority of the Soviet MI-24 helicopters was neutralized, deeply demoralizing the Soviet troops and hastening victory for the Mujahedeen fighters.

Azzam and his two sons were killed in a car bomb attack in Peshawar, Pakistan, in November 1989. His radical thoughts and ideology live on, however, through his related paramilitary manuals and a London-based media organization, Azzam Publications.

Azzam combined hatred for the West, Christians, and Jews, whom he routinely accused of carrying out diabolical conspiracies against Islam, with nostalgia for the days of the Islamic Caliphate, when non-Muslims were still treated formally as second-class citizens. It was the United States that seemed to epitomize for Azzam the ongoing Jewish-Christian conspiracy. Ironically, it was in the United States that Azzam was able to raise huge amounts of money, enlist new fighters, and, most important, provide the political freedom to freely coordinate with other top radical Islamic movements. Azzam helped bring about the mobilization of the Muslim Brotherhood Movement more than did any other leader. Today, the military wing of Hamas in the West Bank is called the Abdellah Azzam Brigades.[8]

PREPARATIONS FOR 9-11

Germany was the major launching pad for the four primary members of the 9-11 suicide plot developed by Osama bin Laden in Afghanistan. The recruits were well versed in Western society and held fervently anti-West ideologies and would suit bin Laden's needs for the attack on America. Mohamed Atta, Hani Hanjour, Marwan al Shehhi, and Ziad Jarrah completed their foundational training in Kandahar in 1999 and came to the United States in early 2000 to begin flight training. By now, al Qaeda possessed leaders who were able to evaluate, approve, and supervise the planning and direction of a major operation; a personnel system that could recruit candidates, indoctrinate them, vet them, and give them the necessary training; communications sufficient to enable planning and direction of operatives and those who would be helping them; an intelligence effort to gather required information and form assessments of enemy strengths and weaknesses; the ability to move people great distances; and the ability to raise and move money necessary to finance an attack.[9]

The planning stage inside the United States involved financing and training operatives for the 9-11 attack. The team members began training at flight schools in Florida and Oklahoma. All of the students were in the United States on "visitor" visas. According to the 9-11 Commission Report, the flight training was paid for by funds wired from Dubai between June and September 2001. Al Qaeda had assembled pilots but determined they would also require other teams to assault the cockpits and subdue the crews of the targeted flights. Twelve of the thirteen who were selected for this task came from Saudi Arabia; the thirteenth came from the United Arab Emirates. In assessing these teams, a Saudi investigation noted that members came from a variety of backgrounds:

- All were between twenty and twenty-eight years old;
- Most were unemployed;
- Most had little more than high school education;
- Most were probably unmarried; and
- Four came from a cluster of towns in an isolated and underdeveloped region of Saudi Arabia.

All of the hijackers who made the trip to the United States were not hindered by immigration or customs. None had arrived through Canada, as originally thought. Al Qaeda trained all of these terrorists in Afghanistan for this specific operation.

Throughout the summer months of 2001, the hijackers, including the trained pilots, undertook surveillance flights across the United States in the types of aircraft that they planned to hijack. At the same time, they tested the security system by carrying box cutters either on their person or in carry-on baggage.

Following the 9-11 attacks on the United States, there was an immediate outcry for a response in kind and to determine where to direct such a response. Osama bin Laden and his support network in Taliban-controlled Afghanistan came quickly to the forefront of targets. A meeting was held on September 13, 2001, between Richard Armitage, deputy secretary of state; Maleeha Lodhi, Pakistan's ambassador to the United States; and Mahmud Ahmed, the head of Pakistan's intelligence service. The deputy secretary stated that the United States wanted Pakistan to take the following steps:

- Stop al Qaeda operatives at its border and end all logistical support for bin Laden;
- Give the United States blanket overflight and landing rights for all necessary military and intelligence operations;
- Provide territorial access to the United States and allied military intelligence and other personnel to conduct operations against al Qaeda;
- Provide the United States with intelligence information;
- Publicly condemn the terrorist acts; and
- Cut off all shipments of fuel to the Taliban and stop recruits from going to Afghanistan.

The United States also wanted Pakistan to break relations with the Taliban government if the evidence implicated bin Laden, and al Qaeda, and the Taliban continued to harbor them.

Combined and improved dissemination of intelligence has been credited for many successes in the aftermath of 9-11, and Britain and Europe have been in the forefront of information sharing and cooperation. The British experience with homegrown terror and the openness of the threat posed by Islamic clerics, such as the hook-handed Abu Hamza al-Masri, a credible cleric yet, alone, was not immediately recognized, as a security threat to either Britain or its allies. However, Masri is currently wanted in the United States for his formation of a terrorist training camp in Oregon in 1999 and for his involvement in a kidnapping in Yemen. While he languishes in a British prison, the justice system in the United Kingdom has authorized his extradition to the United States once he completes his sentence for soliciting murder and inciting racial hatred. Al-Masri openly praised the success of the 9-11 attacks, and one of his young and impressionable students at his London mosque was Richard Reid, the shoe bomber.

The threat from within the United States will continue to focus on the minds of the security and intelligence community. Attempts by citizens to assemble and procure items to make bombs, both conventional and nonconventional, such as that by U.S. citizen Jose Padilla, will remain a high priority. He was arrested at Chicago O'Hare Airport on suspicion of plotting a dirty bomb attack. With the U.S. ability to hold such persons as "enemy combatants" continuing to be challenged, he was eventually indicted in 2005 and, although not charged with plotting to detonate a dirty bomb, was convicted along with three others in 2007. The fact remains that he is in prison and also cooperating with the FBI about any involvement he may have had with al Qaeda while outside of the United States.

THE AFTERMATH

There have been many questions on whether the U.S. authorities could have prevented the attacks on 9-11. However, the training for the crews operating on those flights worked against them and in the hijackers' favor, in that the crews did what they were trained to do—keep the passengers calm and do as the hijackers instructed. Unfortunately, they were never to know the true intentions of the hijackers, until it was too late.

The intelligence community knew that Osama bin Laden had threatened to "cut off the head of the serpent" (the United States) and cause mass casualties; it also knew that bin Laden was planning to do something with aircrafts. An FBI Field Office knew that several pilots were in training, but even with all of this information, the "dots were never connected." Could we have then expected anything else? Hindsight is always 20/20, and intelligence gathering is not a finite art, and it is invariably the case that after an event takes place, previously gathered information contributes a substantial evidence trail to the terrorist. In 2001, passenger screening was one of the lowest-paid and most menial tasks at airports, particularly in the United States. Aviation security suffered a major blow to its performance and credibility—and rightly so. For more than two decades, the industry has lacked any desire to beef up security—a fact clearly laid bare on 9-11. Airline crew training programs had never covered how to tackle determined terrorists, and the cockpits had an almost "open-door" policy for visitors. No one suspected that dedicated terrorists would commit mass suicide in such a ghastly manner as occurred on 9-11. Historical terror events and "dots" pointed clearly to a buildup by internationalized terror fanatics from the Islamic world, with serious planning for inflicting attacks against U.S. targets. So, it was purely a matter of *when* and not *if* an attack would come to the U.S. shores. However, the United States and the rest of the world were not prepared for the outcome or the reaction to it. The failure of the United States and other intelligence organizations to correctly intercept the 9-11 operatives could be blamed on historical events. Since the end of the Cold War, the need for covert operatives had been in decline. Many CIA specialists were moved to different areas of activity, such as the Balkans or Africa. Further, the levels of new recruits to the CIA continued to decline. By the end of the last decade of the twentieth century, the CIA was virtually stripped of any incoming new recruits. Recruits to the CIA typically took a period of seven years of training to become fully effective.

Chronology of Events of September 11, 2001

08:46:40	Hijacked American Airlines Flight 11 flew into the upper portion of the North Tower of New York's World Trade Center. The aircraft cut through floors 93–99.
09:03:11	Hijacked United Airlines Flight 175 flew into the South Tower of the World Trade Center. The aircraft cut through floors 77–85.
09:37	Hijacked American Airlines Flight 77 crashed into the west wall of the Pentagon in Washington DC.
09:40	The FAA suspends all U.S. air traffic. This is the first time that this drastic action has been undertaken.
09:58:59	In a period of ten seconds, the South Tower of the World Trade Center collapses.
10:10	A portion of the west side of the Pentagon collapses.
10:10	United Airlines Flight 93, also hijacked, crashes in Shanksville, Somerset County, Pennsylvania.
10:28	The North Tower of the World Trade Center collapses.

More than 2,600 people died at the World Trade Center; 125 died at the Pentagon; and 256 died on the four aircraft. The death toll on 9-11 surpassed that of the surprise Japanese attack on Pearl Harbor in December 1941.[10]

The War on Terror materialized through a pre-9-11 directive concerning al Qaeda and evolved into National Security Presidential Directive 9 entitled, "Defeating the Terrorist Threat to the United States." This directive would extend to a global war against terrorism—not just aimed at al Qaeda but also at nations that harbored terrorists and terror groups and organizations.

In October 2001, U.S. forces began their attack on Afghanistan, along with a coalition of forces, aimed at dislodging the Taliban and capturing Osama bin Laden. In August 2006, the U.S. government issued its National Strategy for Combating Terrorism document. The document makes its central platform that to win the War on Terror, the United States must

- Advance effective democracies as the long-term antidote to the ideology of terrorism;
- Prevent attacks by terrorist networks;
- Deny weapons of mass destruction to rogue states and terrorist allies who seek to use them;
- Deny terrorists the support and sanctuary of rogue states;
- Deny terrorists control of any nation they would use as a base and launching pad for terror; and
- Lay the foundations, and build the institutions and structures needed to carry the fight forward against terror, and help ensure ultimate success.

The next step is to understand how the radicalization of Muslims has taken place and how that threat may exist in the United States. The 2005 attacks in the United Kingdom were from radicalized young men who were either born in the United Kingdom or immigrated at a young age. The fact that all were unremarkable and had drawn little or no attention is something that the United States will have to consider when attempting to define how the next attack will materialize from inspiration and ideology—inspiration gathered from the spectacular events of 9-11 and ideology from the al Qaeda leader Osama bin Laden preaching a global jihad, turning young men into inspired "Holy Warriors." One of the main perpetrators captured by the United States as one of the masterminds of the 9-11 attacks was Khalid Sheikh Mohammed (KSM). Born in Kuwait, he attended and graduated from North Carolina A&T State University in 1986 with a degree in mechanical engineering. He spent time in Afghanistan fighting the Soviets and joined with Ramzi Yousef in the Philippines in 1994 to organize the "Bojinka" plot, which was to target at least a dozen commercial airliners with simultaneous bombings over the Pacific Ocean. Intelligence agencies disrupted the planning for this attack, and Yousef was subsequently captured in 1995. Between 1995 and 2001, KSM was in hiding but had persuaded Osama bin Laden to provide him with operatives and logistical support for a new airliner attack. The culmination of the planning was the attacks on New York and Washington on September 11, 2001. KSM headed the Al Qaeda Media Committee from 2000 and helped build ties and close operational support between Al Qaeda and Jemaah Islamiya (JI), which was plotting against U.S. and Israeli targets in Southeast Asia.

As we see in so many events involving terrorism, the terrorists take every opportunity to exploit deficiencies in security systems, and it is particularly so when it comes to aviation. The terrorists have a particular fascination for attacking both airliners and airports. The "Bojinka II" plot stands out as a more sophisticated version of the plot to detonate bombs on airliners over the Pacific in the mid 1990s; it, was foiled in Britain with the arrest of twenty-four British-born Muslims in August 2006. Although it's never been determined exactly how many aircraft were to be targeted in this attack, the explosives were to be brought onto aircraft in liquid form and disguised as sport drinks. These improvised explosive devices (IEDs) would then be assembled and detonated in midair believed to be on aircraft departing the Great Britain for the United States. It is obvious that had the plot succeeded, the death toll could well have reached the number of deaths witnessed on 9-11. The plot was far reaching with terrorist planning and operational cells spread around the world and is believed to have originated in Pakistan.[11]

RADICAL ISLAM AND THE UNITED STATES

As we look to the future, we have to determine what threats are posed to the U.S. homeland from radicalized Muslims. Jihad is a flourishing ideology, and while it thrives, those wishing to embrace such an ideology continue to pose a threat. The experiences in Britain and Europe from radicalized Muslims could well be the example for attacks in the United States. Governments cannot protect every building and every citizen and therefore cannot protect every target. The threat from the homegrown jihadist comes from a reality that those trying to enter the United States will use whatever legal and illegal means they can employ, whether they originate from countries in the U.S. Visa Waiver Program or have entered illegally through either Canada or Mexico; they may also be current U.S. citizens presently conspiring to attack the country from within. It is a tactical reality that these individuals exist and are already on U.S. soil.

In review of the terrorist attacks by homegrown terrorists in the United Kingdom in 2005, we can begin to get a picture of a radicalized jihadist. He is invariably the child of moderate Muslim immigrants and aged under thirty-five. The jihadist comes from a varied ethnic background and, contrary to popular belief, is not economically destitute, but rather has a full-time job and is well educated. There is little evidence to suggest that they have any criminal background, therefore making them more unremarkable! Mohammad Siddique Khan, one of the 2005 London bombers, was in fact a family man; he had studied business at Leeds

Metropolitan University from 1998 to 2001 and was working as a teaching assistant with young children. So what transformation did this young man undergo that would lead him to become a suicide bomber in his country of birth?

The jihadi-Salafi ideology is the driver that motivates young men and women, either born or living in the West, to carry out "autonomous jihad" via acts of terrorism against their host countries. This ideology has served as the inspiration for groups such as those that carried out the Madrid train attacks in 2004, The Dutch Hofstsad Group, the 2005 London bombers, as well as the eighteen Canadians arrested in Toronto in 2006 (see Chapter 4). The New York Police Department (NYPD) Intelligence Division undertook a review of radical Islam to better understand the phases that went into the process of radicalization, and their review paper identified four specific phases in the process:

1. Pre-radicalization
2. Self-identification
3. Indoctrination
4. Jihadization

Although the NYPD model is sequential, individuals do not always follow a perfectly linear progression; however, those who do pass through the entire process are quite likely to become involved in the setup and organization of terror attacks.

PRE-RADICALIZATION

This is the point of origin for individuals before they began this progression. It is their life situation before they were exposed to and adopted jihadi-Salafi Islam for their own ideology. The majority of the individuals involved in plots came from unremarkable backgrounds and jobs and lived seemingly normal crime-free lives. The Toronto eighteen terror suspects reportedly were well integrated into Canadian society.

SELF-IDENTIFICATION

This is the phase where individuals, influenced by both internal and external factors, begin their exploration of Salafist Islam, gradually gravitate away from their old identity and begin to associate themselves with like-minded individuals and adopt this ideology as their own. In the Toronto case, the suspects had struggled with their identity, and some had formed a religious club and chat groups; they had also adopted the traditional Muslim style of dress, and some grew beards. The catalyst for this religious seeking is a cognitive opening or crisis, which shakes one's certitude in previously held beliefs and opens an individual to be receptive to new world-views. What those worldviews are and what specific event sparks the religious changes could be many varied events, be it social, economic, or world events involving Muslims, or even a family member's death.

INDOCTRINATION

This is the period when the individual progressively intensifies his beliefs and wholly adopts Salafist teachings and ideology and concludes that the conditions and circumstances exist for action to further and support the cause of jihad. In most events, this phase is driven by a "spiritual sanctioner." While the initial self-indoctrination process may be an individual act, association with like-minded individuals is an important factor as the process deepens. By the indoctrination phase, this self-selecting group becomes increasingly important as radical views are encouraged as well as reinforced by the religious sanctioner.

Another example of homegrown threats against the United States, successfully investigated by FBI, is the "Lackawanna Group," a reference to the working class town of Lackawanna, south of Buffalo, where the Islamist conspirators came from, and is home to 3,000 Muslim Americans, whose families come from the Republic of Yemen, on the Arabian Peninsula. The inspirational leader of the Lackawanna Group was Kamal Derwish who, although born in Buffalo and raised in Saudi Arabia, is steeped in that country's fundamentalist breed of Islam, known as Wahhabism. Derwish had trained in al Qaeda camps in Afghanistan and fought with Muslims in Bosnia. After returning to Saudi Arabia in 1997, he had been jailed for extremist activities. He returned to the United States in 2001 and began to inspire a group of like-minded young Muslims at his local mosque. This can be likened to the events that happened at London's Finsbury Park mosque, where Abu Hamza al Masri preached his hatred of the West. In the spring of 2001, the following group members flew to Afghanistan for training: Mukhtar al-Bakri, Sahim Alwan, Jaber Elbaneh, Faysal Galab, Yahya Goba, Shafal Mosed, and Yasein Taher. Juma Al Dosari, who it is believed had fought with other Muslim fighters alongside Kamal Derwish in Bosnia, arrived in the United States in early 2001 and joined the Lackawanna Group. The Buffalo FBI Field Office was alerted to the Yemeni group via an anonymous letter, and, although the group was investigated, no charges could be substantiated. Following the 9-11 attacks, Al Dosari left to fight with the Taliban in Afghanistan and was captured while doing so sometime in the fall of 2001.

He was declared an enemy combatant and sent to the U.S. Naval Base on Guantanamo Bay, Cuba, where he was questioned. Al Dosari's interrogation confirmed that the Lackawanna suspects were the targets of an al Qaeda recruitment operation. Mukhtar al-Bakri was arrested by Bahraini Police in September 2002 and subsequently interviewed by the CIA. He revealed the names of the other members of the Lackawanna Group; Sahim Alwan, Faysal Galab, Yahya Goba, Shafal Mosed, and Yasein Taher were arrested. In early November 2002, Kamal Derwish was killed in Yemen by a CIA Predator Drone while tracking the al Qaeda plotters of the USS *Cole* attack. Although Derwish was an American citizen, the government would not discuss his death or any connections he may have or have had with al Qaeda. This very brief example indicates the very real problems that exist within the Muslim communities in the United States. The Lackawanna Group was sentenced to between seven and ten years in prison in 2003 and has been cooperating with the government.

The Lackawanna case is just possibly the tip of an as-yet-undiscovered iceberg of terrorist cells that, although unlikely being directed by al Qaeda, are inspired by the terrorist movement to act independently.

How Muslims integrate and how they view themselves not only in the United States but also in other Western countries is an ongoing concern not just to religious groups but to governments as well. The overwhelming view from research companies such as Pew Research point out that many Muslims feel better off in Western society, although their standard of living is often not comparable to that of the general population in the host country.

The widespread appeal of Islamic extremism in the United States is certainly being taken seriously—the problem applies to many European countries as well as the United States. The ability of young Muslim men to become influenced through Internet chat rooms as well as travelling to areas of North Africa and Afghanistan will continue to pose a security threat to the homeland. The list below typifies the activities that are taking place and the very real threats they pose:

- July 2009: Daniel Patrick Boyd—conspiracy to commit murder. From North Carolina along with his two sons accused of discussing violent jihad and possession of weapons. The U.S. Marine Corps Base at Quantico Virginia was the suspected target.
- September 2009: Najibullah Zazi from Denver—plotting to set off a bomb on the New York subway system.
- October 2009: Colleen LaRose from Philadelphia—online name Jihad Jane, allegedly agreed to kill a Swedish artist who drew a picture of the prophet Mohammed with the body of a dog.
- November 2009: Eight Somali Americans charged with attending camps and training with Al-Shahab in Somalia.
- November 2009: A man of Palestinian descent but born in the United States, Major Nidal Malik Hasan, a U.S. Army psychiatrist accused of killing 13 people at Ford Hood, Texas.
- December 2009: Five men from Alexandria arrested in Pakistan charged in an extensive plot that included possible attacks in the United States and fighting troops in Afghanistan.
- May 2010: Faisal Shahzad, born in Pakistan but became a U.S. citizen, allegedly tries to set off a car bomb in Times Square, New York.[12]

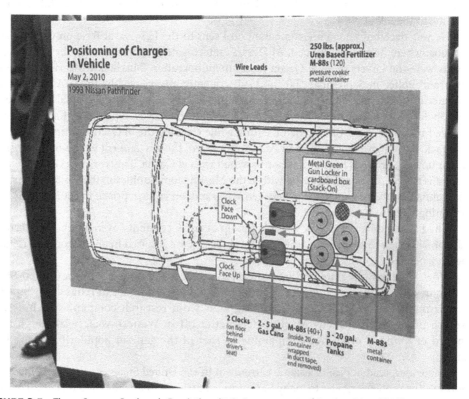

FIGURE 3-5   Times Square Car bomb Depiction (U.S. Department of Justice, May 2010).

Terrorist Group: Pakistani Taliban (influenced/sponsored)

Case Facts: At around 6.00 P.M on May 1, a Nissan SUV was abandoned in Time Square; subsequently smoke was seen to be coming from inside the vehicle. A male of Asian origin was seen removing his shirt before leaving the SUV. An NYPD Mounted officer was alerted by street vendors; on investigation, he noticed smoke coming from the vents, the SUV engine was running, and there were canisters inside the SUV. The immediate area was evacuated and bomb disposal teams were called in.

Investigation: An Nissan SUV had been parked in Time Square where large number of tourists were gathered. The bomb had been primed to explode and had failed to do so. Had the bomb detonated, it would have caused significant loss of life and damage. The investigation and forensic evidence gathered from the vehicle led the FBI Joint Terrorism Task Force to Faisal Shahzad. In December 2009, Shahzad received explosives training in Waziristan, Pakistan, from explosive trainers affiliated with Tehrik-e-Taliban, a militant extremist group based in Pakistan. On February 25, 2010, Shahzad received approximately $5,000 in cash in Massachusetts sent from a coconspirator (CC-1) in Pakistan whom Shahzad understood worked for Tehrik-e-Taliban. Approximately six weeks later, on April 10, 2010, Shahzad received an additional $7,000 in cash in Ronkonkoma, New York, which was also sent at CC-1's direction.

On March 15, 2010, Shahzad purchased a semiautomatic 9 millimeter Kel-Tec rifle in Connecticut. This rifle was found, loaded, in Shahzad's car on the day of his arrest. In April 2010, Shahzad contacted the seller of a Nissan Pathfinder after seeing an advertisement posted on a website. Thereafter, on April 24, 2010, Shahzad and the seller of the Pathfinder agreed to meet in a supermarket parking lot in Connecticut, where Shahzad paid the seller $1,300 for the Pathfinder. In April 2010, Shahzad also purchased components for the improvised explosive and incendiary devices that he loaded into the Pathfinder on May 1, 2010. On May 1, 2010, Shahzad drove the Pathfinder, loaded with the improvised explosive and incendiary devices, to Manhattan and parked the Pathfinder in Times Square in the vicinity of 45th Street and Seventh Avenue. After parking the Pathfinder, Shahzad attempted to begin the detonation process of the improvised explosive and incendiary devices. Thereafter, Shahzad abandoned the Pathfinder and returned to his residence in Connecticut.

On May 3, 2010, Shahzad drove from Connecticut to JFK Airport as he attempted to flee to Dubai. He was arrested later that same day at JFK. After his arrest, Shahzad admitted that he had recently received bomb-making training in Pakistan. He also admitted that he had brought the Pathfinder to Times Square and attempted to detonate it. He was convicted on October 5, 2010, and sentenced to life in prison without parole.

FIGURE 3-6 Terrorist attack brief: Time Square—New York, May 1, 2010—Car bomb. *Source*: U.S. Department of Justice—Office of Public Affairs.

WATCH LISTS

Testimony before the Committee on Homeland Security and Governmental Affairs, U.S. Senate, October 2007

Pursuant to Homeland Security Presidential Directive 6, the Attorney General established Terrorist Screening Centers (TSCs) in September 2003 to consolidate the government's approach to terrorism screening and provide for the appropriate and lawful use of terrorist information in screening processes. TSC's consolidated watch list is the U.S. government's master repository for all records of known or appropriately suspected international and domestic terrorists used for watch list-related screening.

- When an individual makes an airline reservation, arrives at a U.S. port of entry, or applies for a U.S. visa, or is stopped by state or local police within the United States, the frontline screening agency or airline conducts a name-based search of the individual against applicable terrorist watch list records. In general, when the computerized name-matching system of an airline or screening agency generates a "hit" (a potential name match) against a watch list record, the airline or agency is to review each potential match. Any obvious mismatches (negative matches) are to be resolved by the airline or agency. Page 3 GAO-08-194T.

  The National Counterterrorism Center and the FBI rely upon standards of reasonableness in determining which individuals are appropriate for inclusion on TSC's consolidated terrorist watch list. In general, individuals who are reasonably suspected of having possible links to terrorism—in addition to individuals with known links—are to be nominated. As such, inclusion on the list does not automatically prohibit an individual from, for example, obtaining a visa or entering the United States. As of May 2007, TSC's watch list contained approximately 755,000 records.

- From December 2003 (when TSC began operations) through May 2007, agencies encountered individuals who were on the watch list about 53,000 times. Many individuals were encountered multiple times. Actions taken in response included arresting individuals and denying others entry into the United States. Most often, however, agencies questioned and then released the individuals because there was not sufficient evidence of criminal or terrorist activity to warrant further legal action. Nevertheless, such questioning allowed agencies to collect information on the individuals, which was shared with law enforcement agencies and the intelligence community.

- Screening agencies do not check against all records in the consolidated watch list, partly because screening against certain records (1) may not be needed to support the respective agency's mission or (2) may not be possible owing to the requirements of computer programs used to check individuals against watch list records. Not checking against all records may pose a security risk. Also, some subjects of watch list records have passed undetected through agency screening processes and were not identified, for example, until after they had boarded and flew on an aircraft. Federal agencies have ongoing initiatives to help reduce these potential vulnerabilities.

- The federal government has made progress in using the consolidated watch list for screening purposes, but it has not (1) finalized guidelines for using watch list records within critical infrastructure components of the private sector or (2) identified all appropriate opportunities for which terrorist-related screening should be applied. Further, the government lacks an up-to-date strategy and implementation plan—supported by a clearly defined leadership or governance structure—which are important for enhancing the effectiveness of terrorist-related screening.

Several actions have been recommended to promote a more comprehensive and coordinated approach to terrorist-related screening. Among them are actions to monitor and respond to vulnerabilities and to establish up-to-date guidelines, strategies, and plans to facilitate expanded and enhanced use of the list. The Department of Homeland Security and the FBI generally agreed with GAO findings and recommendations.[13]

EXTRAORDINARY RENDITION

After more than a decade of the "War on Terror," state-sponsored terrorism, homegrown terrorism and religiously inspired terror groups and individuals continue to pose a threat to democracies around the world. Afghanistan has been largely forgotten as the United States and other nations begin to withdraw from that devastated region. Iraq continues to stagger under the burden of Islamic sectarian fighting as varying militia groups vie for control, and the country is more reminiscent of a "failed state" than a new democracy. In the United States, the question of dealing with terrorists and the need to gather much needed intelligence became a major priority for the former Bush Administration. The U.S. government did not recognize those captured in both Afghanistan and Iraq as being prisoners of war, but rather as "enemy combatants." This led to speculation surrounding treatment of the detainees in Guantanamo Bay, as well as the well-documented 2006 abuses at Abu Ghraib prison near Baghdad by U.S. Military Police and other agencies of the U.S. Government. The stories of abuse became front-page media stories in the Middle East with You Tube videos depicting military personnel engaging in degrading and abusive attacks on Iraqi prisoners.

Back home, the need for solid intelligence continued. Complaints have been made by Amnesty International and others that the United States, in its race and determination to go to extraordinary lengths to gather information, is violating both U.S. and international laws. By categorizing detainees as enemy combatants, the United States does not apply the rigorous standards required under the Geneva conventions. What is taking place and being driven in secret, presumably by the CIA, is an activity referred to as **extraordinary rendition**, which has been defined as "the transfer of an individual, with the involvement of the United States or its agents, to a foreign state in circumstances that make it more likely than not, that the individual will be subjected to torture, or cruel, inhuman, or degrading treatment."[14] This practice has not had much press in the United States, likely because of the secret manner in which it is being conducted. However, there are cases of "rendition" that took place prior to 9-11, and certainly the practice has been even more widespread since that tragic event. Specifically, critics claim the United States is violating international conventions that ban the use of torture. Since 9-11, dozens of "enemy combatants" have been sent to third-party countries such as Morocco, Saudi Arabia, Yemen, Egypt, and Jordan. All of these countries—in particular, Egypt and Jordan—have close ties to the CIA, and all have been cited by the U.S. State Department as using torture in interrogations. Detainees have been taken often under cover of darkness and transported by private jet to these countries for interrogation. The interrogation tactics used would be illegal if conducted inside the United States. The Convention against Torture prohibits torture carried out at the "instigation of or with the consent or acquiescence" of officials. Handing someone over to a foreign intelligence service with the knowledge that the person will be tortured fits within the prohibitions of the convention. It also appears that U.S. officials engage in the treatment of detainees that may include torture. Witnesses have reported that captives are "softened up" by the U.S. military. The detainees are said to have been blindfolded and thrown into wells, bound in painful positions, subjected to loud noises, and deprived of sleep. There is growing resistance to the use of torture even from law enforcement officials.[15] Article 3 of the United Nations Convention against Torture, to which the United States is a signatory, states that "no party shall expel, return ('refouler') or extradite a person to another State where there are substantial grounds for believing that person would be in danger of being subjected to torture. For the purpose of determining whether there are such grounds, the competent authorities shall take into account all relevant considerations including, where applicable, the existence in the State concerned of a consistent pattern of gross, flagrant, or mass violations of human rights."

Maher Arar—Canadian Citizen

While the number of cases and the extent to which the government is involved in rendition is uncertain, there is a significant case that has embarrassed both the U.S. and Canadian governments for the manner in which a Canadian citizen, transiting through JFK en route back into Canada, was detained and sent on to Syria. Arar came to Canada with his family and had no intention, according to him, of returning to Syria. In the wake and paranoia of 9-11, it is entirely probable that mistakes were made in targeting individuals for this form of treatment. Failings by the Canadian intelligence service and the RCMP led to an individual being forcibly removed from an in-transit location to Syria, where he remained incarcerated and, according to Amnesty International, was severely tortured. He was released on October 5, 2003, 374 days after first being deported to Syria. No charges have been brought against him by Syria, the United States, or Canada even though it was alleged that he had contact with al Qaeda sympathizers.

USA Patriot Improvement Act

On March 9, 2006, President Bush signed the USA PATRIOT Improvement and Reauthorization Act of 2005. Since its enactment in October 2001, the Patriot Act has been vital to winning the War on Terror and protecting the American people. The legislation allows intelligence and law enforcement officials to continue sharing information and using the same tools against terrorists already employed against drug dealers and other criminals. While safeguarding Americans' civil liberties, this legislation also strengthens the U.S. Department of Justice (DOJ) so that it can better detect and disrupt terrorist threats, and it also gives law enforcement new tools to combat threats. America still faces dangerous enemies, and no priority is more important to the U.S. president than protecting the American people without delay.

THE PATRIOT ACT CLOSES DANGEROUS LAW ENFORCEMENT AND INTELLIGENCE GAPS

The Patriot Act Has Accomplished Exactly What It Was Designed to Do

- It has helped us detect terrorist cells, disrupt terrorist plots, and save American lives.
- The Patriot Act has helped law enforcement break up terror cells in Ohio, New York, Oregon, and Virginia.
- The Patriot Act has helped in the prosecution of terrorist operatives and supporters in California, Texas, New Jersey, Illinois Washington, and North Carolina.

The Patriot Act Authorizes Vital Information Sharing to Help Law Enforcement and Intelligence Officials Connect the Dots Before Terrorists Strike   The Patriot Act enables necessary cooperation and information sharing by helping to break down legal and bureaucratic walls separating criminal investigators from intelligence officers.

The Patriot Act Eliminates Double Standards by Allowing Agents to Pursue Terrorists with the Same Tools They Use Against Other Criminals   Before the Patriot Act, it was easier to track a drug dealer's phone contacts than a terrorist's phone contacts, and it was easier to obtain a tax cheat's credit card receipts than to trace the financial support of an al Qaeda fund-raiser. The Patriot Act corrected these double standards—and America is safer as a result.

The Patriot Act Adapts the Law to Modern Technology   The Patriot Act allows Internet service providers to disclose customer records voluntarily to the government in emergencies involving an immediate risk of death or serious physical injury and permits victims of hacking crimes to request law enforcement assistance in monitoring trespassers on their computers.

The Patriot Act Preserves Our Freedoms and Upholds the Rule of Law   The legislation signed today adds over thirty new significant civil liberties provisions.

THE PATRIOT ACT REAUTHORIZATION SAFEGUARDS OUR NATION

The Patriot Act Reauthorization Creates a New Assistant Attorney General for National Security   By creating a new Assistant Attorney General for National Security, this legislation fulfills a critical recommendation of the Commission on the Intelligence Capabilities of the United States regarding Weapons of Mass Destruction. This allows the Justice Department to bring its national security, counterterrorism, counterintelligence, and foreign intelligence surveillance operations under a single authority.

The Patriot Act Reauthorization Tackles Terrorism Financing   This bill enhances penalties for terrorism financing and closes a loophole concerning terrorist financing through "hawalas" (informal money transfer networks) rather than traditional financial institutions.

The Patriot Act Reauthorization Protects Mass Transportation   This bill provides clear standards and tough penalties for attacks on our land- and water-based mass transportation systems, as well as commercial aviation.

THE PATRIOT ACT REAUTHORIZATION COMBATS METHAMPHETAMINE ABUSE

The Patriot Act Reauthorization Includes the Combat Methamphetamine Epidemic Act of 2005   This bill introduces commonsense safeguards that will make many ingredients used in methamphetamine manufacturing more difficult to obtain in bulk and easier for law enforcement to track. For example, the bill places limits on large-scale purchases of over-the-counter drugs that are used to manufacture methamphetamines and requires stores to keep these ingredients behind the counter or in locked display cases. It increases penalties for smuggling and selling methamphetamines.[16]

INTERNATIONAL TERRORISM

After 9-11, foreign terrorists of every stripe could not but now think of the United States as being vulnerable—an easy priority target. Despite the rapid mobilization efforts by Homeland Security on land, rail, and in the air, terrorists and their supporters continue to live in and travel with relative ease throughout the United States. Ironically, the U.S. drug-using population still continues to help finance terrorism around the world by being a major consumer of the entire spectrum of illegal drugs. These narco-dollars continue to fill the war chests of terrorist groups around the world. Narco-terrorists purchase cut-down cocaine shipped from Colombia through Mexico and the Caribbean, and brown tar heroin, marijuana, and, increasingly, methamphetamine from Mexico. The American user continues as a consumer of high-quality Southeast Asian heroin from the Golden Triangle regions. America is a major illicit producer of its own cannabis, depressants, stimulants, hallucinogens, methamphetamine, and designer drugs such as Ecstasy. This creates a multibillion-dollar need for drug money–laundering centers. And then the cycle repeats itself, on and on.

U.S. citizens worldwide killed as a result of incidents of terrorism: 15; U.S. citizens worldwide injured as a result of incidents of terrorism: 9; U.S. citizens worldwide kidnapped as a result of incidents of terrorism: 0.

TERRORISM DEATHS OF PRIVATE U.S. CITIZENS IN 2010 (BY COUNTRY)

Terrorism Deaths of Private US Citizen in 2010 (by Country)

Country	Date of Death	Number	Location
Afghanistan	Saturday, July 10, 2010	1	Kandahar, Afghanistan
	Thursday, July 29, 2010	1	Sheberghan, Afghanistan
	Thursday, August 5, 2010	6	Faizabad, Badakhshan, Afghanistan
	Monday, September 6, 2010	2	Kandahar, Afghanistan
	Monday, September 6, 2010	2	Kabul, Afghanistan
	Tuesday, September 7, 2010	1	Kandahar, Afghanistan
Iraq	Friday, July 23, 2010	1	FOB Kasul, Iraq
Uganda	Sunday, July 11, 2010	1	Kampala, Uganda

Terrorism Injuries of Private U.S. Citizen in 2010 (by Country)

Country	Date of Injury	Number	Location
Uganda	Sunday, July 11, 2010	7	Kampala
Philippines	Thursday, August 5, 2010	1	Manila
Germany	Friday, March 12, 2010	1	Berlin

The term "Private U.S. Citizen" refers to any U.S. citizen not acting in an official capacity on behalf of the U.S. Government; therefore, these figures do not include, for example, U.S. military personnel killed or injured in a terrorism-related incident while on active duty or employees of the Department of State and other federal agencies. Members of U.S. government employees' households are considered private U.S. citizens.

Although every effort was made to include all terrorism-related deaths and injuries involving private U.S. citizens, the figures above reflect only those cases reported to, or known by, the U.S. Department of State, and may not reflect actual numbers of injured, which may not always be reported depending on their severity. As NCTC also notes, in the cases of Iraq and Afghanistan, it is particularly difficult to gather comprehensive information about all incidents and to distinguish terrorism from the numerous other forms of violence.

FIGURE 3-7 Terrorism Deaths, Injuries, Kidnappings of Private U.S. Citizens, 2010. *Source*: Provided by the Bureau of Consular Affairs, U.S. Department of State.

RELIGIOUS EXTREMISM

Jamaat al-Fuqra

There resides, somewhat eerily, a network of possible terrorists-in-waiting within a little-known organization called **Jamaat al-Fuqra**, which has the literal translation, "community of the impoverished." This group's Islamic roots in the United States date back as far as 1980, when it was founded by Sheik Mubarak Ali Gilani, a Pakistani cleric, who incorporated the group under the name of "Muslims of America." The organization has tax-exempt status in the United States and an educational section that supports student training in Pakistan. The group has done little to draw attention to itself in mainstream United States and all but denies its very existence. One of al-Fuqra's first members was Stephen Paul Paster, who had converted to Islam and was convicted of bombing a hotel that was owned by an Indian cult in Portland, Oregon, in 1983. On his release from prison, Paster went to Pakistan, where he joined Gilani and other instructors teaching advanced courses in Islamic military warfare. On a broader scale, al-Fuqra members are believed to have been involved in fighting in Chechnya, Bosnia, Afghanistan, Kashmir, and Lebanon. U.S. sources believe some of its members are affiliated with the al-Kifah Refugee Center in Brooklyn, New York. Following the first attack on the World Trade Center in 1993, the FBI determined that Muslim men, including participants in the attack, had been recruited at the al-Kifah refugee office in Brooklyn and sent to training camps in Afghanistan—first to fight the Soviet army and later to engage in a jihad against the United States. In 1993, the FBI also learned of a plot to blow up bridges, tunnels, and landmarks in New York. That investigation led to the conviction of Omar Abdul al-Rahman, the "Blind Sheikh," for soliciting others to commit all of those acts of terrorism in 1993. A further connection linked the infamous "shoe bomber," Richard Reid, to the Brooklyn office. Moreover, *The Wall Street Journal* reporter Daniel Pearl was investigating Gilani in Pakistan when he was kidnapped and murdered.

Islamic Extremism—A U.S. Military Case

The Fort Hood shooting in November 2009 could have been put down to a workplace violence incident or as is often referred to as someone "going postal." The alleged perpetrator was a serving military officer and psychiatrist Major Nidal Malik Hasan. His activities and possible disillusionment with not just the military but also his adopted country first surfaced in 2008 when he came to the attention of the **Joint Terrorism Task Force (JTTF)**. So what was it that could have turned this professional soldier and doctor against his country? To many observers this was a case of terrorism but maybe that oversimplifies the issues. We find the following testimony provided by Brian Jenkins before the Senate Homeland Security and Governmental Affairs Committee on November 19, 2009, to be both intuitive and instructive in evaluating terrorist incidents.

Again, based solely upon what has been publicly reported, the path that takes Hasan to the Fort Hood slayings includes many of the signposts identified in the radicalization process: his search for meaning and spiritual guidance, his engagement via the Internet with jihadist ideology, his adoption of the jihadist view that the West and Islam are irreconcilably opposed, the broadening of his sense of grievance from the personal to what he saw as a besieged Muslim community, his reported online encounter with an enabler—a jihadist imam whose writings would morally validate and reinforce Hasan's own feelings of anger and aggression, his expression of extremist views, and at some point, his decision to kill. If some of the markers of radicalization and recruitment are missing, it is because, except for Hasan's reported correspondence with the imam, Anwar al-Awlaki, his journey may have been entirely an interior one.

We seek the comfort of certain categorization. Precision is a prerequisite of the law. But human behavior is more complex and provides no bright line between murderer and terrorist. In 1997, a seventy-year-old Palestinian immigrant opened fire on the observation deck of the Empire State Building, killing one person and wounding seven others before taking his own life.

He carried with him rambling, confused letters denouncing Zionists, France, and the United States, but there were also claims that he had been bilked by con artists who left him penniless. Although his motives reflect a tangle of personal and political grievances, his action is generally classified as an incident of terrorism.

In 2002, an Egyptian chauffer opened fire on passengers at the El Al counter at LAX. Again, there was no evidence of radicalization, but his choice of target made him a terrorist in the eyes of many. The factors that drove these two men to kill are murky. We do not know how much to credit personal distress or political intent. As with Major Hasan, the underlying motives may have been personal, but they were acted out in a political realm. Within the ranks of true terrorists, we also find those who became terrorists in response to profound personal crises, rather than deep political convictions, muddled individuals who were swept along by others they happened to meet or who radicalized themselves, sociopaths attracted by the practice of violence. Terrorism, by its very nature, does not attract the well adjusted. Mass killings like the one at Fort Hood invariably prompt the question, Could it have been prevented? Seen through a rearview mirror, the clues appear tantalizingly obvious—if only we had been able to connect the dots. That famous phrase sometimes seduces us into overestimating what is reasonably knowable. While I await the government's own inquiry, in this case I remain skeptical. We do not, nor would we want, to live in a police state where every dubious remark, questionable correspondence, or relationship deemed suspicious is noted, recorded, and scrutinized for signs of dangerous deviancy. As a practical matter, it cannot be done. Communist East Germany's Stasi kept several hundred thousand officials busy poring over dossiers on its citizens; it is an obsession and a fate we would not want to emulate.... Some analysts say that al Qaeda is currently following a strategy of "leaderless resistance." Leaderless resistance envisions an army of autonomous terrorist operatives, united in a common cause, but not connected organizationally. Although it is difficult for authorities to destroy a leaderless enterprise, leaderless resistance is a strategy of weakness. Outside of Pakistan and Afghanistan, its leaders can do little other than exhort others to violence. However, leaderless resistance does enable terrorist leaders to assert ownership of just about every homicidal maniac on the planet, thus projecting an illusion of strength. Major Hasan's Internet imam was quick to praise the Fort Hood murders as another jihad victory. Since 9-11, authorities in the United States have uncovered nearly thirty terrorist plots involving "homegrown terrorists." This total includes plots to carry out attacks in the United States or abroad, as well as support for foreign terrorist organizations. Although not all of the plots, if undiscovered, are likely to have resulted in successful attacks, very little separates the ambitions of jihadist wannabes from a deadly terrorist assault. The essential ingredient is intent. Domestic intelligence collection remains a necessary and critical component of homeland security. Authorities uncovered eight of these terrorist plots in 2009; adding two actual attacks (the shooting in Arkansas and the Fort Hood case) puts the level of activity in 2009 much higher than that of previous years. Apart from common inspiration, there is no evidence of any organizational connection between these events. They appear to be individual responses to jihadist propaganda in the context of U.S. policy decisions. American foreign policy should not be determined by a handful of shooters and would-be bombers, but we must accept the fact that what America does in the Middle East, Afghanistan, and Pakistan may provoke terrorism in the United States. Wars are no longer confined geographically.

Six of the plots since 9-11 targeted American soldiers or military facilities in the United States: (Torrance, 2005; Fort Dix, 2006; New York City, May 2009; Arkansas, 2009; North Carolina, 2009; and Fort Hood, 2009), which could reflect in part jihadist exhortation and in part the plotters' own perceptions that attacking military targets is more legitimate than attacking civilians. However, the majority of the plots appear to have been aimed at causing mass civilian casualties, especially in public transportation venues. What does the Hasan case tell us about the radicalization of Muslims in America? Not a lot. In all, roughly 100 individuals in these plots have been charged with crimes related to terrorism. These include Muslim immigrants, native-born Muslims, and converts to Islam. Almost all were here legally. Most are U.S. citizens. A few, like Nidal Hasan, were veterans of military service. Some of the terrorist plotters uncovered in the United States began to radicalize before 9-11, while others, like Hasan, are more recent converts to jihadist worldviews. Almost all were recruited locally—we have no evidence of terrorist sleeper cells being established in this country.

The plots show that radicalization and recruitment to terrorist violence is occurring in the United States and is a legitimate security concern. It has, however, yielded very few recruits. With roughly 3 million Muslims in America, although some estimates run much higher, 100 terrorists represent a mere 0.00003 percent of the Muslim population—fewer than one out of 30,000.

Terrorist violence is not a new phenomenon. Al Qaeda and its jihadist followers did not bring terrorism to the United States. Along with its immigrant communities, the United States has imported numerous terrorist campaigns. Cuban, Puerto Rican, Croatian, Serb, Palestinian, Armenian, Taiwanese, and Jewish extremists have all carried out attacks on U.S. soil, in addition to the homegrown terrorist campaigns of the far left and far right. In fact, the level of terrorist violence was greater in the United States in the 1970s than it is today. The lack of significant terrorist attacks on the United States since 9/11 suggests not only intelligence and investigative success but also an American Muslim community that remains overwhelmingly unsympathetic to jihadist appeals. Modern communications, especially the Internet, offer access to violence-exalting narratives, but there is absolutely no evidence to show that attempts to exploit the dismay of some Muslims at policies that can be portrayed as an assault on faith or community have interrupted the integration of immigrant communities. What authorities confront are tiny conspiracies or the actions of individuals, which in a free society will always be hard to predict and prevent.[17]

Summary

You may want to recall the early events of Bill Clinton's regime when the United States suffered a "Fire fight from Hell," as it was described in *Newsweek Magazine*. We of course refer to the debacle in Somalia when the United States had the objective of seizing Somali warlord Mohammed Aidid. What had started out as a peacekeeping mission in Mogadishu turned into a race to capture Aidid, who had been undermining UN humanitarian aid in the region. The resulting loss of life to American Marines was starkly played out on TV screens around the world. The Mogadishu failure brought back haunting memories from the failed attempt to rescue U.S. hostages in Tehran two decades earlier and had subsequently cost President Carter the 1980 election. Bin Laden believed the cost in military deaths would again be too unpalatable for the U.S. public, and he taunted a receptive global media with that fact until his death in 2011. In reality, the United States has not suffered from an al Qaeda-inspired attack since 9-11, but there have been numerous close calls. No doubt the increase in homeland security and good old-fashioned police work has gone a long way to delay, deter, and disrupt Islamist elements readying themselves for attacks on U.S. targets. That another attack is on the way is a certainty, but predetermining when and where the attack will come from is the major challenge for authorities. The next chapter discusses terrorism in Canada.

Review Questions

1. Discuss why militias and right-wing extremists are labeled hate groups and are rarely tagged as terrorist groups or organizations.
2. What political and economic circumstances do you consider may give rise to the increased number of right-wing militias in the United States?
3. Discuss the impact that the social media may have in aiding homegrown terror.
4. Why are homegrown terrorist or lone-wolf attacks so difficult to detect and prevent?
5. Discuss how the PATRIOT Act has helped close the intelligence gaps.

Websites

1. **Anti Defamation League**—*www.adl.org*
2. **The Rand Corporation**—*www.rand.org*
3. **The NEFA Foundation**—*www.nefafoundation.org*
4. **Society for Terrorism Research**—*www.societyforterrorismresearch.org*
5. **U.S. Department of Homeland Security**—*www.dhs.gov*

End Notes

1. Rex A Hudson. *The Sociology and Psychology of Terrorism: Who becomes a Terrorist and Why?* A report prepared under an Interagency Agreement by the Federal Research, Library of Congress (September 1999).
2. Department of Justice News Release United States Attorney Southern District of New York (November 17, 2010).
3. Amir Lechner. "Home Grown Radicals." *Intersec. The Journal of International Security*, vol. 20, no. 5 (Chertsey, UK: Albany Media Ltd., May 2010, p. 13).
4. *The Movement.* http://www.pbs.org/independentlens/weatherunderground/movement.html.
5. *Washington Post.* www.washingtonpost.com/wpdyn/content/article/2005/09/28/AR.htm.
6. Sheikh Abdullah Azzam. *Defence of the Muslim Lands.* www.religioscope.com/info/doc/jihad/azzam_defence_1_table.htm.
7. Clark Staten. *Domestic Terrorism: The enemy from Within.* www.emergency.com/domsterr.htm.
8. Steve Emerson. *Abdullah Assam: The Man before Osama bin Laden.* www.iacsp.com/itobli3.htm.
9. Executive Summary 9-11 Commission Report (July 22, 2004).
10. 9-11 Commission Report and Executive Summary of the 9-11 Commission Report (July 22, 2004).
11. Report #15 in a NEFA series. "Target America." *Bojinka II: The Transatlantic Bomb Plot* (April 2008), http://www.nefafoundation.org/newsite/file/FeaturedDocs/Bojinka2LiquidBombs.pdf
12. Home-grown Terror. http://www.washingtonpost.com/wp-dyn/content/article/2010/06/06/AR2010060603996.
13. U.S. Government Accountability Office.
14. Association of the Bar of the City of New York and Center for Human Rights and Global Justice. *Torture by Proxy: International and Domestic Laws applicable to "Extraordinary Renditions"* (New York: ABCNY and NYU School of Law, 2004).
15. Michael Ratner. *War on Terror: The Guantanamo Prisoners, Military Commissions and Torture* (February 2005), www.ccr-ny.org/v2/viewpoints/viewpoint.asp.
16. The White House. www.whitehouse.gov/news/releases/2006/03/20060309-7html.
17. Brian Michael Jenkins. *Going Jihad: The Fort Hood Slayings and Home-Grown Terrorism* (The RAND Corporation: Testimony before the Committee on Homeland Security and Governmental Affairs United States Senate, November 19, 2009), http://www.rand.org/pubs/testimonies/CT336.html.

Canada and the Caribbean

You have enemies? Good. That means you've stood up for something, sometime in your life.

—WINSTON CHURCHILL (1874-1965)

LEARNING OBJECTIVES

After studying this chapter, the student should be able to:

1. Discuss how support for terrorism and fund-raising in Canada poses a threat to the United States.

2. Understand that Canada's liberal attitude to immigration has helped the spread of the threat of terrorism.

3. Discuss how Sikh terrorism has been on the rise in western Canada.

4. Explain how effective the Tamil Tigers have been at raising funds from within Canada.

KEY WORDS TO NOTE

Babbar Khalsa International (BKI)—A Sikh terrorist group sponsored by expatriate Indian Sikhs demanding an independent Sikh state called Khalistan (Land of the Pure) from Indian territory

Canada Security and Intelligence Service (CSIS)—Investigates and reports on threats to Canada's national security

Dal Khalsa—A militant Sikh political movement based in Amritsar

FLQ—Front de Liberation du Quebec a Canadian extreme separatist movement active in the 1960s and 1970s

Multiculturalism—Official Canadian government policy since its introduction in the 1970s on the social importance of immigrants and their integration

Omar Khadr—A Canadian of Pakistani origin captured in Afghanistan and detained in Guantanamo; tried, convicted, and sentenced under U.S. Military Commissions Act 2009 after pleading guilty to killing U.S. serviceman Christopher Speer

Papa Doc—Francois Papa Doc Duvalier—notorious ruler of Haiti throughout the 1960s

Talwinder Singh Parmar—Considered part of the plot group that bombed Air India Flight 182 in 1985, killing over 300—also leader of the Babbar Khalsa terrorist organization. Killed by Indian police while in custody in 1992

OVERVIEW

Canada is associated with terrorist activity and has been a home base for terrorist organizations dating as far back as the 1980s. The country's first experience with terror was strictly a homegrown affair with the French separatist movement in Quebec in the 1970s, but a much more violent form of terrorism during the 1980s was a direct result of events taking place on the Indian subcontinent. This chapter looks at the Sikh terrorist movement that downed an Air India Boeing 747 aircraft off the coast of Ireland and Canada's inability at the time to recognize the threats being posed by external forces. After 9-11, there was considerable criticism from politicians in the United States concerning the porous border between the two countries. The Canadian government has always fostered a liberal approach to immigration policy in contrast to the United States. In a 2002 security report by Canada's Security and Intelligence agency, it was stated that there were more terrorist organizations active in Canada, with the possible exception of the United States, than anywhere else in the world. There were believed to be more than forty such organizations, although not directly involved with violence within Canada, that were involved in terror-related activities, including fund-raising; lobbying through front organizations; providing support for terrorist operations abroad; procuring weapons and material; intimidating and manipulating immigrant communities in Canada, such as Tamil/Sri Lankan migrants in Toronto; and, the obvious concern to the United States, the facilitating of access to the United States.

We will discuss Canada's multiculturalism and how weak immigration and refugee controls have allowed terrorist groups to plan, coordinate, and attack targets on a global scale. Canada is considered to be the easiest country in the developed world in which to obtain refugee status.

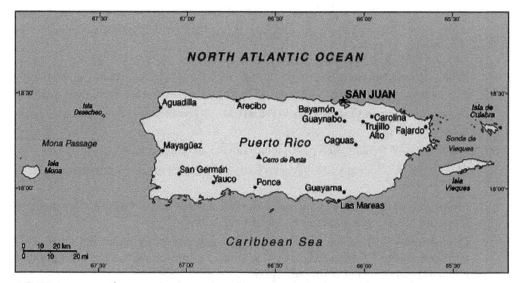

FIGURE 4-1 Map of Puerto Rico (Central Intelligence Agency, *The World Factbook, 2008*).

PUERTO RICO

Puerto Rico is closely aligned with the United States, and the island's inhabitants possess all the rights and obligations of U.S. citizens, except for the right to vote in U.S. presidential elections. The United States also governs the Virgin Islands, Guam, and American Samoa. Puerto Rico is slightly less than three times the size of Rhode Island. The Taino Indians, who inhabited the territory originally, called the island Boriken, or Borinquen (a word that, with various modifications, is still popularly used to designate the people and the island of Puerto Rico). The Taino Indians, who came from South America, inhabited a portion of the island when the Spaniards arrived. While the post-Colombian native language is Spanish, the status of official languages has been a central issue in Puerto Rican education and culture since 1898. Until 1930, U.S. authorities insisted on making English the primary language of instruction in the schools, the intent being to produce English-speaking persons of American culture. But strong resistance to the policy finally brought about a change to the use of Spanish as the basic school language, with English becoming a second language studied by all students. In 1991, the Puerto Rican legislature, following the lead of the pro-Commonwealth Popular Democratic Party and Governor Hernandez Colon, endorsed a bill that made Spanish the island's official language, thus reversing a 1902 law that gave Spanish and English official recognition. In 1993, pro-statehood Governor Pedro J. Rosello signed legislation restoring equal status to English and Spanish for a population of close to 3.9 million.

It is estimated that some 2 million Puerto Ricans have migrated to the United States over the years and had they remained in Puerto Rico, the island would be so densely populated that there would be virtually no room for people to live. Because of massive migration to the United States, more Puerto Ricans are now said to live in New York City than in San Juan.

Besides slaves from Africa (Sudan, Congo, Senegal, Guinea, Sierra Leone, and the Gold, Ivory, and Grain coasts), other ethnic groups brought to work on the plantations joined the island's rich racial mix. Fleeing Simón Bolívar's independence movements in South America, Spanish loyalists fled to Puerto Rico, a fiercely conservative Spanish colony, during the early 1800s. French families flocked to Puerto Rico from both Louisiana and Haiti. As changing governments or violent revolutions depressed the economies of Scotland and Ireland, many farmers from those countries also journeyed to Puerto Rico in search of a better life.

While Puerto Ricans have had a fairly peaceful existence, they have seen some incidents that were considered terrorism in nature, or close to it. In January 1981, the most notable incident occurred when a quasi-terrorist group, the Macheteros, blew up eleven jet fighters of Puerto Rico's National Guard near San Juan. Ronald Fernandez, professor of sociology and author of *Los Macheteros: The Violent Struggle for Puerto Rican Independence*, has spent many years researching Puerto Rico. He writes of the Macheteros's frustrations and susceptibility to lashing out:

> On August 25, 1989, Filiberto Ojeda Rios, acting as his own attorney, gave his closing argument to the jury in a U.S. court in San Juan. The indictment, drawn in the name of the United States of America, charged that Ojeda Rios had shot at and assaulted agents of the Federal Bureau of Investigation. President Reagan had appointed the prosecutor, and President Carter, the American flag standing in the courtroom, had appointed the judge, but the jury was all Puerto Rican.
>
> Far from denying his actions, Ojeda Rios embraced them, and asked the jury to uphold the right of the Puerto Rican people to use force in self-defense against the unwanted, foreign presence of the United States. There are no American heroes (in this

story), nor is there a happy ending. Yet, it is imperative for Americans to know our own contribution to the perpetuation of colonialism. When the sun rose on October 12, 1992, marking 500 years of colonialism, Americans would have done well to take a look at Puerto Rico and the destruction wrought there in the name of "democracy."

The island today has a per-capita income less than one-half that of Mississippi, the poorest state in the United States. Its rates of suicide, mental illness, drug addiction, crime, alcoholism, and sterilization of women are among the highest in the world.[1]

The hotly contested issue of the eventual status of Puerto Rico continues. In 1991, in an islandwide vote, Puerto Ricans rejected an amendment that would have "reviewed" their commonwealth status. In the referendum, commonwealth status was reaffirmed by a very close vote, with statehood, 788,296 (46.3 percent); commonwealth, 826,326 (48.6 percent); independence, 75,620 (04.4 percent); and nulls, 10,748 (00.7 percent). This issue has caused tempers to flare up, but those in opposition fall short of forming newer terrorist groups.

We have seen that the United States still seems to be "the land of the free and the home of the brave." But its very freedom, in a world of terrorism, can be an "Achilles' heel." As the world economic situation continues to destabilize and the American economy has gone into steady decline, the gap between those who can get ahead (haves) and those who cannot (have-nots) continues to widen. As that gap widens, the disenchanted and disenfranchised of both left and right movements in the United States, and around the globe, will become a more active threat to its peace and tranquility. Chapter 15 will discuss U.S. efforts to provide coordinated and effective homeland security to a nation that has felt too secure and, for too long, protected by two oceans had no fears of international terrorism.

CANADA

In November 2002, Osama bin Laden listed Canada as a state to be attacked by his followers. Bill C-36 of Canada's Anti-terrorism Act provides the Government of Canada with the ability to create

FIGURE 4-2   Map of Canada (Central Intelligence Agency, *The World Factbook, 2008*).

a list of "entities." Through Canada's criminal code, the term *entity* is defined as a person or group, trust, partnership, or fund, or an unincorporated association or organization. The government can therefore list an entity as a terrorist organization if it satisfies the following legal test that there are reasonable grounds to believe the entity

- Has knowingly carried out;
- Has attempted to carry out;
- Has participated in, or facilitated, a terrorist activity; or
- Is knowingly acting on behalf of, at the direction of, or in
- association with an entity that has knowingly carried out, attempted to carry out, participated in, or facilitated a terrorist activity.[2]

Canada has one of the longest "undefended borders" in the world, but that may not be the case any longer. After the United States declared war on terror, it realized that its northernmost neighbor could pose a threat to U.S. national security—from terrorist groups within Canada's leaky borders. The United Nations Human Development Agency heralds Canada as the best country in which to live. Unfortunately, terrorist elements read UN material as well, and the country has become a haven for terror groups actively campaigning and fund-raising for terrorism around the globe. The undefined border between Canada and the United States no longer exists, and since 9-11 the United States no longer believes the border with Canada can continue to remain undefended. After the attacks, U.S. National Guardsmen were rushed to the border, and the number of border control officers along the 4,000-mile border has more than tripled.[3]

Juliet O'Neill, of the *Ottawa Citizen*, said in 1996, "You're more likely to be struck down by lightning or die in a car crash than find yourself victim of a terrorist attack in Canada."[4] Although that remark might have seemed appropriate at the time that is certainly not the case now. Canada must assume that it is a target for terrorist attacks even if that premise is based solely on a decade-old edict from Osama bin Laden. The Front du Liberation de Quebec (**FLQ**) crisis in 1970 was the first time that Canada came face-to-face with terrorist violence. Then, the mid-1980s Armenian attacks on Turkish diplomats in Ottawa occurred. And lastly, Sikh extremists were involved in the crash of an Air India jet that blew up over the coast of Ireland, killing 329 passengers, who were mostly Canadians. This incident occurred in June 1985 on the same day as an explosion in the baggage collection hall at Tokyo airport from a bag arriving on a Canadian Pacific airliner from Vancouver.

Canada is a nation founded on immigration, and tolerance as well, and, as such, admits more than 300,000 immigrants plus 25,000 asylum seekers a year. Thanks to liberal attitudes and policies, Canada rarely incarcerates those who claim refugee status and invariably releases them out into the ethnic communities of Toronto, Montreal, and Vancouver, where they become invisible.

The major concern is that Canada is being used as a base for organizing, fund-raising, consciousness-raising, transport, and logistics for international terrorists from among the many refugees as well as honest immigrants there. These groups range from the Tamil Tigers and Islamic extremists to Protestant and Irish Catholic paramilitaries, although that threat has significantly decreased; even Latin American, African, and Asian extremists are present. Canada stays on the alert for homegrown terrorism from a list that is referred to as "issue group extremists." Examples of these are animal rights extremists, armed Indians, antiabortion radicals, neo-Fascists, bikers, and skinheads.

IMMIGRATION AND CANADA

The opportunity for terrorists to sneak into the country under the guise of refugees has distinct concerns for **Canada's Security and Intelligence Service (CSIS)**. A report issued by CSIS in 2002 stated, "...there were more international terrorist organizations active in Canada than anywhere in the world. This can be attributed to Canada's proximity to the United States...and to the fact that Canada is a country built upon immigration, represents a microcosm of the world...terrorist groups are present here whose origins lie in regional, ethnic, and nationalist conflicts, including the Israeli-Palestinian one as well as those in Egypt, Algeria, Sudan, Afghanistan, Lebanon, Northern Ireland, the Punjab, Sri Lanka, Turkey, and the former Yugoslavia."

Of course, potential violence and disputes over land and politics—should Quebec someday choose separation in a referendum—are always on the agenda of Canadian counterterrorism agencies. Among tactics used by low-level terrorist groups in recent years are consumer-scare threats, mail bombs, shootings, and vandalism. Canada has major problems with illicit production of cannabis for the domestic and U.S. drug market. Use of hydroponics technology permits growers to plant large quantities of high-quality marijuana indoors. With its links to the Far East and a long coastline, Canada has a continuing and growing role as a transit point for heroin and cocaine entering the U.S. market. There are many connections between organized crime and terrorism—while high-quality Canadian hash travels south to the vibrant California markets, the return route brings weapons and cocaine, and thus links to terrorism. The trade in illegal drugs between Canada and the United States is significant, and the terrorist group that may be involved in this trade would likely be the Tamil Tigers with bases of operation in Toronto and Montreal; however, the trafficking of people, which gets little news coverage, is of more concern to Homeland Security in the United States. Canada's liberal attitude to immigration sets the stage for a two-tier system of legality and illegality. Few of the people who traveled here through the conventional system should be regarded with suspicion (although this system is in desperate need of reforms), while the refugee system is subjected to considerable and unending abuse. Canada's immigration and refugee system needs a radical overhauling, and the Canadian government appears to recognize that, but few changes have been made to make it happen. Evidence of frontline corruption has been evidenced in Hong Kong and Eastern Bloc countries where Canadian authorities have "failed" to properly verify the backgrounds of immigrant applicants. It would be easy for potential terrorists or their supporters to beat this style of such casual scrutiny. As the past is always so often an indicator of what may happen in the future, we need only look at the threats posed from the failure to check student visas and the abuse that they are subject to in the United States. Many al Qaeda terrorists, who operated successfully in Europe, and the United States, did so, on student visas. Canada is certainly no better at screening these applicants than its Western allies, or at tracking down those that have overstayed their visas or welcome. The abuse of the refugee system is one that Canada is currently living with, and yet seems ill prepared to combat with any degree of diligence. During the 1980s, a surge in illegal immigrant activity from India, Sri Lanka, Vietnam, and Cambodia saw the Canadian immigration and refugee system under continuous assault. False and counterfeit documentation is a central process in people-smuggling operations. Groups of up to twenty travel through major international airports, possibly being escorted. After they have managed to successfully get by the airline's cursory passport check, the passports or immigration documents are returned to the escort during flight for reuse on the next mission, or are flushed down the aircraft toilets; on arrival in Canada, the undocumented traveler then presents himself or herself to be a refugee claimant. Your authors spent a number of years in the United Kingdom intercepting a large number of these illegal immigrants/refugees during the 1980s, the majority originating from across the globe and, in many cases, from Sri Lanka, Afghanistan, Saudi Arabia, Somalia, Algeria, and the Sudan. A number of terrorists have been caught entering Canada with false passports—Mokhtar Haouari and Ahmed Ressam both did that in February 1994 (Ressam had arrived in France with a fake Moroccan passport in the name of Nasser Ressam in 1993, arrived in Montreal with an altered French passport in the name of Tahar Mejadi, and subsequently traveled to Afghanistan for terrorist training under a Canadian passport in the name of Benni Noris). Mohamed Zeki Mahjoub, a Toronto-area convenience store clerk, who is also suspected of being a major "fixer" for Islamic jihad, came to Canada with a doctored passport. Aynur Saygili, a PKK member, who came to Canada to take over a Kurdish cultural organization, also had a doctored passport when entering Canada.

Babbar Khalsa International (BKI) member Iqbal Singh arrived in Canada in 1991 as an undocumented refugee (after hopping through several countries with false documentation).[5]

CANADA'S DOMESTIC TERRORISM

Front de Liberation du Quebec (FLQ)

Liberal and extreme-thinking young Quebecers were eager for change and to establish a separate, French-speaking sovereign state within Canada. Terrorism in such a liberal country as Canada has been rare, but the turbulent days of the radical 1960s saw terrorism come to Central Canada in the shape of a separatist movement, the Front de Liberation du Quebec. From early in 1963 its goal was the separation of Quebec from the rest of English-speaking Canada. Canada is part of the British Commonwealth, and in the 1960s, French-speaking Quebec wanted separation to create its own sovereign state within Canada. A somewhat muted debate on separation and sovereignty continues to this day. The left-wing FLQ espoused a workers' revolution as a means of achieving its goal of separation. They along with many French-speaking Canadians strongly resented the control that English Canada exerted on both politics and the economy in Quebec. The Parti Quebecois, still a political party today, has actively pursued an agenda of separation.

The political boost that the FLQ needed came from an unexpected direction. On a visit to Montreal in 1967, the French President General Charles De Gaulle, in what has become a famous speech, ended with the phrase, "Vive le Quebec Libre" (Long live free Quebec). Throughout the 1960s, the FLQ targeted Anglophile areas of Montreal for bomb attacks.[6]

More than 200 explosions took place between 1963 and 1970, with both Federal and Provincial governments seemingly powerless to intervene. They used robberies in the traditional fashion for financing their operations and also as a reason to hit any Anglophile businesses. The major terrorist event that spelled the end for the FLQ was the kidnapping of the British trade commissioner James Cross and the Province's labor minister Pierre Laporte. The kidnapping produced little value to the FLQ but gave the prime minister, Pierre Trudeau, the reason he needed to use a firmer hand against all subversive elements, not only in Quebec but also throughout the rest of Canada. The two were kidnapped in October 1970 and the dead body of Laporte was found days later in the trunk of a car. Canadians were appalled that the FLQ would go to such drastic lengths, and Laporte's brutal murder turned public and political opinion sharply against them. James Cross was located in a suburb of Montreal by the Royal Canadian Mounted Police (RCMP). After protracted negotiations, the kidnappers were allowed to fly to Cuba in exchange for the release of James Cross. They had also demanded the release of colleagues serving prison sentences for FLQ offenses, but these demands were never met. One of the founder members of the FLQ, Raymond Villeneuve, was convicted of planting a number of bombs and was sentenced to twelve years in prison. A national referendum in October 1995 saw a narrow defeat for the separation movement; however, by then Villenueve had been released from prison and was again assisting with a new, younger breed of Quebec separatists, also hell-bent on tearing up the Canadian Constitution. The Movement de Liberation Nationale du Quebec is deemed extremely small with only a couple of dozen die-hard activists and consists of some former militant members of the defunct FLQ.[7] This terrorist movement, the only one of note in normally reserved and peaceful Canada, has shown that this country is not immune to such social violence.

INTERNATIONAL TERRORISM—SIKH TERRORISM

Canada has had an official multicultural policy since 1971, which in so many regions has had the negative effect of ghettoizing non-English speaking communities in the major Canadian cities of Montreal, Toronto, and Vancouver. Canada has been home to numerous generations of hardworking Sikh immigrants for most of the twentieth century, but it was political events and actions of Indian Prime Minister Indira Gandhi that was to have a profound effect on Sikhs and Canadian security services. Gandhi had been convicted of corruption in 1975, but had stead-fastly refused to resign. Following more than a year of emergency rule, Gandhi was defeated in the country's next General Election. By using dirty politics to aid her return to politics, Gandhi needed to target the alliance between the party that represented Sikh interests and the Hindu party in the Punjab region. Akali Dal (AD), which represented those Sikh interests, had to be seriously undermined by Gandhi's political machine. Financing of all Sikh temples in India was controlled by the Shiromani Gurdawara Prabandhak Committee (SGPC), an organization that was also backing the Akali Dal party. The temples were fabulously wealthy, and influential, and having control and influence with the temples meant power. Gandhi and her political party determined to undermine the AD by supporting and promoting a more radical Sikh movement. The intent of Gandhi's Congress Party was to show AD simply as soft supporters of Sikh ideals. The man targeted to lead the political embarrassment of AD was the now infamous Jarnail Singh Bhindranwale, at the time a relative unknown but nonetheless a popular religious leader. The Congress Party helped promote a new Punjab-based Sikh party, the **Dal Khalsa** (Party of the Pure), for Bhindranwale. The Congress Party was also aware that Bhindranwale was a power-ful advocate for an independent Sikh homeland and was not immune from using violence to achieve his goals. Bhindranwale quickly established his religious standing and manipulated the various Sikh teachings to his own ends, and through this evolved a dedicated armed following of his ideals. By the start of the 1980s, the Dal Khalsa movement was implicated in several murders of religious opponents, and it was now clear to most political observers that Indira Gandhi and the Congress Party had lost what little control they thought they may have exercised over Bhindranwale and his Dal Khalsa movement. Dal Khalsa had begun to establish training camps at some of the Sikh temples and formed an alliance with the All India Sikh Students Federation, which had a violent history in its own struggle to determine a separate Sikh state.

Numerous failed attempts by the Indian government's intelligence service to infiltrate Dal Khalsa accounted for the deaths of more than 100 operatives from the security services. Subsequently, the central government took control of the state of Punjab, and in retaliation the Dal Khalsa movement took control of the Golden Temple, with several hundred of its armed militants. The Sikh religion holds the Golden Temple as its holiest of temples and central to the religion. Indian security police surrounded the temple in an operation named Operation Blue Star in June 1984 and demanded that Bhindranwale surrender. He refused and was killed during the fierce assault that followed. The number of those killed in the assault included many innocent pilgrims, and although the death toll has never been confirmed, it is believed to have run to several thousand. Bhindranwale's Dal Khalsa movement had attracted global support in Sikh communities that were in favor of an independent Sikh homeland and none more so than Dal Khalsa members in British Columbia. The assault on the Golden Temple in Amritsar gave the Sikh radical element all the legitimacy they required. The temple storming gave rise to Sikh extremism in Canada and many street protests in Vancouver; Canada's Pacific coast turned violent. Moderate Sikhs within the Sikh community were attacked and beaten, and although demonstrations were observed by the police, they failed to take any actions or sanctions, and the beatings went unprosecuted. On October 31, 1984, two of Indira Gandhi's Sikh bodyguards attacked and killed her, blaming her for the desecration of the Golden Temple. Rioting ensued throughout India, and many Sikhs fled to the safer Punjab area. In Western Canada, among the Babbar Khalsa International movement, there was elation. However, the Sikh extremists were planning another attack against the Indian government.

Babbar Khalsa (BK)

The Babbar Khalsa was founded in India in 1978. Originally, its founder, Sukhdev Singh Dasuwal, was a follower of Bhindranwale, but he broke away to form his own group and later tried to kill Bhindranwale. Within several years, branches of the BK were established in a number of Western countries, being most active in Canada and Britain. Outside India, they operate as the Babbar Khalsa International (BKI). The BK was present at the Golden Temple in June 1984 with Bhindranwale and his armed followers. A number of Babbars left only days before the assault on the holy complex, putting intergroup rivalries above the defense of the temple.

Philosophically, the Babbars concentrated on changing or, more accurately, controlling the lifestyles of individual Sikhs and were never hesitant about using violence and murder as a way of enforcing a strict fundamentalist code of discipline. So strict are they in the interpretation of Sikh doctrine and practices that observers have often noted their similarity to a religious cult. By the early 1990s, the Canadian-based Talwinder Singh Parmar had broken away from the BKI and formed the Azad Babbar Khalsa ("Independent Babbar Khalsa").[8]

Sikh extremists were to become a major concern to Canada's Security and Intelligence Services. The Air India disaster, which claimed more than 300 lives, was the single-largest loss of life to aircraft terrorism prior to the attacks on September 11, 2001. Of those who plunged so needlessly into the Irish Sea, 154 were Canadians.

Sikh extremism was not new to Canada, and CSIS was actively watching the various Sikh extremists, particularly in Toronto and Vancouver. Sukhdev Singh Babbar and Talwinder Singh Parmar founded Babbar Khalsa International. The first cell or unit of BKI, led by Talwinder Parmar, was discovered in Canada in 1981. BKI has branches in not only Canada but also the United States, France, Germany, Switzerland, and Pakistan. The group's objective is for an independent Sikh state that would be named Khalistan. Parmar was a prime suspect in the Air India bombing, and his associate, Inderjit Singh Reyat, the bomb maker, indicated under interrogation that he had been making a bomb for Parmar for an attack in India. Parmar's rise to significance came after he returned from a trip to India in May 1982. The Indian government requested his extradition for the murder of two police officers in Punjab in November 1981. Parmar remained out of Indian custody, but was detained in Europe in May 1984 just as Operation Blue Star was being mounted by government troops against the Golden Temple in Amritsar. Followers of Sikh separatist Jarnail Singh Bhindranwale had occupied the temple, and when negotiations between police and the separatists failed, Prime Minister Indira Gandhi ordered troops to clear the temple. The resulting loss of life accounted for 83 soldiers and 490 Bhindranwale followers. Indira Gandhi was to die soon after at the hands of her Sikh bodyguards. Almost as if it were a war cry, the attack on the Golden Temple generated significant support across Canada for the Sikh separatist movement, and demonstrations were coordinated from Montreal to Vancouver.

Speaking Out Against Sikh Terrorism

Apart from some very diligent members of the local press, some influential Sikhs have stood up to the extremist Sikh movements in Western Canada—unfortunately the fight has been taken straight to them with devastating consequences. Tara Singh Hayer, Order of British Columbia (OBC), was one such Vancouver businessman who was outspoken against the extremist movement. As a symbol of the struggle for human rights, peace, and freedom of expression, Mr. Hayer paid an enormous personal price for his beliefs. Aware that discrimination thrives on ignorance, Mr. Hayer worked tirelessly to promote understanding between ethnic and cultural groups.

After immigrating to Canada in 1970, he worked as a miner, teacher, truck driver, and a manager of a trucking firm before becoming a full-time journalist. In 1978, he established the community newspaper *The Indo-Canadian Times* and has built it into the leading Punjabi language newspaper in North America.

In August 1988, he survived an attempt on his life, which left him in a wheelchair. Despite this attack, Mr. Hayer has never wavered in his commitment to tolerance, peace, and understanding between cultural communities.

In 1992, he was honored with the Commemorative Medal for the 125th anniversary of Canada and a Certificate of Appreciation from the RCMP Among his other awards, Mr. Hayer received the Journalist Award from the Municipality of Surrey, a city just south of Vancouver, for courageous and outstanding contribution to Punjabi journalism in Canada. He also received the International Award of Distinction for Journalism from the International Association of Punjabi Authors and Artists.

Tara Singh Hayer continued, even when faced with violence, to be a voice of moderation and reason.

In the early and mid-1980s, Hayer was affected by the "nationalist fervor" of Sikhs. The aftermath of Operation Blue Star at the Golden Temple in Amritsar made an indignant Hayer a Khalistan supporter. But his mental makeup and liberal mind-set did not allow him to remain a Khalistan supporter for long. He was revolted by the violence and mayhem associated with the movement. He returned to the path of moderation. The 1985 explosion on an Air India plane drew fearless criticism from Hayer. Thereafter, Hayer remained estranged from the Sikh extremists and their supporters in Canada. Tara Hayer was shot to death as he got out of his vehicle and into his wheelchair at his home in Surrey, British Columbia, on November 18, 1998.[9]

Talwinder Singh Parmar

News reports showed Parmar inciting crowds in Vancouver with his rhetoric and threats of death to Rajiv Gandhi. By 1985, reports and intelligence from CSIS indicated that a Sikh backlash for the Amritsar attacks was probable but could not specifically identify a target. What was to become the target was the Boeing 747, Air India Flight 182 from Montreal to London, which had originated in Vancouver. Parmar returned to India in 1988 and was subsequently shot by Indian police in 1992. After the Air India bombing, Parmar was the prime suspect in the downing of Air India Flight 182 as revenge for the Golden Temple attack by the Indian government.[10]

In November 2007, a prominent Liberal politician, Ujjal Dosanjh, called for tougher laws to combat the rise of extremism in Canada. Dosanjh, a former attorney general and premier of British Columbia, had himself been the victim of Sikh extremism before and after the Air India bombing. Moderate Sikhs residing in British Columbia endured death threats, physical attacks, and fire bombings from the extreme Sikh movement throughout the 1980s and 1990s. The resulting climate of fear and intimidation was not taken seriously enough by the police or politicians, which paved the way for the Air India bombing. Dosanjh believes that if the authorities had taken action, more witnesses would likely have come forward with more information.[11]

In March 1984, the Indian government appealed for the extradition of **Talwinder Singh Parmar** from Canada. The request was refused on the technicality that Canada could not extradite fugitives to a country that did not recognize the Queen as its head of state. In November 1985, the RCMP conducted a raid on the homes of suspected Sikh radicals, Talwinder Singh Parmar, Inderjit Singh Reyat, Surjan Singh Gill, Hardial Singh Johal, and Manmohan Singh. Following the sweep, Parmar and Reyat were arrested on weapons, explosives, and conspiracy offences. The charges against Parmar were dropped owing to lack of evidence. Reyat paid a fine for the weapons' offences, but investigators initially failed to link him to the Air India bombing. Reyat then moved to Coventry, England.[12]

THE BOMBING OF AIR INDIA FLIGHT 182

Two Canadian Sikhs—Ripudaman Singh Malik, a fifty-seven-year-old millionaire business-man, and Ajab Singh Bagri, a Sikh preacher and sawmill worker from the British Columbia interior—were charged with eight counts, including conspiracy to murder, for the downing of Air India. The third conspirator and confidant to Talwinder Parmar was Inderjit Singh Reyat, who pleaded guilty in 2003 to manslaughter for supplying the bomb-making materials that destroyed the Air India flight. The court sentenced Reyat to a term of five years in prison following his plea bargain. The Air India investigation and trial has lasted over twenty years. On March 16, 2005, both men were found not guilty on all eight counts in British Columbia Supreme Court and, as a result, were set free. The verdict stunned the British Columbia Sikh community and divided it as well. This was considered the worst act of terrorism in Canadian history: 331 people were killed in two decisive and deliberate explosions—one in a Japanese airport, another aboard Air India Flight 182. When Air India was downed, Canada relied on the newly created CSIS for its intelligence gathering, and in the twenty-plus years since then, the Canadian Security Intelligence Service has been at the forefront of this investigation along with the RCMP. There have been claims of interference and total mismanagement of the entire case, and for over twenty years, Canadians have grappled with this unsolved crime for which no one has yet been brought to justice.

Only one person has so far been sentenced for involvement in this bombing. What went wrong? How did these two men manage to be found not guilty? In his 600 pages of judgment, presiding judge Justice Ian Josephson, pointed to evidence that was "markedly short" of reason-able doubt. Much of the evidence presented against Malik and Bagri came down to evidence provided by unreliable and often unbelievable witnesses supplying hearsay evidence. There was also condemnation for the actions of CSIS, who had the main suspects under surveillance when

TERRORIST ATTACK BRIEF

Terrorist Group: Sikh extremists (Khalistan)

Case Facts: A suitcase containing an explosive device was loaded onto an Air India flight—the passenger was not on board the aircraft. The bomb detonated at around 0700 off the southern coast of Ireland. The flight data recorder and voice recorder were subsequently recovered from the bed.

Investigation: The bombing of Air India Flight 182 on June 23, 1985, represents the worst terrorist attack in Canadian history. The attack planned and executed in Canada by Sikh extremists—claimed the lives of 329 innocent people—280 of them Canadian. In the immediate aftermath of the bombing, and in the years that followed, the largest, most complex and expensive investigation in Canadian history failed to bring those responsible for the bombing to justice. Subsequent reviews also failed to provide answers to the families of the victims on how this tragedy could have been prevented.

FIGURE 4-3 Bombing—Air India Flight 182—June 23, 1985. *Source*: The Government of Canada Response to the Commission of Inquiry into the Investigation of the Bombing of Air India Flight 182 publicsafety.gc.ca.

they were testing the explosives. CSIS subsequently destroyed surveillance tape evidence. Judge Josephson singled this out as "unacceptable negligence." In addition to the problems of lack of physical evidence, the prosecution called Reyat as one of its star witnesses. The judge found him to have "patently and pathetically fabricated" his testimony. At the end of twenty years, Canada, unfortunately, has little to show for this investigation. The immediate effect of the 1985 disaster was the introduction of the requirement to match passengers with their bags. Of course, where a human element is involved, there is always room for error. The terror scenario played out again in the 1980s with the bombing of a Pan Am 747 over Lockerbie, Scotland, by agents of Colonel Qaddafi's Libyan regime.

LIBERALISM AND REFUGEES

How Canada accommodates its refugee problems is well documented, and many take extreme advantage of the liberal program that allows convicted terrorists to remain within this safe haven. One example of abuse of the refugee system is the case of Mahmoud Mohammad, who immigrated to Canada in 1987 with his family from Lebanon. Mohammad is a former member of the Popular Front for the Liberation of Palestine (PFLP) who, in 1968, attacked an El Al aircraft on the tarmac at Athens International Airport. Mohammad and an accomplice fired more than eighty rounds and threw six hand grenades at the aircraft, killing one passenger in the attack. He was sentenced to eighteen years in jail but released after only two years when Palestinian terrorists hijacked a Greek airliner and demanded his release. Since then, Mohammad has resided in southern Ontario, having lied on his immigration application. The Canadian Immigration Service has been trying to deport him since 1988. His lawyers argue that he should not be deported owing to his poor health.

The story of Mahmoud Mohammad is a classic example of why Canada is often seen as a liberal haven for organizations looking to raise funds without government interruption. Canada is one of the few Western governments that did not recognize and list the Tamil Tigers from Sri Lanka as a terrorist organization until a change in government in 2006 saw as one of its first acts a Conservative government listing the Tigers as a "terrorist organization." Thousands of Sri Lankan refugees and immigrants have come to Canada over the last few decades. As we noted earlier, Canada tends not to incarcerate refugees but rather allows them into society until their status hearings take place. In many instances, this can take several years and often results in an amnesty and the granting of landed immigrant status. With Canada's vast numbers of illegal/ refugee entrants/claimants, it is virtually impossible to check backgrounds to find out how bona fide the claims really are.

The Liberation Tigers of Tamil Eelam (LTTE) is a violent separatist organization that had been fighting in Sri Lanka for nearly four decades until the death of their leader Velupillai Prabhakaran and subsequent defeat by the Sri Lankan military in May 2009. The government of Sri Lanka believes that of all funds raised by the LTTE annually (Canadian $120 million), 25 percent originated through funding from front organizations, proceeds of crime, and drug activity, as well as from Tamil residents located in Canada. The LTTE has been associated with trafficking people into Canada on forged travel documents for more than two decades. The influx into Canada has meant that a huge Tamil community has built up, allowing LTTE to levy war taxes on Tamils. On arrival in Canada many Tamils find that much of their community life is controlled by LTTE front organizations. In Canada, the term *multiculturalism* is used to define almost anything that is not white and Anglo Saxon to such an extent that the government has unwittingly funded many of the Tamil Tiger front organizations involved in immigrant settlement services, as well as Tamil media and housing. From a fund-raising perspective, Canada must be viewed as a choice destination because any opposition voiced publicly is invariably met with claims of racism and intolerance. In 2000, two Liberal Cabinet members, including the finance minister and former Liberal Prime Minister Paul Martin, attended a fund-raising event for a group identified as a front for the Tamil Tigers. When opposition members questioned the pair about the event in Parliament, the Liberal response was to smear the questioners as racists.[13]

The Case of Omar Khadr

Terrorist organizations require the support of networks able to fund activities in other theaters of conflict—Canada is seen by a host of organizations as a rich breadbasket in which to gather funds, and al Qaeda's support network has been operating effectively through the Khadr family in Ontario, close to the U.S. border. It is believed that millions of dollars have been accrued for the al Qaeda network from within Canada. When the Soviet Union invaded Afghanistan in 1980, Khadr (senior) went to Afghanistan, where he met Osama bin Laden. Khadr became involved with Human Concern International (HCI), which purported to raise funds for refugees from the Afghan war. As a Canadian, Khadr sought out funding to support HCI, and funds were channeled to it from the Canadian government through the International Development Agency (CIDA). Much of the money has funded an al Qaeda training camp through offices in Peshawar. Injured by a land mine, he returned to Canada in 1992 for medical aid. Upon recovery, he returned to Pakistan. There, police arrested him in 1995 for his part in the car bombing of the Egyptian Embassy in Islamabad. Fortune was on Khadr's side—Canada's prime minister, Jean Chretien, interceded personally with the Pakistanis on his behalf. Khadr was released and returned to Canada. After the 9-11attacks, Khadr disappeared. Khadr was believed killed in Afghanistan in 2002 during a gun battle. His fourteen-year-old son Omar was captured after that action in which the younger Omar mortally wounded a U.S. Army medic.[14]

Related activities of the immediate family include the following:

- Wife Maha Elsamnah took son Omar from Canada to Pakistan in 2001 and enrolled him in al Qaeda training.

- Daughter Zaynab, twenty-three, was engaged to one terrorist and married another al Qaeda member in 1999. Osama bin Laden was present at the nuptials. Zaynab endorses the 9-11 atrocities and hopes her infant daughter will die fighting Americans.
- Son Abdullah is an al Qaeda fugitive constantly on the move. Canadian Intelligence states he ran an al Qaeda training camp in Afghanistan during the Taliban period, something Abdullah denies.
- Son Abdul Karim, half-paralyzed by wounds sustained in the October 2002 shootout that left his father dead, is presently a prisoner in a Pakistani hospital.[15]

Omar Khadr was captured and sent to the Guantanamo Bay detention camp where he was eventually tried by a Military Commission Tribunal after a plea agreement. In October 2010, he pleaded guilty to murder in violation of the laws of war, attempted murder, conspiracy, and two counts of providing material support to terrorism and spying. His plea deal meant that he would spend the following year in prison and possibly be repatriated to Canada to serve the remainder of his eight-year sentence there. He is the youngest prisoner to have been held at Guantanamo Bay and the first since World War II to be prosecuted by a military commission for war crimes while a minor.[16]

Refugee System under Pressure

The Canadian refugee claimant system is under considerable strain, not to mention abuse from those countries' citizens seeking to implant terrorist sleepers in Canada. Notable examples follow. Mohamed Harkat arrived in Canada from Malaysia on a forged Saudi passport. He was initially unassuming and found casual work in the Ottawa region of Ontario once his refugee application was granted in 1997. He later wed a Canadian woman. Since 1997, CSIS has scrutinized Harkat and claims he was involved with al Qaeda in Pakistan and also other Islamist terror groups before coming to Canada. In 1994, Abdul Jabarah arrived as a refugee claimant with his family from Kuwait. Said to have been recruited by al Qaeda in 1990, he was killed in a police raid in Saudi Arabia in 2003 after his terror cell was involved in truck bombings. Nizar Ben Muhammed Nawar was one of 1,300 Tunisian students who entered Montreal in 1999. He and 100 others dropped from sight after the 9-11 attacks. A suspected al Qaeda recruit, he has returned to Tunisia, where he is actively involved in terror attacks. A member of Hezbollah, Omar el Sayed was arrested in Edmonton, Alberta; he had entered Canada on a forged Dutch passport in 1998. He was arrested for possession of fake identification papers and was wanted on drugs and weapons charges in Germany. A judge granted bail in 2002, and el Sayed vanished.

Canada's relaxed approach dates from the 1951 United Nations Convention of Refugees, which, in simple terms, defined a refugee as someone fleeing a country for a well-founded fear of prosecution for his beliefs in his home state.

Canada lacked a defined policy on refugees until the late 1960s. It had expected a dwindling number of refugees, chiefly Europeans, following World War II. However, Canada accepted around 3,000 refugees per year between 1960 and 1979, and from 1979 to 1998 that figure changed to almost 25,000 accepted refugee claims per year. Canada sees itself as a predominantly liberal state founded on immigration, to a certain degree. Thus, Canada's approach and its almost open-door policy on refugees opened the flood gates—while the vast majority settled well in Canada, some refugees came for different reasons and used Canada's liberalism to help fund their stay in the country. In *Regina v. Singh* in 1985, the defendant, facing deportation for ties to Sikh terrorism, successfully argued Canada's Charter of Rights and Freedoms extended to applicants such as him, and he was entitled to the same rights and freedoms as any Canadian citizen. This meant that however weak or ridiculous the case, every case had to be heard, and since mostly all refugees could claim indigence, they were entitled to have their case publicly funded by the Canadian taxpayer.

CUBA

The Republic of Cuba is the largest country in the Caribbean. It is located between the Caribbean Sea and the North Atlantic Ocean, just ninety miles south of Florida, and is slightly smaller than Pennsylvania. The United States leases the U.S. Naval Base at Guantanamo Bay. The base remains a geographical part of Cuba, and only mutual agreement of the two nations or U.S. abandonment of the area can terminate the lease. This has been a contentious issue in U.S.-Cuban relations for decades. The population is almost 11 million with 51 percent being Mulatto, 37 percent white, 11 percent black, and 1 percent Chinese.

Fidel Castro

Kim II-Sung, Deng Xiaoping, Peron, Khrushchev, Kadar, Franco, and Tito are all famous dictators, long departed. Castro had all but destroyed his country with iron-fisted leadership, yet managed to stay in power until his resignation due to ill-health in February 2008. Born on August 13, 1926, Fidel Castro led a revolt against the Batista dictatorship and became the president of Cuba in 1959.

Castro was the "classic" dictator in that he emerged not from the historical center of his society but from its physical and moral peripheries. His father was a rough and deceitful "Gallego" from the impoverished north of Spain. Like Napoleon the Corsican, Hitler the Austrian, and Stalin the Georgian, who came from similar backgrounds, Castro has a perversely captivating combination of seductiveness and violence. As a boy, he tried to burn down his parents' house and burn up his father's car. Legend says that young Fidel would regularly hang over a canyon while the trains thundered by. Above all, he was always the perfect Machiavellian, naturally mastering every technique of political, physical, and psychological manipulation over the Cuban people, his troops, and leaders around the world.

When he was at the Jesuit high school, Castro was fascinated with reading about the European Fascists. From Mussolini, he took the Italian's hysterical rhetorical gestures. From Hitler, he borrowed his lessons in the sociology of revolution. Hitler had created a power base from the alienated and devastated German lower classes. Castro created his own base from poor workers and farmers. When he marched into Havana in January of 1959, he immediately began using his unique system of revolutionary control. He brought down the upper classes, and the middle classes, by seizing their lands and removing their privileges, or by simply terrorizing them. He removed any and all of his competitors to either by sending them to places where they would surely die (Che Guevara in Bolivia, 1967; Frank Pais on the streets of revolutionary Santiago de Cuba, 1957) or, when that did not work, by executing them (General Ochoa in Havana, 1989). His military and intelligence organizations assured, and still assure, control over the island. Castro has been extraordinarily adept at using the traditional Cuban fear of the "Miami Cubans" and the hated "Americanos" to hold his own people ignorant and in check.[17]

"Hatred is an element of struggle; relentless hatred of the enemy that impels us over and beyond the natural limitations of man and transforms us into effective, violent, selective, and cold killing machines. Our soldiers must be thus; a people without hatred cannot vanquish a brutal enemy."

Thus spoke Che Guevara in 1967. Guevara was one of the most radical of Castro's entourage who was, as mentioned earlier, sent by Fidel to die in Bolivia. Guevara used hatred or, as he put it, "relentless hatred" to "impel us over and beyond the natural limitations of man." This use of hatred to encourage the dehumanization of one's enemy is but another manifestation of the doctrine found throughout the centuries to justify mass murder and torture. It has been used to apparently great success in Cuba, keeping Castro in power for more than forty years.

A State Sponsor of Terrorism

Cuba has been on the U.S. Department of State list of State Sponsors of Terrorism since 1982. Castro stated that the September 11, 2001, terrorist attacks in the United States were in part a consequence of the United States having applied "terrorist methods" for years[18]. The Castro regime has been a supporter of revolutionary groups in Latin America for the past thirty years. Most notably with regard to Colombian guerrilla group members in Cuba, the State Department annual reports on global terrorism for 2002 and 2003 acknowledged that Colombia acquiesced to the presence of Colombian guerrillas in the country and has publicly said that it wants Cuba's continued mediation with the ELN in Cuba. The Cuban government maintains that it has been actively involved in hosting peace talks and that its contributions to peace talks have been acknowledged by Colombia and the United Nations[19].

THE DOMINICAN REPUBLIC AND HAITI

These two small countries share an island and have been involved in strife, war, rebellion, and terrorism in the Caribbean to some extent, although minor. We shall examine them briefly as a possible source of future problems in that region.

The Dominican Republic

Noted more for its major league baseball players in the United States, the Dominican Republic is located on the eastern two-thirds of the island of Hispaniola, between the Caribbean Sea and the North Atlantic Ocean. It is slightly more than twice the size of New Hampshire, with a population of about 7.9 million. The ethnic mix is a reflection of past developments, with whites, 16 percent; blacks, 11 percent; and mixed races, 73 percent. The population is 95 percent Roman Catholic.

Economic reforms launched in late 1994 contributed to exchange rate stabilization, reduced inflation, and strong GDP growth in 1995–1996. In 1996, there was increased mineral and petroleum exploration; a new investment law that allows for repatriation of capital dividends has drawn more investment to the island. President Leonel Fernandez Reyna, who came to power in August 1996, inherited a trouble-ridden economy hampered by a pressured peso; a large external debt; nearly bankrupt, state-owned enterprises; and a manufacturing sector hindered by daily power outages. The Dominican per capita purchasing power is $3,670—three times that of its neighbor, Haiti. The Dominican Republic has been very quiet in the wake of the events of 9-11 and seems to be satisfied with staying out of the kinds of conflicts it has engaged in the past.

The Republic of Haiti

The Republic of Haiti occupies the western one-third of the island of Hispaniola, bordering on the west of the Dominican Republic. It is slightly smaller than Maryland and has a population that is predominately black (95 percent), with mulattos and whites making up 5 percent. These more than 6.5 million people are crowded into one-half the land space of their neighbor, the Dominican Republic. Haitians are predominately Roman Catholic (80 percent), and an overwhelming majority also practices voodoo.

Haiti is one of the poorest countries in the world. About 75 percent of the Haitian population lives in poverty. Nearly 70 percent of all Haitians depend on the agriculture sector, which consists mainly of small-scale, subsistence farming and employs about two-thirds of the country's workforce. Haiti has experienced little or no job creation since President Rene Preval took office in February 1996. Failures to reach agreements with international sponsors have denied Haiti badly needed budget and development assistance. Meeting aid conditions in 1997 was especially challenging in the face of mounting popular criticism of reforms.

François **Papa Doc** Duvalier was the absolute dictator of Haiti from 1957 to 1971. His nickname came from his career as a physician. He became director general of the Haitian National Public Health Service in 1946 and, subsequently, served as minister of health and of labor. After opposing Paul Magloire's coup in 1950, he hid in the interior, practicing medicine, until he was granted a general political amnesty in 1956. In 1957, with army backing, "Papa Doc" was overwhelmingly elected president. Reelected in a sham election in 1961, he declared himself "President for Life" in 1964. His regime, the longest in Haiti's history, was a brutal reign of terror; political opponents were summarily executed, and the notorious Tonton Macoutes (secret police) kept the populace in a state of abject terror and fear. Under Duvalier, the economy of Haiti continued to deteriorate, and the illiteracy rate remained at about 90 percent. Duvalier nevertheless maintained his hold over Haiti. His practice of voodoo encouraged rumors among the people that he possessed supernatural powers. He died in 1971, after arranging for his son, Jean-Claude ("Baby Doc"), to succeed him.

Jean-Bertrand Aristide became president of Haiti in December 1990, only to be ousted seven months after taking office. He went into exile in Venezuela and later the United States. In 1993, a 20,000-member U.S.-led multinational force intervened to forcibly disband the army and restore Aristide to power.

Aristide was a radical Catholic priest who defended liberation theology. He worked among Haiti's poor and was part of a group of progressive priests who opposed the Duvalier dictatorship. Expelled from his religious order in 1988 because of his revolutionary teachings, he became the candidate of a coalition of leftist parties in the 1990 presidential elections and was elected with an overwhelming majority. Party infighting plagued Aristide toward the end of his five-year term, however, and continued for the new administration of Rene Preval, who took over in February 1998.[20] In the relative safety of the new UN-protected Haiti, Aristide launched a new umbrella movement to invigorate and unify the governing Lavalas coalition. Many Haitians had hopes of seeing Aristide back in the National Palace 2000. He has insisted that his latest efforts are not a challenge to Preval, a friend and activist whom he belatedly endorsed for president in 2002. By law, Aristide could not seek a consecutive term as president of Haiti.

To emphasize that the appearance of safety in this battered nation is not necessarily reality, in 1998 unknown gunmen opened fire on the National Palace and police headquarters in the latest apparent effort to try to destabilize Haiti's government. At least one person was killed, a civilian working at the police station, and a policeman was slightly injured. UN soldiers and

Haitian police officers returned fire, but no casualties were reported. UN helicopters also took to the air and patrolled the city. There have been death threats against Preval, former president Aristide, and several liberal Haitian legislators.

Preval has blamed the attacks on soldiers from the army that ousted Aristide in 1991. The army was reformed after an American-led military intervention restored the exiled Aristide in October 1994. Preval has also speculated that the subversion could be connected to his controversial plan to privatize some state-owned enterprises. The fate of this beleaguered, poor, and downtrodden country is far from settled. The state terrorism created by the two despotic Duvaliers, and a combination of violence and voodoo, has left a legacy of former state terrorists ready to leap into the vacuum created by the departure of the UN operation. Time will tell if this dire prediction will come to pass.[21] The twenty-first century has not been kind to Haitians: first the devastating earthquake and then the sudden return in January 2011 of "baby-doc" Duvalier after twenty-five years of exile in France. Exactly what effect his presence will have is yet to be seen, and it must be borne in mind that nearly 50 percent of Haitians are under the age of eighteen and would likely have no knowledge of the man and his notorious Ton Ton Macoutes. Human rights groups such as Amnesty International and Human Rights Watch urged Haiti to prosecute Mr. Duvalier, saying he should be held accountable for the torture and killing of civilians under his rule[22]. Like so many dictators, the Duvaliers used their own personal militia who were directly responsible only to Duvalier; they were given virtual license to torture, kill, and extort. They murdered hundreds of Duvalier's opponents, sometimes publicly hanging the corpses as warnings. After Papa Doc's death in 1971, his son changed their name to the National Security Volunteers, though they continued to terrorize the citizenry. After the overthrow of Baby Doc (1986), although officially disbanded, the group continued to spread terror. It remains to be seen as to whether any remnants remain.

Summary

Canada, thanks to liberal policies on immigration and refugees, continues to experience a flood of thousands of "refugees" from Third World countries. No doubt, many of the refugees are genuine, but some have only escaped from the view of their "oppressive regimes" and continue to foster and promote terrorism from within Canada. The downing of an Air India Boeing 747 off the southern coast of the Republic of Ireland on June 22, 1985, was the worst ever single terrorist attack prior to 9-11. Most of the people on board Air India Flight 182 were Canadian citizens. Canada's only previous brush with an organized attack using terror tactics had been Quebec's experience with the FLQ. Whether the cause of separation will see any resurgence of an FLQ-styled organization is not yet apparent. Sporadic problems in the Caribbean and in Cuba continue to flare. Most of the terrorist and insurgent problems in the islands have been as a result of economic downturns and inefficient and corrupt governments. Cuba remains firmly under the control and dictates of the Castro family, and their power continues to dominate in the region as well as covertly influence Latin American states. As the events of 9-11 recede to form part of history, we must expect the new generation of terrorists to come from the ranks of extreme Islam—those terrorists with designs on launching jihad against both Canada and the United States will very likely come from within our own borders. Canada, as a center for terrorism support and financing, is a continuing problem as it relates to the expatriate Tamil community. Britain, as we shall see in Chapter 5, has experienced and suffered from attacks by home-grown terrorists, those who immigrated to a new homeland only to repay their adopted country with terror and death.

Review Questions

1. Describe how the political climate in Canada may help foster terrorist organizations.
2. How has the influx of migrants to Canada both legal and illegal played a role in terror events globally?
3. How has the LTTE been able to raise funds so easily in Canada for almost the last twenty-plus years?
4. Discuss why Cuba remains on the list of countries designated as a state sponsor of terrorism.
5. Describe methods used by Cuban and Haitian dictators to control their populace and to ensure their political office.

Websites

1. **The Mackenzie Institute**—*www.mackenzieinstitute.com*
2. **Canadian Security and Intelligence Service**—*www.csis-scrs.gc.ca*
3. **Department of Justice Canada**—*www.doj.ca*
4. **Anti-Defamation League**—*http://www.adl.org/terror/tu/tu_0401_canada.asp*
5. **Ministry of Defense**—*http://www.defence.lk/new.asp?fname=20080416_03*

End Notes

1. U.S. Department of State. *Background Notes: Geographic Entities and International Organizations.* http://www.state.com.
2. *Canada Gazette*, Part II (June 19, 2003). Published by the Queen's Printer for Canada.
3. John Bissett. Troubled Borders, Canada, The United States and Mexico, John Bissett, former Executive Director Canadian Immigration Services speaking at the 2nd North American Meeting on the Trilateral Commissions New York (November 14–16, 2003).
4. Juliet O'Neill. *The Ottawa Citizen* (August 3, 1996).
5. *The Mackenzie Institute: The Sub Committee on Immigration and Claims* (January 2000).
6. George Rosie. *The Directory of International Terrorism* (New York: Paragon House, 1987, p. 123).
7. Canadian Press. "Neo-FLQ Group to Fight for Breakup." (December 3, 1995).
8. John Thompson is President of the Mackenzie "Overseas Terrorism in Canada" *Terrorism in Canada's History*, Chapter 2. www.mackenzieinstitute.com.
9. Government of British Columbia (2004). www.protocol.gov.bc.ca.
10. Stewart Bell. *Cold Terror, How Canada Nurtures and Exports Terrorism Around the World* (Etobicoke, ON: John Wiley & Sons, 2004, p. 19).
11. Kim Bolen. "MP calls for tougher laws to deal with extremists." *The National Post* (November 22, 2007).
12. CBC archives. www.cbc.ca.
13. John Thompson. "How the Tigers Came to Canada," *The National Post* (February 28, 2005).
14. Daniel Pipes. "The Khadrs: Canada's First family of Terrorism." *New York Sun* (March 11, 2004).
15. Ibid.
16. Jane Sutton. "Guantanamo Canadian to Serve Eight More Years in Prison" (November 1, 2010). Reuters. http://uk.reuters.com/article/idUKTRE69R01Q20101101.
17. Santo Domingo. "Offices of the General Customs Receivership" (Courtesy National Archives, 1907).
18. Andrew Cawthorne. "Cuba's Castro Urges U.S. to Keep Calm." *Reuters* (September 11, 2001).
19. Cuban Ministry of Foreign Relations. "Declaration by the Ministry of Foreign Affairs: Cuba Has Nothing to Hide, and Nothing to Be Ashamed Of." (May 2, 2003).
20. *The Columbia Encyclopedia*, 5th ed. (New York: Columbia University Press, 1993). Licensed from Inso Corporation. Aristide, Jean-Bertrand. http://bartleby.com.
21. Michael Norton. Associated Press Writer (Port-au-Prince, Haiti, August 19, 1996).
22. Ingrid Arnesen and Jose Cordoba. "Haiti: Ex Dictator Duvalier Returns." *Wall Street Journal* (January 17, 2011), http://online.wsj.com/article/SB100014240527487045114045760866314002081 52.html. Retrieved February 27, 2011.

5

Great Britain and Northern Ireland

This heinous attack upon America was an attack upon us all.
With America, Britain stands in the front line against Islamist fanatics
who hate our beliefs, our liberties and our citizens. We must not falter.
We must not fail.

—MARGARET THATCHER (STATEMENT ON FIFTH
ANNIVERSARY OF 9-11 ATTACKS)

LEARNING OBJECTIVES

After studying this chapter, the student should be able to:

1. Describe the organizational structure of Irish terrorist groups.

2. Discuss the sectarian issues that have divided Ireland for over a century.

3. Identify the methods used by the British government to destabilize and confront the Irish terrorists.

4. Discuss the threat that homegrown terrorism poses to the United Kingdom.

KEY WORDS TO NOTE

Abu Hamza al Masri—Radical Egyptian Sunni Muslim cleric who preached at London's Finsbury Park Mosque

Active Service Units (ASUs)—Small and secretive terror cells that operate autonomously

Black and Tans—British paramilitary force recruited to assist the Royal Irish Constabulary; members wore black and tan uniforms

Decommissioning—Provision in the Northern Ireland Peace Agreement that puts weapons beyond the use of Irish terror organizations

Diplock Commission—Set up in 1972 to consider legal measures against terrorism in Northern Ireland, which led to the establishment of courts without jury; named after Kenneth Diplock

Good Friday Agreement—Plan for devolved government in Northern Ireland signed on April 10, 1998; included terms of early release of prisoners and decommissioning of weapons

IICD—Independent International Commission to oversee the decommissioning of paramilitary weapons under the provisions of the Northern Ireland Peace Accord

Internment—Confinement, often used in wartime; in this case, used in Northern Ireland during the 1980s to combat Irish republican terrorism

Operation Crevice—U.K. Police operation in 2004 to uncover Islamist terror cells operating in England

Orange Order—Originating in the seventeenth century, this is the largest Protestant organization in Northern Ireland and regards itself as defending civil and religious liberties of Protestants and seeks to uphold the rule and ascendancy of a Protestant monarch in the United Kingdom

Scheduled Offenses—Offenses such as terrorism tried in "Special Courts"

Sinn Féin—Led by Gerry Adams—left-wing Irish republican political party that seeks an end to British rule in Northern Ireland

Special Category Status—A de facto prisoner-of-war status for Irish prisoners convicted during the Troubles

OVERVIEW

Britain has been no stranger to acts of domestic terrorism from Irish terror groups during the last thirty years of the twentieth century. Successive British governments have allowed an influx of Islamic extremists into the country, who have inspired, trained, and funded radical elements to fight *jihad* abroad and at home. We examine what is still considered to be one of the most successful and logistically well-organized terror groups of the modern era—the Provisional Irish Republican Army (PIRA)—as well as other factions operating in both Northern Ireland and mainland Britain. Attempts to disarm Irish terror groups continued to be a major political challenge for the Labor government of former Prime Minister Tony Blair. The Good Friday Agreement, or Belfast Agreement, signed on Friday April 10, 1998, came as a major sticking point in achieving a measure of independence for Northern Ireland. We examine how Irish terrorists have turned away from the gun and toward political strategies to attain their goals.

In 2005, the Irish Republican Army (IRA) formally renounced violence and instructed its active units and volunteers to cease all activities and "assist the development of purely political and democratic programs through exclusively peaceful means." The long-term effects of this on Northern Ireland will be apparent only with the passage of time. Of concern to Britain in particular but also the rest of Europe has been the growth of "homegrown" terror cells inspired by radical Islamists. Since the terror attacks of 9-11, Britain has gone to draconian lengths to deter and defeat the rise of Islamic extremism. This chapter examines the rise of Islamic extremism in Britain, reviewing the measures being taken to limit and track down those that have become involved with suspected al Qaeda terrorist operations. Britain has become a recruiting

FIGURE 5-1 Map of Great Britain and Northern Ireland (Central Intelligence Agency, *The World Factbook, 2008*).

haven for young Islamic radicals. These connections, in the wider context of the 9-11 attacks and the workings of the al Qaeda network, will also be discussed. Britain's "special relationship" with the United States, as well as being its staunchest ally, continues to make it a target for Islamic extremism. The bomb attack outside the British Embassy in Turkey in 2004 was al Qaeda's first specific, targeted attack against British interests abroad. New laws aimed at curbing terrorism have meant a tenuous return to an internment-type process used unsuccessfully in Northern Ireland in the 1970s and 1980s. Britain struggled with the realization that Islamic terror had come to its shores, and Britons were ill prepared for the reality that the attacks were the work of young British men who were educated and raised in England. The type of terror they were now witnessing was more commonly associated with terror attacks in the Middle East rather than London!

IRELAND: EARLY HISTORY

In the early sixteenth century, James I, King of England (1566–1625), provided Irish land to Scottish (Protestant) settlers in hopes of establishing the Protestant church in Ireland. He hoped to convert the Irish to Protestantism and persuade them to forfeit their lands, thus assuring Protestant ascendancy to the throne of England. King James II's (1633–1701) inability to work with Parliament and his appointments of Catholics into prominent positions led to both King William and Mary, who ruled from 1689 to 1702 and were staunch Protestants, being "invited" by Parliament to invade England and seize the throne. In November 1688, in what was termed the "Glorious Revolution," William (a Dutchman from the House of Orange), with a predominantly Dutch army, invaded England and was victorious in a bloodless coup. James II was captured while fleeing from London, but William ensured his safe passage to France where he would live in exile. However, by 1689, William III and Mary II coruled England, while James amassed an army in France with which to oppose them.

In 1690, James II,[1] supported by French and Irish armies, fought William III at the "Battle of the Boyne." James II was defeated, and Protestant rule prevailed throughout Ireland. Protestants were the landowners of Ireland, while the Catholics held on to a tenuous existence, suffering great deprivations and poverty. Today, Protestants continue to celebrate the victory of William III over King James II's Catholic army. Orange Lodges, named after William of Orange, still hold annual marches and celebrations in the Protestant regions on July 12. The first Orange Lodge was founded in Loughhall, County Armagh, in 1795. (See "Protestant Marching Season" for more on this fraternal organization.)

IRELAND'S CIVIL WAR

With a history of nearly 800 years of strife, the early decades of the twentieth century would be pivotal for events that would shape its people's destiny for the next century.

Michael Collins, an Irishman born in the south, entered the British Civil Service and joined the Postal Office in London in 1906. It was during this time that he joined the secretive Irish Republican Brotherhood (IRB). In 1912, the British government introduced an Irish Home Rule Bill giving Ireland a separate parliament but with limited autonomy. The Catholic Irish nationalists welcomed the proposed bill, but Protestant unionists in the north saw it as a threat. With the outbreak of World War I in August 1914 and the passing of the act in September, the IRB saw this as an ideal opportunity to strike at the British while they were vulnerable. The act was not implemented due to the outbreak of war.

Germany in turn saw an opportunity to destabilize the British by providing support to the Irish independence movement. While the German offer was readily accepted by members of the movement, little of material assistance actually reached Ireland. In 1916, Michael Collins returned to Ireland and joined the Irish Volunteers, the nationalist's paramilitary wing. On Easter Monday 1916, the IRB made it's move. Led by Padraic Pearse and James Connolly, 1,600 Irish rebels, mostly members of the Irish Volunteers, rose up in Dublin and seized key points in the city. The rebels proclaimed an independent Irish republic but failed to garner popular support. The rebellion lasted for five days and resulted in the destruction of large portions of the city before it was crushed by the British military. Fifteen of its leaders were arrested, summarily tried, and sentenced to death. All were executed by firing squad. Widely reviled during and after the failed rebellion, the dead men quickly became martyrs to the Irish, with their executions turning popular sentiment against the British. Michael Collins participated in the Easter Rising and was subsequently interned at Frongoch Prison Camp, Wales. He returned to Ireland after his release and began setting up an underground intelligence organization. In 1918, the Sinn Féin political movement received strong support, winning 73 of the 105 allotted seats for Ireland. None of those elected including Michael Collins took their seat in the House of Commons in London and, instead, pledged to constitute themselves as the legislature of an independent Ireland. Twenty-seven of the elected members met in Dublin and declared the first Irish Assembly (Dáil Éireann). It declared itself as the sole law-making authority for the Irish people and demanded that Britain leave the country.

IRISH WAR OF INDEPENDENCE, 1919–1921

British attempts to subvert and destroy the **Sinn Féin** government were the starting point for the Anglo-Irish War of 1919–1921 (also known as the Irish War of Independence) and led to the formation of the Irish Republican Army (IRA), the Dáil Éireann's militia. Collins was made commander of the new force. Collins' success in infiltration of British security services was combated by a group of British intelligence agents dubbed the "Cairo Gang." Collins' Irish forces squad executed nineteen British agents (the "Cairo Gang") on November 20, 1920, and he was placed at the top of Britain's most wanted list, with a £10,000 reward on his head. At the end of the year, the British Parliament passed the Government of Ireland Bill, separating the six predominantly Protestant counties in the north (Northern Ireland) from the remaining twenty-six counties in the Catholic south. As a means of combating the growing dissention in Ireland, the British established a militia force known infamously as the **Black and Tans**. They were best described as an auxiliary to the Royal Irish Constabulary and staffed by soldiers returning from the war in Europe. The Black and Tans were synonymous with brutality in their efforts to contain the Republican insurgency. They symbolized the harsh and repressive British rule over the country. There were many reprisal attacks. When Michael Collins' men killed fourteen British undercover agents, the Black and Tans by way of reprisal surrounded a Gaelic football match in Croke Park Dublin, and when shooting broke out, twelve spectators and players were killed and a further sixty injured. This became known as the First Bloody Sunday.[2] The Black and Tans got their nickname from the mixed style of uniform they wore that comprised khaki trousers and dark vest and shirts. This militia organization were given free license as they rampaged through Irish villages and towns; but their actions so outraged the British public that they were recalled and subsequently disbanded in 1921.

While the bill (the Government of Ireland Act 1920) was welcomed in the north, the south continued to call for full independence from Britain. By July 1921, a truce was in place and Collins was part of the negotiating delegation sent to London to discuss peace. On December 6, the

Anglo-Irish Treaty was signed and established the Irish Free State as a dominion within the British Commonwealth and partitioned Northern Ireland from the rest of the country, leaving it as part of the United Kingdom and with limited self-government. The treaty granted the twenty-six counties greater independence than Ireland had enjoyed in over 700 years, and most impartial observers regarded it as a stepping stone to full independence within a generation or two. Compared to the modest Home Rule Act of 1914, the treaty was a gigantic step forward for Republicans. But the true hard liners—including the IRA's Cathal Brugha—found three fatal flaws:

(1) It excluded six counties in Ulster, thereby abandoning Catholics and nationalists in that part of Ireland;

(2) It did not establish a truly independent Republic, only a semiautonomous state in which Britain controlled harbors in times of emergency; and

(3) It required an oath of fidelity to the Crown from elected officials.

The treaty was ratified by the Dáil Éireann on January 7, 1922, by a vote of 64–57. Pro-treaty candidates won 92 out of 128 seats in the Free State general elections held in June. A provisional government was formed with Collins as chairman, but effective administration was obstructed by the anti-treaty faction, which formed a rival government led by Eamon de Valera.

Some IRA units supported the treaty and transformed themselves into the army of the new Irish Free State, giving up the name *IRA*. Other IRA units were anti-treaty and, under Brugha, continued to function under the name *IRA*. They promptly commandeered the Four Courts building as IRA headquarters. Five months later, another election was held and the pro-treaty faction received a safe majority (58–36). They immediately formed a permanent "Irish Free State" government.

The Irish Civil War began almost immediately. Using artillery borrowed from Britain, the Free State government, which proved to be highly authoritarian, bombarded IRA headquarters (the Four Courts building) with artillery fire, killing Cathal Brugha in the process. Then, with military assistance from Britain, it brutally and methodically set about destroying the rebellious opposition. The government used the same tactics that had been most effective against them when they were rebels. It executed seventy-seven anti-treaty advocates, some with cause, some without. It burned down homes and imprisoned over 11,000 anti-treaty citizens. Eventually, the numerically superior Free State Army overwhelmed the IRA.

Collins took command of the army in mid-July and was replaced by William Thomas Cosgrave as chairman of the government. In August, Collins visited his troops in the South and, on his return, was killed during an ambush at Béal na Bláth (Mouth of Flowers) in West Cork on August 22, 1922. Collins was the only fatality and is believed to have died from a ricochet bullet.

The Civil War ended on May 24, 1923, although de Valera, as political leader of the anti-treaty faction, refused to give Cosgrave's government the satisfaction of a formal surrender. Instead, he simply sent a message to the IRA troops and other supporters that further resistance was futile and the effort was being abandoned.[3]

In 1937, a new constitution drafted by de Valera was adopted, and the name of the state was changed from "Irish Free State" to "Eire." In 1948, Republicans attained their 150-year-old dream, at least for the twenty-six counties: In name as well as in substance, the twenty-six counties became a full Republic outside the Commonwealth, pursuant to legislation sponsored by John A. Costello (1891–1976), a Fine Gael leader who succeeded de Valera as prime minister in a coalition government. The same legislation renamed the state from "Eire" to the "Republic of Ireland," its current name.[4]

"THE TROUBLES," 1968–1998

In the early days of "The Troubles" (the term for fighting between Catholics and Protestants), the Provisional Irish Republican Army (PIRA) was considered to be more of a nuisance than a terrorist threat to the security of Ireland. "The Troubles" began with civil rights marches in Northern Ireland. In October 1968, the newly formed Northern Ireland Civil Rights Association organized a march in Londonderry demonstrating its strength and frustration at the discrimination of Catholics by a Protestant majority. The Catholics in the North, probably in copycat fashion of the civil rights marches in the United States led by Dr. Martin Luther King, Jr., demanded better access to jobs, housing, and a fairer share of the economy; the marches and marchers quickly turned violent, and, in an attempt to quell the situation, the British government urged the Northern Ireland Prime Minister Terrence O'Neill to make far-reaching reforms to prevent further outbreaks. The British Home Secretary James Callaghan later wrote, "Ulster had arrived in the headlines."[5] Without the ability to sway the Unionist politicians, however, reforms were doomed to failure. Rioting again broke out in the summer of 1969, and this time troops were sent in to restore order and protect the Catholic enclaves. The end of 1970 would count the triggering of 153 bombs and incendiary devices against Protestant businesses in Northern Ireland.

In the thirty-plus years of "The Troubles," more than 3,000 people on both sides of the religious divide have been killed. To place some meaning and dimension to that figure—if one were to do a comparison-based population size with a comparable terrorist campaign in the United States, the resulting death toll would have reached over 600,000! The enormity of "The Troubles" should not be minimized for its effect on several generations of Irishmen and women. The first Catholic death of the "Troubles" was a teenager, struck on the head by a baton wielded by a member of the Royal Ulster Constabulary (RUC) during street demonstrations and violence on July 14, 1968.

Religion and discrimination have been the battleground, stemming from centuries of social injustice—a region divided by a dominant Protestant presence over a Catholic minority. This led to discrimination against Catholics in almost every facet of everyday life, from finding employment to housing. For instance, almost exclusively, Protestant members staffed the Royal Ulster Constabulary. (It is important to note that the service was always open to the Roman Catholic minority, but those who chose to join were, along with their families, victims of intimidation from within their own community.)

The Independent Commission on Policing for Northern Ireland set up in 1998 (more commonly known as the Patten Report), an act of Parliament—the Police (Northern Ireland) Bill of May 2000—led to a rebirth of the RUC as the Police Service of Northern Ireland (PSNI) on November 4, 2001. Divested of its antiterrorism role, it was to be brought back into a more all-encompassing community-style policing role.

Other changes finally came into effect at the end of the twentieth century, including the removal of the word "Royal" from the police department's title, as well as other recommendations unpopular with the Unionists, who viewed the change as pandering to the Republican movement.

Much criticism was leveled at the RUC; however, the sacrifice made by the men and women who served in the force cannot be overlooked. During the Troubles, 302 officers lost their lives, and many thousands were injured; the force received a vast number of awards and commendations:

- 16 George Medals
- 103 Queens Gallantry Medals
- 111 Queens Commendations.

On April 12, 2000, Her Majesty, the Queen, in presenting the force with the George Cross (awarded for acts of great heroism or for the most conspicuous courage in circumstances of extreme danger) said in part of her speech:

> Due, in no small measure, to the bravery and dedication over the years of the men and women of the Royal Ulster Constabulary, Northern Ireland is now a much more peaceful and stable place in which to live.

The 1960s were a decade of change, with the British Empire seen to be giving up its colonies without a fight. Britain had just withdrawn from one of its last colonies—Aden, in the Persian Gulf—after a total breakdown of law and order achieved through terrorist violence. The IRA concluded that it could topple the British government, which it thought would back down if confronted by the kind of violence that had occurred in Aden. As a result of a split in the ranks of the IRA, the Provisional IRA was formed in 1969 as the clandestine armed wing of Sinn Féin, a legal democratic socialist political movement dedicated to the removal of British forces from Northern Ireland. The Official IRA, which had been in existence for more than forty years, declared a cease-fire in 1972. A further split in the Provisional Movement resulted from the policies of the Sinn Féin leader Gerry Adams between 1994 and 1998. In the fall of 1997, one faction accepted the **Good Friday Agreement**, and the other, a newly formed splinter of PIRA, the Real IRA (RIRA) (or New IRA, as it is sometimes called), continued armed resistance against British occupation of Northern Ireland. Together with the civil rights issues, and the American debacle in Vietnam, the PIRA aimed to make good use of what it considered positive factors. To the PIRA, Northern Ireland was seen as just another British colony, waiting its turn for independence. With this and recent history in mind, they believed that the killing of British soldiers would quickly influence the decision-making processes of the British government and public opinion.

POLITICAL OBJECTIVES

In order to appreciate and understand the kinds of terror campaigns that have been waged by the IRA, PIRA, and Loyalist paramilitaries in the province, it is important to acquire a basic understanding of the political goals of these groups. The IRA of the 1920s demanded, and continues to demand, one united Ireland, and separation from the United Kingdom. In support of this, the Nationalists turned to using campaigns of terror. The Easter Uprising was among the first in a long chain of terrorist incidents conducted throughout the twentieth century. In the early 1920s, bands of IRA men were relentlessly pursued by the Black and Tans. In the 1960s, Cathal Goulding, the Army Council's Chief of Staff for the IRA, considered and then established a position toward shifting the IRA away from violence as the only means to achieve its ends. His idea was the formation of both a Catholic and a Protestant workers group, aimed at the overthrow of capitalism and achieving a united Ireland. As a result, the end of 1969 found a situation rampant with internal disarray and a split in the IRA ranks. Goulding's ideas offended many Catholics who saw themselves as the defenders of the Catholic enclaves of the North, as well as IRA members. When renewed fighting broke out in 1969, following the civil rights marches, the IRA's lack of weaponry rendered it incapable of protecting the northern Catholics. At a special IRA convention held in Dublin in August 1969, it was voted, predominantly by the southerners, to adopt a policy of political activism. Further, it allowed election of Sinn Féin members to both the Dublin and British parliaments. To the men of the North, this was viewed as recognition of partition, or "sleeping with the enemy." Led by Sean

McStiofain, the Provisional Irish Republican Army (PIRA) was formed the following month. Rory O'Brady, Leo Martin, Billy McKee, Francis Card, and Seamus Twomey led the PIRA in 1969. They believed that violence could solve their political problems. Splinter groups were formed from the ranks of the IRA. The PIRA was formed as a splinter group from the IRA as well as a smaller group, the Irish National Liberation Army (INLA).

Sinn Féin,[6] the name of the political party representing the original IRA, was adopted by the splinter Provisionals as their "political wing." Gerry Adams, a prominent civil rights advocate, had long been suspected of being involved directly with the PIRA Council; however, he was responsible for Sinn Féin's rise to power over the past three decades as the political party that would achieve the goal of separation. A sense of fear surrounded the Sinn Féin party, in truth, because so many of its members had gravitated from the ranks of the PIRA and its active service units. The PIRA had effectively used terror campaigns in Northern Ireland against its Protestant neighbors, members of British Army units, and the mostly Protestant RUC. Sectarian reprisals by Loyalist paramilitaries had targeted Catholic families, mainly in Belfast and Londonderry, with Protestant groups targeting innocent civilians purely on the grounds that they were Catholics. PIRA carried out indiscriminate attacks on the British mainland against a broad array of targets. Many were military and government establishments, but the brutal sophistication and indiscriminate nature of the attacks caused widespread death and destruction. Targets ranged from pubs frequented by soldiers, to shopping centers, business districts, airports, and the official London residence of the British prime minister—10 Downing Street. The objective was to successfully attack British military, political, and economic targets with the

FIGURE 5-2   Since the early 1990s, higher levels of protection have been provided with armed police presence to protect the residence of the British prime minister, following PIRA attempts to attack it (Photo by Sian Evans).

aim of undermining the political will of the government, frightening the citizens, and sapping the British economy. They also attacked prominent British subjects and, in 1975, assassinated Ross McWhirter, the coauthor of the *Guinness Book of Records*, who had offered a reward for the capture of IRA terrorists.

The political aims of Sinn Féin/Irish Republican groups continue to be the complete removal of British rule and the establishment of a united Ireland. How could that objective be achieved? In their minds the only way to reach their goal was to wage war. After more than thirty years of "The Troubles," there still is hope for long-lasting peace, but the Irish people ask, "Must it be peace at any price?" The bombs and guns have had the effect of motivating the political leaders on all sides toward a peace agreement. This has been achieved—but, again, at what cost? As noted, more than 3,600 people, both military and civilian, have died during the long course of "The Troubles." Groups that have split away from the IRA to form the Provisional IRA, the Continuity IRA (CIRA), and the Real IRA cannot be seen as having lost total contact with the political organization, Sinn Féin.

Protestants believe that both Gerry Adams and Martin McGuiness have had a long association with the IRA and PIRA and view them as terrorists-turned-politicians. The political "end game" has seen the prominent rise to political power of both Adams and McGuiness. Both men held positions of considerable influence during the negotiations with Britain's Labour government. Both men have been elected to sit in the British House of Commons. However, neither has taken his seat to date, as that would require the men to swear an allegiance to Her Majesty, the Queen of England—an act they view as repugnant. A landmark date for these two men came on January 21, 2002, when they were greeted in London by British Prime Minister Tony Blair and then occupied their new offices in the Palace of Westminster. Although the peace process has achieved a lot, the PIRA has never really "gone away." The tenuous cease-fire has been breached time and again by both the Loyalists and the Republicans, with punishment beatings and attacks. Sinn Féin continues to be seen as the party that can make significant inroads in Westminster. However, during the period since the signing of the peace accord, the Loyalist paramilitaries have not moved their political base and have no real representation in the political arena.

Other paramilitary players have stood for government election in Northern Ireland; during the hunger strikes in 1981, Bobby Sands, a Republican prisoner in the Maze Prison, began his hunger strike "until death." The press coverage that the prisoners garnered allowed his name to become so prominent that he was nominated to run in a local by-election; however, he died in prison in May the same year, three weeks after being elected as MP for Fermanagh and South Tyrone. A further nine hunger strikers would die in the Maze Prison.

Internment

Modern-day **internment** relates to the attempts to contain the fervent Irish Republican movement. However, this style had previously been tested from 1939 to 1945 and again from 1956 to 1962. For terrorist organizations to have success, they must first achieve political recognition, or at least gain some kind of special status. When reintroduced on August 9, 1971, it resulted in the rounding up of 342 mainly Republican sympathizers drawn from a list supplied by the RUC Special Branch. They were placed in detention indefinitely without trial (ability afforded to the Unionist government of the time under the Special Powers Act, 1922) in an old and disused former Royal Air Force base at Long Kesh outside Belfast. The introduction of internment by Northern Ireland's prime minister, Brian Faulkner, failed to decrease the levels of violence in Northern Ireland. In fact the violence soon escalated.

The rounding up of civilians from Republican areas of Belfast and Londonderry placed more than 400 persons in detention in August 1971, and those numbers swelled to over 900 by 1972. What was remarkable was that no Loyalist suspects were rounded up for internment, but neither were many members of the Provisional IRA, the majority of whom had fled south. The effectiveness of this process was soon questioned when it was clear that no significant Republicans were among those interned; however, this may, in part, have been due to poor and outdated intelligence. The deteriorating events in the North led the British government to suspend the Northern government in Stormont Castle and use direct rule from London. Housed in Long Kesh (renamed the Maze Prison), detainees were incarcerated with convicted paramilitary prisoners. Paramilitary prisoners began demanding special status, which, at the time, was applied only to internees. The Republican prisoners viewed themselves as political prisoners and demanded to be recognized as such. In 1974, the British government, under the direction of the secretary of state for Northern Ireland William Whitelaw, granted **Special Category Status** to paramilitary prisoners as well as the internees. Special Category Status gave prisoners the following privileges:

FIGURE 5-3 Mural memorializing paramilitary members killed in Northern Ireland's 30 years of the "Troubles" (Photo by Tony Forward).

- Freedom of association with others in the prison (previously available only to internees);
- One prison visit per week;
- The option of wearing prison uniforms;
- Weekly food parcels; and
- No requirement to perform prison work.

The Maze Prison became a fertile training ground for Republicans, and with more than 1,000 Special Category prisoners, the ability of prison staff to control their activities soon became questionable. Special Category Status was ended in 1976 by Merlyn Rees, the secretary of state. The Maze Prison had constructed new blocks to house Republican prisoners. Their design in

FIGURE 5-4 Mural memorializing paramilitary members killed in Northern Ireland's 30 years of the "Troubles" (Photo by Tony Forward).

the shape of an "H" had them aptly named as *H-Blocks*. Those prisoners moved to the H-Blocks claimed they were political prisoners and not criminals and therefore had a right to Special Category Status. Their demands were not met, and they escalated their action by refusing to wear prison clothes or to wash. If one looks at the hypocrisies of terrorism (which is mostly oppression committed in the name of freedom), we will see there are several:

- Terrorists unilaterally suspend democracy for their own acts.
- Terrorists expect democratic principles to be fully applied to them if they are captured.
- Terrorists seek special recognition from governments they do not recognize.
- Terrorists avoid mentioning violation of their victims' human rights.[7]

When Special Category Status ended in 1976, Republican prisoners were moved into the H-Blocks within the Maze Prison. With their status now revoked, the Republican prisoners took internal action by refusing to wear prison clothing and wearing only a prison blanket. The prisoners' actions fell on deaf ears of the British government, led by "the Iron Lady," Margaret Thatcher. The culminating events of the protests were the hunger strikes and the associated deaths, which made headline news around the world. The hunger strikes ended in October 1981, after which the British government allowed the prisoners to wear their own clothes.

After the 1998 Good Friday Agreement, when more than 400 paramilitary prisoners—both Republican and Loyalist—were released, the remaining half-dozen were scattered to different prisons. During the period of internment—August 9, 1971–December 5, 1975—1,981 people had been detained: 1,874 were Catholic/Republican, and the remaining 107 were Protestant/Loyalist.

By 1970s, the PIRA campaign was operating at full capacity; one of the most violent days was in July 1972, when they detonated a total of 27 bombs in Belfast, killing 7 and wounding 130 others. The bombs were indiscriminate and injured both Catholics and Protestants.

FINANCING OF TERROR

For the PIRA of the 1970s and beyond to have any success against the British Army, it had to establish an arsenal of weaponry to fight its campaign. The obvious method of raising funds for terrorist activities had often been bank robberies. While this method was used in the early days of the campaign, it was not the PIRA's only avenue for funds. Terrorism is clearly not just a cost-effective means of political representation at a broad level, but terrorist tactics can be inexpensively implemented in terms of finance. Fertilizers and other commercially available chemical compounds found in household products will, for the foreseeable future, remain part of the basic arsenal of even the most powerful terrorist groups.[8]

The PIRA has been successful in raising funds by committing armed robberies, kidnappings, extortion, money laundering, smuggling, and drug dealing. It also raises funds through foreign aid and legitimate business ventures. The most spectacular robbery, and possibly the largest in Northern Ireland's history, involved the Northern Bank of Ireland and the theft of more than £20 million in December 2004. Intelligence pointed toward this being a PIRA operation owing to its sophistication and the logistics required to carry it out. Indications are that armed backup units were in place, should police units stumble onto the raid. Why would PIRA risk this kind of activity while delicate talks were ongoing with respect to the Peace Accord? From a historic point of view, the PIRA had previously carried out spectacular operations when events such as peace talks involving the British government had to be disrupted or otherwise stalled. For example, shortly after a breakout from the Maze Prison, one of the escapees was part of a PIRA cell that detonated a bomb in the Grand

Hotel in Brighton on October 12, 1984. The nighttime bombing (when the explosive was planted at least a month before the event and placed on a long-term timer) was aimed at Margaret Thatcher's Conservative Cabinet. Patrick McGee was convicted of planting the bomb in the Grand Hotel three weeks earlier. (McGee was released in 1999 as part of the Good Friday Peace Agreement.) The explosion killed five people and injured more than thirty. The PIRA later issued a statement claiming that it had placed the 100-pound bomb in the Grand Hotel:

> Today we were unlucky, but remember, we only have to be lucky once; you will have to be lucky always. Give Ireland peace and there will be no war.

Financing also comes from the Northern Aid Committee (NORAID) and from the Friends of Sinn Féin—both fund-raising operations that have operated successfully in the United States.

Kidnapping for ransom has been used less by the Republican terrorists than we would probably expect. Most of the notable kidnappings for ransom occurred in the 1970s and involved wealthy industrialists or members of their immediate family. Kidnappings have also involved racehorse stock. In February 1981, Shergar, the British Derby winner, was taken from the Ballymoney Stud Farm. The horse was owned by a syndicate led by the Aga Khan, and although it was believed that no ransom was ever paid by the syndicate, the horse was never recovered.[9]

Revenues generated from illegitimate sources have funded legitimate business interests in the North, from nightclubs to taxi companies and security companies. Broadening the scale of legitimate business interests allows the terrorists the opportunity to permeate all levels of Northern Ireland society.

Extortion was an early method employed by PIRA in the 1970s. They demanded money "with clear menace" from local clubs, pubs, and businesses. This evolved into more sophisticated applications when PIRA established legal security companies that businesses would need to hire to protect themselves from threats by Loyalist terror groups. As the years have rolled by, PIRA has managed to skillfully continue less overt forms of extortion in such a way as to distance itself from the thuggery image, often seen as the hallmark of Loyalist groups. The Ulster Defense Association (UDA) and its methods are often reviled for their thuggery. The public image of this group is that of thugs out for easy money to fund a lavish lifestyle rather than support a political campaign.

It remains unclear just how involved the terrorist groups, both Republicans and Loyalists in the North, have been in the drug trade. Certainly, the PIRA has acted as escorts to certain international drug shipments, but its involvement in the supply chain remains unclear. Anyone wishing to buy drugs in PIRA-controlled neighborhoods would likely need approval from the PIRA leadership. Figures are not currently available in regard to the scale of the drug trade and its specific connection to terrorist activities. There have certainly been punishment beatings, and even killings of citizens, both for drug use and for selling drugs. It is safe to assume that if there is an abundant supply of drugs, this kind of activity will finance terrorist activity.

Weapons procurement has been a major project for the PIRA. Its accumulations of weaponry are largely owing to the support it has received from rogue states, none more so than Libya, enabling the PIRA to stockpile considerable quantities of weapons, ammunition, and explosives over the last thirty years. Libya under Colonel Qaddafi was drawn toward the PIRA most likely as a result of the hunger strike deaths of the ten PIRA members. Libya saw itself as a country emerging from colonialism and had considerable sympathy for the

Revolutionary Movement in Northern Ireland. Libya's support in the early 1970s is believed to have been about $3 million in hard currency, including weapons and explosives. One notable incident involved a shipment containing at least five tons of Russian-made weapons that was intercepted by Irish authorities in 1974. The shipment was destined for the PIRA and was hidden in the hold of the freighter *Claudia*. Authorities intercepted her off the coast of Ireland. The number of prior shipments has never been fully confirmed, but sources believe at least three others successfully reached the terrorists.[10]

Although the PIRA had a representative in Tripoli, the relationship began to sour, the amount of the funds dwindled with the seizure of the *Claudia*, and arms shipments from Libya ceased. Libya's interference was seen by both the U.S. government of Ronald Reagan and the British government of Margaret Thatcher as acts of a state that clearly sponsored terrorism. The eventual destabilizing of the Qaddafi regime by whatever means was a likely goal of the CIA under the leadership of William Casey. Libya had been linked to terror attacks in Europe, and increasing numbers of public protests by dissident Libyan exiles were causing embarrassment to the Libyan regime. Bombings of the Libyan Consulate in Germany and the assassination of the Libyan ambassador in Rome in 1984 created a tense atmosphere within Libyan diplomatic missions in Europe. In April 1984 a group of anti-Qaddafi protesters demonstrated outside the Libyan Peoples Bureau in central London. With police in attendance to ensure public order, automatic gunfire erupted on the crowd from the Libyan Peoples Bureau.

FIGURE 5-5   The Libyan Peoples Bureau, London. Shots were fired at demonstrators outside the building, killing Metropolitan Police Officer Yvonne Fletcher (Photo by Sian Evans).

A police officer, Yvonne Fletcher, lay dying in the street. Relations between Britain and Libya and the United States and Libya deteriorated even further when the United States asserted its right to have ships in the Gulf of Sirte, an area claimed as sovereign by Libya. In 1986, U.S. warplanes, with cooperation from Britain, bombed Tripoli with the intent of "removing" Qaddafi. Although forbidden by the United States, assassination was clearly on their minds. The bombing killed more than eighty, including Qaddafi's adopted baby daughter. Qaddafi and PIRA now had a common enemy, and both sides had cause to despise the Thatcher government. The PIRA held Margaret Thatcher responsible for the hunger strikers' deaths in 1981, and Qaddafi held her complicit in the Tripoli bombings. Arms shipments resumed, and PIRA acquired huge shipments of weapons and Czech-made Semtex explosives. In the fall of 1986, 105 tons of weapons arrived from Libya, including 40 general-purpose machine guns; 1,200 AK 47s; 26 Russian-built DHSK heavy-duty machine guns; RPG-7 grenade launchers; and a large quantity of Semtex high explosives.[11]

In August 1979, in one of their more sensational attacks, the PIRA targeted the British Royal family, detonating a bomb in a small fishing vessel being operated by Lord Louis Mountbatten, cousin to the Duke of Edinburgh, husband of Queen Elizabeth II. The bomb also killed eighty-two-year-old Lady Brabourne, mother-in-law to Mountbatten's daughter, and three teenage boys. Lord Mountbatten was seventy-nine years old. On the same day, the PIRA also killed a patrol of eighteen British soldiers in a roadside bombing at Warrenpoint, County Down.

THE IRISH REPUBLICAN ARMY AND PROVISIONAL IRISH REPUBLICAN ARMY

Official records do not indicate the exact membership numbers of the many Northern Ireland paramilitary groups, but it is widely believed that the number of IRA members reached a peak of around 1,500–2,000 active members in the war-torn years of the 1970s. Membership declined over the next fifteen years until the announced cease-fire in 1994, at which point membership was probably only 300–500. Still one of the most powerful and effective terror

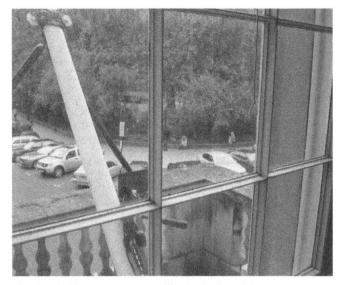

FIGURE 5-6 View from inside the Libyan Peoples Bureau from where shots were fired into demonstrators, killing WPC Fletcher (Photo by Sian Evans).

organizations of the last century, the IRA traces its roots to the Easter Rebellion of 1916 in the Republic of Ireland and gets its name from the first "volunteers" who fought for a free Irish State. The birth of the Provisional IRA came when the IRA split in December 1969, between the "Officials" and the "Provisionals." Confusion was rampant, as both organizations had a military wing, the "Official" and "Provisional" IRA, and both had a political wing, the "Official" and "Provisional" Sinn Féin. It was the "Official" IRA that declared a cease-fire in the summer of 1972, and, from then on, the term *IRA* was

used for the organization that had developed from the "Provisional" IRA. From a splinter group of a small and badly equipped paramilitary grouping, the "Provisional" IRA developed into a well-financed, well-equipped guerrilla/terrorist organization that was involved in what it called "an armed campaign" for almost three decades. The IRA's development of wider connections in countries like Libya, Spain, North America, and South America for logistical and weaponry support expanded it into a truly international terrorist organization.

The IRA has been known to conduct activities outside of Northern Ireland and mainland Britain. It has been active in Europe and had set up safe houses during the early 1990s for operations aimed at military and government targets in the Netherlands, France, and West Germany. Ease of movement and lack of border controls in the Benelux countries made opportunities just

FIGURE 5-7 Memorial to WPC Yvonne Fletcher, who died from gunshot wounds outside the Libyan Peoples Bureau in London (Photo by Sian Evans).

that much simpler. Weapons seizures in Europe in the early 1990s and two **active service unit (ASU)** arrests likely slowed down any advances that PIRA may have contemplated for extensive operations in Europe. The PIRA has more or less observed the cease-fire put in place since the end of 1990s. In August 2001, the credibility of the PIRA and Sinn Féin was brought into question when Colombian security forces arrested PIRA's head of engineering while he was developing mortars for the Revolutionary Armed Forces of Colombia (FARC) guerillas. Three suspected members of PIRA were arrested on August 11, 2001, at Bogotá's El Dorado International Airport, charged with training FARC in explosives handling and urban terrorist tactics. Of the three Irishmen arrested, one was identified as Niall Connolly, who had been in Latin America for at least a decade, according to Colombian and British officials.

Since 1996, however, Connolly had lived in Havana under the pseudonym David Bracken and acted as the Sinn Féin ambassador to the Fidel Castro government. He reportedly traveled frequently to Venezuela, Panama, Nicaragua, and El Salvador, where he is believed to have established contacts interested in arms smuggling, drug trafficking, and supporting the FARC's expanding insurgency in Colombia. Sinn Féin denied having any relationship with Connolly or knowledge of his activities in Latin America, but Cuba's foreign ministry released a statement on August 17, 2001, stating that Connolly had lived in Cuba for five years as Sinn Féin's Latin American representative.[12] Ulster unionists feared that the IRA was, on one hand, talking peace and decommissioning, while on the other, conducting training and seeking high-powered weapons. The other two suspects were identified as James "Mortar" Monaghan and Martin McCauley. Monaghan was a former member of Sinn Féin's ruling executive body and according to Garda Commissioner Pat Byrne, both were experts in the design and manufacture of increasingly effective homemade mortars. The two were also skilled in the use of mercury-tilt switches designed to blow up people in cars and radio-controlled "command" bombs for use against armored vehicles. These are technologies that would have significantly enhanced FARC's explosive-handling capabilities. Remote-controlled explosive devices have been a key feature of terrorist operations in Northern Ireland, particularly in the border regions.

The U.S. Central Intelligence Agency reportedly supplied the Colombian government with satellite footage of the three suspects training FARC rebels inside a demilitarized zone. Colombian officials have described the FARC–PIRA link as a "business relationship," in which the PIRA trades advanced explosives-handling techniques for illegal drugs, cash, or weapons. The three PIRA men spent three years in jail and were released on condition that they remain in Colombia pending an appeal from the Colombian government of their convictions. They were convicted of training Marxist rebels, in December 2004. They have since disappeared, and the Colombians have requested the support of Interpol to track them down. The men could face up to seventeen years in prison. PIRA members most likely schooled FARC rebels in how to mix high-powered synthetic explosives to extend the range of homemade gas cylinder mortars. The FARC needed to extend the roughly 400-meter range of its homemade mortars because of better defenses at military compounds built with American assistance.

Soon after the 9-11 attacks in New York City, David Trimble, the former first minister of the Northern Ireland Assembly, made the following statement about PIRA's head of engineering in the British Parliament on Thursday, October 4, 2001:

> Terrorism is terrorism, and requires no further qualification, so could I ask you (the Prime Minister) to reject the spurious distinction some people seek to draw between international and domestic terrorism... recent events all show that the Irish Republican Movement is part of an international terrorist network, and that there is still no sign that it is making the changes required by the Belfast Agreement.[13]

It is no surprise that the PIRA is one of the most ruthless and well-organized terror groups in history. It has achieved success against significant odds, and by the late 1960s and early 1970s, it had changed dramatically in its makeup. By the end of the 1960s, the Catholic minority was under increasing pressure and assault from Protestant gangs. Catholic enclaves needed protection from Protestant gangs who were burning, shooting, and bombing Catholic housing districts. Out of necessity and pressure from the authorities, the PIRA evolved from a loosely knit organization to one with a military structure, employing geographically based brigades, battalions, and companies. The PIRA reorganized to form cells based on the continental cellular structure and better adapted to modern-day terrorist activities. Autonomous Active Service Units were formed within these cells, becoming almost impossible to penetrate or identify, as each cell had only three to four members. They were given code names and directed by controllers. It was difficult to operate in the Catholic housing districts of Belfast and Londonderry, as everyone knew everyone else. The PIRA owed much of its success to the effectiveness of the cell system.

As part of its mainland campaign after the collapse of the 1974–1975 cease-fires, it centered its attacks on London. Londoners were unfazed by the bombing campaign and stoically went about their business. The PIRA was always concerned about the activity of the British SAS, and in one now-famous incident, the Balcombe Street siege, the PIRA cell gave up without a fight when news was leaked that the London Metropolitan Police were handing over to the SAS. What had started out as a botched raid on a London restaurant saw the four-man PIRA team chased down by uniformed police officers. The gang holed up in a residential area, Balcombe Street, and took an elderly couple hostage for six days before surrendering peacefully. The gang was also responsible for the death of Ross McWhirter and a number of bomb attacks.

CONTINUITY IRISH REPUBLICAN ARMY

The Continuity IRA was a breakaway, or splinter, group of Republicans from the mainstream Provisionals. CIRA may have been in existence in the South for several years. In 1986, some of those Republicans attending the Sinn Féin Ard Fheis (party conference) walked out in protest, but they never presented the threat to the organization posed by the dissidents in 1969. The group was led by Ruairí Ó Brádaigh, who went on to form the Republican Sinn Féin, and other veteran activists. Despite the purity of their beliefs, the Ó Brádaigh wing failed to persuade enough Provisionals to join them. The split was small and contained. The fear of reprisals from PIRA was ever present, and it was years before the Continuity IRA revealed its existence. That, in itself, was a comment on the group's frailty.[14]

DIRECT ACTION AGAINST DRUGS

Sometimes PIRA used the name Direct Action Against Drugs (DAAD) when it wanted to claim responsibility for certain operational activities in Northern Ireland. It is basically a cover name for the Provisionals and not a separate or distinct terror group in the North.

REPUBLICAN SINN FÉIN

The Republican Sinn Féin (RSF) is a breakaway group from Sinn Féin, formed in 1986. The party decided to end its traditional abstention policy, and those who opposed the move walked out to form the RSF. The group was led by Ruairí Ó Brádaigh, former president of Sinn Féin, and Dáithí Ó Conaill, former chief of staff of the Irish Republican Army (IRA). At the 1988 RSF

Ard Fheis, or annual conference, the party reaffirmed its support for the "armed struggle." RSF rejected the 1993 Downing Street declaration and was also squarely against the peace process.[15] RSF saw itself as forming part of a wider Republican Movement with a number of organizations sharing similar ideological and political perspectives including the Continuity IRA, Cumann na mBan, Fianna Éireann, Cabhair, the National Commemoration Committee, and the Republican Prisoners Action Group. RSF strenuously rejected the allegation that it was the "political wing" of the Continuity IRA, as it denied any assertion that the latter was its "military wing."

REAL IRISH REPUBLICAN ARMY

The Real IRA split from the Provisional IRA in 1998 over political differences, forming an armed counterpart to the political 32-Country Sovereignty Movement. The group shares the common IRA goal of reunifying Northern Ireland and Ireland, but rejects the PIRA cease-fire and the Belfast Agreement, continuing to direct violence against the British government in Northern Ireland.

Viewed as one of the most dangerous groups in existence after the Good Friday Agreement, one of its most devastating accomplishments was the bomb attack of the town center of Omagh on August 15, 1998. Twenty-nine civilians were killed in this bombing, and more than 200 were wounded. It was, singly, the worst terrorist attack in Northern Ireland history. Following this atrocity, the group was forced to call a cease-fire. In spite of this, the group remains in existence and gets its support from those not aligned with the peace process. As long as there is a modicum of deadlock and lack of progress, this group is likely to continue to try to sway support away from the PIRA. The Real IRA 2008 New Years Statement published in the Sovereign Nation newspaper was very clear about their intent moving forward:

> The Irish Republican Army will continue to carry out armed attacks against the British military and political apparatus in Ireland, and those who assist in anyway their illegal occupation. Once again the constitutional nationalist and establishment parties are attempting to sell the lie that the RUC/PSNI are a civic police force, and this has been borne out by recent events, that the RUC/PSNI are primarily a political police force whose primary function is to protect British interests in Ireland. It is for this reason that the IRA have carried out a number of attacks against the British police in Ireland, these attacks will continue.

RIRA operates in the same way as does the PIRA, with bomb attacks on security forces and commercial locations and targeting mainland Britain. Its leadership includes Bernadette Sands Mckevitt, the sister of Bobby Sands, a PIRA member who died from a hunger strike, and Francie Mackey, a one-time Sinn Féin counselor for Omagh. Its weapons and explosives likely come from PIRA sources, and there is concern that the group is purchasing weapons through Balkan states.

OTHER IRISH TERRORIST GROUPS

Irish National Liberation Army

Also called People's Liberation Army (PLA), People's Republican Army (PRA), and Catholic Reaction Force (CRF), this small group is an offshoot of the breakup of the IRA in the late 1960s. They reject the ideology of both the official IRA and the Provisional IRA and are considered more Marxist in orientation than the PIRA. Formed in the early 1970s with a small membership of about thirty, it is headquartered in Dublin. Its goals and activities have centered in the Belfast and Londonderry areas. Their political objectives being the formation of a thirty-two-county Socialist

Republic in Ireland, the forced removal by any means, including violence, of British troops from Northern Ireland, and the overthrow of the elected government of the Republic of Ireland. They express solidarity with other national liberation and terrorist organizations around the world. Its leadership consisted of Harry Flynn, Gerard Steenson, Thomas Power, and Dominic McGlinchey. McGlinchey, Steenson, and Power were all killed in bitter feuding between INLA and the PIRA in the late 1980s. Their most audacious act of terror remains the 1979 assassination of Airey Neeve, the British Conservative Party spokesman on Northern Ireland. Neeve was killed when a powerful bomb destroyed his car as he was leaving the Houses of Parliament in London. A highly decorated World War II veteran, he wrote a study of the Nuremberg trials. In his study's final chapter, he was to reflect on the impact the Nuremberg trials had had on his life and the fight between good and evil; his words are extremely telling: "Before our eyes the problems of race and terrorism are a frightening reminder of Hitler's example. Those who use terror to gain their political ends are the heirs of his Revolution of Destruction however much they may claim to represent opposing doctrines."

This assassination marked INLA's first operation outside Ireland. The group was decimated in the 1980s as a result of the "Supergrass" trials. The word *supergrass* is an outgrowth of an eighteenth-century slang term, *copper* (meaning *informer*), which rhymed into *grasshopper*, later shortened to just "grass." "Super" was added to precede "grass" in the late twentieth century to imply informing on a truly grand scale. In the context of Northern Ireland, the Supergrass strategy involved "reforming" terrorists by allowing them to divulge information in court about fellow terrorists and current prisoners in exchange for a new identity in a new country. Police in Northern Ireland used this strategy, and the evidence at that time was admissible in court. Supergrasses were responsible for a number of arrests and convictions of Irish terror suspects; the evidence provided was not required to be corroborated. Uncorroborated testimony is among the more dubious practices in a court of law. These Supergrassers were designated as such by INLA and PIRA militants for those who informed on their former comrades. By the end of the decade, the problems with admission of Supergrass evidence as part of the court process led to the release of many imprisoned INLA and PIRA members. The result—a bloody feud between the INLA and PIRA—killed many militants. INLA still remains brutal and unpredictable. The organization was responsible for the murder of Billy Wright, a Loyalist Protestant and Maze Prison militant, on December 27, 1997. The result of this assassination was a spate of sectarian attacks, in which eight Catholics were murdered. The INLA has been observing a cease-fire since August 1998.

Ulster Volunteer Force (UVF)

A loyalist paramilitary group that also operated under the names *Protestant Action Group* and *Protestant Action Force* in the 1970s with around 1800 members. By 2006, that number had dwindled to a hard core of several hundred supporters. UVF was considered to be the largest of the Loyalist paramilitary organizations. Formed at the outset of "The Troubles" in 1966, it takes its name from its Irish forefathers—the original UVF was formed in 1912 to oppose, by force, the Home Rule Bill for Ireland. In 1914, the volunteers smuggled 35,000 rifles into Larne, County Antrim. Later, men of the UVF joined the British Army en masse as the 36th Ulster Division, which suffered huge losses at the Battle of the Somme. As they went over the top that day and charged the enemy lines, the Ulster soldiers shouted, "No surrender," echoing the same cry used by the apprentice boys in the siege of Londonderry of 1688. Its limited goals are aimed at securing the North's constitutional position within the United Kingdom and to aggressively defend its Protestant heritage.

The endless cycle of violence that has typified Northern Ireland life for more than a quarter of century can be laid squarely at the doorsteps of both Protestant and Catholic paramilitaries.

On many occasions, these groups use different names of ally groups to claim responsibility for attacks. The Loyalist paramilitary groups invariably did not claim specific responsibility for their murders—they moved and operated under various subgroups in their terrorist structure.

The UVF has been responsible for scores of assassinations in Northern Ireland, mostly of innocent Catholics. The UVF leader in the 1960s was Augustus (Gusty) Spence, who killed a Catholic man in a pub on the Shankill Road, Belfast, in June 1966 and was sentenced to life in prison. They are also credited with the simultaneous bombings of Dublin and Monaghan on May 17, 1974, killing thirty-three civilians.

Throughout the 1970s, their main battleground was the Shankill Road area of Belfast and parts of County Antrim. The group was proscribed in 1974, making it an illegal organization. They continued their bloody sectarian attacks, killing twelve people in October 1975. Raids by security forces in 1977 saw twenty-six suspects arrested for the killings. Their convictions resulted in a total of 700 years imprisonment. Their decline came about mostly from informers, whom the British security services were able to skillfully manipulate for information on past attacks, resulting in further arrests and convictions throughout the 1990s. In spite of these setbacks, the UVF continued sectarian attacks against Catholics throughout the 1990s. In 1996, a number of disaffected members of their mid-Ulster brigade formed the Loyalist Volunteer Force (LVF). For its political influence, the Progressive Unionist Party (PUP) is considered as its front in much the same way as Sinn Féin and PIRA.

Along with many other paramilitary groups, the UVF did declare a cease-fire in 1994. Later in the decade, the UVF was frequently accused of violating the cease-fire agreement. As late as August 2005, the UVF continued its sectarian attacks. Gusty Spence announced that the UVF and the Red Hand Commando would "assume a nonmilitary, civilianized role." The UVF contin-ued to feud with other loyalist groups, which caused the British government to announce in 2005 that it no longer recognized the UVF's 1994 cease-fire. Since 2005, the group's leadership has attempted to distance the UVF from criminal activities, although with very questionable results. The Independent Monitoring Commission, formed in 2004 to monitor paramilitary organiza-tions in Northern Ireland, in its April 2006 report stated that the UVF remained an active and violent paramilitary organization. By May 2007, with most other groups either out of commission or having declared a permanent cease-fire, they declared that they were renouncing violence and ending their terror campaign. They also stated that UVF was not disarming but, like the PIRA, was simply putting their weapons and explosives beyond reach.

Ulster Democratic Party (UDP)

The UDP also uses the name Ulster Loyalist Democratic Party. The group was formed in 1989 as a political front for the Ulster Defense Association. The ULDP was the original political mouthpiece of UDA in 1981. This organization had little or no political gains and successes. PIRA assassinated its leader John McMichael with a car bomb at his Lisburn home in December 1987. The UDP strategy was to outwardly portray itself as a distinct political movement and was not aligned with the UDA; we have seen this with PIRA and Sinn Féin. The government banned membership of UDP in 1992. Under the terms of Section 30(3) of the Northern Ireland Emergency Provisions Act of 1996, the following Loyalist groups were proscribed:

- The Red Hand Commandos
- The Ulster Freedom Fighters
- The Ulster Volunteer Force
- The Ulster Defense Association

The following are the proscribed Republican groups:

- The Irish Republican Army
- The Irish National Liberation Army
- The Irish Peoples Liberation Organization
- Women's Wing of the Irish Republican Army (Cumann na mBan)
- Youth Wing of the Irish Republican Army (Fianna na hEireann)
- Saor Eire (Free Ireland)

The UDP was finally dissolved in November 2001. It seems logical that infighting and disagreement over the Good Friday Agreement was the cause of the disbandment of the organization.

Ulster Defense Association (UDA)/Ulster Freedom Fighters (UFF)

The Ulster Defense Association is also one of the largest Loyalist paramilitary groups in Northern Ireland. They also use the name *Ulster Freedom Fighters* as a cover for terrorist actions. An abundance of Loyalist defense associations sprang up in the first years of "The Troubles," which saw numerous attacks in the 1970s on Catholics. Members of the UFF claimed responsibility for these attacks, but they were effectively being conducted by UDA members. The two groups should be viewed as one and the same, and it is difficult to understand why the UDA was not proscribed until August 1992. Along with the UVF, the UDA had significant numbers located in Belfast and was a commanding force to either attack Catholics or challenge the British army presence.

Their aim was to create an independent Northern Ireland, both within the European Union and the Commonwealth. To create the correct political mind-set, it needed to create a viable political forum and thus formed the New Ulster Political Research Group (NUPRG) in 1978. In June 1981, the Ulster Loyalist Democratic Party (ULDP) was established, replacing the NUPRG. The ULDP also proposed independence for Northern Ireland within the British Commonwealth. The UDA was politically savvy and was able to create a document by 1987 that set out its vision for a new political settlement and structure for the North. In spite of UDA's obvious links with terrorism, the proposal document did receive some favorable reviews from politicians and the British government's Northern Ireland Office. UDA leader, John McMichael was killed by a PIRA bomb, but the UDA/UFF continued its attacks on Catholics and Republican supporters into the 1990s. The UDA/UFF joined in the 1994 cease-fire, and members of the Ulster Democratic Party were involved in the multiparty talks in 1996. The Good Friday Agreement remained a political football throughout the remainder of the century. Many groups on both sides were opposed to various sections of the agreement, particularly policing and power sharing.

UDA/UFF continued to feud with other loyalist groups and also maintained its campaign of attacks on Catholics. The ongoing feud and the attacks forced the government to announce that UDA/UFF, the UVF and the Loyalist Volunteer Force (LVF) had ended their cease-fires. Sporadic feuding continued within the UDA, and on February 22, 2003, the UDA declared a cease-fire. The LVF was formed in 1996 as a breakaway group from the Loyalist UFF. LVF is a violent, anti-Catholic movement, strongly opposed to the 1994 cease-fire agreement. Its membership is likely small and accounts for maybe three dozen active members. The British government proscribed the LVF in 1997. Its leader Billy Wright was murdered inside the Maze Prison by members of the Republican Irish National Liberation Army (INLA) in December 1997. As has been the case throughout "The Troubles," no terror act by one side goes without retaliation from the other. In the two weeks following Billy Wright's death, sectarian violence accounted for the murders of eight Catholics by members of the LVF and UFF.

The LVF agreed to a cease-fire in May 1998, but continues to oppose the peace process. In 1998, under the auspices of the Independent International Commission on Decommissioning (IICD), it began to decommission some of its arsenal of weapons. Any weapons and explosives it may have limited access to are likely under the control of other Loyalist groups. It is believed that no other Loyalist groups have decommissioned any weapons or explosives; however, the UVF has claimed to put their weapons "beyond reach."

The LVF, at its peak, had around 300 members, and the group has not been credited with carrying out any attacks since February 2003. Billy Wright was "succeeded" by Mark Fulton, a close acquaintance who reportedly idolized the founder of the LVF; Fulton has been described as Wright's hit man and is thought to be personally responsible for over a dozen sectarian murders. While in jail, awaiting trial on charges of conspiracy to murder a rival loyalist, Fulton died of strangulation on June 9, 2002, in an apparent suicide. He was found in his jail cell in the isolation wing of the prison with a belt wrapped around his neck.[16]

Red Hand Defenders

The Red Hand Defenders (RHD) formed in late 1998 from a group of Loyalist paramilitaries disaffected by the Good Friday Agreement. There has been speculation that RHD is simply a cover name for UDA and LVF members to carry sectarian violence. This would be to their benefit, as only those paramilitaries on formal cease-fire were able to benefit from the early prison-release program within the Good Friday Agreement. If this is the case, clearly the RHD is established as a cover and has no real existing members as they would be considered members of either the UDA or the LVF.

During the 1998 marching season, RHD conducted what seems to be a revenge bomb attack, killing an RUC officer. This attack followed the RUC decision to restrict the Orange Order from marching along the Garvaghy Road in Portadown, County Armagh. They had also claimed responsibility for the killing of Rosemary Nelson, a Catholic human rights lawyer, in Lurgan in March 1999. RHD and the Orange Volunteers (OV) seemed to surface around the same period, and it is thought that the OV may be another cover for Loyalists.

Orange Volunteers

The Orange Volunteers is a Protestant Loyalist paramilitary with ties to the Orange Order. The group originated at the outset of "The Troubles." It was at that time second only to the UDA and the UVF in size and support. The group was believed to be inactive by the end of 1980, but its name came up once again in 1998 at the same time as the Red Hand Defenders. Like other paramilitaries of the time, OV was made up of those disaffected by the Good Friday Agreement and is likely closely linked with the same membership as the RHD. The operational effectiveness of this "new" group is unsophisticated and has utilized homemade blast bombs (pipe bombs) and hand grenades. It may be that this small group of dissidents is also involved in crime, most particularly drug dealing.

TURF WARS

The early 1970s could be described as turf wars among the warring factions of the IRA, the Irish National Liberation Army (INLA), the Ulster Freedom Fighters (UFF), and the Ulster Volunteer Force (UVF). Tit-for-tat murders and revenge killings of both Catholics and Protestants were common, driven mostly by pure hatred.

This was epitomized by the infamous "Shankhill Butchers," a gang of UVF members led by "The Master Butcher" Lenny Murphy, operating in West Belfast and intimidating the

Catholic community and carrying out merciless, cutthroat killings. In those early days, there was a struggle for supremacy in the housing districts and ghettos of West Belfast. The feuding was partly ideological and partly material in that they were fighting for control of the criminal rackets in Belfast and Londonderry. Since the Good Friday Agreement came into force, much of the continued violence has related to criminal activities within the paramilitaries, both Protestants and Catholics.

One Protestant fighter stands out among all others for his audacious attacks against Republicans. In March 1988, the crack British counterrevolutionary warfare unit from the Special Air Service (SAS) Regiment killed three PIRA members on the island of Gibraltar. At their funeral in Milltown Cemetery, with the world's press watching, a man approached from the road and hurled grenades at the assembled Republicans, including Gerry Adams. In the ensuing mayhem, the Protestant Michael Stone was arrested; he was charged and sentenced and was subsequently released in 2000 under the terms of the Good Friday Agreement. His actions did not end there; in 2006, he single-handedly stormed into the foyer of the Northern Ireland Assembly, carrying a bomb and waving a handgun and knife, before being tackled by security staff.

Civil Liberty Issues

Civil rights and civil liberty issues have aided and confused the processes of both peace and terror. The British government has used human rights violations as a tool, both legislatively and as a method of controlling the violence in Ulster.

The Catholic marches of the late 1960s sparked the rioting and bloodshed that led to larger and larger troop deployments in Ulster. Internment was introduced in the 1970s by the British government to curtail the actions of the paramilitary groups. Internment had little strategic effect, but provided PIRA members with significant public sympathy—they were seen as "martyrs for the cause."

With the increase in sectarian violence, judges and juries also became targets for the terrorist groups. The **Diplock Commission**[17] was set up to look at ways of dealing with the legal aspects of controlling a terrorist in a democratic society. Ensuring the safety and integrity of the security forces and giving them the unfettered ability to bring the terrorists before the courts, the Northern Ireland Emergency Provisions Act was passed in 1973. The measures, seen as draconian, served the security services well. The act provided for terrorist offenses to be listed as "scheduled" offenses:

- **Scheduled offenses** were to be tried by a senior judge sitting alone, with more than the rights of appeal;
- Bail was prohibited for scheduled offenses unless granted by the High Court, with stringent conditions attached;
- Persons could be held on police arrests without warrant for seventy-two hours;
- Suspects arrested by the military could be held for four hours;
- Security forces had extensive powers for search and seizure;
- Those arrested for weapons and explosives offenses had the onus of proof reversed for them to prove their innocence; and
- The secretary of state could issue detention orders from information gathered if the security forces believed the information and evidence to be valid.[18]

Nonjury trials were introduced in Northern Ireland in 1972 as a response to witness intimidation by paramilitary groups. The introduction of "Diplock Courts" were opposed by civil liberty organizations and both nationalists and Republicans. At their peak, more than 300 trials per year were held without a jury. Some of those operating the system were targeted by the IRA and, in 1987, Lord Justice Maurice Gibson and his wife were killed by a bomb. The government technically abolished Diplock courts in 2007, but nonjury trials can be used if jurors are believed to be at risk of intimidation. Between August 1, 2008 and July 31, 2009, thirteen nonjury trials were held, down from twenty-nine in the previous year.

With many convictions for terrorist offenses gathered through this sweeping legislation, the PIRA still managed to make both political and publicity points for its predicament. Once in prison, the terrorist took controlled and intimidated prison officers both inside and outside the confines of jail. These laws were adopted in the early 1970s and since then have undergone frequent reviews and amendments. In 1988, fifteen years after it was enacted, the Prevention of Terrorism Act, providing sweeping powers to security forces in Britain, was challenged in the international court. The provision within the act to detain terrorist suspects for up to seven days was determined to have violated the European Convention on Human Rights. In 1999, the home secretary announced the establishment of a review group comprising representatives of the Northern Ireland Office, the Northern Ireland Court Service, the Attorney General's Office, the Director of Public Prosecutions (Northern Ireland), and the then Royal Ulster Constabulary. Underlying the work of the review group was the general consensus that normalization should occur as soon as possible and that the restoration of jury trial would be seen as a normalizing event. In a report to the secretary of state for Northern Ireland in May 2000, the review concluded that the time was not yet right for an immediate return of jury trial. The principal reason for this was the conclusion that the risk of jury intimidation remained significant.[19]

The Terrorism Act of 2000 reformed much of the mechanisms and powers dealing with terrorism. The provisions of this act extended to all forms of domestic and foreign terrorism within the United Kingdom. Certain provisions of previous terrorism legislation, applicable only to Northern Ireland, could be extended for a maximum of five years. The act broadened the definition of terrorism to include actions or threats of action that are designed to

- Influence the government;
- Intimidate the public;
- Advance a political, religious, or ideological cause;
- Involve serious violence against a person or serious damage to property;
- Endanger a person's life;
- Create a serious risk to the health or safety of the public; or
- Interfere with an electronic system.

Special powers within the act include special entry, arrest, and search and seizure authority without a warrant under certain circumstances.

Periodic reviews of the emergency powers specifically relating to Northern Ireland have been undertaken. While the perception may well be that life has returned to a level of normalcy, this is not necessarily expressed by the judiciary in its reviews. Examples of the powers available to both police and military forces came from Schedule 5, Sections 81–88 of the act. Lord Berriew, in his review, concluded that Section 81 allows a police officer to enter and search any premises if he or she has reasonable suspicion that a person is or has been concerned in the commission, preparation, or instigation of acts of terrorism. Section 82 provides that any police officer may arrest, without warrant, any person he or she has reasonable grounds to suspect is committing, has committed, or is about to commit a scheduled offense, or an offense under the Act that is not a scheduled offense, and may enter and search any premises or other place for that purpose.

Section 82(3) empowers a police officer to seize and retain anything that he or she suspects is being, has been, or is intended to be used in the commission of a scheduled offense. Section 83 provides a power of arrest and detention for a period not exceeding four hours to a member of Her Majesty's Forces on duty who reasonably suspects that a person is committing, has committed, or is about to commit any offense, together with corresponding powers of entry and seizure.

This act was further supported with the enactment of the Antiterrorism Crime and Security Act of 2001, which addressed terrorism and foreign nationals. Civil rights movements have objected to provisions in both of these acts, specifically in sections where the burden of proof is reversed in suspected terrorism cases. In reflecting on 9-11, the legislation was also aimed at those Britons involved with attacks overseas. For instance, the British press reported that in December 2000, a British Muslim from Birmingham, England, was alleged to have conducted a suicide attack on an Indian army barrack in Srinagar; in another, a Briton was reportedly plotting a terrorist attack, earlier the same year, against Israel.

NORTHERN IRELAND'S PROTESTANT MARCHING SEASON

The Reverend Ian Paisley

Ian Paisley has been the public face of Protestant reaction to Republicanism (Catholics). Paisley is the leader of the Democratic Unionist Party of Northern Ireland and moderator of the Free Presbyterian Church. As the mouthpiece of the Unionist movement, he was often sentenced for unlawful assembly as he conducted marches and protests around the province in the years leading up to the "Troubles." He even coined a battle cry first heard at the siege of Londonderry in 1688, "No surrender," when thirteen apprentice boys closed the gates of the city on the Jacobite army. In his hard-line Protestantism, he loudly proclaimed opposition to any and every concession offered to the Catholic community. He was an outspoken opponent of the Good Friday Agreement. However, in 2007, Ian Paisley was sworn in at Stormont Castle as Northern Ireland's first minister and was photographed alongside the other senior member of the power-sharing executive and his old archenemy, Martin McGuiness from Sinn Féin. With the guns silent and politics the order of the day, Paisley announced he would retire from politics in March 2008.

The Loyalists, including the entire Orange Order, were determined not to be part of any Republic. It seems almost incredible to people outside of Northern Ireland that the act of marching, seemingly so irrelevant to most, should cause such widespread anger and revulsion. Marching in military style has been a part of Protestant history in for over 200 years. The lore and beliefs have been passed down from generation to generation. To understand what motivates such sectarian hatred between the Catholics and Protestant communities requires a review of the historical roots of marching.

Marching season falls between Easter Monday and the end of September, when more than 2,000 marches are held throughout the North. There are, however, specific march dates in history that create more flashpoints on the calendar than do other marches. The Protestants celebrate the victory of Protestant King William over Catholic King James I at the Battle of the Boyne, on July 12, 1690. But this is more than just the celebration of a victory; for Protestant Orangemen, it is the need to display their allegiance to the Crown and Protestantism. Sometimes referred to as "Orangeism," it could also be described as Ulster Unionism on the march. The **Orange Order** and the Ulster Unionist Council constitute an integrated political movement that is determined that Northern Ireland will remain within the United Kingdom along with England, Scotland, and Wales and will never be absorbed by a Catholic-dominated, all-Ireland republic.[20] Both the Orange Order and the Apprentice Boys say that marching is an essential part of their Protestant culture. The Apprentice Boys is a Loyalist organization similar to the Orange Order. This group annually commemorates the ending of the 105-day siege of Londonderry in 1688. They march with a crimson flag first carried by Protestant supporters of William of Orange who were besieged in Londonderry by an Irish Jacobite army.

The challenges to peace during marching season are many, as the marchers wind their way through long-established routes in Catholic enclave such as the Garvaghy Road in Portadown and the Lower Ormeau Road in Belfast. Both areas have been rife with outbursts of violence in recent years. The Independent Commission on Policing in Northern Ireland made a recommendation in 1998 that it should be a condition for the approval of a parade that the organizers provide their own marshals. This should include, as appropriate, representatives of the neighborhoods involved along the parade route. The Catholic communities, through which Protestants demand the right to march, have so much hostility to marching because it would take but one small incident to provoke an outbreak of serious sectarian violence.

The Loyal Orange Institution, or Orange Order, was founded in 1795 after a Protestant victory at Loughgall, County Armagh. This is referred to as the "Battle of the Diamond." In September 1795, several hundred Defenders (Catholics) assembled at a crossroads called the Diamond, near Loughgall in County Armagh. They had come to attack the house of one Dan Winter, where they were convinced the "peep-o-day boys" (Protestants) stored their guns and met to conspire against Catholics. The Battle of the Diamond, on Monday, September 21, lasted a brief fifteen minutes. The "peep-o-day boys" suffered no losses, but as many as forty-eight Defenders were said to have been killed. The first Orange Lodge was established that evening. One James Sloan, an innkeeper, became the first grand secretary, with power to issue warrants to whichever group of Protestants that wanted to follow his rule and set up Orange Lodges. They were required to swear an oath of allegiance to "His Majesty, King George III, and his successors so long as he and they support the Protestant ascendancy."[21]

Sectarian Violence

The terror groups on both sides of this complex situation have targeted the police and the military as their legitimate targets. The long-established hatred and revulsion of some Catholics for Protestants, and vice versa, has caused the senseless deaths of many innocent civilians. People have been killed purely for their religious affiliations, whether they are from PIRA or a Loyalist paramilitary. Tit-for-tat killings have been a hallmark of Northern Ireland's history through most of the twentieth century and into the twenty-first. (An obvious parallel is the conflict between the Israelis and Palestinians.) This dates back as far as June 17, 1922, when the IRA issued an order for the destruction of property owned by Orangemen. According to police reports, at 2:30 that morning, IRA men executed six unarmed Protestants and a policeman. The attack was motivated purely along religious lines and had no significance in the struggle for the IRA. Five decades later in 1976 a similar, but far more gruesome, attack took place in the Kingsmills area in South Armagh and claimed the lives of ten Protestant workers, who were stopped on their bus ride home from work and executed in a hail of bullets by members of the PIRA. Marching season is the time of year when sectarianism comes into play. Protestants have viewed the treatment of Sinn Féin and the Republican movement as an erosion of their own political and economic power base. As they lose ground, this violence, sectarian in nature, has begun to spread. In 2001, in the weeks leading up to the 9-11 attacks in the United States, Protestants pelted Catholic primary schoolchildren with rocks and verbal abuse as they made their way to school through the Protestant Ardoyne district of Belfast. These scenes were more reminiscent of an earlier age in the southern United States involving bussing of black students to school. The Holy Cross School in Ardoyne district has existed for more than thirty years, but the demographics of the area around it have changed. Mainly a Protestant area when "The Troubles" began, many of the middle-class Protestants moved away throughout the 1990s, and more Catholic families have moved into the area, to the chagrin of Protestants.

THE PIRA AND INTERNATIONAL TERROR

The Sinn Féin and Irish Republican terror groups had a problem, and that problem was credibility. The Peace agreement required weapons to be decommissioned and although some decommissioning had taken place, there was a double standard—the PIRA turned in the old weapons, but then actively pursued acquiring new ones. In May 2002, the PIRA purchased a quantity of Russian-made AN-94 assault rifles. In April 2002, the Israelis identified pipe bomb devices made by PIRA terrorists in the hands of Palestinian terrorists. Paul Collinson, a former officer with the Royal Engineers Bomb Disposal, who worked for the Red Cross at the Jenin refugee camp in Palestine, commented, "The pipe bombs I found in Jenin are exact replicas of those in Northern Ireland. The size of bomb, the way they put the nail in, the way of igniting it with a light bulb filament, where they drilled the holes through, the use of a command wire and the means of initiating the bomb; these are all the same."[22] As we can tell from this report, the PIRA continues to ply its terrorism trade on an international scale not only in the Middle East but also, as mentioned earlier, in South America. This broader involvement of the PIRA on the international stage was also a focus of the U.S. House of Representatives International Relations Committee. This committee concluded that Irish, Iranian, Cuban, and Spanish terror groups had probably been sharing techniques and honing their terror skills, while using illicit drug proceeds for payment. Gerry Adams, as the president of Sinn Féin, not surprisingly turned down an invitation to testify before the congressional committee on the topic.

How closely linked are Sinn Féin and the Irish terror groups? There is little doubt that Adams and McGuiness have the ability to exert significant pressure, whether direct or implied, on the workings of the PIRA and the Army Council. In early 2002, a daring raid was made on the Northern Ireland Police Special Branch offices at Castlereagh. The PIRA managed to seize highly confidential documents that named police informants and undercover operations. To most observers in the security services, it is highly probable that the PIRA Army Council ordered and conducted this seizure. Most, if not all, terror groups come to the table to talk peace only when they are in such a desperate situation that signing a deal or calling a cease-fire is all that is left to them. In 1994, the PIRA called a cease-fire—not when they were winning the battle, but when they were losing it. Both Adams and McGuiness are survivors, and to control the dissidents within the Republican movement, it would seem wholly logical for the PIRA to continue as before, but allowing Sinn Féin the freedom to express concern, sometimes outrage and, more frequently, denial of knowledge of PIRA activities when it comes to the thorny topics of bomb making and weapons acquisition.

There are many differences between the struggle for peace in Northern Ireland and the struggle for peace in the Middle East. In Northern Ireland, there are still many political problems to be resolved, as well as centuries of fear and distrust standing between Catholics and Protestants. However, for Northern Ireland there is a tunnel, and there even appears to be some light at the end of it.

THE NORTHERN IRELAND PEACE PROCESS

It seems almost improbable that the devastation from the 9-11 attacks on New York's World Trade Center prompted many terror groups, particularly the PIRA, to begin some decommissioning and moves toward peace. It is generally agreed that the peace process was developed from a combination of factors: A realization, by both the PIRA and the British Army, that the war could not be won militarily, and the decision by the PIRA to develop political strategies through Sinn Féin, as an alternative way to fight for its goals:

- The willingness of the Social Democratic Labour Party (SDLP) to engage with Sinn Féin in pursuing common nationalist political goals by peaceful means;
- A changing social and economic context in which many of the discriminations against Catholics was addressed and in which a legal and social infrastructure to address issues of inequality, equality, and respect for diversity began to be developed;
- An increased willingness by many within civic society, for example, among businesses, trade unions, and community groups, to actively engage in the process of contact and political leverage for peace;
- The development of some new (albeit small) political parties by the Loyalists, and by the Women's Coalition, which enabled some new thinking on the political landscape; and
- A changing international context, including proactive involvement from the U.S. government, and many U.S. businessmen and politicians, as well as assistance with developing peace processes from South Africa.[23]

In August 2001, just a few weeks before 9-11, the Good Friday Agreement was on the verge of collapse and PIRA had failed to decommission its weapons. The events of 9-11 appear to have had a sobering effect on the men of violence in Northern Ireland. With endless bombings and more than 3,600 killed in sectarian violence, both main players—the British government, which has endured with an occupying army for over three decades, and the Irish terror organizations— eventually came to the conclusion that the fighting must end. From the terrorist standpoint, the use of the gun, albeit used to good effect, has not had its desired effect of removing British occupying forces from Northern Ireland. Early attempts at peace settlements in the two decades preceding the Good Friday Agreement were doomed to failure. Events that would hinder any lasting peace have principally been the decommissioning of weapons in the possession of the paramilitary groups and the PIRA's foreign involvement in Colombian and Middle East terrorism. For many decades, the romantic image of Irish freedom fighters taking on the British was lore in the Irish-American communities of New York and Boston. Media coverage of terrorism— played out on U.S. television screens—has required a fundamental shift in the PIRA's attitude toward decommissioning of weapons. The PIRA has received significant amounts of financial aid from U.S. organizations and support groups; however, in the aftermath of 9-11, the romantic view of the cause for most Americans faded quickly.

Decommissioning

The decommissioning of weapons was a central issue in the peace deal/accord.

In September 1997, the **Independent International Commission on Decommissioning (IICD)** was established to oversee the decommissioning of paramilitary weapons from both sides.

The 1998 Belfast Agreement committed all participants to the total disarmament of all paramilitary organizations. The agreement called on all sides to work constructively with the decommissioning teams to use any influence they may have to achieve the decommissioning of all paramilitary arms within two years of the referendum, in May 1998. Although this target was never met, progress was nonetheless made. The first act of decommissioning was witnessed by the IICD in December 1998, when the Loyalist Volunteer Force (LVF) decommissioned a quantity of weapons.

Caches of weapons and explosives have been stockpiled through the last two decades of the twentieth century. These arms shipments came from state sponsors of terrorism, specifically Colonel Qaddafi of Libya. This support would surely be repugnant to the American public still recovering in the aftermath of 9-11.

In October 2001, the PIRA, under the scrutiny of IICD, "put beyond use" (a term used by the PIRA to signify destruction) a large quantity of weapons and explosives. The first round of PIRA decommissioning was orchestrated shortly after the arrest in Colombia of two senior members of the Republican movement and FARC guerillas. This can only have been an embarrassment to the Sinn Féin leadership and something that would likely damage relations between the Republicans and their U.S. support networks. On the other side of the equation, the Ulster Democratic Unionist Party, led by the Reverend Ian Paisley, was not satisfied with the manner in which the destruction of the weapons and explosives had taken place and was demanding a full listing of weapons destroyed. However, the decommissioning was viewed as a landmark event that gave the British government a further opportunity to announce the removal and closure of the network of army watchtowers along the border with the Republic.

On October 23, 2001, the IRA issued the following statement on the BBC regarding the subject of disarmament:

> The IRA is committed to our republican objectives and to the establishment of a united Ireland based on justice, equality, and freedom. In August 1994, against a background of lengthy and intensive discussions involving the two governments and others, the leadership of the IRA called a complete cessation of military operations in order to create the dynamic for a peace process. "Decommissioning" was no part of that. There was no ambiguity about this. Unfortunately, there are those within the British establishment and the leadership of Unionism who fundamentally opposed to change. At every opportunity, they have used the issue of arms as an excuse to undermine and frustrate the process. It was for this reason this decommissioning was introduced to the process by the British government. It has been used since to prevent the changes that a lasting peace requires. In order to overcome this and to encourage the changes necessary for a lasting peace, the leadership of Oglaigh na hEireann (IRA) has taken a number of substantial initiatives. These include our engagement with the Independent International Commission on Decommissioning (IICD) and the inspection of a number of arms dumps by the international inspectors, Cyril Ramaphosa and Martti Ahtisaari. No one should doubt the difficulties these initiatives cause for our volunteers, our supporters, and us. The political process is now on the point of collapse. Such a collapse would certainly, and eventually, put the overall peace process in jeopardy.

There is a responsibility upon everyone seriously committed to a just peace to do our best to avoid this. Therefore, in order to save the peace process, we have implemented the scheme agreed with the IICD in August. Our motivation is clear. This unprecedented move is to save the peace process and to persuade others of our genuine intention.

SIGNED: P. O'NEILL.[24]

The PIRA's reluctance for verification of arms decommissioning continued to be a stumbling block for Republicans and Loyalists.

Further decommissioning took place in 2003 and 2004, but the PIRA still retained the ability to use force. While they may have decommissioned all of their arms, they had not actually disbanded, and no one except the PIRA has any definitive knowledge as to the number and types of weapons that remain cached. This being said, in 2005 PIRA issued the following statement:

The leadership of Oglaigh na hEireann (IRA) announced on 28 July that we had authorized our representative to engage with the IICD to complete the process of verifiably putting arms beyond use. The IRA leadership can now confirm that the process of putting arms beyond use has been completed.

SIGNED: P. O'NEILL.

(Ret) General John de Chastelain (IICD Commission Chairman) has indicated that the following estimates are an accurate representation of the PIRA arsenal that was decommissioned:

- 1,000 rifles
- 2 tonnes of Semtex
- 20–30 heavy machine guns
- 7 surface-to-air missiles (unused)
- 7 flame throwers
- 1,200 detonators
- 11 rocket-propelled grenade launchers
- 90 handguns
- 100+ grenades.[25]

The peace process, starting with the Good Friday Agreement, has stumbled along for more than half a decade. The aim of a coalition of parties was to lead what might be termed a "joint assembly" made up of all "interested parties," including Sinn Féin. The inclusion of Sinn Féin, and the perception that its leaders still have links and influence over PIRA activities, has had a definite impact on the power-sharing process. Unionist parties were adamant that they could not work out a government with Sinn Féin so long as the Provisionals retained possession of their weapons and munitions. But, with the final decommissioning of the PIRA arms, a power-sharing government for Northern Ireland has become a reality. In May 2007, Ian Paisley and Martin McGuiness were sworn in at Stormont Castle as Northern Ireland's First Minister and Deputy First Minister, respectively, and both Republican groups (Catholics) and the Unionists (Protestants) now make up the power-sharing executive in Northern Ireland.

The "Agreement" is a document th at goes a long way in addressing political, social, economic, and judicial inequalities that, to many, would seem to have been root causes of the thirty years of "The Troubles." Three of the most common points, decommissioning, security and policing, and justice have been cause for not just debate, but at times the near breakdown of the whole Agreement. The following sections taken from the Agreement form some of the most contentious points:

PRISONERS

1. Both governments will put in place mechanisms to provide for an accelerated program for the release of prisoners, including transferred prisoners, convicted of scheduled offences in Northern Ireland or, in the case of those sentenced outside Northern Ireland, similar offences (referred to hereafter as qualifying prisoners). Any such arrangements will protect the rights of individual prisoners under national and international law.
2. Prisoners affiliated to organizations that have not established or are not maintaining a complete and unequivocal ceasefire will not benefit from the arrangements. The situation in this regard will be kept under review.
3. Both governments will complete a review process within a fixed time frame and set prospective release dates for all qualifying prisoners. The review process would provide for the advance of the release dates of qualifying prisoners, while allowing account to be taken of the seriousness of the offences for which the person was convicted and the need to protect the community. In addition, the intention would be that, should the circumstances allow it, any qualifying prisoners who remained in custody two years after the commencement of the scheme would be released at that point.
4. The governments will seek to enact the appropriate legislation to give effect to these arrangements by the end of June 1998.
5. The governments will continue to recognize the importance of measures to facilitate the reintegration of prisoners into the community by providing support both prior to and after release, including assistance directed toward availing of employment opportunities, retraining and/or re-skilling, and further education.

As mentioned earlier, the decommissioning of weapons by paramilitaries has been a major stumbling block for politicians, particularly from the Unionists.

DECOMMISSIONING

1. Participants recall their agreement in the Procedural Motion adopted on September 24, 1997, "that the resolution of the decommissioning issue is an indispensable part of the process of negotiation," and also recall the provisions of paragraph 25 of Strand 1 above.
2. They note the progress made by the Independent International Commission on Decommissioning and the governments in developing schemes that can represent a workable basis for achieving the decommissioning of illegally held arms in the possession of paramilitary groups.
3. All participants accordingly reaffirm their commitment to the total disarmament of all paramilitary organizations. They also confirm their intention to continue to work constructively and in good faith with the Independent Commission and to use any influence they may have to achieve the decommissioning of all paramilitary arms within two years following endorsement in referendums North and South of the agreement, and in the context of the implementation of the overall settlement.
4. The Independent Commission will monitor, review, and verify progress on decommissioning of illegal arms, and will report to both governments at regular intervals.
5. Both governments will take all necessary steps to facilitate the decommissioning process to include bringing the relevant schemes into force by the end of June.

1. The participants note that the development of a peaceful environment on the basis of this agreement can and should mean a normalization of security arrangements and practices.
2. The British government will make progress toward the objective of a return as early as possible to normal security arrangements in Northern Ireland, consistent with the level of threat and with a published overall strategy, dealing with
   i. The reduction of the numbers and role of the Armed Forces deployed in Northern Ireland to levels compatible with a normal peaceful society;
   ii. The removal of security installations;
   iii. The removal of emergency powers in Northern Ireland;
   iv. Other measures appropriate to and compatible with a normal peaceful society.
3. The Secretary of State will consult regularly on progress and the response to any continuing paramilitary activity with the Irish government and the political parties, as appropriate.
4. The British government will continue its consultation on firearms regulation and control on the basis of the document published on April 2, 1998.
5. The Irish government will initiate a wide-ranging review of the Offences Against the State Acts 1939–85 with a view to both reform and dispensing with those elements no longer required as circumstances permit.[26]

The power base for the PIRA and Sinn Féin had rested as much on the gun and the bomb as it did on the vote. The governments of both Dublin and London have believed that terrorism cannot be defeated but must be appeased, and this has caused them to waver in negotiations—first, demanding concessions from the PIRA, next backing down or withdrawing the demand, and then pressuring the democratic parties not to make the same demands. Success in the elections has gone to those parties that have openly opposed serving in government assemblies with armed terrorists. Appeasement will surely win in the end!

POWER-SHARING EXECUTIVE

The peace process has been long and protracted and has at times almost crashed and burned! The appetite for a power-sharing government follows nearly forty years of sectarian violence and political posturing and squabbling. In the history of Northern Ireland's "Troubles," May 8, 2007, was a landmark day—a power-sharing local authority had been brokered and recognized by the governments of both the Republic of Ireland and the United Kingdom. The Reverand Ian Paisley, leader of the dominant party among Northern Ireland's Protestant community, and Martin McGuiness, the deputy head of Sinn Féin Republican Party, were both sworn in as leader and deputy leader, respectively, to lead the new Northern Ireland government. The events would end political and direct rule from London, which had been in effect since the Northern Ireland Assembly was suspended in 2002. Looking back over the last thirty-five years, it's almost inconceivable that these two men, Paisley and McGuiness, would ever speak to each other let alone form the leadership nuclei of a new power-sharing government—in the past, Paisley had long accused McGuiness of being an IRA terrorist and that he had acquired the nickname of "Dr. No" for his continued rejection of the Good Friday Agreement. The May 8 oath that both men took also included a commitment to the Northern Ireland Police, something the Republicans had long resisted as the police were viewed as part of the Union enemy. The Troubles are officially over in Northern Ireland, but what remains of the men of violence? They have certainly not disappeared but have continued to act as organized crime units, controlling drugs and other illegal activities. It is hoped that with cooperation, with the police now enshrined in the new government approach to business, the police service will be able to curb the actions of former terrorists now engaged in criminal activity.

The Police Service of Northern Ireland

The Police Service of Northern Ireland—historically, the Royal Ulster Constabulary (RUC)—has long been composed disproportionately of Protestant and Unionist members. The total percentage of Catholics within the force is only about 7 percent. Over the last three decades, the RUC has been identified with political control, formerly from the Unionist government in Stormont and latterly during the periods of Direct Rule from Westminster, not as upholders of the law, but seen as defenders of the state, and the nature of the state itself has remained the central issue of the political argument.

In 1998, the British government appointed the former governor of Hong Kong, Chris Patten, to head the Independent Commission on Policing in Northern Ireland. The commission's report made 175 recommendations for change. When the recommendations were presented, the Sinn Féin party was adamant that the only way forward for the peace accord was a full implementation of all the recommendations, including the striking of the word "Royal" from the police title. The police force has always had a predominantly Protestant flavor and has lost some 300 officers, who were killed in terrorist acts, and over 9,000 injured during the "Troubles." Policing in the North cannot be likened to the work of any other police force operating in a Western democracy. In 1985, INTERPOL stated that the RUC was the most dangerous force anywhere in the world in which to serve, even surpassing that of Colombia. The Patten Report, entitled "A New Beginning: Policing In Northern Ireland," covered every region of the force from recruitment, IT, size of force, composition by religious affiliation, culture and ethos, public order policing, and human rights. The aim of the recommendations was to attract and sustain support for the new organization from the entire community. The problems faced by the police service in Northern Ireland are, in a sense, unique in a divided society, each side with its own particular history and culture. But many problems are similar to those confronting police services in democratic societies elsewhere. The Independent Commission studied policing in other countries, and while it could discover no model that could simply be applied to Northern Ireland, it was able to find plenty of examples of police services wrestling with the same challenges. The challenge for the police service in the North was how it could be accountable to the community it serves if its composition—in terms of ethnicity, religion, and gender—is vastly different to that of its society. In the words of the founder of the British police service, Sir Robert Peel, the police service's main objective is the prevention of crime rather than the detection and punishment of offenders. The end of the 1990s saw a debate in Britain on policing as it affected ethnic minorities and communities and the police service's relationship with those communities. There is obviously no perfect model for Northern Ireland, and there is no example of a country that, to quote one European police officer, "has yet finalized the total transformation from force to service." The commitment to a fresh start gives Northern Ireland the opportunity to take best practices from elsewhere and to possibly lead the way in overcoming some of the toughest challenges of modern policing.[27]

COUNTERING IRISH TERRORISM

Through necessity the British government developed wide-scale antiterrorist and counterterrorist measures against the terror groups in Northern Ireland. Never before in its history had a British government to deal with internal terrorist activities on the scale that emerged from Northern Ireland. On many occasions, Britain has met violence with violence and has had some innovative ideas to counter the terrorists. Among those innovations are its reputed shoot-to-kill policy, internment, removal of a defendant's right of silence during judicial proceedings, and the prohibiting of news media broadcasting statements of PIRA and Sinn Féin. With the "Irish question" appearing now to be answered after a near century of political and sectarian violence, one has to question how effective the countermeasures really were. The hostility shown by and to Prime Minister Margaret Thatcher helped to fuel the terror campaign against British economic, military, and political targets. She constantly reiterated that she would "never give in" to the IRA. Each side's inability to achieve a military victory should be obvious to the other. The lessons for the rest of the world from Northern Ireland's conflict would seem to be the following:

- Authorities must pursue every effort to make political compromises with dissidents before violence becomes institutionalized.
- Authorities cannot achieve a military victory over terrorists and still maintain civil liberties and democratic institutions.
- Counterterror techniques by authorities that kill, injure, or frighten noncombatants provide support for terrorist groups. Indeed, revolutionary terrorist groups depend on the authorities to perpetrate provocation and outrages against noncombatants.
- Terrorist groups can be devastatingly effective with very few members, given the worldwide availability of sophisticated weapons and explosives.
- Terrorist groups can sustain community support by using both the latent sympathy of citizens, as well as intimidation.
- Even the most technologically sophisticated, well-organized, well-financed, and highly motivated counterterrorist methods can be frustrated by a small group of terrorists that have some community support.[28]

Britain's counterterrorism organizations have had notable successes. The Special Air Service Regiment, which continued to thwart and strike at Republican terrorists through the 1980s and 1990s, was instrumental in preventing terrorist attacks and setting up offensive traps, resulting in the capture and often the death of terrorists. The SAS has had significant success against the PIRA and has been responsible for a number of successful ambushes against them. Many ambushes, spectacular in nature, resulted in heavy loss of life to the terrorists. Most notable was an ambush in March 1988 on the island of Gibraltar of an unarmed ASU that British and Spanish intelligence had determined was about to carry out an attack on the British colony. The terrorists' target was the ceremonial band of the 1st Battalion Royal Anglian Regiment, which had arrived in Gibraltar after a tour of duty in Northern Ireland. Army intelligence officers have been expecting a PIRA attack on a military target for some months. The SAS unit gunned down the PIRA cell in broad daylight; killed were Daniel McCann, thirty, and Sean Savage, twenty-four, both known PIRA activists, and Mairead Farrell, thirty-one, the most senior member of the gang who had served ten years for her part in the bombing of a hotel outside Belfast in 1976. A car used by the PIRA cell was found two days later containing 140 lbs of Semtex with a device timed to detonate during the "changing of the guard" ceremony. An inquest the same year concluded the three had been lawfully killed; but in 1995 the European Court of Justice ruled that the SAS soldiers had violated the fundamental right to life of the PIRA members.

Britain was widely criticized at the time for this action. In the post 9-11 environment, one wonders whether the same criticism would be applied now.

Judicial process was the primary weapon against the terror groups in Northern Ireland, and Britain's early response in sending in troops to protect Catholics from Protestants did not have its desired effect. The PIRA was up against the entire intelligence resources of a major Western government. The brigade and battalion structures of the PIRA, established at the latter end of the 1960s, became targets for penetration by the RUC. Informants were placed within the organization, and several senior PIRA members were arrested. As noted previously, the PIRA remodeled its battalions into smaller cells where only a minority of people knew who was who. The British government was prepared to meet violence head-on with its special counterrevolutionary warfare force, the British Special Air Service Regiment.[29]

DOMESTIC TERRORISM IN MAINLAND BRITAIN

The Angry Brigade

Totally forgotten by many, however, is a small terror group that came to life in the 1960s—the decade that saw the Beatles, widespread drug use, and fundamental changes in societal views and values. The Angry Brigade was Britain's only noteworthy, homegrown terror group.

Their members were dissimilar in almost every way to the Irish terrorists and had no clearly defined enemy to focus on, other than wealthy, middle-class Conservatives running business corporations. Unlike the terrorists in both Northern Ireland and the mainland, the Angry Brigade was a loosely formed group of Communist-style workers' party members. Angry Brigade was a left-wing revolutionary movement, militant and pro-labor. They came to some prominence in the late 1960s. With no military knowledge or background, the Angry Brigade espoused Marxist theories in the hope that workers would find them acceptable in the 1960s. Britain was a changing society with a strong Conservative government under Alec Douglas Hume. Modernization and growth in the factories, particularly in the auto industry and the dockyards, were the order of the day. The leaders of the Angry Brigade sought to change government policy and usher in a new era of socialism by murdering politicians and bombing public buildings.

Activist or Terrorist

As activists in a workers' party struggle against the state and big business, the Angry Brigade issued communiqués and proclamations stating their cause. The brigade hoped to gain recognition by professing support for the Irish Nationalist Movement and such mirror-image revolutionaries as the Symbionese Liberation Army (SLA) in the United States. Closer to home, the group espoused support for the activities of the Red Brigade in Italy and the German Red Army faction. There is no recorded information that the group received any support, either financial or militarily, from either of these terrorist organizations. What is certain is that the brigade caused explosions aimed primarily at political and business figures. The group was tracked down by London's Metropolitan Police and prosecuted for its terrorist and criminal acts. The Angry Brigade's members believed that they were engaged in a workers' struggle that could only come to fruition if the working masses rebelled against their masters. This altruistic goal was never realized, however, possibly owing to the atrocious nature of the brigade's attacks. Little has been heard of the group since the main protagonists were jailed in 1972. They could be termed a "copycat," as they likened themselves to the Weathermen in the United States and, in a later period, to the German terrorist group Baader Meinhoff. The ringleaders, who became known as the Stoke Newington Eight, were sent to prison for long terms in 1972.

Angry Brigade Terrorist Acts

The Angry Brigade is believed to have been involved in a number of bombings in London aimed at banks, corporations, and foreign interest businesses, such as the Bank of Bilbao. The Brigade supported the Basque Separatists in Spain. It is unclear what this group hoped to achieve by attacking the homes of the commissioner of the Metropolitan Police and a member of parliament. Certainly, these actions demonstrated an ability to coerce and intimidate, but their overall effectiveness can be dismissed as having minimal effect in making any changes in the political arena. Unlike the PIRA, the Brigade had no political machinery similar to that of Sinn Féin, or any media support.

Wales and Terror for the Tourist

The region of the United Kingdom known as Wales seldom conjures up visions of terrorist activity. In fact, Wales is better known for its tourist attractions at Caernarvon Castle, the Mountains of Snowdonia, Welsh choirs, famous actors, mining, and the sport of rugby. So, is Wales a nest of terror groups or a convenient hiding place for the indigenous terrorist? Over the past three decades, there has been the odd discussion of an independent Welsh homeland, which occasionally has been brought to the attention of Britons by acts of arson. These acts were usually aimed at unoccupied holiday homes and cottages in the Wales countryside. Claiming responsibility for these acts of arson is a group calling itself the Miebion Glyndwr, or Sons of Glendower. This group takes its name from Owen Glendower, a Welsh leader from the fifteenth century, who vowed to fight the English and their rule over Wales. The arson attacks on remote cottages resulted in more than 100 having been destroyed since the first attack in 1979. The group appears disorganized and factional, with no political platform for its support. About twenty Welsh activists have been convicted and jailed for some fifteen of the attacks. A group calling itself Cadwyr Cymru (the Defenders of Wales) has claimed responsibility for some of the arsons.

Animal Rights Militia

Animal rights activists have been prevalent in Great Britain for several decades, but the Animal Rights Militia is the only one of their many groups to have moved toward terror tactics aimed at companies and research institutes. In 1986, bombs were planted under cars, and at the homes of prominent research scientists and animal importers. Although adequate warnings were given, this marked the group's trend toward violent action. This group, while perhaps using what could be terrorist tactics, is still considered more like criminals than true terrorists. The Antiterrorism Act of 2000, although aimed at curbing Northern Ireland terror groups, could also be focused on the Animal Liberation Front, an activist organization that is believed responsible for a number of bomb attacks against animal research establishments and the agricultural industry. Attacks on fast-food establishments in Belgium appear to have been the work of the same group.

ISLAMIC EXTREMISM

Over the last three decades, Islamic groups have managed to relocate to the United Kingdom as a sanctuary or base for various activities for fund-raising, and primarily to escape their own repressive regimes. Britain's liberal policies have made it easy for Islamic groups to set up official charities to raise funds for their own causes. Terrorists wanted in other countries were given safe haven in the United Kingdom and left free to foment hatred against the West. Extremist groups such as Hizb ut-Tahrir remained legal despite being banned in many European and Muslim countries. Radicals such as Abu Qatada, who is wanted in Jordan on terrorist charges, Omar Bakri Mohammed, who left the UK for Lebanon in 2010 and has not been allowed back in; Abu Hamza, currently in a UK prison but also wanted in the US; and Mohammed al-Massari were allowed to preach incitement to violence and jihad![30] As early as 1998, Osama bin Laden was quoted in *Time* magazine: "Our work targets world infidels. Our enemy is the crusader alliance led by America, Britain, and Israel. It is a crusader-Jewish alliance." Britain's military presence in Afghanistan also makes the country a prime target. The Muslim population in Britain runs to just over 2 million and a constant inflow of refugees—both legal and illegal—crosses into the country from Europe on an almost daily basis. So, how deeply entrenched were Muslim fanatics within the Muslim faith in Britain? The answer is quite startling; according to British officials, up to 16,000 British Muslims are either actively engaged in or support terrorist activities, while up to 3,000 are estimated to have passed through al Qaeda training camps, with several hundred thought to be primed to attack the United Kingdom.[31]

Islamic groups operating within mainland Britain are often from terrorist organizations that appear on the U.S. State Department list of overseas terrorist organizations. These groups include Gama'a al-Islamiyya, Hamas, Shining Path, the Liberation Tigers of Tamil Eelam, Hezbollah, and the Kurdistan Workers' Party. All of these groups had been actively recruiting and raising funds freely in the United Kingdom until September 11, 2001.

The West began to take serious note of al Qaeda in the days after the 1998 attacks on the U.S. embassies in Nairobi and Dar es Salam and the waterborne suicide attack in 2000 on the USS *Cole* in Yemen. It became clear that the reach and spread of al Qaeda and its ideology throughout the world, and particularly in Europe, would pose one of the most significant risks to Western democracies.

Britain, long viewed as one of Europe's most liberal societies; but that view may be changing following the introduction of tough antiterrorism legislation in 2001.

United Kingdom—Religion

There are just over 1.5 million Muslims residents in the United Kingdom; the following breakdown from the U.K. Office of National Statistics drawn from the last countrywide census in 2001 is important in recognizing the change society undergoes with high levels of migration from Third World countries.

Population of Great Britain: by religion, April 2001

	Total population (Numbers)	Total population (Percentages)	Non-Christian religious population (Percentages)
Christian	41,014,811	71.8	
Muslim	1,588,890	2.8	51.9
Hindu	588,342	1.0	18.3
Sikh	336,179	0.6	11.0
Jewish	267,373	0.5	8.7
Buddhist	149,157	0.3	4.9
Any other religion	159,167	0.3	5.2
All non-Christian religious population	3,059,108	5.4	100.0
No religion	8,596,488	15.1	
Religion not stated	4,433,520	7.8	
All population	57,103,927	100.0	

FIGURE 5-8 Religious populations christianity is main religion in Britain.   *Source:* Office for National Statistics licensed under the Open Government Licence v.1.0.

Christianity is the main religion in Great Britain. There were 41 million Christians in 2001, making up almost three-quarters of the population (72 percent). This group included the Church of England, Church of Scotland, Church in Wales, Catholics, Protestants, and all other Christian denominations.

People with no religion formed the second-largest group, comprising 15 percent of the population.

About one in twenty (5 percent) of the population belonged to a non-Christian religious denomination.

Muslims were the largest religious group after Christians. There were 1.6 million Muslims living in Britain in 2001. This group comprised 3 percent of the total population and over half (52 percent) of the non-Christian religious population.

Hindus were the second-largest non-Christian religious group. There were over half a million Hindus (558,000), comprising 1 percent of the total population and 18 percent of the non-Christian religious population.

There were just over a third of a million Sikhs (336,000), making up 0.6 percent of the total population and 11 percent of the non-Christian religious population.

There were just over a quarter of a million Jewish people (267,000), constituting 0.5 percent of the total population and 9 percent of the non-Christian religious group.

Buddhists numbered 149,000 people in 2001, comprising 0.3 percent of the population of Great Britain.

The religion question was the only voluntary question in the 2001 Census, and 8 percent of people chose not to state their religion.

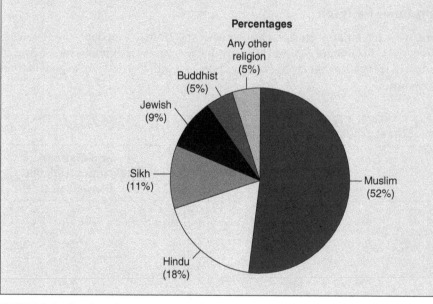

FIGURE 5-8 Continued

London remains a haven for young Muslim immigrants and asylum seekers, and with diminishing prospects for work, they have managed to adapt to the generosity of a welfare state that provides for their physical well-being. Many resorted to attending institutions such as the Finsbury Park Mosque, where many observers would say that they were brainwashed into global movements such as al Qaeda and then sent throughout the world to carry out jihad. Evidence has been uncovered linking Richard Reid, who attempted to detonate an explosive device in his shoes on board a U.S. trans-Atlantic flight in December 2001, Zacarias Moussaoui, the so-called twentieth hijacker (9-11), as well as the millennium bomber, Ahmed Ressam. The Finsbury Park Mosque on St. Thomas's Road, Finsbury Park, was among London's first purpose-built mosques when it was opened in 1993. It was managed by a registered charity but due to disagreements among the trustees, the institution became poorly managed. In the resulting vacuum, one **Abu Hamza al Masri**—a disabled Afghan war veteran—through intimidation and strong-arm tactics was able to take over the mosque in 1996, creating no-go zones for the trustees and physically removing them from the building. Abu Hamza al Masri collected around him supporters, including those dabbling in petty crimes and forgeries. The trustees pressed the charity commissioners to intervene, but action became protracted over the years. Legal moves failed to dislodge Hamza and his band. The mosque was subject to an early morning raid in January 2003. The police did not take action when Abu Hamza al Masri and supporters commenced conducting prayers on the street outside.

The one-eyed, hook-handed Imam Sheik Abu Hamza al Masri continued to be outspoken in his support for Osama bin Laden. In a television interview, he made no apologies and showed no remorse for the 9-11 attack on the World Trade Center. So, was Finsbury Park Mosque a fertile and covert breeding ground for al Qaeda? The mosque itself attracted many Muslims from the London area, namely, Pakistanis, Bengalis, Egyptians, and Algerians. Abu Hamza, himself an Egyptian, has been in the United Kingdom for more than twenty-five years. His presence was imposing—a missing eye and a hook in place of his right hand—to young and impressionable Muslims who would see little future for themselves in the Western democracies and be easily indoctrinated by the Imam and his cohorts. A Canadian Broadcast Corporation (CBC) documentary on recruiting al Qaeda in Britain focused squarely on the Finsbury Park Mosque. Their exposé included hidden videotaping of recruiting activities inside the mosque, as well as videos of terrorist training tactics, even how to slit a person's throat. The problem for British police lay in its inability to pinpoint any crime that the Imam may have committed. When the mosque was forcibly closed in 2002, that did not stop the one-eyed Abu Hamza from preaching on the street outside the mosque, with dialogue such as, "Seek the way of death . . . if you die to defend your religion, you are a martyr . . . die honorably, don't die humiliated."[32] The United States has been trying to build a case against the cleric, on evidence of his involvement in setting up a training camp in Bly, Oregon, in 1999–2000, with the intention to stockpile weapons there for jihad training. He has also been charged in the United States with conspiracy for his involvement with an Islamic group in Yemen that took sixteen tourists hostage in 1998. It's alleged that he provided a satellite phone to the Islamic Army of Aden and spoke to the conspirators before the attack. On May 27, 2004, British police arrested Abu Hamza. He remained in custody, while the United States attempted to have him extradited, and in October 2004, the British charged him on ten counts ranging from inciting racial hatred to soliciting or encouraging the murder of others—"namely, a person or persons who did not believe in the Islamic faith, in particular the Jewish people." He is currently serving a prison sentence for soliciting murder and inciting racial hatred.

Al-Masri faces eleven charges in the United States, including charges related to a 1998 kidnapping in Yemen and the formation of a terrorist training camp in Oregon in 1999. In 2006, a British court ruled that he could be extradited once he has completed his sentence in the United Kingdom.

HIZB UT-TAHRIR (HT) (THE ISLAMIC LIBERATION PARTY), AL-MUHAJIROUN, AND ISLAM 4UK

Hizb ut-Tahrir (HT) is a global organization that is banned in numerous countries. From 1986 to 1996 the group was led by Omar Bakri Muhammed. The organization is antidemocracy and strives to make Islamic caliphates. While despising the democracy of the United Kingdom, its leaders have been more than content to relish the rights, freedoms, and latitude provided under just such a democracy, and with a U.K. location, they also take advantage of the world press availability. In viewing their website, they define a clear message to the politicians—even with events unfolding in Libya in the spring of 2011, they called for the intervention to be by Muslim countries and not from the empire seeking countries of Europe. A 2010 assessment made by the government of this organization determined that individuals who were members did not necessarily progress to violence. The Cabinet Home Affairs Committee stated, "*We do not believe that it is accurate to regard radicalization in this country as a linear 'conveyor belt' moving from grievance, through radicalization, to violence.... This thesis seems to both misread the radicalization process and to give undue weight to ideological factors.*" Before government considers the legitimacy of such groups, it is also worthy of note that at least nineteen terrorists convicted in Britain have had links with al-Muhajiroun, including Omar Khayam, sentenced to life imprisonment as leader of the "fertilizer bomb" plot, and Abdullah Ahmed Ali, the ringleader of the airliner "liquid bomb" plot, who is serving a life sentence. HT also like to debate their side of the political spectrum in the United Kingdom, specifically when it comes to labeling Muslims as moderates or extremists. The following statement was released by HT on January 20, 2011:

> Ignoring the role of politicians, including David Cameron, Cabinet Minister Sayeeda Warsi has sounded a warning about the rise of Islamophobia in Britain..... She argues that Islamophobia is a prejudice that has now become normal and accepted in many parts of society; and that trying to divide Muslims into 'moderates' and 'extremists' creates more intolerance towards Islam and Muslims. Taji Mustafa, Media Representative for Hizb ut-Tahrir in Britain said: "It is hardly surprising that prejudice and hatred towards Islam and Muslims is on the rise when leading politicians ignore political grievances of the Muslim world, rooted in western foreign policy, instead equating Islam with violence saying 'The driving force behind today's terrorist threat is Islamist fundamentalism' (David Cameron 2005); or that the Shariah and Caliphate are 'an evil ideology' (Tony Blair 2005); or when they refer to Islamic scholars visiting from overseas as 'foreign hate preachers' (Theresa May 2010); or when David Cameron demonizes the Muslims of Pakistan during his trip to India saying they cannot 'look both ways on 'terrorism'; or when niqab and Pakistani men are demonized following comments by Jack Straw. These, and other statements, add to the deliberate smears, misinformation and propaganda peddled by some politicians and sections of the British media." "Sayeeda Warsi's statements will come as no surprise to ordinary Muslims. The intolerance she mentions, created by the categorization of Muslims by politicians into moderates and extremists, according to traditional Islamic beliefs and values, is an old colonial—'divide and rule'—strategy that is being played out at a community level under the government's on-going 'Prevent' policy". "Our message to Muslims in the UK is to resist the pressures to compromise on Islamic values, and to carry these noble values to others, redressing the propaganda and smears that will likely continue in future."[33]

HT says it opposes terrorism and condemned the 9/11 and 7/7 attacks. However, it regards integration as "dangerous," orders all Muslims to keep apart from nonbelievers and says that "those [Muslims] who believe in democracy are Kafir," or apostates. A British would-be suicide bomber, Omar Sharif, was radicalized partly by HT activists at his London University.[34] In 1996, Omar Bakri Muhammed split away from HT in disagreement of policy and direction and formed Al Muhajiroum (AM). Omar Bakri came to Britain when the Saudi Arabian government banned AM in 1986 and lived on government handouts throughout his time in the United Kingdom. He left to go to his native Lebanon in 2005, and the home secretary took immediate steps to ban his return as it was alleged that his presence was "not conducive to the public good."

AM provided backing to Abu Hamza, at the Finsbury Park mosque, and in advertising a conference held in the mosque in 2002, AM leaflets described the 9/11 hijackers as the "magnificent 19." Al-Muhajiroum was also known for its intimidation of Jewish university students with inflammatory leaflet drops and radical campaigns that included distributing posters nationwide in 2000 claiming: "The last hour will not come until the Muslims fight the Jews and the Muslims kill the Jews." As a result, it was outlawed on campuses by the National Union of Students in 2001.

AM disbanded in 2004 when Muhammed shut it down fragmenting into two smaller groups, the Saviour Sect and al-Ghurabaa, both later proscribed by the home office for the "glorification of terrorism." AM probably still exists but under different colors as its supporters simply set up new groups, some overt and some covert, and not yet proscribed by the government. Islam 4UK is one such group to emerge and being run by Muhammed's former al-Muhajiroun cohort Anjem Choudary. Its public appearances have not endeared them to the wider British public for their attempts to march in Wotton Basset to disrupt the funeral processions for fallen U.K. soldiers returning from Afghanistan.

TABLIGHI JAMAAT

Tablighi Jamaat, an Islamic revivalist organization that has spread from its origins in India in the 1920s to the broader Muslim world is believed to have many thousands of members in the United Kingdom.

Considered an extreme Islamist movement; its European headquarters in the northern English town of Dewsbury has been in situ since 1978. It has its own extreme views on Islam's place in the world and is considered by British security experts to be the leading force in Islamic extremism and a fertile recruiting ground for young men—Mohammed Siddequ Khan, the leader of the London bomb plot in July 2005, has links to Jamaat. The number of adherents that come to the Dewsbury mosque is quite startling—they come from all over England and Western Europe to meet and be preached to in Dewsbury. To the many law-abiding Muslims in Britain, it is fair to say that their religion is often hijacked by those with an extremist agenda, and it is unfortunate that the voices of moderate Muslims are seldom heard, let alone listened to. With the influx of Muslims in the 1970s came their highly traditional faith influenced by Sufism, passive and quiescent. Over the years, theirs became an increasingly activist faith centering on the mosques that were now generating a highly radicalized ideology, and according to the Pakistani Bishop of Rochester (Christian), a whole generation of Muslim children was indoctrinated with a set of inflammatory ideas about the need for Islam to achieve primacy over the non-Islamic world.[35] The fuel for the radicalization process came from two important events in the 1980s and 1990s. First, the Soviet invasion of Afghanistan, which saw British forces training and equipping Afghan fighters (mujahedeen) against the Soviets whom they eventually drove out of their homeland; these Muslim fighters had now found a cause and a vocation—holy war. Second, the Bosnian war in which a steady media stream depicted the massacres of Muslims by Christian neighbors. Thousands of Islamic fighters from both Afghanistan and Bosnia found their way West.

The Prevention of Terrorism Act 2005

A system of control orders under the Prevention of Terrorism Act 2005 has replaced the Part 4 powers under the Antiterrorism, Crime, and Security Act 2001. The Prevention of Terrorism Act allows for control orders to be made against any suspected terrorist, whether a U.K. national or a non-U.K. national, or whether the terrorist activity is international or domestic. The home secretary is required to report to Parliament as soon as reasonably possible after the end of the relevant three-month period on how control order powers have been exercised during that time.

The facts about Control Orders

- Control orders enable the authorities to impose conditions upon individuals ranging from prohibitions on access to specific items or services (such as the Internet) and restrictions on association with named individuals, to the imposition of restrictions on movement or curfews. A control order does not mean "house arrest."
- Specific conditions imposed under a control order are tailored to each case to ensure effective disruption and prevention of terrorist activity.
- The home secretary must normally apply to the courts to impose a control order based on an assessment of the intelligence information. If the court allows the order to be made, the case will be automatically referred to the court for a judicial review of the decision.
- In emergency cases, the home secretary may impose a provisional order, which must then be reviewed by the court within seven days.
- A court may consider the case in open or closed session—depending on the nature and sensitivity of the information under consideration. Special advocates will be used to represent the interests of the controlled individuals in closed sessions.
- Control orders will be time limited and may be imposed for a period of up to twelve months at a time. A fresh application for renewal has to be made thereafter.
- A control order and its conditions can be challenged.
- Breach of any of the obligations of the control order without reasonable excuse is a criminal offence punishable with a prison sentence of up to five years, or an unlimited fine, or both.
- Individuals who are subject to control order provisions have the option of applying for an anonymity order.
- To date, the government has not sought to make a control order requiring derogation from Article 5 of the European Convention on Human Rights.

Terrorism Act 2006

The Terrorism Act contains a comprehensive package of measures designed to ensure that the police, intelligence agencies, and courts have all the tools they require to tackle terrorism and bring perpetrators to justice.

The act was not a direct response to the July 2005 attacks on London, as new terrorism legislation had already been planned.

After the attacks, consultations with law enforcement and intelligence agencies were held to make sure that their views were considered when developing new legislation.

Content of the Terrorism Act

The act specifically aims to make it more difficult for extremists to abuse democratic freedoms and encourage others to commit terrorist acts.

It created a number of new offences:

- **Acts preparatory to terrorism**—This aims to capture those planning serious acts of terrorism.
- **Encouragement to terrorism**—This makes it a criminal offence to directly or indirectly incite or encourage others to commit acts of terrorism. This will include the glorification of terrorism, where it may be understood as encouraging the emulation of terrorism.
- **Dissemination of terrorist publications**—This will cover the sale, loan, or other dissemination of terrorist publications. This will include those publications that encourage terrorism and those that provide assistance to terrorists.
- **Terrorist training offences**—This makes sure that anyone who gives or receives training in terrorist techniques can be prosecuted. The act also criminalizes attendance at a place of terrorist training.

The act also makes amendments to existing legislation, including

- Introducing warrants to enable the police to search any property owned or controlled by a terrorist suspect;
- Extending terrorism "stop and search" powers to cover bays and estuaries;
- Extending police powers to detain suspects after arrest for up to twenty-eight days (though periods of more than two days must be approved by a judicial authority);
- Improved search powers at ports;
- Increased flexibility of the proscription regime, including the power to proscribe groups that glorify terrorism.

Laws in Britain have been created and amended to accommodate acts of terrorism, and those laws have been subject to Human Rights challenges. In 2006, the Law Lords issued a declaration that Section 3 of the Terrorism Act 2005 was incompatible with the right to a fair trial under Article 6 of the European Convention on Human Rights. In 1989, the European Court of Human Rights had extended the scope of the provision in the European Convention on Human Rights that prohibits torture and degrading treatment. For Western countries attempting to deport illegal immigrants, including suspected terrorists, they were now prohibited from doing so if the judge thought that abuses might be practiced in the country to which the suspect was being deported. The very liberal interpretation by British judges has made removal from Britain an onerous prospect and ultimately playing into the hands of the terrorists wishing to seek out a safe haven.

The government believes it is under attack from Islamic extremists and has gone to extraordinary lengths to inform the public that it is not a case of *if* an attack will happen, but *when*. The government's resilience has relied on draconian measures to hold at bay those it feels have been or may likely be involved or connected to terrorism. To get a greater understanding of how widespread the threat of radical Islam is to the social fabric of Britain, one needs to also appreciate that immigration has played a major part in all this. Travel the streets of London and you will witness a melting pot of languages and people from around the world that have made not only London but also provincial towns and cities their home. But immigration does not always translate into integration. Britain has long been referred to as a multicultural society, but the official view on that is changing in the most part due to radical Islamic extremism in Britain. For years, proponents of multiculturalism have branded their critics as racists, but radical Islam has managed to shock to consciousness

TERRORIST ATTACK BRIEF

Terrorist Group: Syrian Intelligence Operation

Case Facts: An Irish woman Anne-Marie Murphy was befriended by a Jordanian Nazer Hindawi. She subsequently became pregnant, and Hindawi proposed and suggested they marry in Israel. He would travel separately and meet her in Tel Aviv. He placed an explosive device in her hand luggage set to detonate several hours into the flight from London to Tel Aviv. When Murphy arrived at Heathrow, she answered all security questions and showed no signs of emotion or distress. On further examination of her hand luggage, it was found to contain a Semtex bomb (see drawing below).

Investigation: Hindawi had been in the pay of the Syrian intelligence service and had agreed for a sum of money to place a bomb on an El Al flight. He was provided with a safe house in London and also with a Syrian passport. After the bomb was discovered, Hindawi panicked and was concerned that he may be killed by his Syrian minders. He contacted his brother, who called the police. At his subsequent trial in 1986, he was sentenced to forty-five years in prison.

Blue "Trolley Bag"

FIGURE 5-9 Attempted bombing El Flight—London Heathrow Airport—April 17, 1986.

Europe's brain-dead politicians, and now the insidious multicultural model is open to public scrutiny. During a February 2011 security conference in Munich, Germany, Prime Minister David Cameron declared Britain's long-standing state-sponsored policy of multiculturalism an abysmal failure. The British government is responsible for creating a generation of global citizens who thoroughly despise their nation's heritage and have no loyalty to their country whatsoever. Even if the government would abandon its multicultural policy tomorrow, it would take at least a decade to negate multiculturalism's deadly, divisive effects. David Cameron stated, "[W]e've allowed the weakening of our collective identity. Under the doctrine of state multiculturalism, we have encouraged different cultures to live separate lives, apart from each other and the mainstream. We have failed to provide a vision of society to which they feel they want to belong."[36]

To many observers, Britain became a target for Islamic extremists only after its support for the U.S. campaign in Iraq. In reality, Muslims from around the globe have relocated to the United Kingdom and have been doing so for more than forty years. In Britain, hundreds of thousands of Muslims lead law-abiding lives and live and work in peace and harmony. Nevertheless, moderation among the majority appears to be a highly relative concept considering their widespread hostility toward Israel and the Jews, for example, or the way the very concept of Islamic terrorism or other wrongdoing is automatically denied.[37] Long before the events of 9-11 unfolded, and the coalition invasion of Taliban-controlled Afghanistan, and then Iraq, the United Kingdom was home to radical Muslims. One example is the case of Dhiren Barot, who, as far back as 1999, was plotting an attack on London's Heathrow airport. Barot was an airline ticket agent, and his plans included detonating a bomb on a bus in the tunnel connecting the arterial roads to the center of the airport, and exploding a bomb in a tube train under the River Thames with the intent to flood the underground chamber and cause an untold number of deaths as a result. Barot was grammar school educated, and had converted from Hinduism to Islam, and in 1995, long before George Bush became president he attended a training camp in Kashmir. He is a staunch believer that terror works, and that it is a religious duty of all Muslims. So, if we believe that foreign policy can dictate a sea change in Muslim terrorist actions, we need to think again. It is purely a convenient excuse for the Muslim extremists to use and cite both Iraq and Afghanistan. Change can only come from within the Muslim community itself, and removing troops from Iraq or Afghanistan will only convince the impressionable young extremists that terror does work.

SPECIAL IMMIGRATION APPEALS COMMISSION (SIAC)

Non-U.K. nationals detained under the draconian measures of the Antiterrorism Crime and Security Act had only one avenue for appeal open to them. Set up by the British Government Home Office Department, the SIAC was a legal in-camera forum presided over by three High Court Judges. Under international human rights law, the presumption of innocence applies to all persons charged with a criminal offense, even during times of emergency, and requires the state to prove such charge "beyond a reasonable doubt." In these cases, there is no charge being laid; however, the detainee has no rights under this legislation to know firsthand why he or she is being detained. The requirement for the Crown in these cases—to prove beyond a reasonable doubt the probable guilt of any detainee—is not required. Groups such as Amnesty International claim that this legislation is a perversion of justice.

The SIAC has ruled that under the Antiterrorism, Crime and Security Act 2001 (United Kingdom), ATCSA, the burden of proof that the Home Secretary has to meet in order that the SIAC may confirm the certification of individuals as "suspected international terrorists" falls well short of "beyond reasonable doubt." According to the SIAC, under the ATCSA, the onus upon the home secretary is lower than that needed in a civil case, such as cases involving contractual disputes. The SIAC stated: "The standard of proof is below a balance of probabilities (i.e., the standard in civil cases) because of the nature of the risk facing the United Kingdom, and the nature of the evidence which inevitably would be used to detain these appellants."[38]

Like the U.S. detention in Guantanamo Bay, British suspects are held indefinitely at London's Belmarsh Prison, a top-security facility. Fighting terrorism in a democracy is no easy task, and the application of the rule of law makes the problems dangerous and far reaching. The effects that this type of legislation may be having on migrants from the Middle East and North Africa, and their attitude to their host countries are easy to imagine. If these minorities felt any sense of marginalization prior to the events of 9-11, is it any wonder that some would find sympathy with extreme Islamic ideals? The Antiterrorism Act gives the home secretary powers to detain foreign nationals who are thought to be a potential danger to the United Kingdom; however, the challenges for the government here is that they cannot be deported to their country of origin because they face persecution there and no other country will accept them. Under normal circumstances, detainees would be charged with a criminal offense and brought to court. Since 9-11, Britain has detained suspects based on intelligence provided by MI5 and MI6, giving rise to the suspicion that they are linked to international terrorism. It would therefore seem that British authorities do not have any hard evidence with which to lay criminal charge against its detainees, and that the government is unwilling to divulge such information and the sources of such information.

The targeting by police of young male Muslims was inevitable. This has had the effect of pushing some young Muslims, who are resentful of the treatment, toward such figures as Abu Hamza. Are the draconian measures creating wider alienation and actually nourishing hatred? An example of this is Omar Bakri, the head of Al-Muhajiroun, an Islamic extremist group, and the self-proclaimed representative of Osama bin Laden in the United Kingdom. In May 2004, Bakri was linked with suicide attacks in Israel. The psychology of suicide and bombings is one of his more extreme teachings. Young Muslims are also taking their extreme views and actions to other locations—Richard Reid (the "shoe bomber") currently resides in a U.S. jail after his attempt to destroy an aircraft in flight in December 2001. Omar Sharif and Asif Hanif, two young British Muslims, ended up on a suicide mission for Hamas. They detonated a bomb in an Israeli restaurant in April 2003, killing three and injuring fifty-five. Hamas subsequently issued a video of the two young men in which they are seen urging others to follow their example. Omar Sharif's bomb failed to detonate and he was discovered dead a week later off the coast of Israel. Many young radicals were mobilized by the invasion of Afghanistan and the ousting of the Taliban. Hassan Butt, a spokesman for AM, had traveled to Pakistan and established himself there as a facilitator for those Westerners traveling to Pakistan wanting to fight with the Taliban. Butt told the British Broadcasting Corporation (BBC) in a 2002 interview that he had recruited 200 Britons for combat with the Taliban and went on to warn that "if they do return, I do believe they will take military action within Britain."

LONDON—JULY 7, 2005

As previously noted, London has become home to a network of extreme Islamist groups that have consistently used the liberal society in Britain to preach hatred abroad. The mass immigration of Muslims to Europe was an unintended consequence of the post-World War II guest worker programs. Backed by friendly politicians and sympathetic judges, foreign workers, who were supposed to stay temporarily, benefited from family reunification and became permanent residents. Muslims now constitute the majority of immigrants in most Western European countries. Jihadist networks span Europe, thanks to the spread of radical Islam among the descendants of guest workers. The threat of an attack on the British capital has been an increasing security concern since the invasions of Afghanistan and Iraq. Britain is one of the core groups of countries that bin Laden and his fanatics listed for an attack, so it was no surprise to authorities when it eventually came. However, the method of delivery in the London subway attacks was what most disturbed the authorities.

July 7, 2005, heralded the start of the G8 Economic Summit in Edinburgh, Scotland, which was attended by world leaders and the world's press. Thursday, July 7, was the day after London had been awarded the 2012 Summer Olympic Games, and most Londoners were in a celebratory mood. That would all change at 8:50 A.M. at the height of "rush hour."

Terror Attack Timeline—July 7, 2005

08:50—A bomb with approximately 10 pounds of high explosives is detonated by a suicide bomber aboard a westbound Circle Line Underground train about 100 yards into a tunnel after departing Edgware Road station.

08:50—A second explosive device detonates on a Piccadilly Line Underground train just after it left Kings Cross Station. This bomb also was estimated to contain approximately 10 pounds of high explosives.

08:50—A third explosion occurs on a Circle Line Underground train as it approaches Liverpool Street Station. This device is also believed to have contained about 10 pounds of high explosive.

09:47—A fourth explosion takes place on the upper deck of a Number 30 London Transport bus traveling from Hackney Wick to Marble Arch. The bus had been diverted from its normal route, and the explosion occurred outside the offices of the General Medical Council in Russell Square. The blast destroyed most of the upper deck, killing thirteen people.

The bombings from all four attacks left fifty-seven dead and more than 700 injured. The timing of the attacks shows that this was well planned and scripted and intended to cause maximum casualties and make the statement that Islamist extremists have the capability to strike at the heart of the British capital. This may have been a symbolic gesture on the part of the bombers, as it has become clear that all four attacks were the acts of suicide bombers. The motivations for the attacks will be the subject of months of analysis and investigation; however, it is clear that the bombers were all male, and three of the four were born in the United Kingdom and were of Pakistani descent. The fourth, who came to Britain from Jamaica with his parents when he was a baby, had been a recent convert to Islam. All four fit into the age and education level characteristic of Hamas bombers in Israel. In London, unlike the United States and Canada, the motorway system, the streets of most major cities, and the transportation systems are lined with closed-circuit television (CCTV) cameras. Shortly after these attacks, CCTV footage showed the bombers gathering as a group at a regional train station before embarking on their journey to London. The vehicle they traveled in was recovered and valuable evidence gathered. It now seems that the intelligence community had identified at least one of the bombers as a potential Islamic extremist; however, a risk assessment did not determine that this target was a sufficient risk to warrant in-depth surveillance. This might seem strange, but we believe this is all part of connecting the dots. Does this possible miss indicate a tactical error on the part of Britain's security services? The sheer numbers of British-born Muslims now make the task of identifying those who may pose a risk far more complex than simply keeping close tabs on foreign nationals visiting the country. As we mentioned in Chapter 3, the fairly lax U.S. Visa Waiver program allows virtual unrestricted access by British and other European nationals to the United States. This attack would likely have been organized by external forces that supported the cell by providing the ingredients for the bomb, timing devices and detonators, as well as the expertise to construct such a device. Tracking down the support network will be the main role for the police investigators. The British police have a wealth of experience in dealing with terrorism through their activities with Irish terror groups, but this is the first instance of a terror attack carried out by suicide bombers and marks a dramatic turn in events. If suicide missions have the aim of disrupting transportation and sending fear through the traveling public, then the events that took place exactly two weeks after these attacks are worthy of discussion. On July 21, 2005, reports came in around 12:30 in the afternoon of more bomb attacks on the London Underground system and bus transportation. In similar circumstances, three backpack bombs were left on trains at the Oval Kennington, Shepherd's Bush, and Warren Street Underground stations. A small detonation appeared to have taken place in each case, but no injuries were reported. The fourth bomb went off on the top deck of a Number 26 bus in Hackney, again without causing injury. This second round of attacks is likely to have been the work of al Qaeda-inspired Islamist sympathizers willing to make the statement that the threat remains and that the security and police service are powerless to prevent future attacks.

The July 21 Failed Bomb Attack Timeline

- **12.25 P.M.**—Mukhtar Said Ibrahim, Yassin Hassan Omar, and Ramzi Mohammed are believed to have entered Stockwell tube station.
- Yassin Hassan Omar traveled north on the Victoria Line.
- Mukhtar Said Ibrahim traveled to Bank station on the Northern Line.
- **12.34 P.M.**—Ramzi Mohammed went north on the Northern Line attempting to detonate his improvised explosive device before reaching the Oval Kennington station; he ran out of the station.
- Yassin Hassan Omar attempted to detonate his improvised explosive device (IED) on the Victoria Line train as it approached Warren Street Station; he too ran out of the station.
- **1.06 P.M.**—Mukhtar Said Ibrahim left Bank Station and boarded Number 26 bus to Hackney Wick and attempted to detonate his device as he disembarked at Harrow Road.
- Hussein Osman is believed to have embarked at Westbourne Park onto a Hammersmith and City Line train heading west. He attempted to detonate his device near Sheppards Bush Station; he ran from the station.
- July 23—Unexploded device is found in Little Wormwood Scrubs Park.
- July 25—Yassin Hassan Omar is arrested in Birmingham.
- July 29—Said Ibrahim and Ramzi Mohammed are arrested in West London.
- Hussein Osman is arrested in Rome by Italian police.

The bombs all failed to detonate and, this, as it turned out, was more owing to luck than ineptitude on the part of the terrorists. The bombs consisted of hydrogen peroxide mixed with chapatti flour, and detonators created out of high-strength hydrogen peroxide, acid, and acetone, which were placed in tubes of cardboard with light bulbs wired to batteries. U.K. forensic experts believe that they failed to detonate because the initiator was not sufficiently powerful to set off the main charge.

In July 2007, four men were jailed for forty years each for attempting to carry out suicide bomb attacks on London's transport system. Muktah Said Ibrahim, the group's leader, had traveled to Pakistan in December 2004 to hone and learn his bomb-making skills at the same time as two of the July 7 bombers, Mohammed Sidique Khan and Shehzad Tanweer, were there. There was no evidence that the two attacks in London were linked, but the judge believed that both attacks were masterminded in Pakistan.

OPERATION CREVICE

In April 2007, five men were convicted of conspiracy to cause explosions using homemade devices, and although the group had discussed many targets and had acquired the fertilizer base for their bomb, they appeared not to have formulated a target or a defined target plan for their operation. **Operation Crevice** was a combined operation between the British, U.S., Canadian, and Pakistani security services, which ultimately led to the arrest of the five men. All were born and raised in Britain and had become radicalized in local mosques and had then traveled to Pakistan for training. The convicted men, Salahuddin Amin, 32; Omar Khyam, 25; Anthony Garcia, 25; Jawad Akbar, 23; and Waheed Mahmood, all received life sentences. The group came together in 2002, and several of them traveled back and forth between the United Kingdom and Pakistan to facilitate training. Following training, they began to focus on assembling an explosive device, but appear to have abandoned the idea of smuggling components for their bomb in favor of a homemade version. In September 2003, Anthony Garcia purchased 600 kilograms of ammonium nitrate, which they kept in a self-storage lockup in West London. In February 2004, staff at the depot notified police of the suspicious amount of fertilizer being stored. It appears that at this time several of the conspirators were already under surveillance. Members of the group were bugged, and conversations about target selection were recorded. Waheed Mahmood had previously worked for the National Grid and had stolen discs detailing the location of high-pressure gas pipelines. Having decided to use fertilizer, the group was having difficulty acquiring detonators, and it is alleged that they contacted a Canadian citizen, Mohammad Momin Khawaja, to supply them. Khawaja flew to the United Kingdom and met with Khyam; he did not bring detonators with him, but they discussed using remote long-range detonators for their attack. The group then bought airline tickets to Pakistan, and it was at that juncture that the group was arrested as the police and security services feared that the plot to detonate a bomb was now at an advanced stage. The authorities had in fact exchanged the fertilizer for another inert substance. This conspiracy was being hatched at the same time as the July 7, 2005, attack on the London Underground system was taking place. It seems quite remarkable that this group that had traveled to Pakistan, and had actively trained and were highly motivated to carry out a mission, had only received rudimentary training and little or no direction from al Qaeda about how and where to target their attack. It became clear at their trial that Omar Khyam was training in Pakistan at the same time as the July 7 bomber, Mohammed Siddique Khan who, together with Shaheed Tanweer (July 7), were picked up on surveillance in the U.K. meeting with Khyam and Garcia.[39]

Shoot to Kill Policy

This was mentioned earlier in relation to an SAS assault on a PIRA active service unit in Gibraltar in the 1980s. Now, some two decades later, we are witnessing police on the streets of London carrying automatic weapons. They have the authority to shoot first if a suspect fits a profile of a suicide bomber and to ask questions afterward. The danger in this is that innocents can and do get killed—in the SAS case, the ASU in question was known to the security services; however, they were not armed. In London, on Friday, July 22, 2005 (as Scotland Yard detectives were still investigating the failed suicide bombs of July 21 in London), a young, olive-skinned man ran from police in Stockwell after being repeatedly ordered to stop. He was wearing a heavy overcoat in 70-degree temperatures and ran down into the Underground station and onto a waiting train. Police officers shot him in the head a total of seven times and once in the shoulder (according to autopsy reports). Later, it was determined that the man was not a suicide bomber, but a Brazilian electrician Jean Charles de Menezes, who had no connection to any ongoing terrorist investigation or activity. Life on the streets of London has changed. Our archetypical view of the friendly British Bobby is now gone. In November 2007, the London Metropolitan Police were found guilty of endangering the public over the shooting death of Menezes and fined £175,000 with £385,000 in costs. The London Metropolitan Police Commissioner, Sir Ian Blair, was forced to resign in September 2008 by the Lord Mayor of London, who informed Sir Ian that he had lost confidence in him to continue in his position as Commissioner.

Points for Consideration

While the scheduling of the G8 Summit, with world media attention, may be significant in the timing of the London attacks, the announcement of London's selection to host the Olympics would be far too recent an event for the terrorists to have planned for. It did, however, give added opportunity to the attackers. The complete lack of a specific, credible threat for another attack, either in the United Kingdom or Europe, does little to alleviate the threat. The London Underground and bus attacks are shown to be consistent with al Qaeda's approach to taking traditional terror tactics and using them on a scale not seen before. Consistent with current insurgent attacks in Iraq, the bus bombing may have been a required element in order to video the actual attack sequence. This attack has the hallmarks of an al Qaeda or al Qaeda-inspired attack, as it is the only group currently executing this type of atrocity on a global scale.

Although prior attacks have not taken place in London, al Qaeda-affiliated groups have targeted British interests in both Europe and the Middle East:

November 20, 2003—Simultaneous car/truck bomb attacks occur on Hong Kong Shanghai Bank Corporation (HSBC) Headquarters and the British Consulate in Istanbul, Turkey.

June 6, 2004—A British Broadcasting Corporation (BBC) film crew is attacked in Riyadh, Saudi Arabia.

September 15, 2004—A British national is gunned down in Riyadh, Saudi Arabia.

March 19, 2005—A car bomb is detonated outside a British-operated cinema in Doha, Qatar.

An Ongoing Threat

We have detailed some of the major events that have involved radical homegrown Islamists; however, the threat has not diminished. At the end of June 2007, a car bomb was detected by authorities in the heart of London; before it could explode, a second vehicle was found a few hours later—the treasure trove of evidence that these unexploded vehicle bombs were able to provide put the police hot on the trail of resident Islamists. Within twenty-four hours, another attack took place at the International Airport in Glasgow, Scotland. At around 3.00 P.M., two men in a Jeep SUV rammed the entrance doors to the terminal; they had soaked themselves in gasoline, and the rear of the Jeep contained propane tanks. The driver and passenger were Bilal Abdullah and Kafeel Ahmed, respectively, both twenty-seven-year-old doctors. Kafeel Ahmed died from 90 percent burns to his body in August 2007. The terrorists were highly qualified and respectable doctors; a third doctor was arrested the following day. Although the attack and the improvised bombs were crudely made, there was the possibility that had all three vehicles detonated as planned, there would have been a significant injury count. There is speculation that due to the failure of the two bomb-laden vehicles in London, the Jeep (used in the Glasgow attack) may have been at a third unknown location, somewhere in London. When the two primary vehicles failed to detonate, it's probable that the cell decided to relocate away from London and aim at a softer but nonetheless spectacular target. At the time, the Labor Party had a new prime minister in Gordon Brown, a Scotsman; so this may have been an attempt to send the new prime minister a harsh message. As for the perpetrators, it seems that the reach of extreme Islam knows no bounds in its ability to radicalize even these professional young men. It could also be that they were inspired and not directed by al Qaeda and had no organizational links to transnational jihadist networks. If it is determined that they did have jihadist links, it seems clear that the organization is incapable of supplying skilled terrorists, which in part will likely be because of counterterror activities of the security services. The threat to the United Kingdom is definitely not from external forces but from internal, and the comment by Prime Minister Gordon Brown that Britons face a threat that is "long-term and sustained" in nature would seem appropriate.

Cold War Returns to Britain—Death of Alexander Litvinenko

In November 2006, a former Russian spy, Alexander Litvinenko, died an agonizing death in a central London hospital from radiation poisoning. It was determined that Litvinenko had been exposed in some manner to Polonium-210. The dose he was administered could only have been prepared or manufactured in a nuclear facility and given to him through his food in a lethal dose. The radiation killed his cells causing his organs to shut down. According to a 2000 database produced by Stanford University's Institute for International Studies, approximately 88 pounds of radioactive material including weapon-usable uranium and plutonium were removed without authorization from nuclear facilities in the former Soviet Union. While on his deathbed, Litvinenko, an outspoken critic of Russian leader Vladimir Putin, accused Putin of being complicit in his poisoning. Polonium poisoning is a very unusual method of assassination unless it was intended to send a message to the wider expatriot Russian community in London. While the Russian leader and his government have strongly rebuffed any suggestion of government involvement, the British authorities believe Litvinenko was killed by a former KGB agent, Andrei Lugovoi, and have unsuccessfully sought his extradition from Russia to stand trial in the United Kingdom—a request that has been denied by Russia.

EXTREME RIGHT-WING GROUPS

The issues of immigration and violence by right-wing groups against immigrants are not new phenomena for Britain. Hate crimes have been prevalent throughout the twentieth century. The British National Party has a political agenda that demands Britain become independent from Europe and stop the influx of immigrants. The party also calls for the deportation of criminal and illegal immigrants. While this party maintains this stance, it has attracted a hooligan element that attacks indiscriminately persons of foreign origin. The loosely knit group at the center of these attacks—the Skinheads—is associated with football violence. Skinheads first appeared in Britain around the early 1970s and could be found in almost every city in the country. This group is definitely a cult rather than an organization with any political aspirations. Skinhead youths have changed little since those early days of the 1970s: shaved heads, Nazi insignias, tattoos, checked shirts, blue jeans, and steel-toed "bovver" boots in the Doc Martens style. They were easily spotted as angry young men who symbolized a tough, working-class background. The Skinheads were known for their violent rampages and became synonymous with extreme nationalism. Their favored targets for violent attacks were Jews, homosexuals, and Asians. Their style of dress soon went out of fashion; however, a small hard-core movement along the lines of neo-Nazi exists today. Their hate attacks target Jewish cemeteries and Asian shopping areas. Many of the attacks appear random in nature, but there is a belief that some attacks involving English soccer clubs are planned in advance. They are often seen at marches and parades with the British National Party, although there is no evidence to suggest that any Skinheads are members. The ebb and flow of this cultlike movement has endured for almost thirty years and has spread its aggressive attitudes toward Jews and immigrants across Europe and North America.[40]

Summary

The nature of the terrorist threat in Northern Ireland has changed significantly in recent years, with the Provisional IRA (PIRA) and the main Loyalist groups ceasing their terrorist campaigns and engaging with the political process. On May 8, 2007, the devolved Northern Ireland Executive was successfully restored with the creation of a new government under a power-sharing agreement between Nationalist and Unionist political parties. Devolution was completed on April 12, 2010, when policing and justice powers were transferred to the Northern Ireland Assembly from Westminster. The ongoing threats from Islamic extremists has pushed Irish domestic terrorism threats out of our focus, but the threat to security both in Northern Ireland and the British mainland from Irish terrorists has not gone away, it still exists.

The suicide attacks by Islamic extremists in 2005 on the London Underground and subsequent attempts in 2007 to suicide bomb Glasgow airport are an indication of the lengths to which these committed individuals will go to prosecute their cause. While the attack in Glasgow was far less sophisticated and well planned out, it leads observers to the belief that good intelligence is disruptive to their cause. The threat remains, and further attacks cannot be discounted. Britain views itself in the forefront of threats from al Qaeda and jihadist groups, whether from Islamist groups for its Afghanistan involvement or from resident Islamists with aims to turn the country into an Islamic Caliphate.

Review Questions

1. Discuss the factors surrounding the Irish problems of the early twentieth century and why it took nearly a century to redress the issues.
2. Discuss the varying measures used by the British to combat Irish terrorism.
3. What is the importance of marching season in Northern Ireland and why does it provoke such hostility?
4. Discuss how Britain's vision for a multicultural society may be failing and what could be done to help inculcate foreign and in particular Muslims into British society.
5. Why have Islamist movements been so successful in setting up in the United Kingdom when many of them are banned overseas?
6. Discuss the possible effects the Terrorism Acts are having on Muslim groups.

Websites

1. **Sinn Fein**—*http://www.sinnfein.ie/*
2. **Global Security**—*http://www.globalsecurity.org/military/world/para/ira.htm—http://cain.ulst.ac.uk*
3. **Jane's Information Group**—*www.janes.com*
4. **The Bloody Sunday Inquiry**—*http://report.bloody-sunday-inquiry.org/volume08/chapter147/*
5. **Muslim Public Affairs Committee**—*http://mpacuk.org/*
6. **The Jamestown Foundation**—*http://www.jamestown.org*

End Notes

1. *The World Book Encyclopaedia*, vol. 11, S.V. "James II."
2. *The World Book Encyclopaedia*, vol. 10 S.V. "Home Rule."
3. Desmond's Concise History of Ireland, 2000 http://jerrydesmond.tripod.com/index-2.html
4. Ibid.
5. Quote taken from *The Troubles—The Background to the Violence in Northern Ireland*, Edited by Taylor Downing, a Channel Four Book.
6. Strategic Forecasting. http://www.stratfor.com/standard/analysis_view.php.

7. Paul Medhurst. *Global Terrorism* (New York: United Nations Institute for Training & Research Program of Correspondence and Instruction, 2002, p. 70).

8. John Horgan and Max Taylor. "Playing the Green Card—Financing the IRA." *Terrorism and Political Violence*, vol. 11, no. 2 (Summer 1999, pp. 1–38).

9. *Press Association News*. "New hope of Solving Shergar Mystery." (April 4, 1996).

10. U.S. Department of State. Libya/PIRA background paper (July 1998).

11. Brendan O'Brien. *A Pocket History of the IRA* (Dublin: O'Brien Press, 2000, p. 108).

12. Strategic Forecasting. http://www.stratfor.com/standard/analysis_view.php.

13. *BBC News Service* (October 4, 2001, 13.09 GMT).

14. Ed Moloney. *A Secret History of the IRA* (Toronto Canada: Penguin Books, 2002, , p. 289).

15. Gayle Olsen-Raymer. *Terrorism: A Historical and Contemporary Perspective* (New York: American Heritage Custom Publishing, 1986, p. 197).

16. *MIPT Terrorism Knowledge Base*. http://www.mipt.org/

17. *The Diplock Report: Report of the Commission to Consider the Legal Procedure to Deal with Terrorist Attacks in Northern Ireland*. Cmnd.5185 (London: HMSO, 1972, p. 13).

18. Jim Smyth. "Stretching the Boundaries: The Control of Dissent in Northern Ireland." *Terrorism: An International Journal*, vol. 11 no. 4 (Queens University, Belfast; Taylor and Francis, 1988, pp. 289–295).

19. *Report on the Operation in 2003 of Part VII of the Terrorism Act 2000*, sec. 5, Nonjury Trial Section, 74, 75.

20. Andrew Boyd. *The Orange Order, 1795–1995* (1995), www.history.com.

21. Ibid.

22. *The Weekly Telegraph*, London (May 7, 2002, p. 13).

23. CAIN: http://cain.ulst.ac.uk.

24. IRA Statement on Decommissioning: www.cnn.com/world.

25. Force Estimates—Janes Intelligence Review.

26. Extract Northern Ireland Peace Agreement: http://www.nio.gov.uk/agreement.htm.

27. *A New Beginning in Northern Ireland*, Extract 1.3 and 1.4 London: 2, 3.

28. John W. Soule. "Problems in Applying Counterterrorism to Prevent Terrorism: Two Decades of Violence in Northern Ireland Considered." *Terrorism: An International Journal*, vol. 12, no. 1 (1989).

29. Jonathan R. White. *Terrorism: An Introduction* (Pacific Grove, CA: Brooks/Cole Publishing, 1991, pp. 220–221).

30. Melanie Phillips. *Londonistan* (London: Encounter Books, 2007, p. xi).

31. *Draft Report on Young Muslims and Extremism*, UK Foreign and Commonwealth Office, 2004; Robert Winnett and David Leppard. *Sunday Times* (July 10, 2005).

32. Mathew Mcallester. "Islamic radicals draw attention in Great Britain." (May 23, 2004), www.startribune.com.

33. http://www.hizb.org.uk/press-releases/it-is-the-westminster-political-system-that-sayeeda-warsi-is-part-of-that-has-fuelled-islamophobia-in-britain, (January 2011) retrieved April 3, 2011.

34. Andrew Gilligan. "Hizb ut Tahrir is not a gateway to terrorism." *Claims Whitehall Report—Telegraph* online http://www.telegraph.co.uk/journalists/andrew-gilligan/7908262/Hizb-ut-Tahrir-is-not-a-gateway-to-terrorism-claims-Whitehall-report.html.

35. Ibid, p. 9.

36. Jerry Kane. "The Milestone Dairies," *Britain's Prime Minister calls for an end to Multiculturalism* (February 10, 2011). *http://imkane.wordpress.com/2011/02/10/britains-prime-minister-calls-for-an-end-to-multiculturalism/*

37. Melanie Phillips. *Londonistan* (London: Encounter Books, 2007, p. 6).

38. *The SIAC judgment*. 29 October 2003, p. 14, para. 48. In making this ruling, the SIAC relied on the precedent set in the case of *Secretary of State for the Home Department v Rehman* (2001) UKHL 47, in which the House of Lords concluded that no particular standard of proof was required of the secretary of state in reaching his judgment or assessment that an individual's deportation was conducive to the public good.

39. Janes. "Terrorism and Security Monitor." (June 2007).

40. Anti-Defamation League. *The Skinhead International, A Worldwide Survey of Neo-Nazi Skinheads* (New York: Anti-Defamation League, 1995). ADL, 823 UN Plaza New York. http://www.nizkor. org/hweb/orgs/american/adl/skinhead-international.

6

Western Europe

Fighting terrorism is like being a goalkeeper. You can make a hundred brilliant saves but the only shot that people remember is the one that gets past you.

—Paul Wilkinson—Author

LEARNING OBJECTIVES

After studying this chapter, the student should be able to:

1. Discuss the challenges facing freedom of speech and freedom of the press as they relate to religious depictions.

2. Understand how international terrorist groups and cells can operate in Europe.

3. Describe how state terrorism was practiced by nations during the mid-twentieth century.

4. Discuss how right-wing and Islamist extremist terror groups or individuals might use current attack methods as operational lessons for the future.

5. Compare the failure of the ETA campaign in Spain with the success of its Republican cousins in Northern Ireland.

KEY WORDS TO NOTE

Army for the Liberation of Armenia (ASALA)—The Armenian Secret Army for the Liberation of Armenia (ASALA) was a Marxist-Leninist extremist organization that operated from 1975 to 1986

Armata Corsa—An underground separatist movement established in 1999 opposing the links between nationalists and the Corsican Mafia

Dev Sol—Revolutionary People's Liberation Front, formed in 1978 following a split with the Turkish People's Liberation Front, is a Marxist organization that is violently anti-NATO and anti-USA

Euzkadi Ta Azkatasuna (ETA)—Founded by young nationalists in 1952, it is a Basque separatist group fighting for independence from Spain

EOKA—National Organization of Cypriot Fighters—dedicated to the ending of British colonial rule in Cyprus

Executive Order 13224—An executive order signed into law by former U.S. president George W. Bush on September 23, 2001, in response to the September 11, 2001, attacks

Holocaust—Mass extermination of mainly European Jews during World War II by Nazi Germany

Jyllands-Posten—Danish morning newspaper that published cartoons of the Prophet Mohammed

November 17—Revolutionary organization November 17, a Greek Marxist terror group—its operations were ceased around 2002

RAF—Red Army Faction—left-wing German militant group that morphed from the Baader-Meinhof gang in the 1960s.

Shumukh al-Islam—A jihadist forum that posts information related to jihadist ideology

Theo Van Gough—Dutch filmmaker murdered on the street in Amsterdam

Union of Islamic Communities and Organizations in Italy (UCOII)—Islamic revivalist organization

OVERVIEW

Domestic terrorism in Spain had been the exclusive domain of the **Euzkadi Ta Azkatasuna (ETA)** terror organization in the Basque region until May 2004. ETA has continued its bombing campaigns, in spite of an earlier ceasefire agreement and concessions in areas of local government and education. This chapter examines the effects of Islamic extremism: the attacks of March 2004 in Madrid and the broad implications for Europe. Over the past three decades France has contended with sporadic attacks from dissident Algerian factions, Islamic militants trained in the tribal regions of Waziristan as well as homegrown Corsican terrorists and immigrant jihadists joining the war in Iraq and fighting against the United States. Germany, unused to being viewed as a terror haven, was the launching pad for the planning of some of the suicide hijackers of 9-11. Germany also contends with terror of a subtly different kind—from that of secretive al Qaeda cells, some with plans to attack U.S. interests in Germany. This chapter also discusses terror by hate groups that target ethnic minorities such as the neo-Nazi Skinhead factions. In the broad battle for the suppression of terrorist acts, we examine the role played by the European countries in freezing monetary assets of terrorist support networks. Italy has also seen the effects a free society has on the abilities of terror cells to propagate and pursue their mission of terror. Greek terrorism has been the exclusive province of the shadowy **November 17** group. Until the spring of 2002, authorities had made no headway in managing, or even attempting, to arrest any of its members.

SPAIN

Spanish Nationalism and the Basques

The Basque region spills north across the Pyrenees and into southern France, with an estimated half a million Basques living on French soil, and approximately 2.5 million living within the borders of Spain. The origins of the Basque people are uncertain; however, they have been living in this region since long before the Gauls and Iberians settled in Spain and France. They have their own language called Euskera that is not derived from any other European language or dialect. With the size of the region's population, it would be logical to expect that Basque territory

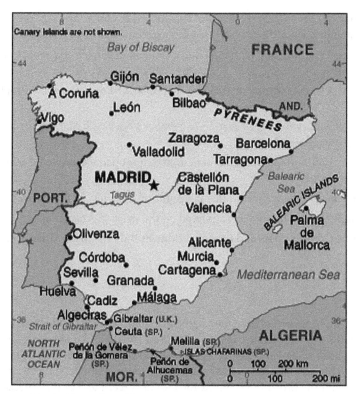

FIGURE 6-1 Map of Spain (Central Intelligence Agency, *The World Factbook, 2008*).

might be a self-governing principality, similar to Monaco. The Basque people do not have their own homeland and, in similar fashion to the Irish Republican movement, have been fighting for self-government and their own homeland since the first quarter of the twentieth century. General Francisco Franco came to power during the Spanish Civil War of 1936–1939 and ruled Spain as an iron-fisted dictator until his death in 1975. In the intervening years, Spain achieved rapid economic growth and prosperity.

Basque Separatism

As the twentieth century drew to a close, there were only two European regions of nationalist conflict. The most notable nationalist conflict and the most documented has been the terrorist campaign waged in Northern Ireland. The Basques of the Pyrenean region of Spain have waged their own internal struggle for a national identity and have not enjoyed a separate homeland or autonomy since the twelfth century. They have indeed managed to maintain and protect their own language and culture over the centuries. General Franco's approach to dealing with the Basque Nationals was to suppress them at all costs by incorporating the Basque region into Spain at the end of the Spanish Civil War and outlawing both their culture and their unique language. Franco's actions led to a rebirth of Basque Nationalistic fervor in the late 1950s. Spain continued to suffer from the scourge of terror attacks perpetrated by ETA into the twenty-first century. In 1999, ETA broke its "unilateral and indefinite" cease-fire and recommenced a bombing and assassination campaign. Since the turn of the century, attacks have increased and, like the attacks by Irish Republicans, the Basque separatists favor the indiscriminate use of remotely detonated bombs in public places, as well as assassination of local and state officials. Following the 9-11 attacks in the United States, the U.S. government, which re-designated ETA every two years as a Foreign Terrorist Organization, went one step further in October 2001 and designated ETA under former President Bush's September 23, 2001, **Executive Order 13224**, as a "Specially Designated Global Terrorist Organization." Executive Order 13224 was specifically aimed at those persons and groups that provide financial support and assistance to terrorist organizations. More specifically, the order further blocked property and prohibited transactions with persons who commit, threaten to commit, or support terrorism. In February 2002, under Executive Order 13224, the U.S. Department of the Treasury designated twenty-one Spanish nationals as members of, assisting in, sponsoring, or providing financial, material, or technological support for, or financial and other services to, or in support of ETA's acts of terrorism, and are otherwise believed to be acting for, or on behalf of them. These twenty-one individuals were identified by the European Union on December 21, 2001, for their involvement in terrorist acts.[1]

Euzkadi Ta Azkatasuna

In 1959, the Basques formed the Euzkadi Ta Azkatasuna (Basque Fatherland and Freedom). It was dedicated to promoting Basque independence. ETA was not originally formed as a terrorist group…but, following General Franco's vicious oppression of the Basques, the group was left with no option but violent retaliation. ETA, much like the Republican IRA, gathered its support from the working classes. Their members come from regions that identify with the strong and unique ethnic identity of the Basque people. They are invariably young, frustrated nationalists with deep anger against their lack of autonomy. The majority of Basques favors nationalism, but do not support the terrorists' violent "any means to an end" approach to resolve a political goal of self-government and determination. ETA has, over the past twenty-five years or more, been a fragmented organization that has seen many offshoots of the original groups formed, disbanded, and re-formed again.

A political report, commissioned in 1986 by the Basque regional government, described the region as being amenable to political solutions. It also described ETA as "an unfortunate child of the Franco Dictatorship." Much of the report suggested political solutions such as how to accommodate Basque Nationalism within the framework of Spain and the European Economic Community (EEC). One of the recommendations was that Basque terrorists, who under Spanish law were tried in Madrid's "special courts," should instead be tried in their Basque courts. And further, they recommended that policing of terrorists should come under the control of Basque police and not Spain's National Police.[2]

Since the 1950s, ETA has been riddled with internal squabbling, bitter dissension, and discontent. The group split in 1966, into what was known as ETA-Zarra (or old ETA) and ETA-Berri (or young ETA). ETA-Zarra was further divided into two subgroups: ETA-5 and ETA-6. The subgroup ETA-5 was then divided further into ETA-Military and ETA-Politico Military, and the most hardened and seasoned campaigners for armed action come from the subgroup ETA-Military.[3] These splits have caused confusion and consternation among the Basque people as to which of these proliferating schisms…to support or oppose. "Actions Unite–Words Divide" is the slogan adopted by ETA-Military, and their terrorist members adopted the same cell-like structure as that used by the Provisional IRA. ETA-military commandos, or irurkos, were made up of three-man cells called "Sleeping Commandos" and were organized in the late 1970s by the ETA-Military commander, Miguel Apalategui.[4] The "sleepers" were to be called up from the Basque community to perform a single terrorist act and then return to their jobs under relative anonymity. To finance its campaign, ETA used robbery and extortion.

Development of the ETA Organization

ETA's growth, and its Youth Movement, is traced back to the Basque Nationalist Party (PNV). The party had been in exile since Franco's defeat of Spain's Republicans in the 1939 Civil War. The Basque Youth Movement was determined to ensure that the Basque's unique language and culture would not die. ETA's political position was purely democratic and in 1957, a group of young Basques traveled to France to convince the exiled PNV government to organize and lead an armed struggle against General Franco. PNV leader, Jose Maria Leizaola, and his government, flatly rejected the idea. ETA's First Assembly came about in May 1962 when a small group of university students and activists gathered to discuss how to go forward and gain support for their ideals. Much of what they discussed at that First Assembly was the example set by other groups struggling for a national identity against such regimes as Fidel Castro in Cuba and others struggling against colonial rule in Africa and the Middle East. These became the first few steps along ETA's path toward terrorism. Determined not to be captured by the police, they set up their own three-man cell structure and defined ETA as a "Revolutionary Movement for National Liberation."

The works and writings of Mao Tse-tung played a significant role in ETA's development. Impressed by Mao, a young Basque, Jose Ortiz, studying in Paris, attempted to rouse others in ETA to the same level of understanding that he had found in his readings of Mao. The Second ETA Assembly, in 1963, set about attempting to rid itself of Maoist influences. No split occurred after the Second Assembly, but shortly thereafter, the Maoist militants within produced their own mini-manual, *Insurrection in Euskadi.* The tract brought forth the Basque determination to embark on a war of revolution. A Third Assembly in 1964 broke away from the old, established Nationalist PNV and, influenced by the Maoists, redefined the group as being anti-capitalist and anti-imperialist. An ETA leader defined the new direction as follows: "The primacy of the human person and of his rights is the basis for any political action." As ETA ideology veered toward the left, the French government took action against ETA founder members on French territory and removed them from the frontier region with Spain.

Eustakio Mendizabel Benito headed up ETA at the start of 1970. Benito's group was known as the "Military Front of ETA." He believed passionately in securing a homeland for the Basque people and preserving their language and had a deep concern about the future. Benito financed his terrorist operations by resorting to criminal activities including armed robbery, extortion, and kidnappings. They had no training in the art of weaponry or the use of explosives while members actively purchased arms through the underground arms networks and bought, as their first consignment, 500 new, 9-mm Firebird Parabellum pistols. They also stole explosives from local factories and quarry operations.

ETA members are known to have received training from the Popular Front for the Liberation of Palestine (PFLP) at its base in South Yemen. One of ETA's most audacious acts was the assassination of Luis Carrero Blanco on December 20, 1973. From 1967 till his death, Carrero Blanco served as the vice president of Spain under General Franco. When General Franco stepped down from office in June 1973, Carrero Blanco succeeded him as Spain's prime minister. ETA has become more advanced and well equipped, and has formed alliances with the Revolutionary Armed Forces of Colombia (FARC) terrorists and members of the PIRA (Northern Ireland). With the peace process holding firm in Northern Ireland, ETA may be hard pressed for support from the Irish republican movement. In prior times, they would have traded explosives to the PIRA in exchange for training in bomb making.

New Century—New Campaign

The previously mentioned cease-fire, which ended in 1999, had probably been misread and likely misunderstood by both the Spanish government and the media. It was widely reported that ETA was severely weakened and ready to capitulate. At a secret meeting between ETA and the Spanish government in 1999, the government presumed that ETA was ready to deal. What actually took place at that meeting has never been revealed; in fact, ETA quickly resumed hostilities against the Spanish government. Similar cease-fires had taken place in Northern Ireland, and many observers have felt that these cease-fires, far from being the death knell for ETA, were a time for covert rebuilding and recruiting. The Basque Socialist Coalition, known as the Herri Batasuna (Peoples Unity) Party led by Arnoldo Ortiz, officially denies any links or involvement with ETA. Throughout the spring and early summer of 2002, ETA engaged in a prolonged campaign targeting Spain's lucrative tourist industry. The ebb and flow of terrorist success is most often measured by the organization's ability to remain at large and to function in a cohesive manner. Spanish authorities, in a cooperative effort with France, have had some spectacular successes in capturing ETA's leadership. In October 2004, French police arrested seventeen Basque separatists in the Pyrenees region of France. Not only were the arrests a blow to ETA, but at the same time, they uncovered caches of arms and more than 700 kilograms of explosives, including potassium chlorate, an ingredient used in the manufacture of bombs. Subsequently, the Spanish government passed legislation that made political parties that supported terrorism illegal. Following this through, the government officially declared the Herri Batasuna Party illegal in 2003. The law also ensured that there could be no resurgence under a new name, so that when former members of the banned group reappeared with the intention of running in local elections in 2003 under the name Autodeterminaziorako Bilgunea (AuB), these lists were determined to be nothing more than Batasuna in a new guise and were similarly banned by Spain's Constitutional Court. ETA continued to seek out new targets to attack and one such target was the lucrative Spanish holiday market, and in its effort to attack the tourists visiting Spain during summer months, it planned a bombing attack on a cross channel ferry; fortunately, the authorities disrupted these plans and no attack has taken place yet. The group also attacked Madrid airport over Christmas season in 2006.

On November 4, 2004, Ortiz attended a mass in San Sebastian and called for an end to the violence. The War on Terror had caught up with Batasuna, and by June 2003, the organization's name appeared on both the European and U.S. Department of State lists of terrorist organizations.[5] Although Batasuna does have considerable Basque support, the appearance of Islamic extremism in Europe no doubt had a significant effect on the Spanish population and particularly since the bombings of the Madrid train stations in March 2004. The president of the mainstream Nationalist Party and also one of the fathers of Basque Nationalism, Xavier Arzalluz, commented publicly, "The time has come to fight for the independence of the Basque region in the streets!" Ostensibly, the appeal that set the Herri Batasuna Party apart from others was that it conjured up memories of the repressive regime of General Franco. The legislation may have had the markings of a bygone era, but Herri Batasuna's political influence would continue to exist in some format and, along with it, some 200,000 voters, many of whom could become willing supporters of a separatist movement. Many observers compare the ETA movement to the Irish Republican Army and Northern Ireland "Troubles." ETA's campaign was actually markedly different from the PIRA's, as it specialized in kidnappings and extortion. This had rarely been a trademark of the PIRA.

In spite of the fact that large numbers of the Herri Batasuna Party had been arrested for their involvement and support of ETA attacks, the party continued to maintain its position by publicly stating that it had no ties, neither institutional nor political, to ETA. Spanish Judge Baltazar

TERRORIST ATTACK BRIEF

Terrorist Group: ETA/ISLAMIC JIHAD

Case Facts: ETA steps up its campaign and targets a restaurant frequented by U.S. servicemen. The bomb killed eighteen and wounded eighty-two, including fifteen U.S. personnel.

Investigation: The attack was presumed to have come from ETA; however, claims for responsibility were also coming in from Islamic Jihad in Lebanon. Evidence uncovered in the wide-ranging investigation failed to conclusively identify who the perpetrators were in this incident—today the case remains unsolved and was at the time the first unsolved major terrorism case in Spain.

FIGURE 6-2   Bombing—Madrid, Spain—April 12, 1985.   *Source*: Paul Medhurst, Global Terrorism— UN Institute for Training and Research.

Garzon has stated that Herri Batasuna was inextricably linked to legal groups and organizations that continued to provide economic and political support to ETA. From these groups it finds new recruits for the possibly ailing ETA ranks. Although there are no valid estimates of ETA strength, it still continues to use indiscriminate bombings.[6]

Similar to its Irish counterparts, ETA has not been able to maintain a long and lasting peace accord. The five-decade-old battle for a Basque homeland has cost more than 850 lives, and the cease-fire proclaimed in the summer of 2006 came to an end within six months—with an ETA bomb attack on Madrid Airport on December 30, and although they did not declare the ceasefire over, the Spanish government most certainly considered it over. Formal notification by ETA came on June 5, 2007, with an announcement that their "permanent ceasefire" was over, stating "minimum conditions for continuing a process of negotiations that do not exist."[7] The Spanish, who may have had some lingering sympathy toward ETA's struggle, were turned away with the diet of violence that was unleashed in the Madrid railway attacks of 2004, and although the ETA organization has not been as active as in pre-Madrid or 9-11 years, they still pose a threat. For a peace process to evolve, the same conditions as in Northern Ireland would likely be required to include a cessation of violence and a verified decommissioning of weapons and explosives. The parallels to Irish terror are quite often drawn, but in essence there are fundamental differences between the two conflicts. There is no equivalent sectarian divide of Catholics and Protestants and neither is there dual involvement of the two governments, the British in London and the Republic of Ireland in Dublin.

While ETA sporadically returned to violence, the Irish issue is settled with a power sharing administration between the two major protagonists. The Basque region has had more power devolved to it than Northern Ireland, and current attitudes to any separation of any region of Spain is pathologically opposed by politicians in Madrid, while at the same time the democratic processes in the United Kingdom, which frequently debates the separation of Scotland and Wales, is based on the wishes of the general public. For any resounding political success with ETA, there must first be consensus on what the common ground is for a peace process among the ruling parties in Madrid—something that is nonexistent at the moment.

Opposition to ETA

Accion Nacional Espanila (ANE), Spanish National Action, was a right-wing terror movement that targeted Basque separatists. ANE was formed in the 1970s and operated against the Basques in northern Spain. It is known to be responsible for reprisal killings of many ETA terrorists and sympathizers, and has also been active in bombings on both sides of the Spanish border. A joint Spanish and French operation in 2001 led to the arrests of thirty-seven ETA members residing in France. Going along with the United States in its war against terror, the French agreed to extradite immediately to Spain any ETA members who had warrants issued against them. In the past, the stumbling block for the French had been the political issue surrounding nationalism, which invariably led to interminably long delays in the extradition process.

Spain has combated terrorism with its paramilitary Special Operations Group, Grupo Especial De Operaciones (GEO). GEO is part of Spain's National Police and is stationed in Guadalajara, near the capital, Madrid. It has special response capabilities and is responsible for VIP protection duties, as well as countering and responding to terrorism. It was designed along the lines of many other European specialist counterterrorism units and is specifically focused on dealing with aircraft hijackings, maritime threats, and hostage taking. The GEO can also be utilized in a support role for Spanish police operations outside the realm of terrorism and is trained and active in protecting visiting heads of state and providing security for high-profile events such as the Olympic Games held in Barcelona in 1992.

GEO has had some noteworthy successes and was responsible for foiling the assassination attempt on King Juan Carlos in 1995 and an attempt by ETA to attack the Barcelona Olympics in 1992. GEO remains the foremost threat to terror cells and activity on the Spanish mainland.

ETA History Timeline

1959—Euskadi Ta Askatasuna (ETA), or Basque Homeland and Freedom, founded during dictatorship of General Franco to fight for self-determination.

1968—Police chief murdered in ETA's first planned killing.

1973—Franco's prime minister, Luis Carrero Blanco, killed when his car passes over ETA explosives in Madrid.

1980—ETA's bloodiest year. Almost 100 killed, despite Spain's return to democracy.

1985—First ETA car bombing in Madrid. American tourist killed while jogging and sixteen Civil Guards wounded.

1987—ETA supermarket bomb attack in Barcelona—twenty-one shoppers killed. ETA apologizes for "mistake."

1995—The Popular Party opposition leader, Jose Maria Aznar, later prime minister, escapes ETA bomb. Saved by vehicle's armor plating.

1998—ETA announces truce. It lasts fifteen months.

2000—A former Socialist health minister, Ernest Lluch, shot dead in Barcelona.

2004—Al Qaeda train bombings in Madrid kill 191 people and reinforce Spanish revulsion against violence. ETA's suspected leader and twenty-one suspects arrested.

2005—Spain's parliament gives government permission to open peace talks with ETA if the group lays down its arms.

2006—Permanent cease-fire announced, lasts approximately six months.

2006—December—ETA sets off car bomb at Madrid's newly opened International Airport Terminal killing two.

2007—ETA cease-fire at an end.[8]

2009—ETA fiftieth anniversary—celebrated with bombs in northern city of Burgos and on the Island of Majorca.

2010—ETA again announces another cease-fire.

2011—ETA announces a permanent and general cease-fire.

ETA's declaration of an end to hostilities on January 10, 2011, recognizes that the solution to the Basque conflict will come "though a democratic process that takes the will of the Basque people as its maximum point of reference, and dialogue and negotiation as its tools." And by noting that the cease-fire will be verifiable, it seems to be opening the door for outside observers to confirm that it is no longer making or purchasing weapons or engaging in the extortion it has used in the past to raise funds.

Frente Revolucionario Anti-Fascista Y Patriotico (FRAP)

Although little remembered today, Spain suffered from other terror groups, one of which was the left-wing Maoist group, FRAP.[9] In an ironic twist, FRAP received worldwide recognition when members were sentenced to death in 1975 for killing a Spanish policeman in Madrid. The worldwide outcry led to demands for Spain to be thrown out of the United Nations. Unmoved by these outbursts for clemency, the Spanish government followed through with the executions as planned on September 27, 1975.

Grupa De Resistencia Antifascista Primo Octobre (GRAPO)

The Anti-Fascist Resistance Group of October First (GRAPO)[10] was another left-wing terror group active in the 1970s at about the same time as FRAP. Four Spanish police officers were killed in a retaliatory action over the execution of five left-wing terrorists. The group takes its name from this action on October 1, 1975. GRAPO was also responsible for at least one attempt on the life of King Juan Carlos. Juan Carlos Delgado de Codex led the group until his death in 1979, while attempting to evade arrest.

Islamists and Spain

After 9-11, Spain embraced the global assault on international terrorism and strongly supports mutual assistance as a strategy to deny safe haven to terrorists. Mutual agreements and cooperation with the French have enabled both countries to root out ETA suspects on the French side of the border. Spain has also been responsible for the break-up and arrest of two suspected al Qaeda-affiliated cells in late September and November 2001. In July 2002, Spanish police continued to chase down suspected al Qaeda members operating on the Spanish mainland. In July 2002, the Spanish police arrested three men who were alleged to be of Syrian origin: two were naturalized and the third held Spanish residency. The police found videotapes from a 1997 visit to the United States in the suspects' possession. The footage shows various angles of the New York World Trade Center towers. Spain's interior minister, Angel Acebes, stated that the footage "was obviously not what a tourist would make." In addition, other high-profile locations had been taped, including San Francisco's Golden Gate Bridge, the Sears Tower in Chicago, the Empire State Building, and the Disneyland theme park in California. While this footage was filmed some four years prior to the 9-11 attacks, it gives considerable weight to the theory that al Qaeda in the late 1990s was very well organized and meticulously planned its attacks down to the smallest detail. Photos of the bridges focused on the construction of the bridge supports, while another two videos showed violent mujahedeen "terrorist training," fighting, and suicide bombers.[11]

The suspected cell leader was Syrian-born Imad Barakat Yarkas, also known as Abu Dahdah. Yarkas is believed to be an organizer and financer for Islamic extremists operating in Spain. Along with two other suspects charged in connection with the 9-11 attacks are Moroccan-born Driss Chebli and Syrian, Ghasoubun. Spanish prosecutors are seeking 74,000 years of jail time for each of the accused and fines of €893 million.[12] The wider prospects for international terrorism in Spain have focused mainly on Algerian nationals residing in or visiting the country. Since 9-11, Spanish authorities have made significant headway in this respect when Mohammed Atta, one of the 9-11 suicide pilots, met with an Islamic cell operating in Madrid in the summer of 2001. Atta's motives and his activities in Spain have not been established, but one may draw the inference that he was meeting and strategizing for terrorist attacks. Spain has established that Atta tried to visit an Algerian who was serving a prison term for forgery. In trying to determine how widely spread the Osama bin Laden network is, Atta would seem able to give the most direct evidence of links among activities in France, Spain, and the United States. Atta was present in Spain at the same time as Tunisian immigrant and former pro soccer player Nizar Trabelsi, who was later arrested in a plot to bomb the U.S. embassy in Paris. If Atta met with Trabelsi, the next rational conclusion would be that the attacks in New York and Washington were to be coordinated with bombing attacks in Europe.[13] As the investigation and links continue to be investigated, the widespread nature of the cell structure in Europe appears to infect France, Spain, Italy, Germany, the Netherlands, as well as Eastern European countries. Spain's significance also indicates that Ahmed Ressam visited Spain prior to his arrest in the plot to blow up the Los Angeles International Airport on New Year's Eve in 1999.

SPAIN'S 9-11

The characteristics of the attack on Madrid's rail system on March 11, 2004, bear further discussion. First, this was the worst act of terrorism on Spanish soil since the end of its civil war more than sixty years ago. Second, the Conservative government was quick to blame ETA for this attack. History tells us the United States made a similar quick response when it initially blamed Islamic extremists for the attack on the Alfred P. Murrah building in Oklahoma City in April 1995, and it was later determined to be the work of homegrown terrorists. The Madrid bombs bore none of the similarities of ETA's previous attacks and for the following reasons:

1. ETA has usually claimed responsibility for its attacks, but did not do so on this occasion.
2. ETA has invariably given advance warnings of its attacks, often to minimize civilian casualties.
3. The leader of the banned Batasuna Party publicly denied any ETA involvement and indicated an Arabic involvement (this was considered an unusual comment on Batasuna's part).

The ten, almost simultaneous, attacks in Madrid were immediately blamed on ETA, which would have meant that ETA had changed its targets away from the police, judiciary, and politicians, and was now targeting the public in general. It was not long before authorities found a videotaped message outside a mosque and, thus, the wider political implications for both Spain and the rest of Europe were about to be realized.

Up until the Madrid bombings, Spain's ruling Conservative government led by Jose Maria Aznar was a committed ally and supporter, not just of the U.S. and British War on Terror but also of deploying Spanish troops to the war in Iraq. To the Spanish voter, the realization was clear—three days before a general election an Islamic extremist cell had detonated bombs in Madrid, killing 191. A disillusioned public that did not support the war in Iraq was now going to turn what was likely to have been a Conservative victory into a stunning defeat. Spain returned the Socialist Party under the control of Jose Luis Rodriguez Zapatero to power. The power to openly change the direction of a nation was about to be shown to the men of terror. The first act by the Socialist government was to pull Spanish troops out of Iraq. Many Spaniards viewed this as a cowardly reaction to terrorism. What is also becoming apparent is that the Islamic extremists who attacked the Spanish public were supporters of the al Qaeda movement. This devastating attack changed the political will and direction of a nation, and its effects caused Spain to turn its back on a previously stated commitment in Iraq. Does Spain's about-turn mean that the country is bending to the will of the terrorists? Some would say yes; however, since the Madrid attacks, the Spanish have managed to unearth a considerable number of Islamic extremists operating within its borders. Iraq aside, the threat is clear and the cause is also clear: Islamic extremism is not on the decline, but is increasing and particularly so in Europe.

MADRID—MARCH 11, 2004   The fanaticism of the terrorists and their will to destroy not only innocents but also themselves was evidenced in the Madrid suburb of Leganes in April 2004. The group that had claimed responsibility for the Madrid train station bombing had stated that it would turn Spain into an inferno if it did not pull its troops out of Iraq and Afghanistan and cease its support for the United States. The letter containing this threat was supposedly from a group calling itself "Abu Dujana Al Afgani" (Ansar Group, al Qaeda in Europe). Concern for Europe, and not just Spain, is the link believed between this group and Abu Musab al-Zarqawi, the Jordanian terrorist conducting his insurgency campaign in Iraq at the time. While this may be speculation, what is known is that Ansar al-Islam is an extreme Islamic terrorist organization that has been responsible for numerous attacks in Iraq, Turkey, and Jordan. The Spanish police cornered the main suspects in the Madrid train station bombings in an apartment in Legenes. Before the raid could begin, the terror cell in the apartment building detonated a bomb that destroyed part of the building. In the ensuing confusion, several of the suspects may have fled the area. The explosion killed three people. To Spaniards the term "11M" is as significant and distressful as 9-11 is profoundly disturbing for Americans. It symbolizes the March 11, 2004, Madrid station bombings that killed 191 and injured nearly 2,000 other commuters. The culmination of the investigation saw a number of radical Islamists in a Madrid court in October 2007. The three lead suspects convicted of murder and attempted murder each received sentences of 34,000–40,000 years in prison; however, Spain does not have death penalty and the longest a prisoner can serve is 40 years, so the 34,000-year term was largely symbolic. A total of twenty-one out of twenty-eight defendants were convicted of the lesser charge of belonging to a terrorist organization.

FRANCE

A Long Acquaintance with Terrorism

On the face of it, France has not seen the same level of terrorist activity as have, perhaps, other major European countries but with its large immigrant population it is very clearly threatened by jihadists trained and indoctrinated in the tribal regions bordering Pakistan and through indoctrination via jihadist websites. France has not been left out of the problems facing other governments in dealing with terrorism. However, European terrorists and Middle Eastern terror groups have always needed bases, not only safe houses but also safe countries from which to mount their terror

FIGURE 6-3   Map of France (Central Intelligence Agency, *The World Factbook, 2008*).

campaigns without too much political or police interference. Until the Madrid bombings, Europe was perceived to be a logistics base for terror groups and cells. The twenty-first-century reality is that Europe (France included) has become a fertile recruiting ground for the likes of Abu Musab al-Zarqawi, the Jordanian leading the insurgent attacks in Iraq. The country of choice for many terrorist groups and terrorists has often been France. From a strategic point of view, terror groups have considered the country an ideal location from which to strike and then return to hide. It has borders with Spain, Italy, Germany, Switzerland, Belgium, and Luxembourg, plus an efficient transportation network of roads, air, sea, and rail systems.

France has not been immune to terror. History books are full of atrocities perpetrated during the French Revolution. (The word "terrorism" was born from that time.) What needs more consideration and discussion surrounds the type of terror groups that utilize France for their base of operations and their reasons for doing so. The next section discusses some specific groups that have successfully used France as a base to mount terror operations and even to carry on turf wars outside their own countries.

The Popular Front for the Liberation of Palestine (PFLP) in France

In the late 1960s and 1970s, France became the European safe haven for the beleaguered PFLP organization. The PFLP was one of the most militant and aggressive Palestinian groups linked to the Palestine Liberation Organization (PLO). Wadi Haddad controlled and led the "external" operations from a secure base, in Aden, now South Yemen, and directed PFLP operations in Europe. They had set up safe houses in Paris for planned attacks in Europe. The audacious attacks carried out by the group include some of the most spectacular attacks in recent history: the attacks at Zurich Airport in 1969, the Dawson Field hijackings in 1970, and the attack on OPEC (The Organization of Petroleum Exporting Countries) headquarters in Vienna in 1975, led by Ilich Ramirez Sanchez, better known as Carlos the Jackal,[14] who now resides in a French prison cell. The Jackal was linked to the following attacks:

- **1972**—Massacre of eleven Israeli athletes by Palestinian gunmen at the Munich Olympic Games.
- **1973**—Edward Sieff, whose family owned Marks and Spencer's department stores, was attacked and wounded.
- **1974**—Armed assault and takeover of the French Embassy in The Hague by members of the Japanese Red Army.
- **1975**—Two French intelligence agents were killed while investigating the Orly Airport attack on an Israeli airliner.
- **1975**—Attack on the OPEC headquarters in Vienna in which three people died and eleven were taken hostage.
- **1976**—Air France, airliner hijacked to Entebbe, Uganda.
- **1982**—Bombing attack on the Paris—Toulouse Express.
- **1983**—Bombing attack on Marseille's main railway terminal killing five people.

The justification for terrorism has been argued vigorously. However, since the end of World War II, the use of terror as a means to an end has had several primary benefits: (1) to receive local and, in most cases, worldwide attention for a specific cause or causes; (2) as an outlet for political impotence and frustration; and (3) to carry out combative measures for countries or states not in the financial position to take direct action themselves. In the political arena, the latter would occur where a state did not wish to take direct confrontational action but rather use the cloak of terror, for which it could always deny any involvement in the aftermath of the event. The Palestinian cause will be dealt with under a separate chapter; however, many organizations like the PLO, and various offshoots, used France in the 1960s and 1970s as a friendly base for operations.

Japanese Red Army (JRA)

The Japanese Red Army terror group was also prominent in France in the 1970s. This group was pledged to a worldwide Marxist revolution and actively supported and was very much involved in the Palestinian struggle in the Middle East.[15] The group was formed in the early 1970s based on feudal Japanese Samurai warrior traditions, as well as Marxism. The JRA operated globally and has been involved in major international terror attacks in support of the Palestinian cause. They participated in the ferocious attack on Lod Airport in Israel,[16] killing Puerto Rican pilgrims in the departure lounge. The group also murdered two U.S. sailors in Italy in 1988. In continuous worldwide support of its Palestinian brethren, the group also hijacked an airliner and held the passengers hostage, demanding the sum of US$6 million in ransom.

Action Direct (AD)

France is a center of operations for international terrorism, but it also has had its own brand of internal terrorists. AD was a Marxist terrorist group unlike many of its other European and Middle Eastern counterparts. It evolved, not out of the 1960s, but the late 1970s and early 1980s.

Considered a left-wing revolutionary group, it began as a Communist revolutionary organization and limited its focus to virulent anti-American sentiment. One of its more audacious attacks was a raid on the Goldenberg Restaurant in Paris in August 1982 when gunmen opened fire, killing six patrons and injuring a further twenty-two other diners.

With its strong views on American interference in European affairs, it adopted the anti-American rhetoric of the Palestinian cause and began attacking Israeli and Zionist targets and those associated with capitalism and imperialism, such as the North Atlantic Treaty Organization (NATO). As AD evolved, it began to build a network of other left-wing terror groups operating in Europe, particularly in Germany, France, and Belgium. The Communist Combatant Cells (CCC) in Belgium,[17] the Red Brigade (RB) in Italy, and the German-based Red Army Faction supported AD's campaign against NATO. With its original base in Paris, AD also became an international terror organization.

There is skepticism in official quarters that this group had to feed off and be supported by the other left-wing groups. Since the unification of East and West Germany, the level of left-wing violence and terror has decreased. This, however, does not indicate that the group has split up or disintegrated, and AD will most likely continue, in some form, to espouse and support its philosophical goals.

Alien Invaders

In recent times, France has been the breeding ground for unwelcome guests from the European and Middle East theaters of terrorist conflict. On the home front, there has been the Front de la Liberation Nationale de la Corse (FLNC), a group of Corsican separatists, as well as the extreme left-wing AD group. Another is the Armee Republicaine Bretonne (ARB). The ARB and the FLNC are distinct in their aims as compared to the AD. They are purely regional French factions with the goal of local autonomy. AD, on the other hand, has somewhat fuzzy international ideological goals. Confusingly, to the casual or the uninformed observer, AD has gone after anti-Jewish interests, which, one would normally associate with the extreme right wing as opposed to the extreme left. France's tolerance for the number of groups active within its borders is probably born out of its own realization of how the French Republic was created. This tolerance has led many other groups to use Paris as a primary base for internal and external operations. The Corsican Army (**Armata Corsa**) set up in 1999 to oppose links between nationalists and the Corsican Mafia on the other hand, has its roots in the criminal classes of Corsica and seems to function partly on the nationalist scene and partly on the criminal side of life. It does, however, denounce the Mafia-style activities that have plagued the island of Corsica. Its attacks have been mostly symbolic as Armata Corsa seeks to create an island state independent from France, and also the return of Corsican terrorists imprisoned in mainland France. The group has been mainly involved in attacks against public figures and buildings as well as tourist locations, and has concentrated nearly all the attacks on Corsica.

With the disintegration of the empire of the Shah of Iran, students in Paris took control of the Iranian Embassy to show their support for Ayatollah Khomeini. The city was a tolerant host to both sides, with both pro- and anti-Khomeini supporters making their protests public. Both groups clashed during a street protest.

The Army for the Liberation of Armenia (**ASALA**) represents another region of Europe. This French group of exiled Armenians was intent on promoting its cause and airing its grievances against the government of Turkey. ASALA's grievances go back in history to 1915–1922, when the Turks massacred more than 1 million Armenians headquartered in the Middle East; its actions are aimed at securing a homeland of its own. Most Armenians lived within former Soviet Bloc countries.

The most aggressive groups operating out of Paris have been the Palestine Liberation Organization (PLO) and the Algerian Islamic terrorist group known as the Armed Islamic Group (GIA). The PLO's headline-catching events included the rocket attack at Orly Airport, when in broad daylight two Lebanese Palestinians calmly parked their car near the runway and, armed with a RPG-7 rocket launcher, fired at an El Al flight taxiing for take-off. Fortunately, the rocket missed the El Al aircraft and hit an empty Yugoslav jetliner.[18] The two terrorists escaped capture at the airport. Not to be outdone by the failure, another attack was scheduled for Orly Airport six days later. By this time, the airport was strongly protected by military security. The group entered the airport with an assembled bazooka, much to the astonishment of the armed police, and a furious gun battle between police and terrorists ensued amid hundreds of passengers and spectators in the airport building. As for the GIA, their actions in France in the mid-1990s included attacks on the Paris Metro subway system. Approximately 5 million Muslims live in France out of a total population of 58 million. GIA's actions in France resulted in bombings throughout 1995, and, in July of that year, a gas canister bomb exploded in the subway, killing seven and injuring eighty-six. Algeria, a former French colony, had been fighting a rising tide of Islamic radicalism. Rather than accede to it, the Algerian government, at that time under Liamine Zeroual, used military force to repress GIA. Because of its support for the Algerians, the French became a legitimate target for the GIA, who hoped France would withdraw its support for Algeria. Aircraft hijackings, by GIA terrorists, seem to be almost a prediction of the tragic events of 9-11. In December 1994, armed terrorists disguised as police officers boarded an Air France jet in Algiers and hijacked it to France. The aircraft was reportedly packed with explosives to be detonated over the capital city of Paris. The aircraft landed in Marseilles and was stormed by members of the crack antiterror group Groupe d' Intervention de la Gendarmerie Nationale (GIGN), which ended the fifty-four-hour siege that culminated in the death of three of the hostages and all of the terrorists. Following 9-11, the French government has been unstinting in its support of the War on Terror. French officials expressed their determination to eradicate the "perverse illness" of terrorism and have offered military and logistics support. France played a leading role and supported the invoking of Article 5 of the UN Treaty, which covers a mutual defense clause. As part of Operation "Enduring Freedom," the French provided logistical support with its army, navy, and air force.

In April 2001, Fateh Kemal was sentenced in Paris for operating a support network believed to be linked to al Qaeda. He was sentenced to eight years in jail. The French were able to establish links between Kemal's operatives and Ahmed Ressam, the millennium bomber arrested by U.S. Custom agents when he was crossing from Canada into Washington State with a bomb intended for a terrorist attack at the Los Angeles International Airport. On the day before the 9-11 attacks, French authorities began to investigate a group linked to al Qaeda that planned to attack U.S. targets in France. The group's leader, Djamel Beghal, was extradited from the United Arab Emirates (UAE) to France in October 2001 as part of that investigation. It was very patient intelligence work that revealed that Kemal was an expert document forger, head of the network of which the Roubaix gang was a part, and had also spent time in Afghanistan, where he'd been in contact with Bin Laden. The French authorities believe it is clear that in the decentralized, compartmentalized, and intersecting root system of Islamic networks, Kemal had been given the responsibility for creating and transporting false ID documents to be used by militants being assembled in Turkey, Bulgaria, Belgium, France, Bosnia, and North America.

Kemal and twenty-three associates were convicted for activities related to association with terrorist enterprises. There was no demonstrative proof of their service or allegiance to Bin Laden, although such links would be impossible to verify given the dispersed, cellular nature of these operations (thus organized precisely to prevent police from following a linear trail back to the top) and their vague hierarchy and direction.[19] Kemal was released from prison in 2005 and returned to Canada, where proceedings were launched to have his citizenship revoked and for his deportation back to his native Algeria.

Under Executive Order 13224, French authorities froze $54 million, the assets of the former Taliban government of Afghanistan. Although France has been a strong UN ally, the U.S. desire to seek death penalty for Zacarias Moussaoui, the only man arrested in connection with the 9-11 attacks, has meant a lack of cooperation between the French intelligence services and those of the United States. Both the French and German governments have been supplying evidence to the United States concerning Moussaoui, but not material that could lead to his execution. In spite of this, the French have been party to counterterrorism discussions at the G-8 summit meetings.[20]

AL QAEDA IN FRANCE

With France's close ties to the North African continent during its colonial era, it is not surprising that many immigrants from Morocco and Algeria migrate to France. The planning and recruiting for the 9-11 attack did not take place in Muslim countries, but mainly on the continent of Europe—in Germany, France, and England in particular. The security and intelligence failures can be linked back to Europe and a failure to follow up on specific intelligence reports from the French security services.

As for al Qaeda, most of its French cells were made up of second-generation immigrants, and as investigations have shown, most of the combatants showed little or no interest in Islam in their own countries. It seems the seeds of Islamic radicalism may have been planted in the mosques of Europe. Radical Islamic beliefs are not the sole domain of Muslims. Richard Reid, the infamous "shoe bomber," and two French-native brothers, David and Jerome Courtailler, are converts to Islam. Lionel Dumont, a French citizen from the northern French town of Roubaix, and also a convert to Islam, saw military service with the French in Somalia. In the early 1990s, he went to the former Yugoslavia and joined a mujahedeen group, the Takfir wal Hirja, in Bosnia. He returned to France and formed an organization with others from the North African communities, called the Gang of Roubaix, which was involved in several terrorist attacks. His links to al Qaeda have never been confirmed, and so far he has evaded arrest from French authorities.[21]

During former president Bush's reelection campaign in 2004, he commented, "More than three quarters of al Qaeda have been brought to justice." This may well have sounded great for the electorate, but, as we have seen, al Qaeda is becoming a rallying cry movement for young and impressionable Muslims around the globe, more particularly those in Western countries such as France, Germany, and the Netherlands. The first prominent example is British citizen Richard Reid, who boarded an American Airlines flight in Paris bound for Miami on December 22, 2001, and attempted to detonate a bomb hidden in his shoes. Richard Reid may seem an unlikely candidate for an Islamic convert—nevertheless his troubled youth brought him into contact with those who would ultimately set him on a path to terrorism:

> **1992–1994**—The British Home Office says Richard Reid was twice incarcerated at Feltham (Middlesex) Young Offenders Institution in West London—for ten days in 1992 and a month in 1994. It was not known what charges led to Reid's incarceration there.

> **Late 1998 and early 1999**—Brixton Mosque chairman Abdul Haqq Baker says Reid and Zacarias Moussaoui—the only person so far charged with conspiracy in the 9-11 terrorist attacks on the United States—attended the same South London mosque during this period, though it is not known if they were there at the same time.

July 2001—Israeli government officials say Reid travelled to Israel for "around ten days" before traveling by land to Egypt.

August to December 2001—Reid reportedly lives in Amsterdam, working in restaurants.

Early December 2001—Reid allegedly spends ten days in Brussels, Belgium, staying at the Dar Salam hostel in an Arab and North African neighborhood.

December 5 and 6, 2001—Reid tells Belgian authorities he'd lost his British passport. The British Embassy issues him a new one.

December 15, 2001—Reid reportedly checks out of the Brussels hostel and arrives in Paris, France, the next day.

December 17, 2001—Reid buys round-trip ticket from Paris to Miami, Florida, to Antigua. Police say he appears to have spent his entire time in the area around the Gare du Nord, one of the city's major train stations.

December 21, 2001—French authorities question Reid after a security agent becomes suspicious because Reid is traveling without checked luggage. Authorities eventually say Reid can board his flight, American Airlines Flight 63, but by then it has already left Paris.

December 22, 2001—Reid boards American Airlines Flight 63, which is following the same route as the flight he'd missed a day earlier. Ninety minutes later, he allegedly tries to use a match to light explosives hidden in his shoes and is subdued when passengers and crew jump on him and strap him to his seat. Doctors aboard the aircraft sedate him. Plane diverts to Boston, Massachusetts, and Reid is arrested and charged with interfering with a flight crew.

December 28, 2001—A federal judge denies Reid bail and remands him to jail in Plymouth, Massachusetts.[22]

Reid was sentenced to life in prison in Federal Court in Boston on January 30, 2003. To many, Reid has been cast as a bungling amateur when in fact the opposite is the case, as there is ample evidence that he had been in contact with other jihadists and had received terror training. With respect to Moussaoui, the intelligence sources on both sides of the Atlantic should have picked up on his activities. French intelligence tracks nearly all North Africans traveling from France to Pakistan and/or Afghanistan. British newspapers reported that the French Directorate of Territorial Security repeatedly informed its counterparts in Britain that Zacarias Moussaoui, who was residing in London in the early 1990s, had made trips to both Afghanistan and Pakistan. Further, he was considered to be involved in terrorism. As part of the investigation into the murder of three French Consular staff in Algeria, Moussaoui's name was found in an address book that was seized. Unfortunately, information provided to the British appears to never have been acted upon.[23]

The FBI had been warned in advance of the 9-11 attacks, and that Moussaoui was associated with Osama bin Laden. Moussaoui was arrested on an immigration violation; the French intelligence report was never acted upon.[24] Zacarias Moussaoui was born in France and, like other suspects arrested in Germany, was not known as an Islamic extremist. In 1992, he went to England and shared an apartment with the French Courtailler brothers while he studied for a degree. Sometime during this period he came under the spell of the fanatical Muslim cleric, Abu Qatada.

Europe is currently the recruiting haven for Islamic militants and social media are fast becoming the route extremists are using to spread their message and recruit jihadists. In 2011, we saw how effective the use of the Internet and social media forums can be in rallying popular support for uprisings as evidenced in Egypt, Tunisia, Libya, Yemen, and Syria. Terrorists and radical Islamist groups continue to use the Internet as a recruiting tool, and now social media as well forms part of their arsenal. In a message posted to the Shumukh al-Islam jihadist forum, a forum member called for supporters of al Qaeda to prepare attacks, including assassinations, suicide bombings, and chemical and bio-weapons attacks, against French individuals in retaliation for enforcing the law banning face veils. The April 13, 2011, poster encouraged forum members to "annihilate them and extirpate them, horrify and terrorize them, do not leave them one place without terrorizing them and making them horrified by you."[25]

Muslim associations are common in most European countries, and Italy has more than 1 million Muslims and 10,000 native Italians who have converted to Islam. The **Union of Islamic Communities and Organizations in Italy (UCOII)** is heavily influenced by Islam and has a Syrian-born head, Mohamed Nour Dachan. Italians and Europeans are increasingly concerned about the rise of extreme Islamic fundamentalism. In 2002, Randa Ghazy, a fifteen-year-old Italian girl who lived and studied in Milan, aroused considerable controversy. The girl wrote a book, *Seguundo Palestina* (*Dreaming Palestine*), which was published and has sold tens of thousands of copies. The book glorifies Arab teenagers who have embraced the jihad against the "Zionists." The book, which is characterized by an anti-Semitic and Islamist approach to the Arab-Israeli conflict, praises suicide attacks against the Jews. The youngster also appeared on TV and radio talk shows and has reached a level of notoriety and even respectability. Although UCOII has, in the past, condemned fundamentalist terrorism, its influential secretary, Hamza Roberto Piccardo, has repeatedly expressed his approval of suicide attacks within Israel.[26] The growth of such extreme organizations and the recruiting of European Muslims for the global jihad have only been exacerbated by the war in Iraq and Afghanistan. European countries have reported mainly second-generation immigrants from Middle Eastern and North African countries where the young and often disillusioned are seen as excellent candidates for radical recruiters for the jihad. The French connection to jihad is also relevant. Jihad is being spread by young Algerian immigrants to France, many of whom are second-generation Algerians. Several European countries were targeted by a French-Algerian named Jamal Beghal, who was arrested in July 2001 in the United Arab Emirates as he was about to transfer from a flight from Pakistan to a flight to Europe. The truly transnational nature of jihad is evident here: This man, with links to al Qaeda, had lived in London and attended the Finsbury Park Mosque along with Richard Reid (the shoe bomber), the Courtailler brothers, Zacarias Moussaoui, and Nizar Trabelsi. Beghal had attended training camps in Afghanistan and recruited mostly young Algerians living in France for the cause of jihad. Beghal's network conducted surveillance and plotted to attack the U.S. embassy in France and a U.S. Air Force base in Belgium. It is highly probable that all had links through the Algerian Salafist Group for Preaching and Combat (GSPC) to al Qaeda. Members of Beghal's group considered themselves to be takfiris (i.e., extreme religious literalists who view anyone who does not subscribe to their extreme and literal interpretation of the Koran as unbelievers and worthy of attack).

France as a secular nation also has Europe's largest Muslim community and faces a dilemma between accommodating Islam and maintaining secularism. In 2004, it passed a law banning headscarves or any other "conspicuous" religious symbols in schools to uphold a separation between church and state. France is currently the only state in Europe to have such a ban. In April 2011, it banned the wearing of the Muslim veil in public places, which provided a focus for al Qaeda-inspired groups to target French interests.

The threat to Western Europe comes from the Middle East and North African immigrant population and the threat in the United Kingdom comes from second-generation immigrants and converts to Islam. In Paris during November 2005, two Muslim youths died while being chased by French police, which sparked a week of rioting. Many Muslim migrants live in slum areas of the major cities and finding work is difficult at best. The presence of so many disgruntled youth, both immigrant and second generation, provides ample fodder for radical Muslim extremists to recruit from. The attacks in the French city of Toulouse in March 2012 showed how the intelligence community is often unable to prevent what on the surface appears to be a "Lone Wolf" attack from a committed jihadist. This was low-cost terrorism involving either a small cell of dedicated jihadists or an individual indoctrinated and trained for such an attack; the attacks saw three French paratroopers gunned down in a street by a lone gunman, to be quickly followed by the daytime massacre at a Jewish school where the same gunman killed the head teacher and three children. The perpetrator was alone for the attacks but was a committed jihadist who had travelled extensively to Asia and like his counterparts in the United Kingdom received training in the tribal regions of Pakistan's border area. Such was the premeditated nature of the attacks that the assailant Mohamed Merah even used a camera to record his killings and post them on the Internet. His attacks were calculated and well planned, and he was well known in jihadist circles in France. Also, he undoubtedly received material support from other jihadists in this operation. Merah was known to French intelligence and also was on a No-Fly list and still managed to execute this attack. The spectacular attacks on Madrid, New York, and London may be for the history books, but his modus operandi will cause serious concern for the intelligence communities on how best to counter this growing threat.

GERMANY

A Mixed History of Fascism, Terrorism, and Democracy

Germany has survived two world wars, was divided into two nations, paid the price of Nazism as well as Communism, and, at the end of the twentieth century, rose as a major industrial power in Europe. History clearly describes the years between the two world wars as being economically harsh for Germany. However, it is important to look back at some significant periods of the twentieth century that affected the German people as well as neighboring countries. Between the two world wars, Germany saw the rise of the Nazi Party and the ultimate power of its leader, former Austrian corporal, Adolf Hitler. Humbled by its reparation payments and crippled by the devastation of the Great Depression of 1929, the Germans faced unemployment and starvation. The reparation repayment was renegotiated under the terms of the Young Plan, against which Adolf Hitler campaigned long and hard throughout Germany. By July 1932, the Nazi Party held 38 percent of the seats in the German Parliament (Reichstag).[27] Hitler's passionate, self-appointed mission was to lead a depressed Germany back to greatness, rid it of Communist and other influences, and purge the society of its ills. To achieve this, he had to gain absolute power and control. In 1933, Paul Von Hindenburg, president of Germany, proclaimed Hitler as chancellor (prime minister). With total control, Hitler proclaimed his government as the "Third Reich." With that, Germany's dictator began his own reign of terror on Germany. By the end of July 1933, through legal processes, Hitler had destroyed the German constitution and outlawed freedom of the press, unions, and all political parties with the exception of the National Socialist Party (the "Nazi" Party). His own breed of police, the Gestapo, hunted down all opponents of his government. Many were arrested on suspicion alone and, more often than not, were jailed or shot.

The Nazis used terror tactics to gain control over the populace. All German children, boys and girls, were required to join the Hitler Youth or the Society of German Maidens. These children

FIGURE 6-4   Map of Germany (Central Intelligence Agency, *The World Factbook, 2008*).

of Germany were indoctrinated into the Nazi philosophy and military discipline and were used as spies to inform on family members who did not embrace National Socialism. A sophisticated network of spies monitored and reported on the German people and fostered an atmosphere of physical and psychological terror.

Germany's New Order

There have been hundreds of accounts about Hitler's "Final Solution" for the "Jewish problem." He believed that the German people were a genetically superior race and that his country had to be purged of the impure, non-Aryan peoples. Those groups singled out for special treatment were Jews, Gypsies, Poles, homosexuals, and Slavs. The term *Holocaust* is widely used to define the mass murder of over 6 million Jewish people. Hitler and his Nazi Party members began their reign of terror on the Jews as early as 1933, almost immediately after Hitler came to power. Sometime in early July 1933 (the date has never been precisely confirmed), beginning around the ninth of the month and lasting for about forty-eight hours, Nazi Party members destroyed thousands of Jewish businesses and synagogues throughout Germany, killed dozens of Jews, and sent almost 40,000 to concentration camps. The night is referred to as *Kristallnacht* (night of the broken glass).

When German armies rolled across Europe, a similar fate awaited Jews in those countries that Germany had conquered. The names of the camps still strike terror into many communities: Belsen, Auschwitz, Buchenwald, Dachau, and others. Hitler's brand of terror, which accounted for the mass murder of millions of Jews and others considered non-Aryan or those who did not fit his Aryan picture of perfection, was a simple means to an end. The Nazi leadership saw it as the cleansing of a nation and those it had conquered. Such use of political terrorism was considered a weapon of psychological warfare.

Post–World War II Germany and Terrorism

After the end of World War II, a long period of rebuilding and healing took place. By the 1960s, the Federal German Republic was experiencing three different types of terrorism: (1) Left-wing terrorism came from the imported views of radical students and their opposition to the U.S. war in Vietnam. (2) Right-wing terrorists opposed the left-wing radicals in a continuation of the anti-Communist past. (3) Criminals also adopted the terror group's actions and copied and mimicked their attacks for personal criminal gain.

The 1960s were the decade of widespread student unrest, although in Germany there was no real catalyst to take the protests to the next stage. Student protests were prevalent on many university campuses in Europe as a platform for anti-Vietnam War protests. Modern terrorism, in Germany's case, has been typified by indiscriminate violence, sensationalized by the murder of innocents.

The student left-wing radicals at the Berlin Free University, in a somewhat copycat style, protested against American involvement in Vietnam. The protests were restricted mainly to marches and the distribution of leaflets, but there was no catalyst in place to take any serious action at a higher level of violence. Two main protagonists came to the forefront of the student protests: Andreas Baader and Gudrun Ensslin.[28] As in many university campuses of the 1960s, both Communism and Marxism were prevalent in the Berlin Free University. Baader, Enselin, and, later, Meinhof were all committed Marxists. The German Red Army faction was formulated at Berlin University led by Gudrun Ensslin and by the freewheeling Andreas Baader, who presented more of a playboy image than that of a terrorist.

Kidnapping for ransom was a hallmark of many of the terrorist groups operating in Europe and the Middle East during the 1960s and 1970s. The kidnapping of a prominent German industrialist Herr Hanns-Martin Schleyer by the Red Army Faction is an example of how desperate the various groups were for media and government attention. Schlayer and his entourage were attacked in a Cologne suburb and his bodyguards were killed.

Red Army Faction (RAF)

This group of committed Marxists sought to engage the United States in a combative role by extending the Vietnam War to German soil. They achieved this by attacking U.S. interests in West Germany, and particularly U.S. servicemen and military bases. Many books describe Andreas Baader as more of a delinquent and a follower than a committed terrorist. He seemed, in many accounts, to draw pleasure from being at the center of an infamous criminal network. To finance its program of violence, the group resorted to a series of bank robberies and other crimes.

The igniting factor that sparked this group into action on a grand scale was, in fact, an eloquent German lawyer, Horst Mahler, who joined the student movement to give it impetus toward a violent action. In 1968, Ensslin and her boyfriend Baader attempted to destroy two Frankfurt department stores with firebombs. They were both captured and sentenced and, a year later, temporarily released during an amnesty for political prisoners. When the amnesty was over, they fled to France as fugitives. They returned to West Germany to join with Horst Mahler, but Baader was again arrested. At this point in the group's development, Ulrike Meinhof came into the picture.

Meinhof was the editor of an underground newspaper called *Konkert*.[29] The paper had been launched in the 1950s, sponsored and supported by Communist groups in East Germany.

Meinhof is reputed to be a close friend of Gudrun Ensslin, and it was Ensslin who persuaded Meinhof to assist in Andreas Baader's prison breakout. The jailbreak on May 14, 1970, resulted in changing the name of the group to the Baader-Meinhof Gang. Over the following two years, Meinhof spent time in Jordan not far from the capital, Amman, and received training in weaponry from the Palestinians. Meinhof and colleagues became skilled in the use of their favorite weapon, the Russian Kalashnikov (the AK-47 assault rifle). After training with the PLO, the group was involved in the attack on the Organization of Petroleum Exporting Countries (OPEC) headquarters in Vienna, Austria, on December 21, 1975. At this point, the RAF joined forces with a group that called itself the "Arab Revolution," a cover name for the Popular Front for the Liberation of Palestine (PFLP).[30]

Ilich Ramirez Sanchez, better known as "Carlos the Jackal," led the assault on the OPEC building in Vienna in 1975 that targeted the oil-producing countries and was more a case of raising money than having a significant political impact. The Saudi Arabian and Iranian governments are believed to have paid a ransom of $50 million for the safe return of their nationals. Among the five strong groups that attacked the building were two German terrorists—Gabrielle Tiedemann and Hans-Joachim Klein. During a gun battle with Austrian security officers, Klein was captured and seriously injured. No political demands were made except the demand that the Austrians broadcast a political statement for the Baader–Meinhof group. The Austrians allowed the terrorist and a number of the hostages to fly to Algiers and then to Tripoli. The large amount of ransom money was transferred to a bank in Aden to bankroll further terrorism.

German authorities arrested the principals of the Baader–Meinhof Gang, which numbered about 100 active supporters. In May 1972, Baader, Gudrun Ensslin, Holger Meins, and Jean-Carle Raspe placed three pipe bombs near the entrance to the I.G. Faben building, which houses the US Army Corps. Both bombs detonated within minutes of each other. The officers' mess was destroyed, and Lt Colonel Paul Bloomquist, a decorated Vietnam War veteran, died from his injuries. The Baader–Meinhof Gang, calling themselves the Petra Schlem Commando, claimed responsibility for the attack and demanded an end to the U.S. mining of Vietnam harbors. Baader and others of the group were captured and sentenced in 1972.

The group was housed in the maximum security Stammheim Prison. Ulrike Meinhof, suffering from acute depression, hanged herself in her prison cell on May 9, 1976. As for the remainder of the group's members, it is something of a controversy as to how they met their ends. On the night of October 18, 1977, several members of the Baader–Meinhof group died from self-inflicted gunshot wounds in their prison cells.[31] Many have asked how guns could have been smuggled into a top-security prison. The most likely answer to that is lawyers for the group brought in the weapons to attempt a breakout.

The deaths coincided with news of a dramatic rescue by the antiterrorist group Grenzschutzgruppe-9 (GSG-9) in October 1977. The GSG-9 stormed a Lufthansa aircraft at Mogadishu, Somalia, killing three hijackers and rescuing the ninety passengers. It would seem to be entirely logical that the Red Army Faction, or as it was usually called, the "Baader–Meinhof Gang," would cease to exist. However, it exists to this day and its growth has not been stemmed by arrests of prominent members over the past two decades. With arrests of successive leaders and gang members, the RAF has continued to rise like a phoenix from its own ashes. It is believed that its growth in the 1970s and 1980s was due, in part, to an elaborate communications system and network set up among the imprisoned terrorists, their lawyers, and the activists still working for the cause. Public opinion soured toward the RAF in 1977, an opinion that had generally held them up as romantics fighting for a misunderstood cause. This was naturally embellished by the popular press, which continued to sensationalize the group's criminal activities and misdeeds.

However, the previously mentioned hijacking of a Lufthansa airline to Mogadishu, Somalia, by terrorists supported by the RAF resulted in the murder of the aircraft's pilot, Jurgen Schumann. This single act helped turn public opinion against the group.

TERRORISM AND THE OLYMPIC GAMES MOVEMENT

High-profile targets will always be on a terrorist groups' agenda, and one of the most significant and historic attacks against innocent civilians is encapsulated in the massacre of Israeli athletes at the Munich Olympic Games, September 5 and 6, 1972. At a time when European countries relied on their police as frontline troops to handle criminal attacks of all nature—the attack by members of the Palestinian terrorist group Black September began an evolution in police response tactics to terrorist threats. In West Germany, they created, through the Federal Police, the Grenzschutzgruppe-9, the crack counterterrorism group. The Black September attack was intended to force the Israeli government to release more than 200 Palestinians being held in Israeli jails, including RAF members being held by West German authorities. The initial attack resulted in the death of several athletes and coaches, and over the next twenty-four hours the police negotiated with the terrorists to get them and their hostages to a local airfield. It was at this point that the German police attacked in an attempt to rescue the hostages. The resulting firefight saw all nine hostages and their captors killed.

The **RAF** reached the pinnacle of their existence toward the end of the 1970s. The group was responsible for the assassination of the West German attorney general, Siegfried Buback, and Hans-Martin Schleyer. They went so far as to attempt to murder the head of NATO in Europe—U.S. Army Four-Star General Alexander Haig. They remained active into the 1980s and by then had joined forces with a little-known German terror unit called the June Second Movement and another called the Red Cells. Little is known of their members or numbers; it seems likely that the groups continue to operate independently of each other. The significance of the date June 2, 1967, is in remembrance of Benno Ohnesorg, who was killed on that day during a student protest that turned into a riot. RAF's most notorious act was the abduction of Peter Lorenz, a candidate for the post of mayor of West Berlin. The ransom paid was for the release of four of the group's compatriots who were then flown to South Yemen.

A Reawaking of Germany's Past

Germany had relied on an influx of foreign immigrant workers for the post–World War II rebuilding of its destroyed infrastructure. The *Gastarbeiter* program, in which Turkish immigrants were brought into Germany strictly for use as menial laborers, celebrated forty years of its introduction in 2011. Some Germans continue to be openly hostile to immigration policies, especially since the events of 9-11. Integration by large numbers of immigrants to German society over the last three decades has clearly failed.

Anti-Semitic behavior still lurks as haunting reminder from Germany's past. Invariably, the message and threats of belligerent intolerance continue to come from radical German Skinhead and neo-Nazi factions. It would be incorrect to label every Skinhead as a racist, as many are from varying religious denominations that are nonracist and are not purveyors of hate crimes. Much of the bigoted violence in Germany has been directed against foreign workers, particularly poor and desperate Turkish immigrants. However, throughout the 1990s and into the new millennium, Jews and Turks became the Skinheads' target of choice. Year after year since, starting in 1990, there has been a steady increase in the number of hate crimes associated with Skinheads and attacks on members of Jewish and Turkish communities. They are most likely to be in their teens and early twenties. Skinheads usually operate in gangs and much of their hatred and violence is spewed after bouts of binge drinking. The gangs roam the streets looking for likely victims to attack. The collapse of the Communist regime in East Germany significantly affected the Skinhead situation. The emergence of the eastern Skinheads radicalized the movement in both numbers and militancy. Skins tended to move in with the extreme right-wing movements in Germany, namely Michael Swierczek's National Offensive, Frank Huebner's German Alternative, The National Front, and Christian Worch's National List.

German authorities were originally either slow or reluctant to respond to the right-wing threats being posed by the Skinhead's hate movement and propaganda; however, in the last decade or so, German authorities have banned some of the neo-Nazi groups and confiscated their propaganda materials. Skinheads have traditionally not aligned themselves with any particular political party, as they view the parties as being part of the "system."

Skinheads also view imprisonment as a badge of honor. Evidence indicates that Skinheads are receiving a thorough indoctrination in neo-Nazi ideology at "comradeship evenings" held in prison. Much of this is provided by the Relief Agency for National Political Prisoners and their Dependants, a right-wing group that sends a steady stream of propaganda to incarcerated neo-Nazis and Skinheads.[32]

Germany in the Twenty-First Century

The unification of Germany, was one of the most unexpected turning points in Germany's modern history, brought with it doubts about a new Germany's ability to cope with the depression and despair suffered by its people in the former East Germany. By the end of 1997, there were growing signs in German cities of right-wing neo-Nazi groups (Skinheads) fostering hate campaigns against immigrants living in Germany. With most European communities lowering the barriers on movement between countries and with the fall of the Soviet Union, many thousands of ethnic groups surged westward for a "better life." What they found in Germany was a growing resentment, mainly by extreme right-wing groups, to the rising tide of ethnic groups seeking jobs in a struggling economy. Skinheads and others saw the immigrants as responsible for the high rate of unemployment and the economic conditions. In many cities, extremists took the law into their own hands and, in shows of nationalist strength, began abusing and intimidating immigrants.

By the spring of 1998, immigrants had virtually disappeared from some cities, having been frightened away by the fearsome onslaughts of neo-Nazism. No specific group or organized terror campaign is being sustained, although special police units are being utilized to break up obvious gangs of Skinheads. No one can predict how far—or if—Germany will regress toward a neo-Nazi influence, or whether this type of incident has been a mere pothole in the rough road to unification. What most observers are watching for from the German government is a signal that it fervently opposes the nationalist movements. With a growing number of incidents involving ethnic groups and neo-Nazi influences at various levels inside Germany's military, it is no surprise that there is a feeling of unease and terror in those who see the unsettling prospect of a rise in the nationalist movement yet again.

AL QAEDA IN GERMANY

Since 9-11, Germany has come to the realization that it has become not only a safe haven but also a recruiting country for radical dissident Muslim youths. Imams in Germany's mosques were calling for a jihad against the United States. Students from North African and Middle Eastern countries were studying in university campuses throughout the country. Evidence points to Germany as being a staging post for Islamic extremists wanting to gain access to North America via forged travel documents, either directly or through Canadian ports of entry. This is a practice that has been ongoing for more than two decades. Many questions still remain, one of the most baffling being, "Why did the intelligence communities fail to detect the planning and steps toward 9-11?" Undoubtedly a very difficult question, as we can now see that all the signs were there and the intelligence on certain individuals were available. Clearly, it simply was not recognized as significant or it was ignored. *The 9-11 Commission Report*, published in 2004, makes considerable mention of the involvement of the Hamburg cell and its growth and training in Afghanistan, its members' ability to move around Europe and the United States, and ultimately, its ability to plan and carry out, undetected, the largest terrorist event in recent history. A successful attack on the United States involving the members of the Hamburg cell would require complex planning and exceptional execution. *The 9-11 Commission Report* puts forward the following list, which it believed al Qaeda would have required to fulfill:

- Leaders who were able to evaluate, approve, and supervise the planning and direction of the operation.
- Communications sufficient to enable planning and direction of the operatives and those who would be helping them.
- A personnel system that could recruit candidates, vet them, indoctrinate them, and give them necessary training.
- An intelligence effort to gather required information and form assessments of enemy strengths and weaknesses.
- The ability to move people.
- The ability to raise and move the necessary funds.

The information on the planes operation presented in *The 9-11 Commission Report* shows that by the spring of 2000, al Qaeda was able to meet these requirements. By late May 2000, two operatives assigned to the planes operation were already in the United States. Three of the four Hamburg cell members would arrive soon after.

Intelligence gathering and covert activities by Western governments was not at Cold War levels, and, although the intelligence community and security services recognized the threat of al Qaeda, they undoubtedly underestimated the tactical capabilities of the group to strike deep into the heart of America. Germany had been more preoccupied with domestic issues and the revelation that planning for 9-11 had taken place within their country came as a surprise to most Germans. Two prominent members of the 9-11 hijackers, Mohammed Atta and Marwan Al-Shehhi, who are believed to have been the pilots that flew the aircraft into the two World Trade Center towers, spent a significant amount of time in Germany. Atta had studied at the Hamburg University for eight years; it appears that he attracted no suspicions from German authorities. He was not openly hostile and did not espouse radical or extreme Islamic views, at least not publicly. Since the fall of the Third Reich and Germany's rebuilding, the German government has been reluctant to interfere with individual rights and civil liberties. In Atta's case, subsequent investigations have revealed that he developed a small religious studies group that is now suspected of being a cover for his principal terrorist planning operations. In Germany, a religious freedom law forbids the government from banning or restricting any group that it recognizes as a religious group. Scientology is restricted under this law, as Germany has ruled that this is, in fact, a commercial enterprise, not a religion. As in the United States, German prosecutors must overcome a high standard of evidence to effect a prosecution. Germany's ability to gather and disseminate intelligence within its borders is also somewhat self-defeating. Law enforcement is decentralized, so police in one of Germany's sixteen states may not share information regularly with police in another region. Germany rarely conducts nationwide criminal investigations or passes information from international agencies to local police.[33]

The third pilot involved in the 9-11 attacks also spent considerable time in Germany. Ziad Zamir Jarrah was born in the infamous Bekka Valley in Lebanon, a stronghold of Hezbollah extremists. Jarrah and his immediate family were not religious fanatics by any means. His parents appeared genuinely shocked and surprised that their son would be involved in a suicide attack on the United States. Jarrah received a monthly allowance from his father that was more than adequate. However, Jarrah's involvement may have stemmed from his friendship with local radical Muslims in Aachen. Jarrah's transformation from an easygoing youth to an Islamic fanatic is puzzling to many. It appears that he drank alcohol and partied at college in Germany. His transformation to more radical ways evidently began around 1996 after he returned from a trip to Lebanon. He changed course in 1997 from dentistry to aircraft engineering for no specifically identified reason. At the same time, he was becoming more steeped in traditional Islamic ways. He grew a full beard and avidly read about jihad and debated the merits of Holy War with his friends. During the latter months of 1999, he told his girlfriend that he was planning to wage a jihad because there was no greater honor than to die for Allah. Radical Muslims in Aachen were involved in fund-raising through local mosques for the Hamas terror group to aid suicide missions in the Middle East.[34]

As part of the coalition against terrorism, Germany has also banned a network of radical Islamic groups centered on the Kaplan organization based in Cologne. German police raided some 200 residences in seven separate German states in connection with the ban and seized the headquarters of the Kaplan group. Metin Kaplan, the Caliph of Cologne, is serving a prison sentence for calling for the murder of a rival religious leader. German authorities have characterized the Kaplan group as being anti-Semitic and antidemocratic and have also banned Kaplan's associated foundation, the "Servants of Islam," as well as other groups totaling 1,100 members.[35]

Kaplan was extradited to Turkey in November 2004, but with his group's only 1,000-odd members, it was hardly able to influence the many Muslim immigrant workers in Germany. However, another more diverse group may well be a wolf in sheep's clothing. The Milli Görüs, which has a translation meaning of "National Vision," is the largest Muslim organization in Germany, with over 27,000 members. Its influence is felt within the tight-knit Muslim communities, particularly in the Turkish Muslim areas. German authorities believe that the group is the foreign wing for Islamist leader and former Turkish premier Necmettin Erbakan and that it secretly seeks to dismantle Germany's democratic structures. Milli Görüs, however, describes itself as an apolitical, unaffiliated lobby for the interests of Muslims living in Germany. German domestic intelligence believes that despite all the public posturing from Milli Görüs, it is apolitical and seeks to help Muslims to integrate into German society, but it is in fact, indoctrinating Muslim youth. In an August 2007 interview, Erbakan made the following statement:

> When we look at the map of the world, we see about 200 countries painted in colors, and we think that there are many races, religions, and nations. The fact is that for 300 years, all these [200 nations] have been controlled from one center only. This center is the racist, imperialist Zionism. Unless you make this correct diagnosis for the illness, you cannot find the cure to it. You will ask, 'What is this belief, this racist imperialism that destroys happiness in this world?'

'Do you know what the safety of Israel means?' It means that they will rule the 28 countries from Morocco to Indonesia. Since all the Crusades were organized by the Zionists…since it was our forefathers the Seljuks who stopped them, according to the Kabbala there should be no sovereign state in Anatolia. This is these people's [i.e. the Jews'] religion, their faith. You can't argue or negotiate with them. This is their religion, and it comes from the Kabbala.[36]

The activities of Milli Görüs have attracted the attention of Germany's Office for the Protection of the Constitution (BFV), one of three national intelligence services in Germany that is charged with gathering information on domestic as well as foreign extremist and terror groups. BFV considers Islamic terrorism poses the biggest security threat to Germany in modern times.[37] Islam is the third-largest religious denomination in Germany, but because it lacks a centralized structure like the Catholic and Protestant churches, it doesn't have the same rights and privileges as the Christian churches. Milli Görüs wants to be recognized as an Islamic church and, thus, unite the splintered Islamic community in Germany. The group has not been banned and neither has it been identified as being involved in crime and terrorism. The German intelligence agencies will, no doubt, continue to monitor the group's activities and development. According to a recent German report the fear within Germany is from Islamists who follow the model of jihad, or Holy War. Germans feel this is one of the most potent dangers to their country. The report also mentioned the militant Islamist Abu Mussab al Zarqawi, whose al Qaeda-affiliated, Jordanian-based al Tawhid group was accused of carrying out attacks on Jewish targets in Berlin and Düsseldorf. Jihadists continue to focus their efforts on attacks in European centers, and many use the justification that NATO countries are supporting and waging war in Afghanistan to legitimize their attacks. Germany has also become a fertile recruiting ground for homegrown converts to Islam to wage jihad. In late 2006, a man was spotted carrying out a surveillance operation on U.S. military installations in an around the city of Hanau. For almost a year German authorities kept the suspect under surveillance, which also led them to other conspirators. The Germans were convinced that an attack was being planned against a U.S. or British installation in Germany. The operation culminated in September 2007, when the German GSG-9 counterterror force raided a house in Oberschledorn and arrested the suspects who were planning to move a large quantity of hydrogen peroxide. The cell had been trained in Pakistan and had amassed almost 700 kilograms of chemicals to make explosives. On March 2, 2011, Arid Uka an Albanian Muslim boarded an American military bus carrying soldiers to the Frankfurt airport and opened fire, killing two and injuring an additional two soldiers who were on their way to Afghanistan. There are indications that Uka, an ethnic Albanian Muslim from Kosovo who was born and raised in Germany, had recently become radicalized and sought to carry out a terrorist attack against American forces in retaliation for the American presence in Afghanistan; his motivation remains unclear. Regardless of whether or not Uka is revealed to have been motivated by jihadist sympathies, small-scale attacks by individual Muslims against American and Western targets, of the type that Uka carried out, have been strongly encouraged by leading jihadist ideologues and on English-language jihadist forums for jihadist sympathizers in the West.

Incitement for jihadists in the West to engage in individually planned and executed attacks as well as attacks against American military targets around the world have been widespread in recent messages from al Qaeda leadership and posts and discussions on influential English-language jihadist forums. In an audio message released on February 27, 2011, al Qaeda second in command Ayman al-Zawahiri called for attacks against American targets in retaliation for alleged American support for despotic leaders in the Arab world. In the third audio message of his series "A Message of Hope and Glad Tidings to Our People in Egypt," Zawahiri incited Egyptians and Tunisians against the United States. The message was preceded by another audio message, released on February 24, 2011, in which Zawahiri exhorted followers to develop innovative methods for attacking Western targets.[38]

Islamic Jihad Union and German Mujahedeen

For Germany the growth of the Salafist movement may pose significant threat to its internal stability. Records of the numbers of Salafists in Germany range up to about 5,000. Those Germans who joined al Qaeda and IJU in Pakistan began their radical road in Salafist mosques. This is where they were radicalized and recruited. Visiting the al-Nur mosque in Berlin, the al-Quds mosque in Hamburg, or the multicultural house in Neu-Ulm was the first step toward jihad.

Like so many Western democracies, Germany is under threat because al Qaeda, IJU, and others aim at perpetrating attacks in Germany to force the German government to withdraw its troops from Afghanistan. A large group of radicals have now received their training and are returning to Europe to carry out lone-wolf attacks. The fear from a security perspective is a Mumbai-style attack happening on German soil. Official sources indicate over 200 Germans may have received training in bomb making and weapons training at camps in Pakistan and Afghanistan. The popular use of social media better defines the current activities of the German Mujahedeen (Taliban) providing a stream of propaganda. It is an offshoot of the IJU and formed in 2009 after an increasing number of Germans arrived at IJU in Mir Ali, North Waziristan. However, the organization never consisted of more than a dozen. Some were killed and some joined the IJU, with some returning to Germany. There remaining activists are likely situated in Berlin area.

Does al Qaeda want to strike Europe? YES. France and Belgium have banned the Burqa; Germany, the United Kingdom, and Italy all took part in Afghanistan occupation; Denmark and Sweden have insulted the prophet; and the Netherlands are home of Geert Wilders—the list of reasons for al Qaeda to attack the European Union countries is growing and so too is the number of terror recruits coming to Waziristan for training.

Under the Council of Europe Framework Decision of June 13, 2002, on combating terrorism, terrorist offences are international acts, which, given their nature or context, may seriously damage a country.

Terrorist offences are committed with the aim of

- Seriously intimidating a population or
- Unduly compelling a government or international organization to perform or abstain from performing and act or
- Seriously destabilizing or destroying fundamental political, constitutional, economic, or social structures of a country or international organization.

Terrorist offences include

- Attacks upon a person's life that may cause death.
- Attacks upon the physical integrity of a person.
- Kidnapping or hostage taking.

- Causing extensive destruction to a government or public facility, a transport system, an infrastructure facility, including an information system, a fixed platform located on the continental shelf, a public place or private property likely to endanger human life or result in major economic loss.
- Seizure of aircraft, ships, or other means of public or goods transport.
- The manufacture, acquisition, possession, transport, supply, or use of weapons, explosives, or nuclear, biological, or chemical weapons, as well as research into and development of biological and chemical weapons.
- The release of dangerous substances, or causing fires, floods or explosions, the effect of which is to endanger life.
- Interfering with or interrupting the supply of water, power, or any other fundamental natural resource, the effect of which is to endanger human life.
- Threatening to commit any of the acts listed above.[39]

The German government continues to target persons supporting terrorist networks, and this is exemplified in the 2011 conviction of the wife a jihadist. The German-Turkish wife of convicted terrorist Fritz Gelowicz was found guilty of collecting up to $4,000 for terrorist groups, the Islamic Jihad Union, the German Taliban Mujahedeen, and al Qaeda, between November 2009 and February 2010. She was also convicted of publishing propaganda texts on the Internet that solicited members for terrorist groups. German prosecutors had characterized the woman as a "fanatical militant" who labeled "infidels" as enemies of Islam and called for their "annihilation." Her husband had been arrested in 2007 while preparing 800 lbs of explosives to detonate at the German parliament as it voted on its NATO force in Afghanistan the following month; he was sentenced to twelve years in prison in March 2010.

ITALY

By 1954, under Mussolini, Italy was the most likely Western country to turn Communist. Following World War II and the formation of a democratically elected government in Italy, the opportunity naturally presented itself for the Communists to come to the fore. A strong, Communist-indoctrinated, left-wing group with some fairly imaginative goals to steer Italy onto a different path than that established by the allied powers rose up. As the new millennium arrived, the transnational terrorism from al Qaeda and its associated cells became a frustrating reality for the Italian government and security services. Terrorist plots would be planned and executed by foreign terror operatives residing in Italy.

Terrorism and Italy

The only significant terrorist movement to emerge from Italy has been the Red Brigade, which has its origins in the early 1970s and grew out of an established, left-wing political party, The Metropolitan Political Collective. They aimed to bring about a Communist revolution in Italy, which it believed would spread throughout Europe. At the other end of the spectrum was a smaller and little-known group, the Ordine Nuove (New Order), an extreme right-wing and Fascist movement. Like the Red Brigade, Ordine Nuove embarked on a campaign of terror to establish its goal of a strong Italian state, supported by a powerful Fascist structure. Throughout the 1970s, both groups used bombings and assassinations as their modus operandi, and it was not often evident which group was responsible for what specific attacks. Italy, like Germany, France, and Spain, is also contending with Islamist threats.

FIGURE 6-5 Map of Italy (Central Intelligence Agency, *The World Factbook, 2008*).

THE RED BRIGADE

The left-wing Red Brigade (RB), like its German compatriots in the RAF, had its origins on the Italian university campuses in the latter half of the 1960s. The group might be considered as a fledgling of the World War II Volante Rosse, formed during the campaign against Nazi Germany as a Communist resistance movement. It continued its campaigns until the end of 1949 and had ongoing links to the Italian Communist Party, no doubt spawning the next generation of left-wing extremists to emerge on the campuses of the 1960s.

After World War II, Italy moved toward a governing style modeled on the political and economic example of the United States. Between 1950 and 1962, the industrial growth and success of the Italian government lay in the hands of coalitions of political parties—the Republicans, Liberals, Social Democrats, and Christian Democrats, all apparently trying to move beyond the Fascist past. While exploiting the need for industrial growth and foreign trade, Italy had neglected the social structure of the country. The bubble burst in 1968 with a cultural-style revolution in the universities and schools and was quickly followed in 1969 with the worst union unrest in the industrialized north that Italy had ever experienced. The unions could not be placated and factories were seized and occupied by both workers and student demonstrators. Workers and management were intimidated and attacked. All of this became the fertile ground for the emerging RB.

The founding members of the RB, Renato Curcio and Margherita Cagol, came from the sociology department of Trent University.[40] They began to target the symbolic nature of the Italian state by attacking senior executives, politicians, and parts of Italian society perceived as being repressive by nature. RB did not burst onto the Italian scene but rather confined itself to incubation, largely in Milan's industrial heart. The period from 1969 to 1972 was a time of building, training, and testing of the RB's objectives. Minor fire bombings and destruction of property were the order of the period. Their support structure outside of Milan at this time was considerably weak. From 1972 to 1974, the RB entered a new phase of expanding to the adjacent areas of Turin and Genoa while experimenting in kidnapping and extortion. During this same time frame, Italian security forces were able to capture Renato Curcio after a gun battle in which his wife, Margherita Cagol, was killed. Observers predicted the imminent demise of the Red Brigade, but that was far from reality. The next generation of RB was on the scene and ready to continue the fight with the Italian government and society in general. The RB has, to some length, emulated the tactics laid out by Carlos Marighella in his *Mini Manual of the Urban Guerrilla*, published in 1969. Attention to detail and technical knowledge, as well as logistical and intelligence information, became a hallmark of the RB. Contained in the *Mini Manual* is Marighella's definition of assaults:

- Assault is the armed attack, which we make to expropriate funds, liberate prisoners, and capture explosives, machine guns, and other types of arms and ammunition.
- Assaults can take place in broad daylight or at night.
- Daytime assaults are made when the objective cannot be achieved at any other hour, as, for example, the transport of money by the banks, which is not done at night.
- Night assault is usually the most advantageous to the urban guerrilla. The ideal is for all assaults to take place at night when conditions for a surprise attack are most favorable and the darkness facilitates flight and hides the identity of the participants. The urban guerrilla must prepare himself, nevertheless, to act under all conditions, daytime as well as nighttime.

The RB perfected the art of kidnapping throughout the 1970s. Mainly symbolic in its action, the group did go beyond kidnapping prominent business personages when it kidnapped Genoa's assistant attorney general, Mario Sossi. They demanded the release of RB prisoners from jail and, in particular, Renato Curcio. Sossi was held captive for a month before his release. The concessions received from the government were the promised release of RB members. However, the attorney general would not permit the release, which had been bargained under duress.[41] The RB also believed that the concessions they received had sufficiently undermined the state. On June 8, 1974, the RB struck down Genoa's Attorney General Francesco Coco in an armed ambush, which had a twofold effect. The first was a confirmation of the RB's retaliatory ability against the figure that had blocked the group's earlier attempts to free its colleagues; and, the second was that RB's threats to selected jurors in the Turin trial of Curcio led to a delay in the trial. Further attacks on members of the bar association had the desired effect of delaying the trial. The intimidating effect of terrorism was working well.

RB Structure

The RB utilized the tried-and-tested cell structure to prevent infiltration and detection. Working from large industrial areas, it had widespread support among the working classes, who provided logistical support to the group.

At its peak it is believed there were more than 500 active members, with a support structure possibly in the thousands. It seems likely that by the last decade of the twentieth century, the RB was reduced down to around fifty active members.

As the twenty-first century dawned, it was not clear that the movement had not undergone resurgence as in late 2003 more than 200 pounds of high explosives and detonators were discovered during a police raid of a known RB house. The police discovered documents claiming responsibility for several attacks including the assassination of a government consultant in 2002. Some 140 of the original RB activists are still sought by Italy, many thought to be living in France.

With its Communist Marxist/Leninist ideology, its early support would have come from the Soviet Union, which in the Cold War years would have provided support for such organizations operating in the West.

Kidnapping

Italian terrorists perfected the art of kidnapping and, in fact, enhanced it. It enabled corporations to get kidnap insurance, turning the crime into a growth industry. This shortsighted provision made it possible for kidnappers to get their money and, for those who were kidnapped, to be released. The RB, on the other hand, kidnapped for different reasons and rarely for money. Two kidnappings stand out for their sheer audaciousness and the brutality with which they ended. These two kidnappings were significant watersheds for the RB. The first, which resulted in nothing more than the symbolic execution of the president-elect, Aldo Moro, was to turn public opinion against the RB. Several communiqués were issued prior to his murder, and the RB made every effort to exploit the media coverage of this atrocity. During Aldo Moro's captivity, the RB showed its strength of purpose and its ability to continue with other operations and carried out two murders and six shootings in Rome, Turin, Milan, and Genoa, in spite of the massive police search and crackdown on the RB and any known members.[42] It was a significant demonstration of the RB's ability to conduct several simultaneous operations.

The second was the release of General James Dozier, the Italian police force's first successful rescue of a kidnap victim from the RB. By the mid-1980s, the number of terrorist incidents committed by RB was down significantly, following a decline in support from the left. By the mid-1990s, RB was distributing communiqués to indicate a cessation of all operations.

GAP AND NAP

Two other groups on the fringes of the Italian terrorism scene in the 1970s modeled themselves on the same style of clandestine activities and systematic violence as the RB. The Partisan Action Group (GAP) originated in Milan at about the same time (1969) as the RB. Their inception is believed to have involved the wealthy Italian publisher Giangiacomo Feltrinelli, who was the group's paymaster and sponsor. Feltrinelli believed that right-wing extremism was on the rise and a return to Fascism was a real possibility. He believed that the only way to confront the risk was to form an urban guerrilla movement. His approach was to form the GAP, a resistance/partisan movement modeled on the resistance fighters of World War II. This model differed from that of the RB, which probably accounts for the nonmerging of the groups in the early days.[43] In the days of student and union unrest, which had also spread to Italy's prison system, another movement sprang up. The Armed Proletarian Nuclei (NAP) came to life from a left-wing prison movement—the Movement of Proletarian Prisoners and the Ongoing Struggle (Lotta Continua).[44] Unlike the RB, this group gained little acknowledgment. Coming from the ranks of Naples prison inmates, the membership immediately began the "armed struggle," financing its movement primarily by robbing banks.

Its main base of operation started in Naples and spread to Rome. The group used explosives to bomb prisons and also attacked prison officials. Unlike the RB, all NAP members were easily traceable from their criminal records. Their modus operandi, coupled with their lack of attention to their own security, resulted in numerous arrests. With no ideological base, NAP'S recruitment of criminal elements led to its eventual downfall. The remainder of the group's membership joined the ranks of the RB. Throughout the terror campaigns, the majority of NAP targets were either political or paramilitary by nature. Indiscriminate attacks against the Italian populace were uncommon.

The Mancino Law

In 1993, the Italian government issued Decree No. 122 as an emergency measure to control, restrict, and limit attacks of a racial nature. Two months later, it was transformed into Law No. 205 by the then interior minister Nicola Mancino. The law enabled the state to prosecute individuals for "incitement to violence for a broad range of hate crimes" that included the use of symbols of hate.[45] Hundreds of youths have been charged under this legislation. Two Italian names have become associated with hate crimes in Italy: Maurizio Boccacci, a Skinhead organizer, and Dr. Sergio Gozzoli, an outspoken anti-Semite and a Holocaust denier.

Skinhead Organizations

The Italian Skinheads, following the example of the Germans, had by the early 1990s, organized themselves under the leadership of the Movimento Politico Occidentale (MPO, Political Movement of the West), founded by Maurizio Boccacci and headquartered in Rome. The group had links to other far-right Skinhead groups in France, Germany, and Great Britain. A notable incident that was bound to become a flash point was the painting of yellow stars on more than 100 Jewish businesses and shops in Rome. Jews attacked MPO skins as a result. The MPO has been banned by the government but has since renamed itself with the Fascist trappings of "I Camerati," a term used by Mussolini to address his fascist followers.[46]

In its effort to become more politically acceptable, delegates at a convention of the neo-Fascist Movimento Sociale Italiano (MSI, Italian Social Movement) voted to move toward the mainstream political parties and to dissolve the MSI. They merged with Alleanza Nazionale (National Alliance), and it was hoped this would make the overall far-right movement more respectable. The delegates also agreed on a strong position against anti-Semitism. The extremists in the organization—many of them Skinheads—broke away from the alliance and reestablished their own version of the MSI.

Ideology

The Italian Skinhead ideology and that of the far-right extremists echo the sentiments of a past generation of neo-Fascists. Their ideology is loosely based:[47]

- The denial of Nazi genocide against the Jews; "historical revisionism."
- Fear and hatred of foreigners, based on the myths of Aryan purity and supremacy.
- The fear and demonization of the Jews in a context of a sinister plot to rule the world.

With the breakdown of the symbolic, and all-too-real, Berlin Wall, the influx of Russian and Eastern nationals to the west—particularly Germany and Italy—has fueled the far right into action.

International Terrorism

Italy has been no stranger to acts of terrorism, with the result that post-9-11 Italy, with its excellent police and intelligence services, has not only aided the U.S.-led War on Terror with its strong military contributions, but has had successes in tracking down and arresting suspected al Qaeda cells. International terrorism requires funding, and in the weeks after 9-11, the Italian government established the Financial Security Committee. This group comprised senior ministry officials from finance, justice, and foreign affairs, whose aim was to stem the flow of funding to terrorist groups in Europe. Even prior to 9-11, Italian security services had targeted such institutions as the Islamic Cultural Center in Milan because they suspected that an al Qaeda lieutenant, Sami Ben Khemais Essid, who had spent time training as a terrorist recruiter in Afghanistan, was active in Italy. The Italians were monitoring the Cultural Center to discover evidence of traffic in arms and explosives and discovered that Ben Khemais was, in fact, in contact with other extreme terrorist groups throughout Europe.

Among those seen at the Cultural Center were terrorists associated with the New York World Trade Center bombing in 1993 and the bombings of the U.S. embassies in Tanzania and Kenya in 1998. The apparent ease with which international terror groups, and particularly those associated with Osama bin Laden, have been able to operate with comparative freedom in Italy is a lesson that security services are now beginning to appreciate. Ben Khemais was sentenced to eight years in prison for his activities. His activities also give us an insight to what may be al Qaeda's next style of terror attack. During their investigation, Italian police intercepted Khemais conversation with another terrorist, which detailed the use of a deadly poison gas attack. Al Qaeda sympathizers and Euro converts to radical Islam will continue to attempt attacks. With a vast population of immigrant workers throughout Europe and with no solid border defenses, the movement between countries by al Qaeda-inspired cells will be a challenge for the foreseeable future. The presence of extreme thinking imams has also been at issue for Germany as it has been for the British authorities. In June 2003, the imam of the Rome mosque began inciting his own congregation to jihad in much the same manner as has taken place at London's Finsbury Park Mosque.

GREECE AND TURKEY

Terrorism is no stranger to these two countries; however, the actions of respective indigenous terrorist groups are restricted for the most part to actions within their countries, rather than out in the international arena. Both countries have had their own regional differences over the years and at times have come close to all-out war—both countries are members of NATO. Their differences centered on territorial claims to a group of islands in Aegean Sea and the divided status of Cyprus, occupied by both Greeks and Turks. Turkey aspired to join the European Union, and its application was actually supported by the Greek government. Their belief being that if Turkey could change its attitude and be accepted into "Europe," it would no longer pose a threat to Greece; however, Turkey's likelihood of joining all but vanished when Cyprus joined the EU in 2004 and with its veto could effectively prevent Turkey from joining. The two are not currently in open conflict and that is probably because of two eastern bloc countries joining the European Union, Bulgaria and Romania. This means that Greece now has a land link to the rest of "Europe" without worrying about a hostile Turkey. To cement a lasting peace between them, the Greek Prime Minister Costas Karamanlis visited Turkey on officially in January 2008—the first visit by a Greek minister to Turkey in almost fifty years.

GREECE

Revolutionary Organization November 17

After twenty-eight years, twenty-three assassinations, 345 bombings, and no arrests, the rest of the West viewed the Greek attitude and its inability to prevent and deter terrorism with a modicum of cynicism. The EU placed considerable pressure on the Greek government for the security of the Olympic Games, held in Athens in 2004. Reacting to fears that Greek authorities could not prevent another Olympic Games attack, the Greek government arrested almost 75 percent of the believed membership of the November 17 group. In December 2003, fifteen members were convicted and sentenced: Five members received life sentences, and imposed sentences on the others totaled 244 years.

The November 17 group had operated in Greece with almost total immunity until the arrests and convictions in 2003. Police and security services had been unable, or unwilling, to identify or arrest any members of November 17. This group of left-wing extremists is considered Marxist-Leninist, anti-imperialist, anti-United States, anti-Europe, and anti-NATO. Their first terrorist action was the assassination of U.S. diplomat, Richard Welsh, in 1975. They have their origins in the university campuses of Greece, much like other left-wing groups in the 1970s. The group's name, November 17, commemorates the date of the attack on the students, NTUA (National Technical University of Athens), on November 17, 1975. Greek military and police, under the control of the ruling colonels, killed several student activists and captured and tortured many more.

FIGURE 6-6   Map of Greece (Central Intelligence Agency, *The World Factbook, 2008*).

The Greek Military Junta was overthrown a few short months after the university incident. November 17's actual membership number is not known, but it can be assumed that it is a small group, with approximately twenty to thirty hard-core members. It did not participate in low-level operations to test its own ability; rather, it burst onto the world stage with a high-visibility terrorist attack on a U.S. diplomat.

In its early years, they committed relatively few attacks; in fact, between 1975 and 1985, November 17 carried out only six attacks. Perhaps the length of time between operations was relative to the fact that police arrested no one. One of its earliest attacks was on the CIA station chief Richard Welsh, who was shot outside his Athens residence several weeks after his identity had been published in the press.

The failure to track down November 17 was a sad reflection on the internal workings of the Greek government and its security services. Over the last twenty years, the group has carried out 345 bombings, resulting in 61 deaths and 250 injuries. Until 2003, no November 17 terrorist had ever been arrested and charged with offenses in connection with those incidents.

They did expand operations after 1985 and, by 1990, had carried out about forty attacks including bombings, assassinations, and shootings, often targeting U.S. military personnel stationed at NATO bases in Greece, Greek industrialists, and politicians. They have been critical of the Greek government for its position in respect to U.S./NATO bases in Greece as well as Greece's membership of the EEC (European Economic Community). The largest number of attacks carried out by the group was directed at internal targets and foreign targets residing on Greek soil. To ensure that no other group claimed responsibility for November 17's terror acts, the group used handguns of the same caliber in consecutive attacks against Greek targets.

They viewed themselves as the people's vanguard and protector ... to lead the working class in an armed struggle. It makes its point with ideological communiqués and actions in support of its cause. Attacks are geared to making the subverted classes more abstractly aware of what is taking place in the political and economic processes in the country. The group fervently holds the United States responsible for complicity with Turkey over the Cyprus crisis, thus making the United States a legitimate military target in its war for the oppressed. Their early attacks were primarily symbolic; the first was against the United States, and subsequent attacks were against the Greek police hierarchy and representatives of the Greek Military Junta. An example of the group's hatred toward the United States can be seen from the content of one of the November 17 communiqués: "The American military forces in our country are an occupation force, and we are going to hit anybody who is a member of it or an agent of its secret services. These actions are going to continue and are going to increase until the last Turkish soldier leaves Cyprus and the last American soldier leaves our country."[48]

In Greece's internal struggle with domestic terrorism, the break for Greek authorities came in 2002, with a botched bombing attack that seriously injured a terrorist bomber. As strange as this may seem, this was the first November 17 terror suspect that Greek authorities have been able to apprehend. The bomber in this instance was Savas Xiros, who was carrying a device that detonated prematurely as he approached the ticket office of a hydrofoil company in Piraeus. In the explosion, Xiros lost a hand and was blinded. The ensuing investigation found a 38 Smith and Wesson revolver in his possession, which had never been fired, but its rightful owner was a Greek police officer who was killed in a 1984 robbery. The bomber's fingerprints also matched those on the getaway car used in the assassination of a British/Greek tycoon. Greek police have had, and continue to have, a mutual assistance program with both the British police and the U.S. FBI as a result of the Greek government's signing of a joint memorandum on combating crime.

Espanastatikos Laikos Agonas (ELA)

The second-most destructive group operating on Greek soil, Espanastatikos Laikos Agonas (ELA, Revolutionary Peoples Struggle), is also committed to the overthrow of the Greek system and is a violent Marxist-Leninist organization. That is where any similarity between it and November 17 probably ends. It also grew out of the university campuses of the 1960s and early 1970s. Its fundamental aims and philosophy were directed at the state, imperialism, and capitalism. Most, if not all, of its targets for terror were of a symbolic nature. Unlike the secretive nature of November 17, which seeks to communicate its positions via communiqués or e-mail, ELA actually utilizes and operates an underground newspaper to forward its aims and political viewpoint. In May 1990, ELA announced that it had merged with another left-wing group, the revolutionary organization May 1. Up to this point the strategy of the ELA had been to avoid death and injury to Greeks as well as foreigners on Greek soil. It had conducted a low-level style of campaign and had not ventured into the more dangerous world of remotely detonated bombs. A communiqué to the Greek government in 1993 appeared to be the turning point in ELA's violent methods in its dealings with the state. It perceived all police officers to be the "local representatives of the CIA."[49]

    On September 19, 1994, the ELA remotely detonated a bomb alongside a police bus, killing one officer and injuring ten others, as well as a passerby. The ELA gave no warnings, which had previously been a signature for the group. Detonating the bomb without prior warning signaled a new and more virulent strain in Greek terrorist behavior. Successive and continuous failures by the Greek government to effect any cohesive response to domestic terror has allowed the organizations to continue to operate with impunity. While neighboring countries in Europe, Germany, Italy, France, and Belgium, had, for the most part, decisively dealt with left-wing violence and terrorist threats with a strong and dedicated response force established by powerful political mandate, it seemed to be lacking in Greece until 2001.

    Much of the blame for the lackluster and feeble efforts of the Greek police must rest on the shoulders of those in political circles. The Pasok Party had held onto the reins of power in Greece for the last two decades, up until the 2004 elections when their popularity had waned. The Conservative New Democracy Party had an easy victory in the 2004 general elections.

Revolutionary Cells/Revolutionary Nuclei (RN)

Revolutionary Cells, also known as Revolutionary Nuclei, has its beginnings from a wide spectrum of anti-NATO, anti-United States, and anti-European Union left-wing groups in the mid-1990s. The group is believed to be the successor to the ELA. ELA has not been credited with any attacks since 1995, and many believe that RN (from the manner and style of its communiqués showing much of the same style as used by ELA) has now taken its place. RN's attacks in the 1990s were considered low level and were aimed mainly at companies that had NATO defense contracts as well as Greek government buildings. The RN has been most active in the Athens area and has also targeted European banks. The size of this terror group is believed to be relatively small, drawing support mainly from the Greek militant left.

Minor Terrorist Groups

The number of terrorist actions in Greece increased in 1998, not only against the state but also aimed at Jewish and anti-Semitic groups, foreigners, as well as politicians. The source of the terror appears to be previously unheard-of organizations operating in Greece. Firebombing has been the hallmark of the attacks, which have been aimed at vehicles and buildings. The government of Greece has indicated that these attacks are coming from various quarters—the New Group of Satanists, the Children of November, Anarchist Street Patrol, and Conscientious Arsonists, all previously unknown before 1998. With the ineptitude of the Greek security services already a well-established fact, only time will tell if their newly formed special task force of more than 1,000 undercover police officers will be effective. As Greece depends heavily on its tourist trade for much-valued foreign currency, this style of attack, which seems so indiscriminate, will do a lot to drive that trade elsewhere.

CYPRUS

Situated in the Eastern Mediterranean Sea, this small island has a population of some 650,000 people and consists of 78 percent Greek-Cypriots, 18 percent Turkish-Cypriots, and 4 percent Maronite and Latin-Cypriots. The Turks and Greeks have lived together on the island for the last five centuries, and mosques and churches can be found almost side by side in many communities.

National Organization of Cypriot Combatants (EOKA)

Cyprus had long been under the control of the British Empire, which by the 1950s was well into its decline. The vast majorities of Cypriots were of Greek origin and, in the 1950s, were under the leadership of the Greek Cypriot Archbishop Makarios. Similar to the operations of the Stern Gang in Palestine, the **National Organization of Cypriot Combatants (EOKA)** terrorist organization and its followers began to strike at the occupying influences of Great Britain. EOKA was established in 1954 as an underground movement with the blessing and approval of Makarios. The revolt began in earnest with the bombing of the Cyprus Broadcasting Station on April 1, 1955. The British government had declared a state of emergency on the island and the Archbishop went into exile in the Seychelles. Makarios returned to Cyprus in 1959 and was elected president of the Cyprus Republic; the Founding Agreements made Turkey, Greece, and Great Britain "guarantor states" for Cyprus. Both the Turkish and Greek communities reached an agreement on a constitution for Cyprus, resulting in a Greek-Turkish Republic. Great Britain retained sovereignty over two military bases on the island. Within three years, Archbishop Makarios was preparing constitutional changes that would abrogate the power-sharing agreements that were contrary to the Constitution. The resulting intercommunal violence was to have a lasting effect on the island.

On July 20, 1974, Turkey invaded the island to "protect" the minority Turkish-Cypriot community. The international community quickly condemned the action. UN Resolution 353, adopted on the day of the invasion, called for all states to respect "the sovereignty, independence and territorial integrity of the Republic of Cyprus." It further demanded an immediate end to foreign military intervention in the Republic of Cyprus. Turkey ignored the United Nations and the international community and seized control of at least one-third of the Republic's territory and since then has engaged in a type of terrorism that we now refer to as "ethnic cleansing." More than 1,600 Greek Cypriots are still unaccounted for, following the invasion, and more than 20,000 lost their homes and possessions. This was a constant and festering sore for the November 17 terrorist group, which continued to blame the United States for failing to act on behalf of the Greek Cypriots. Turkish forces enforced a partition of the island, and Turkish Cypriots fled to the north into Turkish-occupied Cyprus, while Greek Cypriots fled south to the Greek side of the line. Since the 1970s, there has been little terrorist activity and plenty of political posturing with both Greece and Turkey claiming their side of the island as the legitimate Republic of Cyprus. In December 2004, Turkey agreed that it would recognize Greek Cyprus as a European Union (EU) member; however, the Turkish prime minister warned the EU that the Cyprus problem must be solved justly for both sides.

TURKEY

The history of the Turkish Ottoman Empire stretches back to when the Ottoman Turks invaded and captured Constantinople in 1453, bringing an end to the Byzantine Empire. The Ottoman Empire stretched across Eastern Europe and into regions of the Middle East, as we know it today. It stretched as far south as the western reaches of Saudi Arabia and to Yemen at the southern end of the Red Sea. Its conquests stretched through North Africa, from Cairo in the east and Algiers in the west. By the dawning of the eighteenth century, the Turkish Empire was commonly termed "the Sick Man of Europe" and was beginning to lose its huge territorial gains of the previous centuries. The empire lost Algeria to French rule in 1830, and by the end of 1880, Great Britain had taken control of Cyprus and Egypt. France seized Tunisia in 1881. With its empire crumbling, the Turks had to contend with disruptions on the home front as well, ruled by the dictatorship of Sultan Abdul-Hamid II. His rule was one of fear and violent repression of religious groups and stimulated the first covert organization set up to oppose the dictator. The Young Turks, as they were known, were dissatisfied students and disaffected military personnel opposed to Hamid. The group staged a successful coup in 1908 with the aim of restoring democracy to Turkey. The replacement for Abdul-Hamid was his brother, Mohammad V. The Young Turks had envisioned returning the Ottoman Empire to its former greatness; however, the populace was less concerned with aspirations toward empire building and more concerned with its own democratic rights and freedoms. With the empire crumbling, Turkey entered World War I on the side of Germany in the hopes that it would win back much of its losses of the past half century.

FIGURE 6-7   Map of Turkey (Central Intelligence Agency, *The World Factbook, 2008*).

Kemal Ataturk

As has been witnessed throughout history, many inspirational freedom fighters and military heroes with nationalist aspirations have risen to take control over and to form popular governments. Mustafa Kemal was one such leader. Kemal's origins in the Turkish military and his exploits as a natural leader of men brought him to the forefront of politics in Turkey. He formed the provisional government in 1920 after the invasion of the country by forces from Britain, France, and Greece. The Ottoman government was unable to protect the country, so the country turned to its nationalist leader, Kemal. The Sultan's powers weakened and the nationalists grew stronger and were able to forcibly evict the Greeks from Turkish soil. Turkey today is formed around the boundaries outlined in the Treaty of Lausanne signed by the nationalists in 1923. The word "Ataturk" is the surname given to Kemal and means "Father of the Turks."[50]

Separating religion from state has been a hallmark of Turkish politics, and Atatürk nearly removed Islam from public life in the period 1923–1938. Over the decades, however, Islamists fought back, and by the 1970s, they formed part of a ruling coalition; in 1996–1997, they even headed a government. They took power following the elections of 2002, when winning a third of the vote secured two-thirds of the parliamentary seats. Ruling with caution and competence, they got nearly half the vote in 2007, at which point their gloves came off and the bullying began, from a wildly excessive fine levied against a media critic to hare-brained conspiracy theories against the armed forces. The ruling party handily won the 2011 elections returning Recep Erdogan who began his politics as an Islamist in the 1990s, and under his tenure, the once all-powerful military has yielded to civilian politicians.[51] That Turkey is close not only in proximity but also in step with Iran is disquieting—Turkey is showing signs of moving along the same ghastly path as Iran—introducing strict adherence to Sharia law. In the coming years, Turkey may pose a significant threat to peace in the region.

Revolutionary Left (Dev Sol)

A left-wing Marxist group that has its origins in the Turkish Peoples Liberation Army split off in the late 1970s to form **Dev Sol**. This group is vehemently anti-NATO and anti-United States. The aims of this group are to foster an uprising or popular national revolution among the Turkish working classes. The group is financed primarily from armed robberies and extortion from businesses carried out in Turkey.

During the 1980s, the group restricted its area of operation to the domestic scene, mainly in Izmir, Istanbul, and Ankara. With the Middle East crisis and the Desert Storm Operation against Iraq, the group began attacks on the U.S. military personnel. The group launched a rocket attack at the U.S. Consulate in Istanbul in 1992. Since the early 1980s, the group has suffered from internal factional fighting and has carried out limited operations at home. From the training perspective, it is believed that the membership, which is considered to number several hundred, received training and indoctrination at radical Palestinian camps. By the end of 1998, this group was not particularly active in Turkey, but there are indications that it is beginning to resurface and may threaten U.S. commercial interests and Turkish government figures.

Kurdistan Workers Party (PKK)

The leadership and organization of the Kurdistan Workers Party originated from the student movement at Ankara University. Abdullah Ocalan, the leader—now behind bars in Ankara but still the leader—set up the organization with the specific aim of liberating the Kurds. Ocalan was considerably brutal in his methods and used his version of terrorism on his own followers and fellow Kurds. By executing the dissenters, any dissent in the group was put down. It is believed that Ocalan killed more than 10,000 Kurds during the 1980s. His actions had some sobering effects on the Kurdish people—they showed them that PKK was strong and that the people should side with PKK in the struggle for freedom from Turkey. Any failure to actively support the movement was perceived as siding with the Turks. Operating in southeastern Turkey, this Kurdish terror group seeks to set up a Kurdish state fashioned on Marxist lines. Mainly composed of Turkish Kurds, PKK has been in operation since 1974.

Large numbers of Turks migrated to Germany during the last half century, and this, has added to the financial viability of the PKK, an organization responsible for the death of at least 45,000 people since 1984. Turkey, home to 12 million Kurds; the neighboring countries of Iraq, Syria, and Iran have substantial but smaller Kurdish populations. To finance operations, PKK uses a variety of tried-and-tested methods. It is involved in the lucrative trade in illegal immigrants from Iraq into European centers. PKK also controls a lucrative portion of the drug traffic from the East into Europe. Its other levels of fund-raising include extortion from Kurds residing in France, Germany, Belgium, and Romania. PKK also receives aid from state sponsors, such as Iran and Syria. From Syria's perspective, the destabilization of the Turkish regime plays an important economic role.

It had been felt that the group was trying to become more mainstream politically, and has reformed itself with name changes—from the Kurdistan Freedom and Democracy Congress (KADEK) in 2000, and then to the People's Congress of Kurdistan (KONGRA-GEL). From a wider viewpoint, Turkey's support for the U.S. War on Terror has not endeared it to the Syrian regime, nor has its support of Israel. As the War on Terror continued, PKK was declared a "terrorist organization" by the European Union in May 2002. PKK continues to receive support from Iran and also maintains bases in the Bekka Valley, Lebanon. Abdullah Ocalan, imprisoned under sentence of death in a Turkish prison, declared in 2000 that his group, the PKK, which has for so long sought an independent Kurdish state through violent struggle, had changed its stance and would now seek, through a political campaign, only guarantees of Kurdish political, economic, social, and cultural rights in a democratic Turkey. PKK membership, which probably ran to more than 5,000 in 1999 at the time of Ocalan's capture, was diminished down to around 1,000, with Kurdish fighters moving to neighboring Iraq following the U.S. invasion there. Small pockets of PKK members, who had by spring of 2005 changed the name back to PKK from KONGRA-GEL, became active in southeastern Turkey. With the United States occupied in Iraq and Turkey acting a role of neutrality in the region, the United States was faced with Iraqi Kurds that actually supported the invasion. The Kurds' designs for an autonomous region adjacent to the Turkish border area were a matter of national security for Turkey. The United States most certainly wanted to protect the Kurds against any aggression from Turkey's military in the border region. The fact remains that the Kurds have been sheltering PKK separatists.

PKK launched its first attacks in 1984: the twenty-eight-year conflict has caused about 45,000 casualties. However, the turmoil caused by Operation Iraqi Freedom in 2003 provided a safe environment for PKK to regroup and reorganize. Since then, it has gained new strength and power—extending its network on European soil, creating broadcasting platforms for propaganda purposes, and securing new means of funding. In 2010, it launched an impressive number of effective attacks against Turkish troops, infrastructures, and cities. At the peak of its eight-month-long campaign, PKK declared a unilateral cease-fire at the beginning of Ramadan, subsequently extending it until 2011's Turkish general elections. The cease-fire has been mainly respected by PKK. By all accounts 2010 was a successful year for the PKK, with an audacious attack on the Iskenderun Naval base on the Mediterranean Sea, 30 miles from the Syrian border. This attack location was a significant distance from their usual areas of operation. With their proximity to Iraq it came as no surprise that they perfected the use of IED's against military patrols with over a dozen such attacks. PKK also began attacking strategic infrastructures such as gas and oil pipelines. They carried out one attack on the Kirkuk-Ceyhan pipeline, carrying crude oil from Iraq to Turkey followed by the Tabriz-Ankara pipeline, which transports natural gas from Iran to Turkey. Although the attacks caused minor damage and inconvenience, the intent of the attacks may have been to embarrass Turkish efforts to become an energy hub within the EU-funded Nabucco project. The Nabucco consortium comprises leading European energy companies from Austria, Hungary, Germany, Bulgaria, Romania, and Turkey.

Of broader concern will be Turkey's plan to develop nuclear plants and its ability to protect them. The pipeline will carry 31 billion cubic meters of gas per year, but this maximum capacity will only be reached in 2018.

Turkish Hezbollah

The Turkish Hezbollah should not be confused with Hezbollah in Lebanon as it has no known alliance with or connection to that organization. The group established its name in 2004 more or less as a pseudonym while defending propaganda around its terror campaigns.

The group was founded in the 1980s by student activists of Kurdish origins and led by Hüseyin Velioğlu. In the early 1908s, members traveled to Iran and were supported by elements of the Iranian government and learned their terror trade that way. There is no evidence to suggest that the Iranians used Hezbollah as its proxy for operations in Turkey. In fact, Velioğlu appears to have run the organization as a highly centralized autocracy, making every decision himself and insisting that his subordinates present him with detailed reports on all of their activities.

During the late 1980s and early 1990s, Turkish authorities ignored the organization's propaganda activities in the Kurdish areas of southeastern Turkey. At the time, the first insurgency of the Kurdistan Workers Party was at its height and the Turkish security forces appear to have regarded the propagation of any form of Islam as providing an ideological bulwark against the PKK's atheistic Marxism. They did not react when Velioğlu decided to initiate the jihad by targeting rival organizations in the region, starting with the PKK. In the early 1990s, Hezbollah is estimated to have killed over 400 PKK militants and played an important role in preventing the organization from supplementing its rural insurgency by establishing an effective urban cell network in southeastern Turkey. Many mainstream Turks have long believed the Turkish Hezbollah to be an instrument of the state that was being used as its clandestine security force to tackle PKK[52].

TERRORIST ATTACK BRIEF

Terrorist Group: PKK (Kurdistan Workers' Party)

Case Facts: A convoy carrying military personnel was targeted by PPK—a fragmentation grenade was remotely detonated killing five and injuring a further eleven on the bus.

Investigation: The Turkish authorities had been expecting a ramp up in PKK activities in the Turkish cities. As a result of the increase in insurgent attacks, the government has realigned its intelligence service to better combat the threats that seem to be escalating with PKK. The PKK attacks are mostly targeted at the military and police units and also against Kurds living in Turkey who PKK claim are collaborating with the authorities.

FIGURE 6-8 Bombing—Turkey—June 22, 2010.

Hezbollah had a three-stage phase to their overall plans:

- Phase 1: Communication—period of propaganda and indoctrination
- Phase 2: Community—establishing a popular base within society
- Phase 3: Jihad—overthrow of the secular government and establishment of an Islamic state

After a series of raids on Hezbollah safe houses in southeastern Turkey in 1999, Velioğlu and the rest of the organization's leadership relocated to Istanbul. On January 17, 2000, Velioğlu was killed during a police raid on a Turkish safe house in Beykoz, a suburb on the Asian shore of Istanbul.[53]

Assassination has been Hezbollah's most common tactic, usually involving a daylight attack, often by pairs of young assassins using pistols of Eastern European manufacture.[54] The numbers killed in such attacks between 1992 and 1995 amount to over 1,000. Not only did Hezbollah attack the PKK, but by the end of the last decade it was targeting specific senior security officials who were responsible for arresting Hezbollah members. Hezbollah, apart from its normal tactic of assassination, had also resorted to extreme levels of torture, including burning and burying its targets while they were still alive. Turkey continues to view PKK as a threat far greater than Hezbollah; however, a crackdown did eventually materialize and more than 1,000 Hezbollah members have been arrested. In concluding the future of terrorism in Turkey, the answers to its spread lie clearly with the government and its ability to improve the social-economic well-being of young Turkish Islamists. In January 2011, Turkish Hezbollah members were released from custody following a new law that limited the term of detention to ten years. Eighteen were released from custody after having been arrested following the mutilation assignation of Kurds in the south back in 2000.

Armenian Terrorism

Like the Kurds, the ethnic Armenians of northeastern Turkey have, since 1974, been fighting for their own homeland and autonomy in the region. Two terror groups have come to the fore: the Armenian Secret Army for the Liberation of Armenia (ASALA) and the Justice Commandos of the Armenian Genocide. Both groups have targeted diplomats from Turkey in Europe and the United States as part of their terror campaign. Their attacks became more violent when they started to detonate bombs at airports in the 1980s. They set off a bomb at Orly Airport in France adjacent to the Turkish Airlines check-in counters, killing ten and wounding more than seventy in the process. The leader of ASALA, Hagop Hagopian, was shot to death on an Athens street in 1988, and since then the group has been silent.[55]

The Nationalist Threat

The Turkish Revenge Brigade is a previously unknown group that sprang up in 1998, in opposition to Kurdish movements. Considered to be ultranationalist, the group has targeted Kurdish and left-wing journalists who support the Kurdish movement. In May 1998, two members of the group attempted to assassinate a leading Turkish human rights activist, Akin Birdal. The motive for the attack is uncertain, but the head of the Human Rights Association claimed at the time that Birdal had received prior death threats and had asked for protection from the government, but to no avail. How the nationalist movement will develop and who is backing and financing its operations is unclear. No doubt, previous reports of Turkish death squads and their involvement earlier in the decade come back into question.

AL QAEDA IN TURKEY

Al Qaeda's presence in Turkey was likely a foregone conclusion after U.S. and British forces invaded Iraq. Both Britain and the United States are obvious and defined targets for al Qaeda and its splinter groups. In the first direct attack against Great Britain, an al Qaeda cell based in Turkey attacked the British Embassy compound in Istanbul in November 2003. In determining that al Qaeda was responsible, authorities looked at what was spread before them—simultaneous attacks, within seconds of each other; and the targets, the British Embassy and the HSBC Bank in Istanbul.

The method of attack in both instances was by suicide bombing. One has to speculate on what the terrorist cell hoped to gain by attacking during the holy month of Ramadan and killing mostly Muslims. Could it be that the cells involved believed that such an attack would radicalize the Muslim population and encourage others to join their apocalyptic fight against the Western democracies so long hated by al Qaeda? Or was this the start of a broader campaign being waged by al Qaeda against British interests in Europe? For the last two decades, Turkish authorities have concentrated almost exclusively on the PKK and more recently on Turkish Hezbollah and al Qaeda. The week prior to the British Embassy blast had seen suicide bombers target two synagogues in Istanbul. Authorities identified the bombers as Turks from Bingol. Al Qaeda and its affiliates will continue to threaten U.S. interests in the region, given its continued use of a Turkish Air Force base outside Adana. In April 2011, Turkish Intelligence authorities uncovered a plot to use rockets to attack U.S. military aircraft at the base in southeastern Turkey. According to the General Directorate of Security (Emniyet Genel Mudurlugu), the plot was to be carried out by two Syrian members of al Qaeda identified as Abu Muhammad al-Kurdi and Salih Battal.

BELGIUM

Belgium, and its involvement with terrorism, was of considerable internal concern during the 1970s and 1980s. In a country with a population of only 10 million, political violence had been unheard of compared to the troubles besieging its neighbors. Belgian terrorism was not widely publicized by the world press and probably received little or no mention in the U.S. press. However, terrorist incidents have taken place on Belgium soil from external terror groups. These attacks dating back to the 1970s and 1980s were basically anticapitalist in nature. Palestinian terrorists, from the Black September group, hijacked a Belgium state (Sabena) airliner to Israel in 1972, and PLO terrorists also attacked the Iraqi Embassy in Brussels in 1978.

Belgium's internal troubles in the 1980s appeared to come from the direction of neo-Fascist terror gangs, who up until then had not been active but had aligned themselves with other terror groups in Europe. Considered to be more of a criminal gang element on the outer fringes of violent political struggle was the right-wing DARE, the New Force Party, and the West New Post. All were considered extreme Fascist movements, but they had been nonviolent in comparison to the activities of such groups in the rest of Europe.

Ongoing criminal terror attacks were causing a crisis in the government and panic in the country, with innocent bystanders being killed. By the mid 1990s, Belgium became one of those EU countries favored by migrants from Turkey and North Africa who brought with them their own brand of Islamic extremism. In Belgium today some 50 percent of newborns are Muslim—a third of Muslims in the United Kingdom and Belgium are under fifteen versus a fifth of the native population. Counting all age groups, they're a minority. But in generational demographics, Muslims are swiftly becoming a majority.

The country began its flirtation with extremism when an Algerian terror cell of GIA was discovered in the mid-1990s. During the 1970s, members of the Muslim Brotherhood had fled

FIGURE 6-9 Map of Belgium (Central Intelligence Agency, *The World Factbook, 2008*).

from North Africa and the Middle East and were comfortably residing in European countries including Belgium. Mainly focused on propaganda and fund-raising they would form part of what would become a global jihad movement in the new millennium. In 1998, a jihadist network known as the Mellouk Network and led by Fared Mellouk was broken up in a coordinated crackdown by EU intelligence agencies. The period 1998–2001 represented the apex of al Qaeda–dominated jihad; with cells Europewide, the movement was led by the two main protagonists, Osama bin Laden and Ayman al Zawahiri. However, that would soon change with the U.S.-led attack on Afghanistan and the Iraqi invasion following 9-11 and the obvious disintegration of the al Qaeda, centralized style of administration. Many of its members fled Afghanistan and its veterans took up station in Europe. Once in Europe, they launched their local jihad on European soil, creating and maintaining sleeper cells, recruiting, and preparing and plotting terror attacks. Most of the cells and activists were not necessarily directly linked to but were inspired by the potent al Qaeda mythology.[56] There can be little doubt that self-radicalization is the current format for recruiting being used by extreme Islamic groups globally. With a vast array of online tools available to such extreme groups, the recruiting and self-radicalization will continue to provide either individual "lone-wolf" jihadists or small-cell structures made of small groups of like-minded friends. While Belgium may seem to be well advanced in its recognition of the threats posed by jihadist organizations, it is not going to be immune from the global threats that they pose. In 2003, Belgium authorities arrested and sentenced Nizar Trabelsi, a thirty-seven-year-old Tunisian, to ten years in prison for planning to drive a car bomb into the cafeteria of a Belgian air base where about 100 U.S. military personnel were stationed. Trabelsi claims to have met Osama bin Laden and been trained in an al Qaeda camp in Afghanistan in the months prior to the 9-11 attacks.

Revolutionary Front for Proletarian Action (FRAP)

The terms *revolutionary* and *proletarian* are often used as much by European neo-Nazis as they are by leftist groups. Contemporary Nazis also hate European links to the United States. The Revolutionary Front for Proletarian Action (FRAP) conducted its first action on April 20, 1985, a date universally celebrated by European Nazis as the birthday of Adolf Hitler. This was a bombing attack on the North Atlantic Assembly (NAA) in Brussels and was followed the next day by an attack against the offices of AEG-Telefunken. The first reaction by authorities to these attacks and also from the media was that it was the work of an ultraleftist group. The initial arrests were made from among members of leftist groups in Belgium. The attacks on these two establishments suggested that FRAP was as likely to be have been rightist as Communist, although the ambiguous circumstances of these attacks meant that it would be the left that would be stigmatized.[57]

Communist Combatant Cells (CCC)

Pierre Carette was the leader of the Belgian CCC group and became politically active when establishing a committee to gain the release of imprisoned members of the German Red Army Faction. In October 1984, CCC conducted a series of attacks on political and military targets, and Carette was subsequently arrested the following year. He was sentenced to life in 1988 for an attack on the Federation of Belgian Enterprises in Brussels in 1985, which resulted in the death of two firefighters. He was released after fifteen years in 2003.[58]

Carette and the CCC began their short-lived campaign in October 1984. They attacked offices belonging to Litton Data Systems and two months later attacked a NATO oil line near Brussels. Other attacks took place against symbolic property targets in Brussels and Antwerp. Carette's 1985 arrest spelled the end of the CCC. It is still not clear who or what was involved in the destabilizing attempt of Belgium. Was it all an attempt by the left, or was it some other form of terrorism with an as-yet undefined rationale? Whatever the case, there are some underlying aspects to the Belgium political structure that are relevant. One should not dismiss a theory that an agent provocateur may have been involved in the Belgian experience.

NETHERLANDS

The perceived threat that overpopulation from immigration may have on a liberal society is evidenced in the assassination of Pim Fortuyn and **Theo Van Gough**. Fortuyn was a blunt-speaking, anti-Muslim politician, who became better known in death than in life. His comment, "The Netherlands is full," was one of his famous slogans. His viewpoint criticized the fact that the Netherlands was home to 1 million Muslims, the vast majority from Turkey and Morocco. He referred to Islam as a "backwards" religion that censored freethinkers and mistreated homosexuals and women. His assassination, the first in Holland in 300 years, generated widespread sympathy for freedom of speech. Perhaps, surprisingly, it was not at the hands of a fanatical Muslim extremist that he met his death in a hail of bullets. His murderer was Volkert van der Graaf, an animal rights activist; however, van der Graaf's motives for the assassination are not readily clear. The wake-up call for the Netherlands, and the knowledge of the presence of Islamic extremism there, was brought home with the broad-daylight assassination in Amsterdam of Theo Van Gough on November 2, 2004. Mr. Van Gough, an avid and public critic of Islam—using his position as a filmmaker, columnist,

FIGURE 6-10   Map of the Netherlands (Central Intelligence Agency, *The World Factbook, 2008*).

and television talk-show host as his platform—was attacked by a Moroccan with dual Dutch-Moroccan citizenship. The attacker, a member of an extreme Islamic group that has been named by the Dutch Intelligence Service as the Hofstadgroep, repeatedly shot Mr. Van Gough and then proceeded to stab him and slash his throat, to the point where his head was almost severed. The Netherlands was shocked by this public display of Islamic fanaticism on its streets, in a country where radical extremists account for a very small minority of the 1 million Muslims living there. The assassin, Mohammed Bouyeri, was sentenced to life in prison on July 26, 2005. After the killing, Bouyeri attached a note and his knife to the body of Van Gough. The note stated: "I surely know that you, Oh Europe will be destroyed." The Hofstadtgroep is also believed to be linked through its wider network with al Qaeda.[59] Soon after the attacks on 9-11, the Dutch Intelligence Services noted that the global recruiting of young Muslims was moving ahead in the Netherlands. The service believed that several dozen Muslims had been recruited for suicide missions in the Middle East.

Dutch teenager Samir Azzouz was cleared of planning attacks on Amsterdam's Schiphol Airport, a nuclear reactor, and government offices. He had been found in possession of machine gun cartridges, mock explosive devices, electrical circuitry, maps and sketches of prominent buildings, and chemicals that could be bomb ingredients. Such cases raise a difficult question: In the absence of an actual attack, how close must a suspect be to detonating a bomb before prosecutors can demonstrate guilt?[60] The difficulty for European countries is their inability to convict for terrorism offenses that are in the planning stage. Police and security agencies will be sounding alarm bells as Europe gets set to become the new theater for attacks from Islamic groups with worldwide jihad in mind.

DUTCH CARTOONS—FREEDOM OF THE PRESS

The publication of a dozen cartoons depicting the Prophet Mohammed in the Dutch national paper *Jyllands-Posten* resulted in at first localized protest and then open street riots. The violence might have been contained in Holland if it had not been for imams taking a tour of the Middle East and stirring up Islamic fervor by distributing the same cartoons. The press will and do argue that political satire is what they do and many cartoons are seen in national papers on a regular daily basis. Islam forbids any depiction of the Prophet Mohammad; so when these cartoons appeared in 2005, the tensions in the European Muslim communities were raised. The rioting and deaths that ensued seemed totally out of context from any message the cartoons may have been intending to portray to a wider audience. The Netherlands has a large Muslim immigrant population not dissimilar to other European countries, but it seems that any newspaper that prints any controversial commentary does so at its own risk.

Insulting a religion is despicable if that is what this is—or is it freedom of the press; however, in February 2006, more than three months after the original publication, the imam of the Peshawar mosque in Pakistan, one Mohammed Yousef Qureshi, offered 1.5 million rupees (US$30,000) reward for killing one of the cartoonists who portrayed the Prophet Mohammad. There was no outcry from Western democracies or from the Dutch government for that matter. The way to resolve differences with the press has, in Western society, rested with the courts. In October 2006, a Danish court dismissed a lawsuit brought by a group of Muslim organizations against *Jyllands-Posten.* "It cannot be ruled out that the drawings have offended some Muslims' honor, but there is no basis to assume that the drawings are, or were conceived as, insulting or that the purpose of the drawings was to present opinions that can belittle Muslims," said the city court in Aarhus. *Jyllands-Posten* called the decision a victory for freedom of the press, while the Muslim groups who jointly filed the lawsuit say they plan to launch an appeal.[61] The integration of Muslims has not been helped by the growth of Islamaphobia in the Netherlands due to the many acts of jihadist violence around the world. This has led the non-Muslim population to distance itself. This, in turn, has led many Muslims to reorient themselves toward their own communities and cultural and religious backgrounds. As a result, polarization between Muslims and non-Muslims has been on the rise for the past few years, a trend that can accelerate radicalization processes.[62]

SWEDEN AND NORWAY

Neither of these two countries is synonymous with terrorism, but by Christmas 2010 and July 2011 both came to terms with bombings and massacres. In both countries, it would assume the form of a "lone-wolf" attack: in Stockholm, on shoppers in early December 2010, and in Oslo, a bomb attack against the government buildings in the center of the city, and a massacre on an island retreat for Youth Party members on the same day claiming over eighty lives. Sweden's only prior association to a major terror event dates back to the February 1986 assassination of Swedish prime minister Olof Palme. He was shot in the back by a lone gunman while walking with his wife on a Stockholm street. His attacker has never been identified and motive for the attack not clarified.

In the December 2010 Stockholm attack, an online jihadist forum, **Shumukh al-Islam**, was first to identify the Stockholm suicide bomber Taymour Abdulwahab al-Abdaly. Al-Abdaly, a twenty-nine-year-old Iraqi from Baghdad with a wife and two daughters, had moved to Sweden but was currently living in England. In a message left behind, he stated "Briefly, to Sweden and the Swedish people, because of Lars Vilks and his drawings of the Prophet Muhammad, Allah's peace and prayer be upon him, your soldiers in Afghanistan, and your silence over all this, your sons and daughters and brothers and sisters will die just as our brothers, sisters and children are dying.

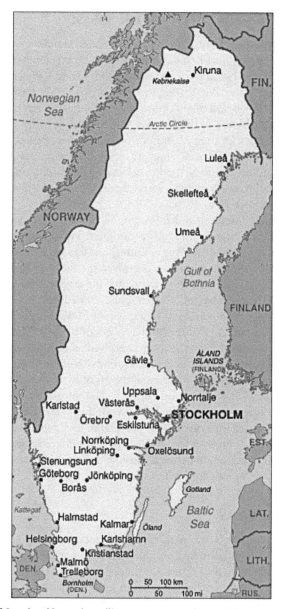

FIGURE 6-11 Map of Sweden (Central Intelligence Agency, *The World Factbook*).

Now the Islamic State has fulfilled what it had promised you, for now we are here in Europe and Sweden, and we are a fact, and not a mirage." The investigation linked his comments to those made by Abu Omar al-Baghdadi in 2007, when he broadcast a threat against specific European companies including Scania, Volvo, IKEA, and Electrolux, as well as threats against Lars Vilks. Al-Abdaly had left Iraq in 1991 and lived in Stockholm and the United Kingdom and was studying at university. He frequented the Luton Islamic Centre where he was vociferously outspoken in his views. How and when he became radicalized has not been determined. His explosive device malfunctioned, which accounted for him being the only fatality on this date. In the Oslo attacks, jihadi forums were praising the executers and warning other European countries including France and England that this was what they should expect as well—in this instance, the jihadi forums were well wide of the mark, as the suspect in this instance was a right-wing extremist who wanted to create a new order and purify Europe of immigrants, hardly something for jihadists to cheer about.

The Norway attacks were apparently the work of an extreme right-wing Christian and vehemently anti-immigration Norwegian named Anders Behring Breivik. He was able to mount two almost simultaneous attacks—one a large car bomb detonated outside government offices in the center of Oslo. He made his way dressed as a police officer to a resort island of Utoya, which was hosting the youth movement of the (left wing) Norwegien governing party. He was able to get on the

FIGURE 6-12 Map of Norway (Central Intelligence Agency, *The World Factbook*).

island in disguise and then calmly executed as many men of the youth movement as he could; his rampage was not stopped for over an hour—the time it took the Norwegien Police to acknowledge the attack and get a response team to the island. In all, Breivik killed over eighty people that day.

Before the attacks were credited to this extreme right-wing Norwegian, the jihadist websites were glorying the action in the belief that it was carried out by an Islamist group, but on this occasion, the killer is best described as a somewhat deranged individual—Breivik had written his own manifesto—"*2083. A European Declaration of Independence*"—which provided insight into his motivations. His ideology appears to be a form of reactionary Christian fundamentalism, fuelled by hatred of Islam, Marxism, and nonwhites. He posted his manifesto on the Internet just prior to the attacks—the details describe his attack plan as being a number of years in the making, and he subscribed to many far-right Islamaphobic websites and forums. Far-right extremists have kept a low profile in Norway. Norway's intelligence services have warned of potential problems from far-right extremists, but the population and the media were more focused on the possibility of Islamist violence. Breivik was also able to remain under the intelligence radar by owning his own farming company, which allowed him to purchase large amounts of commercially available fertilizer that was used to manufacture his car bomb. Publishing the manifesto only on the day of the attack gave scant opportunity for the intelligence services to react. One probable outcome of this attack is that terrorists and particularly al Qaeda–inspired groups will study it to learn lessons. Al Qaeda has been particularly adept at adopting techniques developed by other terror groups. Monitoring of jihadist Web forums where we expect that jihadist propagandists will point to the attack in Norway is an example of an operation that an individual or cell could conduct in the future.

Summary

Terrorism has been synonymous with Europe for more than fifty years and, discounting the levels of genocide practiced by the Nazis in World War II, has been the battleground for both the right and the left and now Islamist extremists. While anticapitalist terrorism marked much of the 1960s era with Baader Meinhof and RAF, and the 1970s and 1980s with November 17, ETA, and PKK, a transformation has taken place. With the fall of Communism came the influx of migrants from the former Soviet republics to Germany, Italy, France, the Netherlands, and Spain. From North Africa the influx came from the Muslim countries of Morocco, Tunisia, and Algeria, with universities accepting students from the wider swath of Islam from the oil-rich Persian Gulf states. The War on Terror firmly rooted in a Western attack on the Islamic nations of Iraq and Afghanistan has led to young, disaffected migrants, many of whom are second generation, taking up calls to jihad. These immigrants may have had no prior interest in their own Muslim faith, but were drawn back into it by skilled Islamic recruiters for a worldwide Jihad against Western democracies. The United States and Great Britain are prime targets, but European nations will also have to contend with the broad specter of jihad in such metropolitan centers as Paris, Berlin, Brussels, Amsterdam, Madrid, and Rome, as the second generation of marginalized youths from Islamic countries become the suicide bombers and terrorists of tomorrow. Europe's future security relies heavily on the network of security and intelligence agencies and their ability to identify the threats from Islamic extremism and the capacity and capability to prosecute. There can be no doubt that Europe is a target for Islamic extremism for recruiting, training, organizing, and spreading jihad. The Madrid train bombings of 2004, the attempt to destroy a flight from Amsterdam to Detroit in 2009, and lone-wolf attacks in Sweden and France are but a harbinger of more attacks to come. In Chapter 7, we will again see the threat of al Qaeda as radical Islam takes its toll in the east in Chechnya and the former Soviet Republics.

Review Questions

1. Discuss how free speech and freedom of the press have become a target for Islamic extremists.
2. Review some of the causes that have led to the spread of global jihad in Europe.
3. Discuss how the Munich Olympic Games would affect the responses to countering terror attacks by European authorities.

4. Compare terrorist ideologies of the 1970s and 1980s with events taking place in Europe since 2001.

Websites

1. **Foreign Policy Association**—*http://www.fpa.org*
2. **Council on Foreign Relations**—*http://www.cfr.org*
3. **Washington Institute**—*http://www.washington institute.org*
4. **Militant Islam**—*http://www.militantislammonitor.org*
5. **Federation of American Scientists**—*www.fas.org/irp/eprint/calahan.htm*

6. **Danish Cartoons**—*http://www.militantislammonitor.org/article/id/1635*
7. **Executive Intelligence Review**—*http://www.larouche-pub.com/other/1995/2246_eta.html*

End Notes

1. U.S. Department of State Information Programs (2009) www.usinfo.state.gov.
2. Intel Brief, courtesy U.S. Department of State (2009) archives on ETA, http://www.state.gov/s/ct/nls.
3. William Gutteridge, ed. "Contemporary Terrorism," an article by Peter Janke, (The Institute for the Study of Conflict, 1986), p. 152). Facts on File, Inc.
4. George Rosie. *The Directory of International Terrorism* (New York: Paragon House, 1987, p. 111).
5. Http://en.wikepedia.org/wiki/Batasuna.
6. "Spain: Move to Outlaw Separatist Party May Fail," *Strategic Forecasting* (July 5, 2002), www.stratfor.com/premium/analysis.
7. "BBC World News." *ETA Declares Ceasefire.* (2007), http://search.bbc.co.uk/cgi-bin/search/results.pl?q=eta+ceasefire.
8. A History Written in Blood. http://www.telegraph.co.uk/news/main.jhtml?xml=/news/2006/03/23/weta223.xml.
9. Rosie. *The Directory of International Terrorism*, p. 135.
10. Pino Arlacchi. *Men of Dishonor* (New York: William Morrow and Co. Inc., 1993, p. 27).
11. Disk News Service. *Spain Arrests al Qaeda Suspect with WTC Footage* (July 16). http://news.bbc.co.uk.
12. Reuters Madrid. *Prosecutor Seeks 220,000 Years for al Qaeda Suspects* (February 14, 2005).
13. ZDF (German TV). Elmar Thevessen and Ulf Roller, "Das Netzwerk des Terrors." (October 24, 2001).
14. David Yallop. *Tracking the Jackal* (New York: Random House Inc., 1993, pp. 48–49.
15. Philip Jackson. "Under Two Flags: Provocation and Deception in European Terrorism." *Terrorism: An International Journal*, vol. 2 (New York: Taylor and Francis, 1988, p. 280).
16. Grant Wardlow. *Political Terrorism, Theory, Tactics and Counter-measures* (London: Cambridge University Press, 1982, p. 38).
17. Philip Jenkins. "Strategy of Tension: The Belgian Terrorist Crisis 1982–1986." *Terrorism: An International Journal*, vol. 13 (New York: Taylor and Francis, 1990, p. 299).
18. Yallop. *Tracking the Jackal*, p. 98.
19. *Fighting Terrorism: Lessons from France*. http://www.time.com/time/nation/article/0,8599,176139,00.html.
20. U.S. Department of State Web site, Patterns of Global Terrorism. http://www.state.gov.
21. *TF1.Fr (French TV)*. "Gang de Roubaix: La Jeunesse de Dumont a l'Etude." (October 4, 2001); "Bin Laden's Invisible Network." *Newsweek*, International edition (October 29, 2001, p. 50).
22. Timeline—The Shoe Bomb Case. (July 1, 2002), http//edition.cnn.com/2002/us/01/07/reid.timeline/index.html.

23. Adam Sage and Daniel McGory. "French Agents Knew of Hijack Suspect in 1994," *The London Times* (October 3, 2001, p. 4).

24. *BBC World* "Moussaqoui" (December 13, 2001); *CNN Inside Europe* (December 16, 2001).

25. SITE Monitoring Service—Jihadist Threat. "Forum Member calls for chemical and biological attacks in France." (April 2011), https://news.siteintel-group.com/

26. *Italy Anti-Semitism Worldwide* (2003). http://www.ac.il.

27. *The World Book Encyclopedia,* vol. 9, S.V. "Reichstag." (1990, p. 254).

28. Richard Huffman. "Motivations from an Internet Article." *Terrorist motivations* (1997). www.Baader-meinhof.com.

29. Ibid.

30. Rosie. *Directory of International Terrorism,* p. 220.

31. Ibid.

32. Anti-Defamation League Website, *The Skinhead International*: A Worldwide Survey of Neo-Nazi Skinheads (New York: Anti-Defamation League, 1995), www.Nizkor.org.

33. Donna Leinwand. *Germany Tightens Security in Sleeper Search, USA Today* (November 26, 2001), 13A.

34. Emerson Vermaat. "Occasional Paper" (Toronto: The Mackenzie Institute, 1993, pp. 129–131).

35. U.S. Department of State, *Patterns of Global Terrorism,* released by the Office of Coordinator for Counterterrorism (May 21, 2002), Europe Overview.

36. A Turkish Flash interview. (2007). http://www.mil-ligorusarsiv.com/videolar/file.php?f=5.

37. "German Intelligence says Islamists Present Major Threat," http://www.dw-world.de/dw/article/.

38. SITE Monitoring Service—In Frankfurt attack, echoes of Jihadist Propaganda https://news.siteintel-group.com/

39. EUROPOL—TE-SAT 2010 EU Terrorism Situation and Trend Report www.europol.europa.eu

40. William Gutteridge, ed. *Contemporary Terrorism. A Challenge to Italian Democracy*, by Vittorfranco S. Pisano (London: The Institute for the Study of Control 1986, p. 167).

41. Ibid.

42. Ibid.

43. Ibid.

44. Ibid.

45. Anti-Defamation League Website, *The Skinhead International*.

46. Ibid.

47. Ibid.

48. Andrew Corsun. "Revolutionary Organization November 17 in Greece." *Terrorism: An International Journal*, vol. 14, no 2 (London: Taylor and Francis, 1991, p. 86).

49. G. Kassimeris. "Greece: Twenty Years of Political Terrorism." *Terrorism and Political Violence,* vol. 7 (London: Frank Kass, 1995, p. 81).

50. *World Book Encyclopedia*, vol. 19, S.V. "Kemal Ataturk," p. 511.

51. Barin Kayaoglu. "London School of Economics: Election 2011, The More Turkey Changes, The More its Political Parties Stay the Same." (June 1, 2011) http://blogs.lse.ac.uk/ideas/2011/06/election-2011-the-more-turkey-changes-the-more-its-politi-cal-parties-stay-the-same/

52. Gareth Jenkins. "Back with a Vengeance—Turkish Hezbollah—Global Terrorism Analysis." *The Jamestown Foundation Terrorism Monitor*, vol. 6, no. 2 (January 25, 2008) www.jamestown.org

53. Ibid.

54. Human Rights Watch. "What is Turkey's Hizbollah?" (February 2000). http://www.hrw.org.

55. Ibrahim Cerrah and Robert Peel. "Terrorism in Turkey," *Intersec,* vol. 7 (West Byfleet, England: West Byfleet, 1997, p. 19).

56. Rick Coolsaet and Tanguy Struye de Swielande. "Belgium and Counter terrorism Policy in the Jihadi era (1986-2007)." *Working Paper 40* http://www.docstoc.com/docs/40615492/Belgium-and-Counterterrorism-Policy-in-the-Jihadi-Era-(1986-2007), retrieved April 22, 2011.

57. Philip Jenkins. "Strategy of Tension: The Belgian Terrorist Crisis 1982–1986." *Terrorism: An International Journal* (London: Taylor and Francis, 1990, p. 304).

58. Http://en.wikipedia.org/wiki/Pierre_Carette.

59. Daniel Pipes. "Theo Van Gough and Education by Murder in Holland." *The New York: Sun* (November 16, 2004).

60. Http://www.reuters.com (April 8, 2005).

61. CBC News Online October 26, 2006: Muhammad cartoons: A Timeline http://www.cbc.ca/news/back-ground/islam/muhammad_cartoons_timeline.html.

62. "Home-Grown Terrorism and Radicalisation in the Netherlands Experiences, Explanations and Approaches." Testimony by Lidewijde Ongering, *Deputy National Coordinator for Counterterrorism*: U.S. Senate Homeland Security and Governmental Affairs Committee (June 27, 2007).

7

Eastern Europe and the Balkans

A fanatic is a person who won't change his mind and won't change the subject.

—Sir Winston Churchill (1874–1965)

LEARNING OBJECTIVES

After studying this chapter, the student should be able to:

1. Trace the history of Russian terrorism from the early twentieth century to the breakup of the Soviet Union.

2. Understand how Russia has as a result of the Chechen crisis been subjected to terrorism from Islamists in the Caucasus region.

3. Describe how the Balkan region became an area for ethnic cleansing.

4. Appreciate the difficulty in defining terrorism relative to events in the Balkans and Chechnya.

KEY WORDS TO NOTE

Boevaya Oranisatsia (BO)—"The Fighting Organization"; terror suborganization within the Russian Social Revolutionary Party; given autonomy under the party

Bolsheviks—Extreme left-wing radicals, who favored revolution

Cheka—Communist secret police organization established during the Russian Revolution in 1917

Gulags—Forced labor camps set up by the Soviet internal police for dissidents and politicians

HEU—Highly enriched uranium

IMU—Islamic Movement of Uzbekistan—militant Islamist group formed in 1991

International Criminal Tribunal for the Former Yugoslavia (ICTY)—United Nations court of law handling war crimes

KLA—Kosovo Liberation Army—A Kosovar Albanian group that sought to break away from the Federal Republic of Yugoslavia in the 1990s

Mehmet Ali Agca—A Turkish assassin who attempted to kill Pope John Paul II in Saint Peter's Square in 1981

OVERVIEW

Terrorism in the former Eastern Bloc and the now Soviet Republics is not a new phenomenon. Repression by the former Soviet Union, with its pitiful and sad history, was depicted by famous novelists of the nineteenth century. Tolstoy, author and creator of *War and Peace* in 1869, captured the horrors of the French invasion of Russia in 1812. Reforms by Czar Alexander II were strongly opposed by his son Alexander III, who succeeded him after his assassination. It was this repressive approach that slowly nurtured the seeds of revolution, which were at first written about as themes of desperation, discontent, and bitterness by the many great intellectuals of that era.

This chapter reviews those early terror theories that were at work in Russia and the Slavic states and also examines how the Soviet Union promoted state-sponsored terrorism. Many of the nineteenth-century Russian writers, such as Maxim Gorky, wrote short stories and plays that reflected the theories of a Communist state in Russia. The early seeds of terrorism grew out of the appalling conditions in which the people of Russia existed under the Czars and out of a need for social and political change. After the breakup of the Soviet Union in 1991, the new millennium continued to witness unrest and the relentless abuses of human rights by Chechen rebels and Russian security forces.

We begin with a review of well-known historic events, and then examine others that occurred in the central and eastern Europe. We will find how the War on Terror has played out in the Chechen Republic and how actions of Chechen rebels are labeled as terrorism by Russia. The availability of nuclear weapons, and their accessibility to terrorists through the Czech Republic, will also be carefully considered.

RUSSIA AND THE SOVIET UNION

Narodnaya Volya (NV) (1878–1881)

Roughly translated Narodnaya Volya[1] means "the people's will." NV was a highly effective terrorist organization that existed for only four years. NV grew out of other clandestine Russian movements and had been formed by the intelligentsia. Hard-liners from several of these groups formed the Narodnaya Volya. Like other terrorist organizations, the NV used terrorism as a means to a political end. It aimed to cause the ruling Romanovs so much distress and turmoil that their actions would shake the Russian Empire's political foundation. Surprisingly, its membership was drawn from the Russian elite, and numbered probably no more than 500, with some fifty or more extremists. It set out to overthrow the tyranny of the Czars and declared a death sentence on Czar Alexander II. The group made several unsuccessful attempts upon his life.

One of its most fanatical members was twenty-seven-year-old Sophia Perovskaya, who succeeded in planting a bomb that killed Czar Alexander II in 1881. A fanatic, as well as the daughter of a Russian General; she was arrested along with five others and publicly executed. The NV was also responsible for the death of General Mezentsev, head of the Third Section of the Czarist OKHRNA (secret police) and also the Governor General of Saint Petersburg. NV members were hunted down and arrested by Czarist authorities, and terrorism in Russia diminished significantly over the next twenty years.

The inspiration for Lenin to form the Social Democratic Labor Party was born from NV's theories. Lenin's views of, and appreciation for, NV had taught him important lessons— that a revolutionary organization cannot be limited to terrorism, but must seize total autocratic and bureaucratic power. The NV symbolized the general social crisis that existed in nineteenth-century Russia, and later during the **Bolshevik** Revolution, which replaced the old

FIGURE 7-1 Map of Russia (Central Intelligence Agency, *The World Factbook, 2008*).

order in Russia. Terrorism faded quickly with the passing of the NV, until the formation of the Social Revolutionary Party at the turn of the twentieth century. Members of NV took extreme care in planning and carrying out their assassinations to avoid killing innocent citizens. Targets for retribution were those deemed guilty of acts of corruption and offences against the people.

Terror and revolution are two words that would be used frequently and interchangeably for Russians over the first twenty years of the twentieth century. The prime objective for terrorism in early twentieth-century Russia was to awaken the masses to the potential for sociopolitical change. The philosophical view of this approach is seen today by events unfolding in North Africa and the Middle East with the masses attempting to overthrow existing authority.

Within the Social Revolutionary Party was a terrorist subgroup that was given autonomy under the party—**Boevaya Oranisatsia (BO)**, or the Fighting Organization. Whereas the NV was more aligned with the educated Russian hierarchy, the BO appealed to a wider Russian audience than just the elite. Within the revolutionary movement, widespread dissent continued over the use of terror tactics, and with the emergence of the class struggle, terrorism as a weapon of that period became redundant.

Russian orator Mikhail Bakunin traveled widely throughout Europe promoting his revolutionary ideals. His ideals were based on the destruction of the prevailing social order, as it existed. His approach to anarchy conflicted greatly with that of Karl Marx, and the two were bitter rivals. Bakunin put forward no useful or thoughtful ideas for a future social order. Marx saw him as a dangerous fanatic. Bakunin's view was that the state had to be overthrown, but Marx believed that it was capitalism that had to be purged. Marx's theory and ideology were that violence was necessary to transform the nature of the working class and that violent insurrection was the only means to change society.

Opposition to the Bolsheviks' rule came from the intelligentsia, as well as from opposition newspapers. The Russian Republics were deeply involved in a civil war in the years from 1918 to 1921. In March 1918, Lenin dissolved the constituent assembly when it failed to recognize the leadership of the Bolshevik government. The protests from the socialist left went unheeded by Lenin, so much so that the group withdrew from the coalition. The Bolsheviks then began a period of terror and repression against all groups that voiced opposition. Hundreds of artists and intellectuals were arrested, who were simply aghast at the attitude of the Bolsheviks and had expected a society based on freedoms in the wake of the overthrow of the Czarist government. The Bolsheviks dealt with nationalists, social revolutionaries, as well as members of the intellectual levels of society (professors, writers, and artists) in the harshest of manners. The church in Russia also became a target of Communist terror and oppression. A systematic campaign by the Communists to deny the Russian Orthodox Church any voice in the Soviet Union started in the 1920s, and by 1939, all the clergy, and many of the church's followers, had been shot or sent to forced labor camps. Of the 50,000 churches in Russia, only about 500 remained open.

Joseph Stalin

To many, the name "Stalin" conjures up scenes of sheer despotic terror. In the first quarter of the twentieth century, his name was synonymous with the word "terror." This chapter is not presented to teach the student the fundamentals of the Russian Revolution, but to explain that the intricate use of terror tactics, practiced by Lenin's Bolsheviks, had the unspoken, unanimous support of the Communist Party. Were the Bolsheviks considered to be terrorists, or were they revolutionaries fighting for their political beliefs for a new Soviet Republic? In hindsight, and because popular movies such as *Doctor Zhivago* seemed to glorify the hostility and man's inhumanity to his fellow man, should we consider the Russian revolution a result of effective terrorism? In later years, and specifically during the Cold War, the United States and NATO allies viewed the Soviet Union as the prime exporter and sponsor of modern-day terrorism. The terrorist "Carlos the Jackal" is believed to have received his indoctrination, training, and funding in the Soviet Union. Although there is some evidence that he did receive part of his university education there, no substantive evidence has ever been unearthed that shows the Soviet Union did, in fact, sponsor him.

Josef Vissarionovich Dzhugashvili adopted the name "Stalin," a Russian word meaning "steel." Following Lenin's death, Stalin became the "Absolute Ruler" of the Soviet Union, from 1929 until he died in 1953. As a young man, he earned a scholarship to study theology but was subsequently expelled for preaching Marxist ideologies. He was a strong political supporter of Bolshevism throughout Europe and is credited with being the first editor of *Pravda*, the newspaper voice of the Communist Party. Stalin used extreme measures on the Russian populace to ensure absolute and blind obedience to his will. Anyone who opposed him was summarily dealt with and either shot or sent to labor camps (**Gulags**) in Siberia. This form of state terrorism was carried out by his head of the secret police, Laurenty Beria.

The Secret Police

Many states where suppression of the masses takes place require a sanctioned police force or security apparatus to do the bidding of a cruel regime. Apart from Adolf Hitler, there have been few other world leaders who have slaughtered and sent to labor camps so many of their own countrymen. The Communist regime under Stalin viewed dissent against the party as a repudiation of the proletarian struggle and a violation of Marxist–Leninist ideology. Any threat to the ideology was a threat to the authority of Stalin and the state. Both the Bolsheviks, and then the Communists, relied heavily on strong, political secret police force to secure their rule. The original secret police, the "**Cheka**," was formed in 1917, with the intention that it would be disbanded after the Bolsheviks under Lenin had consolidated power. The first chief of this secret police force was Feliks Dzerzhinski, who had the power under the Bolsheviks to investigate all or any "counter-revolutionary crimes."

Much has been written of the Russian Revolution, and few would argue that the results of the October 1917 Revolution would surely be felt for decades to come. Even though the Soviet Union has disappeared into history, the difficulty of defining what actions were terrorism becomes problematic. There is no doubt that the Social Democrats of the Lenin era were terroristic in attitude and nature. However, when reviewed and portrayed as a class struggle for worker rights, why are these struggles now termed as "revolutionary actions"? Is it the popular belief that where a common populace supports a cause, whether it is righteous or not, these activities are no longer referred to as merely terrorist acts, but rather a full-blown "popular resistance" or "revolution"?

Western governments have criminalized terrorism and created legislation to deal with specific "acts of violence" against the state, including the banning of terrorist-linked backed or supported groups. Is it reasonable to rationalize that a popular revolution existed within the borders of Spain (ETA) or in Northern Ireland (IRA)? As we strive to understand what terrorism means in each specific category and, indeed, each country, it becomes less easy to define. In Afghanistan, following the Soviet invasion in 1979, no doubt the rebels fighting for the freedom of their country out of the mountains around Kabul would most likely be termed as "terrorists" by the Soviet Union. It is equally fair to believe that to the Afghans these "terrorists" are better described as "freedom fighters"? It is ironic that one of those freedom fighters, who were provided support in the form of training from both the United States and Great Britain, would turn and bite the hands that fed him. We are referring to Osama bin Laden. U.S. Special Forces and Britain's Special Air Service Regiment (SAS) trained Afghan freedom fighters and equipped bin Laden and his followers for covert-style operations against their new "enemies" in the West. Some of those fighters, no doubt, were eventually involved in fighting alongside the Taliban and al Qaeda against coalition forces in Afghanistan.

The Great Terror

Throughout modern history, there have been many dictators who have purged their respective societies of all opposition, both from within and outside their own political structures. The murder of a senior Politburo member on December 1, 1934, was to set in motion a chain of events that resulted in the "great terror." Sergei Kirov was leader of the Communist Party in Leningrad and an influential member of the ruling elite. Popular as he was in Leningrad, in support of workers' welfare, he disagreed with Stalin's policies. Although he was not thought to be a threat to Stalin, he had been approached by some party members to take over as general secretary.[2]

Did Stalin, who was having doubts about the loyalty of the Leningrad apparatus, perceive Kirov as a threat? It seems entirely possible that the People's Commissariat for Internal Affairs (NKVD) could well have planned Kirov's murder on Stalin's instructions. Using the murder of Kirov as the excuse he needed to crack down hard and to purge the Leningrad party structure, Stalin introduced wide-sweeping laws that resulted in millions of Russians being arrested. This purge lasted for approximately four years and Stalin never again visited Leningrad. That four-year period saw millions of Russians sent to labor camps as well as summary executions and show trials. To say the Russian populace was terrified would be an understatement! In view of Stalin's terror tactics, his complete and total domination of the Russian people was further enforced by forcibly resettling more than 1 million people, primarily Muslims from the Northern Caucasus region and the Crimea. Ethnic Tartars, Chechens, Meskhetians, and Kalmyks, as well as Bulgarians, Greeks, and Armenians from the Black Sea coast, were deported.

These deportations took place during and after World War II, with the excuse that all of these deportees were collaborators with the German occupying forces. The forced deportations took place with the use of cattle cars, reminiscent of German deportations of Jews and gypsies to forced labor and extermination camps. The destination for the deportees was Uzbekistan, Siberia, and Kazakhstan—names that today have a ring of familiarity. By the mid-1950s, Nikita Khrushchev denounced the forced deportations. However, many deportees were still not permitted to return to their native homelands until after the collapse of the USSR in 1991.

Estonian Guerrilla Movement, 1944–1955

One guerrilla group that existed after the collapse of the German Axis was an Estonian movement called the metsavennad, which means "guerrilla fighters." With the retreat of the German army, Estonian soldiers who had been drafted into the German army attempted to escape Stalin's discipline, either by leaving the country or fleeing to the forests of Estonia. These men were known as the "forest brethen." German deserters also joined this movement. It formed a protective band around Estonians to prevent violence meted out by the Soviets. The group was well equipped militarily and was also supported by those who sought revenge against the Soviet Union for previous forced deportations associated with collectivization in March 1949. Their cause was the ultimate independence of Estonia, and, although this was a fruitless gesture against the might of the Soviets, they hoped for some relief and withdrawal of the Soviets, possibly with another European theater of war. A post-Stalin amnesty in 1955 saw the movement disappear.

School for Terrorism

The Patrice Lumumba University, also known as "Killer College,"[3] was located near Moscow and established in 1961 as the Soviet Union's educational contribution to the Third World countries of Africa and Asia. It was at this university that the terrorist Ilich Ramirez (Carlos the Jackal) received his postsecondary education. The Venezuelan Communist Party sponsored Ilich's admission and that of his brother Lenin's to this secretive university. Partying played a big part in their curriculum while they were in Moscow and, on several occasions, they ran afoul of their Soviet army and KGB minders. Ilich was arrested while demonstrating for the cause of thirty Iranian students who had lost their passports in a seizure by the Shah's government. Although sponsored by the Venezuelan Communists, neither Ilich nor Lenin were Communist party members, and their ongoing confrontations with the orthodox members of the Venezuelan Communist youth movement at the university finally led to their grants being suspended and their expulsion. Although there have been many books and articles written about Carlos the Jackal, whether or not the KGB recruited him during the period he spent in Moscow will probably never be known. On his own admission, after leaving the Soviet Union in 1970, his next stop was the destination of choice for many international terrorists—Beirut, Lebanon.

Into the Millennium

With the breakup of the Soviet Union, and with many of the Russian Republics seeking to go their own way, separate from the new Russian Federation, Russia found itself in somewhat unfamiliar waters at the end of 1998. No longer controlled by the Communists, and with its people now sampling capitalism, Russia began to see many disaffected youths leaning toward right-wing nationalism. In the summer of 1998, Boris Yeltsin was openly commenting in press reports about the right-wing nationalist threat. What was already surfacing in Russia, now experiencing rampant unemployment, had already surfaced in a unified Germany. Russian youth were even beginning to blame immigrants and Jews for the lack of jobs and the country's other woes. Hate

TERRORIST ATTACK BRIEF

Terrorist Group: Caucasus dissidents (Ingushetia)

Case Facts: A suicide bomber detonated around 15 lbs of explosives inside the arrivals area of the airport killing thirty-six and injuring almost two hundred.

Investigation: The bombing had the hallmarks of extremists from the Caucasus region and the investigation began to focus on the North Caucasus region of Ingushetia. In March 2011, two young brothers from Ingushetia were arrested for their part in the bombing as well as for assisting the bomber make his way to the airport.

FIGURE 7-2 Suicide Bombing—Domodedovo International Airport—Moscow—January 24, 2011. *Source*: RAI Novosti, http://en.rian.ru/russia/20110330/163281446.html

crimes and other violent actions were now commonplace in Russia. Had Russia gone full circle in the last 100 years? At the turn of the twentieth century, Russia was in turmoil with the uprising of the worker classes. By 2006, the threat was clearly being seen from Islamic groups, many living in Russia's neighboring republics.

Russia now allows the press more freedom to report on events as they occur in everyday life than ever before. This new freedom may become part of the lifeblood of any terrorist group starting up in Russia. Under Communist domination, the government-controlled media rarely reported on any anti-Soviet acts. However, since 9-11, there has been a crackdown on what is published and what is disseminated to the worldwide media. This is probably a direct consequence of President George W. Bush's tacit support for Russian president Putin to fight terrorism in the Caucasus. Without these restrictions, a key component in any terrorist arsenal is the ability to present such activities to a broad audience. In the democracies of the West, the suicide bombings in Moscow and the Beslan School attack in 2004, with the resulting loss of life, have made banner headlines. There has been little press freedom to report the true extent of military activities by Russian forces in Chechnya. Russia continues to blame Chechen rebels for bomb attacks in Moscow and continues to use this as a valid reason to carry out military operations against the Chechen state. Chechnya is a small, landlocked state with a predominantly Muslim population of approximately 1 million people. Russian President Vladimir Putin was quick to support President Bush and his declaration of a War on Terror. In dealing with the breakaway Republic of Chechnya, Putin and his government seemed to take the U.S. War on Terror as tacit approval to continue legitimized attacks on Chechnya.

Vladimir Vladimirovich Putin, President of the Russian Federation

Putin was born in Leningrad on October 7, 1952, and after university he worked at the Foreign Intelligence Service and served in Germany. After his return to Leningrad, Putin became an aide to the vice president of the Leningrad State University in charge of international issues. Putin held several key positions until 1997 when he worked as head of the president's Main Audit Directorate and Presidential Deputy Chief of Staff. From July 1998 to March 1999, he was Director of the Federal Security Service. Between March 1999 and August 1999, Putin combined his job as Federal Security Service director with his work as Security Council Secretary. On August 9, 1999, he was appointed First Vice-Prime Minister and, later, Acting Prime Minister. On March 26, 2000, he was elected to the presidency of the Russian Federation.[4]

To ensure support for the U.S. role in attacking terrorism, the Bush administration had essentially ignored the issues surrounding the Russian actions in the south Caucasus region.

With the Cold War over, the enemy was no longer the Soviet Union. Times had changed dramatically, and the threat now came from worldwide terrorism, advanced through the hate and malice of fighters immersed in the Muslim faith, with extremist Islamic justification for their actions. The regions of Dagestan and Chechnya are home to countless Muslims; however, the threat perceived by Russia was vastly different than for that of Western democracies and Islamic extremists. Chechens were fighting for their independence from their former Russian masters, and Russia continued to use its military to maintain control of the region. Chechnya remains an unsettled region, and Russia can continue to expect the unexpected from the Islamic fighters in Chechnya, and perhaps the many other Islamic provinces of Russia. Strange-sounding names like Ingushetia and Beslan are a world away from major urban U.S. cities, and perhaps that is why so little of what exactly is going on in this region gets widely reported. Many observers believe that the Russian security forces are doing little to prevent the spread of terror and, in fact, from their brutal responses, are likely furthering that cause. This observation and criticism continue to be aimed at the U.S. government and its failure to clearly define any foreign policy for the region.

RUSSIA'S FREE-MARKET ECONOMY AND THE RUSSIAN MAFYA

Russia became a "democracy" following the breakup of the Soviet Union. What, one must ask, happened to the KGB after the breakup? The answer to that is, "more of the same—under a different title." The KGB is called the Federalnaya Sluzhba Bezopasnosti Rossiyskoy Federatsii (FSB). From July 1998 until August 1999, Vladimir Putin was the head of the FSB. Over the last thirteen years, the FSB has undergone several structural changes as a result of political power struggles and was changed to reflect five separate departments and eight directorates:

- Counterintelligence Department
- Antiterrorist Department
- Strategic Forecasting and Analysis Department
- Personnel and Management Department
- Operational Support Department
- Directorate of Analysis and Suppression of the Activity of Criminal Organizations
- Investigations Directorate
- Operational–Search Directorate
- Operational–Technical Measures Directorate
- Internal Security Directorate
- Administration Directorate
- Prison System Directorate
- Scientific–Technical Directorate

Organized crime was on the rise in the Russian Federation but the police force was ill-equipped to respond. Interpol, on the other hand, was hard at work, tracking the exploits of more than 400 Russian international criminals. The Office of International Criminal Justice estimated that at least 4,000 organized crime syndicates were operating in the Russian Federation by 1996.

With the breakup of the Soviet Union came the dissolution of the Soviet's intelligence service (KGB). Its agents, however, did not fade into oblivion. Scratching the surface of Russian bureaucracy will uncover layers, like the little Russian dolls, of control dominated by former KGB operatives, many in local government. Organized crime syndicates in the Russian Federation, in collaboration with former KGB officers, is probably a major factor in a booming trade in former Soviet-made weaponry, not the least of which are nuclear capability products.

The "Russian Mafya's" links with former KGB operatives have led to the escalation of weapons sales to terrorist groups. The Mafya has moved from purely internal criminal activities to the exporting weapons to terrorist groups, some with the potential of mass destruction capability. Weapons of mass destruction have been placed on the market for sale to the highest bidder, and some of these sophisticated weapons have ended up in the hands of Third World countries. The potential for global conflict from these sales, while yet to be realized, should not be ignored or minimized.

Russia continues to be at the crossroads on the road to reform—or possibly is taking the long and winding path to anarchy and corruption. Its near neighbors have been embroiled in revolutions throughout the first decade of the twenty-first century; however, a new era of Russian dominance in the region is beginning to assert itself. This lawless society in Russia has led criminal elements to feed on the possibilities of controlling the state and reaping the rewards from corrupt politicians. With the criminal element playing so large a role in the proceedings of daily life in Russia, it is no wonder that these elements will stop at nothing to achieve their goals. On November 22, 1998, the staunch, pro-democracy parliamentarian, Galina Starovoitova, a vocal campaigner for human rights and against political corruption, was murdered in a scene reminiscent of a James Bond movie. She was shot three times in the head at close range as she entered her apartment building. Her campaign had exposed corrupt local politicians, and it is believed that this led to her assassination. Starovoitova was well respected but was among a minority of democracy reformers. The professional hit had all the hallmarks of a gangland-style execution. In a country where few women rise to the heights of local or national politics, her passing was something of a watershed for Russian politics. What the outcome will be is uncertain, but the grip of the underworld on Russia seems to be excruciatingly strong. "Democracy, free-market economy, and the rule of law" are not words or statements that go hand in hand when describing the Russian Federation. Widespread corruption continues to manifest itself in both private and public organizations, and organized crime covers vast areas of the economy, from diversion of collected revenues, a form of money laundering, to the defrauding of overseas aid donors. The illegal trade in arms dealing, and the concern that al Qaeda followers would like to acquire nuclear capability, suggests that Russia may be a prime source for such weaponry. The threat of nuclear terrorism from terror groups, in particular al Qaeda, to fashion a nuclear weapon requires discussion in relationship to the available materials needed to support such an operation. The Russian states have many sites that produced nuclear material during the Cold War years and beyond. Observers and politicians, particularly those in the U.S. administration, believe the only probable method for a group such as al Qaeda to acquire material for such a weapon is through a rogue or hostile state. U.S. policy is fashioned to continuously target hostile states that pose a nuclear supply threat. Maybe this is a sound policy, or maybe it is not. What need concern the world at large are the nuclear stockpiles around the globe and the poor security and accountability that characterize a great many of these sites. To consider fashioning a nuclear bomb, terrorist organizations and nations have different requirements. Nuclear weapons development requires facilities for research and development in the manufacture, control, development, and deployment for conventional means. For the terrorist, the word should be "unconventional." For Osama bin Laden and his al Qaeda-affiliated terror network, using a boat, truck, plane, or car as the means of delivering a nuclear weapon would be their conventional method. The fatwa bin Laden sought and received from a Saudi cleric in 2003 for the use of a nuclear bomb would be permissible under Islamic law, indeed even mandatory, if it were used as a means to stop U.S. actions against Muslims. "If a bomb that killed 10 million of them and burned as much of their land as they have burned Muslims' land were dropped on them, it would be permissible," the ruling held.[5]

According to the International Atomic Energy Agency (IAEA), since 1993 there have been 175 cases of trafficking in nuclear material and 201 cases of trafficking in other radioactive sources (medical, industrial, etc.). However, only eighteen of these cases have actually involved small amounts of highly enriched uranium or plutonium, the material needed to produce a nuclear weapon. IAEA experts judge the quantities involved to be insufficient to construct a nuclear explosive device. However, Mr. El Baradei, Director General of the International Atomic Energy Agency (IAEA), said: "Any such material being in illicit commerce and conceivably accessible to terrorist groups is deeply troubling." There has been a sixfold increase in nuclear material in peaceful programs worldwide since 1970. According to IAEA figures, there are 438 nuclear power reactors, 651 research reactors (of these, 284 are in operation), and 250 fuel cycle plants around the world, including uranium mills and plants that convert, enrich, store, and reprocess nuclear material. Additionally, tens of thousands of radiation sources are used in medicine, industry, agriculture, and research.[6] In respect to Russia in particular, the threat of theft of weapons-grade material such as highly enriched uranium (**HEU**), the compound needed to make a nuclear weapon, is still a major cause for concern. While treaties have been drawn up between the United States and Russia, much work in destroying the stockpiles and securing the existing ones must be addressed. The material for the terrorist to build his bomb is available and currently not that secure. This has been the case since the early 1990s, and either the West has been fortunate or the terrorists have not yet acquired the skill level to manage deploying some form of nuclear strike; a more likely scenario would be a "dirty bomb" or radiological dispersion devices (RDD). The materials for these are more readily available from commercial, industrial, and medical facilities around the world. In 1995, Chechen nationalists placed one such device made up of Cesium 137 and dynamite in Moscow's Ismailova Park. Fortunately it failed to detonate.

UZBEKISTAN AND KYRGYZSTAN

This little understood and recognized region has suffered massively since the breakup of the Soviet Union and is currently threatened by ethnic issues and violence and the obvious reawakening of the threats from Islamic extremism in the region. Violence erupted in Kyrgyzstan in summer 2010 resulting from government largess and corruption. How the violence began and who orchestrated the ethnic attacks has not been determined, but after President Kurmanbek fled the country, the capital Bishek was looted. Tensions continue between Uzbeks and Kyrgyz, and what will be problematic for the region is the Islamic radicals that will try and dictate outcome following decades of cultural repression under the Soviet boot. These two countries are inadequately equipped to handle any levels of terror activity. The spread of militant Islam to the region is reflected in Afghanistan. In 1996, Russia, Tajikistan, Kyrgyzstan, and Kazakhstan signed the Shanghai Treaty with China, designed to demilitarize their mutual borders, and the following year they signed a follow on treaty demilitarizing the 4,300-mile former Soviet-Chinese border. This did not solve the problem, which still exists a decade later of the vast and largely unpoliced borders with Afghanistan.[7]

Islamic Movement of Uzbekistan (IMU)

Uzbekistan eventually became a Soviet republic in 1926 following stiff opposition to the Red Army after World War I. By the twenty-first century, since the end of Soviet control in the 1990s, the Uzbek government had considerably alienated its Muslim population. This may have partly attributed to the rise of the **Islamic Movement of Uzbekistan (IMU)**, renamed the

FIGURE 7-3 Map of Kyrgyzstan (Central Intelligence Agency, *The World Factbook*).

FIGURE 7-4 Map of Uzbekistan (Central Intelligence Agency, *The World Factbook*).

Islamic Movement of Turkestan (IMT), in the mid- to late 1990s, against government actions. The government's response to the terrorist attacks in March 2004 generated a wide negative reaction from the West. Closely affiliated with al Qaeda, IMU is best described as a coalition of Islamic militants from Uzbekistan and other Central Asian states. The group is led by Tohir Yoldashev, a strong anti-Western supporter. The group changed its name in 2001 to the Islamic Party of Turkestan and expanded its goal to that of making Central Asia into an Islamic Caliphate. IMU activities have mainly been against Uzbek targets and the IMU is also supporting actions against foreign troops in Afghanistan.

CHECHNYA

A Mixed Background of Terror and Warfare

In 1991, the presidents of Russia, Ukraine, and Belarus joined together and signed a pact, the Minsk Treaty, which formally broke up the Soviet Union and created in its place the Commonwealth of Independent States. The Muslim states within the former Soviet Union were never consulted and were largely left to fend for themselves. Uzbekistan, Tajikistan, and Kyrgyzstan, or the "Stans," as they are called, have suffered from lack of strong political leadership and over the last twenty years ethnic tensions have come to a head.

After winning the Caucasian War (1817–1864), the Russians deported hundreds of thousands of Chechens. In 1877, 1920, 1929, 1940, and 1943, the Chechens made unsuccessful attempts to topple first the Czars and then the Communists. While most of the Chechen males were fighting against Hitler in the winter of 1943–1944, Stalin ordered that Chechnya be obliterated. Villages were burned, 500,000 people were deported to Kazakhstan and Siberia, and their land was given to non-Chechens. In 1957, the Chechens were allowed to return to their homeland. Dzhokhar Dudayev seized power in Chechnya in August 1991, after a popular vote elected him president that November. Dudayev declared independence from the Soviet Union just a month before its collapse.

Problems in the Caucasus

In February 1994, Russian President Boris Yeltsin and president of the Republic of Tatarstan, Minitimir Shaimiev, initialed a treaty delineating a division of powers between the Russian national government and the government of Tatarstan. The treaty afforded Tatarstan a considerable amount of autonomy and was welcomed by Yeltsin's Nationalities Minister, Sergei Shakhrai, as a "breakthrough." Kabardino-Balkaria and Bashkortostan followed in short order. These treaties represented a fine-tuning of Russia's evolving federation relations, the basic framework of which had been established by the new Russian Constitution of December 1993. The consolidation of Russia's territorial integrity was essential to prevent another Afghanistan failure. The control of the vast group of Islamic states within and without the vast Russian borders was imperative. Above all, there was the explosive situation in the North Caucasus. There, among other problems, the breakaway republic of Chechnya continued to refuse to consider itself a part of the new Russian Federation.

Moscow's previous response to Chechnya's challenge amounted to a policy of benign neglect toward both the republic and its president, Dzhokhar Dudayev. Moscow allowed the republic to go its own way and even attempted periodically to enter into negotiations with Dudayev. The Russian government repeatedly asserted that under no condition would force be used to resolve its differences with the republic and expressed the hope that these treaties would serve as a model for finding a negotiated solution with Chechnya.

Moscow began stepping up financial and military support for opposition forces to the government in Chechnya. Fighting in the republic intensified over the summer, leading to a major attack on Grozny by the combined forces of the Chechen opposition in an effort to overthrow Dudayev. Despite support from helicopters and aircraft with Russian markings, the attack failed. A week later, President Yeltsin decreed the government and military will take all necessary steps to disarm "illegal armed formations" in the republic. Subsequently, 40,000 Russian troops poured into Chechnya. It was a debacle, and the Chechen rebels were able to send the demoralized Russian Army home in defeat.[8] In August 1994, the Russian government began military action to stop Chechnya's secession. Russian troops began aerial bombing and attacked the capital of

Grozny in December and again in February 1995. The rebel Chechen government fled to the hills, and Chechnya was put under armed Russian occupation.

Regardless of whether Russia had a right to use force to defend its territorial integrity against Chechen secession, in hindsight the invasion was a tactical error. The war made it inconceivable that Chechnya would ever become a "normal" member of the Russian Federation, even if it was granted considerable autonomy and a treaty-based relationship with Moscow, like that with Tatarstan. The hostility of the Chechen people toward Russia, deeply rooted before the conflict, has been immeasurably intensified by the brutality of the war and will not be ameliorated by Moscow's promises of financial aid to reconstruct the republic. The Chechen republic will remain a burden on the Russian people, a political nightmare for whatever party is in power in Moscow, and a major and possibly decisive impediment to the preservation of Russian democracy.[9]

Current Situation

The Russian military, in May 2002, openly proclaimed that it was clamping down on the vicious attacks of its soldiers against Chechens; however, this proclamation seems not to have been heeded by the soldiers themselves. Two weeks later, Russian soldiers seized five young men and methodically knifed them to death.[10]

The Russian army has managed to fight two separate wars in Chechnya, the last ending in 2000. Chechens remained undaunted and throughout 2000, the war was still being taken to the Russian public. Bomb attacks continued in Moscow—in the Pushkin Square bombing on August 8, 2000, the bomb was detonated at the height of the evening rush hour, injuring more than ninety and killing twelve. Suicide attacks continued in 2004, with the simultaneous downing of two Russian passenger aircraft and train station attacks in Moscow. Chechnya suffers from a ferocious economic embargo from Russia, which has caused most of its infrastructure to be either destroyed or decaying; thus, Chechnya is barely functioning.

DOKU UMAROV—CAUCASUS EMIRATE GROUP

Doku Umarov, a Chechen Islamist, has called for jihad, but it is somewhat surprising that this group is not engaged in a global jihad but one aimed solely at Russia. Attacks including bombings, suicide attacks, and assassinations have been the hallmark of the campaign of retribution against Russia for its attacks on Chechnya. In March 2010, a suicide attack on Moscow's metro system claimed forty lives and injured over a hundred in two separate suicide attacks. Umarov claimed responsibility and also that the attacks would continue as indeed they have. Further smaller-scale attacks continued in 2010. A Chechen Islamist group claimed credit for the September 9, 2010, bombing in Vladikavkaz, North Ossetia, which killed eighteen people and wounded 140. The Riyadus Salikhin Martyrs' Brigade issued a statement on a website affiliated with Chechen rebel groups saying the attack was part of its jihad in the northern Caucasus. In January 2011, a suicide bomber detonated a suicide vest in the arrivals area of Moscow's Domodedovo Airport, which killed thirty-five and injured dozens more, and again this attack was claimed by Umarov.

Assassinations

Akhmad Kadyrof, the Kremlin-backed president of Chechnya, was killed in a bomb attack in May 2004, along with twenty others when an explosion ripped through a VIP section of a stadium where he was celebrating the defeat of the Nazis in World War II. He was named as the head of Chechnya's civil administration in 2000, and the Kremlin had entrusted him with

TERRORIST ATTACK BRIEF

Terrorist Group: Islamist Militants

Case Facts: Three heavily armed men managed to access the compound housing the Parliament building and stormed the building killing four and injuring at least twenty others.

Investigation: After gaining entry and killing a handful of people, the terrorists sprayed the building with automatic weapons and one terrorist blew himself up—the remaining terrorists also detonated devices killing themselves as Chechen Security Police stormed the building. The tension in the region remains, and although there are almost daily attacks by Islamists focused against the military and police, this was a well-planned attack—although no government deputies were injured in the attack.

FIGURE 7-5   Attack—Chechen Parliament Building—Grozny, Chechnya—October 19, 2010.
Source: Christian Science Monitor, http://www.csmonitor.com/World/terrorism-security/2010/1019/Magnitude-of-deadly-Chechen-parliament-attack-rattles-Russia

organizing a 2003 referendum that would approve a constitution, cementing Chechnya's status as an inseparable part of Russia. Kadyrof was accused of siphoning funds destined for Chechen reconstruction. A former Imam, he had fought on the side of the Chechen separatists but later switched sides in an attempt to lead the republic to some sort of stability following two wars.

The Beslan school attack in North Ossetia in September 2004 was an operation by Basayev, but was more likely to have been promoted and supported by former Chechen president and warlord Aslan Maskhadov. Maskhadov was killed by Russian forces in a shootout in March 2005. He was elected president of Chechnya during its brief period of independence in the mid-1990s.

Shamil Salmanovich Basayev (January 14, 1965–July 10, 2006) was the right-hand man of the former Chechen President Dzhokhar Dudayev who was elected following the breakup of the Soviet Union, in 1991. Basayev was to the Russians what Osama bin Laden was to the Americans. He was responsible for numerous guerrilla attacks on security forces in and around Chechnya as well as terrorist attacks on Russian civilians, including the Russian Theater siege in Moscow and the Beslan School massacre, which resulted in 300 deaths of mostly school children.[11]Most Chechens believed themselves to be Russian and found it difficult to determine exactly how they should react. Terrorist actions led by Basayev were to have an immediate effect in ending the First Chechen War. In June 1995, Basayev led an eighty-plus team of Chechen fighters into Russia and attacked the southern city of Budyonnovsk where they stormed the police station, government buildings, and the city hall. When Russian reinforcements arrived, Basayev and his group retreated and took over a thousand hostages at the local hospital—the ensuing battle resulted in the death of thirty hostages unable to escape the grenades being thrown into the hospital by the special forces. The unsuccessful attempt led to an eventual cease-fire—Basayev managed to negotiate his way out. In exchange for the hostages, the Russian government agreed to halt military actions in Chechnya—on June 18, 1995, Viktor. S. Chernomirdin, prime minister of the Russian Federation, issued the following statement.

To release the hostages who have been held in Budenovsk, the Government of Russian Federation:

1. *Guarantees an immediate cessation of combat operations and bombings in the territory of Chechnya from 05 AM, 19 June 1995. Along with this action, all the children, women, elderly, sick and wounded, who have been taken hostage, should be released.*

2. *Appoints a delegation, authorized to negotiate the terms of the peaceful settlement of conflict in Chechnya, with V.A. Mihailov as a leader and A.I. Volsky as a deputy. Negotiations will start immediately on the 18th June 1995, as soon as the delegation arrives in Grozny. All the other issues, including a question of withdrawal of the armed forces, will be peacefully resolved at the negotiating table.*

3. *After all the other hostages are released, provide Sh. Basayev and his group with transport and secures their transportation from the scene to the Chechen territory.*

4. *Delegates the authorized representatives of the Government of the Russia Federation A. V. Korobeinikov and V. K. Medvedickov to deliver this Statement to Sh. Basayev.*

Prime Minister of the Russia Federation

V. S. CHERNOMIRDIN

18.06.95

However, by the time of the second Chechen war, the stark brutality of the Russian troops toward the civilian population—which has seen more than 250,000 killed, including around 45,000 children—the options became clear: Stay in the towns and be rounded up, kidnapped, or murdered or head for the forests and take up arms. A huge number chose the latter. As a Muslim population, Chechnya has been involved with affiliated terror groups from Muslim countries trained in Afghanistan during the Taliban regime. The Riyadus Salikhin group, under Shamil Basayev, claimed responsibility for the Dubrovka Theater attack in 2002, which led to the deaths of more than 100 civilians. Basayev claimed responsibility for all five major suicide bombings in Russia in 2004 and had stated that he reserved the right to use chemical and toxic substances and poisons against the Russians. Many of his detractors, mostly Russian, considered that he was affiliated with al Qaeda. We suggest that he was not and that his aims were purely within the realm of the domination and establishment of his own fiefdom in the North Caucasus region. As part of its political endgame with the Russians, the United States, through its then secretary of state Colin Powell, made the following comment in 2003 in regard to Basayev: "He has committed, or poses a significant risk of committing, acts of terrorism that threaten the security of U.S. nationals, or the national security, foreign policy, or economy of the United States." This kind of response for a warlord/terrorist who had not likely left Chechnya in the previous ten years may seem somewhat bewildering and confusing. His death in 2006 has been claimed by the Russian FSB.

The Criminal Code of Russia defines terrorism as "any action endangering the lives of people, causing sizable property damage, or entailing other socially dangerous consequences; for the purpose of violating public security, frightening the population, or exerting influence on decision-making."

Russia has continued tightening its antiterrorism and other national security legislation since 2006, leading to concerns that some of the reforms infringe on human rights. The provision banning jury trials for terrorism suspects was approved by Russian Dmitry President Medvedev at the beginning of 2009. The Federal Law on Counteracting Terrorism (2006) targets ideologies as well as practices by including them in the definition of terrorism and terrorist activity.

The law defines terrorism not only as "practices of influencing the decisions of government, local self-government or international organizations by terrorizing the population or through other forms of illegal violent action" but also as any "ideology of violence." One would suspect this is aimed at Chechnya. The definition of terrorist activity, which complements the definition of terrorism, is even broader. The 2006 law includes the following in the definition of such activity: propaganda information that calls to terrorist activity, information that justifies or supports the need for such terrorist ideas, dissemination of materials or activity, and also "informational or other types of aiding and abetting with regard to planning, preparation or implementation of a terrorist act."

This definition can easily be interpreted to include any "alien" or "offensive" ideology or political agenda (e.g., communist) or dissent (e.g., opposition to the Russian government's policies in the North Caucasus).[12]

UKRAINE

Ukraine declared its independence in 1991 after decades of rule by the Soviet Union and the Czars before that. The former Soviet states of Ukraine and Kyrgyzstan have both experienced political unrest and felt the interfering hand of Russia in its attempt to steer both states away from democracy and a return to Communist ideals. Intelligence sources suggest that Russia used every means at its disposal to prevent the election of the pro-democracy, pro-West candidate Victor Yushchenko from succeeding in the Ukraine. Political and outspoken pressure was placed on the Ukrainian public with strongly worded support for the Russian favorite, Viktor Yanukovych. Russia reverted to its old tactics, not of invasion, which it has used so unsuccessfully in recent history, but of assassination. In this case, the popular Yushchenko was the target. Reports indicate that the Russian secret police was involved in supplying the dioxin poison that made the candidate so ill in September 2004. On September 27, 2009, Yushchenko said in an interview aired on Channel 1+1 that the testimony of three men who were at a dinner in 2004 at which he believes he was poisoned is crucial to finishing the investigation, and he claimed these men were in Russia. Ukrainian prosecutors said Russia has refused to extradite one of the men, the former deputy chief of Ukraine's security service Volodymyr Satsyuk, because he holds both Russian and Ukrainian citizenship.[13]

FIGURE 7-6   Map of Ukraine (Central Intelligence Agency, *The World Factbook, 2008*).

GEORGIA

Georgia's Pankisi Gorge area is best described as a lawless region, home to refugees as well as Arab and Chechen terrorists. Successive Georgian leaders have been unable to exert control over this region that has likely been a fertile training ground for Chechens to launch attacks at Russian targets. British authorities suspect Ricin production is established in this region. Controlling terrorism and the scourge of the Pankisi Gorge is a problem not easily solved. The mere threat and obvious presence of Islamic extremist terrorists functioning in the area do nothing to assist the United States in its wider War on Terror. As time passes, government attempts to crack down on this region have, at best, been weak and, at worst, totally inadequate.

In the summer of 2002, Shevardnadze announced that his security forces would be cracking down on terrorists and others in the region of the Gorge; following that announcement, troops moved into the region. A further proclamation from the ministry of the interior was released that simply stated, "The information about the presence of a large number of armed terrorists is invalid." Human intelligence coming from this region indicates significant numbers of Islamic extremists operating in the Pankisi Gorge, so the Georgian claims may be out of line with the reality for this area. The presence of Islamic militants, particularly Chechens, has been an ongoing issue since the mid-1990s On March 22, 2002, Georgian ethnic Chechen journalist, Islam Saidaev of the Caucuses Committee, and fellow Chechen, Zurab Khangoshvili, were arrested on the basis of suspected al Qaida connections. Their arrests were prompted by a letter from the U.S. embassy to Georgian authorities that they were the only two people from Georgia to have performed the pilgrimage to Mecca, Islam's holiest city, that year. This religious act alone was sufficient to raise the suspicion of al Qaida sympathies, a surreptitious argument used by the United States to justify an enlarged military presence in Georgia.[14] The national TV station in Georgia announced in August 2002 that the Pankisi region was home to a few al Qaeda sympathizers, criminals, and bandits.

After 9-11, Georgia supported the U.S.-led War on Terror, and following that support, the United States sent special operations troops to Georgia to ensure that local forces were able

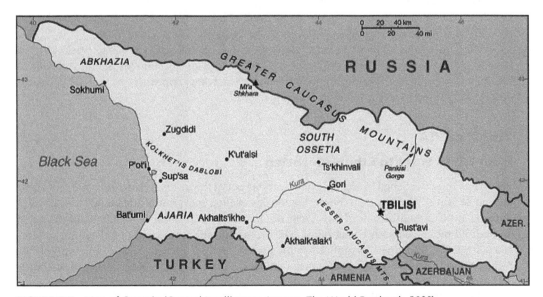

FIGURE 7-7 Map of Georgia (Central Intelligence Agency, *The World Factbook, 2008*).

FIGURE 7-8   Map of Bosnia and Herzegovina (Central Intelligence Agency, *The World Factbook*).

to respond to and root out terrorists in the Pankisi region. What has now turned out to be a fiasco can be blamed on many variables, including corrupt officials and the fear of reprisals from Chechen crime groups who are somewhat aligned with the Chechen extremists, and who are certainly capable of targeting officials in Georgia for reprisals.

With no serious outcome to the attempt by the Georgian security forces to crack down or otherwise disperse any terrorists, the region has become a prime location for Islamic militants to continue to regroup and train for future operations. The reality appears to be that al Qaeda can operate with impunity in the republic of Georgia.

YUGOSLAVIA

From World War I to Ethnic Cleansing

Yugoslavia was established by the League of Nations out of the union of territories dating back to the end of World War I in 1918. Bordering the Soviet Bloc countries of Romania, Hungary, and Bulgaria, the Communist state of Yugoslavia encompassed six separate republics mainly founded on their ethnic or religious background. The area in question has been populated for at least 100,000 years.[15] The first Slavs moved to the area in around the fifth century migrating from regions of southern Poland and the Russian republics. Differing groups of Slavs formed their own enclaves and independent states. Serbians founded Serbia and Croats founded Croatia; however, from about 1,400 onward, the southern Slavs were ruled by foreign powers.

The Turkish Empire controlled Serbian areas, while Hungary and Austria ruled Slovenia and Croatia, respectively. As the centuries moved by, the desire for a united region became a goal of Slovenia and Croatia. The movement to unite sparked an incident that was to change the destiny of Europe and the fate of millions. On June 28, 1914, in Sarajevo, Gavrilo Princip, a Bosnian Serb terrorist, assassinated Archduke Franz Ferdinand of Austria-Hungary, which led to the outbreak of the Great War of 1914–1918. Yugoslavia was so named by King Alexander I, in 1929. The king ruled briefly as an absolute dictator; however, dissident Croat terrorists assassinated him in 1934.

To say that modern-day terrorism played a part in the structure of a nation such as Yugoslavia would not be far from the truth. Two resistance groups fought against each other, as well as against the occupying Germans during World War II. The partisans were led by Josip Tito and his Communist Party and the Chetniks who supported the monarchy under King Peter.

By the end of World War II, the partisans under Tito established a Communist government and on November 29, 1945, the region became the Federal People's Republic of Yugoslavia, thus abolishing the monarchy and sending King Peter into permanent exile. As will be seen throughout this sad tale, many dictators have felt the need to dominate and destroy all opponents of the regime. Yugoslavia under Tito was no different, with many opponents of the Communist government being imprisoned, killed, or exiled. Tito declared a one-party Communist state, but Yugoslavia was not to be a puppet of the Soviet Union. In the late 1940s, Yugoslavia severed all ties with the Soviet Union and became a moderate voice in the region during the Cold War years.

Modern-Day Problems

The people of Yugoslavia were split along ethnic lines into six republics, with Slovenia in the north and Croatia on its southern border. To the south of Croatia was the often-disputed land of Bosnia-Herzegovina. Immediately to the east are Serbia and Montenegro. Civil strife among these ethnic regions has not, until recently, been cause for serious concern. Although nationalist tendencies have been in the forefront of Yugoslavia's political history for the last quarter of the twentieth century, they had not erupted into violent conflict until the civil war of the 1990s. Under Tito's rule, the republics had been forced to keep their nationalist feelings in check. Tito's aim was to eliminate old ethnic divisions and create a united social revolution. When Tito died in 1980, the old nationalist desires of the various republics were reborn. Up to this time Serbs, Croats, and Muslims had lived side by side in a form of peaceful coexistence.

When tough economic times befell them, the Yugoslavs protested Communist Party policy and began to demand changes to a political system that had failed to permit any other political parties to participate. Nationalism was therefore again on the rise in the six republics of Yugoslavia.

Acts of political terrorism have been mostly nonexistent. What had been occurring was a bloody civil war, pitching neighbor against neighbor—almost a Balkanized version of Northern Ireland. All sides in this conflict, however, have used different tactics from those used in the Northern Ireland conflict. Reports out of the various regions cite incidents of "ethnic cleansing," a sanitized term for such extreme measures as the extermination of whole villages (genocide).

The United Nations defines crimes against humanity as crimes committed in armed conflict, whether international or internal in character, and directed against any civilian population:

    a. murder;

    b. exterminations;

    c. enslavement;

    d. deportation;

    e. imprisonment;
    f. torture;
    g. rape;
    h. persecutions on political, racial and religious grounds;
    i. other inhumane acts.[16]

Article two of the United Nations Convention on the Prevention and Punishment of the crime of genocide states:

Genocide means any of the following acts committed with intent to destroy, in whole or in part, a national, ethical, racial or religious group, as such:

    a. Killing members of the group;
    b. Causing bodily or mental harm to members of the group;
    c. Deliberately inflicting on the group conditions of life calculated to bring about its physical destruction in whole or in part;
    d. Imposing measures intended to prevent births within a group;
    e. Forcibly transferring children of the group to another group.[17]

In Bosnia-Herzegovina, the exact number of Muslims killed and displaced remains practically impossible to ascertain. But, by January 1993, between 200,000 and 250,000 people, 10 percent of the Muslim population, are thought to have died, and by early 1994, almost 2 million people were displaced.

Nationalist conflict and resulting civil war have not had the hallmark of terrorist activity as has occurred in other areas, like Palestine and Israel. One exception was the attempted assassination by bombing of Kiro Gligorov, the president of Macedonia, an event that had the clear markings of terrorist action.

Ethnic violence between Albanians and Serbs was illustrated by atrocities committed by both sides. In all respects, the conflict had turned into a regional war. The lightly armed "freedom fighters" were fighting against tanks and heavy artillery. Through the last decade of the twentieth century, Slobodan Milosevic's government had been criticized for its treatment of ethnic minorities, especially in the areas of Vojvodina, Sandak, and Kosovo.[18] Milosevic came to power in 1989 and played a dominant role in the conflict in both Bosnia and Croatia, supplying military and financial support to the Serb nationalist campaigns. He supported proposals from the international community for a brokered peace plan in 1994; however, it was not well-enough received by the Bosnian Serb leadership. This failure prompted Milosevic to close the border between the two republics. In 1995, he signed the Dayton Peace Accord with Bosnian President Alija Izetbegovic and Croatian President Franjo Tudjman. Full diplomatic relations were restored the following year between the former Yugoslavia, now the Federal Republic of Yugoslavia (FRY), and Bosnia-Herzegovina. As for Kosovo, it had resisted the Serbian government since losing its autonomy, and the formation of the **Kosovo Liberation Army (KLA)** in the mid-1990s began attacks on the Serbian police. The response was swift, as the Serbian police and Yugoslav military attacked the ethnic Albanian community in early 1998, forcing a quarter of a million people to flee from their homes. At this juncture, the North Atlantic Treaty Organization (NATO) threatened to use force to curb the assaults by Yugoslavian forces against the ethnic Albanians. Throughout much of 1998 and into early 1999, peace talks were attempted but failed, resulting in a U.S.-led NATO bombing campaign against Yugoslav military targets. This had the opposite effect on the Milosevic government, which hardened its position and intensified its campaign by burning entire villages and forcing the ethnic Albanians in Kosovo to flee to Albania, Montenegro, and

Macedonia. Six hundred and fifty thousand people were forced from Kosovo between March 1998 and April 1999.[19] Many unsubstantiated reports of brutal treatment, rape, and torture of civilians in the Albanian region of Kosovo were beginning to emerge when, by June 1999, the Serbian government agreed to a peace plan for Kosovo. NATO's bombing campaign was suspended on June 10, 1999, and the United Nations Security Council authorized peacekeepers to enter the province. Milosevic lost the federal presidential election in September 2000 to a coalition of opposition parties called the Democratic Opposition of Serbia (DOS). In December 2000, DOS won 176 of the 250 seats in Serbia's National Assembly. In March 2001, the Serbian government arrested Milosevic on charges of abuse of power and embezzlement and in June 2001, following pledges of economic support to the tune of $1 billion by Western governments, Milosevic was extradited to the **International Criminal Tribunal for the Former Yugoslavia (ICTY)** in The Hague, the Netherlands, to stand trial for war crimes.[20] The actions of the Serbian government mirror those of the Nazis during World War II, with the rounding up and arrest of those who have given, or were suspected of giving, any assistance to the so-called rebels. Those arrested were doctors, aid workers, lawyers, and journalists.

Kosovo remained a UN protectorate state; but, in March 2004, there were widespread ethnic clashes across the region. For more than five years, the region has made progress, but the violence certainly laid bare inadequacies of the UN-led mission to Kosovo (UNMIK) and the NATO Peacekeeping Force (KFOR). Much of the violence returned the region to the levels not seen since 1999. Much of this was apparently orchestrated simultaneously by ethnic Albanian groups, possibly with the guidance or control of the Albanian National Army (AKSh), which is known to have launched attacks against ethnic minorities and security forces.

Since NATO intervened in 1999, Kosovo has become the crime capital of Europe. The illicit sex trade is flourishing and has become a major transit point for drugs en route to Europe and North America from Afghanistan. The demobilized Kosovo Liberation Army has not been disbanded or eliminated and is heavily involved in organized crime as well as political intrigue.[21] The majority of Kosovo Albanians saw UN involvement as the major obstacle to independence from Serbia. The geopolitics of the region has changed significantly since 1999—at that time there was no risk involved for a NATO and U.S.-led attack on Yugoslavia—Russia was not a force and was easily ignored. Russia was weak and in no position to challenge the United States and NATO. Putin was rebuilding the Russian sphere of influence in the former Soviet Union. He was meeting with the Belarusians over reintegration and at the same time warning Ukraine not to flirt with NATO membership. He was reasserting Russian power in the Caucasus and Central Asia. His theme was simple: Russia is near and strong; NATO is far away and weak. He was trying to define Russian power in the region.

Kosovo declared its independence on February 18, 2008, and immediately the United States acknowledged Kosovo as an independent state. As of February 2011, seventy-five countries had recognized Kosovo's independence, including twenty-two of twenty-seven EU member states, all of its neighbors (except Serbia), and other states from the Americas, Africa, and Asia.

Notwithstanding the geopolitics of the region, Kosovo is made up of about 2 million people of whom only 120,000 are ethnic Serbs, the remainder are ethnic Albanians. Kosovo is cherished by Serbs as home to celebrated Serb Orthodox monasteries and as the site of the battle of Kosovo in 1389, which resulted in the Serbs being defeated by the Ottoman Empire—the likelihood is that Serbia would retaliate but with political and economic sanctions only. While a majority of EU countries led by Britain, France, and Germany support the Kosovo independence move, some countries such as Spain and Greece are somewhat concerned with recognizing Kosovo as they have their own breakaway groups within their countries. The short term is uncertain, and Kosovo is in much need of support from the EU countries at a time where unemployment is running near 40 percent. It is possible that the declaration could be the cure for the outstanding issue of the Yugoslavia collapse and the signal for economic expansion in the Balkans; alternatively, Kosovo's independence could again stir up conflict between the Albanians and Serbs and result in the destruction of Bosnia.

The International Criminal Tribunal for the Former Yugoslavia

The following is an extract from the indictment against Slobodan Milosevic before the International Criminal Tribunal for the former Yugoslavia:

> Beginning on or about 1 January 1999 and continuing until the date of this indictment, forces of the FRY and Serbia, acting at the direction, with the encouragement, or with the support of **Slobodan MILOSEVIC, Milan MILUTINOVIC, Nikola SAINOVIC, Dragoljub OJDANIC,** and **Vlajko STOJILJKOVIC,** have murdered hundreds of Kosovo Albanian civilians. These killings have occurred in a widespread or systematic manner throughout the province of Kosovo and have resulted in the deaths of numerous men, women, and children. Included among the incidents of mass killings are the following:
>
> a. On or about 15 January 1999, in the early morning hours, the village of Racak (Stimlje/Shtime municipality) was attacked by forces of the FRY and Serbia. After shelling by the VJ units, the Serb police entered the village later in the morning and began conducting house-to-house searches. Villagers, who attempted to flee from the Serb police, were shot throughout the village. A group of approximately 25 men attempted to hide in a building, but were discovered by the Serb police. They were beaten and then were removed to a nearby hill, where the policemen shot and killed them. Altogether, the forces of the FRY and Serbia killed approximately 45 Kosovo Albanians in and around Racak.[22]

Milosevic conducted his own defense against the charges. He suffered from blood pressure and heart problems and died during the proceedings at The Hague on March 11, 2006.

BULGARIA

State-Sponsored Terrorism

The debate on Moscow's level of effort in the arena of state-sponsored terrorism can be theorized at length; however, there is considerable belief that its Communist neighbor, Bulgaria, is active in this area, possibly on Russia's behalf. The extent of Bulgaria's involvement in state-sponsored terrorism is an issue worth discussion. During the Cold War, Moscow's attempts to destabilize the Western democracies involved the use of terror tactics against not only nations but also symbolic personages. In Rome, Italy, on May 13, 1981, a Turkish nationalist attempted to assassinate Pope John Paul II in St. Peter's Square. The Pope was shot and his would-be assassin arrested. The ensuing investigation uncovered a link to Bulgaria. The Pope's assailant, **Mehmet Ali Agca**, is believed to have had an accomplice in place to aid in his escape from Italy. The accomplice, Oral Celik, escaped capture by leaving Italy in a Bulgarian Embassy diplomatic truck. The following year, a Bulgarian State Airline official was charged in Rome in connection with the assassination attempt.[23] Further evidence of Bulgaria's complicity to export terror is seen in the actions of Sallah Wakkas, a Syrian national operating out of Athens. He had purchased more than $50 million worth of Soviet-made weapons and ammunitions from a Bulgarian weapons company, KINTEX.[24]

FIGURE 7-9 Map of Bulgaria (Central Intelligence Agency, *The World Factbook, 2008*).

Further Bulgarian involvement was uncovered when Greek customs seized a ship en route to North Yemen in 1984. The contents of a consignment of oil tankers revealed huge quantities of weapons and ammunitions. The ship's cargo of trucks had been consigned by the Bulgarian State cargo agency, Bulfracht, while the paperwork for the consignment was produced by Inflot, the Bulgarian state shipping agency. It must be assumed that this arms shipment was destined for the Palestine Liberation Organization's training camps in North Yemen. One must deduce that this is just an example of many other shipments that had not been intercepted. In addition, Bulgaria's involvement in drug trafficking has been fairly well documented. Drugs, of course, can be used in the sale or barter for weapons and explosives. KINTEX of Bulgaria has also been known to be a supplier of heroin and morphine to Kurdish dissidents in Turkey, and these drugs have been used as trade for weapons.[25]

Further evidence of Bulgarian attempts at destabilization revolves around the Red Brigade's shadowy involvement in the kidnapping of the American NATO general James Dozier. From evidence deduced by the examining judge at the trial of the Red Brigade ringleader, Antonio Savasta, Bulgaria played a part in the interrogation of the general and offered logistical and training support to the Red Brigade.

Bulgaria's Muslim community has also come under scrutiny since 9-11, in particular the Salafist group Al Wakf al Islami, which has its origins in Eindhoven in the Netherlands. There has been crackdowns by the Bulgarian Police on this group, but so far there has been no indication that Bulgaria is becoming a hot bed of Islamic radicalism.

CZECH REPUBLIC

The Czech Republic and, formerly, Czechoslovakia were well known for being the central clearing point for the arms trade of Eastern and Western Europe. Although the republic is not synonymous with terrorism, its long-standing involvement in the arms business makes its exports very appealing to terrorist groups. Its Communist past and ties with the Soviet KGB allowed it to have extensive networks throughout the world, where it plied the arms trade effectively. The Czech Republic became a full member of NATO in 1999, but this did not necessarily curtail its arms disposal business to countries such as Yemen, which divert their weapons to third countries. The tracking of munitions across international borders, both legally and illegally, continues. *Jane's Intelligence Digest* reported in July 2004 that the Swedish defense ministry had shipped 328 ton of surplus plastic explosives. The material was similar to Semtex. The twenty-trailer convoy had traveled across Denmark and Germany before being intercepted by Czech Customs. What is disturbing about this single shipment was that the material was unmarked (unscented), which would easily allow for it to be smuggled aboard a commercial airliner. Since 9-11, the Czech Republic has raised its voice in the UN to better define terrorism. In 2001, the Czech Republic stated in the UN General Assembly (GA) that the General Assembly could make an enormous contribution if it provided a general definition of terrorism, as this was a missing element in the international legal and political framework. The Czech Republic seemed to believe that when terrorism was defined, the international combat of terrorism was likely to be more successful with abuses of this combat prevented.[26]

FIGURE 7-10   Map of Czech Republic (Central Intelligence Agency, *The World Factbook, 2008*).

Summary

Russia and the former Soviet republics have undergone enormous changes. The Cold War is over and Russia and the United States are on modestly friendly terms in the War on Terror. No longer is Russia a Communist-dominated federation; no longer is it the "Great Bear of the East" that wielded so much power and influence in the world due to military strength and nuclear weapons. Russia is experiencing terrorism from Islamist extremists from Chechnya—not just in the streets of Moscow but also in the air and in its neighboring republics. Organized crime infects Russian society; Russian Mafya-style syndicates permeate all levels of the Russian society. Chechnya remains an ongoing threat to the region's stability as Islamic extremists spread out to neighboring republics. Whether what we are seeing in Chechnya is terrorism or an all-out fight for a country's survival is an open question. Certainly, since the events of 9-11, Russia has seized the opportunity to use military excesses to press home any advantages it can against the rebel state, under the banner of "War on Terror." The region of Macedonia has been devastated by sporadic wars within its borders; the term *ethnic cleansing* is now used again to describe the mass murder of a particular ethnic group. The Kosovo Liberation Army lives to fight another day, and its Albanian support in the region is strong. In the years to come, if the direct fighting ends and some form of lasting peace can ever be achieved, there is no doubt that sporadic terroristic violence, bombings, and assassinations will be a pattern of daily life in these areas. Deep wounds from wars fought based on ethnic lines will take decades to heal. This conflict is an example of how poorly the United Nations has managed to control a region rife with ethnic violence— surely a good example to set for UN involvement in Iraq? For the future, the regions of the north Caucasus may well slip into lawlessness and drift away from Moscow's orbit. Following the disastrous interference in the Ukraine elections, Russia's president now talks of reconstituting the Russian empire. Russia is, in a sense, its own empire. The possibility that it may one day crumble in much the same manner as the former Soviet Union will be Putin's main fear.

Review Questions

1. Discuss why the name Stalin became synonymous with terrorism.
2. How has terrorism evolved in modern-day Russia and how has it been managed?
3. What circumstances led to the atrocities and ethnic fighting in the Kosovo region?
4. Discuss how the nationalist drive for Chechen independence has turned more into an Islamist insurgency.

Websites

1. **Center for Nonproliferation Studies**—*http://www. miis.edu/academics/researchcenters/nonproliferation*
2. **International Criminal Tribunal for the Former Yugoslavia**—*http://www.un.org/icty/*
3. **The Heritage Foundation**—*http://www.heritage.org/ Research/RussiaandEurasia/em844.cfm*
4. **National Academies Press**—*http://www.nap.edu/cata-log.php?record_id=11801*

End Notes

1. *The New Encyclopaedia Britannica*, vol. 8. (1985), 298.
2. "Secret Police." Revelations from the Russian Archives, Library of Congress (1996). http://leweb2.loc.gov/cgi-bin/query.
3. David Yallop. *Tracking the Jackal* (New York: Random House, 1993, p. 20).
4. Courtesy Russian Leadership Directory.
5. Mathew Bunn and Anthony Weir. *The Seven Myths of Nuclear Terrorism* (Philadelphia, PA: Current History, Inc., 2005, p. 153).
6. International Atomic Energy Agency.
7. Anthony Tucker-Jones. "'Flare Up in the Stans' INTER-SEC." *The Journal of International Security* vol. 20, no. 8 (Chertsey, UK: Albany Media, September 2010).
8. Edward Walker. "The Crisis in Chechnya." *Center for Slavic and Eastern European Studies Newsletter* (Spring 1995).
9. Edward Walker. "What's Next in Chechnya." *Association for the Study of Nationalities* http://www.nationalities.org.
10. "Putin's War," *U.S. News & World Report* (May 27, 2002, p. 26).
11. *BBC News online* (July 10, 2006), www.bbc.co.uk.
12. Lev Levinson. "Submission to the Eminent Jurists Panel in connection with public hearings on terrorism, counter-terrorism and human rights in Russia." *Human Rights Institute Governance as a Counter-Terrorist Operation* (Moscow, January 2007) http://ejp.icj.org/IMG/Levinson.pdf
13. Viktor Yuschenko. http://www.absoluteastronomy.com/topics/Viktor_Yushchenko
14. "The Plight of Chechen Refugees in Georgia," (March 21, 2005), www.ihrc.org.uk, retrieved May 1, 2011.
15. Araminta Wordsworth. "Sinking further in a morass of brutality." *Canada's National Post* (December 10, 1998, p. A15).
16. "The United Nations and Human Rights 1945–1995." *UN Blue Book Series*, vol. 7 (1995, p. 424).
17. Ibid.
18. Norman L. Cigar. *The Policy of Ethnic Cleansing* (College Station, TX: A&M University Press, 1995, p. 9).
19. Serbia History-Encarta online Encyclopedia. http://encarta.msn.com.
20. Ibid.
21. Ibid.
22. United Nations. www.un.org/icty/indictment/english/mil-ii990524e.htm.
23. Major General Lewis Mackenzie former commander of UN troops in Kosovo, 1992. "We bombed the wrong side." *The National Post* (April 6, 2004). The prospects for the region under the auspices of the UN are not exceptionally high.
24. Clare Sterling. "Bulgaria Hired Agca to Kill Pope." *New York Times* (June 10, 1984).
25. Philip Sherwell. "NATO planes strike on Kosovo." *The Weekly Telegraph*, Issue #359 (The Telegraph Group Ltd., June 9–15, 1998, p. 19).
26. Jorri Duursma. "Definition of Terrorism and Self Determination." *The Harvard Review* (December 20, 2008). http://hir.harvard.edu/definition-of-terrorism-and-self-determination?page=0,0

8

North Africa and the Middle East

If we ever hope to rid the world of the political AIDS of our time, terrorism, the rule must be clear: One does not deal with terrorists; one does not bargain with terrorists; one kills terrorists.

—MEIR KAHANE (1932–1990)

LEARNING OBJECTIVES

After studying this chapter, the student should be able to:

1. Trace the history of terrorism in Israel.
2. Discuss the profiles of terrorist groups that have operated in the Middle East during the last thirty years.
3. Discuss the involvement of state sponsors affecting the political landscape in Lebanon.
4. Describe the spread of Islamic extremism through North Africa.

KEY WORDS TO NOTE

Abdel Basset al-Megrahi—Libyan Intelligence officer convicted and subsequently released for the bombing of Pan Am flight over Lockerbie Scotland (December 21, 1988)

Al-Fatah—A left-wing nationalist Palestinian political party and largest member of the Palestine Liberation Organization (PLO). It has supported a wide variety of European terrorist groups through the 1960s and 1970s

Ariel Sharon—Israel's eleventh prime minister and former Israeli Army general

Balfour Declaration—1917 declaration pledging British support to a Jewish homeland in Palestine

Black September—A Palestinian terror group that takes its name from the bloody month that saw hijackings of airliners and fighting with Jordanian troops leading to the expulsion of Palestinians from Jordan

Fedayeen—An Arab commando or guerilla unit

Hamas—An offshoot of the Islamic Brotherhood and an acronym for the Islamic Resistance Movement

Hezbollah—Also known as Party of God—a Shia Muslim militant group based in Lebanon

Palestinian Islamic Jihad (PIJ)—Formed by militant Palestinians in the Gaza Strip during the 1970s; committed to the creation of an Islamic Palestinian state and the destruction of Israel

Palestine Liberation Organization (PLO)—Established by Yasser Arafat in 1964 as a political body representing the Palestinian people

Yasser Arafat—August 24, 1929–November 11, 2004) Awarded the Nobel Peace Prize in 1994. Symbolically portrayed as the leader of the Palestinian struggle for an independent Palestinian state; often viewed by outsiders as a corrupt politician and a stumbling block to peace in the Middle East; considered a terrorist by Israel.

OVERVIEW

The late Yasser Arafat stated, "Peace for us means the destruction of Israel. We are preparing for an all-out war which will last for generations." The Peace Accords, and the innumerable sessions proclaiming a new round of talks to resolve the question of Palestinian statehood/homeland and Israeli security, will be examined in detail in this chapter. Resistance to the presence of Israeli settlers in Palestine, the effect this has on Israel's security, and the response by the men of terror in Palestine will also be discussed. Israel's right to exist, and the threats and assaults it has had to withstand, form much of the basis for terror attacks and extreme Islamic movements bent on the ultimate goal—the destruction of the Jewish State.

Palestinians have been depopulated and, for all intents and purposes, terrorized out of their homes to make room for Jewish settlers. This has persisted, contrary to International law, for over half a century. Syria has a role in this problem, under the relatively inexperienced son of the late President Assad. The Gaza Strip and the West Bank have become a flash point for internal fighting between **Fatah** and **Hamas** since the death of **Yasser Arafat**. What effects will the latest accord between Fatah and Hamas have on conditions for peace in the region, a region that is racked by upsurges in regime change driven by so-called democracy movements?

ISRAEL AND ITS RIGHT TO EXIST

"The Middle East Crisis" focuses on the issues of "security" of the State of Israel and "hope" for the Palestinians for their own homeland with ultimate international recognition. Pro-Israel lobbyists in the United States contend that "U.S. aid to Israel enhances American national security interests, by strengthening our only Middle East ally in an unstable, dangerous, and vital region of the world." The ongoing issue surrounding the Israeli settlements in the Palestinian Authority (PA) areas continues. Since 1967, Israel has continued to create settlements in these territories. "The creation of a viable Jewish state, in an adequate area of Palestine instead of in the whole of Palestine would be acceptable," stated then president Harry S. Truman in 1946.[1] The questions regarding Israel's inflexibility, and the Palestinian refugees' having a safe homeland, clearly cannot be viewed as a new phenomenon. As far back as the creation of Israel, the United States has been fielding the criticism, and often the blame, for Israel's intransigence, her belligerence, and her arrogance for coldbloodedness in her attitude toward refugees.[2] The quest for a separate Palestinian state remains as much in focus today as it was over a half-century ago. In 1948, the United States and Britain, appreciated that the 1947 UN partition plan had failed. They concluded that their best political solution was to deny the Palestinians a state of their own. Under this strategy, the Palestinians would simply be absorbed into the neighboring Arab states mainly Transjordan, as it was then known, now the Hashemite Kingdom of Jordan.[3] Land is not the only issue surrounding the Middle East crisis, but the retention of land seized by Israel beyond the UN mandate of 1947, and following the Six-Day War of 1967. This burning issue is still as relevant in 2012 as it was after the Six-Day War. In May 2011, Israel's prime minister Benjamin Netanyahu argued that Israel is ready to make painful concessions in any peace deal but insisted that Jerusalem will not be divided nor will it make concessions on its border security or on the border of a future Palestinian state. In effect, Israel will make no concessions relative to the 1967 borders. Netanyahu refers to Hamas as the Palestinian version of al Qaeda and that for any peace deal to be formulated Fatah would need to rip apart its agreement with Hamas in order to facilitate any Israeli settlement.

Early History

The Jewish people ("Hebrews") settled the region of Palestine about 1,200 years before the birth of Christ. From 70 to 700 A.D., the region was under the control of the Romans, who dispersed most of the Hebrews from the region. With the collapse of the Roman Empire, the Ishmaelite (Arabs) settled in the region and remained there until the Turkish (Ottoman) Empire subjugated them in 1516.

Political Considerations

To understand the complexities of this unique region, we first look at the imperialist influences and designs on this region at

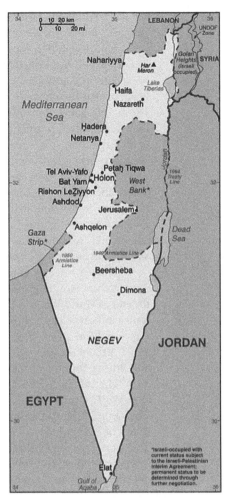

FIGURE 8-1 Map of Israel (Central Intelligence Agency, *The World Factbook, 2008*).

the time of World War I. By the latter part of the 1800s, the Ottoman Empire was in total disarray and internal factional disturbances were continuing within the realm as Turkey's influences waned. The dwindling Turkish Ottoman Empire comprised a significant section of the Arab territories of the Middle East, and this area was, by 1914, an area ripe for the plucking. Britain, France, and Russia all had designs on the Arab lands. Turkey was fighting on the side of the German Empire against Britain and France so it suited Britain to turn the Arabs against the Turks. To sustain the Jews on the side of Britain, the British government issued the "**Balfour Declaration**," named after the highly respected British foreign secretary, Sir Arthur James Balfour. The Declaration read as follows: "*His Majesty's Government views with favor the establishment in Palestine of a national homeland for the Jewish people, and will use their best endeavors to facilitate the achievement of this objective, it being clearly understood that* *nothing shall be done which may prejudice the rights of non-Jewish communities in Palestine, or the rights and political status enjoyed by Jews in any other country."*

This declaration sought to win both financial and political support for the war from Jews in Europe and the United States. The Jews viewed this as tacit agreement for having their own homeland in Palestine. The Arabs, however, read a different meaning into the wording. They believed that they had been forced to agree to any terms put forward, before an agreement on self-determination of lands for the Jews had been realized. The Arabs fought in the belief that they were assured independence; the Jews in Palestine offered to raise troops to fight on the side of the British.

Promising independence to both Zionists and Arabs alike, the British government had unwittingly sown the seeds for an endless succession of wars. In the following decades, the Jews and Arabs would fight conventional wars that would turn into what is now called "modern-day terrorism," a situation that endured for the remainder of the twentieth century. With Arabs and Jews focused on fighting the Turks, Britain achieved its immediate aim of controlling the region and assured support from both. Albeit a shortsighted political decision, it left the Middle East with the distinction of becoming a breeding ground for future generations of terrorists.

The very name "Palestinian" is often seen as synonymous with "Terrorism." This view adequately portrays the problems that beset this area of the Middle East. British strategic aims, at the end of World War I, were to solidify a friendly presence in Palestine to ensure protection of its routes into Africa and to the east into India. Of major importance in this plan would be the Suez Canal and the major shipping route from the Indian Ocean to the Mediterranean. After World War I, Britain set up the Arab kingdoms of Saudi Arabia, Iraq, and Syria in such a fashion that only strong, traditional, family groups controlled them.

The influx of Jewish refugees escaping Europe at the end of the 1930s and during and after World War II was staunchly opposed by the British Conservative Government of Winston Churchill. Despite the desperate need to find a haven for refugees, the doors of Palestine remained shut. The Zionist leadership met in the Biltmore Hotel in New York City in 1942 and declared that it supported the establishment of Palestine as a Jewish Commonwealth. This was a restatement of Zionist aims that went beyond the Balfour declaration and a determination that the British were, in principle, an enemy to be fought, rather than an ally.

Settlements and Terror

Israel's history is founded on its struggle to exist in a hostile environment, surrounded by unfriendly neighbors and Arab refugees. Since the 1948 Arab-Israeli war, the areas that were occupied by Israel have seen countless incursions by Arab refugees and particularly from Jordan and Egypt. Many of these incursions were raids by "foraging Arabs" returning to their home villages and stopping en route to rob and steal. Many attacks on civilians in Jewish-occupied regions resulted, and it is from these early incursions that the Israelis initiated various response mechanisms. To prevent these attacks, the Israelis adopted a policy of destroying abandoned Arab villages along the border region and establishing Israeli settlements in their place. Hundreds of Israeli civilians had been killed by 1953, when the Israeli government established "Unit 101," a special operations/commando unit. Ariel Sharon led this unit in August 1953, on orders from former prime minister David Ben-Gurion. The unit drew much criticism due to its killing of innocent civilians, and in particular the Qibya operation, which left almost seventy civilians dead. However, its extreme methods of attack would eventually form the cornerstones for the development of the Israeli Defense Force (IDF). The brutal nature of the unit's attacks against civilian targets eventually led to its abandonment in 1954, integrating it into the 202 Paratroop Brigade.

THE STERN GANG

The "Stern Gang" was an extreme, right-wing organization and was founded by Avraham Stern in 1940 as a split-off group from the Irgun. Irgun was a Jewish terrorist group organized in the 1930s to defend the Jewish settlers from Arab attacks and, after World War II, used its skills to attack the British in Palestine. Irgun's attacks culminated in the massacre of 250 Arab civilians at the settlement of Deir Yassin, outside Jerusalem in 1948. This action prompted Israeli former prime minister David-Ben-Gurion to call for the Irgun to be disbanded and absorbed into the Haganah Army, the forerunner to the IDFs. Stern was killed by British forces in 1944, but the gang continued under the leadership of Israel Eldad, Natan Yellin-Mor, and Yitzhak Shamir, who became the prime minister of Israel forty years later. Two notable assassinations are credited to the Stern Gang. On November 6, 1944, they killed the British resident minister for the Middle East, Lord Moyne, and on September 17, 1948, the then UN special mediator for Palestine, Count Folke Bernadotte. The Deir Yassin massacre, in 1948, also involved the Stern Gang, but the much larger Irgun was the main perpetrator of that massacre. Both Stern and Irgun were in existence prior to the formation of the State of Israel, and both sought the formation of the Jewish state through actions that are considered terrorism and were mainly directed against the British mandate in Palestine. The Stern Gang's attacks were against the British, not the Arab communities. Discussion of Stern's approaches to the Nazis is controversial due to their very abhorrent nature; maybe it was a case that, in 1939, "his enemy's enemy was therefore Stern's friend." Stern could likely only consider this in terms of the total liberation of the region from British control.

Under the 1947 UN Partition Plan, Israel's original size had been limited to 5,900 square miles. Following the fighting in 1948, Israel's land total became 7,800 square miles. The 1967 Six-Day War dramatically altered the borders of Israel. After this brief war, Israel controlled some 20,870 square miles of newly acquired territory…nearly five times its original size.[4] Settlements continued to be created, and Palestinians were being dispossessed of their land as Israel's expansion continued. Condemnation of Israel came from United Nations resolutions, which, in most cases, were vetoed by the United States. However, in March 1976, the United States finally condemned these settlements as being both illegal and an obstacle to peace. By the time of the U.S. declaration, there were already about sixty-eight settlements in the territories, not counting Jerusalem. William W. Scranton, the former U.S. ambassador to the United Nations, informed the Security Council,

> "Next, I turn to the question of Israeli settlements in the occupied territories. Again, my government believes that international law sets the appropriate standards. An occupier must maintain the occupied areas as intact and unaltered as possible, without interfering with the customary life of the area, and any changes must be necessitated by the immediate needs of the occupation and be consistent with international law. The Fourth Geneva Convention now speaks directly to the issue of population transfer in Article 49. Clearly then, substantial resettlement of the Israeli population in the occupied territories, including East Jerusalem, is illegal under the convention and cannot be considered to have prejudged the outcome of future negotiations between the parties or the location of the borders of states of the Middle East. Indeed, the presence of these settlements is seen by my government as an obstacle to the success of the negotiations for a just and final peace between Israel and its neighbors."[5]

Israeli expansionism has continued in spite of these words spoken over thirty years ago. In February 1989, former Israeli prime minister Yitzhak Rabin assured a "Peace Now" delegation that negotiations (with the Palestinians) were nothing but some "low-level discussions" that avoided any serious issues and granted Israel "at least a year" to resolve the problem (presumably by force). Rabin further stated, "The inhabitants of the territories are now subject to both harsh military and economic pressure; in the end they will be broken."[6]

The Oslo Peace Accords of the 1990s have been so encumbered as to make it impossible to determine what concessions, if any, Israel has made. This is due to the Israeli conditions, entailments, and qualifications, which were so one-sided that Palestinians felt no semblance of self-determination. It is not difficult to see why Palestinians then see terrorism as a tool—and likely their only tool—to make their claims clear to the world at large. The actions of suicide terrorists on 9-11 may have been seen as an opportunity for the Israeli government to bury the Intifada once and for all. In the week following 9-11, the Israelis took their War on Terror directly into Palestinian territory.

The Israeli army killed twenty-eight Palestinians and mounted sixteen incursions into Palestinian Authority areas. The response to the swiftness of the Israeli incursion forced Arafat to declare a cease-fire on all fronts and express readiness to enlist in America's coalition for "ending terrorism against unarmed innocent civilians." Following this, the Palestinian Authority leader warned Islamic Jihad, Hamas, and others not to give "pretexts" that would aid Mr. Sharon's designs. Although these groups heeded the call from Arafat and ended the firing on Jewish settlements from Palestinian areas, they did not agree to end armed actions in their own defense of Palestinian towns still under occupation. These groups also affirmed that they would respond if Israel acted against them or their people. On September 24, 2001, the Israeli army established a twenty-mile "closed military zone" along the West Bank's northern border with Israel. This was ostensibly established to prevent suicide bombers from infiltrating any Israeli Territory.[7] A test of Israel's will came in the subsequent surprising events, which triggered the Second Intifada uprising: attacks by suicide bombers and rioting that continued off and on through 2002. Israeli then prime minister Ehud Barak dispatched a military force, led by then defense minister Ariel Sharon, to the Al-Aqsa compound. Sharon strode into the *Haram al-Sharif* (The Noble Sanctuary) in what was designed to be a gesture to assert his rights as an Israeli to visit this Muslim holy place. This single act sparked the beginning of the Second Intifada. Sharon cannot be described as a statesman whose actions were likely to endear him to Palestinians in general. His reputation was mainly due to his checkered career, in particular his questionable involvement in the Sabra and Shatila refugee camp massacres that took place in Beirut in 1982.

Throughout the latter half of 2001 and 2002, the Israeli government held the Palestinian Authority's leader, Yasser Arafat, "personally responsible" for terrorist and suicide attacks against Israel. Israel adopted the military option to attack specific "Terror" targets inside the Palestinian-controlled areas. In January 2002, the Israeli Air Force used U.S.-made F-16s to drop bombs on Arafat's compound in Ramallah. Most military actions had been in response to Palestinian suicide attacks against Israeli targets. Israel also used targeted assassinations to deter, destroy, and remove Hamas militant leaders.

HAGANAH, IRGUN ZEVA'I LE'UMI, NATIONAL MILITARY ORGANIZATION (NMO)

The Haganah (Hebrew—defense) were established as a Jewish defense force in the 1920s as a response to the lack of protection offered to local Jewish communities by the British from attacks by Arabs. They had no central command in the beginning and were made up mainly of farmers who were poorly equipped. Haganah underwent a quick transformation following riots in 1929 and saw its numbers swelled with Jewish youth from the countryside and the cities. With the British Mandate firmly in place, Haganah participated in actions in defense of British interests to suppress the growing Arab revolts. The British forces in Palestine were actively supporting if not officially recognizing the Haganah. In 1939, the British began to severely restrict all forms of Jewish migration to Palestine, and this would have been a turning point for Haganah and its leadership. The main method of smuggling refugees from Europe was by ship, and although many were intercepted and returned, a large number succeeded in reaching Palestine thanks to the Haganah organization.

NMO, a Jewish underground organization, was founded in 1931 by a group of Haganah commanders who left the Haganah in protest against its defense charter. In April 1937, during the Arab riots, the organization split—about half its members returned to the Haganah. They carried out reprisals against Arabs, which were condemned by the Haganah. The term "Special Night Squads" originates from an invention of the British Army in Palestine in 1938 when Orde Wingate set up plans using British soldiers, members of Haganah, and the Jewish Settlement Police to combat nighttime incursions by Arabs into northern Palestine. Irgun operated exclusively in Palestine as a Jewish group for the establishment of a modern-day Israel. Their main targets were the resident Arab Palestinians and the occupying British Army in Palestine. Bombings were the order of the day, and the two-pronged attacks were designed to have two legitimate aims for the Jews. The first was to destabilize the British presence in the region and make it costly for the British to retain a presence. With the agreement on partition by the United Nations formally granted in 1948, the terrorists of the Irgun began to immediately attack and kill Arab families and individuals who remained in the Jewish sector. The effect on the demoralized Palestinians was to produce a mass exodus from the area. Several notable members of Irgun played an important role over the following years in the development and political status of Israel. Menachem Begin led Irgun activities during the 1940s, and when the State of Israel was official, he entered politics and founded the right-wing Herut Party and became leader of the Israeli opposition party from 1948 to 1967. He became prime minister in 1977 of the right-wing coalition government and took a very hard line against the Arabs. In spite of that he began talks with Egypt in 1977, mediated by then U.S. president Jimmy Carter in the peace treaty of 1979, winning him a share of the Nobel Peace Prize with former Egyptian president Anwar Sadat. Hosni Mubarak, Sadat's successor, would hold that peace in place until the spring revolutions that swept the Middle East and North Africa in 2011. Following the Israeli invasion of Lebanon in 1981 to rid the region of burgeoning terrorist threats to Israel, Begin would resign in 1983 following worldwide condemnation for the invasion.

Ariel Sharon

Until his sudden illness, which has kept him in a virtual coma since 2006, **Ariel Sharon** was viewed with passion by the Israelis. He joined the Haganah and, later, the IDF. After college studies he returned as a major to head up the IDF's Unit 101. The unit was criticized for targeting civilians as well as the Arab armies, resulting in the widely condemned Qibya Operation in the autumn of 1953. More than sixty Jordanian civilians were killed in an ambush of Arab Legion forces. Shortly afterward, Unit 101 was merged into the 202nd Paratrooper Brigade.

Sharon was a member of the Knesset from 1973 to 1974 and, again, from 1977 to the present. He served as the security adviser to then prime minister Yitzhak Rabin and as minister of agriculture (1977–1981) and defense minister (1981–1983) in Menachem Begin's Likud government. During the Israeli invasion of Lebanon in 1982, while Ariel Sharon was defense minister, a massacre of several hundred Palestinians in Sabra and Shatila refugee camps in Beirut was carried out by the Phalanges, a Lebanese-Christian militia allied with Israel. It has been speculated that Ariel Sharon played a significant part in allowing the Christian militia a free hand in the camps and by security the perimeter for them to conduct atrocities within the two Palestinian camps. He was elected prime minister in February 2001 soon after the collapse of Barak's government. His former deputy prime minister Ehud Olmert assumed the role of prime minister on a permanent basis on the declaration of Sharon's permanent incapacity in April 2006.

MOSSAD

The Israeli Secret Intelligence Service

In July 1949, Reuven Shiloah, a close associate of David Ben Gurion, proposed establishing a central institution for organizing and co-coordinating intelligence and security service. The object was to enhance interservice coordination and cooperation. On December 13, 1949, Ben Gurion authorized the establishment of the "Institution for Co-ordination" to oversee the political department and to coordinate the internal security and military intelligence organizations. The institution, Mossad, was born on that day.

The Mossad started out under foreign ministry auspices. In March 1951, with a view to enhancing its operational capabilities and to unifying all overseas intelligence gathering, Ben Gurion authorized its final reorganization. An independent, centralized authority was set up to handle all overseas intelligence tasks. This was called the "Authority" and formed the major part of the Mossad. It included representatives of the other two services at HQ and field echelons. The Mossad broke free of the foreign ministry and reported directly to the prime minister, thus becoming part of the prime minister's office. The Mossad eventually adopted the following verse from the Book of Proverbs as not only its motto, guide, creative awakener, and ideology but also as a dire warning: *"Without guidance do a people fall, and deliverance is in a multitude of counsellors." Proverbs XI/14*[8]

THE PALESTINIAN LIBERATION ORGANIZATION (PLO)

In May 1964, 422 Palestinian national figures met in Jerusalem under the chairmanship of Ahmad Shuqeiri and, following an Arab League decision, founded the **Palestinian Liberation Organization (PLO)**. They laid the foundations and structure of the PLO and, in the early years, followed pan-Arabic ideology. They set up as an umbrella movement for a large number of varied Palestinian interest groups and were regarded by many, the Israelis in particular, as a terrorist organization. The early PLO was not a cohesive organization and contained a broad spectrum of moderate to extremely radical viewpoints. The militant members of PLO were known as **fedayeen** (warriors), prepared to die for Allah. With such diverse opinions, the PLO became splintered and factional. This internecine struggle was much like the many Republican factions in Northern Ireland.

Their driving philosophy was the restoration of Palestine, the destruction of Israel, and the re-creation of an Arab State in Palestine. The PLO is loosely organized under three headings: the Executive Committee, the Central Committee, and the Palestine National Council. The Executive Committee coordinates the major terror activities, and the Central Committee acts as an advisory structure to the Executive Committee. During the 1960s, PLO guerrilla groups carried out sporadic attacks against Israel. However, the new organization then lacked strong leadership, and during this period, they operated from bases inside the Hashemite Kingdom of Jordan, ruled by

British-educated King Hussein. In Jordan, Yasser Arafat laid the groundwork for his operations among the Palestinians. In 1964, Arafat took control of the PLO and turned it from a feeble political movement to one that would be recognized as the only one to represent all the Palestinian people. By 1974, the Arab nations had recognized the PLO as "the sole, legitimate representative of the Palestinian people." In the same year, the United Nations (excluding Israel) similarly recognized the PLO.

Like all good political and terrorist organizations, Arafat's PLO had a senior security advisor, Ali Hassan Salameh (aka Abu Hassan), the "Red Prince." The Israeli intelligence agency, Mossad, believed Salameh to be the PLO member responsible for planning the Munich Olympic Games massacre. Golda Meir, then prime minister of Israel, gave Mossad the task of tracking down the man responsible for the attack. The search lasted seven years. In their attempts to assassinate Salameh, Mossad killed an innocent Moroccan bartender in Lillehammer; such was their fervor to exact retribution on the PLO. Salameh was killed by a remote-controlled bomb, in January 1979, detonated in a stationary vehicle as he drove by with his bodyguards. Arafat worked tirelessly to steer the PLO toward political legitimacy and, in 1988, took the monumental step of announcing the right of Israel to exist and renouncing the further use of PLO terrorism. This commitment, from the man who then spoke for the displaced Palestinians, moved Israel toward discussions on Palestinian self-rule. Young Palestinians, who were frustrated with the slow progress toward self-rule in a homeland of their own, then turned to Hamas or Hezbollah for their leadership.

On September 13, 1993 (in Oslo), the Declaration of Principles between the Israelis and the Palestinians was signed. Palestinian groups formerly under the umbrella of the PLO, such as the Popular Front for the Liberation of Palestine (PFLP) and also the Democratic Front for the Liberation of Palestine-Hawatmeh (DFLPH), suspended their participation in the PLO in protest and continued their campaigns of violence against not only the Israelis but also Americans and members of Arafat's PLO. Arafat remained as the PLO leader until his death in 2004. Arafat had been the specific target of Israel almost unceasingly since 9-11. He endured house arrest in his own compound for much of 2002–2004. Israeli raids into Palestinian areas such as Ramallah and Jenin, to root out terrorists who were targeting civilians, still continued unabated in spite of international condemnation for the use of military hardware in the West Bank and Gaza regions. By the middle of 2002, Arafat was clinging on to the leadership of the PLO, but he faced a mounting challenge from Hamas militants.

The likelihood that a Palestinian/Israeli accord could be brokered between Sharon and Arafat was always in question. Both had a long history of mistrust for each other. Sharon's long-remembered direct or indirect involvement with Christian militias in the Sabra and Shatila camp massacres did nothing to ease the dangers for peace in the region.

Arafat operated more as a dictator than a democratic leader, and some two years after an agreed deadline for democratic elections to be held, Arafat blamed the delay on the Israeli occupation. He stated frequently that this must end before elections could take place.

The world held its collective breath following Arafat's death in a Paris hospital in 2004. Without any viable successor, the vacuum could well have been filled with warring factions that would have done nothing to promote peace in the region. By 2006, the warring and infighting between the various factions of Hamas and the PLO/Fatah became a long-awaited reality. Arafat had been the main player in Palestinian politics and terror for over forty years and held a stranglehold on the PLO and its activities.

Arafat had been chairman of the Palestine Liberation Organization, the titular head of Fatah, then president of the Palestinian Authority, and president of the State of Palestine as declared by the PLO in 1988. Fatah is the name used to describe the Palestinian National

Liberation Movement and is the largest constituent within the PLO. The elections held in 2005 to elect Arafat's successor saw the ascension of Mahmoud Abbas (aka Abu Mazen). Elected on January 9, 2005, as president of the Palestinian Authority, Abbas and then Israeli prime minister Sharon faced some daunting hurdles on both sides of their collective boundaries. Abbas had opposed the Intifada that had lingered since 2000 and aimed to support the U.S.-brokered "road map" to a peace settlement for the region. At an executive meeting on January 16, 2005, the PLO appealed for an end to armed attacks because they would provide excuses to the Israeli position of undermining Palestinian stability. With more than 5,000 deaths since the start of the 2000 Intifada, and two-thirds of that number being Palestinians, the hope was that Abbas would get much-needed support of the Arafat factions within the Fatah movement so that he would eventually have sufficient clout to control the various factions that sought only armed conflict with Israel.

ISRAELI DISENGAGEMENT PLAN

For Israel and former prime minister Sharon's designs to succeed, some serious balancing acts to somehow prevent extremist elements within Israel from disrupting the disengagement plans for the Gaza Strip were required.

The official document distributed by the Israeli Ministry of Foreign Affairs now contains the following:

GAZA STRIP

1. Israel will evacuate the Gaza Strip, including all existing Israeli towns and villages, and will re-deploy outside the Strip. This will not include military deployment in the area of the border between the Gaza Strip and Egypt.
2. Upon completion of this process, there shall no longer be any permanent presence of Israeli security forces or Israeli civilians in the areas of the Gaza Strip territory which have been evacuated.
3. As a result, there will be no basis for claiming that the Gaza Strip is occupied territory.

WEST BANK

1. Israel will evacuate an area in the northern Samaria area, including villages and all military installations, and will re-deploy outside the vacated area.
2. Upon completion of this process, there shall no longer be any permanent presence of Israeli security forces or Israeli civilians in the northern Samaria area.
3. The move will enable territorial contiguity for Palestinians in the northern Samaria area.
4. Israel will improve the transportation infrastructure in the West Bank in order to facilitate the contiguity of Palestinian transportation.
5. The process will facilitate Palestinian economic and commercial activity in the West Bank.
6. The Security Fence: Israel will continue to build the security fence, in accordance with relevant decisions of the government. The route will take into account humanitarian considerations.

Security situation following the disengagement:

GAZA STRIP

1. Israel will guard and monitor the external land perimeter of the Gaza Strip, will continue to maintain exclusive authority in Gaza airspace, and will continue to exercise security activity in the sea off the coast of the Gaza Strip.
2. The Gaza Strip will be demilitarized and shall be devoid of weaponry, the presence of which does not accord with the Israeli-Palestine agreements.
3. Israel reserves its inherent right to self-defense, both preventative and reactive, including where necessary the use of force, in respect of threats emanating from the Gaza Strip.

WEST BANK

1. Upon completion of the evacuation of the northern Samaria area, no permanent Israeli presence will remain in this area.
2. Israel reserves its inherent right to self-defense, both preventive and reactive, including where necessary the use of force, in respect of threats emanating from the northern Samaria area.
3. In other areas of the West Bank, current security activity will continue. However, as circumstances permit, Israel will consider reducing such activity in Palestinian cities.
4. Israel will work to reduce the number of internal checkpoints throughout the West Bank.

Under Sharon's "Disengagement" plan, Palestinians in the Gaza Strip continue to be subjected to the effective control of the Israeli Military. Although Israel will remove its permanent military presence, Israeli forces will retain the ability and inherent right to enter the Gaza Strip at will.[9] Israel will retain control over Gaza's airspace, sea shore, and borders.[10] Under the plan, Israel will unilaterally control whether or not Gaza opens a seaport or an airport. Additionally, Israel will control all border crossings; including Gaza's border with Egypt.[11] Israel will "continue its military activity along the Gaza Strip's coastline."[12] Taken together, these powers mean that all goods and people entering or leaving Gaza will be subject to Israeli control.

Finally, Israel will prevent Gazians from engaging in international relations. Accordingly, if it enacts the "Disengagement" plan as envisaged, Israel will effectively control Gaza, administratively and militarily.[13] Therefore, Israel will remain the occupying power of the Gaza Strip, as contrary to its own assertions. Israel's greatest battle is probably not against "terrorism," but against demography. Statistical analyses project that Palestinian Christians and Muslims will comprise the majority of persons in Israel and the occupied Palestinian territories by the year 2020.[14] If Israel wants to remain a "Jewish State," then it will be very difficult to maintain its Jewish identity if an ethno/religious minority continues to rule over an ethnic majority. Israeli journalist David Landau noted in a statement made to a British journalist that the Gaza plan represents "the simplest, crudest solution [to Israel's demographic time bomb]: to dump Gaza and its 1.3 million Arabs in the hope that that would 'buy' Israel 50 more years."[15]

For any success in the precarious region of Palestine, and for there to be any chance of any kind of settlement, let alone the realization of a separate state for the Palestinians, Mahmoud Abbas must show that his administration will not tolerate corruption and, in doing so, establish the rule of law. Probably more significantly, the leadership of the PA must display a prominent role in disengaging the Israelis from Gaza. The final disengagement and dismantling of Jewish settlements actually went ahead of schedule and for the region in a relatively calm manner. The expected militant Jewish backlash never came about and the militant Palestinian groups, Hamas in particular, celebrated the liberation of the Gaza Strip as being a victory for armed resistance. Israel resides behind its secured Gaza fence line, and the Hamas militants will have to focus more on infiltration operations. Since the August 2005 withdrawal from Gaza, there have been sporadic rocket attacks and the more familiar bus/suicide bombings usually as a response to Israeli security operations.

AL-FATAH

Al-Fatah (or *Al-Asifa*), the fighting organization within the PLO, actually predated the PLO by six years. Under the leadership of Yasser Arafat, it took total control of the PLO after the debacle of the 1967 Six-Day War. It is considered the largest terrorist group under the PLO banner—estimated to have a force of up to 15,000 fedayeen. The group is financed mostly by wealthy Arab states.

Al-Fatah, however, has never managed to prove itself as a military machine against the Israelis in spite of its size and support structure, not even in the occupied territories of the Gaza Strip and the West Bank region of Jordan. Fatah were not able to prevent the Jordanian army from forcibly removing the PLO from its Jordanian training camps around Ajlun and Jerash in 1970, nor could it prevent a repetition in Lebanon, when the PLO was swept out by an Israeli invasion force in 1982.

OPERATION BAYONET

In Chapter 6, we discussed how members of Black September had succeeded in breaching the Olympic Games security at the 1972 Munich Games and massacred eleven Israeli athletes. For the Israeli government there was to be retribution, and the then Israeli prime minister Golda Meir secretly ordered Mossad to track down and kill all those involved in the planning and execution of the raid in Munich. Mossad agents spread throughout Europe and the Middle East and tracked their targets and assassinated them; they made one error—in 1973 in Lillehammer, Norway, they killed an innocent Moroccan waiter who looked like their intended target Ali Salameh. Between 1979 and 1982, Mossad and Israeli military commandos killed more than a dozen members, effectively eradicating the entire group responsible for the Olympic Games attack.

Black September is the name of the al Fatah terror wing and takes its name from the month of the Palestinians eviction from Jordan; **Black September** is the operational military arm of Fatah.

In spite of the extensive Mossad operation in Europe, Black September rebounded as the defense arm of Al-Fatah, protecting it and Arafat from the extremist groups sponsored by Syria and Iraq, who were funding Abu Nidal's Black June.

During the 1960s and 1970s, Al-Fatah offered training facilities to a wide range of the Middle Eastern, European, Asian, and African terrorist organizations, as well as insurgent groups. Reciprocal arrangements within these groups allowed for terror operations to be carried out in each other's names, throughout the world. The arrangements also helped with the financial support required to allow the groups to maintain their operations.

Like the Palestinian people, Al-Fatah is spread throughout the Middle East but is primarily headquartered in Tunisia. Al-Fatah has been provided with aid from Saudi Arabia, Kuwait, and some of the other Arab states in the Persian Gulf region. Al-Fatah members have likewise received training from the former USSR as well as other former Communist Bloc countries.

The tangled web of Middle East terrorism does not start and finish with the PLO. The PLO, like most organizations that are spread over a wide area, will have many different points of political view.

ABU NIDAL ORGANIZATION (ANO)

Sabri al-Banna (1937–2002), also known as Abu Nidal, spent his teenage years in Saudi Arabia and became actively involved in Arab Nationalism by joining the Ba'ath Party. His activities resulted in his arrest and subsequent expulsion from Saudi Arabia. He would become Fatah representative in Khartoum Sudan in 1968 and then in Baghdad in 1970. At the height of his influence in the 1970s and 1980s, he was considered the world's most dangerous terrorist. He rejected any idea of peaceful settlement with Israel and split from Yasser Arafat Fatah faction within the PLO over that issue in 1974. He became increasingly dangerous not only to the West but also to Yasser Arafat's control of the PLO.

Abu Nidal is the cover name for Sabri al-Banna, and the organization uses the following names:

- Revolutionary Council
- Palestinian National Liberation Movement
- Black June
- Black September
- The Revolutionary Arab Brigades
- The Revolutionary Organization of Socialist Muslims
- The Egyptian Revolution; Revolutionary Egypt-
- Al-Asifa (The Storm)
- Al-Iqab (The Punishment)
- The Arab Nationalist Youth Organization

The Abu Nidal Organization was recognized as one of the bloodiest terror groups operating in the Middle East. It certainly became a truly international terror operation by expanding its horizons and ability to strike at its enemies wherever they might be throughout the globe.

Al-Banna was drawn to Baghdad most likely because of what is termed its "rejectionist" approach to those Middle East countries that favored a peace deal with Israel. "Rejectionism" is a Middle Eastern political term meaning unilateral refusal of any peaceful settlement with Israel. Iraq would have been considered one of the most extreme rejectionist states and one that would not sanction any such deals with Israel. This also had the effect of alienating those states in favor of moderation, such as Jordan and Egypt. Al-Banna's goals can be summarized simply: first and foremost, the destruction of Israel; and second, control of the PLO with the support of the rejectionist Iraqi government. It seemed to suit Iraq to have a terrorist group within its boundaries that would do its bidding in return for bases and logistical support. Al-Banna, under the protection of Saddam Hussein, trained about 200 fighters for their joint cause.

Al-Banna believed that by creating terror on a world stage—rather than just the Middle East—he could meet his goals. His ruthless approach to terrorist actions and atrocities focused the world media and political attention firmly on the regional problems. Abu Nidal has carried out attacks in at least twenty countries and is responsible for the deaths of over 900 people. The group has not just targeted Israel but also the United Kingdom, the United States, and France, and those moderate Palestinians with the temerity to seek a peaceful settlement with Israel have also been attacked. Many attacks were spectacular in their audaciousness. The ANO credits itself with the assassination attempt on the Israeli ambassador outside the Dorchester Hotel in London, in June 1982. Three men, Hussein Ghassan Said, Marwan al-Banna, and Nawaf al-Rosan, approached Israel's then ambassador Shlomo Argov as he got into his car after a banquet at the Dorchester Hotel, in Park Lane, London. Said shot Argov in the head. Al-Banna was Abu Nidal's cousin, Said a Jordanian, and the third of Argov's would-be assassins, Al-Rosan, was a Baghdad intelligence colonel.[16]

The ambassador, Shlomo Argov, was seriously injured. This single terrorist attack precipitated another "eye for an eye—tooth for a tooth" revenge response from the Israelis, the 1982 invasion of Lebanon.

The PLO, under Yasser Arafat, denied any involvement in the attack. However, from the Israeli viewpoint, this was sufficient cause to attack, as "terrorism begets terrorism." Israel's response was a military hard line. The Israeli Air Force mounted a bombing raid on Palestinian camps in Beirut, killing at least 50, with 200 injured. It has been speculated that this act provided the Israelis with the excuse to conduct a full-scale invasion of southern Lebanon to purge the region of PLO fighters. The invasion commenced two days after the attack on Argov and was termed "Operation Peace for Galilee." The action was aimed to destabilize Lebanon and force the PLO to flee the country to Syria, Tunisia, and Iraq. As Abu Nidal's notoriety increased, so too did the international flavor of the training camps in and around Baghdad. These training centers attracted radical European elements wishing to learn the trade of terrorism.

SIGNIFICANT INCIDENTS

Abu Nidal was successful in attacking aviation targets. Two such attacks date back to 1985:

December 27, Rome Airport, 08:15—Leonardo Da Vinci Airport is situated on the outskirts of Rome and is the principal international airport in Italy. At 08:15, four young Arabs threw hand grenades at a line of passengers waiting in the check-in line for the El Al flight. El Al's check-in desks are flanked by those of Trans World Airlines (TWA). The four Arabs then opened fire with Kalashnikov AK-47 assault rifles on the American and Israeli passengers waiting in line. Other passengers, including Greeks, Mexicans, and two Arabs, were killed in the attack. El Al has a record of being proactive in aviation security, and at Rome airport, its armed security staff returned fire, along with Italian police, and killed three and injured one of the terrorists. Fifteen passengers were killed and seventy injured.

The terrorists were Arabs, so the PLO was immediately denounced as having orchestrated the attack. In fact, Abu Nidal was the likely culprit; however, the incidents in Rome and Vienna were most likely aimed at discrediting Arafat and the PLO. Both Austria and Italy were well disposed to the Palestinian cause, and this action would have been designed to turn those countries against Arafat.

December 27, Vienna Airport, 08:15—this airport attack was timed to coincide with the Rome attack. There were fewer casualties in Vienna than in Rome: two dead and forty-six injured. The terrorists used the same modus operandi as their colleagues in Rome. However, they were able to fight their way out of the airport and escape temporarily by car, pursued by Austrian police. A gun battle followed, and one of the terrorists was killed and the remaining two surrendered. Again, this attack is attributed to Abu Nidal and his attempt to discredit Arafat.[17]

The ANO has shifted bases periodically from Iraq to Syria and has also had bases in Lebanon, Libya, and the Sudan. Its support network and financial aid came primarily from Iraq and Syria and, more recently, from Libya. Reports of Sabri al-Banna's death came on August 19, 2002, through Middle East news reports that he died of gunshot wounds in Baghdad. He was reportedly suffering from leukemia, and it is not known whether his death was murder or suicide.

Popular Front for the Liberation of Palestine (PFLP)

The PFLP was founded under the umbrella of the PLO in 1967. Its cofounders were George Habash and Wadi Haddad. Habash was born in Lydda, Palestine, in 1925, of a wealthy family that followed the teachings of the Greek Orthodox Church. Wadi Haddad was born in Safad, Galilee, in 1939.[18]

When the British mandate on Palestine ended in 1948, Habash was studying medicine at the American University in West Beirut. He and his family became refugees overnight and fled to Jordan. After completing his studies, Habash set up a clinic with another Palestinian from the Greek Orthodox Church, Wadi Haddad, in Amman, Jordan. It might seem strange that two committed doctors trained to save lives should organize a terrorist group. Both were committed to the belief in the 1950s that Gamall Abdel Nasser (Egypt) was the best hope for the liberation of Palestine. Both were extreme left-wing Marxists. In 1957, Nasser's supporters came close to toppling the Hashemite Monarchy of Jordan; however, King Hussein was able to defeat the uprising. Habash and Haddad fled and relocated their base of operations to Syria. The PFLP sprang from the Arab Nationalist Movement, which the two men had set up. Both viewed Yasser Arafat with loathing for his involvement with the United States and for his efforts at appeasement of the Israelis. Their philosophy espoused terror and was born of the rationale that Israel won its prize by terror, so Arabs should gain Palestine back similarly with terror.

AL-AQSA MARTYRS BRIGADES

This group, unlike Hamas, does not strive for an Islamic state in Palestine but rather uses Islam as a weapon to inspire its struggle for an independent Palestine. The movement is linked to Yasser Arafat's Fatah faction and is responsible for numerous attacks against Israelis, both in the occupied territories and in Israel.

Taking its name from the Al-Aqsa Mosque, one of the holiest of Muslim sites, the group is allied with Fatah. Shortly after the death of Yasser Arafat, they renamed themselves, for a short time, as Brigades of Martyr Yasser Arafat. As a relatively new organization, it did not make it to the U.S. State Department's list of foreign terrorist organizations until after a deadly suicide bombing in Jerusalem in March 2002. Denials of its links to the PLO and Fatah have been commonplace; however, investigative journalists from Britain's BBC exposed documents in November 2003 that showed that the Fatah organizations were, in fact, paying Al-Aqsa Brigades $50,000 a month. Further confirmation came in 2004 from the then Palestinian prime minister Ahmed Qurei, when he stated in an interview in *Ashraq al-Awsat*, a London-based Muslim newspaper: "We have clearly stated that the Aqsa Martyrs Brigade are part of Fatah. We are committed to them and Fatah bears full responsibility for the group." Some of the group's more sensational attacks have been suicide attacks in Israel, most notably:

- **March 2, 2002**—Beit Yisrael suicide bomber kills eleven.
- **January 5, 2003**—Twenty-two killed in southern Tel Aviv bus depot.
- **April 17, 2006**—Two suicide bombers are believed to have carried out the attack at Tel Aviv's Old Central Bus Station. There were at least 19 fatalities and 114 injured and 9 in serious or critical condition.

The group's modus operandi is to employ a suicide belt for the individual bomber. The bomber wears a vest that covers the upper region of the body and is packed, not just with explosives but also nails, ball bearings, and nuts and bolts to inflict widespread injury. Hiding this style of bomb requires a heavy layer of outer clothing as the bomb belt will likely weigh between 10 and 40 pounds, depending on the size of the bomber. Al-Aqsa has been using young teenagers for this activity and, like Hamas, has also used female bombers.

In early 2005, the Al-Aqsa group was respecting the cease-fire truce brokered by the new PA leader, Abbas. As noted earlier, Al-Aqsa is an offshoot of the Fatah's wider organizational structure and has always remained committed to its central cause to end Israeli occupation of Palestine by armed struggle.

The Gaza Strip

The Gaza Strip[19] is an area of 140 square miles. It is home to over 830,000 Palestinians and between 4,000 and 5,000 Israeli settlers. The Palestinian population is concentrated in four cities and eight refugee camps. Ninety-nine percent of the population is Sunni Muslim. Although Gaza City is one of the oldest cities in the world, the borders of the area we know as the Gaza Strip were only created in 1949. With the end of the British mandate in Palestine and the resulting Arab-Israeli battles, eventually two-thirds of this area was claimed by Israel. Egypt claimed the remaining third. After the creation of the Gaza Strip, more than 250,000 Palestinians escaped from the fighting in other areas of the Middle East and came to settle there. Since that time, Israel has refused to allow those Palestinians to return home, in defiance of UN Resolution 141. Most of the current inhabitants of the Gaza Strip are descendants of this group.

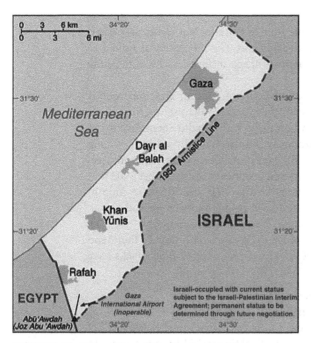

FIGURE 8-2   Map of Gaza Strip (Central Intelligence Agency, *The World Factbook, 2008*).

The Suicide Bomber

The Palestinian terrorists have successfully used suicide bombers to attack targets within Israel during the Intifada. The First Intifada (1987–1993), was a spontaneous explosion of popular resistance to the Israeli occupation. The Palestinians made a conscious and determined choice to consolidate their efforts in the struggle toward independence, regardless of the cost. Since the signing of the Oslo Agreements in 1993, Palestinian terrorist organizations have sent over seventy suicide bombers on missions against Israeli targets. *Yediot Aharonot*, the Israeli daily newspaper, presents a profile of the typical suicide bomber:

- 47 percent of the suicide bombers have an academic education, and an additional 29 percent have at least a high school education.
- 83 percent of the suicide bombers are single.
- 64 percent of the suicide bombers are between the ages of eighteen and twenty-three; most of the rest are under thirty.
- 68 percent of the suicide bombers have come from the Gaza Strip.

In a column published in *The New York Times*, William Safire wrote that "the pride and joy of Arafat's arsenal was a weapon of mass terror that has no known defense: the human missile." Safire describes the suicide bombers as being "brainwashed" and considers the efforts necessary to enable the launching of these "missiles."[20]

HAMAS

The central figure in the establishment of the Hamas organization was Sheikh Ahmed Yassin, a wheelchair-ridden "cleric," whose spiritual ideology fueled the current Palestinian terrorism. Many observers contend that Yassin preached only hatred and attacks on the Israeli state, whereas his comments and ideology would say otherwise. He continually called for suicide terrorism as part of a Muslim's religious obligation and stated in 1998 that "the day in which I will die as a shahid (martyr) will be the happiest day of my life." Yassin most certainly was an IDF target on more than one occasion. He was finally assassinated in a helicopter gunship attack by Israeli forces on March 22, 2004. Yassin had long called for islamist terrorists to join with Hamas in global jihad and to strike at Western interests everywhere if Iraq were conquered. A global jihad involving young and impressionable Muslims from throughout Europe was responsible for the upsurge in suicide bombings in Israel and terrorist attacks and insurgency in Iraq. Yassin had the dubious distinction of providing the first female suicide bombers for his attacks against Israel. It was, in fact, a British suicide bomber who was responsible for the attack on Mike's Place in Tel Aviv in 2003. Although the crippled Sheikh was as much a symbol of Palestinian resistance as was Yasser Arafat, Yassin was operating in a manner totally different from that of the Fatah organization. Yassin was active in sabotaging the peace accords of the 1990s and was hostile to the corrupt and secular PLO of Yasser Arafat. Under Yassin, Hamas aimed to replace the PLO with its own liberation of Palestine from the Jordan River to the Mediterranean Sea by means of violence and armed insurrection and establish an Islamic Palestinian State from the ruins of Israel.

Yassin joined the Muslim Brotherhood while studying at Cairo's Al-Azhar University and adopted the movement's belief that the rule of Islam should be imposed everywhere. After returning to Gaza, Yassin became actively involved in politics. In 1973, he founded the Islamic Center in Gaza, which soon controlled all religious institutions. In 1979, he founded the Islamic Organization; a body that Israeli military initially hoped would reduce the political influence of Yasser Arafat's Fatah movement. At the time, the Islamic Organization dealt mostly with welfare. But the ideology of the Muslim Brotherhood fueled Yassin's belief that the Israelis occupied an Islamic land whose ownership was not negotiable, and the sheikh gradually shifted from social and religious activity to clandestine activities against Israeli rule in the West Bank and Gaza.

Yassin was arrested in 1984 and sentenced to thirteen years in jail for possessing illegal arms, establishing a military organization, and calling for the annihilation of Israel. Yassin acknowledged that he founded an organization of religious activists with the goal of fighting nonreligious factions in the territories and carrying out "jihad" operations against Israel. This organization used monies from Islamic activists in Jordan to acquire large quantities of weapons. He was imprisoned until May 1985, when he was released in a prisoner exchange deal between Israel and the terrorist organization of Ahmed Jibril.

During the First Intifada in 1987, Yassin transformed his Islamic organization into a new body called Hamas. An acronym for the Islamic Resistance Movement, *Hamas* means "zeal" in Arabic. In Hebrew, it means evil.[21]

Ahmad Rashad, a research associate at the United Association for Studies and Research, attributes Hamas's popularity to several factors:[22]

- Its call for the liberation of all of Palestine.
- Its reputation as an efficient organization.
- Its honesty and lack of corruption.
- Its resilience to Israeli crackdowns.
- Its daring and successful attacks against Israeli military targets.
- Its home-based leadership within the occupied territories, as opposed to the PLO's expatriate direction.

Whatever social or political aspiration Hamas may have for the people of Palestine must be then questioned in relation to its neighbor Israel. The Hamas charter speaks to its aims and concepts:

> Israel will exist and will continue to exist until Islam will obliterate it, just as it obliterated others before it.
>
> The Islamic Resistance Movement believes that the Land of Palestine is an Islamic War consecrated for future Moslem generations until Judgment Day. It, or any part of it, should not be squandered: it, or any part of it, should not be given up."
>
> There is no solution for the Palestinian question except through jihad. Initiatives, proposals and international conferences are all a waste of time, and vain endeavors.
>
> After Palestine, the Zionists aspire to expand from the Nile to the Euphrates. When they will have digested the region they overtook, they will aspire to further expansion, and so on. Their plan is embodied in the 'Protocols of the Elders of Zion,' and their present conduct is the best proof of what we are saying.[23]

It is not difficult to see why Hamas is such a serious threat to Israel's continued security and why Israel would want to specifically target its leaders for assassination, as it has done so effectively since 2002.

Organization and Structure of Hamas

Hamas has been heavily involved in the local political scene in Gaza by putting up candidates for union representatives and the board of trade. Its political opponent is the PLO. Hamas dates back to the mid-1980s, when it identified itself as a wing of the Palestinian Muslim Brotherhood. The brotherhood had been seeking to establish a political wing for its organization, and in 1985 and 1986, it issued leaflets in Gaza to encourage a policy of civil disobedience. The leaflets were issued under names such as Harakat al-Kifah al-Musallah (Armed Struggle Movement), al-Murabitoon ala Ard al-Isra (The Steadfast on the Land of al-Isra), and Harakat al-Muqawama al-Islamiyya (Islamic Resistance Movement, IRM). As the tensions grew in the mid-1980s, these communiqués became more and more politicized, and by 1988, the name "Hamas" began to appear.

The military and intelligence wings of Hamas function independently; the intelligence wing gathers information and carries out surveillance operations on collaborators, drug dealers, and other antisocial activities and metes out punishments ranging from warnings to executions. It also distributes literature about Israeli recruitment policy and methods of collaboration and warns the populace about complicity. The intelligence wing also monitors crime in the region. The military wing has different, but well-defined, goals and objectives:

- Establish usar (families) and underground cells.
- Gather information on IDF activities for use in planned operations.
- Carry out training programs in hand-to-hand combat.
- Carry out military-style operations against the IDF.

Hamas military strikes have continued, predominantly against Israeli settlers in the territories, and suicide attacks mainly against civilian targets in Israel. Tactics are of a hit-and-run nature—planting a bomb or a suicide bombing in populated areas of Jerusalem, for example. Despite the PLO agreements with Israel, the Hamas movement declared Arafat a traitor for his agreements with the Zionist enemy. Hamas's response to these agreements has resulted in an increase in disputes with the PLO. Hamas receives its support from other Muslim countries, including Turkey, Iran, Afghanistan, Saudi Arabia and the Gulf States, Yemen, and even Malaysia. Hamas, although similar to the PLO, is willing to settle for a peace agreement with Israel, but has firm objectives that must be met before an agreement can be reached. In 1994, Hamas proclaimed that it was not opposed to peace; however, for it to. "… cease military operations in Gaza and the West Bank…" the following conditions would have to be met:

1. Complete Israeli withdrawal from the occupied territories.
2. Disarm the settlers and dismantle the settlements.
3. Place international forces on the "green line" established in the occupied territories during the 1948 and 1967 wars.
4. Hold free and general elections to determine true representation of the Palestinian people.
5. The Council, which will be composed of electoral victors, shall represent the Palestinians in any negotiations that determine their future and that of the occupied territories.

Many Palestinians lauded the Gaza-Jericho agreement of 1993, as they saw the new prospect of establishing their own legitimate Homeland. However, the slow progress since the agreement was reached and the continued development of the occupied territories by Israeli settlers has led to disillusionment by many Palestinians. This has led to internal strife between PLO and Hamas, with pro-Arafat supporters being assassinated. Israel continued to wrangle over interpretation of sections in the agreement with the PLO throughout the remainder of the twentieth century. It is no surprise that acts of terror aimed at Israeli settlements and at targets in the West Bank and Gaza Strip continued unabated. Hamas has been able to retain sufficient military strength to protect its interests against the Israelis and has a broad political constituency, especially among the young, due to the combination of its fundamentalist religious message and social welfare programs.

Hamas's social programs, such as establishing clinics and schools, are an effective alternative to the PA's own social infrastructure, which was crumbling from corruption and mismanagement even before much of it was destroyed by the Israeli military. The current Intifada, which has continued remorselessly since September 2000, has enabled Hamas to garner and maintain support from other Palestinian factions including Fatah, in what is becoming an unshakeable national consensus.[24] The military wing of Hamas, the Ezzedine al-Qassam Brigades, has continued to carry out suicide attacks against Israel in spite of massive security operations to block all such attempts. Hamas declared an "all-out war" on Israel in January 2002 as a result of an Israeli incursion into the West Bank city of Tulkarem, which saw Israeli commandos shoot dead four Hamas bomb makers and the West Bank leader of Hamas, Yousef Soragji.

The proximity of the Palestinians to the Israeli populous has made for somewhat easy pickings for the Hamas men of terror. Their targets have usually been civilian centers in Tel Aviv, Jerusalem, and other Israeli cities such as seaside resort towns like Netanya. Massive security clampdowns and numerous checkpoints on major arterial roads as well as street checks have not prevented repeated Hamas suicide missions. Each successful attack has resulted in a swift and ferocious response by Israel targeting "suspected" militants in refugee camps in Palestinian territory. The cycle of violence prevailed throughout 2004 and up to the "truce" in early 2005. Israel also reverted to targeted assassination of "suspected" militants, mainly from Hamas. On the night of July 23, 2002, an F-16 fighter aircraft dropped a one-ton bomb on the Gaza home of a Hamas leader. The collateral damage was fourteen civilian deaths. This type of action by the Israeli forces could clearly be defined as a form of state terror. Israel claimed that it had not intended to kill innocent civilians; however, dropping a one-ton bomb in a residential neighborhood would likely have just that effect. In times of war, civilians are often involved in "mistakes." The direct targeting of civilians, as in the World War II German bombings of London and the allies' carpet bombing of Dresden, can be construed as atrocities or terrorism, as they have no specific military objective or significance. In targeting terrorists who hide or live in a civilian environment, such distinctions become blurred. From a Palestinian viewpoint, there is much to be gained in the propaganda war in showing dead civilians to eager news crews. What effect this style of reciprocal attack by Israel will have for peace is uncertain. Although calls for an investigation and wide criticism have ensued in the Israeli media, widespread condemnation has not been long lasting or particularly loud from the international community.

"HAMAS—STAN"

When Hamas won the general election in March 2006, it set itself on a collision course with not only Israel but also Fatah. Hamas had managed through its grassroots social programs and community involvement to solidify its popularity in the Gaza Strip and have it recognized as a viable alternative to the corrupt Fatah-dominated West Bank. No doubt Hamas had watched and mirrored the Hezbollah approach to political power in Lebanon. The West's response to Hamas winning the election was the cessation of funds to the Palestinian National Authority. Hamas may have won the election; it had not won international recognition. Still listed as a terrorist entity, it was not going to be an easy transformation to an internationally recognized legitimate authority in the region. Hamas assumed far more political responsibility than it was capable of assuming, and with the rule of law on the streets effectively being the gun; internal battles followed. The Palestinian security apparatus has always been at the center of power in both Gaza and the West Bank and taking control of that apparatus sparked the start of violence in 2007. Fatah and Hamas sparred in the political arena over control and attempted to come up with a power-sharing agreement through the Saudi Arabia–brokered Mecca Agreement. The deal disintegrated with the battle over control of security forces. In its effort to effectively control Fatah, Hamas mounted an offensive in the Gaza Strip in June 2007.

Hamas believed by doing so, it would be able to negotiate from a position of strength with Fatah over the security forces. This had the effect of two separate states being controlled by warring Palestinian factions, something that Israel would be quick to take advantage of. Hamas gunmen, in one week of June 2007, tore down the portraits of Yasser Arafat from office walls and removed the Palestinian flag, replacing it with the green banner of Islam. Hamas forcibly removed Fatah from Gaza and executed many of its key representatives. Secular nationalism of the sort Fatah has stood for was beginning to look like the weak force and radical Islam as the strong force.[25] In January 2007, Hamas announced that it would never negotiate with Israel and would not be abiding by any of the treaties that Fatah had previously negotiated with the Israelis. The March 2007 kidnapping of a British Broadcasting Corporation (BBC) journalist Alan Johnson in Gaza by members from the shadowy group calling itself the Army of Islam provided the opportunity for Hamas to demonstrate to the international community its ability not to act and control events in Gaza. The Army of Islam is made up of ex-members of Hamas, so it is very likely that Hamas would be able to exercise influence to have the journalist released unharmed. The Hamas-brokered release of Johnson in July 2007 did little to deter the Israelis from making inroads with the Fatah-controlled West Bank to further curtail Hamas in Gaza and prevent any reconciliation between Hamas and Fatah. The Israeli government of Ehud Olmert agreed to a meeting with Mahmoud Abbas and also granted a group of wanted exiled Palestinian leaders including the controversial figure, Nayef Hawatmeh, permission to enter the West Bank for the meeting. Hawatmeh had been the mastermind behind the 1974 Ma'alot massacre. Ma'alot is located in the Western Galilee, 20 km east of Nahariya. Ma'alot was founded in the 1950s when hundreds of thousands of immigrants came to Israel from North Africa, refugees from hostile Arab nations where they were no longer safe. The Israeli Government at that time decided to place new immigrants in development towns such as Ma'alot. On May 15, 1974 (Israel's Independence Day), a group of 11th grade students were on a field trip to the Golan. That night the children were housed at a school in Ma'alot where they slept on the floor. During the night, three Arab terrorists dressed as IDF soldiers attacked the school, killing the guard and some of the children. Some of the children escaped by jumping out of a window on the second floor and the rest were held as hostages.

The terrorists were identified as members of the Democratic Front for the Liberation of Palestine (DFLP) who had infiltrated from Lebanon. They demanded the release of Arab terrorists from Israeli prisons, or they would start to kill the children. The deadline was set at 6:00 P.M. the same day. Israel's policy forbade negotiation with terrorists; the plight of the children forced an exception. By 3:00 P.M., a decision was reached to negotiate, but the terrorists refused a request for more time. At 5:4 5 P.M., a unit of the elite Golani brigade stormed the building. All of the terrorists were killed in the assault, but not before they took the lives of twenty-one children. There were a total of twenty-six victims, including several people murdered by the terrorists on their way to the school the night before. In Beirut, demonstrations honoring the fallen fedayeen as noble martyrs of the cause were ordered by Nayef Hawatmeh, the DFLP leader.[26]

For the Israelis it was crucial to develop a dialogue of sorts with Fatah on the West Bank to prevent Hamas becoming the only Palestinian (Islamist) voice for the region. The Ma'alot massacre maybe over thirty years ago, but it is still fresh in Israeli memories and so is the name of the mastermind behind the attack, Marwan Bargouti. The other concern for Israelis is that any amnesty may also include demands for his release. The Palestinians want a large number exchanged for a captured Israeli soldier, Corporal Shalit. His release is also a precondition to any peace deal being worked out between Israel and the Palestinians. Gilad Shalit, a member of the IDF, was kidnapped by Palestinian terrorists in a cross-border raid on June 25, 2006. Hamas continues to demand the release of at least 1,000 prisoners from Israel in exchange for Shalit including Marwan Bargouti.

WEAPONRY

The ability to strike at Israeli settlements is far easier from the West Bank than it is from the Gaza Strip, which borders an area of Israel that is sparsely populated. The mini civil war that developed briefly over the summer of 2007 did not diminish Hamas's capabilities or their goals of attacking Israel. Hamas's arsenal contains assault rifles and AK 47s, but they have also built up an array of improvised rocket devices, considered highly unstable, which will only get to perfection with more practice. They have developed short-range rockets without any technical guidance system to support target identification. The rockets, named as "Qassam Rockets" after the Syrian Cleric Izz al-Din al-Qassam, have been used extensively by Hamas against Israeli civilian targets. These devices are steel tubes with their stabilizing fins welded to their side using potassium nitrate fertilizer and sugar as the main propellant with TNT as the warhead. The longest-range missile to have struck any target has been 12 kilometers. These missiles have a launch team of between five and ten people dependent on the type and size of the rocket being fired, and this brings the operators into considerable risk of being spotted by Israeli drones in the skies above, or unmanned aerial vehicles (UAVs).

FATAH AND HAMAS—UNITY GOVERNMENT

The Arab spring of 2011 saw widespread popular uprisings throughout the Middle East not least in Egypt. Both Hamas and Fatah met in Cairo in May 2011 and agreed to settle their hostilities—for the time being, but the long- and short-term results of this need further review. The complexity of Middle East politics now has Hamas and its Islamic extreme doctrines calling for the destruction of Israel supposedly aligned with a secular Fatah and the Palestinian Authority, which recognizes the right of Israel to exist. Just how these two groups can coexist and form a unity government is debatable. Maybe the levels of unrest in the Middle East are seen by Hamas as an opportunity for popular demonstrations against Israel. The thirty-two-year-old peace treaty negotiated with Egypt could be in jeopardy—whatever brand of democracy surfaces in Egypt will have a bearing on how Hamas and the PA react. Hamas may not be as militant or as popular with Palestinians as it was six or seven years ago, so it may become a minority in any newly elected Palestinian government. The issues internally for both Fatah and Hamas will revolve around their internal security apparatus. In February 2007, they signed their first unity government agreement in Mecca which lasted less then four months, when in June 2007 Hamas took control of the Gaza Strip and forced Fatah representatives out. On June 14th President Mahmoud Abbas dissolved the Unity Government and declared a state of emergency. The territory is effectively split in two with Hamas controlling the government in Gaza and the West Bank under the control of the Palestinian National Authority.

Palestinian Liberation Front (PLF)

A group best known for pioneering and perfecting the art of international airline hijacking in the late 1960, they split from the PFLP General Command in the mid-1970s and then again into pro-Syrian, pro-Libyan, and pro-PLO factions. Its membership cadre is estimated to be between fifty and hundred.[27] PLF based its operations in Iraq, having moved there from Tunisia after the attack on the cruise liner *Achille Lauro* in October 1985 and the murder of a wheelchair-bound, U.S. citizen Leon Klinghoffer. Abu Abbas, a longtime supporter of Yasser Arafat, led the PLF. Abbas was born in a refugee camp in Syria in 1948. He was a longtime Palestinian terrorist with a price on his head after the murder of the *Achille Lauro* passenger, Leon Klinghoffer. Abbas rose to prominence in the PLO and was elected to the powerful and influential Executive Committee of the PLO in 1982. Until 1985, he operated from Tunisia. After the *Achille Lauro* incident, Italian authorities briefly detained him until he was flown to Yemen.

    Israel remained the prime target of Palestinian terrorist attacks during 1990. Escalating tensions resulted in a number of serious incidents during the year. On May 30, Israeli forces foiled an attempted seaborne assault against the Tel Aviv beachfront. Four terrorists were killed and twelve captured. The attack was carried out by the Palestine Liberation Front, led by Abu Abbas, with substantial assistance from Libya. Former PLO chairman Arafat's failure to take concrete actions against the PLF, a constituent PLO member, led to the suspension of U.S. dialogue with the PLO.[28]

    Abbas was an outspoken supporter of Saddam Hussein during the Gulf War. He was captured by coalition forces in Iraq in 2003 and died in custody from natural causes in March 2004. The PLF gets its support from Syria and has in the past received support from Libya. Along with some presence in Gaza and the West Bank, it has also shown up in Lebanon.

TERRORIST ATTACK BRIEF

Terrorist Group: Palestine Liberation Front (PLF)

Case Facts: On 7 October 1985, the *Achille Lauro*, an Italian luxury liner, with some 100 mostly elderly passengers on board, was hijacked in Egyptian waters by terrorists representing the Palestine Liberation Front (PLF). The ship's captain was ordered to sail for Tartus, Syria. That night, the hijackers informed Egyptian authorities of their action by radio and stated their demand for release of fifty Palestinian prisoners held by Israel. The next day, after being denied docking rights at Tartus by Syrian authorities, the terrorists decided to kill one of their hostages to prove their determination. Pushing the elderly, wheelchair-bound Jewish-American passenger Leon Klinghoffer to the side of the ship, the leader of the terrorists shot him in the head and chest and then threw his body overboard. The Syrians still continued to deny the ship docking rights, but before a second passenger could be killed, the terrorists received a radio message from PLF leaders directing them to leave the passengers unmolested and to head to Port Said, Egypt. Once there, the Egyptian government, unaware that Klinghoffer had been murdered, provided the hijackers with safe passage in exchange for freeing the ship and its passengers.

Investigation: Through clever intelligence work, the National Security Council staff determined that the terrorists were still in Egypt and were about to be flown to Tunisia on an Egypt Air 737 airliner. They reasoned that, with a lot of luck, the United States might be able to intercept the plane before it reached its destination. Saratoga (CV 60), with Commander Task Force (CTF) 60 on board, was steaming northward through the Adriatic Sea toward a port call at Dubrovnik, Yugoslavia, on the afternoon of October 10, following completion of a major North Atlantic Treaty Organization (NATO) exercise in the central Mediterranean.

Suddenly, the carrier received orders from Sixth Fleet headquarters to reverse course and to launch the alert combat air patrol. Despite the ship's "Alert 60" status, two F-14A Tomcats and an E-2C Hawkeye were airborne within twenty-two minutes. Apprised of the emerging situation by Sixth Fleet, Rear Admiral David Jeremiah, CTF 60, immediately alerted his staff that Saratoga was going after the hijackers, even though the plane's exact takeoff time from Egypt, the route it was flying to Tunisia, and its altitude were unknown.

FIGURE 8-3 Achille Lauro Hijacking—The Mediterranean—October 1985. *Source:* GlobalSecurity.org

The Popular Front for the liberation of Palestine—General Command (PFLP-GC)

A secular Marxist group, the PFLP-GC traces its history back to 1959 and the formation of the Palestinian Liberation Front by former Syrian Army Captain Ahmed Jibril. The left-wing PLF led by George Habash merged with the PFLP in 1967. Jabril was actively supported and sponsored by Syria, whereas Habash was seeking a political solution and negotiations with Egypt. The differences between the two were vast and never likely to be settled amicably. In 1968, Jibril split from George Habash and headquartered his new group the PFLP-GC in Damascus. Like its Syrian sponsors, the PFLP-GC wanted armed confrontation with Israel, and Syria was content for them to be their proxy in attacking Israeli interests. They launched attacks internationally to gain broader attention; in 1970, they detonated a bomb on board a Swiss Air flight between Munich and Tel Aviv killing over forty passengers. In 1974, suicide bombers were used for the first time in an attack on Israel, killing eighteen near Kiryat Shimona. While the wider Palestinian movement and groups sought to become more legitimate in dealing with Israel with the eventual goal of Palestinian statehood, the PFLP-GC under Jibril followed the direction of Syria and continued to target Israel. This led to bitter internal struggles and infighting. However, the PFLP-GC continued to openly oppose moves by the PLO to negotiate and make concessions to Israel, joining a rejectionist front of leftist Palestinian groups and resigning from the PLO Executive Committee and Central Council. In 1984, the PFLP-GC was evicted from the PLO and shifted further away from Palestinian interests. In 1986, the PFLP-GC and elements of Syrian military intelligence were implicated in the Hindawi affair—the attempted bombing of an Israeli El Al flight from London. Syria came under fire from the international community, and the United States withdrew its ambassador from Damascus. After that, Syria relied more and more on the PFLP-GC to carry out terrorist operations on its behalf. For a period of time in the 1980s the group was set up in Tripoli and sponsored by Libyan leader Colonel Qaddafi. They remained somewhat marginalized in the mid-1990s as Arafat established the Palestinian Authority that controlled much of the West Bank and Gaza Strip. Since the second Palestinian *intifada* in September 2000, PFLP-GC has tried to reassert itself by attacking Israel. The U.S. State Department classifies the PFLP and PFLP-GC as foreign terrorist organizations.

Democratic Front for the Liberation of Palestine (DFLP)

A strong and vocal opponent to the Israeli peace accord with the PLO; this Marxist group split from the PFLP in 1969.[29] DFLP believes the Palestinians can only achieve their goals by mass uprising. Its political position in the 1980s was somewhere in between those of Arafat and the rejectionists. DFLP again split into two more factions in 1991—one pro-Arafat and one hard-line group headed by Nayef Hawatmeh. This group was suspended from the PLO for opposing the 1993 Declaration of Principles. The DFLP is estimated to have a membership totaling about 500 activists across both groups and has carried out its terror campaign mostly in Israel and the occupied territories. Since 1988, the DFLP has been involved only in cross-border raids into Israeli areas. It receives its funding and logistical support primarily from Libya and Syria.

Palestinian Islamic Jihad (PIJ)

The **Palestinian Islamic Jihad (PIJ)** is a Palestinian Islamic nationalist group with roots among the Palestinian fundamentalists in the Gaza Strip dating back to the 1970s. The founders of the Palestinian Islamic Jihad, Fathi Shaqaqi and Abd al-Aziz Awda, were students in Egypt and members of the Egyptian Muslim Brotherhood until the late 1970s when they decided that the brotherhood was becoming too moderate and insufficiently committed to the Palestinian cause. The PIJ emerged as a separate entity committed to the militant destruction of Israel and the reestablishment of a sovereign Palestinian state. The PIJ, despite being a Sunni group, took inspiration from revolutionary, theocratic Shia ideals espoused during the 1979 Iranian Revolution that established an Islamic regime. The group is much smaller than its Islamic brothers in Hamas and offers no political agenda or social programs. Its ideals continue to be the destruction of Israel and the establishment of a Palestinian.

Ramadan Abdullah Shallah, Secretary General PIJ

Ramadan Abdullah Shallah was born in the Gaza Strip and spent five years at Durham University in northern England, where he reportedly coordinated the activities of Palestinian Islamic Jihad by sending and receiving orders to and from cells of the organization in Gaza and the West Bank. From 1990 to 1995, Shallah lived in Tampa, Florida, where he was a leading member of the Islamic Concern Project (aka the Islamic Committee for Palestine). The organization distributed official PIJ literature used to indoctrinate followers by glorifying PIJ suicide bombers as martyrs.

After PIJ leader Fathi Shaqaqi's death in October 1995, Shallah became the new leader of PIJ and a member of its Shura (consultative) Council.[30] The PIJ strikes at both Arabs and Jews alike and has not limited its area of operation to the territories and the Gaza Strip, like Hamas. In 1991, the group attacked a tourist bus in Egypt, killing eleven passengers, nine of them Israelis. Its method of attack in Israel and the occupied territories has been suicide bombings of bus stations and markets.[31] PIJ continues to front attacks on Israeli targets in both Israel and the territories, although since the 9-11 attacks on the United States and Israel's erection of the security fence it has limited its activities. With respect to any disengagement plan that the Israelis have envisaged, the PIJ network in Northern Samaria has emerged as one of the most tangible threats to the implementation of the disengagement plan, as its leadership questions the value of sticking to the policy of calm (tahadiyah). The PIJ network, encompassing Jenin and Tul Karm and all of the villages in between, was responsible for a major attack within Israel—the suicide bombing at the Stage Club in Tel Aviv on February 25, 2005, in which five Israelis were killed and fifty more were wounded. One of its senior commanders, Luay Saadi, one of Israel's "Most Wanted" terrorists was killed by the Israeli Army in October 2005 in retaliation for his planning of The Stage Club bombing. After the attack, the PIJ leadership in Damascus engaged in evasive tactics designed to escape the Israeli response. Signs were accumulating that indicated that PIJ was back in action, but they were credited with only one attack in March 2007. Israeli intelligence sources also saw evidence that the military wing in the northern West Bank had resumed planning major attacks.[32]

Kach and Kahane Chai (Motto: Terror against Terror)

Kach is a Jewish ultra nationalist group operating in Israel and founded by the late Rabbi Meir Kahane founder of the Jewish Defense League (JDL), a U.S. organization dedicated to protecting American Jews. The JDL became increasingly militant, espousing violence and vigilantism to curb anti-Semitism. The Kach movement (Hebrew for "Thus") emerged from this international JDL office.

In 1984, the Kach and Kahane Chai organization was declared a terrorist organization by the Israeli Government under the 1948 Terrorism Law.[33] Binyamin Kahane, the son of Rabbi Meir Kahane, who was assassinated in the United States in 1990, leads this group. They aim to restore the biblical state of Israel and purge the land of all Arabs. The Kach and Kahane was an outspoken supporter of the terrorist attack on the al-Ibrahimi Mosque by Dr. Baruch Goldstein in February 1994. On several occasions over the last thirty years it has attempted, unsuccessfully, to turn itself into a political movement by running candidates for the Israeli Knesset; however, after the Goldstein attack, the government banned the group from Israeli politics. The group has threatened and attacked Palestinians and Arabs in Hebron and the West Bank and is an embarrassment to the Israeli government. The group was violently opposed to Ariel Sharon's disengagement plan and the dismantling of Jewish settlements in both the Gaza Strip and the West Bank.

The 1993 Declaration of Principles—at its signing seen as breakthrough agreement—has staggered on with no outward resolution of the critical issues in the region; however, it is important to list its main points.

DECLARATION OF PRINCIPLES

Article VI: Preparatory Transfer of Powers and Responsibilities

1. Upon entry into force of this Declaration of Principles and the withdrawal from the Gaza Strip and the Jericho area, a transfer of authority from the Israeli Military Government and its Civil Administration to the authorized Palestinians for this task,

as detailed herein, will commence. This transfer of authority will be of a preparatory nature until the inauguration of the Council.

2. Immediately after the entry into force of this Declaration of Principles and the withdrawal from the Gaza Strip and the Jericho area, with the view to promoting economic development in the West Bank and Gaza Strip, authority will be transferred to the Palestinians on the following spheres: education and culture, health, social welfare, direct taxation, and tourism. The Palestinian side will commence in building the Palestinian Police Force, as agreed upon. Pending the inauguration of the Council, the two parties may negotiate the transfer of additional powers and responsibilities, as agreed upon.[34]

The Declaration of Principles signaled a major breakthrough and a new hope for a definitive solution to the Palestinian question, even peace in the area that, of course, has not been realized. The full text of the Declaration of Principles is not included in this chapter; however, its contents form the basis and fabric for both the Israelis and the Palestinians to move toward the goal of a homeland for the displaced Palestinians. It has been a very bumpy road since 1993, and whether the two sides are able to fulfill the contents of the declaration and meet all that is stipulated remains to be seen. There is considerable resentment in the territories and Gaza Strip of the slow pace toward meeting the goals of the principles.

It is worthwhile to note that the Oslo strategy was to redivide and subdivide an already fractured and fragmented Palestinian territory into three subzones: A, B, and C, in ways entirely devised and controlled by the Israeli side, because the Palestinians were, until very recently, a "map-less" society. At the negotiations, there were no Palestinian representatives with any geographical knowledge who could either argue or contest decisions.[35]

Recruitment and indoctrination into the terrorist cause is believed to continue unabated in the Gaza Strip as the next generation of terrorists are groomed and schooled in hatred aimed at their Israeli neighbors. Children as young as age seven are parading with automatic assault weapons and singing patriotic Palestinian songs that glory in the destruction of Israel.[36] This is hardly a harbinger of a peaceful settlement in the years to come. The core of mistrust between the Palestinians and the Israelis, in both words and deeds, runs deepest in the occupied territories.

JORDAN

The Hashemite Kingdom of Jordan has been a "refuge" for thousands of displaced Palestinians from West Bank villages for the last four decades. Considerable support and sympathy for the Palestinian cause probably exists among Jordanians. Jordan became a safe haven for the Palestinians after Israel's creation, but problems arose with so many extreme elements actively embroiled in terrorist campaigns against Israel. The PFLP had training camps within striking distance of Jordan and for the leadership of the PFLP; the king of Jordan himself became a target. There were open confrontations in the streets of Amman between fedayeen members and the late King Hussein's troops. Wadi Haddad and George Habash were desperate to get the "Palestinian question" into the focus of world attention. It is not certain whether the two men were actually in concert over the operation, but, in July 1970, Haddad was in Beirut with Leila Khaled, a committed member of PFLP, planning one of the most spectacular hijacking events of the twentieth century. The hijacking of international airliners to Dawson's Field in Jordan provoked a reaction around the world, and the traveling public experienced the start of passenger screening security at airports worldwide.

Hijacking of Airliners: A New Tactic?

Over the last half of the twentieth century, there have been so many terrorist attacks that it is sometimes hard to recall them. The spectacular ones seem to be held in our mind: the Munich Olympic Games massacre; the Iranian Embassy siege in London; the destruction of the U.S. Marine barracks in Beirut, Lebanon; the Oklahoma City bombing; Pan Am 103 over Lockerbie; the Air India bombing off the coast of Ireland; and, of course, the New York World Trade Center and the Pentagon attacks are etched in our memories. The hijacking of airliners and hostage-taking has the immediate ability to focus world attention through media coverage.

The actions of the PFLP almost led to a civil war in Jordan and certainly led King Hussein to forcibly remove the PLO from the territory. The hijackings were audacious for their sheer nerve, daring, and lack of any respect for international convention.

The first hijacking took place on a TWA Boeing 707 at 11:50 A.M. on September 6, 1970. The plane was en route from Frankfurt, West

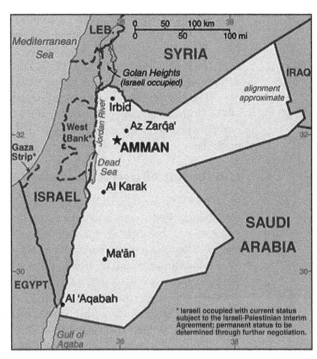

FIGURE 8-4   Map of Jordan (Central Intelligence Agency, *The World Factbook, 2008*).

Germany, to New York. The airliner had a full complement of crew and 145 passengers when it was seized in the skies above Belgium. The pilot was ordered to fly to Jordan. At about the same time, a Swissair DC-8 with a similar number of passengers and crew was seized over France and flown to the same location, Dawson Field, Jordan. At about 2:00 P.M., an attempt was made to hijack a third airliner, an El Al flight en route to Amsterdam from Tel Aviv. Due to confusion at check-in, the El Al hijack team was reduced to three members: Leila Khaled and Patrick Arguello and the third, an Arab. When the pilot refused to obey their instructions, a violent fight ensued and a flight attendant was shot. An Israeli sky marshal killed the Arab hijacker. Khaled and Arguello were overpowered, and the aircraft landed at London's Heathrow Airport, where they were both arrested. The remaining members of Khaled's group who had failed to make the flight hijacked a Boeing 747 operated by Pan American Airlines.

The airliner flew to Beirut, where it refueled and went on to Cairo. The PFLP blew the 747 up on the ground at Cairo Airport, after the crew and passengers were taken off. This action by the PFLP, though aimed at the international arena, was a statement to the Egyptian government about its acceptance of the Middle East peace agreement. With hostages numbering about 300 being held in Jordan, the PFLP laid out its demands to the international community. The hijackers demanded the release of the three members of the PFLP who had been jailed for an earlier attack on Zurich Airport, and who were presently languishing in a Swiss jail. They also demanded the same for terrorists being held in West Germany for the Munich Airport attack. Their third demand involved Leila Khaled's release from police custody for attempting to hijack an El Al airliner over Europe. The British government of conservative prime minister Edward Heath was in utter turmoil over how to deal with this problem, so the PFLP gave it another nudge by hijacking a BOAC VC-10 and adding 110 British passengers to the hostage list. After heavy pressure and diplomatic talks, the PFLP moved the hostages to the comfort of Amman, Jordan. Over the next two weeks, the hostages were moved around Amman in small groups before all were released on September 30, 1970. The PFLP destroyed the British, Swiss, and American airliners at Dawson Field before the watchful lenses of the world's media.[37]

The last British hostages were released on the same day that Leila Khaled was flown out of the United Kingdom and back to the Middle East. Israel has always steadfastly refused to negotiate with terrorists, and it strongly criticized the Western powers for giving in. Britain never made that mistake again.

LOD (Israel) Airport Attack May 30, 1972

In May 1972, a daring attack led by Kozo Okomato, Yasuda Yasuki, and Okudeira Takushi from the Japanese Red Army, possibly acting on the behest of the Black September group, attacked Lod Airport. The team arrived at the airport near Tel Aviv and pulled from their luggage Czech-made 7.62 machine guns. They opened fire indiscriminately in the terminal building and killed twenty-four instantly and injured seventy-seven others. Two of the attackers were killed by Israeli security; Kozo Okomato was tried by Israel and sentenced to life in prison but was released in May 1985 in a prisoner exchange with the PFLP-General Command. Kozo fled to Libya. In February 1997, he was arrested again, this time in Lebanon, but was deported; he eventually disappeared. Today he is rumored to be living in North Korea.[38]

These events pushed the Middle East to the brink of war. The Bonn Summit conference of major Western powers met in 1978 and agreed to sanctions against states that aided and abetted the hijacking of aircraft. The countries agreeing were the United States, the United Kingdom, Canada, France, Italy, Japan, and West Germany.

Jordan in the Twenty-First Century

Jordan's wider role in Middle Eastern affairs is relevant for the fledgling Palestinian government of Mahmoud Abbas, who is considered to be pro-Jordanian. To assist in security, Jordan's King Abdullah has allowed Palestinian fighters to return to the West Bank. Most of these fighters have been trained by the Jordanian military and are pro-Jordan. Abdullah has also requested the Israelis to allow this action to take place. This is Jordan's opportunity to play a major role in the security of the West Bank, a region it considers part of its Hashemite Kingdom. At the same time, any attacks against the stability of the Abbas regime could be tempered with the presence of Jordanian-trained Palestinian fighters. On its other flank are the problems of insurgents from Jordan fighting and supporting attacks against U.S. forces in Iraq. One such fighter was Abu Musab al-Zarqawi, born in Jordan in 1966 of Palestinian parentage. He was named as the link between Iraq and al Qaeda until his sudden death in a targeted bombing by the United States in June 2006. He had been involved with terrorist activities for many years and is thought to have been one of Osama bin Laden's chief supporters. He is believed to have been in Afghanistan in 1990–1991, and while the intervening years record little of his activities, he did surface again in 1999 when he planned the Millennium attack on the Radisson Hotel in Amman Jordan. The plot was discovered and so was his involvement—he was sentenced to fifteen years in prison in absentia. He returned to Afghanistan in 2000 and set up training camps that specialized in biochemical weapons training.

When the Taliban were routed in 2001, Zarqawi was suffering from a leg wound that took him to Iraq, where his leg was amputated. During his recovery in Iraq he set up a base for his training operations, presumably with the blessing of the Iraqi regime. Zarqawi was linked to the assassination of a U.S. official in Jordan in late 2002. He returned to northern Iraq in 2003, and the fruits of his training were discovered in Britain when several suspects, who had direct links to him, were arrested for plotting to put ricin toxin into the military food supply.

Zarqawi continued to focus attacks also on his homeland, Jordan. In November 2005, he dispatched suicide bombers to target three U.S.-owned hotels in Amman, killing fifty-seven and injuring hundreds; all the casualties were Jordanians.

LEBANON

Lebanon has been in existence for centuries and is occupied by both Christians and Muslims. The Christians settled mainly in the mountainous regions, while the Muslims inhabited the coastal region. Like most of the Middle East, the area was under the rule of the Turkish Ottoman Empire until the end of World War I. After the war, the French began to prepare the region for independent status. The French assisted in the creation of the Lebanese Constitution. Lebanon gained its full independence in 1943, and, like its population, the government was designed to reflect the two majority religions, Christian and Muslim. From its very early days as an independent state, Lebanon had close links to Western powers. In the 1950s and 1960s, Beirut was affectionately called the "Riviera of the Middle East." Its hotels and restaurants and vibrant market scene made it a popular spot for tourists and the wealthy. Its location on the Mediterranean Sea helped it flourish as a port as well as a business center. Significant incidents brought about drastic changes in the Lebanese way of life, beginning with what must be termed "an uprising." The first signs of trouble surfaced in 1958, when dissatisfied Muslims violently opposed the government's strengthening of ties to the West. The uprising was tempered when U.S. forces were sent to the aid of Lebanon, and all seemed to return to relative tranquility in short order.

Palestinians Come to Lebanon

With the PLO's reversal of fortunes in 1969—when it was forcefully evicted by King Hussein's Army—vast members spilled into Lebanon. King Hussein's actions were in response to the increasing number of confrontations between the PLO and the Jordanian military. Support for the embattled King came from regular monetary contributions from the United States.

The Arab Muslim population in Lebanon swelled, but its people were treated, at best, as fourth-class citizens. Many lived in the shabby refugee camps around Beirut International Airport. Sabra and Shatila refugee camps and areas of southern Lebanon that were within striking distance of Israel remain in infamy as testament to atrocities committed by Christian militias.

By 1975, the constant warring from the PLO incursions into Israel and the retaliatory strikes by the Israeli air force against Palestinian camps brought the country to civil war. The PLO in Lebanon was widely

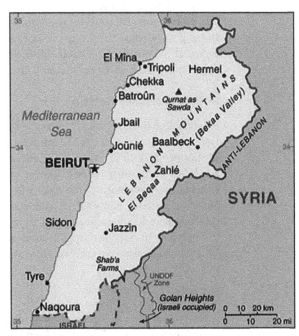

FIGURE 8-5 Map of Lebanon (Central Intelligence Agency, *The World Factbook, 2008*).

supported by the predominately Muslim Arabs, but was opposed by the Lebanese Christians. To the casual observer, Beirut and all of Lebanon have seen a never-ending cycle of violence perpetrated by warring factions from within the country's borders and from unsympathetic neighbors such as Syria, Iran, Iraq, and Israel. Lebanon had become a lawless society with a feeble government unable to restore order or control both internal and external elements bent on its destruction. The style and structure of terrorism to be played out in this theater of conflict can be viewed as political in nature. It is considered to be the oldest technique of psychological warfare—political terrorism may be defined simply as coercive intimidation. It is the systemic use of murder and destruction, or the threat of murder and destruction, in order to terrorize individuals, groups, communities, or governments into conceding to the terrorist's political demands.[39] While Syria had its own agenda to include Lebanon as a part of greater Syria, far more sinister notions were spreading outward from the Persian state of Iran.

The last decade of the twentieth century saw a relative calm return to the streets of Beirut. However, the city continues to echo the problems of a bygone decade. In January 2002, a car bomb killed a Lebanese Christian warlord, Elie Hobeika, who had a dubious past and was a militia leader, armed and equipped by the Israeli military under the control of Ariel Sharon. Hobeika may have led the assault on the refugee camps of Sabra and Shatila near Beirut International Airport in 1982, massacring Palestinian civilians. All of this occurred with the knowledge and connivance of the Israeli military.

Hobeika had served as a Lebanese government minister until 1988 and in 2001 had agreed to give evidence against Ariel Sharon at the Belgian war crimes inquiry. Hobeika's record of involvement in the massacres is somewhat incomplete. Some say he directed operations of Christian fighters from outside of the camps. A 1983 Israeli investigation into the massacres concluded that Sharon bore indirect responsibility and that Hobeika did not enter the camps. Who profits from the death of Hobeika? Many would wish him dead, and not least of all, Palestinians. But the finger could equally be pointed at Israel for the embarrassment his testimony in Belgium would have caused the Israeli government. The group claiming responsibility for his death calls itself the "Lebanese for a Free and Independent Lebanon." However, the group has not been identified by any mainstream opposition groups in the country and could well be a cover name for some other organization.[40]

Political Assassinations

Assassination of anti-Syria politicians in Lebanon has been a feature of the political landscape. Rafik Hariri a former Lebanese prime minister and outspoken opponent of Syria was killed in a massive car bomb attack in February 2005, and in June of the same year a leading anti-Syrian journalist was killed in a similar fashion. George Hawi, the former Lebanese Communist Party leader, was killed in a car bombing in June 2005, and the following month the former defense minister Elias al-Murr was seriously injured in an assassination attempt. In September, an outspoken journalist from Lebanese Broadcasting was also injured in an assassination attack. In December, another anti-Syrian Parliamentarian was killed in a car bomb attack, and in November 2006, Pierre Gemayel, a Maronite Christian and outspoken critic of Syria, was assassinated when his car was ambushed by gunmen.[41]

ISLAM

Before we proceed to discuss the bloodbath that Beirut became, the student should understand some fundamental philosophies about the world of Islam. Islam is a religious faith much like any other. However, it is actually divided into two separate spheres of influence: the Sunni sect and the Shiite sect. There are Five Pillars of Islam:

- *Shehada:* The statement in Arabic says, "There is no god but Allah and Mohammed is Prophet."
- *Salah:* Prayer five times a day. Prayer in Islam is praise of God.
- *Zakat:* The paying of alms to the poor. This is traditionally calculated at 2.5 percent. Different Muslim countries have differing views on Zakat now that income tax is a reality for many.
- *Ramadan:* The month of holy fasting. During Ramadan, Muslims must not eat, drink, or make love from sunrise to sunset.
- *Hajj:* Pilgrimage to Mecca. This is an obligation of all Muslims who can afford it to make the trek to Mecca in Saudi Arabia once in their lifetime.[42]

Sunni Muslims account for about 90 percent of the world's Muslim population; the remaining 10 percent are Shia Muslims. Struggles between the two groups date back to the seventh century; both hold the Quran as their sacred text and Mohammed as the Last Prophet. The Shiites have and believe in their own version of Islamic law and their own theology. The Shiites believe in a chain of leaders, or Imams, who came after Mohammed, and in a structure of spiritual authority through mullahs and a religious establishment.[43] Iran has the largest population of Shia Muslims in the world.

So, with an unstable government and warring factions fighting openly in the streets of Beirut, the country was ripe for the radicals to move in. With the Shah of Iran deposed and an Islamic revolution underway, the actions of fundamentalists spread to the Middle East.

The Shia Sect in Lebanon

Imam Mousa el-Sadr, an Iranian-born cleric, was the undisputed leader of the Shiite community in Lebanon by the end of the 1960s.[44] The Shia community was not, at this point, involved in any type of terrorist activity. Shiites were, however, aligned to politically defend and represent the poor of Lebanon. Together with Gregoire Haddad, a Catholic archbishop, they set up Haraket el-Mahroumeen, or Movement of the Deprived. This group aimed to work within the Lebanese political system to achieve its political objectives. With the passing of time, the Imam found it no easy task to help the poor and oppressed so he changed his doctrine and approach to the government. His party would become rejectionist and take up arms to fight the injustices. The group was known by the acronym AMAL. In stark contrast to its near neighbors in Iran, the Shia sectarian movement continued to operate within the political system after the civil war of 1975. The Lebanese Shia community saw a ray of hope with the formation of a government out of the Iranian Revolution, particularly given the background and birthplace of the Imam. His contacts and involvement with the Iranian movement, as well as the leadership of AMAL, was to end with his abduction and disappearance in 1978. A natural vacuum ensued and the AMAL became the Islamic AMAL, with headquarters in the Bekaa Valley of Lebanon under the auspices of Hussein el-Musawi. Islamic Amal was now foundering. Musawi joined forces to bring AMAL under the umbrella of Hezbollah.

HEZBOLLAH

The origins of the **Hezbollah** movement in Lebanon represent the most important and successful example of Islamic Iran's efforts to export its pan-Islamic brand of revolution beyond its border.[45] Hezbollah is also known as follows:

- Islamic Jihad
- Ansarollah

- Organization of the Oppressed
- Party of God
- Revolutionary Justice Organization

Hezbollah goal remains the establishment of an Islamic state in Lebanon.[46] Their presence in Lebanon was supported and financed by Iran's revolutionary government; and members of the Iranian Revolutionary Guard were sent to the Bekaa Valley to join with the training cadres. It is widely accepted that Hezbollah is controlled and directed by radical Shiite clerics under the central control of Iran through contacts in the Syrian capital of Damascus. Up until his death in 1989, the supreme guardian of revolutionary causes was Iran's Ayatollah Khomeini, who called on "all oppressed Muslims to replace their governments with Islamic Fundamentalist ones." His brand of terror stretched far and wide, and he used terror as his instrument of punishment. His continued diatribes against the "Great Satan,"[47] his term for the United States, and his religious fatwa (of death sentence) against the British author Salman Rushdie for writing a novel called the *Satanic Verses*, constantly stirred the pot of the Middle East politics.

With Hezbollah's rise to prominence in 1982, the group became a further embarrassment to the Lebanese government. Prior to the Israeli invasion of southern Lebanon, which led to the PLO retreating to Tunis, the streets of Beirut were governed by warring militia groups. These included the indigenous Druze populace of the hills around Beirut airport. It was not uncommon for rockets and mortars to be fired over the airport at the Palestinian positions nearby, causing chaos and destruction.

Hezbollah's main targets are the Israeli Jews, but it has also targeted non-Islamic influences in Europe, the United States, and Latin America. Since the withdrawal of the Israeli army from southern Lebanon, Hezbollah has been able to build and recruit combatants for its "Holy War" against Israeli targets. The Al-Manar TV network broadcasts a constant and objective view portraying the values of "martyrdom" (suicide). Al-Manar broadcasts to more than 25 million viewers in the Arab world including Palestinians in Gaza and the West Bank. Their objective is "...to encourage people to martyr themselves," in the words of Nayef Krayem, chairman of the network.[48] Beirut streets are marked with flags displaying the images of martyrs who have completed their suicide missions. Nevertheless, Beirut is still the temporary home to thousands of Palestinian refugees who are denied the same rights as the indigenous population and continue to live in abject squalor. Hezbollah has managed to garner prestige from the Arab states by being responsible for the ultimate Israeli withdrawal from southern Lebanon. The messages being sent to Gaza through the Al-Manar network may sow the seeds for more martyrs from the Palestinian population, but unlike Hezbollah, the Palestinians are unable to retreat to the hills of Lebanon to escape the reach of the Israeli military.

Any discussion of geopolitics in the region will involve both Lebanon and Syria, as Syria has been involved in every aspect of Lebanon's existence for the last thirty years. Both Syria and Iran have trained Hezbollah to be the best military force in Lebanon. Syria has always considered its presence in Lebanon a necessity to prevent civil war breaking out between Muslim and Christians. Syria's presence in the country for more than thirty years is testament to that policy, but its involvement is also crucial to its own economy.

Who killed Rafik Hariri?

The February 14, 2005, bomb attack that killed the former Lebanese prime minister Rafik Hariri has been blamed on Syria and sometimes on Israel, and recently the investigation by the UN Special Tribunal has implicated Hezbollah in the assassination. Hariri had been outspoken of the Syrian presence and interference in Lebanon and had been instrumental in calling for a Syrian withdrawal from Lebanon. It is doubtful whether it will ever be established exactly who or which faction or state ordered the Hariri's assassination, but it was troubling to observe his bodyguard had been significantly reduced and along with it all his experienced protection specialists. Syria denied any involvement and instead pointed the finger at Israel. Syria has been losing its grip on Lebanon since the death of the former Syrian president Hafez al-Assad in 2000. Its attempt to trample the Lebanese constitution by extending the presidency of its hand-picked puppet, Emil Lahoud, by three years was greeted with outrage in Beirut. Assad died just one month after the final Israeli withdrawal from southern Lebanon. The young son of the former president, and his successor, is not necessarily as competent to deal with his father's old guard, who would view any concessions as a sign of weakness. There is always the probability that, in a move to undermine the young Syrian president, forces from within the Syrian intelligence and security apparatus may have conspired to kill Hariri and set Assad up for the ultimate fall. There is no definite evidence to link the killing to Syria; however, the likelihood of it being any other is unlikely. With Hezbollah such an immense force in Lebanon, it is entirely probable that the U.S. demands on Syria to withdraw have a lot to do with the American and Israeli desire to nullify Hezbollah, a group that has been responsible for any number of attacks against both countries' interests.

Kidnapping

The speed and ruthless efficiency with which Hezbollah conducted kidnappings and executions in Beirut took the world completely by surprise. The January 1987 kidnapping of Terry Waite, the Archbishop of Canterbury's special envoy to the Middle East, was remarkable in that it was carried almost live on the major news networks. Hezbollah believed, at the time, that Terry Waite was working for the CIA. However, news bulletins, which showed Waite leaving an aircraft in Cyprus several steps ahead of Colonel Oliver North, provided ample incitement for the kidnappers to justify their actions. The refusal of the British and the United States to deal with terrorists or their demands resulted in Terry Waite and others being incarcerated for several years in the suburbs of Beirut before their eventual release in 1991.

Hezbollah—Structure and Development

From its original inception, Hezbollah operated like a "halfway house" for terrorists. Hezbollah received its guidance and direction from three different people within its hierarchy: Abu Musawi, Hassan Nasrallah, and Sheik Mohammed Hussein Fadollah, the last being Hezbollah's spiritual leader. As a former fighter with the Islamic Amal, Nasrallah's role was to format a terrorist force for the southern Lebanon region.[49]

As noted earlier, Hezbollah was intent on establishing an Islamic state in Lebanon. This would undoubtedly not be welcomed by the style of government established with the creation of Lebanon in the first quarter of the century, which assured that government would predominantly be in the hands of the Maronite Christian majority. As no census had been taken in the country for decades, it was probable that the Maronite Christians were no longer in the majority, a fact not lost on the Beirut militia commanders. With so many different groups fighting for control of the streets and the government, Hezbollah was not content to act like the PLO—as an umbrella for other groups. With Musawi's death Nasrallah turned his terrorist forces toward the same style of revolution as had occurred in Iran and effectively created a regional militia movement. Many other groups had, by 1991, laid down their arms and signed a peace accord. Hezbollah, on the other hand, remained the one major force against the Israelis in southern Lebanon and has been waging a terrorist campaign ever since.

Hezbollah used the suicide bomber to great effect, as did the Islamic Jihad. Hezbollah is blamed for the suicide bomb attack on the U.S. Marine barracks in West Beirut in October 1983, when a suicide bomber drove an explosive-laden truck and detonated it as he crashed into the camp. The bomb killed 241 U.S. Marines. The outcry in the United States was loud and clear: "What are our boys doing over there?" In spite of the outrage, the suicide attacks continued with spontaneous irregularity and with the same devastating results. Intelligence on Hezbollah was scant, and bringing any culprit to trial was almost impossible.

The terror tactics employed in Beirut significantly changed on March 28, 1986, when two British teachers were kidnapped in what had been considered the "safe" area of West Beirut. The following month, Brian Keenan, a British national with dual nationality in the Republic of Ireland, was abducted. The following week, one of the Muslim militia groups operating in West Beirut announced that it had executed a British journalist, Peter Collett. The next day, the three bodies of the Americans—Peter Kilburn, Leigh Douglas, and Philip Padfield—were discovered, and another journalist, John McCarthy, was kidnapped. Beirut had become an extremely hostile place for Westerners. Hezbollah does not confine its attacks against the state of Lebanon exclusively to the Middle East; it is, in fact, an international terrorist group with the ability to strike at targets throughout the world. Through local cell structures in South America, Hezbollah is believed to have been responsible for several large bomb attacks in Buenos Aires in 1994, and a car bombing in London.

Hasan Nasrallah, considered to be one of the shrewdest politicians in Lebanon as well as being the secretary general of Hezbollah, has declared that his movement will not give up its arms, but with the withdrawal of Syrian troops, Hezbollah will continue to defend the interests of Syria and Syria's withdrawal poses the most serious challenge to the Shiite movement since the end of the civil war. Nasrallah's ability to mobilize hundreds of thousands of Shiites, along with those from the thirty or so pro-Syrian factions in Lebanon, threatens to expose the deep rift within Lebanese society—the very crisis the Syrians always maintained their presence prevented. Lebanon's recent history has been one of constant bloodletting as well as of political opportunism by various sects, who have repeatedly hired themselves out to regional powers to advance their sectarian interests. Syria was the last to play such a game.[50]

AT WAR WITH ISRAEL

During the summer of 2006, Hezbollah fighters made an incursion into Israel and captured two Israeli soldiers, setting off a chain of events over the summer months that has had a lasting effect not only on the political fortunes of the Israeli government but also on the Lebanese. The naval blockade of Lebanon, which the Israelis initiated after the raid and bombings of suspected Hezbollah strongholds in Southern Lebanon and the Bekaa Valley, received a response that the Israeli's seemed ill-prepared to handle. The Israeli strategy was a bombing campaign followed up by a conventional ground war with Israeli forces advancing as far as the Litani River. It became apparent that the Israeli government may have severely underestimated Hezbollah's military might as they were well trained, equipped, and entrenched for the Israeli attack. They possessed a huge arsenal of rockets with which they targeted Israel, even reaching the outskirts of Haifa. Although the Israeli response was probably not what the Hezbollah were expecting, while the Lebanese government were powerless to prevent it from happening. As long as Israeli troops are occupying southern Lebanon, there will continue to be a reason for Hezbollah to attack them. Hezbollah gained a certain notoriety and significant Arab sympathy and support for its actions. Hezbollah has a significant political foothold in Lebanon and is heavily involved in community programs. Any attempt by the Lebanese government to curtail the fighters would provoke the Shiite population and inflame many of the sectarian passions that were responsible for Lebanon's long civil war. For the West to have any effect curtailing Hezbollah's popularity in Lebanon, it will have to show and provide aid in significant proportions—as at the moment Hezbollah is filling that void exclusively.[51] What surprised most observers of the war with Israel was that Hezbollah was in a position to operate at will without hindrance from the Lebanese army. Additionally, they were able to prosecute a conventional war thanks to state-of-the-art weapons and supplies they had received from Iran, which included shoulder-launched antitank missiles as well as night vision equipment. Hezbollah was able to benefit from territorial control in southern Lebanon without having to be concerned with the obligations and vulnerabilities that come with governance. It used state-of-the-art missiles to target the Israeli military and Israeli towns and cities. This was the first time a guerrilla army had managed to keep up a sustained bombardment on its enemy's territory, and the psychological effect that this had on the Israeli public was enormous. Hezbollah had managed to maintain its foothold in the south after the Israeli withdrawal in 2000 and gave the rationale that it was the Lebanese resistance protecting the interests of the Shiite populous, and they based this on the fact that in their opinion the Israelis continued to occupy a tiny portion of Israel, the border region of Sheba Farm.

While most of our attention is directed at the Islamic extremists from the Shiite sect, it is also necessary to understand what is happening with the Sunnis in Lebanon. The western section of Beirut is the predominantly Sunni area of the city and since the assassination of al-Hariri in 2005, his son Saad al-Harir has armed and led the Sunni militia with support from Jordan and Saudi Arabia. The Sunnis armed themselves out of a sense of preservation against Shiite aggression. During the Lebanese civil war, the Sunnis looked to the PLO for protection, and since the fighting between Hezbollah and Israel in 2006, the Sunnis have come to realize that they need their own militias for protection.

The successes of Hezbollah are partly due to its charismatic leader, Sheikh Hassan Nasrallah, rather than any inspiration from Tehran, but Nasrallah's stature has far exceeded Iranian expectations and is viewed with some skepticism for his accommodating approach with the Lebanese government. Israel has long sought to have him and others at the top table of Hezbollah assassinated, and the death of Imad Mugniyah in February 2008 indicates that Nasrallah, although no longer openly appearing at public gatherings or party meetings, is considered a target for Mossad. Iran still holds the purse strings and has no doubt insisted that Nasrallah remain out of sight.

SYRIA

Syria has been a major player in the Israeli/Palestinian problems. This Muslim country has a population that is 90 percent Sunni Muslim. Syria gained independence from France in 1946, and by the mid-1960s, the Baath party rose to power with Hafez al-Assad as its president. For years, Syria had been dominated by a succession of military governments. Assad, a former Air Force colonel, died in 2001, and his power passed to his son, Bashar al-Assad, who continues much as his father did. Syria is a longtime supporter of the Palestinian cause and a sworn enemy of Israel. It has fought two unsuccessful campaigns against Israel and lost control of the Golan Heights on its southern border.

Although Syria both sponsors and harbors terrorists, it is likely that any terrorist acts perpetrated on its soil would be quickly suppressed. Assad himself shied away from the public eye and quietly assisted groups such as Islamic Jihad and Hezbollah by allowing Iran to resupply them through Damascus. Assad's government was in open conflict with U.S. forces stationed in Lebanon and, in 1983, shot down an unarmed U.S. reconnaissance flight. Syria tries to maintain

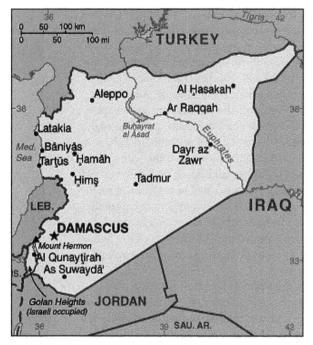

FIGURE 8-6   Map of Syria (Central Intelligence Agency, *The World Factbook, 2008*).

some measure of control over Hezbollah and its actions. It continues to hedge its bets and maintains a thriving business in support of training camps for expatriate terror groups such as the PFLP-GC, led by Ahmad Jibril, the Palestine Islamic Jihad; and the Japanese Red Army. Not far away in the Bekaa Valley are members of the Kurdish Workers Party (PKK), led by the university-educated Abdullah Ocalan, who spent time in Syria before his capture and death sentence in Ankara in 2000.

Syria does not permit homegrown terrorists to perpetrate actions against the state, and Assad's government violently suppresses any attempts, particularly by Islamic fundamentalists, to disrupt the workings of the state. Terrorists, fundamentalists and other political factions are suppressed in the one-party state. Despite this, the Muslim Brotherhood has attempted to raise its banner in Syria.

In 1982, an open revolt in the city of Hama by Islamic fundamentalists resulted in the Syrian army taking decisive action to crush the uprising, which resulted in many deaths and casualties. Syria does, however, continue to provide a safe haven for terrorist groups that are currently active.

Former president George Bush included Syria in his list of countries forming an "axis of evil" in 2002. Al-Assad has openly expressed support for the U.S. War on Terror, but he has done little or nothing in support of it. Only time will tell whether al-Assad has the capability and fortitude to weather pressure from the United States and take some decisive steps against Hamas, the PFLP, and other groups that maintain close terrorist ties. The young president is often viewed as sitting on the fence and, although there is evidence of Syria's involvement in the U.S. practice of "extreme rendition," perhaps as a shrewd attempt to curry favor with the world superpower, he also has managed to disengage his military's visual presence in Lebanon and so far survive.

A Mossad-Targeted Assassination?

A car bombing in Damascus on February 12, 2008, claimed the life of the legendary Hezbollah leader Imad Mughniyah, nicknamed "The Wolf." He had managed to evade capture or death at the hands of the Mossad and the CIA for years. Mughniyah was the head of operations for Hezbollah and was killed after leaving a Syrian intelligence office in Damascus. Israel is obviously the prime suspect in his death but quite naturally is not claiming any responsibility for any action in Syria. Mughniyah had strong ties to the Iranian Intelligence Service and was responsible for a vast number of terrorist attacks including masterminding the U.S. Embassy bombing and numerous airline hijackings. He would have been a major target for the Israeli Mossad.

In the wider events of the Middle East, Syria has become more of a U.S. target—its designation as being part of the "Axis of Evil" could well indicate it is next (after Iraq) for U.S. invasion. Syria enjoys, on its eastern flank, a border with Iraq. Prior to the Iraq invasion by U.S. and allied troops, Syria was likely sending supplies and weapons into the region. Syria has long been a state sponsor of numerous terrorist groups throughout the last forty years and, with the presence of so many foreign troops on Muslim soil, Syria's willingness and ability to prevent insurgents going into Iraq would be questionable. The United States feels it has three main issues with Syria:

- Its ongoing support for Hezbollah.
- Border security, as it affects U.S. troop security within Iraq.
- Its support for Palestinian rejectionist groups.

Syria's close ties with Iran will also make for complex problems in the region. Iran's unabated nuclear program will only strengthen the Bush Administration's resolve to take some sort of punitive action against one or the other—or both—of these state sponsors. Syria remains a constant threat to Israel while continuing its close relationship with both Iran and its regional proxy Hezbollah. Syria, which lies to the immediate south of Turkey, has managed to establish a relationship with that government as it sees the country's anti-U.S. stance as positive for its relationship with Turkey.

Syria expelled PKK leader Abdullah Ocalan in 1998 after threats of military intervention from Turkey. Relationships have changed dramatically between the two countries. In October 2007, Syria openly supported Turkey's decision to mount cross-border military operations to attack Kurdish rebels. The Syrians need the Turks more than Turkey needs Syria. Turkey of course has the respect of other Arab countries in the region and also Israel and the relationship with the United States will only be a temporary issue. Nevertheless Syrian–Iranian relations remain a source of intense concern to Arab countries. Syria also considers itself to be the main power broker on issues relative to Lebanon and its involvement in curtailing some of the insurgent activity in Iraq has achieved international recognition. While Syria takes one step forward, it encumbers itself with two steps backward in its ongoing activities with Hezbollah. Since the U.S.-led invasion of Iraq, the Syrians have facilitated the free flow of Islamist fighters across its border and into Iraq to fight against American troops.

Syrian Unrest—Arab Spring

The unrest sweeping the Middle East and North Africa in 2011 has also affected Syria—a country that has had to endure the same measures of repression as its neighbor Iraq suffered under Saddam Hussein. Unlike Egypt, where the protests were not supported by the military or secret police apparatus, the government forces of Bashar al-Assad went on the offensive. Although hollow promises for reforms were made, they were never likely to be fulfilled; and the Syrian crackdown showed how a dictatorship can engage in tactics to terrify and subdue its own people. During May 2011, the government arrested and tortured more than 8,000 protesters, cut roads and electricity to towns, and arrested journalists and restricted the freedom of the press. The Syrian leadership contends that its actions are to target Islamic extremist infiltrating the cities but the sheer scope of the crackdown along a crescent running from the coast to the Jordanian border suggests a leadership willing and content to use its military might against its own people. Syria's leadership continued to contend into 2012 that terrorist groups were to blame for the internal troubles afflicting the state rather than sweeping unrest from within, with government troops killing dissidents including women and children.

MOROCCO

This North African country, neatly sandwiched between the Atlantic Ocean and Algeria, has been remarkably adept at keeping terrorism at bay. The Moroccan government has rigorously investigated all terrorist acts and threats and has been successful in countering any Islamic radicalism unrest

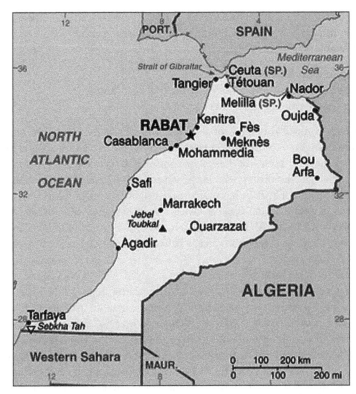

FIGURE 8-7 Map of Morocco (Central Intelligence Agency, *The World Factbook, 2008*).

within its borders. Morocco also arrested a member of the Algerian Islamic Salvation Front in December 1997.[52] Morocco gained its independence from French rule in 1955, after rioting broke out when the French sent the Sultan into exile. The uprising resulted in the sultan being returned to his native Morocco. Sultan Mohammad V changed his title to that of "King" and established a constitutional monarchy to oversee and control all aspects of governing the country. On his death in 1961, his son Hassan assumed the mantle of King and also prime minister. Since its independence, Morocco has laid claims to regions of the Saharan Desert under Spanish mandate. Both Morocco and Mauritania had claims on the region and had to contend with the Polisario Front, an indigenous group operating in the Sahara region. The Polisario Front wanted self-determination and was not likely to accept being consumed by either Mauritania or Morocco. Mauritania dropped its claim to the desert region and, in its place, Morocco claimed the whole area. In its efforts to stave off Morocco, the Polisario Front received military support from Libya and Algeria.

On his death in 1999, Hassan was succeeded by his son. King Mohammed VI has been a strong U.S. ally in the War on Terror, and although many Moroccans have been involved in al Qaeda–style attacks in Europe, the Moroccan regime has hit hard at Islamic extremists attempting to upset the status quo within the country. An attack by Islamic extremists in Casablanca in May 2003 killed more than forty-two, mostly Moroccan civilians, even though the bomb attacks were at five different locations—a Spanish social club, the Belgian Embassy, a Jewish cemetery, a resort hotel, and a Jewish community center. These simultaneous attacks came close after a string of similar events in Saudi Arabia and were likely the work of al Qaeda operatives within Morocco. The important issue here is that al Qaeda is far from being harried and chased out of its support bases in the Middle East. It seems capable of planning and setting up attacks of this scale in two Muslim countries at a time when George Bush was informing the world that al Qaeda might be a spent force—the reality is quite the contrary. For its part, the Moroccan King and his government have hit hard at suspected Islamic extremists within Morocco. Although severely criticized for human rights abuses while doing so, Morocco seems determined to hold down the terror factions within its borders and assist in the U.S. War on Terror. There is growing evidence of increased jihadist activity no doubt inspired by al Qaeda in this region, and in spring 2007, a string of suicide attacks in Rabat had all the hallmarking of an al Qaeda-inspired campaign. Both Algeria and Morocco are cooperating and exchanging intelligence information with Western governments and, particularly, Spain, the United Kingdom, and the United States. Most of the attacks have not been particularly sophisticated in their operational execution allowing authorities to uncover caches of explosives. The stability of both Morocco and Algeria will depend heavily on how much material training these jihadists will get in the coming months. Whether there is capability for training and expertise available from any jihadists returning from actions in Iraq or Afghanistan will no doubt dictate the level of effectiveness of attacks in the future.

EGYPT

The history of Egyptian contributions to modern society is fascinating. Egypt's feat of civil engineering, craftsmanship, and overall attention to detail in developing a dynasty before most of the world became civilized is a matter of historic record. The influences of the Egyptian

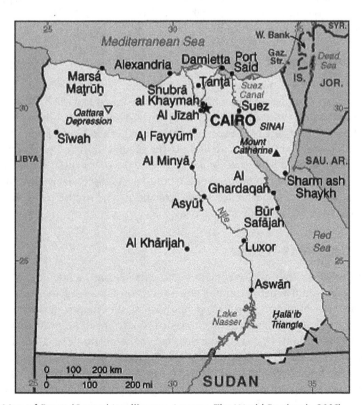

FIGURE 8-8 Map of Egypt (Central Intelligence Agency, *The World Factbook, 2008*).

people and the Pharaohs swept through Africa, the Middle East, and Mesopotamia, dominating societies for centuries. Even now, the study of ancient Egyptian writings occupies the dedication of countless professors and universities. It is believed that the first Egyptian pyramid was built 2,500 years before the birth of Christ. Egypt became a part of the Roman Empire in 31 B.C., and Roman rule dominated Egypt until approximately 395 A.D., when the country was overrun and ruled by Muslims from the Arabian Peninsula.

Twentieth-Century Politics

History sometimes repeats itself and that is the case with Egypt, which had been a country within the Ottoman Empire. The Muslim Brotherhood, which comprises a large percentage of native Egyptians, played a major part in the assassination of then president Anwar Sadat in 1991. Sadat's readiness to make a peace deal with the Israeli government was as much about economics as anything else. Egypt was suffering from excessive military spending and Sadat had promised that this would be lessened with the signing of a peace treaty with the Israelis. At the latter part of the 1970s, Israel considered Egypt its most powerful enemy. A peace agreement between the two countries was being brokered by former U.S. president Jimmy Carter, and, on March 29, 1979, in Washington DC, Menachem Begin and Anwar Sadat signed the accord. In hindsight, this may have been the political action that led to Sadat's untimely assassination. Immediately after the signing of the historic treaty, a summit of Arab League nations was held in Baghdad and Egypt was ostracized both economically and politically from the Arab world. Under the terms of the treaty, the Israelis gave up the Sinai in return for a peace deal and financial support from the United States. Egypt was now an outcast Arab state dependent on the United States for its aid. A large majority of Egyptians welcomed the accord.

The Muslim Brotherhood

Christians and Muslims have occupied Egypt for centuries. Egyptians who are born Christians are referred to as Copts, and number about 5–6 million. Formed in 1922 by Sheik al Banna, the Brotherhood stood solidly as then president Nasser's most vitriolic of opponents in Egypt. There had been an attempt on his life by a member of the Brotherhood, which gave then president Nasser the excuse he needed to round up and jail the membership and proclaim a ban on the movement. The Brotherhood would see an about-face by the presidential office with the arrival of Sadat, and those factions of the Brotherhood willing to support Sadat against his extreme left opponents were themselves supported with large donations. The Brotherhood would eventually bite the hand that fed it, with considerable ferocity.

ANWAR SADAT, 1919–1981

Over time, Anwar Sadat's style of government became increasingly autocratic. Although he had suggested that Egypt would benefit economically from the peace accord, there was no immediate change regarding military spending. In fact, spending in this area increased. Sadat was not gaining any allies among his Arab neighbors as he continued to attempt to keep the peace accord with Israel alive. Israel's attentions, by 1981, were diverted to the northeast and Lebanon. When the Israeli invasion of southern Lebanon began in 1982, the peace process with Egypt became mired in the sand. On the home front in 1981, Sadat was now facing increasing hostilities from the Muslim fundamentalists of the Brotherhood. Far from supporting Sadat, the Brotherhood was now actively challenging his rule. In June 1981, fighting erupted between Muslims and Christians

TERRORIST ATTACK BRIEF

Terrorist Group: Islamic Group - (Al-Gamaa al-Islamiyya) and Islamic Jihad and Muslim Brotherhood

Case Facts: While attending a military parade in Cairo, Anwar Sadat was seated in the VIP stand as military vehicles and troops passed by. Uniformed officers got out of a vehicle at the VIP stand and sprayed the area where Sadat and others were seated with automatic gunfire—Sadat died in a hail of bullets.

Investigation: Sadat's assassin was identified as Lieutenant Colonel Khalid al Islambuli. The conspirators were arrested and tried. In April 1982, two of the conspirators were shot and three hanged. Prior to the assassination Sadat had worked on a peace initiative at Camp David with both Israel and the United States to form a Middle East peace accord. This and his crackdown on opposition to his party in the months before—particularly the Muslim Brotherhood—was the reason for the assassination.

FIGURE 8-9 Assassination—Cairo, Egypt—Anwar Sadat (Former president of Egypt) October 6, 1981.

in Cairo, which resulted in massive property damage and a large number of deaths. Sadat began to suppress the Brotherhood and arrested 1,500 members, including many of the organization's leaders.[53] Clearly out in the cold, Sadat's only close ally was the United States. This alliance fueled the Muslim Brotherhood's hatred of Sadat. This hatred was not aimed at the government, but at Sadat himself. Former president Nasser was, by all accounts, mourned by an entire nation; not so with the passing of Sadat. The Sadat government was seen as increasingly corrupt, with ordinary Egyptians suffering food shortages. Sadat's promise of a better life for Egyptians never seemed to materialize.

Following Sadat's assassination in 1981, there was no spontaneous eruption of violence, no revolution to carry the Muslim Brotherhood forward in Egypt, which had been the intention of the Muslim cell involved in the attack. Although Western world leaders and governments mourned his passing, Egyptians seemed to breathe a collective sigh of relief and, to some extent, regarded Lt. El-Sambouli as a hero. With Islamic fundamentalism on the rise throughout the Muslim world, it seemed probable that a revolt should occur, but this did not happen in Egypt for another thirty years. In elections in 1987, the Muslim Brotherhood allied with two political parties, won 17 percent of the vote, which translated into fifty-six seats in the Egyptian National Assembly.[54] In April 1982, El-Sambouli and his five coconspirators were found guilty of Sadat's assassination and executed for their crimes.

EGYPT'S ISLAMIC EXTREMISTS

Jamaat al-Islamiyya and Egyptian Islamic Jihad, both radical and extreme Islamic groups, have long been associated with Egypt and have made many attempts to violently attack and destabilize successive Egyptian regimes. Mohammed Atta, the supposed leader of the 9-11 attacks and an al Qaeda member, was an Egyptian; many of the al Qaeda leadership come from this hot bed of Islamic extremism. The two groups gained much of their support from the slums of Cairo and the poorer regions of the state. Both have been responsible for the attacks against foreign tourists in Egypt that decimated the lucrative Egyptian tourism economy. Both groups have their roots going back to the Muslim Brotherhood and have been fighting for an Islamic state to replace the secular government of Hosni Mubarak.

Both groups are known to have sent members to Afghanistan for training with the mujahedeen, who fought in Afghanistan against the Soviet Union. Many links exist between these two groups and al Qaeda. To this end, the Mubarak government had suppressed both of them. Claims of torture by human rights groups and criticism from the United States on the topic did not prevent extensive crackdowns on the extremist terror groups. The United States had been a supporter of the Mubarak regime and poured considerable financial aid into the country. Egypt's largest Islamic terror group is Jamaat al-Islamiyya (the Islamic Group). Jamaat al-Islamiyya has a presence both in Egypt and worldwide. Its spiritual leader, the blind cleric Sheikh Omar Abdel Rahman, is serving a life sentence in the United States for his involvement in the 1993 attack on the World Trade Center. (In April 2002, the Justice Department charged that Abdel Rahman had tried to direct further terrorist operations from his cell in Minnesota.)

Following a violent campaign of attacks against the government, Christians, and other targets in Egypt, Jamaat al-Islamiyya has largely honored a March 1999 cease-fire with the Egyptian government. Exiled members of Jamaat al-Islamiyya are known to have joined al Qaeda and trained at its camps in Afghanistan.[55] The Islamic Jihad has close ties to bin Laden's al Qaeda and continues its assault on the Egyptian government. Due to the repressive nature of the Mubarak regime, the group has operated principally outside Egypt and has been turning its Islamic extremist campaign toward U.S. targets. The philosophy of the fundamentalists is to overthrow the government and to replace it with a radical and extreme Islamic government similar to the former Taliban regime in Afghanistan.

Until the fall of Mubarak in early 2011, the Egyptian government continued to support, in principle, the U.S.-led War on Terror and had been an ally of peace initiatives for the Middle East. However, arms continue to be supplied to Palestinian groups through the Sinai Peninsula.

It may be necessary to take a cautious view of a country that has cracked down hard on its Islamic radicals since the assassination of Anwar Sadat and has also seen little respect for human rights. Mubarak's most powerful threat came from the Muslim Brotherhood, even though it was banned from political activity or from participating in government elections; it has members who have stood as independents. Egypt's Parliament approved a constitutional amendment in May 2005 that opened presidential elections to multiple candidates, but opposition figures protested that its stringent conditions would make the September 2005 election a one-man referendum for then president Hosni Mubarak. "This is a political trick which makes a mockery of democracy," said Mustapha K al-Sayyid, a political science professor at the American University of Cairo and a member of the fledgling opposition Kefaya movement, otherwise known as the Egyptian Movement for Change. "The amendment gives veto power to the ruling party to decide who will run in the elections."

In the May 2007 elections for the Shura Council, not one Muslim Brotherhood member was elected. This in a region that was claimed by then president Bush to be a model for democracy—some 800 Muslim Brotherhood members have been arrested since December 2006. In what has become a tradition on voting days in Egypt, riot police surrounded polling stations in districts where Brotherhood candidates looked likely to win. Some stations were simply sealed off, while in others the security cordon opened to let in busloads of government supporters. The demonstrations in Cairo in spring 2011 were not necessarily a popular revolution as the 300,000 demonstrators in Tahir Square represented only a fraction of the population of Egypt. The media attention given to the demonstrations gave the Egyptian military the opportunity to carry out a bloodless coup and remove then president Mubarak from office. What we must learn from these actions in Egypt and elsewhere in the Middle East is that all democratic revolutions do not necessarily lead to a constitutional democracy. Only time will tell what effect the regime change will have on Israel and its peace deal with Egypt, but what is apparent is the continued rise in popularity of the Muslim Brotherhood. Whether the movement has the cohesion to challenge the military remains to be seen; even though the movement has wide support, the constant infighting within the party is leading Egypt into a further period of instability.

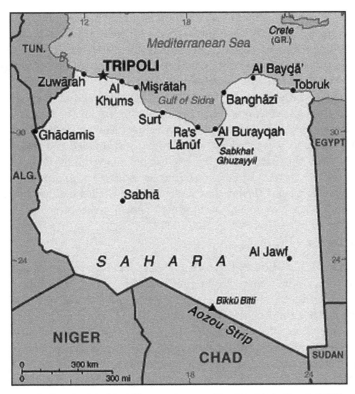

FIGURE 8-10   Map of Libya (Central Intelligence Agency, *The World Factbook, 2008*).

LIBYA

Libya is situated at the northern tip of Africa and has a northern border on the Mediterranean Sea. Its nearest neighbors to the east are Egypt and the Sudan, with Chad and Niger to the south and Algeria and Tunisia to the west and northwest, respectively. The country is made up of 97 percent Sunni Muslims or Arabian Berber tribesmen. In the 1930s, under Italian dominance, there was discrimination against Libyan Jews, who have been persecuted in Libya ever since. Libyans attacked the Jewish sector of Benghazi during World War II and deported about 2,000 Jews. By the time Libya had achieved independence in 1951, nearly all the remaining Libyan Jews had migrated to either Israel or Europe.[56]

COLONEL MUAMMAR EL-QADDAFI

Muammar el-Qaddafi was a man driven by hatred for the state of Israel, the United States, and foreign powers that support them. Up until the late 1990s, Libya did not limit itself to attacking foreign governments, but also sought out and assassinated Libyans opposed to the Libyan leader.

Qaddafi came to power following a military coup that deposed King Idris in 1969 and achieved dictatorial status as Libyan leader. Outspokenly anti-Israeli, anti-Zionist, and anti-Semitic in his public statements, he made no distinction among them. As a mark of his hatred for the Jewish people, he seized all Jewish-owned properties and businesses in 1971. He ruled with an autocratic style and ruthlessly "removed" all dissenters. His control of the government was absolute through the setup of people's committees. As a former military student and officer, he had never been cast in the secular role that he seemed to have adopted in the 1990s. With unrest of the Arab Spring sweeping across North Africa, his regime of terror ended ignominiously. The masses demanded democratic change and fighting broke out across the country. The fighters appealed for international intervention and were supported by NATO with air strikes against Libyan government strongholds. By the end of October 2011, Qaddafi and his hard-line loyalists were all but decimated. Qaddafi's convoy was bombed by NATO jets, and he took cover in a drainage tunnel only to be captured and shot by opposition fighters. The future for Libyans remains very uncertain. NATO support was provided, and Qaddafi was toppled and replaced by Islamists unfriendly to the West. The first pungent signs of disquiet came with the Benghazi desecration of British graves at the War Graves Commission Cemetery in Benghazi in February 2012 committed by an armed group of Salafists. Whether the country slides into failed state and overrun by regional warlords or becomes a safe haven for al Qaeda groups remains to be seen.

Support for Terror

The phenomenon of state-sponsored terrorism applies most appropriately to Libya, Iran, and Syria and forms part of what George Bush termed the "Axis of Evil." The most outspoken of the Arab world leaders, Qaddafi embarked through the 1970s and 1980s on a reign of external terror against the United States and its citizens, specifically those in Europe. Qaddafi supported other terror groups in Europe and allowed them to train on Libyan soil. Qaddafi also provided weapons to such groups as the Provisional Irish Republican Army (PIRA). In one notable incident, Qaddafi supplied several tons of explosives and automatic weapons that were seized by security forces in the Irish Republic. To Qaddafi, the PIRA was fighting a guerrilla war of independence from the dominance of an imperialist power. Libya has been a home and terrorist training ground for more than thirty terrorist organizations, such as Abu Sayeef from the Philippines. However, in order to get sanctions lifted (among other actions taken), Libya expelled members of the Abu Nidal organization in 1998.

There was sufficient opposition to the Qaddafi regime to prompt him to unleash internal assassins to track down and coerce the dissidents into returning to Libya. In 1984, more than thirty terrorist attacks were carried out by representatives of Libyan Revolutionary Committees on Libyans residing in Europe and the Middle East.[57] Not only did Qaddafi focus on his dissidents in Europe and the Middle East, he also sought them out in neighboring Chad and the sub-Saharan African states that were vociferously against his government.

Diplomatic Immunity

To circumvent the interference of foreign customs officials, Qaddafi used diplomatic privileges to move contraband weapons into and out of diplomatic missions in Europe. By the 1980s, Qaddafi had renamed the Libyan embassies as the Libyan People's Bureaus. The problems faced by the British government of Margaret Thatcher and public protests outside the Libyan People's Bureau in St. James's Park, London, would result in the severing of diplomatic ties between the two countries. The following are extracts from the Vienna Convention on Diplomatic Relation, 1961:

ARTICLE 22

1. The premises of the mission shall be inviolable. The agents of the receiving state may not enter them, except with the consent of the head of the mission.

2. The receiving State is under a special duty to take all appropriate steps to protect the premises of the mission against any intrusion or damage and to prevent any disturbances of the peace of the mission or impairment of its dignity.
3. The premises of the mission, their furnishings and other property thereon and the means of transport of the mission shall be immune from search, requisition, attachment or execution.

ARTICLE 29

The person of a diplomatic agent shall be inviolable. He shall not be liable to any form of arrest or detention. The receiving State shall treat him with due respect and shall take all appropriate steps to prevent any attacks on his person, freedom or dignity.

ARTICLE 31

1. A diplomatic agent shall enjoy immunity from the criminal jurisdiction of the receiving State. He shall also enjoy immunity from its civil and administrative jurisdiction.
2. A diplomatic agent is not obliged to give evidence as a witness.

ARTICLE 45

If diplomatic relations are broken off between two States, or if a mission is permanently or temporarily recalled:

a. the receiving State must, even in case of armed conflict, respect and protect the premises of the mission, together with its property and archives;
b. the sending state may entrust the custody of the premises of the mission, together with its property and archives, to a third State acceptable to the receiving State;
c. the sending State may entrust the protection of its interests and those of its nationals to a third State acceptable to the receiving State.

On April 17, 1984, news networks in London showed the dramatic turn of events when gunfire erupted from the Libyan Peoples Bureau into the demonstrators outside. The demonstrators were mainly exiled Libyan students protesting against Qaddafi. The gunfire killed a Metropolitan policewoman, Yvonne Fletcher. Intelligence intercepts of messages between Tripoli and the London Libyan People's Bureau revealed that those inside were ordered to fire on the demonstrators. On the home front, the Libyan-controlled press released a different story about the incident, stating that the police had stormed the building and described the episode as a "barbarous outrage." The standoff at the Libyan People's Bureau ended on April 27, when the occupants agreed to be taken to the Civil Services College in Berkshire to be interviewed by police. Under diplomatic privilege, they refused to help in the investigation and were returned to Libya. The events at St. James's Square were the culmination of a series of bombings and attacks against dissident Libyans in London and the northwest of England.

OPERATION EL-DORADO CANYON

International relations between the United States and Libya were at an all-time low by the middle of the 1980s. Behind the scenes at this time was the Soviet Union, which had been supplying weapons and aircraft to Libya. On March 24, 1986, in an effort to make the Libyans lose face, the

United States began maneuvers with its Sixth Fleet in the Mediterranean in the Gulf of Sirte off the north coast of Libya, in Libya's self-defined exclusion zone.

Libya responded with two terrorist attacks in Europe. In the first attack, on April 2, 1986, a bomb exploded in the cabin of a TWA passenger jet in Greek airspace. Four Americans were killed in the blast; however, the aircraft landed without further incident. Four days later, a powerful explosion ripped through La Belle discotheque in West Berlin, killing an American serviceman. American intelligence indicated that the disco bombing was planned and directed by "diplomats" from the East Berlin Libyan People's Bureau.

The deaths of U.S. citizens became the trigger the Reagan Administration was searching for to launch a previously planned U.S. air strike in Libya. On April 14, 1986, aircraft from U.S. bases in the United Kingdom and aircraft carriers in the Mediterranean bombed targets inside Libya.

Over 100 aircraft took part in the raid in and around Tripoli and Benghazi, causing heavy damage and loss of life. It is believed that then colonel Qaddafi's adopted daughter was one of the fatalities. In all, more than 100 lives were claimed. Was the attack sending a message to other state sponsors of terrorism or was this strike designed to help topple or kill the Libyan leader and allow for a more moderate government to be formed in its place? This was the first time the United States had launched such aggressive military action at a specific country in retaliation for terrorist attacks. Would other terrorist groups heed the example of the attack on Libya and cease activities against the United States? On the political front, members of the United Nations, including France and Italy, the two countries that had refused over flight clearances for strike aircraft from U.K. bases, condemned the United States. Did the French and Italian governments fear some form of reprisal attack from the Libyan leader? The U.K. government, on the other hand, the strongest American ally at the time, had already severed diplomatic ties with Libya over the death of Yvonne Fletcher. A far more serious terrorist attack was being planned, indicating that preemptive military actions may not be successful against determined and fanatical terrorist movements. Some thirteen years later, under a different U.S. administration, spy satellites and long-range smart bombs would again target terrorist sites this time, but in Sudan and Afghanistan.

During the last decade, with the mounting pressure on his country from UN sanctions that were not lifted until 1999, the colonel has had to reevaluate his position in the world. No longer did he have the support of the former Soviet Union. A period of appeasement was definitely the order of the day for Libya's survival. Libya has small stocks of biological agents and the risk that those could fall into the wrong hands or, to be more specific, into the hands of al Qaeda, has been a pressing issue for the United States. In May 2002, the U.S. State Department added Libya to the list of countries that were developing chemical and biological weapons of mass destruction (WMD). Certainly, Qaddafi had no love for the Islamic extremists or al Qaeda, and since 9-11 he had reportedly provided intelligence on Libyan militants outside of the country. This action benefitted Qaddafi as he maintained an iron-fisted approach to Islamic extremists inside Libya.

PAN AM 103

One of the most significant terrorist attacks of the last fifty years has been the destruction of a Pan Am 747–200 over Lockerbie, Scotland, on December 21, 1988. The trial and conviction of a mid-level Libyan intelligence officer still leaves the obvious question as to the complicity of the leader of the Libyan government. In 1999, Libya fulfilled one of the requirements of the United Nations Security Council Resolutions (UNSCR) by surrendering two Libyans suspected in connection with the bombing for trial before a Scottish court in the Netherlands.

One of these suspects, **Abdel Basset al-Megrahi**, was found guilty; the other was acquitted. Al-Megrahi's conviction was upheld on appeal in 2002. In August 2003, Libya fulfilled the remaining UNSCR requirements, including acceptance of responsibility for the actions of its officials and payment of appropriate compensation to the victims' families. UN sanctions against Libya were lifted on September 12, 2003. In August 2009, al-Megrahi was released by Scottish authorities on compassionate grounds based on his apparent illness from terminal cancer. Al-Megrahi died May 20th 2012 nearly three years after his relase on compassionate grounds.

On December 19, 2003, Libya announced its intention to rid itself of WMD and medium-to close-range (MTCR) class missile programs. Since that time, it has cooperated with the United States, the United Kingdom, the International Atomic Energy Agency, and the Organization for the Prohibition of Chemical Weapons toward these objectives. Libya also signed the IAEA Additional Protocol and became a State Party to the Chemical Weapons Convention. In response, the United States terminated the applicability of the Iran-Libya Sanctions Act to Libya and then president Bush signed an Executive Order on September 20, 2004, terminating the national emergency with respect to Libya and ending IEEPA-based economic sanctions. This action had the effect of unblocking assets blocked under the Executive Order sanctions. Restrictions on cargo aviation and third-party code sharing were lifted, as were restrictions on passenger aviation. Certain export controls remained in place and Libya remained on the state sponsors of terrorism list. U.S. diplomatic personnel reopened the U.S. Interest Section in Tripoli on February 8, 2004. The mission was upgraded to a U.S. Liaison Office on June 28, 2004. Libya reestablished its diplomatic presence in Washington with the opening of an Interest Section on July 8, 2004, which was subsequently upgraded to a Liaison Office in December 2004.[58]

Libyan Islamic Fighting Group (LIFG)

Sunni Islamic militants have also been present in Libya but have not managed to engage any popular support for their cause. The LIFG has been in existence for several decades but only publicly announced its presence in a 1995 communiqué following a number of attacks against the Libyan regime. Over the course of 1995 and 1996, LIFG mounted assassination attacks against Colonel Qaddafi; all were unsuccessful. The LIFG leader and its founder, Salah Fathi bin Suleiman, was killed during a battle with Libyan military forces in September 1997. Unable to promote a popular uprising, the LIFG moved to exile in Sudan at a time when Osama bin Laden was setting up his organization in that country. The Libyan government brought significant pressure to bear on the Sudan government to kick out the LIFG members. Bin Laden, as a guest of the Sudan government, was compelled to remove the Libyan fighters from his camps. Many returned to Libya but did not stay long enough to be caught in Qaddafi's crackdown, but instead fled to Europe. Many rejoined al Qaeda in training camps in Taliban-controlled Afghanistan and since 9-11 went on to prosecute a global jihad. Recruits from Libya were heavily involved in the Iraq insurgency. In February 2006, the U.S. Treasury Department took significant steps aimed at nullifying LIFG's base in the United Kingdom, designating five individuals, three companies, and one charity as terrorists for their ties to LIFG. In addition to labeling Birmingham, U.K., resident Abdelrahman al-Faqih as a "senior leader for the LIFG" the Treasury Department also designated Midlands resident Mohammed Benhammedi as a "key financier for the LIFG" and "a member of…. the LIFG economic committee" who was "believed to provide funds for LIFG through Sara Properties Limited, Meadowbank Investment Limited and Ozlam Properties Limited."[59]

The Sanabal Relief Agency was also described as a fund-raising front organization for the LIFG and was designated as a Specially Designated Global Terrorist (SDGT) entity.

Following the ousting of most elements of the former Qaddafi regime and being replaced by a transitional government, there have been moves to restore levels of justice and administration within Libya. Old foes are being hunted and foremost is the former intelligence chief Abdullah al-Senussi who is wanted not only for crime of embezzlement in Libya but also is subject to an arrest following his sentencing in absentia to life imprisonment for the September 19, 1989, terror attack on UTA Flight 772, killing 170 people, including 54 French nationals, when the French airliner exploded over Niger.

SUDAN

Sudan has been fighting an almost endless civil war between Muslims in the north and Christians in the south. Its government appears to have been devastated by the famine and poverty that have wrecked the nation. Sudan has, however, been on the U.S. State Department's list of countries that sponsor and support international terror groups. Safe haven and training grounds have been available to the Abu Nidal Organization, Hezbollah, Hamas, and the PIJ. The UN Security Council passed several resolutions concerning the role of Sudan in sponsoring terror groups; not all have been complied with. One name stands apart from all others at the end of this decade: Osama bin Laden. He was ordered to leave Sudan in 1997, but his legacy was to cause a military confrontation with the United States some twelve months later. Following the bombings of the U.S. embassies in the Kenyan and Tanzanian capitals, which claimed hundreds of lives, the United States struck back. In a reaction similar to that of Ronald Reagan, the Clinton administration retaliated on August 20, 1998. In his address to the nation then president Clinton stated, "Today I ordered our armed forces to strike at terrorist-related facilities in Afghanistan and Sudan because of the imminent threat they presented to our national security ... In recent history they killed American, Belgian and Pakistani peacekeepers in Somalia. They plotted to assassinate the Pope and the president of Egypt. They planned to bomb six United States 747s over the Pacific ...their (terrorist) mission is murder and their history is bloody. The most recent terrorist events are fresh in our memory. Two weeks ago, 12 Americans and 300 Kenyans and Tanzanians lost their lives. Another 5,000 were wounded when our embassies in Nairobi and Dar es Salaam were bombed." The attack against a factory believed to be developing chemical weapons was carried out by a missile attack from U.S. naval ships in the Red Sea. The exact details of the strike were not confirmed; however, news reports seen on television indicated massive damage to the Al-Shifa Pharmaceutical Factory in Khartoum. Throughout the Middle East and

FIGURE 8-11 Map of Sudan (Central Intelligence Agency, *The World Factbook, 2008*).

Asia, there were spontaneous demonstrations against the United States, and the action probably gave impetus to the Islamic extremist movement in Afghanistan. As in the 1986 strike against Libya, this response is not seen as an effective deterrent for terrorism. To many analysts, it is seen as having precisely the opposite effect.

Darfur

Recent memory of atrocities in Rwanda would make many observers wonder why nothing has occurred on an international scale to temper the actions of Sudan's proxy forces in the Darfur region of the Sudan. Much is made of the term *genocide* and whether this is taking place in this region or not. What is definitely taking place is the total destruction of entire villages, including the rape and murder of women and children. As recently as the end of 2004, the Sudanese government made a peace deal with rebels it has been fighting in the southern part of the country for a quarter of a century. The region of Darfur has been in turmoil since 2003, likely as a result of the Sudanese government's fear of being unable to fight two separate insurgent uprisings at the same time and originating in far-flung, impoverished regions of the country.

The National Islamic Front government came to power through a military coup in 1989 and gets its support from Sudan's wealthy and economic interest groups, which reflect only a small minority of the Sudanese population. The peace deal brokered and then signed on January 9, 2005, with the southern rebels from the Sudan People's Liberation Movement/Army (SPLM), gave considerable power-sharing concessions to the rebel movement. The Comprehensive Peace Agreement provided for:

- A new constitution
- Power sharing
- Wealth sharing
- Security throughout the country

According to the agreement, new institutions would be created and a new government of National Unity installed once the constitution was ratified. SPLM Chairman John Garang would become the first vice president of Sudan and the new government of southern Sudan would be established. However, in Darfur, unlike the south, the problems began with the rise of two new movements to challenge the Khartoum regime—namely, the Sudan Liberation Movement/Army (SLA) and the Justice and Equality Movement (JEM). The region had been in conflict at both tribal and regional levels for decades and violent events were not uncommon, but the current levels of attack and counterattack by the government seem to be disproportionate to the problem. UN commissioners reported that the vast majority of attacks on civilians in villages have been carried out by government of Sudan armed forces and Janjaweed. The Janjaweed, or "evil horsemen," comprise mostly Arab ethnic militias. The attacks sponsored by the Khartoum government were aimed primarily at the African, rather than the Arab, population of Darfur.

The international legal definition of the crime of genocide is found in Articles II and III of the 1948 Convention on the Prevention and Punishment of Genocide. Article II describes two elements of the crime of genocide:

1. The mental element, meaning the "intent to destroy, in whole or in part, a national, ethnical, racial or religious group, as such," and
2. The physical element, which includes five acts described in sections a, b, c, d, and e. A crime must include both elements to be called "genocide."

Article III describes five punishable forms of the crime of genocide: genocide, conspiracy, incitement, attempt, and complicity.

EXCERPT FROM THE CONVENTION ON THE PREVENTION AND PUNISHMENT OF GENOCIDE

Article II: In the present Convention, genocide means any of the following acts committed with intent to destroy, in whole or in part, a national, ethnical, racial or religious group, as such:

a. Killing members of the group;
b. Causing serious bodily or mental harm to members of the group;
c. Deliberately inflicting on the group conditions of life calculated to bring about its physical destruction in whole or in part;
d. Imposing measures intended to prevent births within the group;
e. Forcibly transferring children of the group to another group.

ARTICLE III: THE FOLLOWING ACTS SHALL BE PUNISHABLE:

a. Genocide;
b. Conspiracy to commit genocide;
c. Direct and public incitement to commit genocide;
d. Attempt to commit genocide;
e. Complicity in genocide.

It is a crime to plan or incite genocide, even before killing starts, and to aid or abet genocide. Criminal acts include conspiracy, direct and public incitement, attempts to commit genocide, and complicity in genocide.[60] What is clearly taking place in the Darfur region is state terrorism being inflicted on a subgroup and, in this instance, it is the non-Muslim population. The Janjaweed may or may not be practicing genocide, but perhaps the term "ethnic cleansing" could be used to describe the terrible events taking place. To date, we have witnessed that the international community under the auspices of the United Nations will pass resolutions, recommendations, and some sanctions against the government of the Sudan; however, the numbers killed run into the hundreds of thousands with over a million displaced.

ALGERIA

The People's Democratic Republic of Algeria (Algeria) emerged from its French colonial era through a nationalist movement that pitted the FLN (Front de Liberation National) against French security forces, brutally aided by a pro-France terrorist organization known as the OAS (Organisation Armie Secrete). The terrorists' struggle lasted from 1954 to 1962; 1 million Algerians and 17,500 French occupation forces were killed before the Evian Agreement of 1962 ended the FLN's campaign of assassination, bombing, and sabotage and the French's ferocious counterinsurgency campaign of torture, death, and repression.[61] The FLN emerged as victorious revolutionary heroes whose primary sense of political legitimacy lay in throwing out colonial suppressors. Algeria emerged from an effective, two-pronged FLN campaign against the French: the guerrilla war in the cities and rugged countryside of Algeria, and a diplomatic campaign in European and African capitals. France agreed to a plebiscite in 1962 on the issue of independence; 99 percent of the votes were cast in favor of Algerian independence. Ahmed Ben Bella, an FLN political leader during the war of independence, became the first president of independent Algeria. The FLN was in power from 1962 to 1992, when the civilian government was dissolved in a political coup.

Algeria remained officially a one-party socialist country for the three decades of 1962 to 1992, assisted by the French in oil and gas technology, capital fusions, and foreign aid. Population growth increased the size of the nation from 9 million in 1962 to more than 28 million in 1995; 75 percent of Algerians are under the age of twenty-five.

The subsequent rise of a radical Islamic movement in Algeria, which won a round of the parliamentary elections in 1991, caused the FLN to abandon the election process and nullify the results. The party in question, the Islamic Salvation Front (FIS), was immediately banned by the FIS because of its radical Islamic goals. Following the ban, its military wing commenced a campaign of attacks against government and security forces.

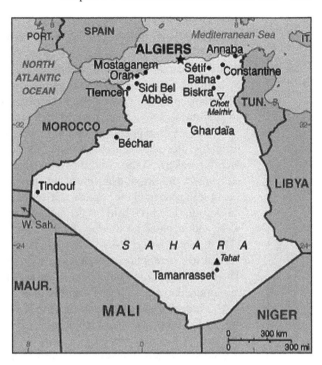

FIGURE 8-12 Map of Algeria (Central Intelligence Agency, *The World Factbook, 2008*).

Economic Crisis

It can be argued that the FLN was ineffective in governing Algeria from 1962 to 1992.[62] A rapidly growing number of young Algerians eager to secure economic positions and hoping for a brighter future encountered bureaucratic inefficiencies of a socialist state economy, coupled with corruption and rigid attempts to control entrepreneurship. A severe housing shortage emerged, along with declining agricultural and industrial production and a devastating drop in oil prices. The economic situation was complicated by a lack of consumer goods, high unemployment, and rising inflation. Servicing Algeria's huge foreign debt (more than $30 billion in 1995) requires almost all of the $9 billion in annual oil and gas revenues. In 1986, an austerity plan was imposed, in part to secure International Monetary Fund assistance.

October 1988 Riots

Algeria's deteriorating economic situation shattered social and economic expectations. Riots ensued and the military responded with excessive repression, firing on and killing hundreds of demonstrators. Thousands were arrested, and rumors began to circulate that security forces were torturing dissidents. Algeria's older citizenry, freedom fighters three decades before in the 1960–1962 era, equated the military's torture to that of the "Colons" (the sometimes-brutal French leaders of colonial days), a similarity that struck a chord and captured some Algerian hearts.

In late 1988, then president Chadli Benjedid, undertook a democratic initiative. Referendums were held in 1988 and 1989, changing the constitution and including more respect for civil rights and a free press. Formation of political associations was permitted, and the one-party (FLN) system was abandoned. By February 1989, at least fifty new political parties were formed, including the Front Islamic du Salah (FIS), recognized as legal in September

1989 (Alexander). The FIS was organized through mosques and, by late 1989, had at least 3 million adherents. FIS political themes included criticizing the state bureaucracy, widespread corruption, and Western secular elites (French influences, primarily). Reflecting Islamic influences, subordination of women was advocated. The FIS sought an Islamic state governed by Islamic law; it proposed to discriminate against ethnic and other minorities (Berbers, Jews, Christians, polytheists, etc.) and French-speakers ("the enemies of God"). Religious extremists sought imposition of Sharia law into all aspects of politics and daily life in Algeria.

These earlier political pronouncements, especially the proposed imposition of puritan codes (drinking, dress, calendar, etc.), alarmed the educated, business people, and intellectuals. Minorities, French speakers, women, and the more educated staged counterdemonstrations. In the June 1990 elections for municipal, department, and provincial assemblies, the FLN was decisively defeated. The FIS won 54 percent of the popular vote cast, which totaled 65–75 percent of the eligible voters. Since no elections had been held for the national assembly, the FLN still controlled the national political scene and prepared for the June 1991 elections by gerrymandering to give more representation to FLN strongholds and districts. In this environment, one FIS leader (Abbassi Madani) called for a general strike, adoption of an Islamic state, and resistance through jihad and civil disobedience. The FIS was, interestingly, openly split over this call. Disruptive events occurred, but not mass revolution; the army declared a state of siege and elections were rescheduled for December.

There is some suggestion that the FIS might not have fared well in the fall 1991 elections, as it had not distinguished itself at local, urban, and municipal administration. It may have been that gerrymandering was an FLN provocation, and the FIS overreaction was triggered, in part, through infiltration of the FIS. In any event, the military declared a state of siege, banning meetings, publications, and demonstrations; suspending activities of political associations; and detaining civilian suspects. The military assumed local arrest authority and military tribunals conducted trials. FIS leaders were arrested en masse and detained in camps and jails. By fall 1991, the state of siege was lifted to permit elections, scheduled by Chadli Benjedid for December 1991 and January 1992.

DECEMBER 1991 ELECTIONS   In the December phase of the national election, the FIS won 189 of 231 National Assembly seats with 47 percent of the eligible vote; the rejection of the FLN was obvious. Faced with a certain FIS victory, the military pressured the president to resign. The National Assembly was dissolved, and the Haut Comite d'Etat (HEC) imposed. On January 11, 1992, the military coup was affected. The HEC banned the FIS (its principal opposition party), jailed almost all the known leaders, detained some 9,000–30,000 FIS members in five detention camps, and cracked down on the press. The latter included searching newspaper premises, expelling resident correspondents of European newspapers, arresting journalists writing for pro-fundamentalist papers, and jailing the editor of an independent weekly.

On January 22, authorities arrested the acting head of the FIS, radicalizing the movement and provoking widespread violence between FIS militants and security forces. A state of emergency was declared that continued until late 1995. By March 1992, the FIS leadership not in detention went underground or into exile, or migrated to adjacent countries. On May 5, military courts sentenced twelve FIS men to hang for the deaths of three army soldiers.[63] Five other Islamic extremist groups emerged and spread through Algeria: Armed Islamic Movement Group (an off-shoot of FIS), Armed Islamic Group, Hezbollah, Repentance and Emigration (*al-Takfir wa'l Hijra*), and Afghans (mostly veterans of the Afghanistan war). Actions were mostly decentralized acts of random terrorism and guerilla warfare. The volume of terrorist events increased sharply and included attacks on security forces, assault on the navy headquarters, and attacks on foreigners.[64] Bombings, assassinations, and attacks on government representatives expanded to include slitting the throats of captured foreigners, FLN members, and journalists. Disco dancers were killed by throat slitting and shooting. Petroleum workers were shot and plants were bombed. In the countryside, with its rugged terrain and desperately poor inhabitants, guerrillas controlled most of the mountain range. Satellite dishes were torn down, newspapers were banned, women were forced to wear traditional veils, men and women were segregated on buses, and Iranian-style enforcement of Islamic law prevailed. Eventually, an Air France airbus was hijacked, resulting in French security forces storming the plane, rescuing the hostages, and killing the hijackers.[65] Four nuns in Algiers were subsequently killed in retaliation. Iran and the Sudan provided arms and military training to the terrorists. To cut French support of the Algerian regime ($1.2 billion in annual aid to the Algerian government, intelligence, and training), a series of bombings in Paris in 1995 and other French cities was undertaken, resulting in deaths and casualties and putting a considerable dent in tourism.

Algerian military undertook brutal and repressive actions in response to Islamic terrorism and violence. Military courts began executing civilians convicted in the three courts that enforced the stringent antiterrorism law; and a strict curfew was declared. Pro-government death squads patrolled both rural and urban areas, and anti-FIS vigilantes took the law into their own hands. Villages formed self-defense groups to ward off FIS terrorism. Riots within prisons were fostered by FIS and other resistance members and were brutally repressed, along with the wholesale slaughter of detained FIS leaders.[66] The army was expanded through conscription, with mandatory military service of eighteen months. The military elite argued that Islamic extremism could be stopped only by force.

By 1994, foreign investment had dwindled to a trickle, families of diplomats were evacuated, embassies had been closed, the official unemployment rate had risen to 20 percent, the Algerian dinar (money) had been devalued by 50 percent, and servicing the international debt was consuming most of the petroleum-generated income. Efforts toward "national reconciliation" by national dialogue were made but failed, primarily by government intransigence in meeting directly with FIS leaders, or FIS boycotting of dialogues in other international sites. Even "secret meetings" appeared to have no appreciable ameliorative effect. It was in this environment that the military regime replaced the HEC with retired General Liamine Zeroual as president, signaling the direct movement of the military into the political arena. The rise of armed Islamic groups came to fruition in 1992 when the military government voided the victory of the Islamic Salvation Front (FIS), the largest Islamic opposition party, in the first round of legislative elections held in December 1991. Islamists were aiming for a pure Islamic state and centered many of their attacks on the civilian population, inflicting countless massacres.

The Armed Islamic Group (GIA)

The **Armed Islamic Group** is an FIS splinter organization that continued the fight against the Algerian military regime in 1992. Since this North African country plunged into a civil war that year, the group has been linked to terrorist attacks in Europe and to the massacres of tens of thousands of civilians in Algeria. The government crackdown has been as fierce in Algeria as that witnessed in Egypt, and, in a similar vein, the GIA seeks to overthrow the current regime and replace it with a radical Islamic one. Many GIA members have joined other groups in Algeria to continue attacks against the secular government. GIA is also credited with the audacious hijacking of an Air France airliner from Algeria to France in 1994, in which the terrorists had planned to set off explosives over the French capital, Paris. The GIA has targeted ex-colonial rulers in particular and has carried out limited bombing campaigns in France. France became the natural target as the Algerian government sought support from France to clamp down on GIA activists operating and raising funds for the overthrow of the secular Algerian government.

Rais Massacre, Algeria

In 1997, Algeria was at the peak of a civil war that had begun after the military's cancellation of the 1992 elections, in fear that it would be won by the Islamic Salvation Front (FIS). The farming village of Rais had been supporting Islamist guerrillas in the region over a period of time but had recently stopped providing them food and money. The attackers arrived at the village in the early morning hours, armed with shotguns, knives, axes, and bombs. They killed the village's men, women, children, and even animals, until dawn, cutting throats and taking the time to burn corpses. They mutilated and stole from the dead and committed atrocities against pregnant women. Estimates indicate more than 400 were killed.[67]

The French government has continued to support the military government in Algeria, much to the opposition and ire of the GIA. Possible links to al Qaeda could relate to Ahmed Ressam, an Algerian national who attempted to cross from Canada to the United States with a bomb destined for Los Angeles International airport in what is termed the "millennium plot." Although Ressam is Algerian and is believed to have met with al Qaeda operatives, this does not necessary widen the ties between the two groups. The GIA's aims are purely internal, as the group advocates the removal of the secular government, whereas the al Qaeda objectives are clearly truly international.

Many Algerians, tired of the poor standards of living, yearn to leave their country. Most who have fled have gone to France, but many have fled to and sought refugee status in Canada. Their ability to speak French makes the Province of Quebec an ideal choice for settlement. The relentless killings and massacres bought little internal support for the GIA, and popular support diminished significantly by the end of the last decade of the twentieth century. The GIA officially rejected a 1999 amnesty law, but not so by its rank and file, who came down from their mountain hideouts, renounced their ways, and returned to their old lives after surrendering their weapons. Although this has meant a significant drop in GIA violence, with over 85 percent of its members deserting, it has likely been eclipsed by a new subgroup. The Salafist Group for Preaching and Combat (GSPC), together with the GIA, both denounce the amnesty of President Bouteflika. Unlike GIA, GSPC has not concentrated its attacks on the civilian population. GSPC has also pledged its allegiance to al Qaeda.

AL QAEDA IN THE LAND OF THE ISLAMIC MAGHREB (AQIM), FORMERLY GSPC

On September 14, 2006, the GSPC formally swore its allegiance to Osama bin Laden and renamed the GSPC "al-Qaeda in the Land of The Islamic Maghreb." With the demise of GIA, AQIM is taking the lead; however, there is again the probability that many within this movement, in similar fashion to the GIA, want to accept the government's amnesty proposals. This has led to factional fighting from within. In November 2004, the government proposed a new cease-fire for GSPC and its members, who total around 500, although significant losses suffered through the relentless actions of the Algerian security apparatus led to a slow but gradual collapse of this particular insurgency. GSPC had set up Islamic training camps in neighboring Chad, and, in 2004, one of the group's significant figures, Amari Saifi, a former Algerian paratrooper, was captured by rebels from the Movement for Democracy and Justice in Chad (MDJT).[68] The MDJT had offered to hand him over to the Algerians, but as time passed, he was handed over to the Libyan government and then to Algeria. Libya's involvement in this incident is probably a direct desire of the Qaddafi regime to show its commitment to the U.S. War on Terror. The Libyans had, in fact, threatened to launch military strikes against the rebels in Chad if Saifi was not handed over. In December 2006 and March 2007, the Islamic Maghreb launched its bombing campaign with roadside bomb attacks targeting foreign nationals in both attacks. This was a significant development and took the focus away from the internecine warfare attacks carried out in previous years and the senseless massacre of civilians. With the new focus on oil exploration and foreign workers, the newly improved and equipped GSPC were seeking to intimidate the West as did the insurgents in Iraq, by attacking oil and gas lines. While the West seeks oil farther away from the Middle East, attention has gravitated to oil rich areas in Africa. On April 11, 2007, the group launched a well-orchestrated suicide attack on the capital Algiers with suicide truck bombings killing thirty and injuring over 200. The attempt at destabilizing the government was the main goal here.

GIA/GSPC's operational presence in Europe is also a consideration, and this expansion was a result of the wave of crackdowns against Islamist militants by the Algerian government in the early 1990s. The Islamists spread to Spain, France, Italy, Britain, and Sweden and beyond. Large numbers of Algerian fighters have turned up in Chechnya and Bosnia as well as Iraq and Afghanistan and more recently in neighboring Libya. The unstable nature of Libya in 2011 posed significant political as well as security concerns for Algeria. The rebels in Libya could easily provide a safe haven for al Qaeda. The recent Arab unrest that swept Tunisia and Egypt and to a lesser extent Algeria did not have the same outcome as the latter two countries and that may be as a result of recent history. It is likely that memories related to the violence of the civil war are still too recent and represent a powerful deterrent to a full-scale revolt. An unstable Libya with a strong AQIM presence would likely engender groups within Algeria to move violently toward regime change. Only time will tell as to the effects of the Libyan uprisings on Algeria.

Summary

Ongoing change continues to be the hallmark of the Middle East and North Africa. Israel's statehood became a reality, and Palestinian statehood did not. In spite of the Oslo Accords, peace seems no closer at hand since the death of Arafat in France in 2004. Israel remains the major power broker in the region and is prepared to use its military might whenever and wherever it sees fit to protect its nationhood. As for Palestine, how the fledgling unity government involving Hamas and Fatah will effectively operate will continue to focus our attention, as will the behavior of any new government in Egypt. What role will Iran play behind the scenes with Syria as well as its continued interference in Lebanon through its proxy Hezbollah? Libya is a country in turmoil; will a strong ruler emerge from the carnage overtaking the country and will that leader be pro-West? The melting pot of the Middle East remains just that; only time will tell whether the kind of democracy being espoused by protesters in Middle East countries turn out to be the kind of "democracy" that can be supported by the West.

Review Questions

1. Terrorism was an early part of Israel's history. Discuss how the various groups were formed to battle the British occupation and how their methods have been adopted to built a strong security apparatus for the Israeli people.

2. Fatah and Hamas have been long-time foes. Discuss the reasons these two groups have been unsuccessful in joining forces against Israel.

3. Discuss the changes that may come as a result of regime change in Egypt and how the Muslim Brotherhood's

attitude to Israel may affect the peace process/accords between Israel and Egypt.

4. Libya has been a longtime sponsor of terrorism for Colonel Qaddafi's own ends. Discuss how the presence

of AQIM in the region may destabilize other countries in this region of North Africa.

Websites

1. **Muslim Brotherhood**—*http://www.ikhwanweb.com/*
2. **Political Analysis, Espionage and Terrorism**—*http://www.debka.com/*
3. **Palestine Facts**—*http://www.palestinefacts.org/pf_1991to_now_hezbollah.php*
4. **Jerusalem Center for Public Affairs**—*http://www.jcpa.org/*
5. **HAMAS**—*http://www.PJTV.com*

End Notes

1. William Roger Louis. *The British Empire in the Middle East 1945–1951* (Oxford: Clarendon Press, 1988, p. 439).
2. Mark Ethridge, U.S. member of the Palestine Conciliation Report to State Department. Top Secret, NIACT (Beirut, March 28, 1949, FRUS 1949, pp. 876, 878).
3. Donald Neff. *Fallen Pillar, U.S. Policy towards Palestine and Israel Since 1945* (Washington, DC: Institute for Palestine Studies, 1995, p. 83).
4. The Foundation for Middle East Peace, Report on Israeli Settlement in the Occupied Territories, Special Report (July 1991); and Richard F. Nyrop, ed., *Israel: A Country Study*, 2nd ed. (Washington, DC: U.S. Government Printing Office, 1979), XIX: Epilogue, p. 185.
5. Jody A Boudreault, et al. (eds). *U.S. Official Statements: Israeli Settlements* (Washington, DC: Institute for Palestine Studies, 1992, p. 15).
6. Noam Chomsky. *The New Intifada, Resisting Israel's Apartheid*, edited by Roane Carey (London: Verso, 2001, p. 13).
7. "The beginning of the end of the Palestinian uprising?" *The Economist* (September 29, 2001, p. 50).
8. *Israel Secret Intelligence Service.* —http://www.mossad.gov.il/Eng/About/History.aspx
9. Sharon's Gaza. *Disengagement Plan,* section III, (May 28, 2004, p. A3).
10. Ibid., section III, p. A1.
11. Ibid., section VI.
12. Ibid., section III, p. A1.
13. Claude Bruderlein. "Legal aspects of Israel's Disengagement Plan under International Humanitarian Law." (Harvard University: Program on Humanitarian Policy and Conflict Research, August 2004).
14. Jonathan Freedland. "A Gift of Dust and Bones: Sharon's Plan for a Pullout Owes More to Demographic Shifts than a Belated Conversion to Peace-Making." *The Guardian* (June 2, 2004).
15. Ibid.
16. *Frosts Meditations.* http://www.martinfrost.ws/htmlfiles/june2009/shlomo-argov.html
17. George Rosie. *The Directory of International Terrorism* (New York: Paragon House, 1987, p. 290).
18. Ibid., p. 36.
19. "An Overview of the Gaza Strip." *Union of Palestinian Relief Committees Journal*, issue no. 25 (March 1997, p. 3).
20. *Israeli Insider.* http://israelinsider.com/home.htm.
21. PASSIA; IDF; Associated Press, and CNN.com (March 22, 2004); Gil Sedan. "Over the years, Sheik Yassin grew in status, violence and radicalism." *Jewish Telegraphic Agency* (March 23, 2004).
22. This material was drawn from an article by Ahmad Rashad, "The Truth about Hamas." http://www.rjgeib.com/biography/milken/crescent-moon/near-asia/palestine/palestine.htm.
23. Mid East Web for Coexistence R.A. http://www.mideastweb.org.
24. "Hamas Has the Peoples' Heart." *The Economist* (December 1, 2001, p. 43).
25. "Martyrs and Traitors," *The Economist* (June 23, 2007).
26. http://www.palestinefacts.org/pf_1967to1991_terrorism_1970s.php

27. MILNET. "Patterns of Global Terrorism." articles maintained by George Goncalves, *United States Department of State Publications* 10321 (1997). http://www.state.gov/r/pa/ei/rls/dos/221.htm

28. Http://www.fas.org/irp/threat/terror_90/mideast.html.

29. MILNET. "Patterns of Global Terrorism." (1997).

30. MIPT Terrorism Knowledge Base. www.tkb.org.

31. MILNET. "Patterns of Global Terrorism." (1997).

32. Http://www.haaretz.com/hasen/objects/pages/PrintArticleEn.jhtml?itemNo = 568735.

33. MILNET, "Patterns of Global Terrorism." (1997).

34. "Israeli Ministry of Foreign Affairs." Main Points of the Declaration of Principles (September 13, 1993).http://www.israel.org/MFA/Peace+Process/Guide+to+the+Peace+Process/Declaration+of+Principles+_+Main+Points.htm.

35. Edward Said. "Palestinians Under Siege." *The New Intifada, Resisting Israel's Apartheid*, ed. Roane Carey (London: Verso, 2001, p. 33).

36. Tom Gross. "Children are indoctrinated into terrorism." *The Weekly Telegraph*, Issue no. 371. (London: Telegraph Group Inc., September 1, 1998, p. 20).

37. Richard Clutterbuck. *Guerrillas and Terrorists* (Athens, OH: Ohio University Press, 1980, p. 80).

38. "Israeli Ministry of Foreign Affairs." www.mfa.gov.il.

39. Paul Wilkinson. *Terrorism and the Liberal State* (New York: New York University Press, 1979, p. 49).

40. Khaled Yacoub Oweis. "Slain Christian Warlord Had No Shortage of Enemies." Article by Reuters, *Daily Telegraph*, (London January 25, 2002).

41. *Daily Telegraph*, London: Lebanon's Victims (November 23, 2006).

42. "The Five Pillars of Islam." *Political Islam Glossary*. http://www.jihadwatch.org/islam101/.

43. "Sunnis and Shiites, the Great Schism." *Political Islam Glossary*, ibid.

44. Ayala Hammond Schbley. "A study of some of the Lebanese Shia's Contemporary Terrorism." *Terrorism: An International Journal,* vol. 12, no. 4 (Basingstoke, England: Taylor and Francis, 1989, p. 220).

45. Magnus Ranstrop. "Hizballah's Command Leadership." *Terrorism and Political Violence* vol. 6, no. 3 (London: Frank Cass, 1994, p. 304).

46. Yonah Alexander. *Hizballah: The Most Dangerous Terrorist Movement,* vol. 4, no. 10 (New York Intersec, Three Bridges Publishing Ltd., October 1994, p. 393).

47. Edgar O'Balance. *Islamic Fundamentalist Terrorism,* vol. 5, no. 1 (New York Intersec, Three Bridges Publishing Ltd., January 1995, p. 14).

48. Guy Lawson. "A Few Good Martyrs." *Time* (January 2002, pp. 89–93).

49. "Patterns of Global Terrorism: 1997." *U.S. State department*, Hellenic Resources Network. http://www.hri.org/docs/USSD-Terror.

50. "Hezbollah: The Real U.S. Target in Lebanon." *Jane's Foreign Report* (Coulsdon, Surrey: Jane's Information Group, Sentinel House, March 10, 2005).

51. Hezbollah (Party of God), "In the spotlight," (August 24, 2006). www.cdi.org.

52. Jonathan. R. White. *Terrorism: An Introduction*, 2nd ed. (Belmont, CA: Wadsworth Publishing Co., 1997, p. 141).

53. Heather Blearney and Richard Lawless. *The Middle East since 1945* (London: B.T. Batsford Ltd., 1989, p. 37).

54. Ibid.

55. International Policy Institute for Counterterrorism. www.ict.org.

56. "Anti-Semitism World Report." (Libya, 1997). http://www.tau.ac.il/Anti-Semitism/annual-report.html.

57. "Patterns of Global Terrorism: 1984." *Terrorism: An International Journal,* vol. 9, no. 3 (Basingstoke, England: Crane Russak & Company Inc., 1987, p. 419).

58. U.S. Department of State.

59. U.S. Treasury Press Release (February 8, 2006). http://www.ustreas.gov/press/releases/archives/200602.html.

60. http://www.preventgenocide.org.

61. George Rosie. *Directory of International Terrorism* (New York: Paragon House, 1986).

62. Martha Crenshaw. "Political Violence in Algeria." *Terrorism and Political Violence*, vol. 6, no. 3 (1994, pp. 261–280).

63. Youssef Ibrahim. "Algeria Sentences 12 Militants to Hang." *New York Times* (May 4, 1992, p. A-3).

64. Rachid Khiari. "Downtrodden Algeria Ruled by Death, Fear," *San Francisco Examiner* (April 4, 1994, p. A-9).

65. Thomas Sancton. "Anatomy of a Hijack," *Time* (January 9, 1995, pp. 54–57).

66. Jesse Birnbaum. "The Prison of Blood," *Time* (March 6, 1995).

67. Rais Massacre. http://en.wikipedia.org/wki/Rais_massacre.

68. *Jane's Intelligence Digest* (November 12, 2004).

9

The Persian Gulf

The terrible thing about terrorism is that ultimately it destroys those who practice it. Slowly but surely, as they try to extinguish life in others, the light within them dies.

—TERRY WAITE—SPECIAL ENVOY TO ARCHBISHOP OF CANTERBURY
(HELD HOSTAGE IN BEIRUT BY ISLAMIC JIHAD, 1987–1991)

LEARNING OBJECTIVES

After studying this chapter, the student should be able to:

1. Discuss the methods used by Saddam Hussein to control the majority Shi'a in Iraq.
2. Describe the methods used by the Shah of Iran to control his people during his turbulent reign.
3. Discuss al Qaeda's presence in the Persian Gulf and their target selection criteria.
4. Discuss the Iraqi insurgency and differentiate between terrorism and insurgency.

KEY WORDS TO NOTE

Abu Musab al-Zarqawi—Jordanian militant who ran terror training camps in Iraq and formed al Qaeda in Iraq—was killed by U.S. forces in 2006

Anwar al-Awlaki—A dual citizen (U.S. and Yemen)—believed to be in Yemen and has acted as a planner and trainer for al Qaeda and affiliates

Ali Hassan al-Majid—Saddam Hussein's cousin known as Chemical Ali, so named for carrying out gas attacks on Kurdish villages in Iraq

Ba'athist regime—Arab nationalist party with a mostly secular ideology that often contrasts with that of other Arab governments in the Middle East

Islamic Revolutionary Guard Corps (IRGC)—Army of the Guardians of the Islamic Revolution—formed in Iran following the revolution to protect the Islamic regime

Mahdi Army—Formed in 2003, the Mahdi Army is an armed group loyal to Muqtada al-Sadr, a Shia leader from a family line of revered clerics persecuted under Saddam Hussein

PETN—Explosive pentaerythritol tetranitrate—difficult to detect—explosive used by Richard Reid, the Shoe Bomber

Qods Force—Part of the Iranian Revolutionary Guard Corps (IRGC) responsible for extraterritorial operations, including terrorist operations. A primary focus is training Islamic fundamentalist terrorist groups

SAVAK—Ministry of state security during the reign of the Shah of Iran

Sayyid Qutb—Egyptian and member of the Muslim Brotherhood

Sharia (Islamic Law)—The Islamic code or laws observed in many Muslim countries

Tabun—Used as a nerve gas in chemical warfare

TATP—Acetone peroxide or commonly called TATP is an organic peroxide and acts as a high-power explosive. It is highly susceptible to heat, friction, and shock. For its instability, it has been called the "Mother of Satan"

OVERVIEW

Recent historic events in the Persian Gulf, the body of water that is surrounded by a number of Arab and Islamic states, is now well known to most students. The oil crises, the exile of the Shah of Iran, the Iraq–Iran war of the 1980s, the hostages at the U.S. embassy in Iran, the Gulf War of the early 1990s, the invasion of Iraq in 2003, and the revolts spreading throughout Bahrain and Yemen have made the "Persian Gulf" a household term. Perhaps one of the most important areas of the world, especially when we consider state-sponsored terrorism, the Persian Gulf is surrounded by some of the biggest players on the field of terrorism. This chapter takes a fast-moving tour through the history and background of the major political and religious events in this region. We discuss how these countries are shaping the future of this region and how their past has influenced the present. These oil-rich countries have the power to bring modern technological societies to their knees simply by cutting off the supply of that most crucial commodity—oil. We begin our visit to the lands of the Arabian nights with the world's largest oil producer, Saudi Arabia.[1]

SAUDI ARABIA

The Kingdom of Saudi Arabia has borders with the Persian Gulf and the Red Sea, north of Yemen. The kingdom is slightly more than one-fifth the size of the United States, but only 2 percent of its land is considered arable. Bordering countries are Iraq, Jordan, Kuwait, Oman, Qatar, the United Arab Emirates, and Yemen. Its petroleum, natural gas, iron ore, gold, and copper have made Saudi Arabia a very rich nation. The Saudis' extensive coastlines on the Persian Gulf and Red Sea provide leverage on shipping (especially crude oil) through the Gulf and the Suez Canal. Its population of only 20 million (which includes 5 million nonnationals) is able to build and support the infrastructure for the Kingdom in grand style. Ethnic groups are limited; 90 percent of the population is Arab and the remainder is Afro-Asian. One hundred percent are Muslim, and the official language is Arabic. As an Islamic monarchy, Saudi Arabia has no constitution. It is governed according to **Sharia(Islamic law)**; a literal translation of the word means the "path" and is also described by theologians as "God's Law." Sharia is supposed to be interpreted, and the law derived, from four sources:

1. The Quran, Islam's holy book, viewed by Muslims as the literal word of God;
2. The *hadith*, or record of the actions and sayings and preaching of the Prophet Mohammed;

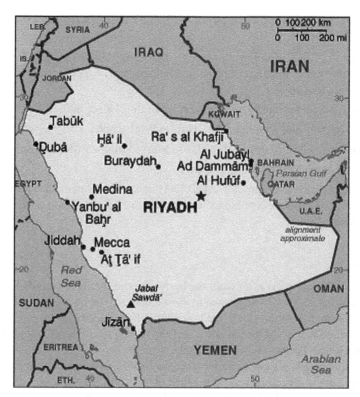

FIGURE 9-1   Map of Saudi Arabia (Central Intelligence Agency, *The World Factbook, 2008*).

3. The *ijma*, the consensus of Islamic scholars; and
4. The *qiyas*, a reasoning that uses analogies to apply precedents established by the holy texts in the Quran to problems not covered by them; for example, a ban on narcotics based on the Quranic injunction against wine drinking.

The Sharia governs all aspects of Muslim life, and some aspects of it have formed part of the current Islamic legal codes. Where there is opportunity to interpret laws, as is the case in democratic legal forums, Sharia has developed through five separate schools since the death of the Prophet Mohammed, four in the Sunni sect and one in the Shia sect.[2] Freedom of religion does not exist. Islam is the official religion, and all citizens must be Muslims. Religious freedom is not recognized or protected under the laws, and basic religious freedoms are denied to all but those who adhere to the state-sanctioned version of Sunni Islam. Citizens are denied the freedom to choose or change their religion, and many noncitizens, including Muslims, practice their beliefs under severe restrictions. The government limits the practice of all but the officially sanctioned version of Islam and prohibits the public practice of other religions.

King Abdul Aziz

The history of modern Saudi Arabia began in 1902, when Abdul Aziz Al-Sa'ud and a band of his followers captured the city of Riyadh, returning it to the control of his family. Abdul Aziz was born around 1880 and spent the early years of his life with his father in exile in Kuwait. After the capture of Riyadh, he spent the next twelve years consolidating his conquests in the area around Riyadh and the eastern part of the country, from where the Turks were expelled. The Arab tribes had never liked the Turks, and they were only too willing to listen to a new ruler, whose ambitions were assisted considerably by the troubles in the Ottoman Empire. In 1933, the lands under the control of Abdul Aziz were renamed the Kingdom of Saudi Arabia, and in 1936 a treaty was signed with Yemen marking it as the southern borders of the Saudi Kingdom.

Abdul Aziz's main preoccupations were the consolidation of his power and the restoration of law and order to all parts of his recently created kingdom. To these ends, he developed a system whereby every sheikh was responsible for his own tribe under the authority of the King, who was empowered to intervene to impose law and order. It was clearly understood that internal anarchy within the kingdom could quickly lead to foreign intervention. All agreed that this was unacceptable. King Abdul Aziz died in 1953, after more than half a century as leader, and King Saud bin Abdul Aziz, his eldest son, succeeded him to the throne. After eleven years, King Saud abdicated in favor of his brother, Faisal, the crown prince. In March 1975, King Faisal was assassinated in Riyadh by one of his nephews. The transfer of power, however, went smoothly, and King Khalid bin Abdul Aziz took power, with Fahad bin Abdul Aziz being made crown prince. King Khalid continued most of King Faisal's popular policies. It was during King Khalid's reign that Saudi Arabia enjoyed the prosperity and enormous wealth of the "petrodollar" boom years.

King Khalid died in June 1982 and was succeeded by Crown Prince Fahad bin Abdul Aziz. King Fahad was well versed in the art of governing, as he had served as the country's first minister of education. King Khalid had been in poor health for much of his reign, so Fahad ruled in all but title. Continuing development within the country and the infrastructure marked King Fahad's reign. On the political front, Iran's open hostility toward Saudi Arabia led the government to strengthen its ties of defense with the United States, Britain, and France.

Within days of Iraq's invasion of Kuwait in 1990, King Fahad allowed U.S. troops into the kingdom to help defend the country. In November 1990, he announced that plans were being made for the formation of a consultative council; there was some feeling that this was done in response to criticism that he had not consulted widely enough before allowing foreign troops into the kingdom. In any case, in March 1992, the king announced that the consultative council would be appointed by year's end, and he made its duties clear. Like other such creations in the Gulf States, the council is a purely consultative body with no legislative powers. Its formation, however, simply put an official stamp on the long-standing system of consultation, which has long been a mark of Arab politics and society. King Fahad suffered a stroke in 1995 and died on August 1, 2005. He is succeeded by his half-brother, Crown Prince Abdullah.

The George W. Bush administration had a primary mission in the region, that of hunting down al Qaeda in the Gulf States. President George W. Bush made some tough statements on June 24, 2002, when he outlined the new U.S. plan for peace in the Middle East and set specific terms for dealing with the Palestinians. He again called on Palestinians to reform and promised that when the Palestinian people have new leaders, new institutions, and new security arrangements with their neighbors, the United States would approve and support the creation of a Palestinian State, whose borders and certain aspects of its sovereignty will be provisional until resolved as part of a final settlement in the Middle East. Since that statement, little has changed, although some positive recognition has come to the Palestinians, they remain mired in conflict between Hamas, controlling the Gaza Strip, and the Fatah-dominated region of the West Bank.

Demanding that the Palestinians essentially replace Yasser Arafat, Washington had substantially improved Arafat's position. Anyone within the Palestinian community (at that time) who had demanded Arafat's resignation was open to the charge of collaborating with the Americans.

The United States was aware of the consequences of its demand. By making reform and new leadership prerequisites for further American participation in a peace process, the United States created the framework for its withdrawal from that process.

The U.S. president was, in effect, washing his hands of trying to solve the Israeli-Palestinian conflict. Washington's challenge, however, was not aimed at the Palestinians but at the country that pushed for greater U.S. involvement in the peace process—Saudi Arabia. Riyadh tried to shift U.S. attention from its war against terrorists and al Qaeda by making clear resolution of the Israeli-Palestinian conflict a key prerequisite for Saudi cooperation in hunting down Osama bin Laden's associates and financiers. Bush's actions were a warning to the Saudis that the conflict between Israel and the Palestinians could no longer serve as a distraction.

FROM THE PALESTINIANS TO RIYADH

Saudi Arabia inserted itself in the peace process when Crown Prince Abdullah used a column written by the *New York Times* writer Thomas Friedman, earlier in 2002, to publicize his own newly created Middle East peace proposal. Abdullah offered Israel complete normalization of ties with all the Arab States in exchange for Israel's full withdrawal to the 1967 borders. Though this was a promise Riyadh actually could not deliver, the tactic worked to buy time and direct the U.S. focus away, albeit temporarily, from Iraq and al Qaeda.

President Bush's Middle East policy appeared to make the United States eager to expand its involvement in the Middle East conflict. It was clear that the Bush administration would be able to achieve reforms only if the Palestinians were willing to work with Washington. However, peace required a new and different Palestinian leadership, and with Arafat's death in 2004, the way should have been cleared for the "road map" to take shape. President Bush indicated that although Washington would continue to be engaged, its focus will change. Specifically, the Bush administration will try to segment its Middle East policy, placing the Israeli-Palestinian conflict in a box to freely adopt a policy to pursue its primary Middle Eastern goals of destroying the al Qaeda and its wider plans of establishing democracy in Iraq and the region. Containing Iran and its designs on nuclear weapons also figures into U.S. strategy for the region. The single most important piece of any U.S. strategy to annihilate bin Laden's terrorist network is to do something about Saudi Arabia. Since Riyadh continues to be a key U.S. ally in the Gulf, whereas the other regional power, Iran, is decidedly anti-American, Washington has resisted placing any blame for 9-11 squarely on the Saudis.

AL QAEDA AND THE SAUDI KINGDOM

Immediately after the events of 9-11, the United States considered that the efforts by the Saudi regime to track down supporters of al Qaeda were insufficient. It is important to note that the Saudi Royal family has over 6,000 princes, including forty-five ruling princes, and it should be no surprise to discover that there are splits within the family as to the support being given and offered to the United States. The ruling princes are mostly progressive in their attitudes toward the West, but there are a growing number within the family who are more conservative. Strong anti-Western sentiment, not just in the Middle East but also in Saudi Arabia, will pose difficulties for the dictatorial governance of the king. The decade of the 1980s was characterized by the rise of ultraconservative, politically activist Islamic movements in much of the Arab world. These Islamist movements, labeled *fundamentalist* in the West, sought the government institutionalization of Islamic laws and social principles. Although Saudi Arabia already claimed to be an Islamic government whose constitution is the Quran, the kingdom has not been immune to this conservative trend.[3]

WAHHABI ISLAM

The term *Wahhabism* is a designation for the religious movement within Islam founded by Muhammad ibn Abd al-Wahhab (1703–1792). Members describe themselves as muwahhidun ("unitarians"), those who uphold firmly the doctrine that God is one, the only one (wahid). This self-designation points to the movement's major characteristic—its opposition to any custom or belief threatening and jeopardizing the glorification of the one God. Wahabbiyyah is not a new sect within Islam but a movement whose purpose is to purify Islam of perceived heretical accretions. The Wahhabis base their doctrines on the teachings of the fourteenth-century scholar Ibn Taymiyya and of the Hanbali School of Law, the strictest of the four recognized in the Sunni consensus. They believe that all objects of worship other than Allah are false, and anyone who worships in this way deserves to be put to death. To introduce the name of a prophet, saint, or angel into a prayer or to seek intercession from anyone but Allah constitutes a form of polytheism. Attendance at public prayer is compulsory, and the shaving of the beard and smoking are forbidden. Mosques should be architecturally simple, not luxurious or ornate. Prohibited are the celebrations of the Prophet's birthday, making offerings at the tomb of saints, and playing music. The injunctions of the Quran are to be taken literally.[4]

Osama bin Laden came from a wealthy Saudi background and yet spent little time immersed in the teachings and preaching of the strict adherence to Wahhabism. From his behavior and comments, it would be more likely to assume he accepted the ideology of Sayyid Qutb. Bin Laden believed that the Saudi Royal family's support for Western interests was a betrayal of Islam. Although the strict adherence to Wahhabism continues in the kingdom, the Saudi approach had always been to encourage those who wanted to spread the word of Islam, and violent jihad to do so elsewhere—but not at home within the Saudi Kingdom. This strategy worked well, with the Saudis exporting militants to Bosnia, Afghanistan, and Iraq. Attacks on Western interests in the Kingdom indicate clearly that the influences of the al Qaeda network are no longer confined to remote locations in Afghanistan and the Russian Republics. Fighters are returning to Saudi Arabia and are targeting the Western influences within the Kingdom. Al Qaeda's ultimate goals for the kingdom are as follows:

- Removal of the Royal family and
- Removal of all Western influences in the Kingdom.

Owing to the U.S. presence in Iraq, anti-Western sentiment grew quickly in Saudi Arabia. To effectively deal with al Qaeda operatives and sympathizers, the Saudis needed to rely on their own security apparatus. Although Saudi security services have arrested many terror suspects, they have been unable to infiltrate al Qaeda, garnering most of their intelligence from arrested suspects. Throughout 2003 and 2004, in almost every shootout that took place, involving attacks against Western targets and Saudi security forces, al Qaeda members were able to escape to fight another day. The availability of well-trained bomb makers returning from Iraq to set up operations in Saudi has had the desired effect on Western companies. So many had been targeted during the last decade that it had a negative effect on the oil economy of the Saudi Kingdom, which is almost totally reliant on Western expertise for its oil production. Al Qaeda's actual strength in the kingdom may be small and limited in number, but it has the sympathy of about 50 percent of the population. This sympathy, coupled with any possible power struggle within the Saudi Royal family, could lead to an eventual collapse of the existing pro-Western regime.

At the end of 2004, bin Laden was calling openly for attacks against his Saudi homeland. However, security forces in the kingdom have been cracking down hard since the string of bomb attacks in 2003. Al Qaeda's leader on the Saudi Peninsula, Fahd bin Faraj al-Juweir, is on record threatening Westerners and also the Saudi regime itself. He led a failed suicide attack on the Abqaiq Oil Refinery on February 24, 2006, and was subsequently killed three days later in a two-hour shootout with Saudi security forces. Two suicide attackers, both on a list of wanted militants, were killed in the refinery attack, which was the first significant strike by al Qaeda militants on oil facilities in the region.

SAYYID QUTB (1906–1996)

Sayyid Qutb joined the Muslim Brotherhood (MB) in 1951 and is probably the one man who could be considered the ideological grandfather of Osama bin Laden and the other extremists who surrounded him. Sayyid Qutb became radicalized on a trip to the United States back in the early 1950s. As Qutb traveled through America, he was shocked at the moral and spiritual degeneracy he observed, stating that "no one is more distant than the Americans from spirituality and piety."

In his home country of Egypt, his outspoken behavior brought him into direct conflict with the pro-Western government. Like so many other young radicals, he was imprisoned for his membership in the banned MB. One of the most important things Sayyid Qutb wrote during his incarceration was his explanation of how a Muslim might justly assassinate a ruler. For a long time, killing political rulers was expressly forbidden in Islam—even an unjust ruler was regarded as better than the anarchy of no ruler. Instead, the religious leaders of the *ulama* (Islamic scholars) were expected to keep the rulers in line. Qutb was hanged in Egypt in 1966.[5] Throughout the discussion in this text, we refer to Islamic extremists and also Islamism, and Islamism can be defined as being extremist political ideologies based on the Muslim religion and claiming that Islam must be the basis of political life. Islamists believe that Islamic law (Sharia) must be the basis for all statutory laws and that Muslims must return to the original teachings and the early models of Islam; and that Western military, economic, political, social, or cultural influence in the Muslim world is un-Islamic. Radical Islamists wish to restore and expand the Muslim Caliphate. Islamism developed originally in the context of the Ottoman Empire, the British Raj in India, and British and Turkish rule in Egypt and was therefore in part a reaction to colonialism. The basis of Islamism as developed by Qutb is virulently anti-Semitic, independent of any issues related to Israel or Zionism. This may also explain the targeting of Jews in attacks by al Qaeda, such as the one in Mumbai in November 2008.

The Saudi wing of al Qaeda has been waging a violent campaign aimed at toppling the pro-U.S. Saudi monarchy and expelling Westerners from the birthplace of Islam. Its most successful year would appear to be 2003, when suicide bombers attacked three Western housing complexes in Riyadh, but since then al Qaeda has been relatively contained. Throughout 2007 and into 2008, al Qaeda's relevance in Saudi Arabia was insignificant, especially by bin Laden's standards. In 2007, al Qaeda attacks were limited to just a single attack on February 26, allegedly by Walid Mutlaq al-Rashadi, one of Saudi Arabia's most wanted terrorists. This was an attack against French and Belgian citizens traveling by car in the northwest of the country, killing four Frenchmen. In April 2007, the Saudis announced that they had arrested 172 suspected militants,

40 foreign nationals and 132 Saudi citizens. Historically, arrests by the Saudi security forces have involved shootouts and invariably loss of life to one or more of the militants. The likelihood is that this latest batch of militant arrests were part of the logistics and planning for a series of attacks and most likely none were frontline actors—so no last-stand shootout or heroics. Looking forward it seems at the present that al Qaeda is having a difficult time trying desperately to maintain some level of relevance in Saudi Arabia. It has tried to appeal to all levels of society, including the security forces, with little or no success. Al Qaeda's leadership is clearly struggling to remain relevant in the ideological realm, a daunting task for an organization that has been rendered geopolitically and strategically impotent on the physical battlefield.[6]

Saudi Counterterrorism

Nineteen of the 9-11 bombers of New York City and Washington DC were born in Saudi Arabia, and it is also the birthplace of Osama bin Laden. Not unnaturally the kingdom had to literally come into the twenty-first century and reform its approaches to terrorism and extremism. It has achieved that by forming liaisons and intelligence-sharing initiatives with Great Britain and the United States.

On a more advanced, focused level, Saudi Arabia has also been conducting two different, yet complementary, programs: "Counter-Radicalization" and "Rehabilitation." Whereas the broader public programs are preventative in nature, each of these programs go directly to the active source of extremism propagation and serve to neutralize it. In creating these programs, Saudi Arabia's ministry of interior drew on the expertise of a group of international social scientists, psychiatrists, psychologists, and other physicians and experts to create strategies tailored to radicalism. In addition, the ministry has been working in conjunction with King Fahad Security College and Naif Arab University for Security Sciences to develop and refine the training activities for public security professionals.

- Counter-Radicalization Program: The purpose of the program is to combat the spread and appeal of extremist ideologies among the general populous. It strives to instil the true values of the Islamic faith, such as tolerance and moderation. Central to this effort is education about the dangers of radical Islam—consisting of school and religious programs and popular pronouncements, and the provision of positive, alternative outlets for at-risk groups—such as encouraging participation in sporting events and athletic programs, social outings, and so on.
- Rehabilitation Program: The rehabilitation program is intended to reintegrate deviants/extremists back into society, change their behaviour (disengage them), and change their beliefs (deradicalize them). It is designed to target deviants who have completed their prison sentences. The program reeducates violent extremists and extremist sympathizers through intensive religious debates and psychological counselling. The goal is for them to renounce ideologies that espouse terrorism. Any individual who has committed or participated in a violent crime, constituting murder, will not be released following completion of the course.[7]

It is also worth noting that although these programs have the possibility to "softly" change the approach to extremism within the kingdom, their security services are continuously criticized for the length of detention without trial and the numerous allegations of ill-treatment and torture of suspects and detainees that pose a threat to the normalcy of the kingdom. The government also operated a rehabilitation program designed to reeducate those arrested for supporting extremism or terrorism, including Saudis formerly held at the Guantanamo Bay detention facility. The program was designed to reintegrate individuals into society and includes educational, social, and religious components to undermine extremist messages and foster a more tolerant attitude. The program builds on family and tribal relations to reinforce the message and speed the reintegration process. Those who complete the program and show evidence of having been rehabilitated are eligible for consideration for release from custody, though not before they have served any prison sentence for their previous crimes. The long-term effects of this program have yet to be evaluated to determine if any "graduates" have returned to their old activities or whether the actual program may be a recruiting area for Islamic extremist.[8]

KUWAIT

The State of Kuwait, a nominal constitutional monarchy, is slightly smaller than New Jersey and lies between Iraq and Saudi Arabia, bordering the Persian Gulf. While its primary natural resource is petroleum, fish, shrimp, and natural gas are also plentiful. It is another Persian Gulf country with almost no arable land and no permanent crops (about 75 percent of its potable water must be distilled or imported). Kuwait has strategic value in its location at the entrance to the Persian Gulf. The small population of only 1,834,269 includes 1,381,063 nonnationals. The ethnic mix is 45 percent Kuwaiti, 35 percent other Arab, 9 percent South Asian, 4 percent Iranian, and 7 percent other. Muslims make up 85 percent of the religious followers, but are split: Shia

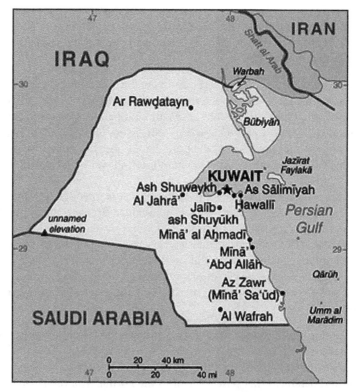

FIGURE 9-2 Map of Kuwait (Central Intelligence Agency, *The World Factbook, 2008*).

30 percent, Sunni 45 percent, and other 10 percent. Christians, Hindus, Parsi, and others make up the remaining 15 percent.

The chief of state is Amir Sheikh Saad Al-Abdullah Al-Sabah (since January 2006), and the head of government is the prime minister. While there are no official political parties and leaders, several political groups act as de facto parties (e.g., Bedouins, merchants, Sunni and Shia activists, and secular leftists and nationalists).

Kuwait has a small and relatively open economy with proven crude oil reserves of about 94 billion barrels, or roughly 10 percent of world reserves. Kuwait has rebuilt its war-ravaged petroleum sector; its crude oil production averages 2 million barrels per day. Petroleum accounts for nearly half of its GDP, 90 percent of export revenues, and 75 percent of government income. Because of its high per capita income, comparable with Western European incomes, Kuwait provides its citizens with extensive health, educational, and retirement benefits. The bulk of the workforce is non-Kuwaiti, and they have a considerably lower standard of living than Kuwaitis. Per capita military expenditures are among the highest in the world. The World Bank has urged Kuwait to push ahead with privatization, including in the oil industry, but the government will move slowly on opening up the petroleum sector. The present Al-Sabah dynasty was established in Kuwait in the mid-eighteenth century, about 1760. Kuwait was nominally a province of the Ottoman Empire, ruled from Constantinople. This was observed on paper but seldom in fact. In 1899, when the Turks threatened to take actual control of the country, the ruling sheikh sought and received British protection.

The Kuwait Oil Company discovered oil in Kuwait in 1938, but because of World War II it was not exported until 1946, after which time Kuwait's economy flourished. Kuwait remained a British Protectorate until 1961, when it became independent under Sheikh Abdullah Al-Salem Al-Sabah. However, when Iraq claimed the emirate in the early 1960s, it once again received British protection. In July 1961, Kuwait joined the Arab League and in 1963 became a member of the United Nations. In February 1963, the first legislative elections were held, and Sheikh Abdullah, the Emir of Kuwait, inaugurated the first National Assembly.

During the 1980s, Kuwait experienced several terrorist attacks by Shiite Muslim extremists, including one in 1985 that attempted to assassinate the emir. Kuwait, like most Arab States, supported Iraq in the Iran–Iraq war (1980–1988). Kuwait played a major role in establishing the Gulf Cooperation Council (GCC) in 1981, consisting of Saudi Arabia, Kuwait, Bahrain, Qatar, the United Arab Emirates, and the Sultanate of Oman. The council held a firm position during Iraq's invasion of Kuwait on August 2, 1990, and its seven-month occupation of the Emirate.

Rather than befriend a tyrant, or surrender to Iraq's Saddam Hussein in the Gulf War, Kuwait stood firm in the heat of all the battles it faced. During the Iraqi occupation, from August 2, 1990, to Kuwait's liberation on February 26, 1991, the Kuwaitis once again gave evidence of their strength and fierce determination. After a decade, a whole generation is growing up with the memory of the Iraq invasion of Kuwait, but the younger teenage generation, with more fundamental, even radical views, seems to be sympathetic to the cause of the jihad in Iraq. Kuwait has a land border with Iraq, and it was one of the main staging points for U.S. troops en route to Iraq. It was also likely a returning point for insurgents escaping from areas such as Fallujah. Kuwait's proximity to the war zone—Iraq—has led to a spread of al Qaeda influence in the country. There are indications that Kuwaitis have been involved in suicide missions in Iraq against U.S. targets. It is also clear that Kuwaiti extremists were training in camps in Afghanistan during the Taliban regime, and the likelihood is that some may have returned to Kuwait to further attack U.S. interest there. Taped messages from the number one terrorist in Iraq, al Zarqawi, called on fighters in 2005 to return to Kuwait and attack not only U.S. interests but also Kuwaiti government officials.[9] Many Muslim groups, particularly those in Kuwait, are still smarting from the 2004 Abu Ghraib prisoner abuse scandal and view it as part of the United States' overall plan to attack Islam and Muslims. Attacks in Kuwait, in comparison to those in Saudi Arabia, have been relatively minor. However, that has not discouraged the authorities from reactivating a 1984 law banning women drivers from wearing a veil covering their faces, on the premise that terrorists could disguise themselves. Unlicensed mosques that were constructed without the proper planning and consent were destroyed to prevent them from being used as militant hideouts. More extensive laws were introduced to search private premises and homes for weapons. Stricter control of extremist websites was also enforced.[10]

The Arab Gulf states, including Kuwait, rely on foreign military support for their defense—as we saw in 1990 when Saddam Hussein invaded and occupied Kuwait. Kuwait's ruling family fled to the sanctuary of neighboring Saudi Arabia. That being said, we need to appreciate that these states need to contain the Shiite political influence in Iraq and prevent the spread of the Shiite militia groups, and they do this by providing a robust Sunni presence in the region. Iraq's Shiite militias are well trained and equipped by Iran's Revolutionary Guard Corps. The other factor that is in the hands of the Gulf states is the control of the world's oil distribution and increasing the amount of oil being produced could seriously damage the Iranian oil industry, which utilizes outdated technology. The Sunni/Shia ethnic divide is a topic to be exploited by both the Saudi influence in the Gulf region and Iran. Iran has gone one up on the Saudis in this regard and has appealed to all Muslims (not only Shiites) to rise above nationalistic and sectarian divisions and called for pan-Islamic unity. This has not become a reality, but it does make the Saudi regime extremely cautious in its dealings with Iran. Saudi Arabia has always seen itself as the leader of the Islamic world and has on many occasions attempted to use the ethnic card to create a rift between Iranian Shia and those in the Gulf states.

IRAQ

Iraq is 97 percent Muslim (Shia, 60–65 percent; Sunni, 32–37 percent) and 3 percent Christian or other. The official languages are Arabic and Kurdish.

The Ba'athist regime, which held power over the last three decades of the twentieth century, engaged in extensive central planning and management of industrial production and foreign trade while leaving some small-scale industry and services and most agriculture to private enterprise. Iraq's economy has been dominated by the oil sector, which has traditionally provided about 95 percent of foreign exchange earnings. In the 1980s, financial problems were caused by massive expenditures in the eight-year war with Iran and damage to oil export facilities by Iran. This led the government to implement austerity measures and to borrow heavily and later reschedule foreign debt payments. Iraq suffered economic losses of at least $100 billion from the war. After the end of hostilities in 1988, oil exports gradually increased with the construction of new pipelines and restoration of damaged facilities. Iraq's invasion of Kuwait in 1990, and subsequent international economic embargoes and military action by an international coalition beginning in January 1991, drastically changed its economic picture. Industrial and transportation facilities, which suffered severe damage, have been partially restored. Oil exports were at only 25 percent of the prewar level because of implementation of UN Security Council Resolution 986 in December 1996. The UN-sponsored economic embargo had reduced exports and imports and contributed to a sharp rise in prices. The Iraqi government had been unwilling to abide by UN resolutions so that the economic embargo could be removed. The government's policies of supporting large military and internal security forces and of allocating resources to

FIGURE 9-3   Map of Iraq (Central Intelligence Agency, *The World Factbook, 2008*).

key supporters of the regime had exacerbated shortages. In accord with a UN resolution, Iraq agreed to an oil-for-food deal in 1996, under which it would export $2 billion worth of oil in exchange for badly needed food and medicine. The first oil was pumped in December 1996, and the first suplies of food and medicine arrived in 1997.

SADDAM HUSSEIN (1937–2006)

Saddam Hussein was born in Auja, near Tirkit, in 1937. He was president and prime minister of Iraq from 1979 to 2003. His political platform was a combination of moderate social democracy, close to the European model, amid a struggle to keep the country of various ethnic and religious groups together. In the West, the image of Saddam Hussein went through a dramatic change, from being one of Europe's and the United State's favorites into the most negatively presented dictator in the world. UN officials confirmed that Iraq had contravened the Geneva Convention by using chemical weapons against Iran. Iraq also used "mustard gas" from 1983 and the nerve gas "**Tabun**" from 1985, as it faced attacks from "human waves" of Iranian troops and poorly trained but loyal volunteers. Tabun can kill within minutes. In 1988, Iraq turned its chemical weapons on Iraqi Kurds in the north of the country. Saddam Hussein's invasion and occupation of Kuwait would cast him as a pariah in the region. At home, he presided over a secular state with relative freedom for the economic sector and freedom for women; there was also free education. He adopted a widespread and intricate system of secret police and spies to keep control on his people. Opposition to the Ba'ath Party regime was unheard of, and those who were seen as plotting against his regime were arrested, tortured, and killed. He was responsible for the deaths of thousands of his own people. Saddam was a Sunni Muslim, and the minority Sunnis enjoyed benefits and positions in Iraqi society, but other groups, especially Shia, were denied these benefits. After the U.S.-led invasion of Iraq, Saddam was captured, tried, convicted, and executed by an Iraqi court for crimes against humanity and his own people, the Kurds, the Marsh Arabs, and thousands of others who suffered under his rule. He was hanged on December 30, 2006. One of his most senior officials, **Ali Hassan al-Majid**, his first cousin, acquired the name "Chemical Ali" as well as the "Butcher of Kurdistan" for his role in leading the al-Anfal Campaign, during which he ordered a toxic gas attack on the Kurdish town of Halabja that resulted in the deaths of thousands of Kurds. He was the regional commander in southern Iraq and was responsible for suppressing the southern uprising of the Shiites. Ali was captured on August 21, 2003, and convicted of crimes against humanity and was executed in February 2010.

Iran and Iraq restored diplomatic relations in 1990 but were still trying to work out written agreements settling outstanding disputes from their eight-year war concerning border demarcation, prisoners of war, and freedom of navigation and sovereignty over the Shatt al Arab waterway. In November 1994, Iraq formally accepted the UN-demarcated border with Kuwait that had been spelled out in Security Council Resolutions. This formally ended Iraq's earlier claims to Kuwait and to Bubiyan and the Warbah Islands. There is still dispute over Turkey's water development plans for the Tigris and Euphrates Rivers. Ironically, the area of the Middle East we now call Iraq, which we have seen in recent decades as a major source for state-sponsored terrorism and constant wars, is also where, many scholars agree, recorded history as we know it began.

Hammurabi was the King and a great lawgiver of the Old Babylonian (Amorite) Dynasty. His legal code was produced in the second year of his reign. Many new legal concepts were introduced by the Babylonians, and many have been adopted by other civilizations. These concepts included the following:

- Legal protection should be provided to lower classes;
- The state is the authority responsible for enforcing the law;
- Social justice should be guaranteed; and
- Punishment should fit the crime.

A copy of the code is engraved on a block of black diorite nearly 8 feet high. A team of French archeologists at Susa, Iraq, formerly ancient Elam, unearthed this block in 1901. The block, broken in three pieces, has been restored and is now in the Louvre Museum in Paris.

Abu Ja'far Muhammad ibn Musa al-Khawarizmi (680–750 A.D.), a great scholar and mathematician, originated algebraic equations. Some credit him with the invention of the concept of "zero." Al-Khawarizmi wrote ten math textbooks that have survived the test of time. His *Kitab hisab al'adad al-hindi* was an arithmetic textbook that introduced Hindu numbers to the Arab world; now they are generally known as Arabic numbers. Christian Europeans at first rejected the Arabic numbers and declared them the work of Satan. His major work is entitled *Kitab (al-jabr) w'al-muqabalah*, whose title gives us the word "Algebra."

In 1936, King Ghazi I formed the Pan Arab movement with the other Arab States, promising kinship and nonaggression. The first coup d'état in the modern Arab world came in 1936, led by General Baks Sidqi. This marked a major turning point in Iraq's history, opening the door for further military involvement in politics. In 1945, Iraq became a founding member of the Arab League and joined the United Nations.

Iraq joined in the war with Israel in 1948, in alliance with Jordan, according to a treaty signed by the two countries during the previous year. The war had a negative impact on the

Iraqi economy. Oil royalties paid to Iraq were halved when the pipeline to Haifa was cut off. The war led to the departure of most of Iraq's prosperous Jewish community. About 120,000 Iraqi Jews immigrated to Israel between 1948 and 1952. In 1961, Kuwait gained its independence from Britain, and Abdul-Karim Qassim immediately claimed the Emirate as originally part of the Ottoman province of Basrah. Britain reacted strongly by dispatching a brigade to the country to deter Iraq. Qassim backed down. In 1963, Iraq finally recognized the sovereignty and borders of Kuwait.

Leading up to 1979 Saddam Hussein was the power base behind the ailing President General Ahmed Hasan Al-Bakr. Bakr had appointed Saddam as his vice president, and when he stepped down due to ill-health, Saddam Hussein took full control as president of Iraq. He immediately began a sustained purge of all his and the Ba'ath Party's political rivals to assure his position and total control of Iraq. Once more, the political situation flared into hostilities with Iran. The Iran–Iraq war, which began in 1980, lasted for eight years and had a crippling effect on the economies of both countries. Neither side gained any territory but an estimated one million lives were lost. In July 1988, Iran accepted the terms of UN Resolution 598, and military actions ceased. Before Iraq had a chance to recover economically, Saddam once more plunged into war, with the invasion of Kuwait in 1990.

The United States declared its interest in protecting Kuwaiti sovereignty. In the ensuing months, the UN Security Council passed a series of resolutions condemning the Iraqi occupation of Kuwait and applied total, mandatory economic sanctions against Iraq. In November 1990, the UN Security Council adopted Resolution 678, permitting member states to use all necessary means, authorizing military action against the Iraqi forces occupying Kuwait, and demanding Iraq's complete withdrawal by January 1991.

Saddam Hussein failed to comply with this demand, and the Gulf War, Operation Desert Storm, began on January 17, 1991. Allied troops from twenty-eight countries participated. The combined air forces of Great Britain and the United States launched an aerial bombardment on Baghdad to start the battle. The war, which proved disastrous for Iraq, lasted only six weeks, but 140,000 tons of munitions were dropped on the country, and as many as 100,000 Iraqi soldiers were killed. Coalition air raids destroyed roads, bridges, factories, and oil industry facilities and disrupted electric, telephone, and water service. Finally, a cease-fire was announced on February 28, 1991. Iraq agreed to UN terms for a permanent cease-fire in April of that year, and strict conditions were imposed, demanding the disclosure and destruction of all stockpiles of weapons, including weapons of mass destruction (WMD).

Insurrections quickly broke out in southern Iraq and in Kurdistan in the north, where rebels took control of most of the region's towns. Units of Saddam's elite Republican Guard that had survived the conflict suppressed protest with extreme brutality to gain control in the Basrah, Najaf, and Karbala regions. In the southern cities, rebels killed Ba'athist officials, members of the security service, and other supporters of the Saddam regime. In Kurdistan, Iraqi helicopters and troops regained control of the cities taken by the rebels, and there was a mass exodus of Kurds to the Turkish and Iranian borders, fleeing from a possible repeat of the 1988 deadly chemical attacks. By the end of April 1991, 2.5 million refugees had fled from Iraq.

The United States, attempting to prevent the genocide of the Marsh Arabs in southern Iraq and the Kurds to the north, established air exclusion zones north of the 36th parallel and south of the 32nd parallel. The attempted assassination of former President George Bush in Kuwait prompted a swift military response on June 27, 1993. The Iraqi Intelligence Headquarters in Baghdad was targeted by twenty-three Tomahawk cruise missiles, launched from U.S. warships in the Red Sea and Persian Gulf.

In October 1994, Iraq again moved some Republican Guard units toward Kuwait, an act that provoked large-scale U.S. troop deployment to deter an Iraqi attack. The move was interpreted as a sign of Saddam's frustration with the continuation of stiff UN sanctions, but he backed down (establishing a pattern of behavior he continued using until the U.S. invasion of Iraq in 2003). He agreed to recognize the existence and borders of Kuwait. In the months that followed, Hussein's position appeared to become more precarious as dissatisfaction with his rule spread in the army and among the tribes and clans at the core of his regime.

In May 1995, Saddam fired his half-brother, Wathban, as interior minister and, in July, demoted his notorious and powerful defense minister, Ali Hassan al-Majid, to give more power to his two sons, Udai and Qusai. It became clear that Saddam felt more secure when protected by his immediate family members. Major General Hussein Kamil Hassan al-Majid, his minister of military industries and a key henchman, defected to Jordan, together with his wife (one of Saddam's daughters) and his brother, Saddam (also married to one of Saddam's daughters), and called for the overthrow of the regime. In response, Saddam promised full cooperation with the UN commission that was disarming Iraq (UNSCOM) in order to preempt any revelations that the defectors might make. Not surprisingly, when Saddam forgave the defectors and they returned to Iraq, other clan members murdered them both, soon after they crossed the border.

The weakening of the internal position of the regime occurred at a time when the external opposition forces were as weak as ever—too divided to take any effective action. At the same time, France and Russia were pushing for an easing of sanctions. The United States and Britain's determination to keep up the pressure on Iraq had prevailed, however. In any case, the apparent weakening of the regime was illusory. In fact, during 1996, the regime's grip on power seemed to have significantly strengthened despite Saddam's inability to end the UN sanctions. There was yet another major buildup of U.S. forces in the Gulf, as a result of Saddam's refusal to allow unrestricted UN inspections of suspected sites for storing weapons of mass destruction. In May 2002, on the eve of signing a historic U.S.-Russian nuclear arms reduction treaty, President Bush spoke strongly to President Putin of the Russian Republic, "If you arm Iran, you're liable to get the weapons pointed at you." Bush considered Russia's dealings with Iran the single, greatest proliferation threat on the globe at the time. On a day that took him from the old East–West divide of Berlin to the heart of the former Soviet Union, a defiant Bush answered critics of his expanding antiterror war plans. He denounced anyone who would appease terrorists or ignore threats to Europe.

Bush and Putin met to sign a ten-year treaty binding the nations to reduce their nuclear stockpiles by about two-thirds—to a range of 1,700 to 2,200 each. The three-page treaty has a preamble and just five articles. Hundreds of Communists and leftists staged a noisy protest at the U.S. embassy in the German capital. Bush responded to antiwar protesters who clogged city streets a day before—and to European leaders balking at his hopes of toppling Saddam.

President Bush came face to face with European opposition when three lawmakers from the ex-Communist party of Democratic Socialism, seated about 20 feet away, held up a banner reading: "Bush, Schroeder, Stop your wars." In a news conference before the address, German Chancellor Gerhard Schroeder declined to join Bush in pushing for a government change in Iraq. Separately, Defense Minister Rudolf Scharping suggested that Germany did not have the resources to participate in military action against Saddam. "We have no room for a new engagement," Scharping told German television. Nuclear proliferation is a sour point in a U.S.-Russia relationship that has flourished since 9-11. On another troubling issue, Bush said Putin understood that a loose nuke could affect his security and was doing what he can to prevent terrorists from getting nuclear materials from Russian stockpiles.

OPERATION IRAQI FREEDOM AND BEYOND

Saddam Hussein's reign came to an end in March 2003 following a demand by U.S. President George W. Bush that Saddam Hussein and his two sons, Uday and Qusay, leave Iraq immediately. Bush promptly provided a forty-eight-hour deadline for compliance. No one expected the Iraqi dictator to comply with such a demand, and the following day, U.S. spokesman Ari Fleischer announced that the United States would invade Iraq whether Saddam and his sons left Iraq or not. Fleisher stated that "the bottom line is, a coalition of the willing will disarm Saddam Hussein's Iraq, no matter what." The U.S. justification for the invasion has been widely debated and challenged. Most importantly, the United States and Britain's action did not have the explicit endorsement of the United Nations. Most scholarly and legal authorities have concluded that the action violated the UN Charter. With the invasion by land and attacks from the air, the Iraqi military machine crumbled, and, on May 1, 2003, George Bush announced an end to major combat. Most of the Iraqi military and the well-trained and well-equipped Iraqi Republican Guard had not fought or been captured, but had simply "gone home." They took their weapons and munitions with them. This would be the starting point for the years of insurgency to follow. Apart from the regular conscript army of Iraq and the Republican Guard, there was a third and vitally important paramilitary group that had been established in the mid-1990s—namely, the Fedayeen Saddam. This organization numbered around 40,000–50,000 members and was staffed by Sunnis and supporters of the Ba'ath Party regime of Saddam Hussein. This group had been variously under the control of both Uday and Qusay Hussein for periods of time. The Fedayeen was responsible for some of the most atrocious acts against Ba'athist opponents. It conducted widespread campaigns of assassination but was loyal to the party. With the removal of Saddam Hussein, this force of fighters was adequately prepared and would have little to lose in fighting the United States and any Shiite-dominated government that came to power.

Deaths of Uday and Qusay Hussein—July 22, 2003

Lt. Gen. Ricardo Sanchez, Commander, Combined Joint Task Force Seven (CJTF-7) said:

> Today our coalition forces, associated with the 101st Airborne Division, Special Forces and Air Force assets, conducted an operation against suspected regime members. An Iraqi source informed the 101st Airborne division today that several suspects, including Qusay and Uday, numbers two and three on the U.S. Central Command's most-wanted list, were hiding in a residence near the northern edge of the city. The six-hour operation began when the division's Second Brigade Combat Team approached the house and received small-arms fire. The division subsequently employed multiple weapons systems to subdue the suspects, who had barricaded themselves inside the house and continued to resist detention fiercely. Four persons were killed during that operation and were removed from the building, and we have since confirmed that Uday and Qusay Hussein are among the dead. The site is currently being exploited.[11]

The minority Sunnis controlled Iraq for the last four decades of the twentieth century and had kept the large Shia majority in check. Saddam's security apparatus—and it was a well-organized one—melted away in the face of the U.S.-led invasion. It has been able to immerse itself back into society to carry on attacks against both the invading coalition forces and the Iraqi Shiites. Much has been broadcast on news media and the Internet about Western hostages and their treatment, including torture and decapitation, but what has not been reported is that kidnappings of Iraqi citizens have far outnumbered those of Westerners. The numbers of insurgent organizations operating in Iraq have multiplied since the official end to hostilities in 2003. Both sides—Sunni and Shia—have developed fronts and insurgent forces to attack each other, the U.S. and coalition troops. The Sunni Islamists are similar to the Wahabi sect in Saudi Arabia and composed of Iraqis belonging to the Salafi branch of Sunni Islam advocating a return to the pure Islam preachings of the Prophet Mohammed and opposes any foreign non-Muslim influence. Hard-line Iraqi clerics and members of the Muslim Brotherhood in Iraq have helped support the militant Islamist movement. The Sunni groups include the following:

The Iraqi National Islamic Resistance: This group wants to establish an Islamic Iraq free from external interference and the forcible removal of U.S. forces. Its activities have centered on Baghdad, and its attacks have been primarily launched against military targets in areas west of Baghdad. It takes account of its activities by distributing information outside mosques at Friday prayers. It has also called on Arab states to send troops to help them in Iraq. In 2004, reports indicated that they were mounting around ten attacks a day, mainly against U.S. and coalition forces.

The National Front for the Liberation of Iraq: This organization was formed soon after the invasion in 2003, and its influence is spread throughout the country. It consists of Islamists and nationalists and carries out attacks similar to those of the Iraqi National Islamic Resistance. In a statement sent to IslamOnline.net, the Front revealed that "after intensive contacts with a number of armed Iraqi groups and Arab volunteers who flocked to the country ahead of the U.S.-led invasion, a unified resistance command has now been forged." It indicated that the contacts made also included elements from Saddam Fedayeen and Ba'athists who were not loyal to Saddam Hussein.

The Iraqi Resistance Islamic Front (JAAMI)/Salah al-Din Brigades (SDB): This group, which formed in mid-2004, brings together a small coalition of resistance fighters. It formed a political party with SDB in 2004, and although it opposes the current political process, it is viewed as a moderate Islamic jihadist movement. Its operations take place mainly in Sunni regions of Iraq and are more military in style of attack; their leader Saif al-Din Mahmoud has pledged that his group will not use booby-trap bombs in cities or engage in the killing of hostages. The group tends to cooperate with all other jihadist groups with the exception of al Qaeda. It takes the stand that by declaring jihad it has the duty to fight the invaders. According to statements issued by the front, JAAMI's military wing, the Salah-al-Din and Sayf-Allah al-Maslul Brigades, has carried out dozens of operations against the U.S. occupation forces.

Imam Ali Bin-Abi-Talib Jihadi Brigades: This Shiite group appeared for the first time on October 12, 2003. It vowed to kill the soldiers of any country sending its troops to support the coalition forces and threatened to transfer the battleground to the territories of such countries if they were to send troops. The group also threatened to assassinate all the members of the Interim Governing Council and any Iraqi cooperating with the coalition forces. The group also announced that Al-Najaf and Karbala were the battlegrounds in which it would target U.S. forces.

In addition to the groups resisting occupation, other armed groups have emerged and resorted to operations of abducting and killing foreigners as a method, in their opinion, to terrorize the enemy and as a political pressure card to achieve their specific demands.

The Islamic Army in Iraq: This group combines Islamism with Iraqi nationalism. It is made up primarily of former Ba'athists and is likely the largest active group; they target Iraqi police and military as well as members of the Shiite **Mahdi Army** and Badr groups.

Ansar al-Islam/Ansar al-Sunnah: Led by Mullah Krekar, this group is based in northern Iraq near the Iranian border and follows a strict form of Sunni Islam similar to Wahhabism. The group grew from the Islamic Movement of Kurdistan and comprises Afghan veterans and foreign fighters. Their aims are to rigorously enforce the concept of Sharia law in Iraq's northern provinces. When in control of villages, the group mandates strict religious observance, destroying a girls' school, outlawing "vice," and enforcing daily prayers at mosques. The group has also made threats against non-Muslims, such as the Kaki'i religious sect, which largely fled rather than convert or live under Dhimmitude laws; (Dhimmitude is the Islamic system of governing populations conquered by *jihad* wars, encompassing all of the demographic, ethnic, and religious aspects of the political system). The group's founder Krekar was arrested in 2010.[12] On March 15, 2004, Ansar al-Islam was named as a "Foreign Terrorist Organization" (FTO) under the Immigration and Nationality Act. On October 15, 2004, the State Department named the "Monotheism and Jihad Group"—the successor to Ansar al- Islam—as an FTO. The designation said that the Monotheism group "was…responsible for the UN headquarters bombing in Baghdad." Later that month, perhaps in response to that designation, Zarqawi changed the name of his organization to "al Qaeda Jihad Organization in the Land of Two Rivers (Mesopotamia—Iraq)," commonly known now as al Qaeda in Iraq, or AQ-I. The FTO designation was applied to the new name.[13]

Al Qaeda in Mesopotamia (AQM), aka Al Qaeda in Iraq: The most well-known and publicized group, led by Abu Musab al-Zarqawi—the second-most-wanted terrorist on the planet after Osama bin Laden. Jama'at al-Tawhid wa'l-Jihad (Monotheism and Jihad Group) was the group's original name; it started operations in Iraq immediately following the coalition invasion. Zarqawi pledged support to bin Laden and renamed the group al Qaeda in Iraq, eventually forming the central core of the Islamic State of Iraq (ISI).

Roadside bombings and beheadings, and posting gruesome videos of his atrocities on the Internet, were the hallmark of his insurgency operations. AQM is a Salafi-Jihadi extremist group that attempted to bring other jihadist groups under its sphere of control and influence during 2006. However, this led to confrontation with other groups, most notably the Islamic Army in Iraq. The group is skilled at IED deployment, kidnapping, and assassination. It has kidnapped and executed numerous Western hostages since 2004. AQM rejects the political process, and any groups working with the government are considered legitimate targets for AQM. AQM's founder, the late **Abu Musab al-Zarqawi**, was born in 1966 a Palestinian Jordanian and had been sentenced to seven years in jail in Jordan in 1992 for plotting to overthrow the Hashemite Monarchy. He was killed on June 7, 2006, when U.S. forces bombed his safe house near the city of Baquba. On June 15, 2006, it was confirmed that Egyptian Islamic Jihad militant Abu Ayyub al-Masri would succeed Zarqawi as head of al Qaeda in Iraq. It has been claimed that at that time Iranian influence was being brought to bear, which precipitated attacks against other Iraqi insurgent groups.

Among AQM's many targets include the bombing of the Jordanian Embassy and the UN headquarters in Baghdad; the Najaf bombings on August 29, 2003, that killed Shiite leader Muhammad Baqir al-Hakim; and the bombing of the Italian military headquarters in al-Nasiria.

Mujahideen Shura Council

In early 2006, al Qaeda in Iraq posted an Internet statement saying it had joined five other insurgent groups in Iraq to form a new umbrella organization, the Mujahideen Shura Council. Two of these groups—the Victorious Sect Army and the Islamic Jihad Brigade—were known, while three were apparently new groups. The Mujahideen Shura Council issues statements and posts videos on a website—including a video showing the executions of two Russian hostages in June 2006. Analysts say moves to build cooperation and a unified strategy among the disparate insurgent groups have had some success. Its leader until his death was Abu Musab al-Zarqawi, and its current leader is believed to be Abu Ayyub al-Masri. The group functions as an umbrella for Sunni insurgent groups.

Mahdi Army

The Mahdi army is a Shia militia movement led by Moqtada Sadr, a radical Shiite cleric, well supported by weapons plundered during the initial weeks of the U.S.-led invasion from Iraq's enormous weapons' stockpile. Analysts also believe that the movement is financed by Iran and also with training from the Shia group Hezbollah in Lebanon.

Sadr's brand of Shia nationalism, opposition to the U.S. presence in Iraq and hostility toward the powerful established Shia political parties, has proved popular among poor, disenfranchised Shia communities, and his key stronghold is the slum district of Sadr City, named after his father, a revered cleric murdered by Saddam Hussein's security forces. Mahdi fighters staged uprisings against U.S.-led forces in April and August 2004, but since then Sadr has become involved in the political process and holds thirty seats in the Shia bloc that dominates parliament.

As insurgent attacks have increasingly targeted Shia areas, the Mahdi army had become one of the major armed forces on the ground in Baghdad, controlling and protecting Shia areas. The Shia population in the Baghdad neighborhoods at first welcomed the Mahdi army as the national police and municipal officials were feeble at best, but they soon changed and began to display a serious appetite for sectarian violence as well as corruption and extortion. Whole areas were "cleansed" of Sunni civilians with many being summarily executed. The Mahdi army took over gas stations and mosques and extorted protection money from businesses. Al-Sadr was unable to control the rogue element within his movement, and they began to lose their grassroots support. The 2007 military surge by the U.S. military further loosened the Mahdi army's control of the streets. Al-Sadr's reputation was severely damaged in August 2007 by fierce fighting in the holy city of Karbala when his men fought pitched battles and were fended off by the Badr Brigade militias of the Islamic Supreme Council of Iraq. While the two main Shia factions were fighting, this was not in the grand scheme of operations for the Iranians who want to have a united Shia movement, not a fractured one. The Sadr movement is pivotal to events, both political and military, in Iraq. In early 2007, the U.S. Commander General David Petraeus called the Mahdi army the biggest single threat to Iraq.[14] By the end of 2011, and with the withdrawal of U.S. troops, militia members of the Mahdi Army loyal to Shiite cleric Moqtada al-Sadr were integrating into positions of influence within the Iraqi security apparatus.

Badr Brigade/Corps

This is a Shiite militia similar to the Mahdi army, composed of Iraqi military officers who escaped, defected, or were captured during and after the Iran–Iraq war, 1980–1988. The movement is supported by the Supreme Council for the Islamic Revolution in Iraq (SCIRI), the most powerful

Shiite party in Iraq. The Iraqi Ba'ath Government began its reign with a brutal suppression of the religious leadership of Grand Ayatollah Sayed Muhsin Al Hakim who was put under house arrest. His son Sayed Mahdi Al Hakim was accused of being a traitor who fled the country and was assassinated in Sudan in 1988.The Badr Brigade waged a low-level war of ambushes, sabotage, and assassinations against the regime, using undercover cells in Iraq and bases in Iran when Saddam Hussein was still in control in Iraq. In 1977, there was a popular uprising when the regime prevented the people from visiting the Shrine of Imam Husain in the holy city of Karbala. Sayed Mohamad Baqir al-Hakim, the leader of SCIRI and the son of Grand Ayatollah Sayed Muhsin Al Hakim, was arrested, tortured, and sentenced to life imprisonment without a trial. In 1980, Ayatollah Mohamad Baqir Al Sadr, who became the religious leader after the death of Sayed Muhsin Al Hakim, was executed with his sister Amina Al Sadr. Saddam's regime issued a decree to execute all the members of the Islamic Movement. After Iraqi forces were removed from Kuwait in 1991, the popular uprising in the south of Iraq was partly coordinated by the secret cells and elements connected to Badr corps and took part in launching and spreading the uprising from the south to other parts of Iraq.

Its members were funded, trained, and equipped by the Iranian Revolutionary Guard Corps. During the U.S.-led-occupation government's crackdown on militia groups in 2003, the 10,000-strong militia changed its name from the Badr Brigade to the Badr Organization of Reconstruction and Development. The group operates mainly in the southern Iraq region, in and around Basra, where a number of regional governments are dominated by SCIRI representatives. SCIRI wants to create a separate Shiite-run region comprising nine provinces in southern Iraq.

INSURGENCY AND TERRORISM

As is often the case, commentators use the words insurgency and terrorism, so it is necessary to know what an insurgency is. Insurgency is a movement, basically a political effort with a specific aim. This sets it apart from both guerrilla warfare and terrorism, as they are both methods available to pursue the goals of the political movement. As we have witnessed in Iraq, the insurgency is aimed at challenging the government for control of specific areas and territory, and as is often the case, external support is often a factor in supporting an insurgency. In the case of Iraq, we see this in support and interference from both Iran and Syria. Insurgency unlike terrorism does not require the targeting of noncombatants, although many insurgencies expand the accepted legal definition of combatants to include police and security personnel in addition to the military. Terrorists do not discriminate between combatants and noncombatants, or if they do, they broaden the category of "combatants" so as to render it meaningless. Deliberate dehumanization and criminalization of the enemy in the terrorists' mind justifies extreme measures against anyone identified as hostile. Terrorists often expand their groups of acceptable targets, and conduct operations against new targets without any warning or notice. Terrorists use methods that neutralize the strengths of conventional forces. Bombings and IED attacks on civilian targets where military or security personnel spend off-duty time, ambushes of undefended convoys, and assassinations of poorly protected individuals are common tactics.

Ultimately, the difference between insurgency and terrorism comes down to the intent of those involved. Insurgencies sometimes adhere to international norms regarding the law of war to achieve their goals, but terrorists are conducting crimes under both civil and military legal codes. Insurgents in Iraq have been responsible for numerous atrocities. In 2004, a four-man private security detail from the Blackwater security company was ambushed near Fallujah; they were killed and their mutilated bodies hung from a bridge over the Euphrates River.

TERRORIST ATTACK BRIEF

Terrorist Group: Islamic State of Iraq

Case Facts: Members of the insurgent group stormed the Central Bank of Baghdad and took a large number of hostages killing at least fifteen and injuring 50.

Investigation: Attacks by dissident insurgent groups are common in Iraq, and in this incident, the Islamic State of Iraq used thirty insurgents to take over the entire building. The siege lasted approximately three hours and ended in a gun battle with Iraqi troops and police killing all thirty insurgents.

FIGURE 9-4   Hostage Taking—Baghdad—Iraq—June 13, 2010.   *Source: The Journal of International Security,* vol 20, no. 7, Incident Brief, Albany Media, Chertsey, Surrey, UK, p.38.

Terrorists routinely claim that were they to adhere to any "law of war" or accept any constraints on their violence, it would place them at a disadvantage vis-à-vis the establishment. Since the nature of the terrorist mind-set is absolutist, their goals are of paramount importance, and any limitations on a terrorist's means to prosecute the struggle are unacceptable.[15]

IRAQI INSURGENCY

The Iraqi insurgency may not have been something that the U.S. administration would freely admit that after the Iraq invasion it had even envisaged. The insurgency has been an ongoing problem for the security of Iraq and is now simmering especially with a Shiite-dominated Iraqi government. Bin Laden's declaration of Jihad in the early 1990s emphasized his desire to secure the withdrawal of U.S. and foreign troops from Saudi Arabia and viewed the Saudi Royal family with disdain for inviting foreign troops to the Arabian Peninsula, which in his mind constituted an affront to the sanctity of the birthplace of Islam and a betrayal of the global Islamic community.[16] In 2004, bin Laden identified the Iraq conflict as a "golden and unique opportunity" for jihadists to engage and defeat the United States. He characterized the Iraq insurgency as the central battle in a "Third World War, which the Crusader-Zionist coalition began against the Islamic nation," he stated, "The whole world is watching this war and the two adversaries, the Islamic nation on the one hand and the United States and its allies on the other. It is either victory and glory or misery and humiliation. The nation today has a very rare opportunity to come out of the subservience and enslavement of the West and to smash the chains with which the Crusaders have fettered it."[17] His endorsement of the activities of the late Abu Musab al Zarqawi as an affiliate of al Qaeda is also representative of al Qaeda's need for a presence in Iraq. Bin Laden also encouraged Muslim Iraqis and non-Iraqis of all ethnicities to cooperate in opposing the Iraqi government. His preferred method of attack on both coalition forces and government was the use of "martyrdom operations," or suicide attacks. Bin Laden and Zarqawi had based their calls for revolutionary change in Islamic societies on a stated belief in a model of governance where Muslim citizens would be empowered to choose and depose their leaders according to strict Islamic principles and traditions of consultation, or shura.[18] Iraq has been used as a training forum for many affiliated al Qaeda groups, so the question on the minds of many is, will this change the focus of attacks on Israel and the Palestinian cause? Al Qaeda leaders have engaged in anti-Israeli rhetoric with varying levels of intensity. While there has been very little evidence to suggest the presence of al Qaeda in the Palestinian territories, it remains a fact that the leadership continues to insist the aims of the preparations being made in both the east and the west include the removal of Israel from the Muslim lands of Palestine.

WEAPONS OF MASS DESTRUCTION

It would be difficult to discuss the problems in Iraq without talking about WMD and possible links to the al Qaeda networks. The reason the United States and its allies are in the region in the first place was that Saddam Hussein was believed to have nuclear weapons capability. In the post-9-11 security environment, the Bush administration had little choice but to assume the worst. Many have charged that the White House either inflated or manipulated weak and otherwise ambiguous intelligence that showed Iraq as an urgent threat and thus make an optional war a necessity. In the two years that U.S. troops had been in Iraq, no sign to support the previous certainty that there were WMD had been uncovered. Large stockpiles of conventional weapons were unearthed but none of the type that suggested there was any urgency in waging a war against Iraq. During the 1990s, when weapons inspection teams were attempting to uncover any evidence of a nuclear program, UN sanctions were in place and had a marked effect on the economy of the country. These sanctions also prevented any upgrade in conventional weapons, and that is likely one reason why the Iraqi army's resistance was so minimal in 2003. The Iraqi military and weapons program had, in fact, steadily eroded under the weight of UN sanctions. The unique synergy of sanctions and inspections eroded Iraq's weapons programs and constrained its military capabilities. These facts are contrary to the Bush administration's contention that Iraq was a "gathering" threat. The renewed UN resolve demonstrated by the Security Council's approval of a "smart" sanctions package in May 2002 showed that the system could continue to contain and deter Saddam Hussein.

Unfortunately, only when U.S. troops invaded in March 2003 did these successes become clear. The Iraqi military had, in the previous twelve years, been decimated by the strategy of containment that the Bush administration had called a failure in order to justify war in the first place.[19] Iraq has been the center and object—almost exclusively—for the U.S. "War on Terror," but your authors and, more widely, the media and politicians have used the term *insurgency* to describe the acts of violence in Iraq since the U.S. invasion in 2003. While the military has been fully engaged in counterinsurgency work, much of the security of foreign nationals has fallen to "global security providers," who have also become legitimate targets for insurgents. There is no doubt that many methods being employed by the factions in Iraq have involved terroristic-style attacks, but there is a distinction between what terrorism is and what insurgency is. An insurgency requires the active or tacit support of at least a minority of the general population. This definition would certainly fit the events taking shape in Iraq involving the minority Sunni groups. While insurgents will frequently describe themselves as an insurgent or a guerrilla movement, terrorists have historically declined to call themselves "terrorists" and have preferred terms such as *freedom fighter*. Terrorists rely on the impact their activities have on the public at large and attempt to avoid the negative connotations of identifying themselves openly as terrorists.

Whether the spread of al Qaeda's influence in Iraq is a direct result of the U.S. presence there or whether there are fighters from the movement circulating throughout the country is unclear. However, the influential Strategic Survey conducted by the London-based International Institute for Strategic Studies quotes that a cadre of at least 18,000 individuals who trained in al Qaeda camps between 1996 and 2001 are today believed to be positioned in some sixty countries throughout the world.

SUPPORT FOR INTERNATIONAL TERRORISM

Prior to the invasion of Iraq, there were a large number of very senior U.S. politicians who could not accept that Iraq was involved in sponsoring terrorism or, for that matter, was a threat to U.S. security. Obviously, the world is a better place without Saddam Hussein; however, it is history that has determined his involvement in sponsoring terror groups. Many dissidents who escaped from Iraq during Saddam's regime claimed that he maintained terrorist training camps outside Baghdad. He had entertained and provided safe haven to Abu Abbas, a former secretary general of the Palestine Liberation Front. It was Abbas who was responsible for the hijacking of the cruise ship *Achille Lauro* in 1985, in which an American citizen, Leon Klinghoffer, was killed. Abbas was briefly in Italian custody but was able to produce an Iraqi diplomatic passport, forcing the Italian authorities to release him. He may have arrived in Baghdad around 1995 and was caught there by U.S. forces in April 2003. He died while in U.S. custody in March 2004.

Saddam Hussein's support for the families of Palestinian suicide bombers is also well known and reasonably documented. Sabri al Banna the leader of Abu Nidal Organization (AN) was supported by the Saddam regime as well as Syria and Libya. ANO was responsible for terrorist attacks in more than twenty countries, the deaths of more than 400, and over 700 injured. Nidal's terror group carried out simultaneous attacks in Rome and Vienna airports on December 9, 1985, killing nineteen. Sabri al Banna died under mysterious circumstances from gunshot wounds while in his Baghdad apartment in 2002.

BAHRAIN

The State of Bahrain is on a scattered archipelago in the Persian Gulf, east of Saudi Arabia. These landmasses are small; totaling only 3.5 times the size of Washington DC. Bahrain has resources of oil, natural gas, and fish. It is close to primary Middle Eastern petroleum sources and located in a

FIGURE 9-5 Map of Bahrain (Central Intelligence Agency, *The World Factbook, 2008*).

strategic position in the Persian Gulf. It has a very small population of 603,318 (including 221,182 nonnationals). Bahrain gained independence from the United Kingdom in 1971.

Bahrain's chief of state is Amir Isa bin Salman Al Khalifa (since 1961), and the head of government is Prime Minister Khalifi bin Salman Al Khalifa (since 1970). The cabinet is appointed by the Amir, who is a traditional Arab monarch. Political parties are prohibited. Political pressure groups and leaders comprise, and represent, several small, clandestine leftist and Islamic fundamentalist outfits. Following the arrest of a popular Shia cleric, Shia activists have fomented unrest sporadically since late 1994, demanding the return of an elected national assembly and an end to unemployment.

In Bahrain, petroleum production and processing account for about 60 percent of export receipts, 60 percent of government revenues, and 30 percent of GDP. Economic conditions have fluctuated with the changing fortunes of oil since 1985, for example during and following the Gulf crisis of 1990–1991. The sultanate continued to be plagued by arson attacks and other minor security incidents throughout 1997, most perpetrated by domestic dissidents.

The State Security Court jailed thirty-six Shia Muslims accused of a pro-Iranian plot to topple the government by force, while acquitting twenty-three others. Unrest in Bahrain has led to at least twenty-eight deaths and hundreds of arrests since December 1994.[20] Shiites suffer from higher rates of unemployment and are barred from employment in the police or security services. The government maintains that the protests plaguing the country are organized by Hezbollah-Bahrain, allegedly backed by Iran.[21] Alleged members of the Bahraini Hezbollah were on trial. In all, fifty-four Shia Muslims in detention and twenty-seven others being tried in absentia are accused of fomenting violence and antigovernment activities.[22] The existence of Bahrain Hezbollah itself is questioned by some who accuse the government of fabricating its existence in order to blame outsiders for the political unrest. Their jail sentences range from five to fifteen years. Some Bahraini Hezbollah members reportedly underwent terrorist training in camps in Iran and Lebanon.

The Sunni Muslim-led government in Bahrain is reforming the political system to pacify a vocal and increasingly discontented Shiite majority. However, these measures are limited in substance and may end up fueling more dissent and unrest in the country.

In February 2002, Bahrain's leader, Sheik Hamad bins Isa Al Khalifa, proclaimed himself king and declared his country a constitutional monarchy. Hamad also dissolved Bahrain's appointed consultative council, paving the way for the establishment of a bicameral parliament following elections scheduled for later in the year. Kuwait is currently the only Persian Gulf state with an elected parliament.

The government's transformation from the emirate system into a constitutional monarchy has been heralded as a step toward democracy. The feeling in the rest of the world is that it is not. Instead, it reflects the battle in an unresolved power struggle between Bahrain's minority Sunni Muslim-led government and the majority Shiite Muslim community. The Shia Sunni imbalance in Bahrain and the unrest sweeping the Middle East during 2011 could impact security in the entire Persian Gulf region. The country is not a major oil producer but does have a vital refining industry that imports crude from neighboring states. It is also an important financial hub for the region, with many foreign banks located in the capital, Manama. Moreover, Manama is also headquarters for the U.S. Navy's Fifth Fleet and a center for U.S. military operations in the Gulf. Cooperation between Bahrain's two religious sects is critical to maintaining the island's calm. The situation in the country mirrors a historical contest between Islam's two largest sects throughout the Middle East, especially in the Persian Gulf. It also reflects the two distinct communities' struggle for control over Bahrain's valuable resources.

OMAN

The Sultanate of Oman borders the Arabian Sea, the Gulf of Oman, and the Persian Gulf, between Yemen and United Arab Emirates. Although small, its natural resources include petroleum, copper, asbestos, some marble, limestone, chromium, gypsum, and natural gas. This parched nation has no arable land and no permanent crops. Oman is strategically located on the Usandam Peninsula and controls the Strait of Hormuz, a vital transit point for world crude oil. Seventy-five percent of Oman's 2,264,590 population is Sunni Muslim, with the remainder Shia Muslim and Hindu. Oman is a sultanate, a monarchy that has been independent since 1650, when it expelled the Portuguese.

On November 6, 1996, Sultan Qaboos issued a royal decree promulgating a new basic law, which clarified the royal succession, provided for a prime minister, barred ministers from holding interests in companies doing business with the government, established a bicameral Omani council, and guaranteed basic civil liberties for Omani citizens. The sultan is the chief of state, the head of government, and a hereditary monarch. Oman's economic performance is closely tied to the fortunes of the oil industry. Petroleum accounts for 75 percent of export earnings and government revenues, and roughly 40 percent of GDP. Oman has proven oil reserves of 4 billion barrels, equivalent to about a twenty-year supply at the current rate of extraction. The earliest settlements in Oman, as in the Arabian Peninsula generally, date from some time in the third millennium B.C. At that time, and for some hundreds of years more, Oman was on the edge of the trade routes linking ancient Mesopotamia to the Indus Valley; however, it does not appear to have profited a great deal from its location.

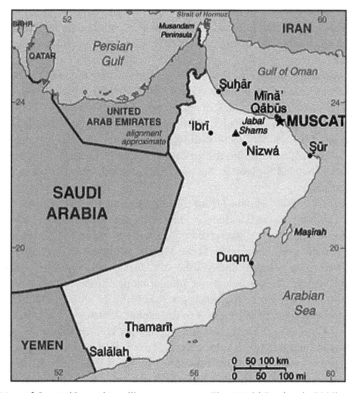

FIGURE 9-6 Map of Oman (Central Intelligence Agency, *The World Factbook, 2008*).

The southernmost region of Oman, modern Dhofar, was responsible for the area's importance. It is one of the few spots in the world where frankincense trees grow. Frankincense is an aromatic gum from certain species of trees that grow only in southern Oman, the Wadi Hadhramaut in Yemen, and Somalia. The incense burns well because of its natural oil content. In addition, it has medicinal uses; these two factors, plus its relative scarcity, made frankincense an extremely sought-after substance in the ancient world. Frankincense was vital to the religious rites of almost every civilization in the ancient world. The great temples of Egypt, the Near East, and Rome itself were all major consumers of the scarce commodity, not to mention the thousands of other temples found in every city, town, and village. Indeed, the writer Pliny, in the first century A.D., claimed that control of the frankincense trade had made the south Arabians the richest people on earth.

In the second century A.D., at the height of the trade, some 3,000 tons of frankincense were transported each year by ship from south Arabia to Greece, Rome, and the Mediterranean world. Although the trade went into a decline after the third century A.D., it still managed to keep south Arabia relatively wealthy for another three centuries.

The tribes in the northern part of Oman were converted to Islam during the first generation of the Islamic era, the middle of the seventh century A.D., and shortly thereafter came under the rule of the Umayyads, whose center was in Damascus. About a century later, the Omanis revolted against the Umayyads and expelled them from their country. The Umayyads themselves remained only a short time as the leaders of the Muslim world, for the Abbasids, whose capital was in Baghdad, soon overthrew them.

Oman managed to remain free of the Abbasids and continued its adherence to Ibadi Islam, which is still dominant in the country today. Because of Oman's remoteness from other Muslims, the Ibadis survived as a group long after they had vanished from other parts of the Muslim world.

By the end of the eighteenth century, the Omanis were in control of an extensive empire. At its height in the nineteenth century, the empire ruled both Mombasa and Zanzibar and had trading posts much farther down the African coast. (Oman's last colonial outpost—Gwadar, on what is now the coast of Pakistan—was not surrendered until September 1958, when Sultan Said bin Taimur allowed it to be reintegrated into Pakistan in return for a payment of £3 million.) In 1749, the first ruler of the present dynasty (Al-Busaid) gained power, and, in 1786, the capital was formally moved from the interior to Muscat. About this same time, Al-Busaid adopted the title of "Sultan," which continues to this day.

The heyday of the Omani Empire occurred in the mid-nineteenth century under Sultan Said bin Sultan, who ruled from 1804 to 1856. He was responsible for bringing Dhofar under the Omani flag, and he also extended Omani influence and control down the East African coast. He had an army of 6,500 men and a navy consisting of fifteen ships. When he died, the empire split in two; one son became the sultan of Zanzibar and the other, the sultan of Muscat and Oman. In the very name of the latter, the perceived difference between the interests of the coast and those of the interior was acknowledged. In fact, they were regarded as two entities ruled by the same monarch, though the writ of the ruler in Muscat sometimes did not extend very far into the interior. Muscat's control depended very much on the regard for the Sultan held by the tribes of the interior. In the early twentieth century, the Sultan's power to control the interior of the country was felt to have decreased.

In February 1932, Sultan Said bin Taimur, father of the present ruler, came to power. When he tried to exercise his nominal control in the interior of the country in the early 1950s, the British, who believed the area had oil, backed him. And, in order to procure it, the British needed the Sultan to have control of the area and Oman's indefinite borders with Saudi Arabia and Abu Dhabi to be clearly drawn. The result was a territorial dispute over the Buraimi oasis involving Oman, Saudi Arabia, and Abu Dhabi. With British help and his own bravado, Sultan Said, in the end, was the winner, and the Buraimi oasis is today firmly within the borders of Oman.

Sultan Said bin Taimur was, in the words of one British writer, an arch-reactionary of great personal charm. He wanted no change of any sort in Oman and did all he could to isolate his country from the world. He issued all visas personally. He forbade travel to the interior by coastal residents and vice versa. Believing education was a threat to his power, he opposed it.

In general, Omanis were not allowed to leave the country, and those who did were seldom allowed to return. The sultan's only contact with the outside world was through his British advisers and Muscat's merchant families. He allowed the latter to establish enormously lucrative monopolies for the import of goods, which he saw as crucial to his survival. In exchange, the merchants stayed out of politics and imported nothing that Sultan Said felt reeked of progress or the West (radios, books, eyeglasses). Through their customs receipts, the merchants provided the Sultan with most of the country's income. Aside from a few rich merchants, most of the population relied on agriculture and fishing.

Oman has been Islamic since the seventh century. From 1932 to 1970, Oman was controlled by Sultan Said bin Taimur, a reclusive and repressive ruler whose policies finally resulted in revolt in Dhofar in 1965. In 1970, his son, the British-educated Qaboos bin Said, overthrew his father and embarked on an ambitious modernization program. This small and tightly controlled country has been bypassed by most of the terrorism and violence in the region and is almost totally unknown in the rest of the world.

Oman, a key U.S. ally in the Middle East, is adjusting its budget to reflect its assistance to the War on Terror, but the oil-rich sultanate is actually reducing defense funding and shifting the savings into social welfare programs. Unlike many other governments in the region, Oman's regime has faced relatively little domestic opposition to its relationship with the United States. This is largely due to strong oil revenues and an extremely tolerant local segment of Islam. Even so, it appears the Omani leadership is investing in preventative measures to keep a lid on unrest, knowing that Washington will guarantee its external security. By addressing domestic security before it becomes an issue, Oman hopes to avoid the problems faced by neighboring Saudi Arabia, where extremist Muslims actively oppose the basing of U.S. military forces there. A pacified population will allow the Omani government to deepen its involvement with the U.S. military, which is likely reexamining its options in the antiterror campaign.

The U.S. military currently uses at least three air bases in Oman as part of operations in Afghanistan. The Navy runs P-3 Orion aircraft patrols out of the Masirah air base, where at least one squadron of AC-130 gunships is based as well. Oman also hosts several Air Force pre-positioning sites, with enough equipment and fuel to maintain three air bases and 26,000 support personnel. Its continuing support of the United States makes Oman a key player in this global effort.

IRAN

One of the most controversial states in the Persian Gulf, the Islamic Republic of Iran borders the Gulf of Oman, the Persian Gulf, and the Caspian Sea, between Iraq and Pakistan. Iran is slightly larger than Alaska and has large resources of petroleum and natural gas. Its estimated population, 67,540,000, includes 917,078 nonnationals and a broad base of ethnic groups (Persian, 51 percent; Azerbaijani, 24 percent; Gilaki and Mazandarani, 8 percent; Kurd, 7 percent; Arab, 3 percent; Lur, 2 percent; Baloch, 2 percent; Turkmen, 2 percent; other, 1 percent) and religious

FIGURE 9-7 Map of Iran (Central Intelligence Agency, *The World Factbook, 2008*).

affiliations (Shia Muslim, 89 percent; Sunni Muslim, 10 percent; Zoroastrian, Jewish, Christian, and Baha'i, 1 percent). This broad spectrum is reflected in languages as well (Persian and Persian dialects, 58 percent; Turkic and Turkic dialects, 26 percent; Kurdish, 9 percent; Luri, 2 percent; Balochi, 1 percent; Arabic, 1 percent; Turkish, 1 percent; other 2 percent). Iran is a theocratic republic, and its constitution codifies Islamic principles of government.

Mujahedin-E Khalq (MEK) Organization

The MEK, also known as the National Liberation Army of Iran (NLA), the militant wing of the MEK, the People's Mujahedin of Iran (PMOI), and the Muslim Iranian Student's Society, was formed in the 1960s by a group of left-wing college radicals opposed to the Shah of Iran and became the largest and most militant group opposed to the Islamic Republic of Iran.

The MEK sought to counter what was perceived as excessive Western influence in the Shah's regime (1941–1979), and in the 1970s concluded that violence was the only way to bring about change in Iran. Since then, the MEK, following a philosophy that mixes Marxism and Islam, has developed into the largest and most active armed Iranian dissident group. Its history is studded with anti-Western activity and, most recently, attacks on the interests of the clerical regime in Iran and abroad. MEK was financed and supported through the Iraqi regime of Saddam Hussein and was actively supporting repression of Saddam's enemies within Iraq.

The MEK directs a worldwide campaign against the Iranian government that stresses propaganda and occasionally uses terrorist violence.

During the 1970s, the MEK staged terrorist attacks inside Iran to destabilize and embarrass the Shah's regime; the group killed several U.S. military personnel and civilians working on defense projects in Tehran and supported the 1979 takeover of the U.S. embassy in Tehran. In April 1992, they carried out attacks on Iranian embassies in thirteen different countries, demonstrating the group's ability to mount large-scale operations overseas. Several thousand fighters with an extensive overseas support structure are based in Iraq. Most of the fighters are organized in the MEK's National Liberation Army (NLA).

In the 1980s, with the outbreak of war between Iran and Iraq, the group fled to Paris and most resettled back in Iraq by 1987. Their attacks were sporadic, and in 1999, they assassinated Iran's Army Chief of Staff Ali Shirazi and, in 2000, launched a rocket attack on the Presidential Palace. Until the U.S.-led invasion of Iraq, MEK had established numerous bases in the country, and these were overrun by the U.S. military in 2003, with the MEK surrendering peacefully and handing over their weapons and munitions. MEK continues to have supporters in Western Europe and also in the United States and Canada, but since its support structure and demise in Iraq, its membership has dwindled significantly.[23]

Maryam Rajavi and Masood Rajavi have been the leaders of MEK since the early 1980s; they joined as students in the early 1970s. Masood has been in charge of MEK's military wing operating in Iraq, and his whereabouts since the U.S. invasion are unknown. When Maryam Rajavi relocated with MEK to Paris in 1981, she was elected to the leadership position. Maryam was arrested by French police on a raid on the group's HQ near Paris in 2003.

Political pressure groups that generally support the Islamic Republic include Ansar-e Hizballah, Mojahedin of the Islamic Revolution, Muslim Students Following the Line of the Imam, and the Islamic Coalition Association. Opposition groups include the Liberation Movement of Iran and the Nation of Iran party. Armed political groups that have been almost completely repressed by the government include Mojahedin-e Khalq Organization (MEK), People's Fedayeen, Democratic Party of Iranian Kurdistan, and the Society for the Defense of Freedom.

In the early 1990s, Iran experienced a financial crisis caused by general financial mismanagement and an import surge that began in 1989. In 1993–1994, Iran rescheduled $15 billion in debt, with the bulk of payments due in 1996–1997. The strong oil market in 1996 helped ease financial pressures, however, and Tehran has so far made timely debt service payments. In 1996, Iran's oil earnings, which account for 85 percent of its total export revenues, climbed 20 percent from the previous year. Iran's financial situation remained tight through the end of the decade. Its continued timely debt service payments depended, in part, on persistent strong oil prices during the following years, a prediction that has failed badly as petroleum prices plummeted in 1998.

Iran is an illicit producer of opium poppy for the domestic and international drug trade. Iran continues to be a key transshipment point country for Southwest Asian heroin going to Europe.

THE SHAH OF IRAN

Mohammad Reza Pahlavi was restored to the Peacock Throne with the assistance of the Central Intelligence Agency in 1953. The CIA assisted in a coup against the left-leaning government of Dr. Mohammad Mossadeq, who had planned to nationalize Iran's oil industry. The CIA also provided organizational and training assistance for an intelligence organization for the Shah. With training focused on domestic security and interrogation, the intelligence unit was taxed with the mission to eliminate threats to the Shah. Formed under efforts of U.S. and Israeli intelligence officers in 1957, **SAVAK** became an effective secret agency. General Bakhtiar was appointed its first director, only to be dismissed in 1961. He was assassinated in 1970 under mysterious circumstances. His successor, General Pakravan, was dismissed in 1966, failing to crush the opposition from the clerics in the early 1960s.

In 1961, Iran initiated a series of economic, social, and administrative reforms that became known as the Shah's White Revolution. The core of this program was land reform. Modernization and economic growth proceeded at an unprecedented rate, fueled by Iran's vast petroleum reserves, the third largest in the world. Domestic turmoil swept the country as a result of religious and political opposition to the Shah's rule and programs, especially SAVAK, the hated internal security and intelligence service.

The Shah turned to his childhood friend, General Nassiri, to rebuild SAVAK to properly serve the monarchy. Mansur Rafizadeh, the SAVAK director in the United States throughout the 1970s, claimed that General Nassiri's telephone was tapped by SAVAK agents reporting directly to the Shah, an example of the level of mistrust pervading on the eve of the revolution. SAVAK increasingly symbolized the Shah's rule from 1963 to 1979, a period of corruption, one-party rule, the torture and execution of thousands of political prisoners, suppression of dissent, and alienation of the religious masses. The United States reinforced its position as the Shah's protector and supporter, sowing the seeds of the anti-Americanism that later manifested itself in the revolution against the monarchy.

Accurate information concerning SAVAK has never been published. Pamphlets issued by the revolutionary regime after 1979 indicated that SAVAK had been a full-scale intelligence agency with more than 15,000 full-time personnel and thousands of part-time informants. SAVAK was attached to the office of the prime minister, and its director assumed the title of Deputy to the Prime Minister for National Security Affairs. Although officially a civilian agency, SAVAK had close ties to the military, and many of its officers served simultaneously in branches of the armed forces.

Another close confidant of the Shah, Major General Hosain Fardust, was deputy director of SAVAK until the early 1970s, when the Shah promoted him to the directorship of the "Special Intelligence Bureau," which operated inside Niavaran Palace, independently of SAVAK.

Originally formed to round up members of the outlawed Tudeh, SAVAK expanded its activities to include gathering intelligence and neutralizing the regime's opponents. An elaborate system was created to monitor all facets of political life. A censorship office was established to monitor journalists, literary figures, and academics throughout the country; it took measures against those who fell out of line. Universities, labor unions, and peasant organizations, among others, were all subjected to intense surveillance by SAVAK agents and paid informants. The agency was also active abroad, especially in monitoring Iranian students who opposed Pahlavi rule.

SAVAK contracted Rockwell International to develop a large communications monitoring system called IBEX. The Stanford Technology Corp. (STC), owned by Hakim, had a $5.5 million contract to supply the CIA-promoted IBEX project. STC had another $7.5 million contract with Iran's air force for a telephone monitoring system, operated by SAVAK, to enable the Shah to track his top commanders' communications.

Over the years, SAVAK became a law unto itself, having legal authority to arrest and detain suspected persons indefinitely. SAVAK operated its own prisons in Tehran (the Komiteh and Evin facilities) and others throughout the country. SAVAK's torture methods included electric shock, whipping, beating, inserting broken glass, and pouring boiling water into the rectum, tying weights to the testicles, and the extraction of teeth and nails. At the peak of its influence, SAVAK had at least thirteen full-time case officers running a network of informers and infiltrators covering 30,000 Iranian students on U.S. college campuses. The head of the SAVAK agents in the United States operated under the cover of an attaché at the Iranian Mission, with the FBI, CIA, and State Department fully aware of these activities.

In 1978, the deepening opposition to the Shah erupted in widespread demonstrations and rioting. SAVAK and the military responded with widespread repression that killed 12,000–15,000 people and seriously injured another 50,000. Recognizing that even this level of state terrorism had failed to crush the rebellion, the Shah abdicated the Peacock Throne and departed Iran in 1979. Despite decades of pervasive surveillance by SAVAK, working closely with the CIA, the extent of public opposition to the Shah and his sudden departure came as a considerable surprise to the U.S. intelligence community and national leadership.

The SAVAK organization was officially dissolved by Ayatollah Khomeini shortly after he came to power. However, it was no surprise that SAVAK was singled out as a primary target for reprisals. Its headquarters were overrun and prominent leaders were tried and executed by Khomeini representatives. High-ranking SAVAK agents were purged, and sixty-one SAVAK officials were among 248 military personnel executed between February and September 1979.[24]

The 1979 Islamic revolution and the war with Iraq transformed Iran's class structure politically, socially, and economically. In general, however, Iranian society remains divided into urban, market town, village, and tribal groups. The clerics dominate politics and nearly all aspects of Iranian life, both urban and rural. After the fall of the Shah, much of the urban upper class of prominent merchants, industrialists, and professionals, favored by the former regime, lost influence to the senior clergy and its supporters. Bazaar merchants, who were allied with the clergy against the Pahlavi Shahs, also gained political and economic power since the revolution. The Shah went into exile and died in Cairo, in July 1980, where he was given a state funeral.

On February 1, 1979, exiled religious leader Ayatollah Ruhollah Khomeini returned from France to direct the revolution, resulting in a new, theocratic republic guided by Islamic principles. Back in Iran after fifteen years in exile in Turkey, Iraq, and France, he became Iran's national religious leader. Following his death on June 3, 1989, the Assembly of Experts, an elected body of senior clerics, chose the outgoing president of the republic, Ali Khamenei, to be his successor as national religious leader in what proved to be a smooth transition. In 1989, an overwhelming majority elected Ali Akbar Hashemi-Rafsanjani, the speaker of the National Assembly, president. He was reelected June 11, 1993, with a more modest majority of about 63 percent. Some Western observers attributed the reduced voter turnout to disenchantment with the deteriorating economy. Iran's postrevolution difficulties included an eight-year war with Iraq, internal political struggles and unrest, and economic disorder. The early days of the regime were characterized by human rights violations and political turmoil, including the seizure of the U.S. embassy compound and its occupants on November 4, 1979, by Iranian militants. By mid-1982, a succession of power struggles eliminated first the center of the political spectrum and then the leftists, leaving only the clergy. There has been some moderation of excesses, both internally and internationally, although Iran remains a significant sponsor of terrorism.

The Islamic Republican Party (IRP) was Iran's dominant political party until its dissolution in 1987; Iran now has no functioning political parties. The Iranian government is opposed by a few armed political groups, including the Mujahidin-e Khalq (People's Mujahidin of Iran), the People's Fedayeen, and the Kurdish Democratic Party.

Khomeini's revolutionary regime initiated sharp changes from the foreign policy pursued by the Shah, particularly in reversing the country's orientation toward the West. In the Middle East, Iran's only significant ally has been Syria. Iran's regional goals include its desire to establish

TERRORIST ATTACK BRIEF

Terrorist Group: Revolutionary Guards and Students

Case Facts: At the height of the Iranian Revolution that saw the overthrow of the Shah of Iran, a large group of students and part of a violent crowd stormed the U.S. Embassy—with the tacit support of the Revolutionary government of Ayatollah Khomeini.

Investigation: Iranian students stormed the embassy in response to U.S. support for the deposed Shah of Iran who had managed to escape to safe haven in the United States. The students were demanding his return. A stalemate ensued, and they held all fifty five embassy staff hostage for 444 days. During this period, there was one failed attempt by U.S. Special Forces to release the hostages. The United States cut diplomatic relations with Iran following the embassy siege. The Shah died the following year in exile in Egypt, and at the same time Iraq invaded Iran. The hostages were released when President Reagan agreed to unfreeze Iranian assets in exchange for the safe return of the hostages.

FIGURE 9-8 Hostage Taking—U.S Embassy Tehran, IRAN—November 4, 1979.

a leadership role, curtail the presence of the United States and other outside powers, and build trade ties. In broad terms, Iran's Islamic foreign policy emphasizes the following:

- Vehement anti-U.S. and anti-Israel stances;
- Elimination of outside influence in the region;
- Export of the Islamic revolution;
- Support for Muslim political movements abroad; and
- A significant increase in diplomatic contacts with developing countries.

Despite these guidelines, however, bilateral relations are frequently confused and contradictory due to Iran's oscillation between pragmatic and ideological concerns. Iran's relations with many of its Arab neighbors have been strained by Iranian attempts to spread its Islamic revolution. In 1981, Iran supported a plot to overthrow the Bahrain government, and the unrest (Arab Spring) that swept the Middle East and Bahrain in 2011 would have been approved by Iran. In 1983, Iran expressed support for Shiites who bombed Western embassies in Kuwait and, in 1987 Iranian pilgrims rioted during the Hajj (pilgrimage) to Mecca in Saudi Arabia. Nations with strong fundamentalist movements, such as Egypt and Algeria, also mistrust Iran. Iran backs Hezbollah, Hamas, the Palestinian Islamic Jihad, and the Popular Front for the Liberation of Palestine-General Command—all groups violently opposed to the Arab-Israeli peace process.

Iran's relations with Western European nations have alternated between improvements and setbacks. French-Iranian relations were badly strained by the sale of French arms to Iraq. Since the war, relations have improved commercially but periodically are worsened by Iranian-sponsored terrorist acts committed in France. Another source of tension was Ayatollah Khomeini's 1989 call to all Muslims to kill Salman Rushdie, British author of *The Satanic Verses*. Many Muslims consider this novel blasphemous to their holy scriptures. The United Kingdom has sheltered Rushdie, and strains over this issue persist. There are serious obstacles to improved relations between the two countries. The U.S. government defines five areas of objectionable Iranian behavior:

- Iranian efforts to acquire nuclear weapons and other weapons of mass destruction;
- Its involvement in international terrorism;
- Its support for violent opposition to the Arab-Israeli peace process;

- Its threats and subversive activities against its neighbors; and
- Its dismal human rights record.

The United States believes that normal relations are impossible until Iran's behavior changes. The United States has made clear that it does not seek to overthrow the Iranian government but will continue to pressure Iran to change its behavior. Iran's continuing support of terrorists and terrorism creates continuing danger for Americans in Iran because of the generally anti-American atmosphere and the government's hostility to the U.S. government. American citizens traveling to Iran have been detained without charge, arrested, and harassed by Iranian authorities.[25]

IRAN AND NUCLEAR WEAPONS

The United States has cast Iran as being an integral part of the "axis of evil" and believes that it has been attempting to assemble the ingredients to manufacture weapons-grade nuclear material. This, of course, has not been confirmed. The Iranians can look at what has transpired since 9-11 and how the United States has reacted: The United States invades Iraq, which did *not* have nuclear weapons; the United States backed away from North Korea, which *does* have a nuclear weapons program. So, from a survivalist standpoint, the need for Iran to have an active nuclear program could be viewed as a method of restraining U.S. aggression. A nuclear Iran under the leadership of President Mahmoud Ahmadinejad pronounced in 2006 that the solution to the Middle East crisis would be the destruction of Israel.

Iran's connections with and sponsoring of terror groups is well documented. Iran was intimately involved in the attack on the Khober Towers complex in Saudi Arabia, and it has been supporting various Palestinian causes that hit at Israel's attempts at peace in the region. The obvious concern is that a nuclear Iran could supply the know-how to subgroups, or even the materials to construct a small nuclear device for delivery within Europe or the United States. Iran's nuclear program dates back to the days when the Shah was in control. By 2012, Iran was nuclear capable, and the control of the entire program rests in the hands of the president. Iran, against all opposition from external forces, continues to build and support the use of chemical, biological, and nuclear programs. The West views a nuclear Iran a threat to stability in the region, a region that descended into even more turmoil during 2011. A nuclear Iran and a nuclear Israel, does this mean equalization? Iran continues to threaten and call for Israel's destruction. However, with popular uprisings across the Arab world and in particular in neighboring Syria, Iran may be better focused on domestic issues that could threaten its own stability.

SPONSORING TERRORISM

Iran is considered by the U.S. State department to be the world's leading sponsor of terrorist groups and particularly those opposed to a Middle East Peace agreement. The Qods Force, the external operations branch of the **Islamic Revolutionary Guard Corps (IRGC)**, is Iran's primary mechanism for cultivating and supporting terrorists abroad. The IRGC has over 100,000 members and was originally formed after the revolution by Ayatollah Khomeni, who conscripted the most fanatical revolutionaries into the organization. He also amended Iran's constitution to give the IRGC the lawful right to "protect the spirit of the Revolution," sending the corps to impose the regime's laws on Iranians through physical violence. The IRGC assassinated many key figures in the opposition during this time.[26] The IRGC are fiercely loyal to the clerical regime and also act as a counter to the militray, which at the time of the revolution may have had loyalties to the Shah. As time passed, the IRGC and its structures operated totally independent of the Iranian military. Constructed along military lines with ground, sea, and air capability, the IRGC also controls the Iranian missle deployment program. The IRGC reports to and is accountable to the supreme leader and maintains complete political and social control and order over Iranian society.

Iran provided weapons, training, and funding to Hamas and other Palestinian terrorist groups, including Palestine Islamic Jihad (PIJ) and the Popular Front for the Liberation of Palestine-General Command (PFLP-GC), and has provided hundreds of millions of dollars in support to Lebanese Hizballah at training camps in Iran. Since the end of the 2006 Israeli-Hezbollah conflict, Iran has assisted Hezbollah in rearming, in violation of UN Security Council Resolution 1701. Iran has equally interfered in Afghanistan and has provided training to Taliban forces, which has allowed them to promulgate successful attacks on U.S. and other forces in the region. The Qods Force, which is best described as a "Special Forces" unit that trains militant organizations and has been in Beirut, Sudan, and other troubled regions, also engages in espionage and assassination. Iran has continued to supply Iraqi militants with Iranian-produced advanced rockets, sniper rifles, automatic weapons, and mortars that have killed Iraqi and coalition forces. Iran was responsible for the increased lethality of some attacks on U.S. forces by providing militants with the capability to assemble explosively formed penetrators that were designed to defeat armored vehicles. The **Qods Force**, in concert with Lebanese Hezbollah, provided training outside of Iraq and advisors inside Iraq for Shia militants in the construction and use of sophisticated improvised explosive device technology and other advanced weaponry. The designation of countries that repeatedly provide support for acts of international terrorism as state sponsors of terrorism carries with it four main sets of U.S. government sanctions:

1. A ban on arms-related exports and sales.
2. Controls over exports of dual-use items, requiring thirty-day congressional notification for goods or services that could significantly enhance the terrorist-list country's military capability or ability to support terrorism.
3. Prohibitions on economic assistance.
4. Imposition of miscellaneous financial and other restrictions, including the following:

   - Requiring the United States to oppose loans by the World Bank and other international financial institutions;
   - Exception from the jurisdictional immunity in U.S. courts of state sponsor countries, and all former state sponsor countries (with the exception of Iraq), with respect to claims for money damages for personal injury or death caused by certain acts of terrorism, torture, or extrajudicial killing, or the provision of material support or resources for such acts;
   - Denial to companies and individuals tax credits for income earned in terrorist-list countries;
   - Denial of duty-free treatment of goods exported to the United States;
   - Authority to prohibit any U.S. citizen from engaging in a financial transaction with a terrorist-list government without a Treasury Department license; and
   - Prohibition of Defence Department contracts above US$100,000 with companies in which a state sponsor government owns or controls a significant interest.

It is quite clear that designating Iran as a state sponsor of terrorism has done little to effect change in Iran or its attitude to the West and the Middle East.[27]

YEMEN

The Republic of Yemen was established on May 22, 1990, with the merger of the Yemen Arab Republic (YAR; Yemen Sanaa or North Yemen) and the Marxist-dominated People's Democratic Republic of Yemen (Yemen Aden or South Yemen). The newly formed republic borders the Arabian Sea, the Gulf of Aden, and the Red Sea, between Oman and Saudi Arabia. Yemen is slightly larger than twice the size of Wyoming, with borders to Oman and Saudi Arabia. Estimates of its population run from 13.9 million to as high as 16.6 million people of Arab and Afro-Arab concentrations in western coastal locations, South Asians in the southern regions, and small European communities in the major metropolitan areas. Muslims, including Sha'fi (Sunni) and Zaydi (Shia), plus small numbers of Jews, Christians, and Hindus practice their brands of religion.

The former Aden (South Yemen) gained independence from the United Kingdom in 1967. The northern city Sanaa became the political capital of a united Yemen. The southern city Aden, with its refinery and port facilities, is the economic and commercial capital. Future economic development depends heavily on Western-assisted development of the country's moderate oil resources.

British and Turkish Domination

The British conquered Aden (Southern Yemen) in 1839, and it became known as the Aden Protectorate. The British made a series of treaties with local tribal rulers in a move to colonize the entire area of southern Yemen. British influence extended to Hadhramawt by the 1950s, and a boundary line, known as the Violet Line, was drawn between Turkish Arabia in the north and the South Arabian Protectorate of Great Britain, as it was then known. (This line later formed the boundary between northern and southern Yemeni states in the 1960s.)

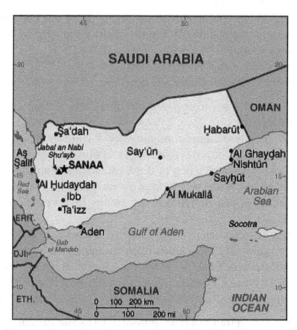

FIGURE 9-9 Map of Yemen (Central Intelligence Agency, *The World Factbook, 2008*).

Separate States and Unification

In the late 1960s, the British presence in southern Yemen was minimal, outside of Aden itself. In 1970, the republic's name was changed to the People's Democratic Republic of Yemen, or PDRY.

Mutual distrust between the two Yemens characterized the 1970s, and tensions flared into a series of short border wars in 1972, 1978, and 1979. Two presidents of the YAR were assassinated during this period. But under the presidency of Ali Abdullah Salah of the Hashid tribe, in the late 1970s and early 1980s, the stability of the YAR steadily improved. By the end of 1981, a constitution had been drafted to implement a merger between the two states. Attempts to consolidate, however, were delayed by political instability in the PDRY, and it was not until 1990 that the merger was made official.

The new country was named the Republic of Yemen. The border was opened and demilitarized, and currencies were declared valid in both of the former countries. Sanaa took major steps during 1997 to improve control of its borders, territory, and travel documents. It continued to deport foreign nationals residing there illegally, including Islamic extremists identified as posing a security risk to Yemen. The interior ministry issued new, reportedly tamper-resistant passports and began to computerize port-of-entry information. Nonetheless, lax implementation of security measures and poor central government control over remote areas continued to make Yemen an attractive safe haven for terrorists. Moreover, Hamas and the PIJ maintain offices in Yemen. A series of bombings in Aden in July, October, and November 1997 caused material damage but no injuries. No group claimed responsibility. The Yemeni government blamed the attacks on Yemeni opposition elements that had been trained by foreign extremists and supported from abroad possibly from Iran. Yemeni tribesmen kidnapped about forty foreign nationals, including two U.S. citizens, and held them for periods ranging up to one month.

Yemeni government officials frequently asserted that foreign powers instigated some kidnappings, but no corroborating evidence was provided. All were treated well and released unharmed, but one Italian was injured while resisting a kidnap attempt. The motivation for the kidnappings generally appeared to be tribal grievances against the central government. The government did not prosecute any of the kidnappers. At the end of 2007, there was a growing Shiite revolt against the Yemeni government, led by the Believing Youth Movement. Attacks from this group and open fighting with the military were primarily centered in the northern region of the country in the Province of Sanaa. The attacks seem to emanate from a complaint that the government had cancelled a Shiite religious celebration.

Attacks against U.S. targets in the Gulf and surrounding states have been limited; however, the State of Yemen has experienced low levels of terrorism for some time. The al Qaeda attack on the USS *Cole* on October 12, 2000, in the Port of Aden, while on a refueling stop, appears to have been a protest against American presence in the Middle East; it was not directed at any particular aspect of U.S. policy, such as Palestine or Iraq.

The al Qaeda attack in the Port of Aden was the first successful suicide attack on a U.S. Naval craft by terrorists. Eyewitnesses said an inflatable speedboat helping the destroyer moor exploded alongside the ship, opening a twenty-foot by forty-foot hole at the waterline on the left side.

Seventeen American sailors were killed and thirty-nine injured in the seaborne suicide attack. The bomb is believed to have been made with a military grade C-4 plastic explosive, and around 400 pounds or more were used in the attack. The investigation has shown that the attack group in this case contained not only Yemeni but also Muslims from other Middle Eastern countries.

By the end of this first decade, the economy in Yemen was almost at the point of collapse, and the crackdown on al Qaeda in Saudi Arabia, in 2009, encouraged members to move to Yemen and forge alliances with militants in the country. By end of 2009, the al Qaeda migrants had merged to form al Qaeda in the Arabian Peninsula (AQAP). While Yemen remains on the brink of collapse and popular uprisings against the government continue, this allows AQAP to operate with little interference and to establish training facilities and support structures in Yemen. AQAP is hierarchical, compartmentalized, and highly decentralized, allowing it to withstand attacks and arrests and still continue to operate. The group has also mastered new recruitment, propaganda, and media campaigns, including a bimonthly AQAP magazine, *Sada al-Malahim* (the Echo of Battles), which offers theological explanations and praise for jihad fighters, tailored to appeal to its Yemeni audiences.[28] The presence of foreign fighters in Yemen and the proximity of other failed states in the Horn of Africa such as Somalia make Yemen a destination of choice for aspiring jihadists. The AQAP has welcomed the presence of the American-born Yemeni-American cleric **Anwar al-Awlaki**, who gained several degrees at U.S. universities and is said to have provided spiritual guidance to the underwear bomber, Umar Farouk Abdulmutallab, and other suspected terrorists. He was a non-Arabic speaker so naturally was drawn to the writings of the U.S.-educated Anwar al-Awlaki. He later met al-Awlaki in Yemen and was recruited to al Qaeda. Umar Abdulmutallab, when arrested after this failed attempt to detonate a bomb in his underwear on board a Northwest flight over the United States, claimed that he had been given direction to do so by al-Awlaki. A month before the attack in November 2009, Abdulmutallab's father warned the U.S. Embassy in Nigeria that his son might be dangerous, a warning that officials failed to connect to other evidence that intelligence officials had gathered.[29] The bomb was made up of a highly explosive mixture of Pentaerythritol Tetranitrate (**PETN**) and Triacetone Triperoxide (**TATP**). TATP was also used by Richard Reid, the Shoe Bomber, in a similar plot to destroy a commercial airliner.

Al Qaeda and affiliates have long been attracted to aviation as a means to deliver bombs to targets and, on October 29, 2010, came close to delivering several bombs concealed in the holds of cargo aircraft. Two freight packages were seized in separate incidents in the United Arab Emirates and the United Kingdom containing IEDs secreted inside computer printers. In both incidents, the printers had been packed inside freight boxes, which also contained personal goods such as clothing, ornaments, and compact discs. Both boxes had been shipped by commercial carriers from Sana'a, Yemen, with final destinations indicated as Chicago. These two devices were not picked up by existing conventional x-ray devices or bomb detection dogs, and again the bomb was made up of PETN. The attention will now be drawn to the levels of security around cargo aircraft. As neither of these packages exploded, it may have been an attempt to test the overall strength and weakness of applied security measures.

Summary

The War on Terror, the invasion and containment of Iraq, and Iran and its designs on nuclear weapons are all subjects that will keep not just the United States but also the rest of the world focused on this region. Wider implications for the whole of the Middle East range from the proliferation of nuclear weapons to the threat of Islamic uprising in such friendly states as Saudi Arabia and Yemen. With maybe tens of thousands of trained al Qaeda fighters at large, this region of the world continues to remain unstable. Iran's political and military posturing and desire to produce WMD will cause more extreme reaction from the United States, Israel, and Europe. The spread of extreme Islam in Iraq and consequences of its spread will have to be considered. Establishing democracies in parts of the world that have never experienced it may take many years, if ever, to reach fruition. Oil may be the prize that the United States seeks in the

Middle East, and the removal of the United States from Muslim lands is the prize the extremists seek. It will be decades before we can look back at this time frame and determine what worked and what failed on the path to democratization and the successes of the "War on Terror" in this region.

Review Questions

1. Why has al Qaeda been unable to gain a strong foothold in Saudi Arabia?
2. Why did the Saudi monarchy begin to purge the kingdom of al Qaeda supporters?
3. Discuss the support that the Saddam Hussein regime provided to foreign terrorist organizations and why.

4. Compare the methods used by the Shah of Iran to control the populace with those used by the current regime.
5. Yemen is heading for failed-state status. Why has al Qaeda been allowed to insert itself into this region and what implications does it have for the United States?

Websites

1. **CDI Terrorism Project**—*http://www.cdi.org/terrorism/menukes.cfm*
2. **Dudley Knox Library**—*http://www.nps.edu/Library/Research*
3. **Strategic Studies Institute of the U.S. Army War College**—*http://www.strategicstudiesinstitute.army.mil/*

4. **Belfer Center for Science and International Affairs**—*http://belfercenter.ksg.harvard.edu/publication/ 2110/combating_terrorism_in_the_horn_of_africa_and_yemen.html*
5. **United States Institute for Peace**—*http://www.usip.org/center-conflict-analysis-and-prevention/publications-and-tools*

End Notes

1. Most of the background data contained in this chapter were extracted from websites such as the following: The U.S. State Department of State, *Patterns of Global Terror Report*; The U.S. Department of State, *Country Reports on Human Rights Practices*; The U.S. Department of State Background Notes; *Geographic Entities and International Organizations*, http://www.state.gov; *The U.S. Central Intelligence Agency World Factbook*, http://www.cia.gov/and other government sources.
2. Sharon Otterman. *Islam: Governing under Sharia Law*, Council on Foreign Relations. www.cfr.org/publications.
3. *Country studies—Saudi Arabia*. http://countrystudiesus/saudi-arabia/
4. General information on Wahhabism. http://www.mb-soft.com/believe/txo/wahhabis.htm.
5. Austin Cline. *Your Guide to Agnosticism/Atheism*. http://atheism.about.com/od/islamicextremismpeople/a/qutb_p.htm.

6. Terrorism Intelligence Report: Fred Burton and Scott Stewart—al Qaeda in 2008 the Struggle for Relevance—Stratfor.com.
7. *The Kingdom of Saudi Arabia Initiatives and Actions to Combat Terrorism*. (Washington, DC: Royal Embassy of Saudi Arabia Information Office, January 2011), www.saudiembassy.net.
8. U.S. Saudi Collaboration on Counterterrorism: — Office of the Coordinator for Counterterrorism U.S. State Department. http://www.susris.com/articles/2009/ioi/090502-saudi-collaboration.html
9. *Arab Times* (February 15, 2005).
10. *Kuwait Times* (February 20, 2005).
11. *U.S. Department of Defense: Press Briefing* (July 22, 2003).
12. *The Mackenzie Institute Profiles in Terror*—http://www.mackenzieinstitute.com/terrorism/ansar-al-Islam.htm, retrieved June 6, 2011.
13. Federation of American Scientists. www.fas.org.

14. "The enigma of Muqtada al-Sadr." *The Economist* (February 28, 2008).

15. Terrorism Research. http://www.terrorism-research. com/insurgency/.

16. Robert Fisk. "Interview with Saudi Dissident Bin Laden." *Independent* (London, July 10, 1996).

17. *OSC Report—FEA20041227000762* (December 2004).

18. *OSC Report GMP20041216000222* (December 16, 2004).

19. George A. Lopez and David Cortright. "Containing Iraq, Sanctions Worked." George Lopez is Director of Policy Studies at the Joan B. Kroc Institute for International Peace Studies at the University of Notre Dame. David Cortright is president of the Fourth Freedom Forum and research fellow at the Kroc Institute. *Foreign Affairs* (July/August 2004).

20. www.cidcm.umd.edu/mar/chronology (Reuters, March 29, 1997).

21. www.cidcm.umd.edu/mar/chronology (Middle East Review of World Information).

22. www.cidcm.umd.edu/mar/chronology (AFP, March 6, 1997).

23. *Global Security.*—http://www.globalsecurity.org/ military/world/para/mek.htm

24. The Federation of American Scientists. www.fas.org.

25. United States Department of State. Public Affairs Washington, DC (July 1994). http://www.state. publicaffairs.gov.

26. Dr. Babek Ganji. "Iranian Strategy: Factionalism and Leadership." (Defence Academy of the United Kingdom: Conflict Studies Research Centre, March 2007).

27. State Sponsors of Terrorism. http://www.state.gov/s/ ct/rls/crt/2009/140889.htm

28. Julie Cohn. "Islamist Radicalism in Yemen Council on Foreign Relations." (June 29, 2010). http:// www.cfr.org/yemen/islamist-radicalism-yemen/ p9369Updated

29. "Abdulmutallab: Cleric Told Me to Bomb Jet." *CBS News* (February 2010). http://www.cbsnews.com/ stories/2010/02/04/national/main6174780.shtml

10

Northeast, Central, and Southern Africa

Germany is the place where when Hitler was the prime minister and supreme commander, he burned over six million Jews. This is because Hitler and all German people knew that Israelis are not people who are working in the interest of the world and that is why they burned the Israelis alive with gas in the soil of Germany.

—IDI AMIN, PRESIDENT OF UGANDA (TELEGRAM TO KURT WALDHEIM, UN SECRETARY-GENERAL, AND GOLDA MEIR, ISRAELI PRIME MINISTER, ON SEPTEMBER 12, 1972)

LEARNING OBJECTIVES

After studying this chapter, the student should be able to:

1. Examine and discuss how failed states such as Somalia have led to an uptick in piracy in the Indian Ocean.
2. Understand that tribalism plays a major role in dictatorships that prey on their countrymen.
3. Discuss how the effects of colonialism have led to a modern genocide in Rwanda.
4. Discuss how al Qaeda-affiliated groups have operated in Africa and been able to attack "soft" targets.
5. Appreciate what little effect the UN can have in preventing genocide from taking place.

KEY WORDS TO NOTE

Al Shabaab—Islamic militant group based in Somalia seeking to create an Islamic caliphate in the region

Apartheid—A government policy of strict racial segregation once practiced in South Africa

Boko Haram—Nigeria-based Islamist terror group demanding imposition of Islamic Law throughout the region

BOSS—South African state security apparatus first established by John Vorster in 1966 and set up to protect national security interests

Front for the Liberation of Angola (FNLA)—Guerilla organization that fought for independence from Portugal and became a political party in 1991

Front for the Liberation of Mozambique (FRELIMO)—Founded in 1962 as a liberation movement that fought for independence from Portugal

Mau Mau—A militant African nationalist movement active in Kenya during the 1950s whose main aim was to remove British rule and European settlers from the country

MEND—Movement for the Emancipation of the Niger Delta, fighting against perceived government corruption and for control of the oil-rich Niger delta

Ogaden National Liberation Front (ONLF)—Separatist group fighting for an independent state in the Ogaden region

The Bakassi Boys—A violent vigilante group that operates with almost impunity as supposed anticrime vigilantes

Unilateral Declaration of Independence (UDI)—A proclamation of independence for a newly formed country or state, in this case declared by the white minority in Rhodesia in 1965

OVERVIEW

This chapter introduces a different source of terrorism—one that evolves over time and turns a state against its ethnic, religious, and historic tribal enemies. Despotic leaders in the northeast, central, and southern regions of Africa have utilized measures they saw fit including genocide. We delve into the rise and fall of some of the vilest rulers and the terror methods they employed— for example, the despicable, modern-day tactician, Field Marshall and President for Life, Uganda's Idi Amin Dada. We shall also examine the historical roots of African terrorism and its progression to modern times, in places like Mozambique, Zimbabwe, the Republic of Congo, and South Africa. Each country has its own significant and unique history.

ETHIOPIA

Ethiopia has undergone dramatic changes since the 1974 overthrow of Emperor Haile Selassie, "The Lion of Africa." In 1935, Ethiopia became the object of Italian colonialism, and the Emperor fled the country to live in exile in England. During World War II, the British, with the help of the Ethiopians, evicted the Italians from the country and returned Emperor Haile Selassie to the throne.

Eritrea is a region of Ethiopia that lies to the north, along the Red Sea coast, which had been under Italian control and influence since the 1880s. The Ethiopian government took control of Eritrea in 1961, and ever since has been fighting an unending battle with Eritrean Nationalists seeking independence. Extremely poor living conditions, coupled with resentment of the Selassie regime's autocratic methods and corrupt government, resulted in a military coup led by Lt. Colonel Mengistu Haile-Mariam in 1974. By 1977, he was the preeminent military ruler, seeking aid from the Soviet Union to establish a socialist People's Republic and was at first successful at fighting off incursions from Somali and Eritrean rebels. After he was elected to the presidency in 1987, Soviet aid along with the economy began to diminish. He abandoned socialism, and unable to mobilize the military resistance, he fled south to Zimbabwe. Trouble also flared up in the south of the country in the Ogaden, which was disputed territory with neighboring Somalia. Many of the

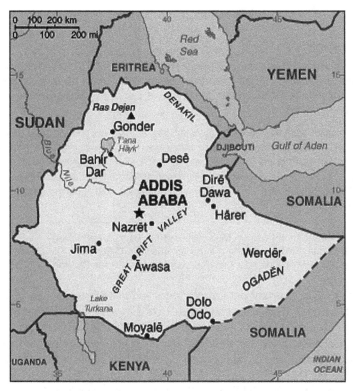

FIGURE 10-1   Map of Ethiopia (Central Intelligence Agency, *The World Factbook, 2008*).

inhabitants are Somalis, and the resulting invasion of the region by Somalia's military in 1977 has been an ongoing and festering sore between the two nations.

By the end of the 1980s, the military rulers were turning toward elected civil government, under a new constitution. Although elections were held, the military leadership continued to control the country. On May 28, 1991, the Ethiopian People's Revolutionary Democratic Front (EPRDF) toppled the authoritarian government of Mengistu Haile-Mariam and took control in Addis Ababa.

A new constitution was promulgated in December 1994, and national and regional elections were held in May and June 1995. The main issue facing Ethiopia at the end of the decade was rebuilding the crumbling infrastructure of the country following years of civil war.

Ethiopia and Somalia still continue to squabble over the Ogaden region in the southern half of the country. The country is also a staging post for the transshipment of illicit drugs from Asia destined for Europe and North America and cocaine for the markets of South Africa.

The disputed Ogaden has seen the rise to prominence of the **Ogaden National Liberation Front (ONLF)**. The group is a nationalist movement formed as far back as 1984 and seeks self-determination for the ethnic Somalis that inhabit this region. The ONLF formed in the wake of the Western Somali Liberation Front (WSLF), which lost the support of Somalis living in Ogaden after the 1977–1978 war in which Ethiopia crushed Somali government forces attempting to gain control of areas with large ethnic Somali populations. They had not been of particular concern to the Ethiopian government until the regime's military invasion of Somalia in 2006, which targeted the Somali Supreme Islamic Courts Council (SICC), which aspired to create a Greater Somalia in the disputed Ogaden. There was obvious collaboration between the SICC and members of the ONLF.

TERRORIST ATTACK BRIEF

Terrorist Group: Islamic Group (Egypt)

Case Facts: Eleven terrorists planned to assassinate Hosni Mubarak—the group was divided in two teams and were provided safe haven in Sudan—nine went to Addis Ababa for the operation and two remained in Khartoum to organize the plot. The plot was uncovered and disrupted by Ethiopian security forces killing five and capturing three of the terrorists.

Investigation: Weapons were flown in to the operation on a Sudan Airways commercial airliner. Passports had been prepared in Khartoum, and implications were drawn that the Sudanese government was involved in supporting the plot—one of the terrorists escaped back to Sudan and joined the other two who had remained behind. Sudan would not confirm or deny their presence and without admitting complicity in the plot dismissed its interior minister, and when extradition was requested of the three suspects by Ethiopia, the request was denied.

FIGURE 10-2   Assassination plot—Hosni Mubarak—Former Egyptian president—Addis Ababa—June 1995 *Source:* Ted Dagne. "Africa and the War on Terrorism." *CRS Report to Congress* (January 2002), Specialist in International Relations, Foreign Affairs, Defense and Trade Division

Since that invasion, ONLF has come out and attacked government forces and foreign oil installations. The government responses to ONLF activity have been broad sweeps by its counterinsurgency troops and centering on villages that have supplied support to ONLF. The Ethiopian approach has seen its troops acting indiscriminately and has come under public pressure for its human rights abuses from the International Red Cross. Faced with mounting pressure to control the insurgency and to protect the oil resources in the Ogaden region, the Addis Ababa regime of Prime Minister Meles Zenawi must do all it can to destroy the ONLF. While the ONLF remains purely nationalist, there will only be concern for the U.S. interests should they become infiltrated or aligned with al Qaeda. In Somalia, Ethiopian soldiers ensure the security of a secular government led by Abdullahi Yusuf, who would be unlikely to survive the onslaught from SICC and Islamist fighters. Ethiopia's fate and that of Somalia lay in the hands of dictators attempting to destroy an Islamist surge in the Horn of Africa.

SOMALIA

Ongoing interclan feuding and a weakened military from the fighting in Ethiopia had left Somalia in desperate straits. In 1969, the clans within Somalia felt that the distribution of wealth only resulted in benefits to very few people. The control of the beleaguered country reverted to military rule, under the banner of the Somali Revolutionary Socialist Party, led by Major General Said Barre. The entire economy, that is, banks, schools, and land, came under the direct control of the military government. This action coincided with one of the major famines of the twentieth century, and the ruling party did essentially nothing to aid the sick, starving, and dying.

Resistance and uprisings finally came with the formation of the United Somali Congress (USC), which ousted Said Barre on January 27, 1991. Since then, the country has deteriorated even further, with no functioning government, anarchy, and interclan fighting and banditry. This situation left one of the poorest countries in Africa to stumble around blindly with no functioning administration, as the various clans vied for power, until the transitional government of Ali Khalif Galaid was voted into power in 2000... and just as quickly voted out by a no-confidence vote a year later. The interim government was recognized by the United Nations but was not held in high esteem by the Somali people. Somalia is all about turf wars, and the possibility of any leader being able to bring the floundering country out of the Middle Ages seems remote.

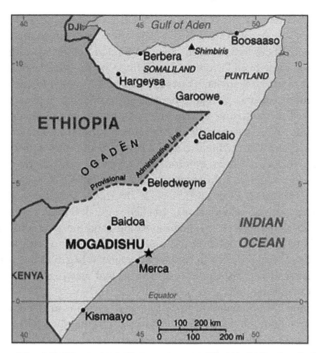

FIGURE 10-3   Map of Somalia (Central Intelligence Agency, *The World Factbook, 2008*).

After U.S. military intervention in Afghanistan, speculation was that its next target would be Somalia as it seemed to fit the bill of a lawless state that draws terrorists like a magnet. Sudan and Somalia remain the only regional countries not allied to the United States. Friendly relations with Kenya, Tanzania, Ethiopia, and Eritrea seem secure, despite some recent conflicts.

Since the U.S. missile strikes on Sudan—after the two U.S. embassy bombings (which resulted in Osama bin Laden being deported), and especially since 9-11, Africa's largest state has been attempting to shed its image as a "sponsor of terrorism," and thus cut back the U.S. support for the southern rebels. The defining moment in relations between the two countries occurred in 1993 with the slaughter of eighteen American Marines and the deaths of hundreds of Somalis in the capital of Mogadishu. The Clinton administration subsequently evacuated and withdrew all U.S. forces from Somalia. This was portrayed as Somali rejection of a peacekeeping mission but, in fact, the deaths were a direct result of a seventh botched attempt to capture the notorious warlord Mohammed Aideed. Aideed was killed several years later by a clan member. However, the hand of bin Laden was also at work as he had issued a "fatwa," calling for Muslims to attack the "soldiers of occupation." The United States has continued to strike at Somalia as it is viewed as a failed state, and this makes the country a refuge for al Qaeda militants. In May 2008, Aden Hashi Ayro, al Qaeda's commander in Somalia, was killed in a U.S. air strike. Ayro had trained in al Qaeda training camps in Afghanistan and was leader of the Islamist group al-Shabaab.

Al-Shabaab (aka Harakat Al-Shabaab al-Mujahidin, the Youth, Mujahidin al-Shabaab Movement, Mujahideen Youth Movement)

Originally the militant wing of the Islamic Courts Union, the group that controlled Somalia prior to the country's invasion by Ethiopian forces, al-Shabaab leaders have claimed affiliation with al Qaeda since 2007. Al-Shabaab is led by "Abu Zubeyr," Sheikh Mohamed Mukhtar Abdirahman.

Formed from clan members of the Hawiye clan, the organization consists of several thousand fighters. How closely aligned it is with al Qaeda is unknown even though they have pledged allegience to al Qaeda. There have been instances of foreign fighters operating with al-Shabaab, including several who came from Europe and the United States. While al Shabaab has controlled much of central and southern Somalia, it does not control the capital Mogadishu, and control of the capital Mogadishu is seen as pivotal to both al-Shabaab and Somalia's Transitional Federal Government (TFG). If the government were to lose control, then the jihadist movement would become de facto rulers of a large swathe of central and southern Somalia. The jihadists have used the conventional terrorist methods to attack government forces with IED and hit-and-run terrorist ambushes. To succeed in an environment where no central government has been in control for two decades requires a different approach. In 2008, al-Shabaab began to reach out to the Somali public with a series of town visits. A December 2008 International Crisis Group report describes these outings as "well choreographed, with clerics addressing public rallies and holding talks with local clan elders." Al-Shabaab would hand out food and money to the poor, give criminals quick trials with "mobile sharia courts," and attempt to settle local disputes. As the group sought to take control of towns in southern Somalia, it began to use political strategies as well. Before a particular town was captured, insurgents had meetings with local clan leaders to convince them that their intentions were good.[1]

Ethiopia has long been Somalia's primary rival in the region, and its foreign policy is aimed at keeping Somalia weak and divided. Ethiopia had been urging the United States to extend its War on Terror to Somalia since 9-11. Ethiopia invaded Somalia in 1996 and 1999 (capturing or killing hundreds of Somalis) and supported antigovernment rebels such as the Rahanwein Resistance Army. In August 2000, a peace conference resulted in the closest thing that Somalia has had to a broad-based national government. However, Ethiopia, it seems, is actively trying to destabilize its neighbor. Somalia nevertheless continues to function and has established clans and subclans with considerable inter- and subclan rivalry. Warlords still control various sections of the country, which is one reason why al-Shabaab may be acceptable with lack of any other central government control. One may have expected that after the removal of the Taliban government from Afghanistan, Somalia would become a prime location for terrorist training camps, and although it had been identified as being involved in the U.S. embassy bombings in Kenya, it does not currently appear to be the "problem state" it most surely aspired to be. However, Somalia has been home to a key player for al Qaeda and one of the United States's Most Wanted Terrorists, Fazul Abdullah Mohammed; he was al Qaeda's longest-serving and highest-ranking operative in East Africa and was killed in a shootout with Somali forces at a checkpoint near Mogadishu on June 7, 2011. Mohammed was the mastermind of the 1998 bombings of two U.S. embassies in Nairobi and Dar es Salam; he was also responsible for aligning al-Shabaab with al Qaeda and coordinating with the al Qaeda in Yemen (AQAP). His death came at a difficult time for al Qaeda, following the death of Osama bin Laden in May 2011, and replacing Mohammed with someone with his level of experience will be difficult. Following the death of Osama bin Laden, the Shabaab movement pledged its support to the new leader of al Qaeda, Ayman al-Zawahiri, in June 2011.

Somalia's location on the Indian Ocean gives it an easy launching platform to the Saudi peninsula. Somalia has a vast coastline, ideal for facilitating the movement of terrorists to operational hot spots in the Persian Gulf. Though mainly a Muslim nation, much of what transpires in that country is not due to religious infighting but interclan differences. The United States also declared the Somali Islamic Movement, al-Ittihad, a terrorist organization. Al-Ittihad emerged in 1991 as one of numerous warring militias; its aim was the establishment of an Islamic state. However, its military operations ended in defeat by invading Ethiopian troops in 1997.

Since then, al-Ittihad has become Somalia's leading provider of education and judicial, health, and welfare services—all scarce and badly needed in a country experiencing an extensive drought in the south and facing severe food shortages elsewhere. The Somali government and the United Nations deny that al-Ittihad undertakes terrorist operations or has any links with al Qaeda.

Recognizing the regional gains made by the United States in its battles in Iraq and Afghanistan, it is not difficult to draw parallels to Somalia, and to understand the deep-rooted fear and suspicion in the Arab and Muslim worlds that behind the "War on Terror" is a strategy aimed at attaining regional dominance and compliant allies, regardless of consequences. The Somalis are basically mistrusting of the tribal politics that disrupt their country. The last government set a course to appease the warlords by offering olive branches in the form of cabinet posts. Some 15,000 militiamen were given positions as police officers. This has cost the government most of its treasury, and it still dares not deploy the new policemen throughout Mogadishu for fear they will return to the ways of their former warlord masters.[2]

The tracking of funds linked to terrorism has identified close ties between Sheikh Ahmed Nur Jimale, the founder of a financial and telecommunications conglomerate, and Osama bin Laden. The company founded in 1989 is involved in wire transfer services, telecoms, currency exchange, and Internet services. The company is believed to operate over 127 offices outside Somalia and sixty within the country.[3]

The TFG is now led by Abdullahi Yusuf Ahmed, who was sworn into office in Kenya in October 2004. The integration of the al-Ittihad members into the social infrastructure, whether as teachers or preachers, means that they may be more difficult to monitor. There is no reason to suppose that they are not quite capable of reorganizing when the time suits them. Somalia is traditionally Sunni Muslim and Islamic extremism is increasing rapidly. The country comprises two dominant clans and the Hawiye clan that gave rise to the SICC and went underground following the invasion and occupation by Ethiopian troops in late 2006. While the SICC remains underground, its two mouth pieces—Sheikh Sharif Ahmed, who at one time was leader of the now-defunct Ittihad, and Sheikh Hassan Dahir Aweys, who leads the SICC's militant wing—have made noises to Ethiopia that they would consider brokering a peace deal. The likelihood that the Hawiye would actually agree to guarantee the security of the existing government is highly questionable. The Hawiye clan wants Ethiopian troops out of the region, who currently take some of the brunt of the attacks in the Somali capital Mogadishu from warring clans on the one hand and Somali and Islamist fighters on the other.

A peace deal in Mogadishu could also impact maritime shipping along the Somali coastline, an area that has seen a rapid increase in pirate activity. Practically no pirate attacks occurred under SICC control in the second half of 2006. Piracy is a means of generating income and not, in this instance, a case of terrorism. Ethiopian forces have cleaned up the SICC in Mogadishu; none of the leadership has been killed or captured but have likely escaped or gone underground. In support of the regime, the United States launched air strikes against SICC strongholds in the southern Somali town of Dobley on March 3, 2008, and intended to target the SICC leadership. The presence of Islamic fighters in this region has continued to build, and as African oil becomes a more precious commodity, we will continue to see U.S. support against Islamist insurgencies, particularly in this region where there is significant oil exploration.

While clan infighting will likely continue with an uncertain outcome for both Somalia and Ethiopia, the religious factor and the aims of the SICC are at odds with most Somalis. The SICC proclaims to want to unite all Muslims; however, Somalis, comprising mainly Sunni Muslims, do not subscribe to the strict Wahhabi and Islamist interpretations of Islam, and many are concerned about the strict applications of Sharia Law.

PIRACY—A SOMALI ISSUE

Attacks on maritime targets have continued with numerous attacks taking place far out into the Indian Ocean and all originating from the coast of Somalia. The pirates have become more sophisticated with every countermeasure that is placed against them. Initially they operated in coastal waters in fast dhows and then from large vessels farther out at sea and have now taken to using hijacked vessels as their mother ships knowing full well that the naval forces will not fire on them if they have hostages on board, which they invariably do. The Rules of Engagement for those navies operating to protect merchant shipping prohibit them from firing on ships known to have hostages on board. By the end of 2010, the Somali pirates were using at least five merchant ships as pirate support vessels to launch attacks on shipping hundreds of miles from the East African coast. By the spring of 2011, estimates of the number of merchant seamen held hostage was more than 700. The threat to shipping and trade for Europe and Africa is at issue, and so far the pirates have the upper hand with the world's navies seemingly incapable of stopping the assault on merchant vessels.

UGANDA

Located in Central East Africa and bordering on Lake Victoria in the south, Uganda, as we know it today, went through a long and turbulent period in its history. Uganda gained its independence from Britain in 1962 and elected Milton Obote to be its first prime minister. In 1966, he was responsible for reordering the Constitution and replacing it with exclusive powers for the

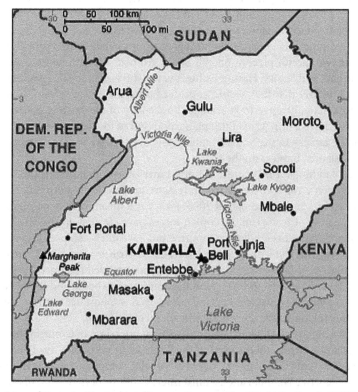

FIGURE 10-4   Map of Uganda (Central Intelligence Agency, *The World Factbook, 2008*).

executive leadership. It was no surprise when the following year he declared himself president and Edward Mutesa, the country's first president, fled into exile in England. Obote placed most of Uganda under emergency laws and severely restricted the powers of the traditional tribes of Uganda's five tribal areas. Obote had extreme socialist views and was not popular with his people, and while at the Commonwealth Heads of State meeting in Singapore in 1971, his Army Chief Idi Amin led a coup against the government. Idi Amin Dada remained in power until 1979.

For Ugandans, the 1970s were horrific—a time when Uganda's self-proclaimed "President for Life," might well have coined the modern phrase "ethnic cleansing." The sheer scope of the terrorism against the Ugandan people during the very dark days from 1972 to 1979 is almost inconceivable. His praise of the work carried out by Adolph Hitler to exterminate the Jews, and his open hostility and demands for the destruction of Israel, spewed from the mind of this deranged psychopath! To try and understand any ideology that Amin may have had is incredibly difficult. He was extremely temperamental and prone to sudden changes of mind and irrational behavior.

What is not in question is the length he went to purge Uganda of any and all opponents, both political and social. His first move was to cleanse the country of any foreign influence and return Uganda and its wealth to the native Ugandans (primarily to himself). The son of a witch doctor, Amin's appetite for wealth knew no boundaries or the incredible lengths he would go to get it. Obote made him responsible for military control of the northern region of Uganda.[4] To achieve his wealth, he engaged in smuggling and murder or, to put it the old-fashioned way, "rape, plunder, and pillage."

Amin created a bureaucracy of state-sponsored terrorism to administer terror to Ugandans. He established two secret state police organizations, the Public Safety Unit and the Bureau of State Research. The Public Safety Unit was empowered to shoot to kill anyone—on just mere suspicion. The Bureau of State Research carried out interrogations and torture, usually also resulting in the death of any hapless prisoner. The actual number of Ugandan citizens killed during Amin's reign has never been accurately documented or accounted for, but it is believed to be as many as 500,000.

As is too often the case in the African continent, tribal rivalries and old hatreds play a large part in the business of selective "genocide." Under Amin (a member of the Lugbara tribe), Uganda set in motion the calculated elimination of all the Lugbaras' historical tribal enemies, especially the *Acholi* and *Langi* tribes. Handpicked secret police and vicious interrogation units from Amin's native *Lugbara* tribe were the implementers of this state-sponsored genocide.

On many occasions, Amin would observe or indulge in torture and other bizarre excesses personally. His presidential palace was linked by a series of tunnels connecting it to the Bureau of State Research in an adjoining building in the capital city of Kampala. He surrounded himself with a team of specially trained Palestinian bodyguards. When it came to executions, one of the methods employed was to provide a hammer to one prisoner who was then commanded, at gunpoint, to smash the skull of the prisoner next to him. This process of execution was then continued until the last prisoner was dispatched with a gunshot. The bodies of many executed prisoners were returned, in badly mutilated condition, to their families or dumped in rivers or in forests. Among other suspected atrocity practiced by Amin and his tribesmen was cannibalism. Killings by the army, where Amin's tribesmen were engaged in a systematic massacre of *Acholi* and *Langi* tribesmen, were the first signs to a watching public of the madness to follow. The expulsion of the Israelis, in 1972, was ultimately a result of their refusal to supply arms to Amin. The Asian exodus was one of the most significant events in Uganda's history. The reason for the expulsion is not clear; certainly Amin was under significant internal pressure to "deliver the goods" of postliberation euphoria and expectation, not just from the civilian population but also from his army. Uganda is only now beginning to heal, after over a third of a century.

Airline Hijacking to Entebbe

The 1970s saw an unprecedented number of airliner hijackings. One of the most notable was the hijacking of an Air France flight en route from Tel Aviv to Paris with 250 passengers and crew. The hijackers consisted of both German and Arab members of the Popular Front for the Liberation of Palestine. The aircraft flew first to Benghazi, Libya, then to Entebbe, Uganda. After negotiations began, the hijackers released 146 hostages but held onto the remaining 106 mainly Jewish passengers. They demanded the release of a large number of Arab terrorists being held in both Israeli and European prisons. As the negotiations dragged on it was clear to Israeli authorities that the Ugandan leader Idi Amin was helping the hijackers. The Israeli government quickly created a plan to rescue the hostages in Operation Jonathan. A force of Israeli commandos in three Hercules aircraft landed at Entebbe, much to the surprise of the hijackers and the Ugandan troops. The Israelis stormed the airport building killing seven of the eight hijackers as well as destroying Ugandan MIG aircraft on the ground. Three hostages were killed in the hour-long operation as well as the leader of the assault team Lt. Col Jonathan Netanyahu. One hostage, an elderly English woman, Dora Block, who had previously been taken to a local hospital suffering from the effects of the hijacking was subsequently murdered by the Ugandans as a reprisal for the attack on Entebbe.

Asians and the British owned and controlled over half of Uganda's wealth, and expelling them was Amin's shortcut to achieving what was expected. In addition, Amin bore some motives for revenge on the British and wanted to teach them a lesson they would never forget. According to Amin, the reason for expelling the Asians was revealed to him in a dream, wherein God decreed that if he didn't do it, the country would be ruined. In 1978, Amin invaded Northern Tanzania in an effort to boost failing morale and wipe out more enemies. The retaliation was supported by expelled Ugandan troops, including the Front for National Salvation (FRONASA), which was led by Yoweri Kaguta Museveni. Museveni had been active since his student days at Ntare School, Mbarara; he studied political science and economics at the University of Dar es Salaam, graduating in 1970 with a Bachelor of Arts. The advance on Kampala was swift against the demoralized, though heavily armed, troops of Amin. The Tanzanian and Ugandan liberators arrived in Kampala in April 1979 under the banner of the Uganda National Liberation Army (UNLA). After a short period of indecision, the Uganda National Liberation Front (UNLF) was formed from an amalgam of several Ugandan political and military groups. Not for the first time in Uganda's history, the people had united against a common enemy.

Milton Obote, who had then returned from exile, would contest elections as leader of the Ugandan Political Coalition (UPC). A third major political party emerged to do battle with the Democratic Party (DP) and UPC. It was the Uganda Patriotic Movement (UPM) and, once more, Yoweri Museveni was prominent in Ugandan affairs. Milton Obote won the disputed election and was sworn in as president for his second term in 1980. Obote's army, under Major General Tito Okello, returned him to power, anxious for revenge on those who supported Amin in 1979.

Dissatisfied with the election results, Yoweri Museveni and twenty-six young men retreated into the Luwero Triangle and started what was to be a long campaign of guerrilla warfare. The National Resistance Army (NRA) was formed under the banner of the National Resistance Movement (NRM). The turning point in the long bush war was the death of the UNLA commander, Oyite-Ojok, who was Obote's cousin. Ojok was a powerful figure, and his death demoralized Obote's troops and caused a power struggle within the *Langi* and *Acholi* army factions. Obote's men rioted in the cities and towns, frustrated at the lack of success against the NRA. Obote consistently resisted appeals to negotiate with the NRA; he gradually alienated the *Acholi*, who felt they were fighting alone against the NRA. This up-swell finally led to Obote being removed from power in 1985; he was granted political asylum in Zambia and died in exile in 2005.

The constitution was suspended, parliament dissolved, and Major General Tito Okello was sworn in as president in July 1985, but violence and lawlessness remained. Gradually, the NRA gained more support and more control in crucial areas. Museveni and Okello met in Kenya and signed peace agreements for a new, equally represented government. Within a month of the agreement, the war intensified and the NRA moved closer to Kampala. Then, on January 26, 1986, the NRA forces overran Kampala.

Yoweri Museveni was sworn in as president of Uganda on January 29, 1986, and announced that his takeover represented a fundamental change in the affairs of Uganda and not a "mere change of guards." He proclaimed a ten-point program wherein NRM would "usher in a new and better future for the people of Uganda." The ten points included issues ignored or maligned by the previous seven presidents, such as democracy, security, and elimination of corruption. To mixed reactions, a large, broad-based cabinet was appointed with friend and foe alike. In an effort to unite every corner of Uganda under one government, Museveni included representatives of previously antagonistic political parties, tribal groups, and religious factions in the government of the day.

Museveni extended personal invitations to exiled Ugandans, offering key government advisory or corporate positions. A significant brain drain had taken place during the war years and Museveni was anxious that these individuals help rebuild a fragmented and broken country. When the NRA arrived in Kampala, it encountered no serious resistance. The victorious soldiers were disciplined and friendly; this army was within the law, not above it.

The task that lay ahead in 1986 was immense. The violent policies of a whirlwind of governments had left Ugandans without belief in their leaders. National pride and identity were essential to rebuild the battered country. One of Museveni's most painful and arduous tasks was to convince the people that a democracy would emerge from a military takeover. The country was in a mess, and only a slow, systematic, and transparent examination of the damage might set wrongs to right again. The NRA reestablished law and order everywhere in Uganda, except for the north and northeast, which had remained bastions of discontent and insecurity. The sporadic lawlessness in the north has been a constant problem to the NRA, and until a national identity emerges, the issue will remain.

Uganda's infrastructure, including its judicial system, the constitution, road construction, agriculture, health care, education, and tourism, had broken down and a system of locally elected government officials was put in place. Every Ugandan is a member of at least one legislative body that gives him or her voice in everyday affairs. This was to be the primary foundation on which a new national identity would be built. The personification of Uganda's malaise has been the magnitude of the AIDS crisis. Uganda was one of the first countries in Africa to recognize and begin to deal with this disease. The results have been very positive—education and awareness have been the key areas targeted.

Although Yoweri Museveni is a man with strong opinions and a keen sense of right and wrong, the reality of the chaotic situation he found in Uganda when he took power in 1986 meant that he had to accommodate people with views and attitudes that sometimes ran directly counter to his own.

In August 2002, humanitarian agencies and Ugandan authorities were working out an emergency plan following a Lord's Resistance Army (LRA) attack on a refugee camp in northern Uganda, which forced thousands of Sudanese refugees to flee into the bush. The office of the UN High Commissioner for Refugees (UNHCR) said plans were in hand to move at least 24,000 Sudanese refugees who had fled from the camp to a safer location, following an LRA attack on the Acholi-Pii refugee settlement in Pader District. UNHCR's information officer for Uganda reported that Ugandan authorities had, at an emergency meeting between humanitarian agencies and senior government officials, agreed to relocate the refugees to a safer location yet to be agreed upon, preferably in Yumbe, Hoima, or Nebii districts, all in western Uganda.

The International Rescue Committee (IRC) for Uganda said it was also planning a response, which would involve transporting food to Rachkoko from neighboring Kitgum District. This was the second LRA attack in a week on the Acholi Pii Camp. The LRA group had first attacked the camp on July 31, 2002, but government soldiers repulsed the attackers, UNHCR said. Earlier, on July 8, LRA fighters had attacked the Maaji refugee settlement, in nearby Adjumani District, killing six refugees and putting another 8,000 into flight. The number of casualties incurred in the first attack remains unclear. Major Shaban Bantariza, the Ugandan army spokesman, told the BBC that about 200 LRA fighters had killed four soldiers and eight civilians, losing eleven of their own in the process. The magnitude of the attack was an indication that the Ugandan government was no longer able to guarantee security in northern Uganda, where humanitarian assistance was becoming increasingly dangerous as a result. The IRC had earlier withdrawn most of its staff from the camp, following the first attack, but redeployed them there after receiving assurances from the Ugandan authorities guaranteeing their security. Since June 2001, the LRA has intensified attacks on northern Ugandan districts in response to the pressure exerted on it in southern Sudan. About 500,000 displaced Ugandans and some 155,000 Sudanese refugees live in camps in northern Uganda, according to the refugee agency.

THE LORD'S RESISTANCE ARMY

The Lord's Resistance Army (LRA) is one of the most ferocious organizations to have emerged in central Africa, yet few Westerners have ever heard of it, since nearly all its violence is perpetrated in the border region between Uganda and Sudan in East Africa.

On a continent plagued with guerrilla warfare, where war crimes are standard fighting fare, the LRA stands apart as an especially odious group. LRA crimes against humanity are so repulsive that its only former ally, the Islamic government of Sudan, jettisoned its relationship with the LRA to improve Sudan's international relations. What began in 1986 as a rebellion against the Ugandan government has metamorphosed into a military millenarian cult. Its reason for existence is to perpetuate the power of its leader, a ruthless witchcraft practitioner named Joseph Kony.[5] The LRA under Kony had a fearsome reputation for its brutality against the people of Northern Uganda, and it is believed the group has managed to abduct and indoctrinate over 20,000 children into its ranks since it was first established in 1987.[6]

Since Museveni came to power in 1989, one of his most significant challenges has come from the Lord's Resistance Army. The LRA has been led since its inception by Joseph Kony Joseph a member of the northern Acholi tribe; Kony was born in 1961 in the village of Odek in northern Uganda. He derived his original power base through his aunt who was the tribal mystic. The first movement in the development of the LRA was called the Holy Spirit Movement with the ideal of overthrowing the government in Kampala in retaliation for the collective violence meted out to the Acholi tribes. Kony had served in the Ugandan Peoples Democratic Army (UPDA) and described himself as a self-styled Prophet sent to save and avenge the Acholi. When the UPDA signed an accord with the Ugandan government in 1988, Kony refused to agree and splintered away with some other disgruntled troops. From this point in 1988, he established the LRA. With his military background and religious zeal, he created the Uganda Christian Democratic Army and began targeting the government. In 1991, he changed the name of the group to the Lord's Resistance Army.

One of the more unsavory factors about the LRA is its propensity to forcibly recruit child soldiers as young as age twelve to either carry out attacks or be used as sex slaves. Human rights groups believe the LRA's ranks consist of 85 percent child soldiers. A large percentage of the children are kidnapped and forced to commit atrocities against their own families, and young girls are held as sex slaves and "wives" for local commanders. Recent attempts by the government to eradicate the LRA have included well-organized operations centered in southern Sudan, with the approval of the Sudanese government. However, there are claims that both sides have used extrajudicial methods to suit their needs. Ugandan People's Defense Forces (UPDF) is also reportedly using and abusing children. The operation inside Sudan, code named "Iron Fist," has displaced more than 1.2 million inhabitants from northern Uganda and seen over 60,000 children being used as soldiers. The phenomenon of "night commuters" has also emerged—an estimated 20,000 children flee their homes each night in fear, seeking refuge from possible abduction by the LRA, and searching for places to sleep in churches and hospitals.[7] Uganda has deployed approximately 8,000 of its troops in the Democratic Republic of Congo (DRC). Again, this is a consequence of the rich reserves of timber and diamonds. A form of trade was developed in the border regions, with shipments transferred through Uganda under the control of the Ugandan military. There is no vested interest for the Ugandans to see any cease-fire or peace within the DRC. Much of the spoils in this conflict originate in the northern city of Kisangani. The LRA was funded and supplied by the government in Khartoum, and the Ugandan government was sponsoring attacks by the Sudan People's Liberation Army (SPLM); but since 2005, SPLM has been playing an official role in government, so the source of financial and material aid has dried up.

Museveni invited the International Criminal Court (ICC) to indict the LRA's leaders for war crimes, arguing that his country's own justice system was unable to deal with cases of such legal magnitude.[8] The warrants against Kony, Vincent Otti, Raska Lukwiya, Okot Odhiambo, and Dominic Ongwen were historic, since they were the first issued by the fledgling ICC, which began work in 2002. Lukwiya was killed in August 2006 during a fight between the LRA and Ugandan military forces. The LRA has suffered from regional political influences as it was often used as a pawn, particularly in the conflict between Sudan and Uganda. However, Sudan is more concerned with settling its grievances with Uganda rather than putting down the LRA. In 2008, with Sudanese and troops from the Congo launched a joint operation, but with feuding and mistrust among the so-called allies, the operation named "Lightning Thunder" foundered. Although the campaign had some short-term successes, they never got near to capturing Kony and his lieutenants. The United States has for several years been training the Ugandan Special Forces; however, this will come to naught if the military is ill-supplied and poorly equipped for a counterinsurgency campaign that requires coordination and long-term commitment. Uganda would possibly need support from European nations and/or the United States to gain an upper hand on Kony and his gang; however, with so many other regional conflicts and uprisings taking place, it's hard to envisage any support coming to this area of central Africa.

ZIMBABWE

Many Black African states were looking to shed the yoke of the British Empire in the 1960s and 1970s. White rule in Rhodesia, under Ian Smith, ended in 1980, when the country gained its independence and Robert Mugabe became the country's first prime minister. However, Mugabe and his government faced violent opposition mainly from the region of Matabeleland. Mugabe's ruling party, the Zimbabwe African National Union (ZANU), was also strongly opposed by the Zimbabwe People's Revolutionary Army (ZIPRA) and the Zimbabwe African People's Union (ZANPU).

FIGURE 10-5 Map of Zimbabwe (Central Intelligence Agency, *The World Factbook, 2008*).

Mugabe used what can easily be termed *state terror* on the peoples of Matabeleland to ensure his own position in Zimbabwe. To do this he used the Zimbabwe Army Fifth Brigade as a vehicle to control, repress, torture, interrogate, and execute all armed opponents in Matabeleland.

UNILATERAL DECLARATION OF INDEPENDENCE (UDI)

November 11, 1965, is the date Ian Smith declared a **Unilateral Declaration of Independence (UDI)** for Rhodesia. If one were to look to the north about the same time, as scenes were being played out in the name of independence, the view was far from gratifying. Millions were dead in Nigeria and the Congo, more than 500,000 in the Sudan, and over 200,000 in Rwanda and Burundi. In nearly all instances, it was black man killing black man, and the countries were in the hands of blood-crazed dictators.[9]

Unfortunately for the rebel government of Ian Smith, the rest of the world, including Britain and the United Nations, would not recognize the new breakaway state and instead enforced strong economic sanctions on the country. In the years preceding the UDI, most forms of terrorism and violent criminal actions were well under the control of the authorities. In that era, when there was a perception of weakness and an opportunity arose to destabilize a region in Africa, the undertones of Communist involvement were never far away. So, too, it was with Rhodesia. Many of the young blacks were lured out of the country on promise of "scholarships" in Zambia and Tanganyika.

In fact, these young men were being sent for Communist indoctrination and weapons training in camps in North Korea and the former USSR. They were returned via such ports as Dar es Salaam on the coast of Africa and then infiltrated back into Rhodesia to fight against the Smith government. Ian Smith was prime minister of Rhodesia and a powerful advocate of white minority rule; his unilaterally declared independence (UDI) from Britain in 1965 would result in a fifteen-year campaign against Communist-backed African nationalists fighting for an independent African state later to become Zimbabwe. The campaign would cost the lives of 40,000 people.

Smith never once backed down from his position that there should never be black majority rule in Rhodesia. The white South African government withdrew its support for Rhodesian UDI, and this was a turning point for Smith. By 1972, the armed African nationalists under Joshua Nkomo and Robert Mugabe were raiding white farms at will. Ian Smith died on November 21, 2007, aged eighty-eight.[10]

With so many ways to define terrorism, would the likes of Nkomo and Mugabe be viewed as terrorists, insurgents, freedom fighters, or just violent criminals? The answer to this question is not easy. From the Rhodesian standpoint, they were certainly seen as terrorists, so the Smith government used the Rhodesian Special Air Service Regiment to good effect in destroying these "terrorists." The task from the military standpoint was almost hopeless, given the makeup of the borders that surrounded the country. The only friendly region lay to the south with the South African government. The numbers of terrorists and insurgents continued to grow in the same manner as that faced by the United States when it fought an impossible-to-win war in Vietnam.

The politics of the day did nothing to inhibit the violence in Rhodesia. On the contrary, to most people in Rhodesia, both black and white, it seemed that the terrorist forces had the tacit support of the British government in the name of African nationalism. The two leaders of the terror groups, Joshua Nkomo and Ndabaningi Sithole, were openly supported in Britain even though they were leaders of the two parties banned by the Smith government. The black nationalists, Robert Mugabe being one of them, formed ZANU as a result of a split with the Nkomo leadership. Nkomo formed the opposing ZAPU movement. Formed along tribal lines, Nkomo's support came principally from the Ndebele tribes of Matabeleland in the west, while Mugabe's support lay in the tribes of Mashonaland in the east of the country.

Serious voting irregularities during the 2002 general election, witnessed by the Commonwealth observers, resulted in an announcement from London that Zimbabwe was to be suspended from the Commonwealth for twelve months. The leaders of South Africa, Australia, and Nigeria made the decision on behalf of the fifty-four-nation group, after studying an observer mission report on Zimbabwe's appalling presidential elections. Announcing the decision in London, former Australian prime minister John Howard said he hoped the international community would encourage reconciliation in Zimbabwe between the main parties. At a summit held before the Zimbabwe election, Howard and the presidents of South Africa and Nigeria, Thabo Mbeki and Olusegun Obasanjo, respectively, were appointed to decide what action, if any, the Commonwealth should take against Zimbabwe. The ballot in Zimbabwe saw the reelection of incumbent president Robert Mugabe amid allegations of violence, terrorism, and intimidation against the opposition, Movement for Democratic Change, led by Morgan Tsvangirai. Western governments severely criticized the fairness of the election, while African governments were less willing to condemn Mugabe.

The Commonwealth Observer Group accused Mugabe of using state powers and institutions to steal his victory. The United States, Britain, and the European Union condemned the elections as "unfair and not free." Before leaving Australia for London, Howard said, "This is quite a moment of truth for the Commonwealth … it's not something that can be swept under the carpet."

Mbeki and Obasanjo held talks with Mugabe to try and seek a compromise. Among the proposals speculated on was a government of National Unity, but both Mugabe and Tsvangirai cast doubt on the plan. Tsvangirai said: "We arrived at the conclusion that the objective conditions do not exist for meaningful discussion because Mugabe's party … ZANU-PF, is embarking on mass retribution against our members in the rural areas."

Mugabe, who has been in power since 1980, was sworn in for another six-year term. He took the victory as a mandate to pursue his land reform program. Zimbabwe's main Labor Federation called for a three-day general strike to protest what it called postelection harassment of workers.

The Harare meeting came on the same day that a white farmer was shot dead by suspected ruling party militants. Terry Ford was the first white farmer killed since Mugabe was reelected and the tenth killed since militants began often-violent occupation of white-owned land two years earlier. Denmark, which is not a member of the Commonwealth, announced it was closing its Harare Embassy and ending further developmental aid to the country and stated that reports from national and international observers clearly showed that the election was neither free nor fair. Denmark withdrew its embassy staff from Harare that summer.

Zimbabwe continues to reel under the effects of Mugabe's dictatorship, with millions facing certain death from disease, starvation, and state-sponsored violence, yet Mugabe's message to the nation was a promissory note for more misery and death. The annual National Heroes' Day in 2002 proved to be no exception. The illegitimate ZANU-PF government has routinely turned this somber national occasion into an indecent partisan junket to spread a message of violence and hatred.

Mugabe fails to connect with the primary concerns of the people of Zimbabwe, which are food, jobs, health, and an end to poverty. He instead concerns himself primarily with rhetorical nationalism. In fact, Zimbabwe now is a country where everything is in short supply except misery, starvation, and death. The regime has reduced innocent citizens to the levels of scavenging animals.

Where Zimbabweans expect a message of hope and decisive leadership to confront the problems bedeviling the country, they are told that their daughters and sons will be forcibly drafted into the so-called National Youth Service and be transformed into killing machines for the perpetuation of Mugabe's dictatorship. Change in Zimbabwe is inevitable, no matter how many innocent citizens are slaughtered by his regime. Evidence at hand demonstrates, beyond any reasonable doubt, the regime's culpability in widespread and systematic incidences of murders, tortures, rape, abductions, arsons, and many other forms of well-organized political violence that have taken place with impunity over the first decade of the twenty-first century. The partisan public media has never exposed nor condemned ZANU-PF violence, but has instead defended it. The police force, on the other hand, has mastered the art of selective harassment, arrests, and prosecution of the opposition, while ruling party criminals who are guilty of heinous crimes are walking scot free. As the 2008 elections came around, there was the real prospect that Mugabe now over eighty years old would relinquish his control and fade into obscurity. On the contrary, the March 2008 elections were a well-rigged affair by the dictatorship—thugs from Mugabe's ZANU-PF party roamed the countryside at will attacking and intimidating voters. True democracy is still not being felt in what was once the breadbasket of Africa.

In addition to the acts of barbarism that have been perpetrated with state sanction and impunity, the regime has sought to legalize the harassment of political opponents and to control what the people read, hear, and see through the enactment of legislation with severe democratic deficits, like Jonathan Moyo's Access to Information Act and John Nkomo's Public Order and Security Act. What is blatantly disturbing and unacceptable about the regime is that at a time when the nation has an avalanche of political and economic crises on its hands—for which the regime is responsible—its ministers, such as John Nkomo, Joseph Made, and Jonathan Moyo, are busy trying to outdo each other in their daily television appearances. The regime's ministers have become obsessed with little things at a time when they should be answering questions about more serious things, like the supplying of salt for Zimbabwean families.

The United Nations has condemned Zimbabwe, Uganda, and Rwanda for actions in the DRC. These three countries initially intervened in the DRC to stabilize the area in the aftermath of Laurent Kabila's overthrow of Mobutu Sese Seko and the subsequent chaos that took place in the eastern half of the former Republic of Zaire.

Both Uganda and Rwanda support the rebels in the east and Zimbabwe supports the government. However, the UN report accuses Zimbabwe, Uganda, and Rwanda of perpetuating the war for their own financial gain, as they exploit the country's rich mineral resources. The DRC is one of the richest countries in the world in minerals. It has gold, copper, diamonds, cobalt, Coltan (a metal ore for use in aerospace telecommunications industries), and timber.

In the rebel-controlled areas, Rwanda is accused of exporting Coltan mineral, which it mines inside the DRC; Uganda is accused of gold-smuggling activities; and Zimbabwe allegedly engages in joint ventures with DRC government officials, which benefit only the ruling elite back in Harare. The armed forces of the DRC have been pushed into the western half of the country, unable to penetrate the areas held by the Tutsi-backed rebels in areas where these three countries' armies are operating, despite receiving military aid from Zimbabwe, Angola, and Namibia.

The governments of Rwanda and Uganda reject the claims that they are prolonging the war for their own gain. Although a UN-monitored cease-fire has been established, there is still fighting between rival armed groups. The result, as is the usual case in Africa, is paid for in civilian suffering and lives. Infant mortality stands at 40 percent. There are reportedly 2 million displaced persons and 16 million people classified as not receiving the basic nutritional levels as stipulated by the United Nations.

ZANU-PF 5 BRIGADE

The PF 5 Brigade came into existence under Prime Minister Mugabe's command. In October 1980, Mugabe signed an agreement with then North Korean president Kim Il Sung that arranged for North Korean training of Zimbabwean troops. Koreans were sent to train this new brigade that Mugabe said would be used to "deal with dissidents and any other trouble in the country." The 3,500 ex-ZANLA troop members that made up the 5 Brigade were supplemented by some ZIPRA troops, which were withdrawn before the end of the training stage. The training lasted until September 1982. At deployment, the 5 Brigade was different from any other army units: It answered only to the prime minister and did not follow the standard military chain of command. It had unique codes, uniforms, radios, and equipment that were not compatible with standard-issue Zimbabwean army tools. The 5 Brigade's most distinguishing feature was their red berets.

The 5 Brigade was deployed twice into Matabeleland—once in Matabeleland North in late January 1983, then in Matabeleland South in January 1984. After this, they were retrained, deployed again, and then in 1986 finally withdrawn, to undergo a conventional training period under the British Military Advisory Team. In late 1986, the 5 Brigade was disbanded and its soldiers spread out between other regular army brigades.

The deployments of the 5 Brigade into Matabeleland in the early 1980s were marked with a reign of terror, with actions meant to draw out antigovernment "dissidents." Within the first weeks of the first deployments, 5 Brigade troops had murdered more than two thousand civilians; beaten thousands more, destroyed property, and burned houses. Civilians seemed to be specifically targeted during those weeks; hundreds of civilians were rounded up, marched at gun point to a central area, like a school or village well, beaten with sticks, and made to sing Shona songs praising ZANU-PF. These gatherings would then end with public executions.[11]

In the clinical sense, starvation has not yet set in Zimbabwe. But the signs are there—people with sticklike arms and legs and swollen bellies. AIDS is wiping out a whole generation of parents. Thousands upon thousands of small children barely exist with no food, no family income, no medicines, and no answers. Over a third of these children have HIV or AIDS. It is not life they are living—they are just waiting to die. Zimbabwe is now facing a major famine that may decimate half of the country's population.

Zimbabwe's 1992 Land Acquisition Act is at the heart of the redistribution of land owned by white farmers and arbitrarily handed over to blacks. The act was intended to speed up the land reform process by removing the "willing seller, willing buyer" clause. This empowered the government to buy land compulsorily for redistribution. From Harare, the word of Zimbabwean officials was that: "White Farmers will live to regret their defiance of government orders to abandon their land." This followed nearly 3,000 white farmers being ordered to leave their property as part of a plan to seize white-owned lands and turn them over to poor blacks. No serious measures have yet been taken against farmers who have defied the deadline, which changes quickly and often. But, then Co-Vice President Joseph Msika, head of Zimbabwe's Land-reform Task Force, told state television about the farmers refusing to leave their land: "Those who are not going to work within the laws of Zimbabwe have nobody to blame but themselves. The law will take its course." A powerful local government minister said: "All the excuses by the farmers show what an arrogant and racist bunch they are. It shows they want to derail the land redistribution program by any means…they will not succeed," according to the state-run *Herald* newspaper. Former vice president Simon Muzenda warned that authorities would act firmly against farmers opposing the, "irreversible" land program. "You are told by government what we want done and you simply do that," he told state radio. In Washington DC, the U.S. State Department denounced Zimbabwe's attempt to evict the farmers and thousands of farm workers as "a reckless and reprehensible act."

While Robert Mugabe continues to rule supreme in Zimbabwe, he continues to target all opposition; in May 2005, he targeted the urban centers that failed to support him during his reelection campaign in March 2005. The country languishes in abject poverty and real fears of famine exist. In late May 2005, Mugabe ordered a "cleanup" that sparked rioting in Harare. Three thousand police supported by the Zimbabwe military destroyed informal settlements and street markets and arrested almost 20,000 hawkers. The government-sanctioned destruction has left tens of thousands homeless with nowhere to repatriate. The opposition Movement for Democratic Change claims that this action is purely a pretext for the government to announce a "state of emergency." Today the Mugabe brand of politics, intimidation, murder, rape, and forced removals of Zimbabweans marks the standard for a failed state that the rest of the world, although condemning it, does little to correct.

SOUTH AFRICA

For the last half of the twentieth century, South Africa operated under a white-dominated apartheid government, using "**apartheid**" as an official method to control the actions, activities, and opportunities of native, black, colored, and African Asians in the Republic of South Africa. The main political party that was set up to fight apartheid was the African National Congress (ANC). Strangely, that party started on a political platform and moved eventually toward armed confrontation with the South African government.

FIGURE 10-6 Map of South Africa (Central Intelligence Agency, *The World Factbook, 2008*).

Color alone, by no means, carries with it a unity of belief, purpose, or ambition. The most virulent and persistent of hatreds in Africa is often those between people of the same color. The black population of South Africa is divided into at least seven distinct ethnic groups, each with its own written language and home area, and each resolved to retain its own identity. That way the groups could develop separately and still remain apart. In the forty years up to the early 1990s, the South African governments set out to regulate this "problem" by the establishment of separate, self-governing "homelands" for each group.[12] To most people, from the outside looking in, apartheid has always had an evil connotation. Although this text is not intended to be a forum for debating the pros and cons of segregation of ethnic groups in South Africa, it is relevant to the South African experience with terrorism.

Britain's involvement in the Cape colony dates back to over three centuries, when the region along the Cape was very important as a refueling and trading post for shipping to and from the Orient and India. The Cape colony was also home to Dutch migrants from Europe who had settled the Colony in 1652. From the middle of the sixteenth century, the Dutch East India Company had executive powers over the Colony, and all its inhabitants, but allowed Dutch settlers to leave the company and start their own farms. These people became known as "Boers." With the migration inland, the white farmers fought the tiny, "San Tribes," people (Bushmen) and either killed or enslaved them for work on their farms.

The Dutch government formally turned the Colony over to Britain in 1834. The first British settlers had arrived in the Cape in 1820, and with control going to Britain, an unpopular decision was made to end slavery. Britain established English as the official language of the Cape to the extreme resentment of the Boers living in the Colony. Unhappy with British rule, the Boers began to move north and settled in regions farther away in the Transvaal, the Orange Free State, and Natal. The move north became a historic event for the Boers and is generally referred to as the Great Trek.

With the discovery of diamonds in the Kimberley region, and gold in the Johannesburg areas, Anglos and Boers would eventually fight the first Anglo-Boer War. Overwhelming force of arms allowed the British to defeat the Boers by 1902, thus bringing about the Orange Free State, Transvaal, and Natal, all under firm British rule. This rule, not surprisingly, included all the Black tribes, most of which submitted peacefully to their new masters. As in most matters, there is always an exception to a rule, and the South African exception was the "Zulus." This warlike tribe would submit to nobody and, in 1879, defeated and destroyed a well-trained British regiment at Isandhlwana. Overwhelming superiority of forces and firepower eventually defeated the Zulus, and by 1888, none of the black African tribes retained independence.

AFRIKANER NATIONALISM

Two famous Boer generals, Louis Botha and Jan Smuts, had a great part to play in the rise of Afrikaner nationalism in South Africa. General J. Hertzog formed the Nationalist Party, which had the ideology that the Boers had a right to rule South Africa and to unite the Anglos and Afrikaners. With a nationalist government coming to power in South Africa for the first time in 1922, nationalists began the changes that would shape the United South Africa of their dreams. This included the recognition of Afrikaans, alongside English, as the official language and also the development of industry less dependent on Great Britain. With the outbreak of World War II, South Africa was already an independent nation within the British Commonwealth, and there was considerable debate as to which side, if any, to support. Hertzog favored neutrality while the Boer General Smuts sided with the British against Germany.

Apartheid

During the war years, the Nationalist Party underwent a rebirth and change of direction under the inspiration of D.F.D. Malan, a strong supporter of the nationalist South African cause. Under his guidance, the adoption of segregation along racial lines (apartheid) was developed and instituted as part of government policy, with sweeping police powers of enforcement. The government had created the power to direct the masses as to where to live and where to work. The struggle against apartheid, or racism, as some observers prefer to call it, became a part of the South African struggle and terrorism for over fifty years. However, one significant incident in March 1960 marked the turning point in the attitude of the international community toward the apartheid government of South Africa and caused the sting of economic sanctions against it. One of the requirements of the apartheid laws was for all blacks to carry ID cards. In protest, blacks went to police stations without their cards and waited to be arrested. The same scene was played out in many locations; however, in Sharpsville, the police opened fire with automatic weapons, and killed sixty-seven and wounded over 200 blacks. From this one incident the ANC formed its military wing, the Umkonto We Sizwe (Spear of the Nation).

Extreme Right-Wing Afrikaner Movement

Extremism in South African politics emerged at the end of the 1960s from splinter groups that broke off from the National Party and called themselves the Herstige Nasionale Party (HNP). By 1971, all the hard-liners of Afrikaner Nationalism had been forced out from the National Party and thus formed the Afrikaner Weerstandsbeweging (AWB), The Afrikaner Resistance Movement. The AWB became known principally for its menacing, but flamboyant, leader, Eugene Terre'Blanche. Likened to Adolph Hitler, his speech-making skills were legendary, although his message was usually disjoined and with little meaning except to menace and threaten. This ability allowed Terre'Blanche to attract large crowds of supporters to his meetings. Not only was he a consummate politician and orator but also an accomplished sportsman. He served in the South African Police Service as a Warrant Officer. After leaving the police service, he went on to form the AWB in July 1973 with another former police colleague, Jan Groenewald. The early movement was extremely small, and the meetings were secret for fear of drawing the attention of the **Bureau of State Security (BOSS).**

BOSS not surprisingly portrayed all the same trappings and uniform style, complete with swastika, as the German Nazi Movement. Albert Hertzog, a former cabinet member of the National Party and founder of the HNP, was at this time outside of the party hierarchy, following the party's disastrous showing in the general election, and was looking for a cause to support. That support, together with his great business acumen, went to Terre'Blanche and the AWB. Although the 1970s were the formative years for the AWB, no specific acts of terror can be attributed to the organization. With the dismantling of the apartheid system in South Africa, that would change over the following seventeen years.

Many observers labeled the AWB as a neo-Nazi organization. Although the leadership of the AWB vehemently denied the label, the group's flamboyant uniforms did not easily dispel this viewpoint. Still searching for its true identity, the AWB went through several different scenarios, usually linked to storm trooper and motorcycle gang-style images with fearsome-sounding names like the Lightening Falcons or Storm Falcons. Most were burly and surly men outfitted with jackboots and helmets.

The first signs of violence came in 1985, when Terre'Blanche proclaimed that the AWB would form into units of guards. These groups were called the "Sentinels" or "Brandwag" and were formed up along the Northern Transvaal border with Zimbabwe. The white farmers in the border areas formed Brandwags to protect against incursions from across the border with Zimbabwe. The AWB equipped itself with its own bodyguard of heavies to "control" and monitor meetings. Most of the white farmers in the more remote regions of the Transvaal were also local commando (army) members, so it was not surprising that they would be well armed with sophisticated weapons. With the extreme right-wing's sympathy, and now sophisticated weapons in its members' hands, the aims of the AWB were to make sure black groups and political organizations would not become targets for action. What made the AWB so popular was its belief in preserving its claims to land and demands for an Afrikaner nation to be formed out of the former Boer Republics.

By the end of the 1980s, it became clear that the enemy of the AWB, apart from left-wing politicians, was also the African National Congress (ANC). Over the years that led up to the first ANC-elected government and the ending of the apartheid system in South Africa, AWB members and supporters carried out various terrorist acts to destabilize the ANC and the elected government. The AWB had hoped to escalate the violence into a full-scale civil war. As we now know, that was never to be the case. However, the bomb attacks were directed mainly at black civilian targets as were the indiscriminate use of bombs in the major cities. The bombing campaign resulted in many AWB arrests and convictions. In 1996, the AWB, still under the control of Terre'Blanche, announced that the movement would now operate underground.

The AWB symbol is the eagle. The group's official guidebook details that: "This emblem enables the AWB to give its full acknowledgement to the symbolism of the eagle which epitomizes the protection of the Lord: Like an eagle that stirs up its nest that flutters over its young, spreading out its wings, catching them, bearing them on its pinions." (*Deuteronomy* 32:11). Terre Blanche was murdered in April 2010 by two of his farm workers while taking a nap at his ranch.

The Future

In April 1994, the African National Congress gained over 60 percent of the vote in the country's first free elections, bringing an end to apartheid and white minority rule. With the public's general acceptance of the new government, UN recognition, and the rapid lifting of international sanctions, it is difficult to see the AWB or a similar nationalist movement emerging in South Africa in any significant fashion for the near future. As long as Afrikaner nationhood is alive and well, however, there will always be the opportunity and threat for a different generation to take up where Terre'Blanche left off.

The African National Congress (ANC)

The quasi-political African National Congress (ANC) movement dates as far back as 1912 and has consistently, along with other liberal groups, opposed the nationalists and their apartheid policies. Garnering support for any action, given the overwhelming numbers (75 percent of the population is black and 14 percent white, with the balance being made up of Asians), would not be difficult. Probably the most famous name connected to the movement is that of the first black president of South Africa, Nelson Rolihlahla Mandela. Born in 1918, the son of a tribal chief, Mandela received an excellent education and became a lawyer. Toward the end of World War II, he joined the African National Congress. Mandela, an outspoken opponent of apartheid, led protests and demonstrations against apartheid and police brutality during the 1950s, for which he was arrested and charged with treason. The charge was not proven, however, and he was acquitted. He was arrested again in 1962, charged with terrorist offenses, and sentenced to life in prison. His release thirty-two years later would become the harbinger and beginning of the new South Africa and a black majority government. The role of the ANC and various acts of terrorism in South Africa are intertwined. The ANC contention is that it had been driven to acts of criminal violence, bombings, shootings, and murder because it lacked any political alternative. With apartheid firmly in place and its leader firmly in jail, the ANC members embarked on a terror campaign aimed at the state, the white minority, and their own black brothers who failed to support them. Intertribal fighting has been a hallmark of fighting in the south. Some of the forms of brutality the ANC used are quite gruesome to describe. One favored method in killing recalcitrant blacks was the "rubber necklace"—a badly beaten victim was placed in a stack of used car tires and then set on fire.

The ANC received external support in its campaign from Communist sources outside South Africa's borders. This led to the government reducing and diminishing the effects of apartheid on the black and colored communities. The ANC had a military wing that advocated revolutionary violence. It further advocated the kind of Communist revolution that swept into Russia at the start of the twentieth century. A 1987 quote from Winnie Mandela, then wife of the imprisoned Nelson Mandela, clearly defined the Communist goals for the ANC: "The Soviet Union is the torchbearer for all our hopes and aspirations. In Soviet Russia, genuine power of the people has been transformed from dreams into reality." Since the middle of the 1980s, the Republic of South Africa has undergone drastic political changes, and with those changes came the fruition of the dream of the overthrow of the regime and the system of apartheid.

Having been banned since 1961, the ANC had been headquartered outside South Africa, in neighboring Zambia. To this extent, one may assume the Zambians gave material support to ANC terrorists crossing into South Africa. The South African police and military were very effective in patrolling and controlling border incursions from neighboring African countries, especially those hostile to the apartheid regime. The neighboring countries of Lesotho, Mozambique, and Botswana have been, at varying times, the locations for terrorist training bases for the ANC and were supported by Russian technicians. The external locations did not prevent the South African security forces from taking preemptive actions against the training base locations in those countries. The ANC also aided in defining the term *terrorism* by declaring in the 1980s that the South African government was a terrorist government and that the ANC was acting in self-defense.

Robben Island University (Isle of Purgatory)

Many historic landmarks have formed central points for penal servitude around the world. Well-known among those landmarks are Wormwood Scrubs in London, England; the Island of Elbe; Devil's Island; and Alcatraz. Not so well known to the world is Robben Island, situated off the southern coast of Africa at Cape Town, with a splendid view of Table Mountain. This island had served as a dropping off point for Cape traders in the sixteenth century. It has been a leper colony, a hospital for the insane, an armed garrison, and the long-time residence of Nelson Mandela and other banned and convicted members of the ANC. Today it is a national monument and tourist attraction. The island was turned over to the South African Department of Prisons when the South African Artillery School vacated it in 1959. The first African political prisoners arrived at the prison to serve their sentences in 1962, along with members of the Pan-African Congress activists, as well as soldiers from an armed group called "Poqo." Members of the ANC, including Nelson Mandela, arrived soon afterward. Many arrived in a state of general illiteracy. However, "B Section," which housed Nelson Mandela and his cohorts, became known as Robben University. Here, many inmates were able to learn and further their political debates and beliefs. The ANC "students" observed a prison code that required they maintain their commitment to changing South African society, and to find positive development through their term of imprisonment. The code also required that none of them were to leave the prison without some education. The last prisoners left the island in 1991, after the ANC finally received political recognition.

Winnie Madikizela-Mandela

Winnie, the estranged wife of Nelson Mandela, the first black president of South Africa, has been described as the "Mugger of the Nation." During the political buildup to her husband's dramatic release from his life sentence on Robben Island, in true charismatic fashion, Winnie surrounded herself with a phalanx of bodyguards. As the ex-wife of the former president, her actions and those of her bodyguard have been questioned. Winnie Mandela, her bodyguards, and a group of tough youths from the Soweto Township became known as the Mandela United Football Club. Jerry Richardson, who was a convicted murderer, was the group's leader. They were involved in beatings of blacks in the townships. Winnie herself was convicted of kidnapping in 1991.[13]

Is South Africa out of the shadow of terrorism? Apart from the Planet Hollywood bombing in 1998, the country has been relatively free of terror attacks. The passage of time and the removal of the apartheid South African government have not seen any sudden improvement in everyday living conditions, hoped for by the millions of black South Africans. Questions are now coming to the table about corruption and incompetence of the highest order under the current government. Weak governments on the African continent have been susceptible to terrorism. However, until recently, South Africa had a strong democratic system of government and had control of its borders and an effective security force. It seems probable that the rainbow of nations in South Africa and their neighbors may someday pale. As whites leave the country in ever-increasing numbers for a safer life outside the Republic, the fabric and wealth of South Africa may suffer from instability.

ISLAM IN SOUTH AFRICA

People against Gangsterism and Drugs (PAGAD)

People against Gangsterism and Drugs (PAGAD) were established in 1996 as a community anticrime force. It originated in a network of hitherto disparate and isolated antidrug, anticrime groups and neighborhood watches frustrated by their inability to tackle problems whose roots extended far beyond their individual localities. Predominantly, but by no means exclusively, Muslim, PAGAD began with a loose organizational structure and an informal, collective style of leadership. It was open to approaches from other anticrime groups and prepared, at least, to consider working with the police. Many of the more violent actions taken against drug dealers, such as the attack on Rashaad Staggie in August 1996, were neither planned nor formally sanctioned by the organization as a whole. PAGAD's development since these early days cannot be seen simply as the unfolding of a master plan conceived and executed by a small group of Islamic radicals. Rather, it has to be viewed as the outcome of the interplay between many internal and external forces…of action by PAGAD and its constituent elements and reaction by the state and its agencies in the specific political, social, and economic context of the Western Cape.

The state's view of PAGAD has changed dramatically over the last decade. From a popular anticrime movement, it has become first a violent, and therefore illegitimate, vigilante organization and then, since 1998, an urban terror group threatening not just the state's monopoly on the use of coercive force but the very foundations of constitutional democracy. In line with these altered perceptions, the state's response to PAGAD has changed from constructive engagement to demonization and repression.[14]

PAGAD has become rabidly anti-Western, as well as antigovernment in its activities. It views the current South African regime as a threat to Islamic values. The group is led by Abdus Salaam Ebrahim. PAGAD's G-Force (Gun Force) operates in small cells and is believed to be responsible for carrying out acts of terrorism and targeting mainly synagogues and nightclubs in the Cape region of South Africa.[15]

PAGAD's activities seem at odds with its value structure. The group's website lists the following as its goals:

- To propagate the eradication of drugs and gangsterism from society;
- To cooperate with and to coordinate the activities of people and people's organization having similar aims and objectives;
- To make every effort to invite/motivate/activate and to include those people and people's organizations that are not yet part of PAGAD;
- To raise funds to realize the foregoing aims; and
- PAGAD is a nonprofit-making movement. All its assets, income, and contributions shall be used to achieve these objectives of PAGAD.[16]

Boeremag (Boer Force)

Since the end of the apartheid regimes, South Africa has had to contend with a small outbreak of extreme right-wing nationalism in the form of the Boeremag movement. This group seeks to overthrow the current South African government and drive the black population north into central Africa and create a Boer (white) homeland. Boeremag's activities in the first four years of the millennium have been to place a number of bombs around buildings and bridges, most often where there is a large concentration of blacks. Bombs went off in the township of Soweto and the group expected the black population to rise up in a race war against the whites. Eighteen of the group's members have been arrested as it continues to demand a separate Afrikaner Homeland.[17]

Both the South African and U.S. governments have officially designated PAGAD as a terrorist organization. South African police efforts and court prosecutions severely damaged the group in the early 2000s. Since 2001, PAGAD has demonstrated a significantly weakened operational capability. Externally, the threat to the RSA comes from extreme jihadists who would focus on U.S. and Western interests in the state. However, RSA is considered somewhat neutral in the War on Terror and supports Palestinian rights.

QIBLA MOVEMENT

The threat comes from highly secretive groups such as Qibla, which was established among the Muslim immigrants in the 1980s and directed and supported by Iranian intelligence. Although Qibla is a purely South African organization, it is manipulated from a safe distance by the Iranian intelligence services, which use the organization not only to propagate the worldview of the Islamic Republic but also as a cover to conduct espionage in RSA.[18] As in other regions of the world, these Muslim movements have basically the same goal of creating an Islamic-controlled state. Qibla is also linked to PAGAD and infiltrates that movement in order to carry out its attacks.

KENYA

Myriad tribal groups, spread throughout the land, have populated Kenya for untold centuries. The Kikuyu is one of the largest tribes of the region, and it works the land alongside the Kamba, Masai, and Luo tribes. The beginnings of colonialism in the nineteenth century saw the erosion of the tribal rights in Kenya. Britain was granted title over the lands now called Uganda and Kenya. Uganda became a British Protectorate in 1885, and Kenya followed shortly after in 1893. Britain, in those days, was interested primarily in the rich natural resources of Uganda and constructed a railway system between Kampala and Mombasa. Much of the work was done by imported labor from the Indian subcontinent. Most of the merchants of Kenya and Uganda are the descendents of these railway workers. By 1915, British settlers had claimed the fertile highland regions for growing crops for export and displaced the tribes of those regions. Africans and Asians were prohibited from being landowners.[19] The British, unprepared to deal with the native issues in Kenya, permitted the growth of Black Nationalist movements, and, in 1929, one of the most prominent African leaders of the twentieth century, Jomo Kenyatta, went to England to negotiate for land rights on behalf of the Kikuyu Central Association. With the onset of World War II, Africans were conscripted, thus providing a trained cadre for what became the **Mau Mau** terrorist group.

Unlike its near neighbors, the population of Kenya has been relatively free of terrorist activity and atrocities. Insurrections and uprisings in Kenya have been perpetrated in living memory by what is still considered one of the most shadowy and frightening organizations to gain a foothold on the African subcontinent, the Mau Mau. This almost mythical, shadowy, and mysterious organization in Kenya came to prominence again as a result of what may be construed as a colonial land grab. In fact, the tribes of Kenya were land farmers and cattle herders who considered the land "everyone's land." But much of their area was "owned" by white families. Kenya became part of Britain's far-flung empire, bringing with it taxation as well as education to the natives of the region. Britain and the settlers were of an unshakable belief that the land was the sole property of the tribal government, and therefore the colonial government had rights to the land. Naturally, such an assumption did not sit well with the tribes of Kenya. The land grab

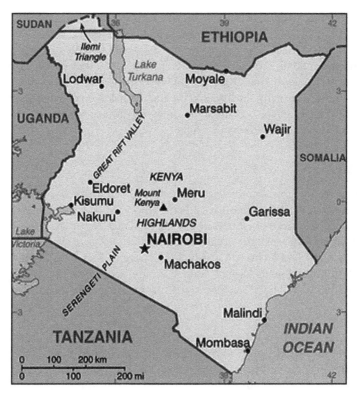

FIGURE 10-7   Map of Kenya (Central Intelligence Agency, *The World Factbook, 2008*).

instigated a rebirth of the Mau Mau. Although the specific aims of the organization have never been detailed, the group flourished in the tribal lands of Kenya.

One of the best-educated tribes of the region was the Kikuyu, and it was from this environment that the Mau Mau found its roots. The Kikuyu, like the other tribes, had been reduced almost to the levels of third-class citizens or serfs in their own country. In a region of the world where superstitions and magic have a considerable foothold, the groundswell of support for a secret society, to fight for the people, quickly became apparent. The Mau Mau had taken an oath—that the Kikuyu took extremely seriously—for the total removal of all whites and those who had supported the colonial British government. In the early 1950s, the Mau Mau began attacking white settlers on their farms in Kenya. The attacks came to a full-scale rebellion in 1956 and were finally forcibly crushed by the British. Many tribesmen were sent to detention camps or were hunted and killed. The Mau Mau leader at the time was Dedan Kimathi, who was executed for leading the uprising. The Mau Mau campaign had a softening effect on the British and sincere efforts were made to stabilize the country; however, from 1956 to 1960, the country was under a "state of emergency." The Kenyan African Union (KANU), led by Jomo Kenyatta, sought independence for the country. In 1963, Britain granted full independence to Kenya. Kenyatta became the country's first president.

INTERNATIONAL TERRORISM IN CENTRAL AFRICA

With the emergence and spread of Islamic fundamentalism throughout the Middle East, and also into regions of Northern and Southern Africa, it is not surprising that a "soft" target, such as an embassy of a foreign superpower, would suffer the brunt of a terrorist attack.

That attack came against the U.S. embassy in Nairobi, Kenya, in early August 1998. The U.S. embassy in Nairobi certainly did not have the levels of security protection afforded to other U.S. legations, particularly in the Middle East. The embassy was considered below the acceptable standards for security, particularly after the bombing of the U.S. Marine Corps barracks in Beirut in 1984, which claimed the lives of 242 marines. Recommendations to tighten U.S. security had not included Kenya; presumably, the threat assessment was considered low for this region of the world. With lax security and the location of the building being in the center of Nairobi, it became too good a target for the determined terrorist to pass up. A massive car bomb decimated the embassy building and caused extensive damage to the surrounding buildings. The bomb claimed 170 lives, mostly Africans, and wounded several thousands. The object of the attack was the U.S. administration, and not Kenya. The attack has been credited to bin Laden and also to Fazul Abdullah Mohamed—both now dead. Abdullah had operated in east Africa and found safe haven in the badlands of Somalia. He was fluent in five languages and was the master of disguise. His death in a shootout at a Somali military checkpoint in June 2011 should have a negative impact on al Qaeda in the region. The United States had placed a "bounty" of $5 million on Mohammed and had attempted to assassinate him at least six times since 2006. The most recent attempts were in 2008 and 2009, when U.S. military used its satellite tracking and eavesdropping capability to track cell phone conversations between al Qaeda operatives and launched a series of cruise missiles at a specific Somali house, killing and wounding several militants but not Mohammed. Again in 2009, a U.S. Special Forces unit targeted another al Qaeda commander Saleh Ali Nabhan—his vehicle was attacked by a helicopter gunship, killing Nabhan and several other al Qaeda members.

Politically Expedient Response

The Nairobi attack caught the Clinton administration almost totally unprepared for a problem of such magnitude, at a time when the president was facing serious personal and legal problems of his own. The attack prompted the same political and military response as the 1986 Libyan attack on U.S. servicemen in Germany. That incident resulted in then president Reagan ordering an attack on Libya, even though there was no verifiable evidence that the Libyans were, in fact, responsible.

If retribution or retaliation is to be meted out, and it seems to have been in this case, governments must be cautious about the levels of violence and the message that they are sending, not only to a small group of determined terrorists but also to whole nations that become the target.

The effectiveness of retaliatory attacks against Sudan and Pakistan has been determined to be marginal at best. The attacks against Libya did not deter the bombers from destroying a Pan Am airliner over Lockerbie, Scotland, in 1988. On the other hand, the suicide attack against the U.S. Marines in Beirut did not deter then president Reagan from ordering his marines to invade the tiny Caribbean Island of Granada a very short time later, responding to fears of an alleged Cuban takeover of the island. In this millennium, the United States seems determined to track down and kill those who have perpetrated attacks on the United States, be they located in Somalia, or Pakistan in the case of Osama bin Laden.

ANGOLA

Angola had been Portugal's prize jewel in Africa for more than 500 years. Portuguese navigator Diego Cam landed in Angola in 1482 and left his mark in the traditional Portuguese shape of the cross. Over the centuries, the Portuguese exploited little, if any, of the natural wealth of the country, which was rich in mineral deposits. With colonial development happening throughout

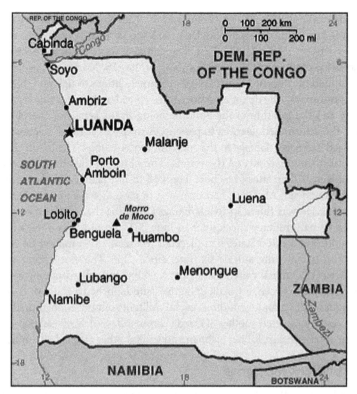

FIGURE 10-8 Map of Angola (Central Intelligence Agency, *The World Factbook, 2008*).

other regions of Africa, Angola continued to languish in quiet slumber. Holden Alvaro Roberto founded Angola's first nationalist movement in 1956 and five years later led the first attack on colonial settlers in Angola. His Union of Angolan Peoples (UPA) drew its main support from his Bakongo ethnic group. In 1962, he transformed the UPA into the National Liberation Front of Angola (FNLA), which operated mainly from Zaire (later the Democratic Republic of the Congo). In 1975, Roberto and the leaders of the other two independence movements in Angola reached an agreement with Portugal and signed a peace treaty that led to the country's independence. Fighting immediately broke out between the three factions, however, and the FNLA, backed by several Western countries, was decisively defeated in 1976 by the Popular Movement for the Liberation of Angola (MPLA), which was supported by the Soviet Union and Cuba. Roberto spent the next 15 years in exile, returning to Angola in 1991.[20]

They killed many villagers and committed atrocities on both the living and the dead. At one location, the victims were put through a sawmill while still alive.[21] They attacked men, women, and children, hacking limbs from bodies and heads from torsos. Roberto died in Luanda in August 2007.

Popular Movement for the Liberation of Angola (MPLA)

The Popular Movement for the Liberation of Angola (MPLA) started in the late 1950s in the Angolan capital of Luanda and, by 1961, had begun to fester into a civil war throughout the country. In the northern region of Angola, the **Front for the Liberation of Angola (FNLA)** was formed, and, in 1966, the National Union for the Total Independence of Angola (UNITA) appeared. The warring factions continued sporadic fighting over the years. However, the Angola military's overthrow of the Colonial Portuguese government in 1974 led to Angola's eventual independence a year later. With the guerrilla army's spread throughout the country, neither of the sides could agree as to which would eventually lead the new government, and fighting resumed. The MPLA was receiving considerable aid from the USSR, as well as Cuba. The Russians supplied weapons, training, and support, while Cuba supplied the fighters to help with the guerrilla war.

By 1976, the battles were over, and the Marxists dominated and influenced the MPLA. With a Marxist government so close to the northern border of Namibia, formerly Southwest Africa, the South African government continued to provide support and weapons to the UNITA rebels fighting against the Marxist government forces of the MPLA. Many of those fighting with the UNITA were South African mercenaries as well as former British soldiers. A cease-fire eventually came into effect in May 1991 and lasted until October 1992.

At that time, UNITA refused to accept the election results and fighting resumed between UNITA and the MPLA government. Sporadic fighting continued over the next two years, and, finally, in 1994, it was agreed that UNITA guerrillas would merge with the Angolan army. All of this took place under the watchful eye of UN peacekeepers, and although the transition was slow, the new government of National Unity came into office in April 1997. Since that time, UN forces have pulled out of Angola.

However, the ongoing decades of violence since Angola's independence from Portugal have now seen a dramatic shift in the fortunes of one of the main protagonist groups, namely the ongoing battle with the National Union for the Total Independence of Angola (UNITA). In February 2002, government troops engaged in a fierce firefight with UNITA rebels led by their patriarchal leader, Jonas Savimbi. During this single action, Savimbi was killed when troops attacked his stronghold in the southern region of the country. The short- and long-term effects of his death will likely mean that there will be a vacuum and those insiders will likely concentrate on a power struggle, thus fracturing UNITA. Whether this means the end of UNITA, it is still too early to say. Much of the funding support for UNITA came from its illegal trade in diamonds. It is probable that the illegal trade will continue and arms will still be traded for them. Savimbi's movement has not benefited from the end of the Cold War when much of its support network came from the Democratic Republic of the Congo, headed up by Mobuto Sese Seko.

MOZAMBIQUE

Sandwiched between Tanzania and South Africa, this legacy of Portuguese colonialism bears the ravages of civil war. Many of Mozambique's problems stem from its nearby neighbors, South Africa and Zimbabwe, the former Rhodesia. Organized along the lines of a one-party state, the current Mozambique government moved out of the realm of a guerrilla/terrorist organization and become a political party. In the early 1960s, many inhabitants were becoming increasingly frustrated with the Portuguese rule, and the **Front for the Liberation of Mozambique (FRELIMO)** was formed.

FRELIMO carried out operations against the Portuguese until 1974, when the country was finally granted independence. FRELIMO was a strong Marxist regime, opposed to the white minority rule (apartheid) of South Africa in the 1980s and also of the Ian Smith minority independence government of Rhodesia (Zimbabwe). When independence was declared, FRELIMO closed its western border with Rhodesia and many dissidents from Rhodesia set up bases in Mozambique to attack the Smith government, assisted by the Russian supported FRELIMO. As the ideological focuses of the surrounding states changed, so did Mozambique. The Samora Machel government in

FIGURE 10-9 Map of Mozambique (Central Intelligence Agency, *The World Factbook, 2008*).

Maputo supported the banned ANC movement in South Africa and supplied weapons, training, and support to terrorists fighting cross-border battles with the South African security forces. Mozambique also had its own internal strife at this time, and South Africa supported the Mozambique National Resistance Movement (RENAMO) in its guerrilla war with the Marxist government. By 1984, South Africa and Mozambique reached an agreement to stop supporting terrorists and guerrillas in each other's country. However, this did not stop RENAMO from continuing its war against apartheid with the FRELIMO. RENAMO's tactics were aimed at totally destabilizing the country, and it began to destroy even schools and medical facilities with over 1,800 schools and 500 health centers destroyed. Close to 100,000 people were killed in countryside villages.

Death of Samora Machel

In 1986, then president Samora Machel was killed when his Russian-made Tupolev aircraft (with a Russian crew) crashed into a hillside on the South African side of the border. What is uncertain about this crash is the manner in which it occurred. Was it an accident or a planned assassination?

There has been speculation since the crash that there was a high-level South African plot to eliminate Machel. Evidence from the crash suggests that external influences somehow tampered with the directional systems of the Tupolev 134A-3 aircraft. Because it was so far off course, it is suspected that a decoy navigational beacon was activated to misdirect the aircraft onto a crash course. South Africa covertly supported the increasing number of RENAMO raids into Mozambique and had increasingly angered Machel. Whether South Africa was involved or not, it is known that there were raised tensions in the previous weeks before the crash, including threatening signals from the SA Defense Ministry. This led to extreme tension between the two countries and continuing distrust on both sides.

By 1992, the two sides reached an uneasy peace and called for an election process that would include RENAMO on the ballot. When voting took place in 1994, FRELIMO had 44 percent of the vote and RENAMO 33 percent. There is no special antiterrorism legislation in Mozambique. Despite the Penal Code of 1886, which is the basis of criminal law in Mozambique, the only existing legislative act, which criminalizes terrorism, is Law No. 19/91 (the Law of Crimes against State Security).

Threat from jihadists in Mozambique is relatively small. As the country is a one-party state and all sides have had a hand in developing the state to what it is today and as many Muslims would be members of FRELIMO, any outside influences from jihadist cells would likely become known to the political leadership. FRELIMO party members rely on the party for their commercial, economic, and political interests and success. As a country situated on the east coast several other landlocked countries use Mozambique to transit to the coast; trade goods as well as people need to transit Mozambique to reach the Indian Ocean. Currently, there is no significant evidence of terrorist training camps within the country and it's very unlikely that the present government would tolerate such camps being set up.

RWANDA

A small, landlocked African state, Rwanda had become infamous with the unexplained murder of Diane Fossey, the famed naturalist and expert on silverback gorillas. In the 1960s, others knew of Rwanda for its fabulous pictorial postage stamps that graced many a philatelist's collection. But, in 1994, it became a killing field for the native Hutus, who eventually massacred well over 500,000 Tutsis.

Rwanda had for centuries been a land of farmers occupied by the Hutu tribesmen and Pygmy hunters. In the thirteenth century, the warrior Tutsis invaded and took control over the Hutus. To the casual onlooker, it might seem logical to assume that the Hutus and Tutsis were sworn enemies. That could not be further from the truth; in fact, Hutus and Tutsis had lived side by side and intermarried for hundreds of years.

There are few differences in the physical characteristics of the two tribes. They look the same, pray to the same Gods, and had peacefully coexisted for centuries. So what happened to cause the genocide that took place in 1994? One must first look at the role played by the colonial forces of Belgium that ruled up to the early 1960s. The Belgian authoritarian control in Rwanda organized and institutionalized the ethnic stereotypes in the country. As it was impossible to physically distinguish between Hutu and Tutsi, the Belgians decreed a system that sounds like it came out of the Dark Ages in order to define in which ethnic group a person belonged. Amazingly, it used these following criteria: If a farmer owned nine cows or less, he was issued an identity card stating he was a Hutu; if he owned ten or more cows, he was a Tutsi. The Belgians had overnight created a class structure dependent on the details of an identity card, and this had been the basis for a social division of the two tribes since the 1930s.

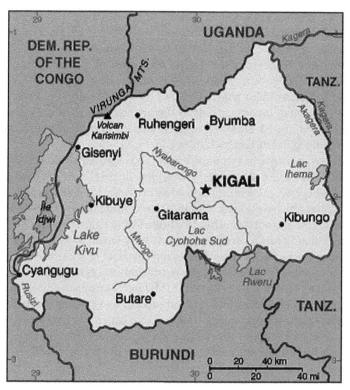

FIGURE 10-10 Map of Rwanda (Central Intelligence Agency, *The World Factbook, 2008*).

The Belgians had created minority elite; they gave privileges and positions on the Belgian colonial administration structure. The Belgians ruled by the grace of the Tutsi minority in Rwanda, who had been schooled and educated by the Belgians. As they grew more powerful, they sought to throw off the mantle of colonialism and demanded independence. To counter the Tutsis' demands, the Belgians began to switch their allegiance to the Hutu majority, producing enough hatred against the Tutsis to start a popular uprising. The uprising brought the Hutu into government and over 100,000 Tutsis were killed. A similar number of Tutsis, fearing further atrocities, fled to neighboring Uganda in the north, where they remained in exile. It was this exiled group and their descendents who returned to begin the civil war in 1990. In exile, the group formed the Rwandan Patriotic Front (RPF), which was made up of displaced Tutsis and Hutus. The RPF aimed to replace the oppressive and repressive government with a new democratically elected government.

The Hutu-dominated government of president Habyarimana was determined to remain in power. The Hutu planned to eradicate the Tutsis in methods not dissimilar to the Nazi extermination of the Jews. The tool of the trade, in this instance, was propaganda. As most of the Hutus were illiterate farmers, the government began to systematically bombard the population with radio announcements that were deliberately and openly anti-Tutsi. It went beyond just denouncements of the Tutsis, but actively demanded that civilian Hutus kill any and all Tutsis they came across. Terror and threat, terror and threat, were repeated over and over in efforts to sow the seeds of total annihilation of the Tutsis. In a format reminiscent of South American death squads, the Hutu government set up civilian militia, training them in weaponry, hand-to-hand combat, and methods to quickly kill their enemy, the Tutsis. This organization was called the Interahamwe, meaning "those who attack together." The Hutu militias began killing Tutsis wherever they found them, and soon it became apparent that to kill a Tutsi would not be considered a crime in that country…it was just eliminating a form of vermin. However, after three years of the civil war and slaughter, a cease-fire was finally reached between the two sides in 1993. Then, under the auspices of the United Nations in 1994, the devastated country prepared to set up some form of transitional government. However, the Hutus continued to arm and train its civilian militia openly, right under the noses of UN observers. It is still not clear to the international community as to why the United Nations made no effort to report these facts or to seek any clarification on how to handle the issues.

Death of a President

Uprisings often need to have a "trigger mechanism" to set them off. In April 1994, the plane carrying then president Habyarimana was shot down as it approached Kigali, the Rwandan Capital, killing the president. This single incident became the "green light" for the genocide to begin once more in earnest. Within hours of his death, the attacks and killings of Tutsis commenced, and within a single month nearly half a million Tutsis lay dead and the rest were scattered throughout the country. Those who were able to escape fled to neighboring countries. The United Nations stood by and observed the genocide and has been criticized for failing to intervene and stop the massacres.

Two months into the killings, the United Nations passed a resolution to send in a UN peacekeeping force of around 5,000 troops. With the killings all but over, and the RPF advancing from the north, many of the Hutu militia escaped across the border to Tanzania and to refugee camps set up inside the border. The point may have been missed in newspaper articles in regard to the genocide in Rwanda and the need for urgent humanitarian aid for the refugees. But most of the refugee camps held only the murderous members of the Hutu, as nearly all the Tutsis had been caught and killed in the preceding six-week period. The country's demand that the Hutus and Tutsis reintegrate within Rwanda is unique in world history. Genocide, civil war, refugee flight, abundant hate propaganda, a culture of impunity, and ongoing insurgency and atrocities—this is Rwanda. The most telling and difficult question is whether the people of Rwanda can rewrite a social contract that will be acceptable to any functioning society. Can they overcome their mutual suspicion and live as neighbors and fellow countrymen again? The Hutus returning to Rwanda must fear retaliatory actions being meted out against them, the same as to the Tutsis in 1994.

In recent history, such a reintegration has never happened. It certainly did not take place in Germany, causing the international community to create Israel, a sovereign Jewish state. Fleeing from the killing fields, the people of Cambodia resettled in other countries. Rwanda today is still a dangerous and suspicious place.

DEMOCRATIC REPUBLIC OF CONGO (DRC), FORMERLY ZAIRE

The Democratic Republic of Congo (DRC) is located in Central Africa and straddles both the equator and the Congo River. With a population of 40 million and rich with mineral resources of gold, copper, zinc, and diamonds, to name but a few. Henry Stanley discovered the region in the 1870s and was asked to set up Belgian trading posts along the Congo River in 1878 by King Leopold of Belgium. The king ruled this African country as his own private fiefdom, and it only fell under the control of the Belgian government in 1908. At that time, it was called the Congo Free State.

By the 1960s, colonial Belgian rule was coming to an end, and, on June 30, 1960, the Belgian Congo became the independent Republic of Congo. The first president of the new Central African Republic was Joseph Kasavubu, with the legendary Patrice Lumumba as his prime minister. Unluckily, for the young, Communist-inspired Lumumba, his position was extremely tenuous in the eyes of the West, particularly the United States.

The 1960s was the height of the Cold War, and the CIA was intent on eliminating Soviet involvement in mineral-rich central Africa. The CIA conspired with factions that were anti-Communist to overthrow the Lumumba government and install a pro-West regime. This was achieved by infiltrating mercenary elements into the country. The CIA had planned to poison Lumumba; however, prior to his assassination, the army mutinied. The army at this time was led by a young Zairian officer Joseph Desire Mobutu. In July and again in September 1960, Mobutu, an army colonel, announced the suspension of all political parties and took control of the country. In November 1960, Lumumba was arrested and handed over to rebel forces and was executed on January 17, 1961. For the next four years the government was in turmoil, until the military coup of Desire Mobutu. The next thirty-two years saw Desire Mobutu rule the country with an iron fist and in a somewhat African tradition plundered the country's central bank for his own personal use and gains, buying homes, villas, and castles in Europe. His leadership was violently anti-Communist and strongly pro-West, which suited the world situation in the Cold War years, and the particular interests of the U.S. Mobutu received vast sums of "development" aid, aimed at preventing the spread of any Communist influences. In the 1970s, he began a period of "Africanization" and changed his name to Mobutu Sese Seko, meaning "He the all powerful warrior." Names of cities were changed; Leopoldville changed to Kinshasa, and the country to the Democratic Republic of Zaire, from Congo. Mobutu has plundered his country to such a state of deprivation that when the Hutu and Tutsi fighting in neighboring Rwanda spilled over into Zaire, he had no military to stop the incursions. The Rwandans were led by an old friend of Patrice Lumumba, namely Laurant Kabila.

Mobutu Sese Seko

Mobutu's tyrannical reign was all about ancient methods of pillage and plunder in a twentieth-century format. He was estimated to be one of the five richest men in the world and was president of one of the poorest nations and lowest standard of living in Africa.

In a country of such enormous mineral wealth, it was not difficult to establish where the wealth had gone. Mobutu lived a lavish lifestyle in Africa and had villas throughout Europe. One of the earliest uprisings against his regime came in 1964, in the area of the eastern Congo. It was led by a young Marxist rebel, Laurent-Desire Kabila, who would later return to lead the civil war against the Mobutu regime. Much of what took place in the Congo was a result of outside influences and internal disputes between the many ethnically diverse tribes that had settled in the region. Refugees from rebel actions and atrocities in neighboring countries also were factors.

Hutu and Tutsi differences in Rwanda played a significant part in the eventual rebellion and civil war that overtook the DRC. Insurgent rebellion was prevalent throughout the long dictatorial reign of Mobutu, but he had always managed to put down the uprisings, either by force or by proclaiming presidential or legislative reforms. The country existed as a one-party state under Mobutu, so challenges to his rule were frequent. Citizenship issues and land rights also added to the tensions of the DRC. The complications of the various regions of the DRC are interwoven within the ethnic groups, who vie for power. The principal groups are located in the province of Kivu, which has a long history of ethnic violence; these groups are the Hunde, Nande, and Banyarwanda.

Banyarwandans are a collection of displaced Rwandans who arrived in the region to work the land, courtesy of their colonial Belgian masters; they comprise both Hutus and Tutsis. Members of this group were not considered to be citizens of Zaire under Mobutu's rule, and that has not changed with the transition to Kabila's government in 1997. The local chiefs in Northern-Kivu Province had rented to the Banyarwandans most of the land they occupied. By 1993, the Banyarwandans were pushing for reforms and an end to the injustices carried out against them. What was to complicate the situation in Zaire was the massive and sudden exodus of Hutus from Rwanda. Included in this exodus was the local Militia Interahamwe, which had been involved in the genocide in Rwanda after the death of the Rwandan president.

An uprising in 1993 escalated into yet another, full-scale ethnic battle. Most of those killed were Banyarwandans. The situation was not improved by the arrival of the Hutu refugees from the fighting and killing in Rwanda. The uprising spread and soon became a national movement to overthrow Mobutu. The rebel forces consisted mainly of Tutsi warriors, and soon Laurent Kabila became their revolutionary leader.

Widespread disillusionment in the Zairian army led to the eventual capitulation of the Mobutu government. On May 16, 1997, with only his personal bodyguard remaining in Kinshasa and the rebel forces on the doorstep, Mobutu left quietly for the safety of Morocco, where he lived in exile until his death in September 1997 from prostate cancer. However, since Kabila came to power, the ethnic violence between the factions has not ceased, and with unprotected borders, the DRC has seen an increase in rebel attacks from outside. From within, the fighting and massacres have continued, particularly in the North and South Kivu provinces. Hutu and Tutsi continue to kill each other. Much of Kabila's support comes from the army, which has been dominated by Rwandan Tutsis.

The Congo can be viewed in much the same vein as Somalia as it, too, is defined as a failed state. Since the start of the cease-fire in 1999, the most contentious issues are still unresolved. The country is variously occupied by six foreign armies and roving bands of militia. Hundreds of thousands have been displaced in the war years and have not yet been repatriated.

The Congo is home to many non-Congolese groups and one, in particular, is the Hutu-dominated Liberation Army of Rwanda (ALiR), which fled from that country after the genocide it perpetrated in Rwanda in 1994. The ALiR continues to be supported by the government in Kinshasa, as the Congo has no effective military force to deal with the occupying forces of Rwanda and Uganda. The Tutsi-dominated regime in Rwanda, afraid of renewed Hutu attacks, maintains its own occupying forces in eastern Congo, refusing to withdraw until the Hutu groups are disarmed. And, for reasons of their own, Angola, Zimbabwe, Namibia, Uganda, and Burundi all maintain a strong military presence in the Congo as well. President Joseph Kabila and his backers, Angola and Zimbabwe, refuse to consider power sharing through dialogue with antigovernment rebels without guarantees of Rwanda and Uganda's full withdrawal. The rebels and their sponsors, on the other hand, refuse to consider withdrawal until a transitional government is established through dialogue and Rwanda's border security is guaranteed. These external demands have to be addressed as part of the Congo's political transition. In total, these challenges appear to present a near-impossible "catch-22." But they can be resolved if the international community, and especially the United Nations, is prepared to make a greater commitment to completing all three parts of the peace process.[22]

NIGERIA

The rise of Islam in Nigeria is not something that should necessarily be a surprise, particularly to the Nigerian public. The country has been subjected to years of government squandering and corruption, so much so that Muslim regions have turned to the strict Sharia to enforce laws. After 9-11, there

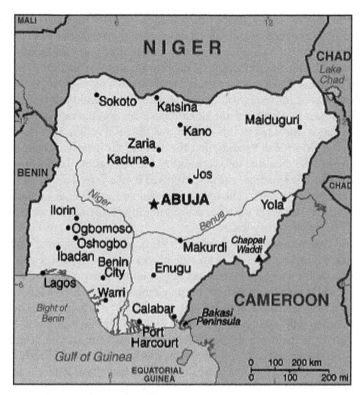

FIGURE 10-11   Map of Nigeria (Central Intelligence Agency, *The World Factbook, 2008*).

were sporadic outbreaks of violence between Muslims and Christians, including burning and looting of Christian-owned shops and restaurants that served alcohol in retaliation for a Christian attack on a mosque. In the many decades since the retreat of colonial powers, Africa has been an unsettled and volatile land. So, it is not surprising that radical Islamic fundamentalism would have a significant foothold in areas of Nigeria as well as other underdeveloped nations in Africa. Does the rise of Islam also mean that there is likely to be an increase in fundamentalist attitudes toward Western democracies and values? Certainly, a minority would seek to use religion as a cover for subversive operations against either the host state or to assist in propagating the fundamentalist movement.

Lawlessness and crime are an everyday problem for most nations of the world; however, the activities noted in Nigeria lend a new twist to the meaning of crime fighting. **The Bakassi Boys** are a group of young men who have taken some measure of control over the lawless southern city of Onitsha. The Bakassi Boys operate a terror subculture working outside of the established law. The Boys' brand of terror is to snatch victims, usually suspects in some crime or wrongdoing, and subject them to interrogation and, in many cases, instant execution. The Anambra state governor, Chinwoke Mbadinuju, has financed the group and provided it with weapons and even police vehicles. Quite clearly, law and order has broken down, and regional southern states have turned to vigilante operations to suppress crime. This can quickly lead to wider regional implications for the formation of private armies to do the bidding of their financial backers. Nigeria is Africa's most populous nation, with more than 125 million people and over 200 distinct ethnic groups, so it is not unusual to have clashes on religious, ethnic, and communal grounds. The violent outbreaks have claimed thousands of lives since the election in 1999 of then president Olusegun Obasanjo, following sixteen years of military rule. That period of military rule was able to contain ethnic and religious violence. More than 900 people died in 2004, and there are many claims that the Nigerian police and military did nothing to prevent the killings from taking place.

In a report on two waves of killings in Plateau and Kano state in February and May 2004, Human Rights Watch said the government's failure to punish the killers was feeding the cycle of violence. Central Nigeria lies on a religious fault-line, dividing the mainly Christian south and the predominantly Muslim north. Tension has been heightened by the adoption of the strict Islamic law, or Sharia, by several state governments elected with the ending of military rule in 1999.

In rural areas, the divide between Muslims and Christians often coincides with a conflict over land use. Violence in Plateau dates back to 2001 when around 1,000 people were killed in less than a week in September during religious riots in the state capital, Jos. Over the next two years, there followed a series of tit-for-tat attacks by Muslim and Christian communities in the hinterland that escalated into large-scale violence again in 2004.[23]

Nigeria is oil rich and has seen such companies as Shell Petroleum Development take an almost 50 percent stake in the oil reserves of the country. Most of the pipeline and development activity is centered on the Niger delta, and it's in this area that a shadowy and violent group has emerged to attack pipelines, kidnap workers, and generally harass and disrupt the supply of crude oil. The Movement for the Emancipation of the Niger Delta (**MEND**) operates in fast inflatable boats along the Niger and began operating in late 2005 with attacks on the oil infrastructure. The Nigerian then president Olusegun Obasanjo had attempted to make electoral reforms that would allow him to preside for a third term; a vote in the Senate supported by then vice president Atiku Abubakar rejected his attempt to make the necessary amendments. Oil wealth and government corruption continue to be the order of things in Nigeria and with oil at $100-plus per barrel and with production set at around 3 million barrels per day, the country would see revenue of around $100 billion. Controls being as weak as they are in Nigeria, it was not surprising that Abubakar would want Obasanjo out of power, and it was he who helped set up the MEND militia organization.[24] Attacks against the oil infrastructure have gone on for several decades; however, the activities of MEND were somewhat different as they focused on political change rather than an all-out assault on the oil patch. Their systematic approach had the desired effect and the third term in office for Obasanjo failed to materialize. May 2007, as part of a new crackdown on the mismanagement and corruption in Nigeria's oil industry, saw a new president in office; Umaru Yar'Adua took office pledging drastic changes and reforms. His vice president was Goodluck Jonathan, an ethnic Ijaw from the Niger Delta Province, who turned out to be an official spokesman for MEND. President Yar'Adua died in May 2010 and Vice President Good Luck Jonathan was sworn in as president.

MEND immediately had concerns that revenues would not be flowing in the manner that they demanded and set about disrupting the pipeline operations and the flow of crude. Many attacks are committed against oil interests and many are attributed to MEND, but in fact are carried out by other like-minded militants operating under MEND's umbrella. As the years have passed, MEND has become more of a loose affiliation of gangs—some operating independently of MEND's authority. To combat MEND, the Nigerian government has used the country's counterinsurgency troops from the Nigerian Joint Military Task Force. MEND continues to be a force in the area despite the heavy military presence to counter their activities.

Boko Haram

Approximately 40 percent of Nigerians are Muslims and the remainder Christians, and like many other African states Nigeria is blighted by corruption and sectarian and tribal fighting. The **Boko Haram** is located in the northern reaches of the country and has embarked on a Taliban-style campaign to force their brand of extreme ideology of Islam on the northern states. This has led to outright confrontation with the government and numerous attacks against the civilian population including Christian churches and Muslims who do not follow their brand of Islam including targeted assassination of imams. The police have often been targets for indiscriminate attacks. Several campaigns to neutralize by force have always led to resurgence by Boko Haram. The fear from many quarters is that they may become infiltrated by fighters from Somalia, Iran, Yemen, and Sudan. In June 2011, the group targeted the police HQ in the capital Abuja with a powerful car bomb. The group is prepared to enter into dialogue with the government but only once the following conditions have been met:

- Unconditional release of all imprisoned members of Boko Haram.
- The immediate prosecution of all those involved in the killing of Boko Haram leader Malam Muhammad Yusuf after he was taken into police custody in July 2009.
- An investigation into the alleged poisoning of Boko Haram suspects awaiting trial.
- Implementation of Sharia in the twelve northern states of Nigeria. These states adopted Sharia codes in 1999, but their current application is not strict enough to meet Boko Haram's standards.[25]

The economic problems facing Nigerians will continue to provide opportunities for groups such as Boko Haram in the north and MEND in the south.

Summary

The rise of Islamic extremism and strict ideology is spreading through northern and central Africa and threatens to destabilize vulnerable and corrupt governments. The threats from the spread of al Qaeda are ever present. Although mineral resource and oil exploration continues unabated, it is in most countries to the detriment of the economy and the population at large, with often only corrupt governments and their supporters benefitting. The establishment of an apartheid-free South African Nation under the presidency of Nelson Mandela had its share of violence perpetrated by both sides. South Africa is still considered one of the richest and most powerful nations in Africa, and its influence over its neighbors over the coming years will be of considerable interest worldwide.

The troubles plaguing the regime of Robert Mugabe and the struggle that brought him to power in Rhodesia/Zimbabwe were all typical of states gaining nationhood in southern Africa. Many of the fledgling countries that fought for independence have suffered under the hammer of tyrannical dictators, whose only real interests were to use capital and foreign investment in their respective countries for bankrolling their personal lifestyles. The influences of Communist involvement in the region over the past fifty years have been considerable and destabilization seems to continue in one form or another.

Review Questions

1. Discuss the reasons as to why Somalia remains a failed state and why piracy being practiced by Somalis is so difficult to defeat.
2. What were the conditions that led to the Israeli Operation Jonathan in Uganda?
3. What are the reasons why the LRA continues to operate at will?
4. What external forces are possibly influencing PAGAD and why does it pose a threat to the stability of RSA?

5. What role did Belgium play in the Hutu versus Tutsi situation in Rwanda?
6. What are the conditions that have given rise to the increase in Islamic extreme ideology in Nigeria and

why are extremist groups targeting oil companies in the Niger Delta region?

Websites

1. **The United States Institute for Peace**—*http://www.usip.org/countries-continents/africa/sudan*
2. **Lord's Resistance Army**—*http://www.globalsecurity.org/military/world/para/lra.htm*
3. **World Defense Review Strategic Interests**—*http://worlddefensereview.com/pham062107.shtml*
4. **The Triumph of Evil**—*http://www.pbs.org/wgbh/pages/frontline/shows/evil/*
5. **The National Security Archive**—*http://www.gwu.edu/~nsarchiv/NSAEBB/NSAEBB53/press.html*
6. **Human Rights Watch ZANU**—PF*http://www.hrw.org/english/docs/2008/04/19/zimbab18604.htm*

End Notes

1. Stephanie Hanson. *A l-Shabaab*, Leadership and Division (August 10, 2011), http://www.cfr.org/somalia/al-shabaab/p18650.
2. "Somalia's Government and Warlords—A Patchwork of Fiefs." *The Economist* (November 3, 2001).
3. "The White House." Office of the Press Secretary (November 7, 2001), http://www.whitehouse.gov/news/releases/2001/11/20011107-11.html.
4. Bruce Quarrie. *The World's Secret Police* (London: Octopus Books Ltd., 1986, p. 104).
5. J. Carter Johnson in Kitgum. "Deliver Us from Kony." *Why the children of Uganda are killing one another in the name of the Lord* (Uganda, January 2006), http://www.christianitytoday.com.
6. Buteera, Richard. "The Reach of Terrorist Financing and Combating It–The Links between Terrorism and Ordinary Crime." *International Society of Prosecutors* (Washington, DC, August 12, 2003).
7. Coalition for Human Rights and Justice Institute for Northern Uganda.
8. Institute for war and peace reporting (AR No. 121, July12, 2007), http://www.iwpr.net/.
9. Douglas Reed. *The Siege of Southern Africa* (Johannesburg, South Africa: Macmillan, 1974, p. 45).
10. Buteera, Richard. "The Reach of Terrorist Financing and Combating It." The Links between Terrorism and Ordinary Crime. Telegraph.co.uk. (Washington, DC: International Society of Prosecutors, August 12, 2003).
11. "Breaking the Silence, Building True Peace." *A Report on the Disturbances in Matabeleland and the Midlands 1980–1989.* (1997), http://www.hrforumzim.com/members_reports/matrep/matreppart1a.htm.
12. Reed. *The Siege of Southern Africa*, p. 95.
13. Peter Hawthorn. "Mugger of the Nation." *Time, Canada Limited* (December 8, 1997, p. 37).
14. Bill Dixon and Lisa-Marie Johns. "Gangs, Pagad & the State: Vigilantism and Revenge Violence in the Western Cape." *Violence and Transition Series*, vol. 2 (May 2001). Bill Dixon is a Senior Lecturer in the Department of Criminal Justice, University of Cape Town, and a researcher at the Institute of Criminology.
15. http://en.wikipedia.org/wiki/People_Against_Gangsterism_and_Drugs.
16. http://www.pagad.co.za/aims.htm.
17. *SCG International Risk.* Terrorist Group Profiles. http://www.scgonline.net/index.htm.
18. Anneli Botha. "PAGAD: A Case Study of Radical Islam in South Africa." *Publication: Terrorism Monitor*, vol. 3, no. 17 (September 14, 2005), http://www.jamestown.org.
19. Kenya, Capsule History. http://www.africanet.com.
20. Holden Alvaro Roberto, http://www.britannica.com/EBchecked/topic/505518/Holden-Alvaro-Roberto.
21. Reed. *The Siege of Southern Africa*, p. 25.
22. "Disarmament in the Congo: Preventing Further War." *InternationalCrisisGroupReport*http://www.intl-crisis-group.org/projects/showreport.cfm?reportid=519.
23. Ibid. UN Office for the Coordination of Humanitarian Affairs, NIGERIA: Rights Group Accuses Government of Letting Religious Killers Off Hook.
24. *Global Market Brief* (May 10, 2007), Stratfor.com.
25. "Nigeria's Boko Haram Issues Conditions amongst wave of Islamist Violence." *The Jamestown Foundations Terrorism Monitor*, vol. 9, no. 25 (June 23, 2011), http://www.jamestown.org/programs/gta/.

11

Southern and Southeast Asia

An eye for an eye ends up making the whole world blind.

—Mohandas Gandhi (1869–1948)
Indian Political Activist

LEARNING OBJECTIVES

After studying this chapter, the student should be able to:

1. Discuss the turbulent history of relations between India and Pakistan and the reasons why the region remains unstable.

2. Describe why terrorism and terror groups are able to flourish along the border of Pakistan and Afghanistan.

3. Explain the role played by the Taliban in the ongoing insurgency in Afghanistan.

4. Discuss the role played by the Pakistani ISI and its involvement over several decades as a supporter to terror organizations.

KEY WORDS TO NOTE

Haqqani Network—Afghan insurgent group closely aligned to al Qaeda and sponsored by the Pakistani ISI

Harakat-ul-Ansar (HUA)—Sunni Islamic militant group based in Pakistan and operating mainly in Kashmir

Inter Services Intelligence (ISI)—Pakistan's intelligence agency established by the British Army in 1948

Khmer Rouge—A Cambodian Communist movement came to power in 1975 and was one of the most violent regimes of the twentieth century; responsible for the deaths of approximately 1.7 million people by execution, starvation, and hard labor

Lashkar i Jhangvi (LJ)—A Sunni sectarian radical group with the goal of establishing a Muslim state in Pakistan, based mainly in the Punjab region of Pakistan and the port city of Karachi

Lashkar-e-Taiba (LeT)—Army of the Righteous—one of the largest Islamist terror organizations in Southern Asia—attacks both civilian and military targets

Liberation Tigers of Tamil Eelam (LTTE)—A separatist group seeking an independent state for ethnic Tamils in Sri Lanka

Madrassas—Islamic religious schools—many found in Pakistan

Mullah Omar—Leader of the Afghan Taliban and leader of the Afghan Government 1996–2001

Pol Pot—Cambodia's leader of the Khmer Rouge

OVERVIEW

Fear, hate, and mistrust for the United States and deep religious divides sum up the problems facing the Indian subcontinent. The situation is further exacerbated by both India and Pakistan having nuclear weapons programs. This remains one of the most complex regions of the world to both Americans and Westerners—a region continuously faced with terrorism and violence. This chapter will introduce some of the major problem areas in the most troubled countries, from the vastness of India, to Pakistan, to tiny Sri Lanka. The chapter discusses ongoing battles for autonomy and freedom, fought largely by terrorism and insurrection and shows how difficult it is to separate the problems into neatly defined categories. In addition, we will take a critical look at the potential threat of the Islamic efforts to unite into a global power stretching from the Persian Gulf to the eastern states of the Russian Republic.

INDIA

The Indian subcontinent has had a civilization since 2500 B.C., when the many inhabitants of the Indus River Valley developed a culture based on commerce and sustained by their agricultural trade. During the second millennium B.C., pastoral, Aryan-speaking tribes migrated from the Northwest into the subcontinent and then settled in the Middle Ganges River valley. The history of this region includes religious discord, violence, and terrorism. India was made up of many kingdoms with often-changing boundaries. In the fourth and fifth centuries A.D., northern India was unified under the Gupta dynasty. During this period, known as India's Golden Age, Hindu culture reached up to new heights.

Islamic influences spread across the subcontinent over a period of 500 years, starting in the tenth and eleventh centuries. Turks and Afghans invaded India and established sultanates in the areas around and near Delhi. Then descendants of Genghis Khan swept across the Khyber Pass in the eleventh century and established the Mogul Dynasty, which lasted from the eleventh to the fifteenth centuries. During this period, there were two major cultural and religious systems—those of the Hindus and the Muslims. These cultures had centuries of mutual contact, trade, and lasting influences on each other. The British appeared on the subcontinent in 1619 and, by the middle of the 1800s, controlled most of present-day India, Pakistan, and Bangladesh. In 1857, a rebellion in north India was led by mutinous Indian soldiers, resulting in the transfer of all political power to the British Crown, which then began administering most of India directly and controlled the rest through treaties with local rulers. By the late 1800s, India had taken its first steps toward self-government. The British viceroy established provisional councils comprised of Indian members to advise the Crown. By 1920, India's Mahatma Gandhi had transformed the Indian National Congress political party into a powerful movement against British colonial rule.

FIGURE 11-1 Map of India (Central Intelligence Agency, *The World Factbook, 2008*).

Following Gandhi's concepts of nonviolent resistance, the party used both parliamentary means and noncooperation to compel the British to give India its independence. In 1947, India was awarded Commonwealth status and Jawaharlal Nehru became India's first prime minister. A period of continuing and escalating bloody conflicts between the Hindus and Muslims finally led to the British partition of India. This division, created on the basis of incompatible religions, resulted in the formation of East and West Pakistan, where there were Muslim majorities. These groups were forcibly moved—Muslims to the north and Hindus to the south—creating anger and animosity that still pervades to this day. After partition, India became a full member of the Commonwealth, and a republic, on January 26, 1950.

Present-day relations between India and Pakistan took a downward plunge when both acquired nuclear weapons capability. Recent tests seem not more calculated to divert attention from economic and international issues, but rather than to "rattle their nuclear sabers." India has long complained about continuing foreign interference from Afghanistan and Pakistan and the menace of escalating terrorism in the region. For years, the most ruthless of the Islamic and other terrorist organizations have been known to use Afghanistan as a base for recruiting, training, and harboring terrorists to carry out operations abroad.

INDIA'S POLITICAL ASSASSINATIONS

January 30, 1948—Mohandas (Mahatma) Gandhi, spiritual leader of the Indian independence movement, was shot to death by a fanatical young Hindu.

October 31, 1984—Indira Gandhi, prime minister of India and only daughter of Jawaharlal Nehru, took her married name from her husband Feroze Gandhi, whom she married in 1942. She was assassinated by members of her Sikh bodyguard as revenge for the Indian Army assault on the Sikh temple in Amritsar in June 1984.

May 21, 1991—Rajiv Gandhi, president of the Indian Congress Party, while campaigning, was assassinated by an LTTE female suicide bomber.

Aircraft hijackings have been a popular modus operandi for Pakistani terrorists. In 1999, an Indian airliner was hijacked on Christmas Eve and continued to fly between India, Pakistan, Afghanistan, and the United Arab Emirates until December 31, at which time they surrendered to UAE authorities. Their demands were for the release of terrorists held in prisons and also a large sum of money. During the standoff, they killed one passenger in an attempt to press their demands. When the ordeal ended, it was determined that the terrorists had links to Pakistan's **Inter Services Intelligence (ISI) agency**.

On many occasions, India has drawn attention to the presence of training camps in neighboring Kashmir and Afghanistan. Terrorists are trained and equipped to carry out operations in India, particularly in the states of Jammu and Kashmir. Many hundreds of thousands of refugees from Afghanistan's war against the Russians were readily recruited by their protectors in Pakistan and used to foment terrorism and to pressure India into granting even more territory in the Kashmir region. In many instances, the ISI is believed to be behind any number of terror attacks in India.

SPECIAL ECONOMIC ZONE

Although fighting between Muslims and Hindus within the country is not uncommon, the Indian government has considerable exposure to internal troubles due to rapid business expansion in its special economic zone—a swath of land stretching almost across the country that has seen phenomenal growth and wealth to the booming IT industry. Land grabs by many unscrupulous politicians have led to large numbers of displaced tribesmen in these areas. India faces militant threats primarily from three sources:

1. Maoist rebels known as Naxalites
2. Tribal-based ethnic separatists
3. Islamist militants fighting in the name of Kashmir

Most militant activity is in the Jammu and Kashmir regions and the northeastern part of the country. The Naxalites have made direct threats against multinational corporations, though they primarily focus their attacks on police stations, locally owned factories, and Indian government officials. The Naxalite movement has created a single command center for the revolution, which clearly means more attacks are to come.

The Naxalites still have a host of problems to deal with, however. India has at least ten Naxalite splinter groups that have broken away from the main movement due to differences over ideology and militant strategy, along with general disillusionment with the movement and war fatigue. Indian media also report Naxalite defections on a nearly daily basis, though these incidents often are exaggerated and in some cases stage managed by the police. This was most recently illustrated in January 2008, when reports came out that as many as seventy-nine Naxalites in Chhattisgarh had defected. Soon enough, allegations emerged that innocent tribal people were forced to "surrender" as Maoist rebels.

ISLAM AND INDIA

Most Islamist attacks have centered in India, and militants have traditionally not been exported from India, and those operating within the country have likely come from and been sponsored by Pakistani-based groups. Al Qaeda seems to have paid scant attention to India as a center for targeting attacks, but India's internal security apparatus and lack of security infrastructure would make certain sectors and particularly the affluent special economic zone a prime, "soft," target for Islamist militant attacks. Osama bin Laden made mention of India in proclamations, and in 2006, he called on the Kashmiri Muslims to rise up against India. Al Qaeda appears to have no Indian base as such and would most likely depend on Kashmiri jihadists to do its bidding in India. Successful attacks have been carried out by Kashmiri militants, and the devastating railway bombings in Mumbai in 2006 and the Mumbai massacre in November 2008 are good examples of the spread of the jihadist threat.

MUMBAI ATTACKS, NOVEMBER 2008

India's version of 9-11 took place in the heart of India's economically rich city of Mumbai, formerly Bombay. As we have witnessed elsewhere in the world, well-planned and coordinated attacks by well-armed and determined individuals or groups can and will succeed in most cases if security is not vigilant; in the Mumbai attacks, the government had intelligence several weeks prior that an attack was probable. However, it is clear that public gathering places, train stations, restaurants, hotels, and the like were totally unprepared for an attack such as this one. At the attack locations, there was little evidence of any security presence established to defend against this onslaught.

The terrorist group responsible for the Mumbai attacks has been identified as Lashkar-e-Taiba, or Army of the Pure. They have targeted Hindus in India and brought India and Pakistan to the brink of all-out war. In 2000, an **LeT** attack on India's Parliament in New Delhi prompted the Indian government to mobilize 700,000 troops to India's border with Pakistan. Whether the Mumbai attack was intended to have the same effect, we do not know, but the rhetoric between Pakistan and India was ramped up. Strategically, the attack may also have been designed to divert Pakistani forces from the western border where the Pakistani Army is fighting Taliban insurgent forces.

LeT was designated by the United States as a Foreign Terrorist Organization, forcing the Pakistan government to similarly ban it. In the past, LeT is believed to have been trained and supported by the Pakistani Inter Services Intelligence agency in exchange for a pledge to target Hindus in Jammu and Kashmir and train Muslim extremists in India. Experts also indicate that LeT is supported by Saudi Arabia as well as Pakistani citizens. It has a network of terrorist training centers and religious schools in Pakistan and has its headquarters in Lahore.

Attack Time Line

The attack in Mumbai lasted from November 26 to 28 and also reminds us of the need for a greater control of the media. The trend for reporting every last detail on every guest or hostage, and every developing issue related to the security presence, greatly assisted the attackers who were able to monitor a vast array of media reports on their own success and progress at the locations they had attacked.

The LeT terrorists left the sanctuary of Pakistan on November 22 and traveled by boat into India's territorial waters and transferred to a larger vessel; the following day they are believed to have sent a distress call that was picked up and responded to by an India fishing vessel.

The crew of this vessel were all killed with the exception of the captain, who navigated them to their destination near the entrance to Mumbai harbor where they transferred to rubber dinghies. The ten terrorists landed in the fishing area and then spread out in five teams of two—all were equipped with AK-47 assault weapons, ammunition, hand grenades, and other types of explosives.

TARGETS   The five teams had a set of priority targets to attack:

- The Leopold Café, a popular restaurant in south Mumbai frequented by foreign businessmen and tourists;
- The Mumbai Central Railways Station and Terminus, always packed with travelers and commuters;
- The Taj Mahal Hotel, visited by foreign businessmen, tourists, and government officials;
- The Oberoi-Trident Hotel, also in South Mumbai and similarly popular with tourists and foreign businessmen;
- Nariman House, a Jewish Outreach Center, also in South Mumbai, owned and operated by a Jewish couple from New York.

The first team attacked the railway station at around 9.30 P.M., firing indiscriminately into the packed station and killing 56 and wounding over 100. The two-man team then fled the railway station and made for a secondary target to cause maximum disruption—the nearby Cama Hospital, where they began to fire at hospital staff and patients. As they left, they were challenged by Indian Police officers whom they shot and killed or injured and hijacked their vehicle and drove away. They were intercepted at a police roadblock; one was killed in the ensuing shootout and the other apprehended.

While the first team began its attack on the railway terminus, the second team attacked the Leopold Café near the Taj Mahal Hotel. They shot and killed ten diners and staff and then headed to the Taj Mahal Hotel, where a third team had already begun to attack staff and diners in the front lobby and the restaurant area. The two teams began rounding up hostages believed to be either British or Americans. The fourth team began a similar attack on the Oberoi Hotel and the fifth attacked the Jewish Center. The government response was to send a team of Naval commandos from Delhi, who arrived on November 27. The siege of the hotels and the Jewish Center lasted for nearly forty hours. The hotels were both badly damaged by fire, and the Rabbi and the other hostages including his wife were all killed by the terrorists. There were a total of 174 deaths and 311 injuries, with the majority of those killed being Indians.

The attackers were all Pakistani nationals, nine were killed and one was captured. The security services also noted that the terrorists carried satellite phones and had been communicating with handlers back in Pakistan during the assault on the five targets.

Motives

Previous terror attacks have pushed these two nuclear powers to the brink of all-out war, and it may be that this was the intention again due to the long-running dispute over Kashmir. Another more probable motive was the targeting of Westerners and in particular U.S. and British citizens as part of the global jihad and the even-more significant target—the Jewish Center. The terrorists also killed specific groups and not indiscriminately—the Jewish Center was a specific killing zone, whereas in the hotels Muslim hostages were set free and those of other nationalities and religions were executed.

Pakistan's ISI has used several organizations in its strategy to destabilize India:

1. Lashkar-e-Taiba (LeT)
2. Harkatul Mujahiden (HuM)
3. Harkatul jihad-e-Islami (HuJI)
4. Jaish-e-Mohammed (JeM)

THE PUNJAB AND SIKHISM

The northern Indian state of the Punjab has seen politics and religion mix with deadly results. In 1984, it led to the assassination of then prime minister Indira Gandhi by her own Sikh bodyguards who believed she had used the politics of religion for her own political gains and to the benefit of the Congress Party in the Punjab. Violence continued in Punjab for years after her assassination. In May 2007, there were clashes between mainstream Sikhs and followers of the Dera Sacha Sauda. The Dera had openly supported the Congress Party in the state assembly elections in 2007; however, Akali Dal, the main Sikh political party, won and since then has encouraged open protests against Dera. The flash point for violence was the heretical behavior of the Dera leader, one Ram Rahim Singh, who dressed up as Gobind Singh, the Sikh's most revered "guru." The weak apology by Singh did little to tone down the acts of violence that followed. A Dera is a temple that conducts educational and social activities, and there are thousands of Deras in Punjab; however, it appears that Mr. Singh may have outgrown the organization with more than 400,000 followers, both Sikhs and lower-caste Hindus. As the Akali Dal and Congress continue to play religion and politics, the likelihood of sectarian attacks is very real. This is also exacerbated by the economic hardship in the Punjab due to overfarming and the falling water table.[1]

PAKISTAN

Tensions between the United States and Pakistan continued through 2011, and though a supporter of the War on Terror, the killing of Osama bin Laden and the implications that he was being protected by Pakistan's spy agency, the ISI, or elite members of Pakistan's military have done little to help Pakistan's fragile political machine. Pakistan has opposed secret CIA operations within Pakistan including the use of unmanned drones inside its territory. From the U.S. perspective, Pakistan is considered a key ally despite the obvious concerns about ISI and the tracking of bin Laden to a military town inside the country.

U.S. NAVY SEALS KILL OSAMA BIN LADEN—MAY 2011

Osama bin Laden has been the U.S. Number One Most Wanted Terrorist since the September 11 attacks on the United States. It took the United States ten years to track down the mastermind behind 9-11 to Abbottabad, not far from the Pakistani capital Islamabad, where he was killed by U.S. Navy SEALS on May 1, 2011. Special Forces units the world over celebrated this successful operation, which is believed to have taken not more than forty minutes to complete and was done without the knowledge or permission of the Pakistan government. Aside from killing bin Laden, the SEALs netted a treasure trove of intelligence, including laptop computers, hard drives, and cell phones. Britain, the United States, and their allies steadfastly attempted to track him and his cohort following the invasion of Afghanistan, but bin Laden along with Ayaman-al-Zawahiri and Taliban leader Mullah Omar had always managed to either hide out in the rugged mountains

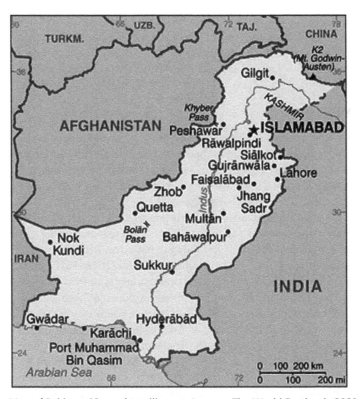

FIGURE 11-2 Map of Pakistan (Central Intelligence Agency, *The World Factbook, 2008*).

or escape into Pakistan. Bin Laden, through his own magnetism, was able to spawn a global movement of al Qaeda spreading through the Middle East to Northern and Central Africa and Europe; while loosely affiliated, these groups held true to his ideology of attacking the West. Many of bin Laden's family fled to the border region with Iran, but the exact location of bin Laden had never been discovered. Intelligence reports suggest that he had been almost housebound in Abbottabad for the five years preceding his death. Although bin Laden has been replaced, the fact of his death will likely have little impact on the spread of Islamic extremism or the attacks on Western targets. Other organizations have lost their leaders; the Taliban leadership has been decimated but still continues to operate and is probably now more extreme than it was prior to the military invasion of Afghanistan. Dead too are Yasser Arafat, Sheikh Yassin, and others, but all their movements continue to operate in spite of their losses. In Pakistan, the leader of the pro-Taliban Red Mosque, Abdul Rashid Ghazi, is dead, as is the Pakistani Taliban leader Baitullah Mehsud, but their deaths have had no noticeable effect on Islamists across Pakistan.

Pakistan's reputation as a terrorist haven has seen many Westerners targeted for kidnapping or assassination.

In November 1997, four U.S. employees of Union Texas Petroleum and their Pakistani driver were murdered in Karachi when their vehicle was attacked near the U.S. Consulate. Shortly after the incident, two separate groups claimed responsibility for the killings, the Aimal Khufia Action Committee, a previously unknown group; and the Islami Inqilabi Mahaz, a Lahore-based group of Afghan war veterans. Both groups cited the motive for the attack as being the conviction of

Mir Aimal Kansi, a Pakistani National, tried in the United States for the 1993 murder of two CIA employees and the wounding of three others. Kansi was found guilty and sentenced to death. Ramzi Ahmed Yousef, who was extradited from Pakistan to the United States in 1995, was convicted in New York in November 1997 for his role in the 1993 World Trade Center bombing in New York City.

BENAZIR BHUTTO

Benazir Bhutto was portrayed as Pakistan's last great hope to bring a level of democracy to Pakistan. Unfortunately, any hope of that died with her assassination in December 2007, when a gunman and suicide bomber attacked her, killing her instantly. Ms. Bhutto had only recently returned to Pakistan from a self-imposed exile of eight years, following President Pervez Musharraf's dropping of corruption charges against her.

Before her return to Pakistan, she had clearly criticized the government of Pervez Musharraf for failing to reign-in and defeat the Islamic militants of al Qaeda and the Taliban. "Pakistan is in a crisis and it's a crisis that threatens not only my nation and region, but could possibly have repercussions on the entire world."[2] Benazir Bhutto was returning to Pakistan as a symbol of hope for the country. She had previously been elected prime minister in 1988 and had immediately ran afoul of the powerful military machine and the Inter Services Intelligence Agency, both of which have significant control and influence. Within two years of taking office, she was dismissed by the military on charges of corruption and misrule. She regained power in the 1993 general election at about the same time as the Taliban regimes were coming into power in Afghanistan. Her party, the Pakistan Peoples' Party, is left-leaning and eschews religious extremism but had recognized in the Taliban the opportunity to secure trade routes across southern Afghanistan. Her difficulty with confronting her own military was also a problem, and she agreed to provide covert aid to the Taliban regime, but denied to the United States that Pakistan was funding or arming the Taliban. In 1996, she was again removed from power by the military and sought exile in London and then Dubai, where from a distance she remained involved in Pakistani politics.

On October 18, 2007, Bhutto returned to Pakistan, and the first attempt on her life took place just after midnight on October 19, 2007. Her entourage was en route from Karachi International Airport to the tomb of Muhammad Ali Jinnah, the country's founder, when it was attacked by suicide bombers in the dense crowd around Bhutto's armored bus. Reports indicated that there were two explosions shortly after one another and that around 140 people were killed—how many were killed by the bombings and how many by the stampeding masses as they escaped the carnage has not been determined. What was clear was that the moment she set foot in Pakistan she would become a target of either the Musharraf supporters or Islamist militants. Prior to her return, she had pledged to take on the Islamists and went so far as to say that if she were prime minister, she would permit the United States to send troops into Pakistan if the situations in the tribal areas were to further deteriorate. Musharraf ordered troops to storm Islamabad's Red Mosque, and Ms. Bhutto came out in strong support of the action.

There has been speculation that the attack on Bhutto was in fact a government conspiracy; however, on December 27, 2007, after attending a political rally in Rawalpindi, she was shot by an assailant as she stood in the well of her vehicle, her head and shoulders exposed through the sun roof, when the assailant then detonated an explosive vest, killing twenty people including Benazir Bhutto.

Pakistan's military is coming under continuous attacks from Islamist militants in the rugged Northwest Frontier Provinces (NWFP). Pakistan's military is a very formidable force and most certainly one to be reckoned with. In the past where assassination attempts against government officials have taken place, swift and violent retribution has been meted out by the military.

The Lal Masjid (Red Mosque)

The Red Mosque in the Pakistani capital Islamabad has been in place since 1965 and is home to fundamentalist teachers with links to global terrorism and jihad in the intervening decades. The mosque leadership had been openly opposed to the government, and after the London bombings in 2005, Pakistani police investigated links between one of the bombers, Shehzad Tanweer, and the Red Mosque. The police were confronted and repulsed by baton-wielding women from the self-styled vigilante, Lal Masjid Brigade.

By the summer of 2007, the mosque leadership had become more and more extreme and speeches from the leadership became far more menacing. Pakistani authorities were of the belief that the mosque had become home to jihadists from the tribal region bordering Pakistan and Afghanistan and had turned the fundamentalist religious institution into an armed military camp. The Chinese government was a significant supporter of Musharraf and his regime and had a large number of its nationals in Islamabad. When the Lal Masjid brigade kidnapped seven Chinese nationals from a massage parlor, this raised the stakes for the mosque to a significant level. The Chinese government demanded that the Pakistani authorities take action to release the kidnapped Chinese. Islamabad is a heavily fortified city, so when President Musharraf proclaimed "surrender or die" as his final message to the inhabitants of the mosque, the ensuing daylong battle was unexpected in its ferocity. Far from being a bastion of education, the Red Mosque was heavily fortified and occupied with trained fighters and militants from banned religious groups and fighters linked to both the Taliban and al Qaeda militias operating in the tribal regions. The week-long standoff at the mosque was followed up by 200 commandos storming the enclave resulting in more than 100 deaths, including another dozen soldiers and the extremist leader Abdul Rashid.

Pervez Musharraf

As chief of the Army, General Musharraf had been in power since the military seized control of Pakistan in 1999 and was a supporter of the U.S. "War on Terror." This has made him a target for Muslim fundamentalists as well as opposition parties. In November 2007, there were challenges to the validity of his reelection as president. His suspension of the Pakistani Constitution did nothing to curry favor with the powerful state judiciary, and his jailing of several key ministers including the Chief Justice Minister would cause a political backlash amid attempts to impeach him. It was with this backdrop that Musharraf resigned as president in August 2008 rather than face impeachment. In September 2008, Asif Ali Zardari—the widower of Benazir Bhutto—who

TERRORIST ATTACK BRIEF

Terrorist Group: Taliban

Case Facts: A young boy aged around fourteen detonated a suicide vest at a military checkpoint in the market town near the Swat Valley killing forty-one people including at least six military personnel.

Investigation: In the weeks leading up to the anniversary of 9-11, there had been increasing number of attacks against military convoys and police post. In this attack, the bomber was a young teenage boy and was on foot near a military checkpoint as an army convoy approached. As the convoy reached the post, the suicide bomber struck. It is believed that this attack is the work of the Taliban but the first such attack in Pakistan using a child as the bomber—in Afghanistan, they use children unwittingly to carry bombs.

FIGURE 11-3 Bombing—Alpuri—Pakistan—September 11, 2011. *Source*: http://www.telegraph.co.uk/news/worldnews/asia/pakistan/6305970/Boy-13-kills-41-in-Taliban-suicide-bombing-in-Pakistan.html was until his wife's assassination not in the political limelight and in fact was better known for his conviction and imprisonment for corruption—was sworn in as president. He had, then, little or no political experience, and only time will tell on his ability to handle the army, which has been and will remain the power base of Pakistan's politics. More importantly, with dwindling support for U.S. action in Afghanistan, his relationship with the United States will be critical to both his survival and ability to handle the Taliban insurgency that threatens the very survival of Pakistan.

Pakistan, Afghanistan, and Islam

Religious differences and a long history of violence and hatred among former brothers and fellow countrymen still separate India and Pakistan. Sponsoring international terrorism, separatist subversion, and insurgency are not new to either side. Since the 1970s, Pakistan has also trained Sikh and Indian separatist movements. The Shiromani Gurudwara Prabandhak Committee (SGPC) is the major Sikh terrorist organization in India. It established tight control over the culture and economy of the Indian state of Punjab in the early 1980s and forced Sikh traditionalism and conservatism on Punjabi society. Pakistan was quick to recognize this as an opportunity to exploit further divisions in India. The Sikh struggle for an independent state attracted Pakistan's attention. Pakistan had long held its own claims to Kashmir and saw some possible benefit from encouraging the formation of a Sikh state, Khalistan, located in the Punjab, as this would weaken India's defense of the remaining portion of Kashmir. Pakistan hoped to exploit the tensions in Kashmir in order to destabilize India and began to provide support and training as terrorist activities of the Sikh militants increased. The Sikhs began to represent such a potential threat that India, in July 1984, launched an assault on the Golden Temple at Amritsar, one of the holiest places for Sikhs. Ultimately the escalation of Sikh separatist terrorism resulted in the assassination of Indira Gandhi the same year. The Sikhs' armed insurrection escalated as high-quality weapons became available. The arsenal included sophisticated bomb-making materials and better training for Sikh separatists in the Afghanistan mujahedeen camps. The long reach of Sikh terrorism further resulted in the bombing of the Air India jet from Toronto that blew up over the coast of Ireland, killing 329 passengers.

A corresponding ideological development in Indian Kashmir then occurred. Almost overnight, the prevailing popular sentiment in Indian Kashmir was the belief that because the targets of Indian security forces were Muslims, Islam was in danger. This had a galvanizing effect on the fanatical Islamic youth of the Kashmir region, who formed new cadres of terrorists. The extent of Pakistani and Afghan influence on the Islamist transformation of the Kashmir insurgency was profound and deadly.

Pakistan's **Inter Services Intelligence (ISI)** began to assume quite a different role from its behind-the-scenes maneuvers. It seemed to be taking over direct control of the Sikh movement. The ISI made the city of Darra, Pakistan, the primary source of weapons for the Sikh, Tamil, and Kashmiri liberation movements. Darra became the storefront for the regional illegal arms market.

Having witnessed the initial impact of the Islamist message in Indian Kashmir, Pakistan began to broaden its horizons and set its sights higher. In 1986, with growing experience in training, organizing, and operating with the Afghan mujahedeen, and with military supplies available, Pakistan began expanding its operation to sponsor and promote separatism and terrorism, primarily in Kashmir, as a strategic, long-term program. Among the most crucial activities of the ISI were the following:

- Religious radicalism was propagated in small, but lethal, doses to promote separatism and communal outlook.
- Training and indoctrination of selected leaders from the Kashmir valley was arranged to create militant cadres.

- A large number of youths from the Kashmir valley and Poonch sector were given extensive training in the use of automatic weapons, sabotage, and attacks on security forces.
- Automatic weapons and explosives were issued to these people.
- Special teams were trained to organize disruption and engineer incidents to damage the myth of a democratic and secular image for India and Kashmir.

The Harakat-ul-Ansar (HUA)

An Islamic militant group based in Pakistan and operating primarily in Kashmir, Harakat-ul-Ansar was formed in October 1993 when two Pakistani political activist groups, Harakat ul-Jihad al-Islami and Harakat ul-Mujahedin, merged. Faroogi Kashmiri is currently leading this group. His predecessor, Fazlur Khalil, supports the al Qaeda doctrine of attacks against the West and the United States. Khalil is the secretary general of the organization.

The HUA has carried out a number of operations against Indian troops and civilian targets in Kashmir and has been linked to the Kashmiri militant group, Al-Faran, which kidnapped five Western tourists in Kashmir in July 1995; one was killed in August 1995 and the other four reportedly were killed in December of the same year. The HUA has several thousand armed supporters located in Azad Kashmir, Pakistan and in southern Kashmir and the Doda regions of India. These areas are composed of mostly Pakistanis and Kashmiris, but include Afghans and Arab veterans of the Afghan war. The HUA uses light and heavy machine guns, assault rifles, mortars, explosives, and rockets.

Based in Muzaffarabad, Pakistan, its members have participated in insurgent and terrorist activities primarily in Kashmir. The HUA trained its militants in Pakistan and in Afghanistan during the Taliban regime, prior to the U.S. airborne attacks of 2001. They collect donations from Saudi Arabia and other Gulf and Islamic states and from Pakistanis and Kashmiris. The source and amount of its military funding are unknown. Khalil was detained by Pakistani forces in 2004 but released later that year. One of HUA's associates is Ahmed Omar Sheik, who was convicted for the abduction and murder of the *Wall Street Journal* journalist Daniel Pearl. HUA began to use a different name in 2003, calling itself Jamiat ul-Ansar (JUA).[3]

The head of Pakistan's ISI political section developed a long-term program called K-2, aimed at castigating the Kashmiri and Sikh subversive efforts by making them appear to be under one umbrella of Sikh and Kashmiri extremists and Muslim fundamentalists. These groups would clearly not become allied with each other because of long-held hatred among them. This program would then intensify acts of violence in Punjab, Jammu, Kashmir, and the Terai region of Uttar Pradesh. Escalation of terrorism and subversion since the early 1990s is widely believed to have been a direct outgrowth of the ISI's implementation of the K-2.

Sikh terrorists were increasingly smuggling weapons from the Jammu and Kashmir areas or from Ganganagar in Rajasthan, where the ISI had its own bases. Clandestine ISI support for the Sikh terrorists continued to improve. By 1992, the ISI was operating thirteen permanent, eighteen temporary, and eight joint training camps for Kashmiris in Pakistan and Kashmir alone. Thus, while these Kashmiris failed to incite or stir up a popular war, they did establish enough popular support to embark on the second phase: a direct and violent confrontation with the Indian security forces, whom they consider to be occupiers. That would not have been possible without Pakistani and other Islamist support.

Many of the factions involved in the Afghanistan civil war included large numbers of Egyptians, Algerians, Palestinians, and Saudis. Many of these factions continue to provide haven to terrorists by facilitating the operation of training camps in areas under their control. The factions remain engaged in a struggle for political and military supremacy over India.

The Indian and Pakistani governments both claim that the intelligence service of the other country sponsors bombings on its territory. The government of Pakistan acknowledges that it continues to provide moral, political, and diplomatic support to Kashmiri militants, but denies allegations of providing any other assistance.

Lashkar-e-Taiba (Army of the Pure)

LeT is an Islamic terrorist organization, active in Jammu and Kashmir. It is the terrorist arm of the Markaz Dawa-Wal-Irshad, an Islamic fundamentalist organization. It came to notice in 1997 during Nawaz Sharif's second term as Pakistan's prime minister. LeT uses "suicide attacks" where small groups of fidayeen (suicide squads) would storm a security force camp and kill as many personnel as possible. They reportedly changed the name to Pasban-i-Ahle Hadith following their inclusion in the U.S. State Department's Foreign Terrorist Organization list. One of its main goals is the destruction of India and the establishment of an Islamic state. Lashkar-e-Taiba was launched during the last days of Afghan resistance against Soviet occupation. Though Lashkar-e-Taiba's entry into Jammu and Kashmir was first recorded in 1993, it came into the picture of Kashmir militancy only in 1997. Its induction to Kashmir is believed to be the result of deteriorating Harkat–ISI relations.

Lashkar's militant activities soon outshone those of Harakat. The group would first use local Kashmiri militants only as helpers and guides, keeping both the armed operations and leadership with nonlocal cadre, generally Punjabis from Pakistan. Today, the outfit is the largest group active in the Valley with a dedicated *Fidayeen* unit (suicide squad) that changed the landscape of militancy in Kashmir.

LeT has 2,200 offices across Pakistan and an estimated two dozen camps along the Line of Control, an unmarked border between India and Pakistan in Jammu and Kashmir. Two LeT training camps are located at Muzaffarabad, the capital of Pakistan-held Kashmir. The training is divided into two phases—Daura Aam (basic phase) and Daura Khaas (special phase). During the first phase, a twenty-one-day period, students are motivated to internalize jihad as an exclusive life-long mission, mainly through intensive exposure to semi-mythical stories glorifying the lives and exploits of Islam's historical martyrs. The second phase lasts for three months and involves weapons training, ambush, and survival techniques.[4]

However, what really drives the organization's ideological indoctrination and the rigors of its jihadist training is a concept evolved by Hafiz Saeed. His unique approach has been to merge Islamic education with modern curricula, thus ensuring a balance between religious and secular training.[5]

LeT has also become a focus for the Pakistan ISI to use it in its campaign against India. LeT played a major role in the planning and execution of the bomb attacks on a train station in the Mumbai financial district in July 2006, when powerful bombs ripped through seven commuter trains killing 174 and wounding nearly 500 others. Like HUA, the LeT is used to pit Muslims against Hindus, and by placing bombs and targeting either of the religious groups they hope to succeed in their objective.

SIKH TERRORISM

Sikh terrorism is mainly sponsored by expatriate and Indian Sikh groups, with designs to create an independent Sikh state called Khalistan (Land of the Pure) from Indian territory. Active groups include Babbar Khalsa, International Sikh Youth Federation, Dal Khalsa, and the Bhinderanwala

Tiger Force. A previously unknown group, the Saheed Khalsa Force, claimed credit for the New Delhi marketplace bombings in 1997. Sikh attacks in India are usually against Indian officials and facilities, other Sikhs, and Hindus. They include assassinations, bombings, and kidnappings. These attacks have dropped markedly since 1992. Indian security forces killed or captured many of the senior Sikh militant leaders and disrupted extremist groups. Many low-intensity bombings that might have been credited to Sikh extremists occur without subsequent claims of credit. Sikh militant cells are active internationally, and extremists gather funds from overseas Sikh communities. The Sikh expatriates have formed a variety of international organizations that lobby for the Sikh cause overseas. Most prominent are the World Sikh Organization and the International Sikh Youth Federation.[6]

KASHMIR

Over the decades, there has been a continuous cycle of declared and undeclared wars between India and Pakistan, with an ever-increasing enmity between the two countries. Protagonists of each country are emphatic about their separate claims to Kashmir and stubbornly proclaim that they will never give up that claim.

The Kashmir problem was created toward the end of British rule in India and still lies at the heart of the instability between Pakistan and India. This issue even affects Afghanistan. In the last years of British rule, all parties agreed to divide India into a Hindu-majority country called India and a Muslim-majority country called Pakistan. Pakistan took its first form as East Pakistan (now Bangladesh) and West Pakistan, about 1,100 miles apart on either side of India.

The state of Kashmir was close to the heart of Jawaharlal Nehru, the first prime minister of independent India; he did not wish to give it up to Pakistan, in spite of its Muslim majority. The departing British, under Lord Mountbatten, made no secret of their dislike for the nascent state of Pakistan and for its leader, Mohammed Ali Jinnah. Britain's Viceroy, Lord Mountbatten joined Nehru in persuading the Hindu Raja of Jammu and Kashmir to accede to India. To afford India with a contiguous connection to Kashmir and make it defensible, the British granted the adjoining Gurdaspur district to India, instead of Pakistan as was originally planned.

The Muslim majority of Kashmir has been unwilling to accede to Indian rule over Kashmir and has been involved in a steady escalation of resistance to India since independence in 1947. As a result, India has had more troops and other security forces per capita in Kashmir than any other nation has had anywhere. The George W. Bush administration referred to all Kashmiri resistance fighters as "Terrorists." Had it not been so tragic, it would have been considered funny that Bush and Russian President Putin stood side by side as they jointly told Pakistan's President Musharraf to stop aiding terrorists in crossing the cease-fire line into Indian Kashmir. George Bush was obviously ignoring the record of his companion, Putin—a man responsible for the killing of almost 100,000 Chechens. In Kashmir, the fact is that Indian forces have long prevented a reign of terror. Kashmiri Muslims disappear after being "detained" by Indian security forces. If they are lucky enough to ever return, it is only after suffering severe torture. Many are killed either "while resisting arrest" or "while attempting to escape"—euphemisms applied with impunity by the occupying forces.

No sooner had India and Pakistan become independent than hostilities began between them for the possession of Kashmir. It is said that the Kashmir dispute has been the cause of two wars between India and Pakistan. In fact, the Kashmir dispute has been the cause of a long, sixty-year war between India and Pakistan; the two nuclear-armed nations have hardly ever had a week without an exchange of some kind of deadly weapons fire along the cease-fire line that exists between Indian Kashmir and Pakistani Kashmir. Huge numbers of soldiers have been killed and wounded in this game of "keep-away," but each side carefully keeps their losses a closely held secret. Billions of dollars have been spent in pursuit of continuing warfare between the two nations attempting to get an upper hand in the battle for Kashmir. At the same time, millions of people constantly face death by starvation and preventable diseases (or even nuclear war!).

India regards Kashmir as a part of India and, therefore, pride and honor are involved; for Pakistan, it is a matter of "survival" because the only major river in Pakistan now originates in Kashmir.

At the time of independence, there were six major rivers flowing through Pakistan. All, except for the Indus River, flowed through the province of Punjab ("five waters") in North Eastern Pakistan. The Ravi, Sutlej, Beas, and Chenab rivers all flow from Indian East Punjab, and the Jhelum flows from Kashmir. In the 1950s, India drew up plans to divert the flow of some of the rivers that passed through Pakistan. After over nine years of negotiations, an agreement was then made that resulted in the "Indus Waters Treaty" of 1960. This treaty gave up three of the rivers, the Ravi, Beas, and Sutlej, for India's exclusive use, while the Indus, Jhelum, and Chenab were determined to be shared with Pakistan.

The mighty Indus, which was used for fishing as well as for river commerce, is no longer mighty, and during the dry months, it becomes almost stagnant in the south, permeating the air with the smell of rotten vegetation. Over 100 miles upstream, one may cross this now-slow river on foot. It is small wonder that Pakistan feels insecure if India should control the headwaters of the Indus, the Jhelum, and the Chenab.

Currently, Pakistan is accused of supporting the "terrorists" in Kashmir. These are all largely Kashmiris supported by Pakistanis who are struggling to remove Indian rule from Kashmir. Pakistan supports them by providing protection, shelter, and military support. This is no different from Indian support of rebels in areas of Pakistan like Baluchistan, the North-West Frontier Province, and so on. In fact, the largest support India gave to any rebel movement in Pakistan (which pales in comparison with anything Pakistan has done in India) was to the Bangladesh Freedom Fighters. This support first began in 1971, when India began providing shelter to the Mukti Bahini, the Bangladesh Liberation Army, until war was declared between India and Pakistan, resulting in Bangladesh independence. In hindsight, this was a just war for India to be involved in, as the Bengalis were oppressed and near-genocidal action was being taken against them by the (Western) Pakistani Army. One could make a similar argument for the Kashmiris of today and for support of their liberation movements.

Since independence, India has dissolved at least three popularly elected state governments of Kashmir. The Muslim governments of Kashmir failed to toe the Indian line by demanding more and more autonomy, so India imposed presidential rule over them, each time lasting for years. During the last sixty years of war and terror between India and Pakistan, only a few voices have been heard demanding Kashmir for Kashmiris—and both sides ignored them. Why did they not vacate Kashmir and leave it for the Kashmiris to rule? Such a step would have led to the first rapprochement between the two warring nations. It would also have allowed the beleaguered Kashmiris their first opportunity to attempt to live and prosper in peace.

A Kashmir with open borders would give people from India and Pakistan opportunities to meet, promote mutual understanding, and invest there in joint ventures. With the elimination of tensions in Kashmir would come a scaling back of arms and, perhaps, demilitarized borders. From there, it may only be a small step toward a closer relationship and, perhaps, even the initiation of a loose federation involving India, Pakistan, and Bangladesh. All three nations spring from the same source; families have been split among the three sides and even culturally the similarities far outweigh the differences. Is there really a reason why these three countries cannot follow the European Community model to come together?

Resolving the Kashmir issue may be the first and greatest step in preventing many future wars and separatist movements in South and Central Asia.

Nuclear Proliferation Threats

There has been much worldwide commentary on whether or not Islamic terror groups such as al Qaeda are searching for the means to develop weapons of mass destruction (WMD). Pakistan has had a thriving nuclear program since the 1970s, and its leading scientist Dr. Abdul Qadeer Khan has also provided much-needed assistance to the Iranian nuclear program. Through the support and financing of the Pakistan government, Khan was in control of the Khan Research Laboratories. The U.S. CIA is of the belief that Khan may have been peddling nuclear technology to unfriendly countries and terrorist groups like al Qaeda. Whether this will ever be confirmed is another matter, as Khan is currently under house arrest in Pakistan, and the government refuses to allow either UN or U.S. investigators to interrogate him. A vast majority of Pakistanis view Khan as a celebrity figure who donated money to charities throughout the country. How far-reaching his black market activities have spread, and how much this activity has spread the threat of nuclear weapons proliferation, is unclear.

ISLAMIC MILITANCY

Since 9-11 and up until his resignation in August 2008, President Pervez Musharraf had pledged support to the War on Terror and had gone on record that he would deal with Islamic terrorists who reside within Pakistan's borders. Most of the arrests of al Qaeda-linked suspects have occurred in Karachi. Official reports target Karachi as being home to more than 417 well-known terror cells and operatives from differing sectarian and militant organizations. Karachi has a population in excess of 14 million with more than 1,000 religious schools and 10,000 mosques. Many former Taliban fighters fled from the Afghan war to the border towns of Pakistan's north-west frontier and spread into Karachi, a fertile recruiting ground for misguided youths for jihad. When the Taliban controlled Afghanistan, a large number of Pakistanis trained for jihad in Taliban-supported training camps and the numbers, which cannot be confirmed, are thought to be over 30,000 such fighters over the years. Following 9-11, the Pakistani government cracked down on militant fund-raising and focused more specifically on those groups supporting jihad in Kashmir. One such terror organization is the **Lashkar i Jhangvi (LJ)**, an extreme Sunni group that has its roots in a sectarian movement calling itself Sipah-I-Sahaba Pakistan. With sectarian violence the group's goal, its main subjects for attack have been mostly those from the Shia religious sect. The group had ties with the Taliban regime in Afghanistan and aided many fighters returning through the northwest frontier cities of Peshawar and Rawalpindi. It was this terror group that had made attempts on former president Musharraf's life.

The Jaish-e-Mohammed (JEM, the Army of Mohammed), an Islamic extremist group based in Pakistan, was formed by Masood Azhar upon his release from prison in India in 2000. Azhar's release resulted from the hijacking of an Indian Airlines flight, which had similar modus operandi to the attacks that took place on 9-11. In the Indian Airlines hijacking, the terrorists slit passengers' throats with knives smuggled onto the flight and then stormed the cockpit. Masood Azhar was released from prison in India in exchange for the 155 passengers on board the flight.

JEM's aim is to unite Kashmir with Pakistan. It is politically aligned with the radical political party, Jamiat-I Ulema-i Islam Fazlur Rehman faction (JUI-F). In October 2001, the United States announced the addition of JEM to the Treasury Department's Office of Foreign Asset Control's (OFAC) list, which includes organizations that are believed to support terrorist groups and have assets in U.S. jurisdiction that can be frozen or controlled. In 2001, JEM was added to the U.S. list of Foreign Terrorist Organizations. The group is located primarily in Peshawar and has its operations in Kashmir. Most of its support members come from Pakistani or are former Taliban/ Afghan fighters. The leadership of JEM has threatened to kill India's prime minister in its bid to rid Jammu and Kashmir of Indian forces. JEM's extensive organization in Pakistan has set up schools for jihad at its offices throughout the country, and with its external links to the former Taliban regime in Afghanistan as well as Sunni terror cells in Pakistan, JEM will continue to be a threat in the region. JEM uses suicide attacks as well as more conventional attacks with light weapons and improvised explosive devices (IEDs). Although banned in Pakistan since 2002, the group appears to operate openly in many areas of Pakistan.

NEPAL

Nepal is a region probably most famously known for Sir Edmund Hillary's conquering of Mount Everest, rather than a hotbed for political violence and insurgency. The insurgency in this poverty-ridden kingdom came from a Maoist movement looking to replace the monarchy with a Communist state. Democratic reforms seemed unlikely and King Gyanendra announced a state of emergency in February 2005, following his dismissal of the government, and has become increasingly reliant on the Royal Army, which had been less than effective in fighting the rebel insurgents. The king had also relied on political collaboration with India, which feared that the insurgency could spread there with support from left-wing groups. In May 2008, the end finally came to the 240-year reign of the Nepal Royal family, following which the Nepalese government reached a peace accord with the Maoist rebels, in a country desperate for peace.

FIGURE 11-4 Map of Nepal (Central Intelligence Agency, *The World Factbook, 2008*).

Nepal was declared a republic by the constitutional assembly, which voted to abolish the Hindu monarchy, which had been in control of the country for over two centuries. King Gyanendra came to the throne soon after a large number of the Royal family was massacred in 2001. Conspiracy theories abounded about his involvement, which would only sour his relationship with his subjects. His sacking of the government and his embarking on a period of autocratic rule can have only hastened his demise. In 2011, most insurgent and terrorist activity faded away and most Maoists laid down their weapons. But problems of a political nature still pose problems for stability, most of which has centered on drafting the country's first Constitution, the terms of which none of the political parties can agree upon. Repeated Maoist announcements regarding the intention to start a "new revolution," and acquisition of capacities for violence by various other political formations, have only added to apprehensions that the political impasse may spiral incrementally into open chaos.[7]

SRI LANKA

The Democratic Socialist Republic of Sri Lanka is an island in the Indian Ocean, south of India. It is slightly larger than West Virginia and was known as Ceylon until 1972. Sri Lanka was the center of Buddhist civilization in the third century B.C. and still has a strong Buddhist majority (69 percent), with minority representation by Hindus (15 percent), Christians (8 percent), and Muslims (8 percent), distributed among an estimated population of more than 18,700,000.

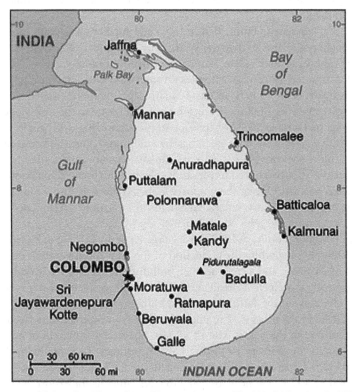

FIGURE 11-5 Map of Sri Lanka (Central Intelligence Agency, *The World Factbook, 2008*).

As of 2001, the Sinhalese constitute 74 percent of Sri Lanka's population, Tamils are 18 percent, Muslims 7 percent and Burghers comprise most of the rest of the population.

The Portuguese first settled on this island in 1505, followed by the Dutch in 1658. The British arrived in 1796 and made it a colony of the British Empire in 1853. Sri Lanka was granted independence in 1948. The Ceylonese government resisted an insurrection by terrorists attempting its overthrow in 1971.

LIBERATION TIGERS OF TAMIL EELAM—LTTE

The Tamils of Sri Lanka constitute a distinct nation and form a social entity with their own history, tradition, culture, language, and traditional homeland. The Tamil people call their nation "Tamil Eelam." Founded in 1976, the **LTTE** was the most powerful Tamil group in Sri Lanka and used overt and illegal methods to raise funds, acquire weapons, and publicize its cause of establishing an independent Tamil state. Frequent episodes of Sinhalese nationalism during this time also limited the ability of many Tamils to find education or employment according to their expectations and the international climate of revolutionary politics and national liberation movements had its attractions. Some of the conditions that generated the conflict have changed, some never will.[8]

The LTTE began its armed conflict with the Sri Lankan government in 1983 and relied on a guerrilla strategy that included the use of terrorist tactics.[9] The armed uprisings began to take shape in 1983 as Tamils complained about discrimination and demanded an autonomous state for Tamils and so began a quarter century of conflict between the Tamils and the Sinhalese-dominated government of Sri Lanka.

As the conflict worsened, Tamils fled to India and further afield with more than 200,000 Tamils having sought political asylum in the West, many in Canada. The Sri Lanka Tamils initially received support from India and Indian Tamil groups in South India.

The LTTE continued its terrorist activities through the 1990s, attacking government troops and economic infrastructure targets and assassinating political opponents. The LTTE's most spectacular terrorist attack in 1997 was a truck bombing directed at the newly opened Colombo World Trade Center on October 15. The explosion injured more than 100 people, including many foreigners, and caused significant damage to nearby buildings. Eighteen people, including LTTE suicide bombers, hotel security guards, and Sri Lankan security forces, died in the explosion. Sri Lankan authorities shot two of the terrorists as they tried to escape, and another three killed themselves to avoid capture. One of the bombers lobbed a grenade into a monastery as he fled the scene, killing one monk. In two separate incidents in June, in the Tricomalee area, the LTTE assassinated two legislators and nine other civilians.

During the summer months of 1997, naval elements of the LTTE conducted several attacks on commercial shipping, including the abduction of the crew of an empty passenger ferry and setting it on fire. The captain and a crewmember, both Indonesian, were released after only three days. The LTTE stormed a North Korean cargo ship after it delivered a shipment of food and other goods for civilians on the Jaffna Peninsula, killing one of the vessel's thirty-eight North Korean crewmembers in the process. The ship's North Korean captives were freed five days later and eventually returned to the vessel. The LTTE also hijacked a shipment of more than 32,000 mortar rounds bound for delivery to the Sri Lankan military. In September, the LTTE used rocket-propelled grenades to attack a Panamanian-flagged, Chinese-owned merchant ship that had been chartered by a U.S. chemical company to load minerals for export. As many as twenty people, including five Chinese crewmembers, were reported killed, wounded, or missing.

The United States designated LTTE a Foreign Terrorist Organization, pursuant to the orders of the Antiterrorism and Effective Death Penalty Act of 1996.[10]

Known Sri Lankan terrorist front organizations included the following:

- The Liberation Tigers of Tamil Eelam (LTTE)
- World Tamil Association (WTA)
- World Tamil Movement (WTM)
- Federation of Associations of Canadian Tamils (FACT)
- The Ellalan Force
- The Internet Black Tigers (IBT)[11]

Of all of these organizations, the LTTE was by far the most powerful Tamil group in Sri Lanka. The LTTE group's elite "Black Tiger Squad" conducted suicide bombings against many important targets, and all rank-and-file members carried a cyanide capsule to kill themselves rather than be caught. The LTTE was insular and highly organized, with its own intelligence service, naval element (the Sea Tigers), and women's political and military wings. The LTTE integrated a battlefield insurgent strategy with a terrorist program that targeted key government and military personnel, the economy, and public infrastructure. Political assassinations included the suicide bombing attacks against Sri Lankan President Ranasinghe Premadasa in 1993 and Indian prime minister Rajiv Gandhi in 1991 (the group's only known terrorist act outside Sri Lanka). The LTTE has detonated two massive truck bombs directed against the Sri Lankan economy, one at the Colombo Central Bank in January 1996 and another at the Colombo World Trade Center, as mentioned previously. The LTTE also attacked infrastructure targets such as commuter trains, buses, oil tanks, and power stations. Its preference was to attack vulnerable government facilities and then withdraw before reinforcements arrive, or to time its attacks to take best advantage of security lapses on holidays, at night, or in the early morning. The LTTE is also known to have recruited approximately 10,000-armed combatants in Sri Lanka, with approximately 3,000–6,000 members that formed a trained cadre of fighters. The group also had a significant overseas support structure for fund-raising, weapons procurement, and propaganda activities.

The Tigers controlled most of the northern and eastern coastal areas of Sri Lanka but conducted operations throughout the island. Headquartered in the Wanni region, LTTE leader Velupillai Prabhakaran established an extensive network of checkpoints and informants to keep track of any outsiders who entered the group's area of control. The LTTE's overt organizations supported Tamil separatism by lobbying foreign governments and the United Nations. They also used international contacts to procure weapons, communications, and bomb-making equipment. The LTTE exploited large Tamil communities in North America, Europe, and Asia to fund its fighters in Sri Lanka. Information obtained since the mid-1980s indicates that some Tamil communities in Europe were also involved in narcotics smuggling. The LTTE learned well from the tactics employed by the IRA in Northern Ireland.

Throughout 2006 and 2007, fighting escalated between elements of the LTTE and the Sri Lankan military in spite of an agreed cease-fire. The Tamil leader, Velupillai Prabhakaran, announced the commencement of the Fourth Eelam War in November 2006, while the Sri Lankan government only made the announcement in January 2008 that the cease-fire was at an end.

Actions by the Sri Lankan military throughout 2007 did little to cause the LTTE to waiver in their demands for a Tamil homeland. The Sri Lankan military gained the upper hand in the Eastern Province and overran rebel positions at Sampur, just south of the port of Trincomalee, plus gaining control of two key coastal towns, greatly restricting the LTTE's ability to resupply its eastern forces from the north. The military launched Operation Definite Victory, clearing the

TERRORIST ATTACK BRIEF

Terrorist Group: LTTE (Tamil Tigers)

Case Facts: In a nighttime attack mounted by members of LTTE, a small craft had mingled with fishing boats near Trincomalee and silently approached a Sri Lankan Naval fast-attack vessel, ramming it and setting off explosives. The Sri Lankan vessel was severely damaged and thirteen seamen were killed in the blast.

Investigation: The incident came at the end of almost four years of cease-fire between LTTE and government forces. The Sri Lankan FAV sank shortly after the explosion and only two seamen were rescued alive. Tamil tigers use not only conventional bombs to target government forces but also their own version of Navy and Air Force to target shipping and Air Force targets. The tigers are known to frequently use suicide bombers both male and female.

FIGURE 11-6   Bombing—Naval attack trincomalee Sri Lanka—January 7, 2005.
Source: Ethnic Conflict History of LLTE attacks, http://sricolama.com/ethnic-conflict.html?start=3

LTTE from the Ampara district before moving on to other rebel controlled towns. The LTTE seemed powerless to respond after their camps were overrun one after the other.[12]

The ebb and flow of success in insurgent operations was reality in this theater of war, and the Tamils continued to attack government forces and use new methods of attack to undermine the government as much as to publicize their presence. In March 2007, the LTTE launched its first aerial attack using light passenger aircraft to carry bombs and successfully attacked an air force base outside the capital Colombo. The same year they launched a commando raid on an air base north of Colombo, and while all the commandos were killed, they managed to destroy a large number of Sri Lankan Air Force aircraft on the ground, including two attack helicopters.

More than 70,000 have died since the conflict started in 1983.

The success of the Tigers was in many ways due to their fund-raising abilities abroad, with a flourishing and loyal Tamil diaspora in Western countries, including Canada, the United States, Australia, and Great Britain. Vast numbers of Tamils have fled as refugees to the West and are "taxed" by the LTTE, who also engage in criminal activities for fund-raising including widespread credit card fraud. Most weapons brought into the area originated from dealers in Southeast Asia and then were smuggled in by a small flotilla of LTTE-operated ships.

Defections from the LTTE leadership and successes on the military side enabled a military campaign in the spring of 2009 to overrun almost all but a small enclave of Tamils in the coastal region. Two Army divisions trapped the Tamils fighters, and their leader, Velupillai Prabhakaran, was killed by the military. On May 17, 2009, the Tigers formally laid down their weapons and twenty-six years of conflict were at an end.

AFGHANISTAN

The Taliban

The Taliban ("Students of Islamic Knowledge Movement") ruled Afghanistan from 1996 until 2001. They came to power during Afghanistan's long civil war. Although they managed to hold 90 percent of the country's territory, their policies—including their treatment of women and support of terrorists—ostracized them from the world community. Put into context of Afghan history, the rise of the Taliban, though not their extremism is unsurprising. Afghanistan is a devoutly Muslim nation; 90 percent of its population is Sunni Muslims. Religious schools were

FIGURE 11-7 Map of Afghanistan (Central Intelligence Agency, *The World Factbook, 2008*).

established in Afghanistan after Islam arrived in the seventh century, and *Taliban* became an important part of the social fabric: running schools, mosques, shrines, and various religious and social services and serving as mujahedeen when necessary.

After the 9-11 attacks, the U.S. government pressed the Taliban government of Afghanistan to turn over bin Laden and the al Qaeda leadership who had sought sanctuary in the mountainous regions of the country. To no one's surprise, the Taliban refused to give him to the United States. Their refusal was the signal for the aerial bombing of Taliban military sites. By November 21, the Taliban had lost control of Kabul, and by early December, had been completely routed. In 2008, more than five years as Afghanistan's leader, President Hamid Karzai came to power; he still had only marginal control over large swaths of the country. The Taliban continues to fund its insurgency through the drug trade. An August 2007 report by the United Nations found that Afghanistan's opium production doubled in two years and that the country supplies 93 percent of the world's heroin.

Islamic extremists from around the world, including of Egyptians, Algerians, Palestinians, and Saudis, used Afghanistan as a training base from which to operate. The Taliban, as well as many of the other combatants in the Afghan civil war, facilitated the operation of training and indoctrination facilities for non-Afghans in the territories they controlled. Several Afghani factions provided logistic support, free passage, and sometimes passports, to members of various terrorist organizations. Many of these individuals, in turn, were involved in fighting in Bosnia and Herzegovina, Chechnya, Tajikistan, Kashmir, the Philippines, and parts of the Middle East. That the Taliban is a ruthless organization is beyond question, and the tribal warlords on the other hand were often as equally vicious. One such leader was Mullah Dadullah, who was described in intelligence reports as being the military mastermind of the Taliban insurgency. Dadullah had, until his death in 2007, been front and center of the military activities of the Taliban. Dadullah traveled to Pakistan to raise money and arms for the insurgency and focused his attention on the **Madrassas** in Karachi to recruit his fighters. In 2003, Mullah Omar released a tape naming him as a member of the new ten-man leadership council that would "confront the occupation." He led the Taliban's day-to-day operations in the south and southwestern Afghanistan, but, more importantly, he was one of the closest links between the Taliban insurgency and al Qaeda. As part of his fund-raising efforts, he was responsible for the increase in kidnappings in the region, which provided a good level of income for the Taliban. He was also the Taliban's spokesman for the progress of the insurgency and was at ease dealing with the news media, especially when it came to detailing his involvement in training suicide bombers, executing suspected collaborators, and beheading hostages. On many occasions in 2006, he was listed as killed in actions against U.S. and Afghan forces. He was a ruthless fighter and particularly so in battles against the Northern Alliance when the U.S. war to remove the Taliban started in 2001. He had been sentenced to life in prison in absentia by a Pakistani Court for attempting to assassinate Maulana Shirani, then a member of the Pakistan Parliament. Mullah Dadullah lost a leg when he trod on a landmine in 1994; however, this did not deter him from his personal involvement in the fighting with the then Afghan government forces and also against the Northern Alliance. He was killed in a clash with British and U.S. Special Forces in Helmand Province on May 13, 2007. He was a close friend and ally of the Taliban leader Mullah Omar and his loss was at the time a serious blow to the Taliban.

The realities of the War on Terror and the Afghanistan campaign that filtered out after the ousting of the Taliban may have punctured the mood that prevailed in October 2001. The idea that the Afghanistan campaign was a possible new strategy for warfare, based on the employment of massive, precision-guided airpower with little commitment of ground troops, has obviously been revisited. Large numbers of Afghan civilians died, owing to less-than-precise bombing, and scores of people allied to the United States were targeted and killed by U.S. forces, acting on sometime faulty intelligence. Relying on Afghan mercenaries to do the fighting on the ground resulted in Osama bin Laden's escape from the Tora Bora Mountains. And when U.S. troops did engage in close-quarters fighting with the Taliban/al Qaeda forces in the Gardez area near Pakistan in early March 2002, an enemy that was assumed to be on the run bloodied them.

Most of the Taliban's leaders were educated in Pakistan's Islamic schools and in refugee camps where they had fled with millions of other Afghans after the Soviet invasion. Pakistan's Jami'at-e 'Ulema-e Islam (JUI) political party provided welfare services, education, and military training for refugees in many of these camps. They also established religious schools in the Deobandi tradition.

AL QAEDA (THE BASE)

Al Qaeda was established in the 1980s by Osama bin Laden, originally recruited by the CIA in its efforts against the Soviet occupation of Afghanistan. Al Qaeda was bin Laden's creation from fighters who had been recruited to confront the Soviet forces in Afghanistan. Assisted by the Palestinian cleric Abdullah Azzam, they recruited thousands of fighters for the mujahedeen. Once the Soviets withdrew, these fighters were dispersed to follow bin Laden's wider goals of a holy war against Western democracies that were invading Muslim lands. Throughout the 1990s, few in the United States or elsewhere knew of bin Laden, but with attacks on U.S. embassies in Africa, the bombing of the USS *Cole* in Yemen, and ultimately the 9-11 attacks on New York and

Washington, bin Laden became the most hunted man on earth. The United States attacked his bases in Afghanistan and invaded the country; at every turn bin Laden was able to escape to the lawless tribal areas bordering Pakistan and even into Pakistan itself. The United States considers al Qaeda to be the biggest terrorist threat that it faces and almost every terrorist attack since 9-11 bears the hallmarks of al Qaeda involvement. Al Qaeda is believed to have terror cells in more than 100 countries with many thousands of sympathizers and supporters in Western countries. It has also inspired al Qaeda affiliates to take up the cause of jihad and adopt the al Qaeda name. It also maintains close ties with the following terror organizations that follow the same Sunni dominated ideology:

- Egyptian Islamic Jihad
- The Libyan Islamic Fighting Group
- Islamic Army of Aden (Yemen)
- Jama'at al-Tawhid wal Jihad (Iraq)
- Lashkar-e-Taiba and Jaish-e-Muhammad (Kashmir)
- Islamic Movement of Uzbekistan
- Al-Qaeda in the Islamic Maghreb (Algeria) (formerly Salafist Group for Call and Combat)
- Armed Islamic Group (Algeria)
- Abu Sayyaf Group (Malaysia, Philippines)
- Jemaah Islamiya (Southeast Asia)

On May 1, 2011, a team of U.S. Navy SEALs tracked bin Laden to a house in Abbottabad in Pakistan, where he was shot and killed; the value of this killing has yet to be felt. Many young and impressionable followers of bin Laden held the view that their inspirational leader was invincible, and having slipped out of reach of the United States for more than ten years; his death will certainly be a blow to many of his followers. His replacement and long-time deputy, Ayman al-Zawahiri, does not have the same charisma as bin Laden, but the global movement may well be capable of overcoming this difficulty. Bin Laden will undoubtedly be considered a martyr, and many more attacks on the West will be carried out in his name. What is clear is that al Qaeda has been able to adapt when faced with adversity and remains a dangerous and adaptive organization. Al Qaeda promotes an ideology that unites a variety of grievances including that there is a global conspiracy led by the United States and Israel against Muslims and Islam. The terrorists draw their inspiration from a global message that has been articulated by figures such as Osama bin Laden. The message is uncompromising and asserts that the West represents a threat to Islam, that loyalty to religion and loyalty to democratic institutions and values are incompatible, and that violence is the only proper response. Al Qaeda members adopt an extreme interpretation of Islamic teaching, which they believe places an obligation on believers to fight and kill to achieve their aims. Most Muslims and the world's leading Islamic scholars reject this position. The terrorists point to the depravations suffered by Muslims and label the United States and Israel (Crusaders and Zionists) responsible for those depravations.[13] They assert that the solution to this problem is to eradicate Western influences from the Muslim world, replace existing governments with a supranational "caliphate" and impose a strict and exclusive form of government based on their particular interpretation of Sunni Islam. The governments of many Muslim states are branded as "apostates" who do not adhere to its definition of "true Islam." Secular republics and religiously based monarchies alike are attacked on this basis. By branding them as guilty of apostasy—an offence for which Islamic law prescribes a death sentence—the terrorists justify taking violent action against the governments and citizens of those states, even though they are coreligionists.

Al Qaeda strongly objects to democratic elections in Muslim lands and in particular in Afghanistan, Iraq, and Palestine. It claims that democracy is a rival "religion" and that principles such as freedom of speech and freedom of religion are equivalent to apostasy, punishable by death. In al Qaida's view, the only acceptable form of government is a "Caliphate" based exclusively on Sharia law.

Al Qaeda is not a monolithic organization, nor is it merely a "brand name." It is, instead, a movement consisting of a "network of networks." The al Qaeda movement can be characterized as comprising three elements:

Al Qaeda core: consists of the surviving members of al Qaeda's senior leadership and other operatives under their direct control. This is essentially the remnant of the original pre-9/11 al Qaeda organization. It has been badly disrupted by the worldwide campaign against terrorism, but it remains active in planning attacks and recruiting operatives.

Al Qaeda-linked networks: consisting of terrorist networks that share al Qaeda's ideology and are in occasional contact with the al Qaeda core. The "fertilizer plot" terrorist cell convicted in April 2007 is an example of such a network; one of its members had travelled to Pakistan for terrorist training and is believed to have had direct contact with al Qaeda figures.

Al Qaeda-inspired networks and cells: consists of groups that share al Qaeda's ideology but do not have current contacts or links with al Qaeda. One such terrorist network carried out the 2004 Madrid train bombings; another such network, the Indonesian terrorist group Jemaah Islamiya, carried out the Bali bombings of 2002 and 2005.[14]

Al Qaeda Operations

A large number of attacks carried out by al Qaeda have been both spectacular and unforgettable for the impact they have created:

- **1998**—simultaneous bombings of U.S. embassies in Nairobi and Dar es Salaam
- **2000**—suicide bombing USS *Cole*—Yemen
- **2001**—airline hijackings in the United States—aircraft flown into World Trade Center and the Pentagon in Washington
- **2002**—attempted to shoot down passenger airliner in Kenya with surface to air missile
- **2003**—car bomb attacks in Riyadh, Saudi Arabia
- **2005**—simultaneous suicide bomb attacks on London, U.K. subway system
- **2006**—attack on Saudi oil refining facility
- **2007**—failed bomb attack on Pakistan's prime minister, Benazir Bhutto
- **2007**—car bomb attacks in London, the United Kingdom, and Glasgow International Airport
- **2009**—attempted and failed suicide bomb attack on Northwest Airliner en route to Detroit

Despite the death of bin Laden, al Qaeda network remains to fight another day. Bin Laden will be remembered by history as the man who revived the idea of pan Islam. This had long been derailed in the Arab world by national self-interest and the great flirtation with socialism. From socialism came secularism and the one-party state where democracy failed. Al Qaeda exemplified bin Laden's jihadist version of Islam and for a while appealed to the poor and disenfranchised. Across the globe, local and regional groups found common cause in the mantra of global jihad. Bin Laden's appeal also rested on the fact that he had brought down one superpower in Afghanistan and could do so again with the United States.[15] Unlike the Soviet Union in the 1980s, the United States would not be so easily assaulted and beaten.

TALIBAN-LINKED INSURGENTS—HAQQANI NETWORK

Groups confronting NATO coalition forces are primarily either al Qaeda or aligned with the Taliban, and one of the most daring and confrontational groups is the **Haqqani Network**, which is based in North Waziristan but within close proximity to the Afghan border. Haqqani is led by Jalaluddin Haqqani and his son, Sirajuddin Haqqani. Jalaluddin fought with the Taliban against the Soviets and rose high up in the Taliban movement after the Soviet withdrawal and is believed to have had close ties with **Mullah Omar**. While the father is believed to be either seriously ill or possibly dead, his son has taken over as operational commander of the Haqqani Network. The methods of attack have been suicide bombings, truck and car bombings, and raids on government and police buildings dressed as either police or military—these raids have also targeted banks and prominent hotels occupied by Westerners. Most always their actions leave a trail of bodies in their wake and appear more concered about a large body count of civilians than military. It is believed the group through the father has support from Arab countries in the Persian Gulf and members travel to those regions. There are concerns also that this group has influence with the Pakistan ISI, which may be providing strategic information to Haqqani. The Haqqani commanders have been targeted and have always managed to avoid capture.

ISLAMIC EMIRATE OF AFGHANISTAN

When the Soviet Union was forced out of Afghanistan in the late 1980s, the country was at the mercy of the tribal warlords. From 1930 to 1978 was likely the most peaceful period in Afghanistan' modern history but that would end with a pro-Soviet communist coup, and their inability to maintain any control, cohesion, or administrative responsibility ultimately led to the Soviet invasion. This, in turn, inspired an American-led counterinterventionist strategy, implemented through Pakistan as the "frontline state," in support of the Afghan Islamic resistance forces (the *Mujahideen*). The Soviets were forced to leave Afghanistan by the end of the 1980s, and their protégé regime collapsed at Kabul in April 1992.[16] A country that had suffered over a decade of deprivation welcomed the control and discipline that the Taliban offered. Mullah Omar with the support of Pakistan's ISI set the Taliban up almost as its proxy militia in Afghanistan. The Taliban imposed its exteme religious doctrine including sharia on the population. When Osama bin Laden fled to Taliban-controlled Afghanistan in 2006, he was welcomed along with his money and Arab influence. During the 1990s, the United States was more preoccupied with accessing oil and gas rights and deny them to Iran, and if it had not been for the bin Laden-sponsored attacks on embassies in East Africa, the Taliban may have continued unabated for many more years to come. However, the subsequent missile attacks on Afghan targets in attempts to kill bin Laden did little to persuade the Taliban from dominating Afghanistan. The Taliban also offered training and support to Chechens seeking independance and even offered to open a diplomatic mission in Kabul. In 1999, Pakistan's General Pervez Musharraf overthrew the government in a bloodless coup. Musharraf orginally agreed to help arrest bin Laden, but his influence failed to make that materialize. General Musharraf urged the international community to reocognize the Taliban as the legitimate government of Afghanistan. As the threats against the West mounted, the United States had sanctions imposed by the UN—none of which had the slightest effect on the Taliban.

In early 2008, Mullah Omar still reigned supreme over the Taliban, who had changed their official name to the "Islamic Emirate of Afghanistan" in communiqués. He managed to avoid capture, but has found a way to appear in videos released to the Middle East media. In December 2007, rifts in the al Qaeda organization started to become public when Mullah Omar sacked Mansour Dadullah, the brother of Mullah Dadullah. Mansour was commander of the southern area of Afghanistan. Although it is unclear why he was removed, his references to "worldwide jihad" reflect an ideology akin to that of al Qaeda, rather than the more traditional Taliban focus on Afghanistan. He also was an advocate of extreme and controversial tactics seen as unpopular in Afghanistan. Dadullah was captured by Pakistan security forces as he and five others attempted to cross into Pakistan's southwestern Province of Baluchistan.

Washington's continued tilt toward Israel has not helped in shoring up the legitimacy of its Arab allies among their people. Israel is the great spoiler of the U.S. effort to manage the Middle East, and Israel can get away with it because it can rely on massive support in the U.S. Congress to blunt pressure from the U.S. Executive Branch. Indeed, the Afghan fiasco and Israel's continued intransigence, it can be argued, have combined to make Washington's strategic situation in the Middle East and the Persian Gulf worse rather than better. There have been no political or military gains in Southeast Asia, with Indonesia maintaining its distance from Washington and the U.S. buildup in the Philippines becoming more controversial by the day. The introduction of U.S. forces in some of the Central Asian republics—the so-called Stans—may, on the surface, seem to be a strategic plus, especially when one takes into consideration the energy reserves of the area. However, with the failure to achieve decisive military or political victory on any front, Washington's Central Asian deployment may actually be a case of overextension.

The impressions (real or imagined) that the United States is now actually working to undermine Islam is being strengthened by U.S. support of regimes in Uzbekistan and Turkmenistan. These regimes, like America's other ally, Turkey, are brutal in their suppression of Muslims and any practice of Islam. As the negative image of the United States grows throughout nonextremist Islam, so do acts of terrorism against Americans and U.S. facilities in Islamic regions.[17]

Drugs and the Taliban

The big question surrounding opium production in Afghanistan, in terms of international drug control efforts, was how to prevent the massive opium poppy harvest in Afghanistan from reaching global drug markets. And the more important question that follows is one of how to end decades of Afghanistan's dependency on opium growing at all. To fully understand the importance of the issue, one only needs to know that as recently as 2004 Afghanistan accounted for a huge proportion of the global production of opiates as well as for most of the heroin found in European markets.

Taliban authorities finally issued a ban on opium poppy cultivation, declaring it "nonIslamic." This ban resulted in a considerable decrease of opium production in 2001. There are plenty of theories as to the motivation of that oppressive regime's decision. Some believe that the Taliban wanted to escape a threat of new sanctions, while others speculate that it wanted to please the international community and relax its isolation. Many have said that the reason for the ban was that the Taliban simply wanted to increase the price of existing stockpiles from the record harvest in 1999, which was 4,600 metric tons and "next-to-the-best harvest" in 2000 of 3,300 metric tons. Whatever its motivation, the Taliban's ban was effective. In 2001, the areas under opium poppy cultivation were reduced by 91 percent. If the ban had been maintained for another year, the existing stockpiles (estimated to amount to two or three years of production) would have melted down with all the predictable consequences: a gradual shortage of heroin in European markets, increase in prices, decrease in purity of the heroin offered, and even a higher demand for treatment. That historic opportunity in international drug control efforts is now in danger of being missed or, at least, delayed.

The period following the events of 9-11, and the subsequent fall of the Taliban regime, coincided with the opium poppy planting season in southern and eastern Afghanistan. Since the

Taliban has been removed from power, the amount of land now used for opium production is larger than the corresponding total for coca cultivation in Latin America (Colombia, Peru, and Bolivia combined). In 2007, Afghanistan produced 8,200 tons of opium, 34 percent more than was produced in 2006, thus accounting for 93 percent of the global opiates market! No other country has previously produced narcotics on such a massive and deadly scale. Quite clearly, opium production in Helmand and Kandahar provinces is being fuelled by the ongoing insurgency, with Helmand accounting for almost 50 percent of the production. In 2007, the Taliban controlled large swathes of Helmand and Kandahar provinces as well as along the border with Pakistan.[18]

Present and Future Challenges

In terms of the country's drug trade, some believe Afghanistan would be better off if the Taliban were still in power. The answer is clearly "no"! It was the Taliban regime that profited from the drug business for years and made Afghanistan a safe haven for international terrorist masterminds and created conditions for drug trafficking in the first place.

The Taliban regime seized control of the major opium producing areas of Afghanistan in 1996 and regularly collected taxes from the drug business (10 percent from producers and 20 percent from traders). It is difficult to imagine that in such a tightly controlled society, producing, selling, and stockpiling of literally thousands of tons of opium could have gone on throughout the 1990s without the complicity of the Taliban. Further proof of the regime's involvement in the growth of opium production is the fact that there were no recorded drug seizures in that country, while 90 percent of global seizures of heroin took place in neighboring Iran.

On January 17, 2001, Afghanistan's new interim authority head, Dr. Hamid Karzai, issued a ban that was even more comprehensive than the one issued by the Taliban. His decree banned not only cultivation but also processing and illicit use, smuggling, and trafficking of opium. At the time of the ban, most opium poppy fields had already been sown.

Afghanistan's interim authorities are committed to drug control, but the fact is, after decades of devastation of the country, the interim government still does not have the capability to enforce its ban. That is why the international community needs to assist the country in building that power. In the short term, the challenge for the international community is how to assist Afghanistan's authorities in preventing the poppy harvest from reaching the world markets. Answers range from destroying the opium poppy crops to compensating farmers by buying their harvest and then destroying it. Proponents of the second option argue that buying opium from producers (at farm-gate prices, which average about $30 per kilo) is much less expensive than allowing it to get into the hands of the traffickers (who sell it, depending on the region, for $230–$300 per kilo). Whatever course of action is finally decided, destroy, buy, or something else, it is a decision that needs to be made on the ground, in full coordination and cooperation with Afghanistan authorities and international representatives. This short-term strategy also needs to include a tightening of the security measures against drug trafficking countries like Iran, Pakistan, Tajikistan, and Turkmenistan. There is an emerging consensus among all involved that unless effective drug control is actually exercised, everything else being done in Afghanistan might be in vain. The illicit trade in opium is likely centered along the border with Pakistan and also involves trafficking in weapons and manpower. The presence of state-of-the-art weapons has not been as evident in Afghanistan as in Iraq. There is little use of missiles or surface-to-air missiles (SAMs) in the volatile Helmand province or around Kandahar. In addition, the numbers of fighters facing NATO troops has not increased, and British military estimates the Taliban insurgents to number in the 5,000–6,000 range.

The Taliban and al Qaeda groups have mounted military attacks against U.S., Canadian- and British troops using varied tactics from hit-and-run assaults to suicide attacks, car and truck bombs, and the more sophisticated IED attacks. There has been little let up in the ongoing battles, and regular surges by U.S. troops serves to move Taliban elements from area to area. During 2011, there were hints and rumors of willingness on the part of the United States to talk terms with the Taliban. With over a decade of military operations failing to remove or dissuade the Taliban, Americans have grown war weary. In a speech from the White House in June 2011, President Obama made the following announcement:

> Al Qaeda is under more pressure than at any time since 9/11. Together with the Pakistanis, we have taken out more than half of al Qaeda's leadership. And thanks to our intelligence professionals and Special Forces, we killed Osama bin Laden, the only leader that al Qaeda had ever known. This was a victory for all who have served since 9/11 .... We do know that peace cannot come to a land that has known so much war without a political settle-ment. So as we strengthen the Afghan government and security forces, America will join initiatives that reconcile the Afghan people, including the Taliban. Our position on these talks is clear: They must be led by the Afghan government, and those who want to be a part of a peaceful Afghanistan must break from al Qaeda, abandon violence, and abide by the Afghan constitution. But, in part because of our military effort, we have reason to believe that progress can be made

BURMA (MYANMAR)

Burma is a mysterious Southeast Asian nation that most people know very little about. Veterans of World War II will recall the Burma Road and the Flying Tigers, but most of us probably know little or nothing of today's Burma. Images of shining pagodas, elephants, and flying fish at play along the mighty Irrawaddy River, from Rudyard Kipling's famous poem "Road to Mandalay," may come to mind. But Burma's reality today has little in common with such romantic legends. For most of its modern history, following independence from Britain in 1948, Burma has been run by a military-controlled socialist regime that has isolated the country, wrecked its economy, and totally repressed its many diverse ethnic populations.

A massive and peaceful "people power" demonstration movement demanded an end to the military dictatorship in 1988 and again in 2008. The army leadership reacted violently and swiftly to repress and quell this movement. To maintain the status quo, a new military junta, the State Law and Order Restoration Council (SLORC), seized direct power to quell any kind of movement toward democracy. Crowds of peaceful protesters were machine-gunned down by SLORC troops, and thousands were killed. For a few days, events in Burma captured world headlines but were soon replaced by sound bites about other world events in some more familiar locales. Global attention briefly picked up again, however, in December 1991, when Daw Aung San Suu Kyi, the long-detained democracy advocate and leading voice of freedom for Burma, was awarded the Nobel Peace Prize.

Still, most of the world has little interest in Burma. To further confuse the situation, the SLORC generals changed the country's long-standing official name (by decree and without public consultation) to Myanmar, a transliteration of the country's Burmese language name. And Burma's democratic opposition and powerful generals outright rejected the name and refused to recognize it. More confusion came in November 1997, when the generals renamed their own junta the State Peace and Development Council (SPDC) in hopes of improving their rapidly deteriorating and well-earned bad international image.

The people of Burma continue to suffer under one of the world's most brutal regimes. The United Nations, world religious leaders including the Pope and the Dalai Lama, many governments, and human rights groups have urged an end to human rights violations in Burma. The military regime's response so far has been intensified abuse, such as murder, torture, rape, political imprisonment, and forced labor. The military regime allows, and probably participates in, the growing explosion of heroin production in Burma. Cease-fires with several ethnic opposition armies that have long traded in drugs have allowed an estimated increase of nearly 400 percent in Burma's heroin production since the junta took power in 1988. Around the world, this flood of cheaper and purer heroin is causing a vast new wave of addiction. In recent years, approximately 60 percent of the heroin reaching the United States has been of Burmese origin. And, in Burma itself, an estimated half million addicts are spreading an AIDS epidemic at a rate that has been seen only in some areas of Central Africa.

Burma plays a pivotal role in South Asia's security, due to its strategic position linking South and Southeast Asia and bordering the continent's two most populous countries, China and India. But independent Burma had long pursued a policy of neutrality. To the alarm of many countries, the military regime is now increasingly dependent on China as a political ally and arms supplier. Fear of Chinese military influence in Burma is helping to spur a costly regional arms race that diverts funds desperately needed for their human development.

People who argue that trade and tourism can help promote respect for human rights are pressing for increased international involvement with the Burmese military regime. Some claimed that "constructive engagement" might convince the junta to fight drug trafficking and to reduce its reliance on China.[19] A few simply declared that business and human rights are separate issues that should not be mixed. The junta itself, backed by a few Asian autocrats, asserts that it respects human rights in an "Asian" or "Burmese" context and such internationally recognized standards do not apply in Burma.

FIGURE 11-8 Map of Burma (Central Intelligence Agency, *The World Factbook, 2008*).

Among these critical human rights issues is the SPDC's continuing detention of opposition figures.

Resolution of the political impasse in Burma will eventually require real, substantive dialogue with the democratic opposition, including Aung San Suu Kyi and representatives of the ethnic groups. Arbitrary detentions are unjustifiable and will only worsen rather than solve the political crisis.

The United States has protested the policies of the Burmese government through its embassy in Rangoon and will continue to work with like-minded countries to press the Burmese government to take positive action, including the release of political prisoners and the initiation of a genuine dialogue with Aung San Suu Kyi and other NLD leaders.

The 1997 explosion of a parcel bomb at the house of a senior official in Burma's military-led government was the country's most significant terrorist event. On his visit to Burma, Bishop Tutu spoke of the blast that killed the adult daughter of Lieutenant-General Tin Oo, second-secretary of the ruling State Law and Order Restoration Council. No group or individual claimed responsibility for the attack, but the government of Burma attributes the act to Burmese antigovernment activists in Japan. The package containing the bomb bore Japanese stamps and postmarks. The Burmese expatriate and student community living in Japan denies any involvement in the incident.[20]

Reports suggest a massive increase in methamphetamine production and distribution from Burma, and although the Burmese government has expanded its counternarcotics efforts over the past few years, the impact has been limited. While part of the problem is that the Burmese government does not control many of the ethnic groups that traffic in drugs, the government also does not make sufficient effort at interdiction. There is also some evidence of corrupt elements in the military that may be aiding the traffickers, and there are signs that the Burmese encourage traffickers to invest in a multitude of development projects throughout the country.[21]

Burma is a poor country, with an average per capita GDP of approximately $406, at a weighted exchange rate, perhaps double that in terms of purchasing power parity. Progress on market reforms has been mixed and uneven. Beginning in 1988, the Burmese government partly opened the economy to permit expansion of the private sector and to attract foreign investment. Though modest economic improvement ensued, since 1993 the pace of economic reform has slowed and major obstacles to further reform persist. These include disproportionate military spending, extensive overt and covert state involvement in economic activity, state monopolization of leading exports, a bloated bureaucracy prone to arbitrary and opaque governance, and a poor education and physical infrastructure. In addition, due to international opposition and to the SPDC's unwillingness to cooperate fully with the International Monetary Fund (IMF), SPDC access to external credit from the IMF, World Bank, and Asian Development Bank continues to be blocked by sanctions. In September 1998, the World Bank announced that Burma had defaulted on its loan repayments. Some analysts think the laundering of drug profits in Burma's legitimate economy is extensive.

At the ASEAN meetings in Manila in July 1998, then U.S. secretary of state Albright, with Foreign Minister McKinnon of New Zealand, led a discussion of the political impasse in Burma. The meetings included representatives from Austria, Australia, Canada, Germany, Korea, Japan, and Great Britain and Burmese Foreign Minister Ohn Gyaw. The ministers expressed their concerns over the deteriorating conditions in Burma and demanded a speedy, peaceful resolution to the situation. They pressed for the immediate commencement of an SPDC dialogue with the democratic opposition, to include Aung San Suu Kyi. Secretary Albright continued to actively promote international constructive engagement with the SPDC toward an improved human rights climate.

It is clear that the SPDC is not eager to release its chokehold on the Burmese people, and the world's attention is often drawn away from such remote areas. In 2010, the military rule formally ended and has since then seen a slow but gradual move toward political reform culminating in Aung San Suu Kyi being elected to parliament in March 2012. A large number of pro-democracy parties took part in the elections, which have been described by observers as relatively transparent and without interference. Nonetheless, the military still retains significant power and presence within the country.

CAMBODIA

Cambodia is located on the Gulf of Thailand, between Thailand and Vietnam. It is a tiny country, slightly smaller than Oklahoma. The country is a land of rice paddies and forests and is dominated by the Mekong River. It has a population of about 11 million, ethnically composed

FIGURE 11-9   Map of Cambodia (Central Intelligence Agency, *The World Factbook, 2008*).

of Khmer (90 percent), Vietnamese (5 percent), Chinese (1 percent), and other (4 percent). The religious preference is overwhelmingly Theravada Buddhist (95 percent). Cambodia was called "Kampuchea" under the disastrous dictatorship of the **Khmer Rouge**.

The economy has been destroyed by decades of war, but it is slowly recovering. Government leaders are moving toward restoring fiscal and monetary discipline and have established good working relations with international financial institutions. Growth, starting from a low base, was strong between 1991 and 1996. Despite such positive developments, the reconstruction effort faces many tough challenges because of internal political divisions and the related lack of confidence of foreign investors.

Rural Cambodia, where 90 percent of about 9.5 million of the Khmer live, remains mired in poverty. The almost total lack of basic infrastructure in the countryside hinders development and contributes to a growing imbalance in growth between urban and rural areas over the near term. Moreover, the government's lack of experience in administering economic and technical assistance programs and rampant corruption among officials slow the growth of critical public sector investment. The decline of inflation from the 1992 rate of more than 50 percent is one of the bright spots in Cambodia's return to a peacetime period. In a somewhat interesting and unusual move, the Khmer Royal Armed Forces (KRAF) was created in 1993 by the merger of the Cambodian People's Armed Forces and the two non-Communist resistance armies (KRAF is also known as the Royal Cambodian Armed Forces, or RCAF).

Offshore islands and sections of the boundary with Vietnam remain in dispute and the maritime boundary with Vietnam is not clearly defined. Also, parts of the border with Thailand are now in dispute, as its boundaries are also not clearly defined. In the Golden Triangle, where Cambodia, Thailand, and Vietnam have mutual borders, heroin is being routed to the West, giving Cambodia the possibility of becoming a major money-laundering center. High-level, narcotics-related corruption reportedly involves the government, military, and police. There are small-scale opium, heroin, and amphetamine production operations in Cambodia and a larger production system of high-grade marijuana for the international market.

Hard-liners based in the Khmer Rouge stronghold at Anlong Veng regularly launched guerrilla-style attacks on government troops. Guerrillas are also suspected in two deadly attacks against ethnic Vietnamese civilians in Cambodia, but they have denied playing a role in the disappearance of two Filipino and two Malaysian employees of a logging company in 1997.

The death of former Khmer Rouge leader **Pol Pot** (Saloth Sar), in 1998, in the Thai-Cambodian border area, brought an end to one of the most chilling and bloody chapters of the twentieth century. During Pol Pot's four years of rule over Cambodia, from 1975 to 1978, the Khmer Rouge was suspected of killing as many as 2 million people through mass executions, starvation, and slave labor.

The genocide in Cambodia was the outcome of a complex historical development in which the pernicious ideological influence of Stalinism came together with the military bloodbath carried out against the people of Indochina. Pol Pot will be little mourned by the people of Cambodia.

The fate of British mine-clearing expert Christopher Howes, allegedly kidnapped by the Khmer Rouge in March 1996, remains unresolved. Unconfirmed reporting suggested Howes was with forces loyal to Pol Pot, and some Cambodian officials expressed fears publicly that he had been killed. In May 1996, Khmer Rouge leader Khieu Samphan denied any knowledge of Howes's whereabouts.

Incidents of terrorism in East Asia continue to increase. Continuing defections from the Khmer Rouge to Cambodian forces reduced the threat from the terrorist group, but guerrillas in the Cambodian provinces have been responsible for deadly attacks on foreigners. The unstable political situation in Cambodia has led to marked political violence. In October 1997, the secretary of state designated the Khmer Rouge as a foreign terrorist organization pursuant to the Antiterrorism and Effective Death Penalty Act of 1996.

Pol Pot

The political activity of Pol Pot (Saloth Sar) began in post–World War II France, when Cambodia was part of its Indochina colony. The son of a relatively well-off peasant family, Pol Pot received a government scholarship in 1949 to study in Paris, where he gravitated with a number of his friends to the Stalinist circles around the French Communist Party. He returned to Phnom Penh in 1953, worked as a teacher, and was involved in the start of the embryonic Communist Party in Cambodia. Police repression under the government of Prince Norodom Sihanouk, the country's first postcolonial ruler, forced the party leaders to flee the capital in 1963 and seek sanctuary in the remote rural areas of the country.

It was only after the American intervention in Cambodia during the Vietnam War that Pol Pot and the Khmer Rouge began to get wider support. From a badly organized force of less than 5,000 men in 1970, the Khmer Rouge expanded to an army of around 70,000. In April 1975, the Lon Nol dictatorship collapsed and Pol Pot came to power. The peasant-based army and Khmer Rouge leaders carried out policies of an anti-working-class character, which had far more in common with fascism than socialism. With an economy in shambles, Pol Pot was unable and unwilling to organize the feeding of the cities; he ordered the evacuation of Phnom Penh and other towns. The entire urban population of workers, intellectuals, civil servants, small shopkeepers, and others was driven into the countryside to harsh labor on irrigation schemes and other grandiose projects aimed at elevating agricultural production.

Under Pol Pot's leadership, the Khmer Rouge conducted a campaign of genocide in which an estimated 2 million people were killed during its four years in power in the late 1970s.[22]

The Khmer Rouge is a Communist insurgency that is trying to destabilize the Cambodian government. It is still engaged in a low-level insurgency against the Cambodian government, Although its victims are mainly Cambodian villagers, the Khmer Rouge has occasionally kidnapped and killed foreigners traveling in remote rural areas. One to two thousand members of the Khmer Rouge operate in outlying provinces in Cambodia, particularly in pockets along the Thailand border.

The Khmer Rouge may not be considered as a serious threat to the destabilization of Cambodia, but, some twenty years and three Cambodian regimes later, the National Army of Democratic Kampuchea, as the Khmer Rouge military is known, continues to wage warfare and terrorism from scattered jungle bases of operation in an attempt to regain control of Cambodia and resume its utopian experiment. Although there have been large-scale defections from the Khmer Rouge to Cambodian government forces since 1996, and the group suffered a significant split in 1997, it still may be considered dangerous.

THAILAND

The ancient Kingdom of Thailand sometimes referred to as "Siam" lies southeast of Burma and borders the Andaman Sea and the Gulf of Thailand. It is slightly more than twice the size of Wyoming. This country has a population of almost 60 million; the ethnic groupings are Thai (75 percent), Chinese (14 percent), and other (11 percent). Religious affiliations are Buddhism (95 percent), Islam (3.8 percent), Christianity (0.5 percent), Hinduism (0.1 percent), and other (0.6 percent). Thailand is independent since 1238 A.D., and has never been colonized. A new constitution was approved in 1991 and amended in 1992.

FIGURE 11-10 Map of Thailand (Central Intelligence Agency, *The World Factbook, 2008*).

History Timeline—Thailand

Some significant dates:

- **June 24, 1932**—King Prajadhipok falls in a bloodless coup, and a constitutional monarchy and parliament are introduced. A succession of military dictators retains power for most of the period until 1973.
- **October 14, 1973**—400,000 student-led protesters topple the military rulers, leading to a brief period of unstable democracy.
- **October 6, 1976**—A bloody crackdown on student protesters ends with the military returning to power.
- **March 1980**—Moderate military ruler Prem Tinsulanond survives several coup attempts.
- **July 1988**—General Chatichai Choonhavan wins general elections.
- **February 1991**—General Sunthorn Kongsompong stages a coup and topples Chatichai's civilian government.
- **May 1992**—Junta member General Suchinda Kraprayoon assumes the prime minister's post, drawing hundreds of thousands of protesters into the streets of Bangkok demanding a return to civilian rule. The king intervenes and General Suchinda agrees to resign.
- **September 23, 1992**—Democrat party leader Chuan Leekpai is elected prime minister.
- **October 11, 1997**—The king signs the country's sixteenth "People's Constitution" into law, in a major development for political reform and democracy.
- **March 4, 2000**—The first senate elections are held under the new constitution.
- **January 6, 2001**—Telecommunications magnate Thaksin Shinawatra wins elections in a landslide to become the twenty-third prime minister.[23]
- **September 19, 2006**—Thaksin Shinawatra is accused of corruption and is ousted in a bloodless military coup and goes into exile in Dubai.

Thailand is one of the more advanced developing countries in Asia. It depends on exports of manufactured goods, including high-technology goods, and the development of the service sector to fuel the country's rapid growth, averaging 9 percent since 1989. Most of Thailand's recent imports have been for capital equipment and raw materials, although imports of consumer goods are beginning to rise. Thailand's 35 percent domestic savings rate is a key source of capital for the economy, and the country is also benefiting from rising investment from abroad.

THAILAND'S INSURGENCY

Since 2001, the level and intensity of Thailand's insurgency has started to increase, with the main problem areas being the southern Thai Provinces of Pattani, Yala, and Narathiwat, home to the majority of the country's Malay Muslims. Statistics from the Thai Ministry of the Interior show that in 2001 there were fifty terrorist-related incidents across the three affected Provinces, with nineteen police officers killed. In 2002, guerrillas attacked several police stations, seizing huge quantities of arms and ammunition. Between January and November 2004, some 573 people were killed and 524 injured.[24] There are no indications that Thailand's insurgents are being exported to other conflicts around the globe and their focus is purely on domestic political grievances. However, as Malay Muslims are known to practice a more moderate form of Islam, but Wahhabi teachings and the increase in religious schools in the south being sponsored and supported by states in the Middle East is a cause for concern to the Buddhist government. The sharp rise in insurgent attacks in 2007 and the types of attack being carried out point to a level of expertise that was not previously evident. This leads analysts to believe that the increased insurgency may be due to the presence of foreign fighters. Thailand has been ruled by a Buddhist-dominated government for decades and is kept in power by a powerful military with unwavering support for the Thai monarchy. The south is home to the poorest of the population, and the Malay Muslim grievances go back decades stemming from discrimination and attempts at forced assimilation by successive ethnic Thai Buddhist governments. The presence of insurgent groups date back to the late 1960s and early 1970s, created to defend against Communist influences spreading across Thailand's borders. In 1971, the Thai Royal family sponsored the Village Scouts, a rightwing ultra-nationalist group established not to be involved in politics but as a group to do the bidding of the Royals. Today they continue to have the support of the Thai Royal family as well as the Royal Thai police and military. In the 1970s and 1980s, the most effective of the groups operating was the Pattani United Liberation Organization (PULO), calling for an independent Islamic state in Thailand.

The government stemmed the unrest with political and economic reforms that undercut support for armed struggle, and hundreds of fighters accepted a broad amnesty. The insurgency looked to be all but over by the mid-1990s.

But new strains then appeared, with four particularly significant groups emerging or re-emerging, with violence erupting early in 2004. The major groups active today include the following:

- BRN-C (Barisan Revolusi Nasional-Coordinate, National Revolutionary Front-Coordinate) the only active faction of BRN, first established in the early 1960s to fight for an independent Patani state. Thought to be the largest and best organized of the armed groups, it is focused on political organizing and recruitment within Islamic schools.
- Pemuda, a separatist youth movement (part of which is controlled by BRN-C), is believed to be responsible for a large proportion of day-to-day sabotage, shooting, and bombing attacks.
- GMIP (Gerakan Mujahidin Islam Patani, Patani Islamic Mujahidin Group), established by Afghanistan veterans in 1995, is committed to an independent Islamic state.
- New PULO, established in 1995 as an offshoot of PULO and the smallest of the active armed groups, is fighting for an independent state.

Major attacks started in January 2004, involved carefully coordinated attacks in which militants raided an army arsenal, torched schools and police posts, and the following day, set off several bombs.

The second, on April 28, 2004, involved synchronized attacks on eleven police posts and army checkpoints across Pattani, Yala, and Songkhla and ended in a bloody showdown at the Krue Se Mosque, when the Thai army gunned down thirty-two men inside. By the end of the day, 105 militants, 1 civilian, and 5 members of the security forces were dead.

The third, on October 25, 2004, began with a demonstration outside a police station and ended with the deaths of at least eighty-five Muslim men and boys, most from suffocation after arrest as a result of being stacked five and six deep in army trucks for transport to an army base.

There are several explanations, none mutually exclusive, for why violence has escalated. Two of the most plausible are the disbanding of key government institutions, and the fear and resentment created by arbitrary arrests and police brutality, compounded by government failure to provide justice to victims and families. Rapid social change has also contributed to insecurity and frustration in Malay Muslim communities and a feeling that their way of life, values, and culture are threatened.[25]

Separatist have continued to wage an insurgency and by 2008 more than 3,000 had died. The government has had little success in putting down or negotiating a peaceful settlement with the insurgents.

The simmering differences between the Thai military and the government will do nothing to resolve the situation in the south. On the contrary, while politicians and generals continue their infighting and political power struggles, it will give the insurgents more opportunity to attack and destabilize the government. The heavy-handed response to the insurgents by both the military and police is fueling the current insurgent attacks.

VIETNAM

The Socialist Republic of Vietnam is a Communist state made up of the former North and South Vietnams, after ten years of the Vietnam War. This country, war torn for many decades, is in Southeastern Asia, bordering the Gulf of Thailand, the Gulf of Tonkin, and the South China Sea, between China and Cambodia. It is slightly larger than New Mexico. After consolidation at the war's end, Vietnam has a population of over 75 million. The ethnic population distribution is Vietnamese (85 percent to 90 percent) and Chinese (3 percent), with Muong Tai, Meo, Khmer, Man, and Cham making up the ethnic balance. Religious affiliations are (in descending order) Buddhist, Taoist, Roman Catholic, indigenous beliefs, Islam, Protestant, Cao Dai, and Hoa Hao. Vietnam won its independence from France in 1945 when the French colonial forces were defeated. Its new constitution was approved in 1992.

Vietnam is a poor, densely populated country that has had to recover from the ravages of decades of war, the loss of financial support from the former USSR, and the rigidities of a centrally planned economy. Substantial progress has been achieved over the past ten years in moving forward from an extremely low starting point. Economic growth continued at a strong pace with industrial output rising by 14 percent during 1996; real GDP expanded by 9.4 percent. Foreign direct investment rose to an estimated $2.3 billion for the year. These positive numbers, however, mask some major difficulties that are emerging in economic performance. Many domestic industries, including coal, cement, steel, and paper, reported large stockpiles of inventory and tough competition from more efficient foreign producers. While disbursements of aid and foreign direct investment have risen, they are not large enough to finance the rapid increase in imports. It is widely believed that Vietnam may be using short-term trade credits to bridge the gap. That is a risky strategy, one that could result in a foreign exchange crunch in the near term.

Vietnamese authorities continue to move very slowly toward implementing the structural reforms needed to revitalize the economy and produce more competitive, export-driven industries. Privatization of state enterprise remains bogged down in political controversy, while the country's dynamic private sector is denied both financing and access to markets. Reform of the banking sector is proceeding slowly, raising concerns that the country will be unable to tap sufficient domestic savings to maintain current high levels of growth. Administrative and legal barriers are also causing costly delays for foreign investors and are raising similar doubts about Vietnam's ability to maintain the inflow of foreign capital. Ideological bias in favor of state intervention and control of the economy is slowing progress toward a more liberalized investment environment.

Vietnam has disputes over maritime boundaries with Cambodia and is involved in complex negotiations over the Spratly Islands in the South China Sea. These are ongoing with China, Malaysia, the Philippines, Taiwan, and possibly Brunei. There are also unresolved maritime boundaries with Thailand and with China in the Gulf of Tonkin, and disputed ownership of the Paracel Islands in the South China Sea, which are occupied by China but claimed by Vietnam and Taiwan. Offshore islands and sections of boundary with Cambodia are in dispute as well. Key growing areas in Vietnam cultivated 3,150 hectares of poppy in 1996, producing 25 tons of opium, making it a major opium producer and an increasingly important transit point for Southeast Asian heroin destined for the United States and Europe. Vietnam has a growing opium addiction problem, plus possible small-scale heroin production in country. While there is little known terrorism in Vietnam, a Vietnamese court sentenced two persons to death and three others to life in prison for carrying out a grenade attack on the waterfront in Ho Chi Minh City in 1994, in which twenty persons, including ten foreigners, were injured. The five were part of the Vietnam Front for Regime Restoration, an antigovernment exile group based in the United States.

Ho Chi Minh

The affectionate name given to him by his countrymen, "Uncle Ho," gives rise to an image as a kindly, humble man. Yet Ho was a lifelong revolutionary, who first led an insurrection against Japanese occupiers. In 1945, Ho's commandos took Hanoi, the Vietnamese capital. In one of the ironies of history, Ho Chi Minh paraphrased a future enemy's benchmark of freedom—the U.S. Declaration of Independence—while addressing an enormous crowd after the success against the Japanese. Ho proclaimed: "All men are born equal. The Creator has given us inviolable rights: life, liberty, and happiness!"

Ho again led revolutionary forces against outside control, fighting an eight-year war that led to the division of Vietnam into two countries, North and South Vietnam. An election that was meant to be held in 1956 to reunite the country under a democratically elected leader was never held. South Vietnam, backed by the United States, refused to participate in the elections, fearful Ho would win.

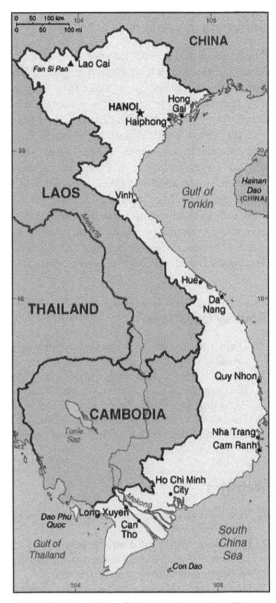

FIGURE 11-11 Map of Vietnam (Central Intelligence Agency, *The World Factbook*, 2008).

Ho's regime in the North became rigidly totalitarian. After the defeated French exited, the United States escalated its involvement, supporting a series of weak governments in South Vietnam.

Vietnamese independence was finally achieved, just six years after Ho's death in 1969. The victory came at a staggering price: An estimated 3 million North and South Vietnamese were killed in the struggle.[26]

Summary

The terrorism and violence generated in Southern and Southeast Asia span a large menu of very complicated and diverse scenarios. These range from individual acts (assassination of two prime ministers named Gandhi), religious hatred (the Hindus, the Muslims, and the Sikhs), political genocide (Khmer Rouge), and state terrorism (Burma) up to conventional and nuclear war possibilities. This complex region, one that is little understood in the Western world and often mysterious, holds huge potential but many problems. Thailand alone stood somewhat calm until 2001, but increasing insurgent problems in the south and an influx of Islamic extremists is giving rise to concerns. The former Indochina tries to recover from decades of suffering from wars, terror, and destruction for over four decades and is beginning to make some progress, but with fits and starts. The situation between India and Pakistan, the involvement of Pakistan's ISI in terrorism, and the U.S. killing of Osama bin Laden in Pakistan will provide ongoing opportunities for terror in the region. Added to that mix is the significant presence of Islamic fighters in the Northwest Frontier Provinces and the flow of fighters either entering or leaving Afghanistan. Time will tell if these great nations will survive, facing a situation every bit as dangerous as any in the Middle East. The incredibly long histories of most of the nations in the region have created long memories and simmering hatreds.

Review Questions

1. Discuss the rise of the al Qaeda movement and its overall ideology.
2. How has the Pakistan Inter Services Intelligence (ISI) agency been involved in the problems facing Afghanistan over the last thirty years?
3. Discuss some of the reasons why Islamic militants conduct operations against Hindu and Christian targets in India.
4. What role did the Taliban play in the development of Afghanistan after the Soviet invasion?
5. What role did al Qaeda play during the Soviet invasion of Afghanistan and how were they supported?
6. What methods did the Pol Pot regime use to combat the economic problems facing Cambodia?

Websites

1. **History Politics**—*http://www.sscnet.ucla.edu/southasia/ History/Independent/Indira.html*
2. **Liberation Tigers of Tamil Eelam**—South Asia Terrorism Portal—*http://www.satp.org/satporgtp/ countries/shrilanka/terroristoutfits/Ltte.htm*
3. **Jane's Islamic Affairs Analysis**—*http://www.janes. com/products/janes/security/news/islamic-affairs- analyst.aspx*
4. **South Asia Analysis Group**—*http://www.southasia analysis.org/*
5. **Musharraf and Terrorism (Archives)**—*http://www. southasiaanalysis.org*
6. **Global Terrorism Analysis**—*http://www.jamestown. org/programs/gta/terrorismfocusgta/*
7. **United States Institute for Peace**—*http://www.usip.org/ publications/terrorism-and-counter-terrorism-web-links*

End Notes

1. The Economist, India's Sikhs, *Heresy and History* (July 7, 2007).
2. Macleans. (December 3, 2007, p. 30).
3. "Patterns of Global Terrorism." *U.S. Department of State* (2005).
4. The Jamestown Foundation. http://www.jamestown.org/publications_details.php.
5. Saeed Shafwat. *The Rise of Dawat ul-Irshad and Lashkar-e-Toiba in Pakistan: Nationalism without a Nation*, ed. Christopher Jaffrelot (New Delhi: Manohar Publications, 2002).
6. "Patterns of Global Terrorism." *U.S. Department of State* (1998).
7. Nepal Assessment 2011.http://www.satp.org/satporgtp/countries/nepal/index.html
8. John Thompson. "The Liberation Tigers of Tamil Eelam: Essential Points."*Mackenzie Institute Briefing Note #25* (2009). http://www.mackenzieinstitute.com/2009/tamil-tigers-040609.htm
9. "Liberation Tigers of Tamil Eelam." http://www.globalsecurity.org/military/world/para/ltte.htm
10. "Patterns of Global Terrorism." *U.S. Department of State* (Washington, DC, 1997). http://www.state.gov.
11. Press Statement by James P. Rubin, spokesman (September 8, 1998). http://www.state.gov.
12. "Tigers Suffer Setback." *Janes Terrorism and Security Monitor* (London, January 2008).
13. "Al Qaeda's Ideology." *The Security Service MI5* https://www.mi5.gov.uk/output/al-qaidas-ideology.html
14. Ibid.
15. Anthony Tucker Jones. "The Fall of Osama bin Laden." *The Journal of International Security* (Chertsey, UK: Albany Media Ltd, May 2011, pp. 6–8).
16. Amin Saikal. "The Taliban, Pakistan's Geopolitical Instrument, America's Problem." —South Asia Terrorism Portalhttp://www.satp.org/satporgtp/publication/books/global/aminsaikal.htm
17. Walden Bello (April 29, 2002), http://www.state.gov.
18. UN Office on Drugs and Crime—Afghanistan Opium Survey, 2007 Report.
19. Editors. "Afghanistan's 2002 Opium Harvest." *Intersec* (March 3, 2002, pp. 78–81).
20. Irrawaddy News Magazine Interactive (Archives), http://www.Irrawaddy.org.
21. "The White House." Office of the Press Secretary (October 27, 1998). http://www.state.gov.
22. The Death of Pol Pot (2008), http://www.wsws.org/news/1998/apr1998/plpt-a18.shtml.
23. http://australianetwork.com/news/infocus/s1745603.htm.
24. *Janes Intelligence Review* (May 1, 2005).
25. "Southern Thailand: Insurgency Not Jihad." *Asia Report #98* (May 18, 2005). http://www.crisisgroup.org/home/index.cfm?id=3436.
26. PBS. www.pbs.org.

12

The Pacific Rim

*Terrorism has become the systematic weapon of a war
that knows no borders or seldom has a face.*

—Jacques Chirac (President of France 1995–2007)

LEARNING OBJECTIVES

After studying this chapter, the student should be able to:

1. Explain how Islamist separatist groups have been linked to al Qaeda in Indonesia and the Philippines and the threat they pose to the West.

2. Understand how a cult organization was effective in deploying a nerve agent in a public transit system.

3. Describe the methods employed by China to suppress a religious cult.

4. Describe the connections between Philippines' terror groups and al Qaeda network.

KEY WORDS TO NOTE

Abu Sayyaf Group (ASG)—A small but effective Islamic terror group that seeks an independent Islamic state along the Sulu archipelago

Aum Shinrikyo—Japanese religious cult founded in 1984 and responsible for the gas attack on the Tokyo subway

ETIM—East Turkestan Islamic Movement—a separatist group demanding independence from China

Falun Gong—A spiritual discipline originating in China—the movement is categorized by China as terrorist in nature

Japanese Red Army (JRA)—Formed in 1970 to foment a global revolution—responsible for airline hijackings and massacre at Lod Airport in 1972

Jemaah Islamiyah (JI)—Indonesian-based Sunni Islamic extremist organization, the stated goal of which is to create an Islamic state encompassing Indonesia, Malaysia, Thailand, and Mindanao in the Southern Philippines

Moro Islamic Liberation Front (MILF)—Formed in 1977, it is an Islamic movement fighting for an independent homeland in the Southern Philippines

New People's Army (NPA)—Military wing of the communist party of the Philippines—a Maoist group formed in 1969 to overthrow the Philippine government

OVERVIEW

The Pacific Rim contains those countries that sweep in a long arc from Australia to Japan. Many have been suffering serious financial crises. As major trading partners to the United States, and the European Economic Community, many have brought the world great turmoil; through wars, insurgencies, corrupt governments, and from right and left-wing terrorism. These problems have a major impact on the other countries of this region. Their financial and political chaos creates opportunities for terrorist groups to take advantage of the turmoil to advance their agendas. This chapter builds upon the previous analysis of Southern and Southeast Asia and discusses how individual countries are reacting in terms of their backgrounds and histories of terrorist actions. We shall start with the biggest country, in terms of population, China.

CHINA

Our examination of the Far East and the Pacific Rim cannot begin without first discussing the People's Republic of China (PRC). Following the fall of the Soviet Union, the PRC has now become the world's second-greatest superpower.

China is bordered by a coastline of over 10,000 miles that includes the East China Sea, Korea Bay, Yellow Sea, and the South China Sea. The country is only slightly smaller than the United States. Its land borders are over 14,700 miles long and include the countries of Afghanistan, Bhutan, India, Kazakhstan, North Korea, Kyrgyzstan, Laos, Macau, Mongolia, Nepal, Pakistan, Russia (Northeast), Russia (Northwest), Tajikistan, and Vietnam. China is the world's fourth-largest country (after Russia, Canada, and the United States), with a population of approximately 1.3 billion. The ethnic makeup of this world giant is as follows: Han Chinese,

FIGURE 12-1 Map of China (Central Intelligence Agency, *The World Factbook, 2008*).

91.9 percent; Zhuang, Uighur, Hui, Yi, Tibetan, Miao, Manchu, Mongol, Buyi, Korean, and "other" make up the remainder. While China is officially atheist, it is traditionally pragmatic and eclectic. Daoism (Taoism), Buddhism, and Muslim religions are unofficially practiced by 2–3 percent of their population, and Chinese Christians number only about 1 percent. But, remember, these are percentages of 1.3 billion people—and 1 percent still represents a very large number!

China was an ancient, and widely scattered, society until it was unified under the Qin, or Ch'ing, Dynasty in 221 B.C. The Ch'ing Dynasty, the last of the dynasties, was replaced by the Chinese Republic in 1912. The People's Republic of China was later established in 1949. Beginning in late 1978, the Chinese leadership began moving the economy from a sluggish, Soviet-style, and centrally planned economy to more market-oriented economy, but still one that is within a rigid political framework and firmly under Communist Party control. The authorities switched to a system of household responsibility in agriculture in place of the older collectivization. It increased the authority of local officials and plant managers in industry, permitted a wide variety of small-scale enterprises in services and light manufacturing, and opened the economy to increased foreign trade and investment. The result has been a quadrupling of China's GDP since 1978. Agricultural output doubled in the 1980s, and industry also posted major gains, especially in coastal areas near Hong Kong and across the Straight in Taiwan, where foreign investment helped spur output of both domestic and export goods. On the darker side, the leadership often experienced in its hybrid system the worst results of socialism (bureaucracy, lassitude, and corruption) as well as those of capitalism (windfall gains and stepped-up inflation). Beijing has periodically had to backtrack, retightening central controls at intervals. From 1992 to 1996, annual growth of GDP accelerated, particularly in the coastal areas, averaging more than 10 percent annually, according to official Chinese figures. From 1995 to 1996, inflation dropped sharply, reflecting tighter monetary policies and stronger measures to control food prices. At the same time, the government struggled to

- Collect revenues from provinces, businesses, and individuals.
- Reduce corruption and other economic crimes.
- Keep afloat the large, state-owned enterprises, most of which had not participated in the vigorous expansion of the economy and many of which have been losing the ability to pay full wages and pensions.

It is estimated that from 60 to 100 million surplus rural workers were then adrift, between the villages and the cities, many subsisting on part-time, low-paying jobs. Another long-term threat to continued economic growth was the deterioration of the environment—notably, air pollution, soil erosion, and the steady dropping of the water table, especially in the north. China still continues to lose arable land, because of erosion and economic development. Furthermore, the Chinese government gives insufficient priority to serious agricultural research. The next few years might see increasing tensions between a highly centralized political system and an increasingly decentralized economic system.[1]

China is also a major transshipment point for heroin produced in the Golden Triangle and is beginning to experience a rapidly growing domestic drug abuse problem.

PAN-TURKIC MOVEMENT—UIGHURS

Terrorism in China had matured long before the 9-11 tragedy, with February 5, 1997, marking the beginning of active terrorism in the country. Terrorist activities have three separate yet interrelated dimensions. First, the insurgent movement has a well-defined political program, aimed at achieving independence through ethnic struggle. More concretely, this program contains a mixture of ideas including the Pan-Turkic movement that spread to Xinjiang at the beginning of the last century. In the 1930s, when Xinjiang was at the height of turmoil, the Uighurs established an East Turkistan Islamic Republic. Although it existed for only three months, its legacy died hard. In the early 1980s, the spirit of independence based on Turkish ethnicity was rekindled, inspiring many Uighurs who resented Chinese domination of local affairs. Ethnic self-determination works in tandem with Pan-Turkism as another motivating factor. Under the banner of human rights and equality, the dissidents use both peaceful means of lobbying in the international arena and violent means by way of protest within China. The movement has generated sympathy from a range of Uighur communities in remote Xinjiang. Second, Jiangdu activists have built base networks both at home and abroad, with extensive foreign connections revolving around three centers of activity, each of them interconnected: Activists launch anti-China campaigns under the name of promoting human rights and ethnic equality in the West. Dozens of Islamic organizations comprising Chinese exiles were legally registered in Central Asia during the mid-1990s, such as the East Turkistan Liberation Movement in Kazakhstan. Although most of them were later outlawed, they continued to engage in covert operations that pose a security threat to Beijing. The third center used to be in Afghanistan, where Xinjiang insurgents received indoctrination and military training from al Qaeda. One Chinese source revealed that more than fifty known terrorist organizations existed in Central Asia and that more than 500 Xinjiang insurgents had been trained in Afghanistan.[2]

Reports from China on terrorist events have been limited, and most events since 1997 have been attributed to separatist attacks by Uighur who continue to wage a campaign of violence. The Uighur, a Chinese-Muslim ethnic minority group, is concentrated in the Xinjiang autonomous region in far-western China. Xinjiang is a resource-rich and strategically important region bordering Afghanistan, Pakistan, and Kazakhstan among other nations. Beijing is intensely sensitive to threats to its territorial integrity both there and in Tibet. Beijing claims that the World Uighur Congress is the front organization for East Turkistan Islamic Movement (**ETIM**).

In February 1997, Uighur separatists conducted a series of bus bombings in Urumqi, which killed nine persons and wounded seventy-four. Earlier Uighur rioting in the city of Yining resulted in as many as 200 deaths. Uighur exiles in Turkey claimed responsibility for a small pipe bomb that exploded on a bus in Beijing, killing three persons and injuring eight. In another incident, Uighur separatists were blamed for killing five persons, including two policemen. The Chinese government quickly executed several individuals who were involved in both the rioting and the bombings. Beijing claims that support for the Uighurs is coming from neighboring Muslim countries, an accusation that has been strongly denied.

The government has tightly controlled the practice of Islam, and official repression in the Xinjiang Uighur Autonomous Region (XUAR) targeted at Uighur Muslims tightened in some areas. Regulations restricting Muslims' religious activity, teaching, and places of worship continued to be implemented forcefully in the XUAR. The government continued to repress Uighur Muslims, sometimes citing counterterrorism as the basis for taking action that was repressive. Chinese authorities detained and arrested persons engaged in unauthorized religious activities. The government reportedly continued to limit access to mosques, to detain citizens for possession of unauthorized religious texts, imprison citizens for religious activities determined to be "extremist," and force Muslims who were fasting, to eat during Ramadan, and confiscating Muslims' passports in an effort to strengthen control over Muslim pilgrimages. In addition, the Uighur government maintained the most severe legal restrictions in China on children's right to practice religion. In recent years, Uighur authorities detained and arrested persons engaged in unauthorized religious activities and charged them with a range of offenses, including state security crimes. Xinjiang authorities often charged religious believers with committing the "three evils": terrorism, separatism, and extremism. Uighur authorities prohibited women, children, Chinese Communist Party (CCP) members, and government workers from entering mosques.[3]

The East Turkestan Islamic Movement (ETIM)

The Uighurs are an ethnic minority group of approximately 8 million. Their ethnicity, language, and culture are more similar to the Turkic peoples of neighboring Central Asian republics. Although the ETIM seeks to establish an independent Islamic regime, the majority of Uighurs are Sunni and do not necessarily support the idea of a separate Islamic state. ETIM is a small but extreme group founded by the Uighurs, whose mandate is an independent state called "East Turkestan." From the Chinese government perspective, it is quite convenient to have this group operating here as it is close to the center of Islamic extremism in Afghanistan and Pakistan and allows the Chinese to claim that they are fighting the "War on Terror" in their own backyard. This allows them to put pressure on the U.S. Administration to "ignore" Chinese human rights issues. In 2002, the U.S. State Department deported two ETIM members to China from Kyrgyzstan for allegedly plotting attacks on the U.S. embassy in the Kyrgyz capital of Bishkek, as well as other U.S. interests.[4]

In January 2007, the government announced that it had conducted raids on a suspected ETIM training base in the Pamir Mountains in Xinjiang Province, an area of rugged mountains bordering Afghanistan and Tajikistan. China claims that ETIM members were being trained, funded, and supported at the base by al Qaeda.

Former president George W. Bush met with the then president of China in October 2001 in Shanghai. During an exchange of views and mutual support on matters confronting the global threat of terrorism, George Bush stated, "… the government of China responded immediately to the attacks of September 11th. There was no hesitation, there was no doubt that they would stand with the United States and our people during this terrible time. There is a firm commitment by this government to cooperate in intelligence matters, to help interdict financing of terrorist organizations. President Jiang and the government stand side by side with the American people as we fight this evil force."[5] The meeting between the two heads of state in October 2001 signaled that China would make the most of controlling those groups that were considered subversive and internal enemies of the state. China's communist regime, which fears that China could splinter if regional separatist movements gain ground, has long called the ETIM a terrorist group. On January 21, 2002, the Information Office of the State Council (China's cabinet) issued a report arguing that terrorist forces from Xinjiang "jeopardized…social stability in China, and even threatened the security and stability of related countries and regions." The report cited four waves of terrorism during which Uighur activists were allegedly responsible for explosions, assassinations, attacks on police and government institutions, and poison and arson attacks both inside China and abroad. From 1990 to 2001, the combined efforts resulted in over 200 incidents, 162 deaths, and more than 440 injuries. During those years, Xinjiang police reportedly broke up 487 terrorist groups and identified 253 major violent terrorist crimes. The most serious threat purportedly came from organizations operating from neighboring countries, such as Afghanistan and Uzbekistan, but the report also alleged that other groups, operating from bases in Turkey, Germany, and the United States also sponsored terrorist activities.

Much of the State Council's report and a subsequent one in September 2002 focused on the East Turkistan Islamic Movement (ETIM), dozens of whose members allegedly trained in

Afghanistan.[6] China continues to state that ETIM is sponsored by al Qaeda, and there maybe some truth to this as at least twenty-two were captured by U.S. forces in Afghanistan and sent to Guantanamo, where they were interrogated and most all were released but not deported to China. It seems likely that although these fighters had received training at Afghan camps, it does not necessarily make them adherents to al Qaeda. From China's perspective it, would make sense to cast ETIM as linked with al Qaeda and global jihad to allow them a freer hand in dealing with internal disputes in that region. As the Chinese press is state controlled it is extremely difficult to get any accurate data relative to activities involving ETIM that can be independently verified.

Falun Gong

While there has been limited reporting on terrorism in China, members of the "Falun Gongs" spiritual group have created cracks in the tight controls of mainland China's leadership. The government's anti-**Falun Gong** propaganda—a new phase in the battle between this group and the government—could possibly pose a bigger threat to the Communist Party, if that country's rate of urban unemployed were to rise up in support of the Falun Gong. The Falun Gong has hacked into Chinese government television broadcasts in Yantai, Shandong Province, and briefly aired a message saying, "Falun Gong is good." The incident was one of a string of broadcast station hackings that hit six cities in six months, primarily in the country's northeastern "rust belt," where unemployment and labor unrest are growing. The group was trying to counter the government's massive anti-Falun Gong propaganda campaign, which centers on the January 2001 self-immolation attempt by a group of Falun Gong followers in which two had died. These new tactics revealed the Falun Gong is technological savvy and may even have pointed to a shift in focus. Since most of the Falun Gong broadcasts were focused on China's northeast, the government fears groundwork may be underway for a new showdown with the group, one that could draw on the urban unemployed. By hacking into state television, taking its case directly to the Chinese people, the Falun Gong is also confronting China's central leadership, a strategy that has thus far used peaceful demonstrations, appeals for dialogue, and attention from foreign media to try to convince Beijing to lift its ban of the movement. The government's inability to crush the group has only reinforced Beijing's perception that the Falun Gong is a serious threat to its authority. Although the group could simply have gone underground after the government outlawed it in 1999, it chose to fight for its rights, which has led it down the path toward confrontation.

The Falun Gong emerged as a semi-religious exercise group in the early 1990s and grew rapidly, crossing all socioeconomic classes, and filled a spiritual void in China at a time of rapid change. In April 1999, after a run-in with a local government, the Falun Gong then confronted Beijing directly in perhaps one of the most impressive displays of civil action in China since the 1989 incident in Tiananmen Square, when more than 10,000 followers and students, converged along the street outside the government compound in Beijing, in a daylong silent vigil. This Gandhi-inspired peaceful demonstration, which faded quietly into the night, unfortunately had precisely the opposite effect on the Chinese Government. Rather than persuading China's leaders to legitimize the Falun Gong, it sparked confusion among the country's elite. The protest showed the Falun Gong's well-developed command and communications structure could be pervasive across Chinese society. After a brief respite, Beijing banned the group, and began a crackdown, rounding up and detaining thousands of Falun Gong's members. Falun Gong quickly appealed for international help. It turned to and drew international media attention at a time when China was petitioning for entry into the World Trade Organization (WTO), and bidding seriously to host the 2008 Summer Olympic Games. Falun Gong then began appearing in Tiananmen Square in peaceful protest. The heavy-handed crackdown by Chinese security forces that followed was captured on foreign media and broadcast worldwide.

In January 2001, the group's strategy fell apart after a group of alleged Falun Gong practitioners arrived in Tiananmen Square and set themselves on fire! Whether these were simply overzealous members of the Falun Gong, or a group of people misled by government infiltrators to take extreme measures, the self-immolation proved a propaganda coup for the Chinese Government.

Whereas previous government claims that the Falun Gong was evil and dangerous were more often brushed aside by many Chinese who felt Beijing was overreacting, the pictures of half-burnt young girls on national television gave credence to the government's argument. Once again, the Falun Gong altered its strategy. Foreigners, rather than Chinese followers in Tiananmen Square, increasingly carried out protests and wherever the Chinese leaders traveled in Europe or Asia, supporters of the Falun Gong were there. In January 2002, they began a new tactic of pirate attacks on government television. The first incident took place in Chongqing, Sichuan Province, and was followed on February 16, in Anshan, Liaoning. In Anshan, three Falun Gong activists tapped into the local cable line but were caught in the process, and security forces shot at least one.

On March 5, Falun Gong activists managed to hack into eight channels in Changchun, Jilin Province, the hometown of Falun Gong Founder, Li Hongxi. They broadcast two twenty-minute films contradicting the self-immolation story and extolling the virtues of the Falun Gong. On April 21, they struck in Harbin, Heilongjiang Province, reportedly airing pro-Falun Gong material for more than an hour.

Two recent cases, in Laiyang and Yantai, both in Shandong Province, were shorter broadcasts, simply relaying the message that "Falun Gong is good." But, in these cases, rather than hacking into cable lines, the Falun Gong managed to hijack the government satellite broadcasts, according to Chinese security officials, cited by the *South China Morning Post*, something quite a bit more sophisticated than splicing a VCR into cable lines.

The most recent Falun Gong activities have three key characteristics: First, they all suggest that what appeared to be a headless organism does have a centralized planning and organization structure. Second, the attacks indicate sophisticated technological savvy, particularly if the group managed to pirate into the state's satellite system. The similarity of the attacks and their dispersal also suggest there is an active training network inside the Falun Gong. Finally, the TV hijackings took place in China's northeast rust belt. Heilongjiang, Jilin, and Liaoning Provinces have been the sites of active labor protests for months, and large-scale demonstrations have rocked Daqing and Liaoyang and broken out in Fushun and Anshan. Although this could be a coincidence, the area is the traditional support base of Falun Gong; it also could be an attempt to bridge the gap between the group and the large pool of unemployed state workers there.

There appears now to be a realization among the Falun Gong leadership that the Chinese government will not change its position on the group particularly after a three-year nationwide campaign denouncing it as an evil cult and a socially destabilizing element. The following is a brief chronology of the reported manner in which China treated a Falun Gong practitioner. A brief chronology of Ms. Gao's suffering under the Chinese government's persecution:

- **July–December, 1999**—Arrested five times in Shenyang and Beijing for petitioning the government to stop persecuting Falun Gong. Suffered beating and force feeding in jail.
- **February 2000–January 2001**—Arrested and detained in Masanjia Labor Camp. Suffered various tortures.
- **June 20–July 7, 2003**—Arrested and detained in Shenyang Detention Center. Suffered electric baton shock, beating, and forced feeding.

- **July 8, 2003**—Sentenced to three years of forced labor in Longshan Labor Camp. Suffered various tortures.
- **May 7, 2004**—Handcuffed to a steel pipe and shocked on the face by two policemen with three electric batons for seven hours. Face was disfigured.
- **July 7, 2004**—Ms. Gao's photos published on a Falun Gong website (http://www.minghui.ca/).
- **May 8–October 4, 2004**—In police custody at a hospital.
- **October 5, 2004**—Escaped police custody.
- **March 6, 2005**—Rearrested.
- **June 6, 2005**—Sent to a hospital's emergency room.
- **June 12, 2005**—Parents informed to come to the hospital.
- **June 16, 2005**—Died in the hospital.[7]
- **70–100 million**—Number of Falun Gong adherents practicing in China before the ban in 1999.
- **450,000–1 million**—Estimated number of Falun Gong practitioners held in labor camps, prison camps, and other long-term detention facilities at any given time.
- **87,000**—Number of reports of torture against Falun Gong adherents to emerge from China since 1999.[8]

HONG KONG

Hong Kong returned to its former status as a province of China on July 1, 1997. High-flying Hong Kong businesspersons and others fled from the island in droves when this move was first announced several years ago. Many are now returning back to be, "where the action is," in Asia.

In a joint declaration, China promised to respect Hong Kong's existing social and economic systems and lifestyle. Hong Kong borders the South China Sea and mainland China, about six times the size of Washington DC, and is scattered over more than 200 islands. The six and a half-million people are an unbalanced ethnic mix of 95 percent Chinese and 5 percent other. They practice religion in an eclectic mix of 90 percent local religions and 10 percent Christians.

Hong Kong has long been the major and most dynamic business and financial center of mainland Asia and a bustling free market with few tariffs or nontariff barriers. Natural resources are severely limited, and food and raw materials must be imported. Manufacturing and construction account for about 18 percent of GDP. Goods and services exports account for about 50 percent of GDP. Real GDP growth averaged a remarkable 8 percent. A shortage of labor continues to place upward pressure on prices and the cost of living. Prospects remain bright but only as long as major trading partners continue to be

FIGURE 12-2 Map of Hong Kong (Central Intelligence Agency, *The World Factbook, 2008*).

reasonably prosperous, and they probably will, as long as investors feel China will continue to support free market practices. While terrorism has been virtually nonexistent there, Hong Kong is a major hub for the Southeast Asian heroin trade and is involved with transshipment of drugs and money laundering. There is also an increasing problem with the indigenous population's amphetamine abuse.

TAIWAN (REPUBLIC OF CHINA)

The Republic of China (usually referred to as Taiwan since the 1970s) on the island of Taiwan has experienced at least twenty terrorist events since 1979, including thirteen aircraft hijackings and five bombings. Factors responsible for the relatively small burden of terrorism on Taiwan in the past include tight military control over political dissent until 1987, a warming relationship with the People's Republic of China in the 1990s, political inclusion of major internal cultural groups, geographic isolation, and a lack of other significant international enemies.

The Republic of China borders the East China Sea, the Philippine Sea, the South China Sea, and the Taiwan Strait. It is north of the Philippines, on a large island off the southeastern coast of China, and is slightly smaller than Maryland and Delaware combined. The population of approximately 21,699,776 is composed of Taiwanese (84 percent), mainland Chinese (14 percent), and aborigine (2 percent). Religion in Taiwan is based on a mixture of Buddhist, Confucian, and Taoist (93 percent), Christian (4.5 percent), and "other" (2.5 percent). Political pressure groups include the Taiwan independence movement and various environmental groups. Debate on Taiwan independence has now become acceptable within the mainstream of domestic politics in Taiwan. Political liberalization and the increased representation of the opposition Democratic Progressive Party (DPP) in Taiwan's legislature have opened public debate on the island's national identity. Advocates of Taiwan independence, including those within the DPP, oppose the ruling party's longtime traditional stand that the island will still eventually be reunited with mainland China. Goals of the Taiwan Independence Movement include establishing a sovereign nation on Taiwan and entering the United Nations. Other organizations supporting Taiwan independence include the World United Formosans for Independence and Organization for a Taiwan Nation.

Taiwan has a dynamic and capitalist economy, with considerable guidance of investment and foreign trade by government officials, and partial government ownership of some large banks and industrial firms. Real growth in GDP has averaged about 9 percent a year over the past three decades. Export growth has been even faster and has provided the impetus for industrialization. Inflation and unemployment are very low. Agriculture contributes less than 4 percent to GDP, down from 35 percent back in 1952. Traditional labor-intensive industries are steadily being moved offshore and replaced with more capital and technology-intensive industries. Taiwan has become an active major investor in China, Thailand, Indonesia, the Philippines, Malaysia, and Vietnam. Tightening of labor markets has led to an influx of foreign workers, both legal and illegal.

Taiwan is involved in long-standing and complex territorial disputes with China, Malaysia, the Philippines, Vietnam, and (possibly) Brunei over the Spratly Islands. The Parcel Islands are occupied by China, but are claimed by both Vietnam and Taiwan. China and Taiwan also dispute claims over the Japanese-administered Senkaku-shoto (Senkaku Islands/Diaoyu Tai). The island nation is tightly controlled, and there is no discernible terrorist activity. Taiwan is considered an important heroin transit point, and there seems to be a fast-growing problem with domestic consumption of methamphetamine and heroin.

JAPAN

Japan is a constitutional monarchy that became an independent state in 660 B.C., through the efforts of Emperor Jimmu. Located in Eastern Asia it is an island chain between the North Pacific Ocean and the Sea of Japan, east of the Korean Peninsula. Japan is slightly smaller than California and has a population of over 125 million. The appetite of the Japanese for fish is contributing to the depletion of this resource in Asia and elsewhere. Ethnic diversity is literally unknown in Japan, where 99.4 percent of the population is Japanese, and only 0.6 percent is other (mostly Korean). Religions are also similarly broken out: Those who observe both Shintoism and Buddhism comprise 84 percent, and other comprises 16 percent.

Japanese government–industry cooperation, a strong work ethic, their mastery of high technology, and a comparatively small defense allocation (roughly 1 percent of GDP) have helped Japan's economy advance with extraordinary rapidity to become one of the most powerful in the world. One notable characteristic of the Japanese economy is the working together of manufacturers, suppliers, and distributors in closely knit groups called keiretsu. A second basic feature has been the guarantee of lifetime employment for a substantially large portion of the urban labor force. But, sad to say, this guarantee has been slowly eroded. Industry, the most important sector of their economy, is heavily dependent on importing raw materials and fuels. The much smaller agricultural sector is highly subsidized and protected, with crop yields that rank among the very highest in the world. Usually self-sufficient in rice, Japan must import about

FIGURE 12-3   Map of Japan (Central Intelligence Agency, *The World Factbook, 2008*).

50 percent of their requirements of other grain and fodder crops. Japan maintains one of the world's largest fishing fleets and accounts for nearly 15 percent of the global catch.

AUM SHINRIKYO   Aum Shinrikyo is fanatical cult that is obsessed with the apocalypse. It was responsible for the Sarin gas attack on the Tokyo subway system in 1995 but since then has not been credited with any further attacks. According to the U.S. Department of State, Country Reports on Terrorism Shoko Asahara established Aum in 1987 and the cult received legal status as a religious entity in 1989. Initially, Aum aimed to take over Japan and then the world, but over time it began to emphasize the coming of the end of the world. Asahara predicted in the late 1990s that the United States would initiate Armageddon by starting World War III with Japan.

Aum Shinrikyo began its public campaign of terror on June 27, 1994, in Matsumoto, a city of 300,000 approximately 322 kilometres northwest of Tokyo; a group of cult members drove a converted refrigerator truck into a nondescript residential neighborhood. Parking in a secluded parking lot behind a stand of trees, they activated a computer-controlled system to release a cloud of Sarin. The nerve agent floated toward a cluster of private homes, a mid-rise apartment building, town homes, and a small dormitory. This neighbourhood was targeted for a specific reason. The dormitory was the residence of all three judges sitting on a panel hearing a lawsuit over a real-estate dispute in which Aum Shinrikyo was the defendant. Cult lawyers had advised the sect's leadership that the decision was likely to go against them. Unwilling to accept a costly reversal, Aum responded by sending a team to Matsumoto to guarantee that the judges did not hand down an adverse judgment. A light breeze (3–5 knots) gently pushed the deadly aerosol cloud of Sarin into a courtyard formed by the buildings. The deadly agent affected the inhabitants of many of the buildings, entering through windows and doorways left open to the warm night air. Within a short time, seven people were dead. Five hundred others were transported to local hospitals, where approximately 200 would require at least one night's hospitalization.

Their next major act of violence would serve as a wake-up call to the world regarding the prospects of weapons of mass destruction and terrorism. On March 20, 1995, packages were placed on five different trains in the Tokyo subway system. The packages consisted of plastic bags filled with a chemical mix and wrapped inside newspapers. Once placed on the floor of the subway car, each bag was punctured with a sharpened umbrella tip, and the material was allowed to spill onto the floor of the subway car. As the liquid spread out and evaporated, the vaporous agent spread throughout the car. Tokyo was experiencing a coordinated, simultaneous, multipoint assault. The attack was carried out at virtually the same moment at five different locations in the world's largest city: five trains, many kilometers apart, all converging on the center of Tokyo. The resulting deaths and injuries were spread throughout central Tokyo. First reports came from the inner suburbs and then, very quickly, cries for help began to flow in from one station after another, forming a rapidly tightening ring around the station at Kasumagaseki. This station serves the buildings that house most of the key agencies of the Japanese government. Most of the major ministries, as well as the national police agency, have their headquarters at Kasumagaseki.

By the end of that day, fifteen subway stations in the world's busiest subway system had been affected. Of these, stations along the Hbiya line were the most heavily affected some with as many as 300–400 persons involved. The number injured in the attacks was just under 3,800; of those, nearly 1,000 required hospitalization—some for no more than a few hours, some for many days; and twelve people were dead.[9] Aum dabbled in many different biological agents. They cultured and experimented with botulin toxin, anthrax, cholera, and Q fever. In 1993, Asahara led a group of sixteen cult doctors and nurses to Zaire, on a supposed medical mission. The purpose of the trip to Central Africa was to learn as much as possible about and, ideally, to bring back samples of

Ebola virus. In early 1994, cult doctors were quoted on Russian radio as discussing the possibility of using Ebola as a biological weapon.

The U.S. secretary of state designated Aum Shinrikyo as a "Foreign Terrorist Organization," pursuant to the "Antiterrorism and Effective Death Penalty Act of 1996." In addition to the murder charges stemming from the Sarin nerve gas attack, Aum's leader Shoko Asahara faced sixteen other charges, ranging from kidnapping and murder to illegal production of drugs and weapons. Nine former Aum Shinrikyo members pled guilty or received sentences from twenty-two months to seventeen years for crimes they committed on behalf of Asahara. One Aum Shinrikyo member was acquitted of forcibly confining other cult members. Shoko Asahara claims to be a reincarnation of the Hindu god Shiva, who promised to lead his followers to salvation when impending Armageddon arrived. Asahara was arrested on Mount Fuji in 1995 and was eventually convicted and sentenced to death in 2004. His final appeal was dismissed in 2006, and he waits execution. He was succeeded by Fumihiro Joyu, a former engineer who was the head of Aum's Moscow operation and Aum was recast as Aleph with the aim of convincing authorities that the remade group posed no threat to Japan. In late 2003, however, Joyu stepped down under pressure from members who wanted to return fully to the worship of Asahara. A growing divide between members supporting Joyu and Asahara emerged. In 2007, Joyu officially left the group and in May established a splinter group called Hikari No Wa, which is translated as "Circle of Light" or "Ring of Light." Japanese authorities continued to monitor both Aum (now called Aleph) and Hikari No Wa. Could Aum Shinrikyo ever again develop the potential to give this so-called catastrophe a nudge? In 1999, Japanese police had unearthed "Sarin precursor chemicals," hidden by Aum Shinrikyo in mountains north of Tokyo, then raising the question, "What else was the cult hiding?" A few months before that, a self-declared Aum Shinrikyo member threatened to release gas at eleven Moscow subway stations.

In its continuing crackdown, police have confiscated more than half a million leaflets. Aum Shinrikyo has never apologized or expressed remorse for its past actions. An apology is vital if the cult expects any chance of normal relationships with Japanese society, but the cult's six leaders have not come to the same conclusion. The Japanese authorities could have outlawed Aum Shinrikyo using a draconian 1952 law against subversive activities, but it decided that the sect did not pose an "immediate and obvious threat" to public safety. And, meanwhile, clumsy policing and political paralysis may continue to provide the conditions for Aum Shinrikyo to rise and thrive once more.

JAPANESE RED ARMY (JRA)

This left-wing terrorist group was first established in the late 1960s and follows the models of similar left-wing student movements of that era. Small and extremely violent they received their training in the Palestinian camps of the Middle East and were responsible for deadly attacks such as the Lod Airport massacre in Israel in 1972, which it carried out on behalf of the Popular Front for the Liberation of Palestine. In 1974, they attacked the French Embassy in The Hague, taking several hostages until the French government released one of their colleagues. Five members were convicted in Lebanon on various charges related to forgery and even illegal residency and sentenced to three years in prison. Another member, Jun Nishikawa, was captured in Bolivia and deported to Japan, where he was indicted for his role in the 1977 hijacking of a Japanese Airliner flight. Four of the five **JRA** members arrested remain in custody in Lebanon. Tsutomu Shirosaki was captured in 1996 and brought to the United States to stand trial for the offenses arising from a rocket attack against the U.S. Embassy in Jakarta, Indonesia, in 1986. He was convicted in Washington DC, of assault with the intent to kill, attempted first-degree murder of internationally

TERRORIST ATTACK BRIEF

Terrorist Group: Japanese Red Army (obo. PFLP)

Case Facts: The JRA carried out a machine gun attack inside the terminal of LOD airport. In the ensuing mayhem the terrorists were able to kill twenty-five and wound a further seventy-six passengers and staff. Two of the terrorists were killed in a shootout with Israeli security and the third was arrested.

Investigation: Cooperation between two terrorist groups was at play in this attack, carried out by the JRA on behalf of the Popular Front for the Liberation of Palestine. All three Japanese members were previously trained in terror tactics in Lebanon. The three terrorists had arrived on an Air France flight carrying slim musical cases. Once inside the terminal they opened the case and using the hidden weapons opened fire. The assault was claimed by the PFLP as revenge for the Deir Yassin attack by Jewish Irgun forces in 1948. Tsuyoshi Okudaira and Yasuyuki Yasuda died in the terminal and Kozo Okamato was seriously injured—he survived and was sentenced to life in prison.

FIGURE 12-4 Assault/shooting—Lod airport tel Aviv Israel—May 30, 1972.

protected persons, and attempted destruction of buildings and property in the special maritime and territorial jurisdiction of the United States. He was also convicted of committing a violent attack on the official premises of internationally protected persons. In February 1998, he was sentenced to thirty years in prison. Seven hardcore JRA members remain at large. Since the late 1970s, the group has been inactive and not operating as a distinct terror group, and it's believed that some JRA members have been operating under the umbrella of a group calling itself the Anti-Imperialist International Brigade.

NUCLEAR JAPAN

By some estimates, the country has enough weapons-grade plutonium from fast-breeder reactors to build as many as 6,000 nuclear weapons, and there is little doubt about Japan's technical ability to build such weapons. A nuclear program in Japan, then, is not limited by technology, as it may be in countries like Pakistan and North Korea, but by political will. And the resistance to changes in Japan's defensive posture is clearly fading fast.

An international outcry followed comments by the former vice minister of defense Shingo Nishimura in a 1999 interview, when he said, "If Japan armed itself with nuclear weapons it may be better off." The minister was then forced to resign, and the public outcry nearly broke apart the fledgling coalition between the ruling Liberal Democratic Party and Nishimura's Liberal Party. Other "provocative" statements by Japanese politicians have been similarly received. Japanese Defense Agency Chief Fukushiro Nukaga resigned in 1998, ostensibly over an agency procurement scandal. His statement that a preemptive strike on North Korean missile sites could be considered as "defense" under Japan's Constitution, but did little for his political longevity. Japanese politicians have suggested that Japan's constitution would be a form of U.S.-imposed pacifism that would force Japan to remain defenseless.

With the 1998 North Korean missile launch over Japan, and East Timor's referendum for independence from Indonesia a year later, Japan's military policy slowly began to evolve.

The 9-11 attacks and the U.S. global antiterrorism campaign have accelerated this ever-growing evolutionary change.

The changing shape of Japan's military in the twenty-first-century world now bears watching carefully. But, even more frightening, is the thought that fanatical groups like the Japanese Red

Army, or the Aum Shinrikyo, or terrorists from rogue states may find ways to up the ante on their terrorism and get at the stockpiles of enriched plutonium to build a dirty bomb. The world continues to change in the wake of 9-11.

THE TWO KOREAS

The Democratic People's Republic of North Korea

Following World War II, Korea was split into two and its northern half had come under Soviet-sponsored Communist domination. North Korea tried to conquer the U.S.-backed Republic of South Korea in the Korean War (1950–1953), but failed. North Korea's president, Kim II-sung, then adopted a policy of diplomatic and economic "self-reliance" as a check against excessive Soviet or Communist Chinese influences. Kim II-sung set out to mold North Korea's political, economic, and military policies around his eventual objective of reunifying the two Koreas under his control.

Kim Jong-II was officially designated as his father's future successor in 1980. He assumed a growing political and managerial role until his father's death in 1994, when he assumed full power without opposition. After decades of sad economic mismanagement and resource misallocation, the North, since the mid-1990s, has relied heavily on international food aid to feed its population while continuing to expend resources to maintain an army of about 1 million. North Korea's long-range missile development and research into nuclear, chemical, and biological weapons, and massive conventional armed forces are still a major concern to the international community. In 1994, North Korea signed an agreement with the United States to freeze and ultimately dismantle its existing plutonium-based nuclear program. The International Atomic Energy Agency (IAEA) was monitoring North Korea to assure its compliance with the agreement. North Korea later was found to be in violation of that agreement, when the world learned that it was pursuing a nuclear weapons program based on enriched uranium. In 2002, North Korea expelled the IAEA monitors and, in 2003, declared its withdrawal from the International Nonproliferation Treaty. In mid-2003, Pyongyang announced it had now completed their reprocessing of spent nuclear fuel rods (to extract weapons-grade plutonium) and was now developing a "nuclear deterrent." Since August 2003, North Korea has participated in six-party talks with the United States, China, South Korea, Japan, and Russia to try to resolve the stalemate over its nuclear programs. Kim Jong-II died of a heart attack in December 2011 and like his father before him power was passed by him to his youngest son Kim Jong-un. A relatively unknown member of the Jong dynasty, he has yet to cement his power base.

FIGURE 12-5 Map of North Korea (Central Intelligence Agency, *The World Factbook, 2008*).

The Republic of South Korea

South Korea has experienced thirty suspected terrorism-related events since 1958, including attacks against South Korean citizens in foreign countries. The most common types of terrorism used have included bombings, shootings, hijackings, and kidnappings. Prior to 1990, North Korea was responsible for almost all terrorism-related events inside of South Korea, including multiple assassination attempts on its presidents, regular kidnappings of South Korean fisherman, and several high-profile bombings. Since 1990, most of the terrorist attacks against South Korean citizens have occurred abroad and have been related to the emerging worldwide pattern of terrorism by international terrorist organizations or deranged individuals. The September 11, 2001, World Trade Center and Pentagon attacks and the 2001 U.S. anthrax letter attacks prompted South Korea to organize a new national system of emergency response for terrorism-related events.

Korea was an independent kingdom under Chinese Suzerainty for most of the past millennium. Following its victory in the Russo–Japanese War in 1905, Japan occupied Korea; five years later it formally annexed the entire peninsula. After World War II, a Republic was set up in the southern half of the Korean Peninsula, while a Communist-style government was installed in the north. During the Korean War (1950–1953), U.S. and UN forces intervened to defend South Korea from North Korean attacks supported by the Chinese. An armistice was signed in 1953, splitting the peninsula along a demilitarized zone at about the thirty-eighth parallel. Thereafter, South Korea achieved rapid economic growth, with per capita income rising to roughly "eighteen-times" the level of North Korea. In 1987, South Korean voters elected Roh Tae-woo to the Presidency, ending twenty-six years of military dictatorship. South Korea today is a fully functioning, modern democracy. In June 2000, a historic, first North–South summit took place between the South's president Kim Tae-chung and the North's leader Kim Jong-II.

The United States planned to withdraw one-third of its 37,000 troops from South Korea by the end of 2005, according to a South Korean government official. The withdrawal of more than 37,000 troops, the first pullback since 1992, included 3,600 American soldiers scheduled to deploy from South Korea to Iraq in summer 2005, stated Kim Sook, head of the North American Division at South Korea's Foreign Ministry, at a press briefing in Seoul. He said the South Korean government was informed of the plan. The American decision to cut troops in South Korea—the only major American military presence in the Asian mainland—caught South Koreans by surprise.

The cutback appears to be part of a wider-planned rearrangement of American troops to be in the Pacific. With Washington's concern growing about monitoring and patrolling international sea lanes in the region, the United States is already investing tens of millions of dollars in expanding Air Force and Navy facilities on Guam, in the Western Pacific.

FIGURE 12-6   Map of South Korea (Central Intelligence Agency, *The World Factbook, 2008*).

"The South Korea lobby in Washington is dying," a conservative American lawyer, John E. Carbaugh, said, referring to the fact that there are no longer any Korean War veterans in the U.S. Congress. On the peninsula, Communist North Korea has 1.1 million soldiers, and South Korea has 690,000. The American contingent of 37,500 troops, about one-tenth the size of the U.S. forces at the peak of the Korean War, is largely symbolic.

THE PHILIPPINES

The Republic of the Philippines is situated in Southeastern Asia, on a long archipelago between the Philippine Sea, and the South China Sea. It is east of Vietnam and is slightly larger than the State of Arizona. The scattered population of more than 76 million has an ethnic mix of Christian Malay (91.5 percent), Muslim Malay (4 percent), Chinese (1.5 percent), and other (3 percent). The major religions are Roman Catholic (83 percent), Protestant (9 percent), Muslim (5 percent), Buddhist, and other (3 percent).

The Philippines has broadly defined terrorism as "the premeditated use or threatened use of violence or means of destruction perpetuated against innocent civilians or non-combatants, or against civilian and government properties, usually intended to influence an audience" with the purpose of creating a state of fear to extort, coerce, intimidate, or cause persons or groups to change their behavior. Terrorist methods are hostage taking, piracy, sabotage, assassination, arson, armed attacks, threats, hoaxes, bombings, and shootings. It is a signatory to eleven of the twelve international counterterrorism instruments and supports the adoption of a Comprehensive Convention on International Terrorism that would supplement the Declaration on Measures to Eliminate International Terrorism. Threats to the stability of the Philippines come from a triangular attack from communist-inspired terrorism (New People's Army) and the Islamic groups of Abu Sayyaf (ASG), **Jemaah Islamiyah (JI)**, and the Moro Islamic Liberation Front. The three Islamic groups are not all aligned but do use one or other as proxy organizations to front their attacks; were they all to be aligned with a singular goal, the threat would be considered far more extreme.

Abu Sayyaf (ASG)

Abu Sayyaf means "bearer of the sword" in Arabic—its roots can be traced back to the Soviet invasion of Afghanistan and the global jihad movement that was created. The group's ideology is to form an Islamic state in the Philippines, and much of that is derived from its leadership that met with al Qaeda leaders in Afghanistan back in the 1980s. ASG was formed by Abdurajak Janjalani, a veteran of the Afghan Mujahidin and originally financed by a Saudi businessman living in the Philippines. Janjalani met members of the al Qaeda hierarchy including bin Laden's brother in law Jamal Khalifa

FIGURE 12-7 Map of The Philippines (Central Intelligence Agency, *The World Factbook, 2008*).

who was the director of the Saudi-based charity Islamic International Relief Organization and in 1991 set up a number of reputable charities in the Philippines that constructed schools and clinics that also supplied fighters for the ASG. In the early 1980s, about 300–500 Moro fundamentalists arrived in Peshawar, Pakistan, to fight with the mujahidin fighting the Soviets in Afghanistan; one of them, Ustadz Abdurajak Janjalani, emerged as a leader. Janjalani was the son of a Basilan ulama and became a fiery Islamic orator himself. He attended an Islamic university in Saudi Arabia, graduating in 1981 before studying Islamic jurisprudence at Ummu I-Qura in Mecca for three years.

He returned to Basilan and Zamboanga to preach in 1984. In 1987, he traveled to Libya and then continued on to join the Mujahidin and fought the Soviets for several years in Afghanistan. In Peshawar, Janjalani befriended a wealthy Saudi supporter of the Mujahidin, Osama bin Laden. Janjalani, and later his younger brother, Khaddafy Janjalani, received training in the late 1980s and early 1990s at a training camp near Khost, Afghanistan, that was run by a professor of Islam, Abdur Rab Rasul Sayyaf, whose belief in the strict Wahhabi interpretation of Islam found him in favor with many wealthy Saudis, including Osama bin Laden.[10] ASG and the Islamist **Moro Islamic Liberation Front (MILF)** have their centers of operation in the same geographic region of the Sulu archipelago and easternmost island of Mindanao, where a rugged terrain has made it difficult for the government to root them out. ASG has become well known for its kidnappings, mainly of foreign tourists, usually for ransom, bombings, and extortion. ASG's trail of terror stretches back to its first bombing attack in 1995, when it carried out an attack on a small town in Mindanao Province. It's most prominent attacks came in 2000, when an armed group of ASG members attacked an upscale resort complex in Malaysia and kidnapped twenty-one tourists. The following year, it continued its campaign of striking high-profile locations and targeting foreign tourists. In 2001, ASG again kidnapped more Westerners from a Philippines' resort complex and subsequently murdered several hostages, including an American citizen, when security forces attempted a rescue operation. A similar fate occurred during a rescue attempt of U.S. hostages in June 2002, which also resulted in the death of another U.S. citizen.

Continued attacks in 2004 included the bomb attack on a ferry in Manila Bay that killed 132 passengers and is believed to have been the work of a faction loyal to ASG. The group's successes were limited when the United States and Australia sent troops to the Philippines to

TERRORIST ATTACK BRIEF

Terrorist Group: ABU SAYYAF

Case Facts: Boat loads of Abu Sayyaf terrorist attacked the upscale resort and without encountering any resistance took a large number of hostages and returned with them to safe territory on Mindanao. The number of hostages including several American missionaries fluctuated as Abu Sayyaf continued to take and release hostages over the next twelve months. During this period, several of the hostages were killed by beheading.

Investigation: The kidnappers had demanded $1 million for the safe return of the American hostages, and a smaller ransom was paid. However, they were not released. In June 2002, U.S.-trained Philippine commandos attempted a rescue operation for the two U.S. captives and a Filipino nurse being held with them. Two of the hostages including an American were killed in the shootout, and the American missionary Garcia Burnham, although injured, was freed. In 2007, the Abu Sayyaf members captured during the shootout were sentenced to life in prison.

FIGURE 12-8   Kidnapping for ransom—Tourist resort, Palawan Island, Philippines—May 27, 2001.

train the army in counterinsurgency techniques. The military onslaught against the ASG reduced its numbers to around 450 by early 2005. However, like so many other insurgent terror groups, ASG managed in February 2005 to launch simultaneous bomb attacks in Manila, General Santos City, and Davao, killing 11 people and wounding more than 100. Janjalani was killed in a clash with Philippine police in December 1998, and his younger brother, Khadafi Janjalani led the group into the new millennium. With the peace agreement between the government and the Islamist Moro Islamic Liberation Front gaining pace, it seems highly likely that the smaller ASG would want to create a level of instability and try to attract hard-line, dissident members of MILF who have little sympathy for the peace deal. The regional extremist group, Jemaah Islamiyah (JI), whose strongest ally until the 2003 peace deal was MILF, has possibly the most to lose in this probable outbreak of peace. The MILF rebels handed over an Italian priest, Luciano Benedetti, to Philippine government officials several hours after he was kidnapped by MILF forces.

The guerrilla arm of the Communist Party of the Philippines (CPP) is an avowedly Maoist group formed in December 1969. It aims to overthrow the government through protracted guerrilla warfare. It is the longest running Communist insurrection in the world and is still the most active conflict in the Philippines. Although primarily a rural group, the NPA has an active urban infrastructure to carry out terrorism, and it uses city-based assassination squads called sparrow units. It derives most of its funding from contributions of supporters and so-called revolutionary taxes extorted from local businesses. NPA is in disarray because of a split in the CPP, a lack of money, and successful government operations. With the U.S. military gone from the country, NPA has engaged in urban terrorism against the police, corrupt politicians, and drug traffickers. The NPA has an estimated strength of several thousand members who operate throughout the Philippines. It is unknown whether it receives any external aid. The CPP-NPA remains a designated terrorist organization by both the United States and Europe. In an interview between The Communist Party of the Philippines spokesman Ka Roger and *Jane's Terrorism and the Security Monitor*, it was evident that the CPP had no intention of laying down arms or coming to any deal with the government, and its posture is still to replace the existing government with a Leninist style peoples' revolutionary government. It views the current ruling system as semi-colonial, semi-feudal, and dominated by foreign capitalist countries. The CPP also accused former President Arroyo of "fixing" the 2004 vote. Ka Roger also went on to explain how the CPP would set up a mass people's militia, reorganize the military, set up a pro-people program, complete the land reform, and nationalize strategic industries and fast track a national industrialization program. Over 40,000 people have died as a result of the Communist-inspired insurgency.[11]

INDONESIA

Indonesia, the former Dutch East Indies, is situated in Southeastern Asia on an archipelago in between the Indian Ocean and the Pacific Ocean. It has a varied population of almost 210 million in a land area slightly less than three times the size of Texas. Independence from the Netherlands came in 1949. The combined islands of Indonesia have the largest Muslim population in the world.

Indonesia enjoyed a decade and a half of peace in the 1950–1960 time frame, but its political fortunes shifted significantly in 1965, following a leftist coup attempt against President Sukarno, the republic's first leader. Within days, the army executed the leaders of the coup, but its aftermath brought a wave of violence. Rightist gangs, encouraged by their military commanders, killed tens of thousands of alleged Communists. By 1966, an estimated 500,000 people had been killed in the violent unrest. The events of 1965 and 1966 left the then president Sukarno severely weakened.

FIGURE 12-9 Map of Indonesia (Central Intelligence Agency, *The World Factbook, 2008*).

In 1966, he was forced to transfer key political and military powers to General Suharto, who led the military defeat of the coup. In 1967, the legislative assembly named Suharto acting president, removing Sukarno from power.

With the backing of the military, Suharto quickly proclaimed a "New Order" in Indonesian politics, concentrating on policies of economic rehabilitation and development. Using advice from Western-educated economists, Indonesia grew steadily, transforming itself from an agricultural backwater to a highly diversified manufacturing and export-driven state. Per capita income levels rose from $70 in 1966 to $900 in 1996, while the proportion of the population living below the poverty line declined from 60 percent to an estimated 11 percent over roughly the same period. The government instituted further economic reforms in the early 1980s, liberalizing trade and finance and expanding foreign investment and deregulation. Trade and investment boomed as a result; Indonesia's economy grew more than 7 percent annually from 1985 to 1996.

Suharto, his family, and his friends benefited greatly from the economic expansion. Critics claim the president regularly used his position to provide subsidies, and regulatory relief, for those companies of his children and friends. Suharto's family controls an empire valued anywhere from $16 billion to $35 billion in industries ranging from hotels and transportation to banks and automobiles.

In the mid-1970s, Suharto moved quickly to stop what he saw as a leftist move, to then force the colony of East Timor to be independent, after Portugal abandoned the territory. Fearing creation of a state that could destabilize surrounding provinces, Suharto sent in troops to crush that movement and annexed East Timor. Thousands of people died during the fighting, or later starved to death.

The United States cut off some military assistance to Indonesia in response to a November 1991 shooting incident in East Timor involving security forces and peaceful demonstrators. In 1996, government forces swept through East Timor again, this time after a series of guerrilla attacks on security personnel. The government takeover of the Indonesian Democratic Party's East Timor headquarters in July of that year triggered serious rioting in Jakarta. Human rights officials say that 5 died and 149 were injured in the attack. Twenty-three other people were reported missing.

Despite the corruption and human rights abuses, Suharto continued to stay in power into 1998. His grip on power started deteriorating the year before, however, when Thailand announced the devaluation of the baht in July 1997. This move caused the value of Indonesia's currency, the rupiah, to drop as much as 80 percent at one point. Foreign investors fled and many companies that were adversely affected by the currency devaluation went bankrupt. Like other Asian countries, Indonesia's banks were hit especially hard; by January 1998, sixteen banks had their operations suspended. As the country negotiated with the International Monetary Fund over the terms of its $43 billion bailout package in early 1998, riots began to erupt over rising food prices, gradually intensifying despite violent police efforts to put them down.

The People's Consultative Assembly, a legislative body that was largely appointed by the president himself, reelected Suharto to a seventh term. Student protests broke out amid calls for him to step down. In May, riots and looting turned violent as tens of thousands of students demonstrated in Jakarta and other parts of the country. Hundreds perished in clashes with security forces in Jakarta. In a show of resistance, students then began to occupy the country's Parliament grounds, demanding the president's resignation. On May 21, Suharto bowed to the pressure and resigned from his office, naming Vice President B.J. Habibie as his successor. There were attempts to charge Suharto with corruption after his resignation but none suceeded and he died in January 2008.

Within days, Habibie pledged to lift restrictions on political parties and hold open elections as part of a package of reform measures intended to liberalize life in Indonesia and revive political activity that had been stifled for more than four decades. The moves, however, did little to quell the unrest. Throughout the summer of 1998, student demonstrators continued to demand the resignation of then President Habibie as well, claiming that the government had done little or nothing to stem the country's economic crisis or spiraling high prices.

In November 1998, student-led protests for greater democracy in Jakarta turned violent after a crackdown on demonstrators killed at least five students and two others. As rioting ensued, demonstrators burned shops across the city and set cars ablaze. At least sixteen were killed over a period of several days.[12]

The United States welcomed the Indonesian government's newly established broad-based fact-finding team in 1999 to investigate the causes of the May riots and the rapes of ethnic Chinese women. In November, the team, which included representatives from the government, the Indonesian military (ABRI), the police, and nongovernment organizations, released its report. Despite the "reservations" of some members, and the fact that investigators, victims, witnesses, and family members faced anonymous death threats and other forms of intimidation, the fact-finding team issued a credible, balanced report under difficult circumstances.

The report determined there were three types of riots: (1) some were local and spontaneous, (2) some were aggravated by provocateurs, and (3) others were obviously deliberate, to include an involvement by elements of the military. The report called for further investigations and even had recommended that Lt. Gen. Prabowo and all others involved in cases of kidnappings of political activists be brought up before a military court. The report also verified that eighty-five acts of violence targeted against women occurred during the riots, including rapes, tortures, sexual assaults, and sexual harassment, mostly being against ethnic Chinese.

To restore confidence, it was crucial that the Indonesian government implement the team's recommendations, including further investigation of military leaders and others alleged to be involved in fomenting or participating in the violence. It was further strongly urged that the Indonesian government take steps to prevent intimidation and threats of violence against investigators, witnesses, and their families and that those responsible for these acts should be held accountable.[13]

Portugal and Indonesia are now in a dispute over the sovereignty of Timor (East Timor Province). The United Nations does not recognize Portugal's claim. Those two small islands are in ownership dispute with Malaysia. Indonesia continues to be an illicit producer of cannabis, largely for domestic use, but has a possible growing role as a transshipment point for Golden Triangle heroin. Separatist groups in East Timor apparently continued to target noncombatants and were involved in several bomb-making activities in 1997. In Irian Jaya, a former province of Indonesia, in April 1997, an alleged attack by the separatist Free Papua Organization against a road survey- ing crew left two civilians dead. If Indonesia cannot get its economic situation straightened out, it is a powder keg for escalating violence and terrorism between the state and opposition groups.

Indonesia has more Muslims than any other region in the world. It is little surprise that Islamic extremism would find a base and sympathy here among some radical minorities. Islamic terrorism has been extensive throughout the region and is led primarily by an al Qaeda "proxy organization," Jemaah Islamiyah (JI). This shadowy Islamist terrorist organization has developed economic and military assets through the use of cells (fiahs), operating throughout Southeast Asia. Guided by its objective of creating an Islamic state ruled by Sharia (Islamic law), JI wishes to create an Islamist theocracy (JI's conception of Dawlah Islamiyah, or Islamic state), which would unify Muslims in Thailand, Malaysia, Indonesia, Brunei, and the Southern Philippines. JI shares a common philosophy with, and has links to, the al Qaeda network. JI has emerged as the most extensive transnational radical Islamist group in Southeast Asia.

It became synonymous with attacks planned against not only Western interests but also Christian churches in Indonesia. The government of Singapore had discovered in 2001 that JI was planning to attack the British and U.S. embassies, as well as Australian interests in Singapore. The JI attack on the island of Bali in October 2002 is often referred to as "Indonesia's 9-11." The attack targeted European, American, and Australian tourists, resulting in over 200 deaths. The bomb attack against the Marriott Hotel chain in Jakarta in August 2003 is also likely the work of JI extremists.

JEMAAH ISLAMIYAH (JI)

JI is an Indonesian-based terrorist group with a strong presence within the Muslim communities of Southern Philippines. The exact timing for when JI came on the terrorist scene is uncertain, although the name dates back to the 1970s. The group's activities were certainly enhanced by links to al Qaeda and its leadership calling for the destruction of the United States, the United Kingdom, Australia, as well as the Philippines. JI has been led by Abu Bakar Bashir, the Indonesian cleric since the mid 1990s. JI goals are to form an Islamic state in Southeast Asia. In 1994, JI set up a training camp to replace its Afghanistan locations, setting up Camp Hudaibiyah, which became its headquarters for the Philippines. JI was linked through Ramzi Yousef to the now infamous Bojinka plot to blow up international flights in 2005. Yousef was based in Manila, and the plot was foiled by British authori- ties. Yousef had targeted dozen aircraft flying across the Pacifc to the United States by bringing bomb parts and liquid explosives into planes and assembling the bombs in flight. The bombers would get off at an intermediate stop and leave the bombs primed and timed to exploded en route to the United States.

The Philippine government continued its strong support for international cooperation against terrorism and actively sought to build a multilateral approach to counterterrorism in some regional and other forums. The government cooperated in providing additional personnel to protect likely targets and to identify, investigate, and act against likely terrorists. The govern- ment quickly responded when a U.S. company experienced what appeared to be a **New People's Army (NPA)** attack on one of its subcontractors in Quezon, and officials at the cabinet level met with company executives to discuss what could be done to improve security.

Who is Abu Bakar Bashir?

An elderly Indonesian cleric of Yemeni descent, stately, if frail, in appearance, Abu Bakar Bashir (also spelled Ba'asyir), hardly comes across as one of the world's most fearsome men. His inflammatory rhetoric, however, has commanded widespread concern. Bashir was released from Indonesian prison on June 14, 2006, after serving out a twenty-five-month sentence. He was found guilty by Indonesian courts in 2003 of being part of an "evil conspiracy" to commit the 2002 Bali suicide bombings, though all charges directly linking him to the attacks were subsequently dropped.

If Bashir's involvement in coordinating the Bali bombing is debatable, as many experts have said, it is also somewhat beside the point. Indonesian officials say a striking number of the more than 200 Jemaah Islamiyah militants arrested in the aftermath of the Bali attacks cited Bashir as their inspiration, the ideological general of their "holy war." Bashir has accordingly been labeled the "spiritual leader" of JI by a number of news sources.[14] He is no doubt the leading and most powerful influence over JI, and he espouses the overthrow of the Indonesian government and the establishment of Sharia Law.

AUSTRALIA

Six separate statements issued by bin Laden or his deputy Ayman al-Zawahiri specifically threatened Australia:

- On November 3, 2001, bin Laden said, "The Crusader Australian forces were on the Indonesia shores…they landed to separate East Timor, which is part of the Islamic world."
- In an interview released in mid-November 2001 concerning the war in Afghanistan, bin Laden said, "In this fighting between Islam and the Crusaders, we will now continue our Jihad. We will incite the nation for Jihad until we meet God and get his blessing. Any country that supports the Jews can only blame itself…what do Japan or Australia or Germany have to do with this war? They just support the infidels and the Crusaders."
- Bin Laden made further reference to Australia in a videotape released in the United Kingdom in May 2002 in which he said, "What has Australia in the extreme south got to do with the oppression of our brothers in Afghanistan and Palestine?"
- On November 12, 2002, bin Laden made a statement that gave much more prominence to Australia than any other non-U.S. Western country and reaffirmed Australia to be a terrorist target: "We warned Australia before not to join in [the war], in Afghanistan, and [against] its despicable effort to separate East Timor. It ignored that warning until it woke up to the sounds of explosions in Bali. Its government falsely claimed that they were not targeted."
- On May 21, 2003, in an audiotape, Ayman al-Zawahiri said: "O Muslims take matters firmly against the embassies of America, England, Australia, Norway and their interests, companies and employees."
- On October 18, 2003, in an audio message addressed to the American people concerning the war in Iraq, bin Laden stated that, "We maintain our right to reply, at the appropriate time and place, to all the states that are taking part in this unjust war, particularly Britain, Spain, Australia, Poland, Japan and Italy."[15]

The Commonwealth of Australia is located on the Oceania continent and is slightly smaller than the United States. It is the world's smallest continent, but is the sixth-largest country. Its population (estimated at about 18,438,850) is concentrated along the eastern and southeastern coasts.

FIGURE 12-10   Map of Australia (Central Intelligence Agency, *The World Factbook, 2008*).

The ethnic makeup is Caucasian (95 percent), Asian (4 percent), and Aboriginal (1 percent), and some other. Religious affiliations are Anglican (26.1 percent), Roman Catholic (26 percent), other Christians (24.3 percent), and the balance unknown. Australia became an independent member of the Commonwealth in 1901 and has a prosperous, Western-style economy. Per capita GDP is above the levels in many highly industrialized West European countries. Rich in natural resources, Australia is a major exporter of agricultural products, minerals, metals, and fossil fuels. Commodities account for about 60 percent of the value of total exports, so a downturn in world commodity prices can have a big impact on the Australian economy. The government is pushing for increased exports of manufactured goods, but competition in international markets continues to be severe.

In May 2004, an Australian citizen Jack Roche pleaded guilty to charges of conspiracy to commit offences against the Crimes (Internationally Protected Persons) Act 1976. Roche was sentenced to nine years' imprisonment. Roche was associated with Jemaah Islamiyah in Australia, trained in Afghanistan, and met with and took direction from Hambali and other extremist identities, including Khalid Sheikh Mohammed. Roche videotaped the Israeli embassy in Canberra and the Israeli consulate in Sydney in June 2000 as a preliminary measure to support a possible future terrorist attack in Australia.

Australia is considered a safe country. Only a few terrorist acts have been carried out over the past sixty years:

1975—A letter bomb that originated in the Middle East injured a press secretary at the Queensland State Premier's office.

1978—A bomb explodes outside the Hilton Hotel in Sydney where the Commonwealth heads of government were staying.

1980—Turkish Consul General, Sarik Ariyak, was assassinated in Sydney by two members of the "Justice Commando of the Armenian Genocide."

1990—Gasoline bomb attack on a Jewish College in Sydney.

1996—A premature explosion of a parcel bomb in a Melbourne mailroom was believed to be intended for a major pro-Yugoslav supporter.

2002—Jack Roche, a British-born convert to Islam, was charged with plotting bomb attacks on the Israeli embassy in Canberra and the Israeli consulate in Sydney. Roche claimed to have been al Qaeda-trained in Afghanistan. In May 2004, he pleaded guilty to charges of conspiracy to commit offenses against the Crimes (Internationally Protected Persons) Act 1976 and was sentenced to nine years' imprisonment.

2010—three Islamists were sentenced in Sydney for plotting an armed attack on an Australian Army camp. All were of Australians of Somlai or Lebanese descent and with links to al Shabaab. The planned suicide attack was in retaliation for Australia's military involvement in Afghanistan.

INTERNATIONAL TERRORISM

Australia has been a staunch ally in the War on Terror and is an outspoken supporter of both the United States and Great Britain. Regionally, its proximity to Indonesia makes it a target for Islamic extremists. Australian nationals were targeted in the Bali attack, so the threat remains a serious one for Australia. Indications are that Australia must reckon on a sustained campaign over many years to diminish that threat. Regionally, terrorist groups like JI show themselves to be capable of adapting to the setbacks following the arrest and prosecution of most of those responsible for the Bali bombing.

JI and al Qaeda retain a potent capacity to inflict harm on Australian interests in Southeast Asia. The Australians cannot discount the possibility of a threat emerging from splinter groups inspired by the jihadist ideology of al Qaeda and JI. The very anti-Western nature of these groups will focus more likely on locations outside the country, where Australians travel for vacations. Areas such as Bali and Bangkok, Thailand, are havens for not only Western tourists but also Australians.

Australia has made specific amendments to its legal frameworks to specifically target terrorist organizations and the membership of such organizations. Under Australian Law there are two ways for an organization to be identified as a "terrorist organization." Either an organization may be found to be such an organization by a court as part of the prosecution for a terrorist offence or it may be specified in Regulations, known as "listing". Before an organization can be listed, the attorney general must be satisfied on reasonable grounds that the organization is directly or indirectly engaged in preparing, planning, assisting in, or fostering the doing of a terrorist act.

The listing of an organization ceases to have effect two years after its commencement, or if the minister ceases to be satisfied that the organization is directly or indirectly engaged in, preparing, planning, assisting in, or fostering the doing of a terrorist act, whichever occurs first. When a court has determined, or by regulation it is determined, that an organization is a "terrorist organisation," it is an offence to

- direct the activities of the organization;
- recruit persons to the organization;
- receive training from or provide training to the organization;
- receive funds from or make available funds to the organization; and
- provide support or resources to the organization.

It is also an offence to be a member of any listed terrorist organization and to intentionally associate with a person who is a member or who promotes or directs the activities of a listed terrorist organization where that association provides support that would help the terrorist organization to continue to exist or to expand. Australia has officially listed seventeen such terrorist groups:

- Abu Sayyaf Group—Listed 14 November 2002, relisted 5 November 2004, 3 November 2006, 1 November 2008, and 29 October 2010.
- Al-Qaeda (AQ)—Listed 21 October 2002, relisted 1 September 2004, 26 August 2006, 8 August 2008, and 22 July 2010.
- Al-Qaeda in the Arabian Peninsula (AQAP)—Listed 26 November 2010.
- Al-Qaeda in Iraq (AQI) (formerly listed as Al-Zarqawi and TQJBR)—Listed 2 March 2005, relisted 17 February 2007, 1 November 2008, and 29 October 2010.

- Al-Qaeda in the Islamic Maghreb (AQIM)—Listed 14 November 2002, relisted 5 November 2004, 3 November 2006, 9 August 2008, and 22 July 2010.
- Al-Shabaab—Listed 22 August 2009.
- Ansar al-Islam (formerly known as Ansar al-Sunna)—Listed 27 March 2003, relisted 27 March 2005, 24 March 2007, 14 March 2009, and 9 March 2012.
- Hamas's Izz al-Din al-Qassam Brigades—Listed in Australia 9 November 2003, relisted 5 June 2005, 7 October 2005, 10 September 2007, and 8 September 2009.
- Hizballah External Security Organisation—Listed 5 June 2003 and relisted 5 June 2005, 25 May 2007, and 16 May 2009.
- Islamic Movement of Uzbekistan—Listed 11 April 2003, relisted 11 April 2005, relisted 31 March 2007, 14 March 2009, and 9 March 2012.
- Jaish-e-Mohammed (JeM)—Listed 11 April 2003, relisted 11 April 2005, 31 March 2007, 14 March 2009, and 9 March 2012.
- Jamiat ul-Ansar (formerly known as Harakat Ul-Mujahideen)—Listed 14 November 2002, relisted 5 November 2004, 3 November 2006, 1 November 2008, and 29 October 2010.
- Jemaah Islamiyah (JI)—Listed 27 October 2002, relisted 1 September 2004, 26 August 2006, 9 August 2008, and 22 July 2010.
- Kurdistan Workers Party (PKK)—Listed 17 December 2005, relisted 28 September 2007 and 8 September 2009.
- Lashkar-e Jhangvi (LeJ)—Listed 11 April 2003, relisted 11 April 2005, 31 March 2007, 14 March 2009, and 9 March 2012.
- Lashkar-e-Tayyiba—Listed 9 November 2003, relisted 5 June 2005, 7 October 2005, 8 September 2007, and 8 September 2009.
- Palestinian Islamic Jihad—Listed 3 May 2004, relisted 5 June 2005, 7 October 2005, 8 September 2007, and 8 September 2009.[16]

Summary

The spread of Islamic militancy has been more over the last decade on China's borders, but the level and type of threats are unclear due mainly to lack of verifiable information from China. In Japan the Aum Shrinkiyo showed how devastatingly effective a small committed group can be when it comes to chemical and biological weapons use and the ease with which to deploy them. Indonesia and the Philippines, which have been supported by military and police training from both the United States and Australia, continue to suffer from Islamist threats as well as from communist groups that may ultimately pose a more significant threat than the likes of ASG and JI.

Review Questions

1. How serious is the threat of terrorism to the stability of the Philippines?
2. What methods did the Aum Shinrikyo cult employ to attack the Japanese public?
3. What are the methods used by Chinese authorities to crack down on subversive groups?
4. What is the link between terrorist groups in Indonesia and al Qaeda?

Websites

1. **International Crisis Group**—*http://www.crisisgroup.org/*
2. **Center for Research on Globalization**—*http://www.globalresearch.ca/index.php*
3. **South Asia Analysis Group**—*http://www.southasiaanalysis.org*
4. **DEBKA**—*http://www.debka.com/*

End Notes

1. Secretary Madeleine K Albright. "Meeting the Far East Crisis: What Should Governments Do?" U.S. Department of State, http://www.state.gov.
2. Dr. You Li. "China's Post 9/11 terrorism Strategy."*China Brief*, http://www.asianresearch.org/article/2047.htm.
3. "Country Report on Human Rights Practices." U.S. State Department (2007) http://www.state.gov/g/drl/rls/hrrpt/2007/100518.htm. The White House: U.S., China Stand Against Terrorism: Remarks by President Bush and President Jiang Zemin in Press Availability Western Suburb Guest House (October 2001).
4. Council on Foreign Relations. (July 2008), http://www.cfr.org/publication/9179/east_turkestan_islamic_movement_etim.html_terrorist_organizat-ions.
5. U.S. China Stand Against Terrorism, Remarks by President Bush and President Jiang Zemin in Press Availability Western Suburb Guest House (Shanghai, People's Republic of China), White House Press Release October 19, 2001.
6. A Human Rights Watch Briefing Paper for the 59th Session of the United Nations Commission on Human Rights. "In the Name of Counter-Terrorism: Human Rights Abuses Worldwide." (March 25, 2003), http://www.hrw.org/un/chr59/counter-terrorism.
7. Falun Gong Human Rights Working Group. http://www.flghrwg.net/index.php?option=content&task=view&Itemid=50&id=1272.
8. The Falun Data Information Center. *Annual Report* (2010), http://faluninfo.net.
9. Kyle B. Olson. Research Planning, Inc., "Arlington, Virginia, USA." *Emerging Infectious Diseases*, vol. 5, no. 4 (1999), US Center for Disease Control, www.cdc.gov.
10. Zachary Abuza Balik. "Terrorism The Return of Abu Sayyaf." *Strategic Studies Institute Paper* (2005, p. 2).
11. Janes Terrorism and Security Monitor (October 2007).
12. Tim Ito. (October, 1998), Washingtonpost.com.
13. George Wehrfritz. *Newsweek* (April 13, 1998, pp. 24–30).
14. Council on Foreign Relations. (June 2009), http://www.cfr.org/publications/10219.
15. *Transnational Terrorism the Threat to Australia.* (2004), Australian Government Department of Foreign Affairs and Trade. http://www.dfat.gov.au/publications/terrorism/.
16. List of Terrorist Organizations. (March 2012) Australian Government and National Security, http://www.nationalsecurity.gov.au/agd/www/nationalsecurity.nsf/AllDocs/95FB057CA3DECF30CA256FAB001F7FBD?OpenDocument?open&query=listing of terrorist organization.

13

Latin America and
South America

*Individually and collectively we will deny terrorist groups the capacity
to operate in this hemisphere. This American family stands united.*

—Declaration by the Organization of
American States, September 21, 2001

LEARNING OBJECTIVES

After studying this chapter, the student should be able to:

1. Discuss how death squads have been used as a tool of the state in Latin America.

2. Describe the rise of the peasant revolt and its causes in Mexico.

3. Discuss why the Tri-Border maybe strategically important for terrorist organizations.

4. Examine the history and development of FARC in Colombia.

5. Understand how drugs have played a role in the political and social instability for Latin American countries.

6. Appreciate why the CIA has been involved in undermining states that were aligned with the Soviet Union.

KEY WORDS TO NOTE

Cali cartel—Drug cartel founded in 1977 in southern Colombia around the city of Cali

Chiapas—Southeast Mexican State where a peasant uprising led by the Zapatista National Liberation Army continues to press for greater autonomy

Morazanist Patriotic Front (FPM)—A radical, leftist Honduran terrorist group that first appeared in the late 1980s; its attacks were in protest of U.S. intervention in Honduran economic and political affairs

Monsignor Juan Gerardi Condera—Guatemalan Catholic priest and human rights activists beaten to death after compiling a report on human rights abuses in 1998

Popular Revolutionary Army (EPR)—A leftist guerrilla movement that advocates armed struggle in order to overthrow the Mexican government

Rebel Armed Forces (FAR)—Guatemalan guerrilla organization established in 1961 and lasting until the peace agreements in 1996

Revolutionary Armed Forces of Colombia (FARC)—Established in 1964 as the military wing of the Colombian Communist Party and is a large well-organized Marxist movement

Sandinista National Liberation Front (*Frente Sandinista de Liberación Nacional* FSLN)—A socialist political party in Nicaragua, named after Augusto César Sandino, leader of the Nicaraguan resistance against the U.S. occupation of Nicaragua in the 1930s. Party members are called **Sandinistas** in both English and Spanish

The Shining Path—Sendoro Luminoso—a left-wing Maoist group that seeks to overthrow the Peruvian government

United Self-Defense Forces of Colombia (AUC)—An umbrella organization for paramilitary groups in Colombia

Zapatista National Liberation Army (ELZN)—A revolutionary leftist group based in Chiapas, the southernmost state of Mexico

OVERVIEW

Geographically, Latin America includes the landmass extending from the Rio Grande border between Texas and Mexico to the southern tip of South America, plus some Caribbean islands. The total landmass is two and one-half times the size of the United States. Brazil alone is larger than the continental United States.

The physical features of this vast expanse present sharp differences: The Andean mountain range, which stretches the full length of South America and has peaks as high as 20,000 feet; the dense, tropical forest of the Amazon basin; the arid desert plains of Northern Mexico; and the fertile, deep grasslands of the Argentine pampas.

Latin America has three primary racial groups: native indigenous Indians, white Europeans, and black Africans. Spanish is generally spoken everywhere, except for Brazil (Portuguese), the Andes (Quechua and other uniquely Indian languages), Guatemala (over twenty Indian languages), the Caribbean (French, English, and Dutch), and Mexico (scattered pockets of Indian languages). By early 2005, the total population of this vast area came to 365,384,570 compared with 295,267,054 million in the United States.[1] Latin American society displays startling contrasts between rich and poor, city and country, learned and illiterate, powerful lords of the hacienda and the deferential peasants, and the wealthy entrepreneurs and desperate street urchins. Politically, Latin America includes twenty-six nations, whose recent experiences range from military dictatorships to electoral democracy. Economically, Latin America belongs to the "developing" world, having been beset upon, and battered by, historical and contemporary obstacles to rapid economic growth. Here, too, there is diversity: from the one-crop dependency of tiny Honduras to the industrial promise of Brazil, Chile, and Mexico.

Throughout modern history, Latin Americans have sought to achieve political and economic independence from colonial, imperial, and neo-imperial powers with only one goal: wealth for the winners. It is a bitter irony that the name "Latin America" was coined by mid-nineteenth-century French, who thought that since their culture, like that of Spanish and Portuguese America, was "Latin" in context (i.e., Romance language speaking), it was destined to assume leadership throughout the continent. As these observations suggest, Latin America resists easy categorization. It is a region rich in paradoxes:

1. Beginning in 1492, its conquest by the Spanish and Portuguese created a new social order based on domination, hierarchy, and intermingling of European, African, and indigenous Indian elements. The European intrusion profoundly altered the Indian communities. Compared with the ancient civilizations of Africa and Asia, these Latin American societies are relatively young. Most nations of Latin America obtained political independence from Spain and Portugal in the early nineteenth century, more than 100 years before successful anticolonial movements in other Third World countries.

2. Throughout its history, Latin America has been both tumultuous and stable. Its tradition of political violence has erupted in coups, assassinations, armed movements, military interventions, and (more rarely) social revolutions. Ideological encounters of liberalism, positivism, corporatism, anarchism, socialism, communism, fascism, and strong religious teachings of every doctrinal hue have sharpened the intensity of struggle. Despite the differing forms of political conflict, old social and economic structures have persisted.

3. Latin America has been independent and dependent and autonomous and subordinate. The achievement of nationhood by 1830 in all but parts of the Caribbean basin represented significant growth and achievement. Yet, this nationhood continued to be affected by colonization originating from Britain and France, and ultimately, the United States.

4. Latin America is both prosperous and poor. Ever since being conquered by the Europeans, the region has been described as rich in natural resources: first, the lust for silver and gold and, today, for petroleum, gas, copper, iron ore, coffee, sugar, soybeans, or for expanded trade in general. But the image of endless wealth lingers. In startling contrast, there is also the picture of great poverty: peasants without tools, workers without jobs, children without food, and mothers without hope.

To understand Latin American history and its many experiences with terrorism, political violence, and insurgency requires a flexible, broad-based approach.

LATIN AMERICAN TERRORISM

Terrorism that has occurred in Central and South American countries tends to be significantly different than terrorism that has taken place in Western Europe, Asia, and the Middle East. Many Latin American countries have suffered from "state terrorism," including the use of death squads by extreme right-wing, authoritarian governments. A definition of "terrorism" worth considering is that put forward by the U.S. Department of Defense:

> The calculated use of violence or the threat of violence to inculcate fear intended to coerce or to intimidate governments or societies in the pursuit of goals that are generally political, religious, or ideological.

This definition was crafted to distinguish between terrorism and other kinds of violence. The act of terrorism is defined independently of the cause that motivates it. People employ terrorist violence in the name of many causes. Insurgency, freedom fighting, or just plain terrorism from both the left and the right continues unabated in Colombia. The tendency to label as terrorism any violent act of which we do not approve is erroneous. Terrorism is a specific kind of violence. It therefore begs the question: Is state involvement in systematic abuse of human rights and a government's tacit support of military junta and the use of unofficial death squads in many Central and South American countries terrorism? The so-called banana Republics, joked about in the early part of the twentieth century, became serious problems when they experienced revolutions and insurgencies in the 1970s and 1980s. The former Soviet Union and other Communist causes often backed efforts to destabilize the area and break the U.S. support of dictators.

We begin with the most prominent terror movements in Central America, from their developmental stages after the Mexican Revolution of 1910 to the changes in typical terror tactics in South America. Drug dealings by Colombian, Mexican, and other drug cartels (referred to as narco-terrorism), and the oppressive regimes in Uruguay, El Salvador, Argentina, and others will be discussed. The horrors associated with Latin American death squads will be explored, along with the conditions, tactics, and distinctive characteristics of Latin American terrorism.

MEXICO

For several decades after independence, Mexico's political life was a prototype of chronic political instability. National governments came and went at gunpoint, threatening the new nation's territorial integrity. By the mid-nineteenth century, Mexico was heading toward a liberal government that would have greatly reduced the power of the church and the corresponding burden of its colonial legacy. Political liberalism, however, gave way to the dictatorship of Porfirio Diaz from 1876 to 1880 and again from 1884 to 1911 and, thus, was confronted by the Mexican Revolution...the first of the world's great twentieth-century revolutions. Out of that revolution, a stable political system arose that has been unmatched anywhere in Latin America. The Wars for Independence left Mexico in abject decay. Actual fighting was widespread and protracted, leaving a severely disrupted economy. Gold and silver mines, once the pride of Spain's overseas Mexican empire, had fallen into disrepair. Insurgents and royalists had made it a point of killing technicians, while thousands of miners had gone off to war, leaving the mines to fall into ruins. Roads had been neglected as well, so the country lacked a workable system of transportation and/or strong

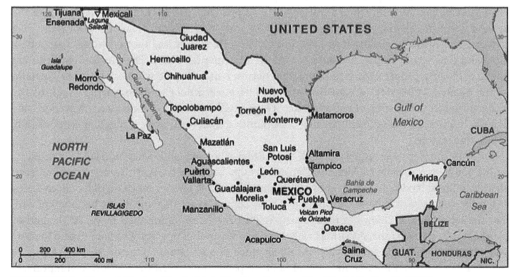

FIGURE 13-1 Map of Mexico (Central Intelligence Agency, *The World Factbook, 2008*).

communication capability. Travel by stagecoach was difficult and hazardous, and transport, often by pack saddle, was costly and slow. This was a serious obstacle to economic progress. It was estimated that over 30 percent of the entire adult male population in Mexico was unemployed, often angry, and usually well armed. They posed not only an economic problem, but a social and criminal threat as well. Some of these veterans did find work while others turned to crime (highway robbery being a particular favorite). Some stayed on in the military while others drifted into unofficial, quasi-military police units that provided support for local political bosses, generally known as *caudillos*, who were soon to play a dominant role in Mexico's political scene.

There were two institutional power bases in Mexico after independence—the Catholic Church and the Mexican military. The church had come through the independence wars with most of its wealth intact. The second power base was the military, which dominated national politics during the forty-year period from 1821 to 1860. Mexico had at least fifty separate presidencies, each lasting an average of less than one year! Army officers led thirty-five of these ill-starred regimes. The usual means of winning the presidential office was through a military coup to get rid of the sitting president. Looming through this period was the powerful figure of General Antonio Lopez de Santa Ana, who held the presidency on nine separate occasions and who installed figureheads at other times. Santa Ana was one of Mexico's most famous caudillos. These strongmen assembled their armed followers (miniature armies), who were primarily seeking wealth. Once they fought their way into national power, they participated in the further draining of national reserves, until the next reigning caudillo, armed with new followers, fought his way into power. The caudillos themselves did not bother too much with the job of governance. That was left up to a cadre of lawyers and professional advisors, many who described themselves as *licenciados*, meaning licensed, degreed, or in some way considered to be certified individuals.

General Porfirio Diaz assumed power after the death of Benito Juarez in 1872, who had himself overthrown Maximilian von Hapsburg of Austria (1863–1867). The Diaz Era (1876–1911) signaled progress, but at a stiff price. For the thirty years of his reign, Diaz proved himself to be a master of political intrigue. He began by creating a broad coalition of his military colleagues and followers. Building his army was one of his major goals, and he forged ahead while maintaining control of a vast countryside, where the large majority of Mexicans lived. Diaz relied heavily on a force of *guardias rurales*, or rural police. In short, Diaz patiently built up the power of the federal government where it counted, in military and police power. A shrewd politician, Diaz avoided ever presenting himself as a corrupt dictator. He simply had the constitution amended, time and time again, so that he could be reelected to the presidency. The Mexican government made economic progress by building a vast network of railroads whose costs were partially supplemented by private foreign investment. The government took to seizing much of the railway land in the interest of nationalizing. These regular seizures of land also involved private homes, businesses, villages, and farming communities, many who were struggling economically under this regime.

Emiliano Zapata emerged as a rock-hard leader of former landowners and landless peasants in the southwestern state of Morelos. Zapata's groups were the country dwellers who had seen their traditional land rights taken away by the smooth-talking lawyers and a myriad of licenciados using the new laws of "liberal" inspiration. These Zapatistas (as they inevitably became known), saw the rebellion as a chance to restore justice. That meant regaining their lands. At the end of World War II, Mexico looked to industrialization as a way out of poverty. The man to lead the way was Miguel Aleman, the first civilian president since the Revolution. One of Aleman's first acts was to reorganize and rename the official political party, now called the Partido Revolucionario Institucional (PRI). Adding the word "institutional" signaled a turn toward pragmatism, which has also been described as leftist in its leanings. The party was made up of three sectors: peasant, worker, and popular. The format is still retained. PRI emerged as a dominant official party, different from any other in Latin America. This era signaled a start of what became Mexico's legacy of political dominance through a one-party system. In 1964, Mexico's other political party, known as Partido Autonomista Nacional (PAN, a right-wing-oriented party), began to win seats in the Mexican congress, although it was still overwhelmingly outweighed by PRI representation. In 1971, guerrillas appeared on the scene, calling for violent action against the PRI. They staged a series of bank robberies and kidnappings. The latter reached into the diplomatic corps, and their victims included the U.S. Consul General in Guadalajara and the daughter of the Belgian ambassador. In 1974, the father-in-law of the president was seized and held for ransom by militant guerillas. In the state of Guerrero, an ex-school teacher, Lucio Cabanas, led a guerrilla army that began to strike at will. Cabanas had turned revolutionary soon after his 1962 election as general secretary of the Federation of Socialist Peasant Students in Mexico. He fled the city for the Guerrero mountain region where he led his Army of the Poor and Peasant's Brigade against Injustice. It kidnapped the official PRI candidate for governor and defied the army by direct attacks on isolated outposts. It took a 10,000-man army more than a year to hunt down and kill the rebels and their leader. Despite predictions on the left, Cabanas had no successor in Guerrero or elsewhere, as the guerilla threat soon faded. To avoid capture, Cabanas committed suicide.

In the late 1960s, student-initiated protests in Mexico shook the Western world. The precipitating factor was Mexico's hosting of the summer Olympic Games in 1968. The Mexican government went all out to "sell" Mexico to the world. The Mexican Left, always strong among students, was upset that the government might succeed in this public relations venture. There began a test of wills. A secondary school clash in Mexico City in 1968 was met by brutal force from the riot police. Protest spread to the national university in August, culminating in a strike. The government thought it was a "subversive conspiracy" bent on disrupting the Olympic Games. President Diaz Ordaz responded by sending army troops onto the campus, thereby violating its historic sanctuary status. The battle was quickly joined. Could the student left stop the Olympic Games? The tragic pattern of confrontation between students and troops continued. On October 2, 1968, a rally of students in the Mexico City section of Tlateloco drew an unusually heavy contingent of security forces. An order to disperse was not observed and the police and paramilitary forces moved in. Later they claimed to have taken sniper fire from surrounding buildings. They began shooting, and the crowd was caught in a murderous crossfire, as hundreds fell dead and many more wounded. The massacre at Tlateloco sent a shudder throughout Mexico. There was no inquiry and no convincing explanation from the military or civilian authorities responsible for the slaughter. Many critics said the massacre proved the bankruptcy of the PRI monopoly on power. By the same token, the brutal show of force convinced everyone that mass challenges to authority would only bring more death and destruction. The effect was then very chilling.

On January 13, 2005, Special Prosecutor Ignacio Carillo announced that Mexico would be bringing charges of genocide against two dozen former officials for the 1968 leftist dissident student massacre at Mexico City's Tlateloco Plaza, just days before the Olympic Games opened. Former president Luis Echeverría, who was interior minister at the time, was under investigation for his role in the tragedy. In July 2004, the prosecutor sought to bring genocide charges against Echeverría and twelve others in a different case, a 1971 attack on students that left at least a dozen dead. The charges were dismissed based on the statute of limitations, and the Supreme Court is reviewing Carillo's appeal. He pledged to file charges in the Tlateloco case even if the Supreme Court has not ruled in the 1971 killings, though the High Court's decision is seen as crucial to establishing a framework for prosecuting similar cases.

In June 2006, eighty-four-year-old Echeverría was charged with genocide in connection with the massacre. He was placed under house arrest pending trial. The following month he was cleared of genocide charges, as the judge found that Echeverría could not be put on trial because the statute of limitations had expired.

President Vicente Fox, of the Partido de Accion Nacional (PAN), took office in 2000, ending seventy-one years of single-party rule by the PRI party. He pledged to expose Mexico's repressive, secret past. From the 1960s to the 1980s, 100 or more Mexicans are reported to have died at the hands of government security forces in a so-called dirty war against dissidents. Rights groups hailed Fox's appointment of Carillo in 2002 as an unprecedented step toward ending official impunity. But limited resources, court maneuvers, and resistance by police and military have hampered the prosecutor. Of eleven "dirty war arrest warrants," just three suspects have been arrested and face trial. Genocide, normally associated with slaughters like the Nazi killing of the Jews, is increasingly being used in human rights cases around the world. In Mexico, genocide can apply if victims were targeted as members of a group, such as a student movement.[2]

North American Free Trade Agreement (NAFTA)

Mexico's emergence from a colonial past has been conditioned by one factor that no other Latin American nation shares: a 2,000-mile border with the United States. That proximity has produced benefits and liabilities. Harvard-educated economist Carlos Salinas de Gortari, at the age of thirty-nine, was elected president of Mexico in 1988. He quickly moved toward an economy based more on free market principles than on state control and toward better economic relations with the United States. He is, perhaps, best known for his role in negotiating the North American Free Trade Agreement. Salinas was a técnico, a competent technocrat with little, or no, grassroots political experience. Technically, he was highly qualified to deal with the nation's problems. Politically, however, he had to define himself on the campaign trail. Salinas won with only 50.4 percent of the vote—his victory marred by allegations of fraud. As president, he worked to revive Mexico's economy by curbing inflation and reducing government regulations. He became the major promoter of NAFTA, and in signing the accord (in 1992), reversed Mexico's historical resistance to foreign investment and to U.S. involvement in its affairs. Although Salinas's administration was praised for its economic reforms, it lost some of its luster when his brother, Raúl, was arrested in 1995 for the 1994 murder of a PRI official and was later (1996) accused of massive financial misappropriations. After Carlos Salinas responded by criticizing the Mexican government, he was pressured into de facto exile, only returning to Mexico in 2000. All the optimism resulting from the NAFTA accord promptly came under assault. On January 1, 1994 (the day after NAFTA came into effect), a guerilla movement in the poverty-stricken state of **Chiapas** rose up to denounce the free trade accord, the Salinista economic model, and the undemocratic character of the political regime.

Zapatista National Liberation Army (ELZN)

A major issue facing the Mexican government has been the land dispute surrounding the Chiapas region in southern Mexico. Mexico has experienced almost unprecedented economic growth in the past few decades, but there has been a clear failure to equitably distribute that wealth due to a lack of social reform. As a result, Mexico remains a country of "haves and have-nots." In addition to Chiapas, other regions have experienced guerrilla warfare. These are located in the regions of Oaxaca, Hidalgo, Vera Cruz, and Puebla. Immortalized from the days of the revolution, Emilio Zapata who had been conscripted into the army and served for seven years fought passionately for restoration of confiscated land; his Plan of Ayala, called for the seizure of all foreign-owned land, all land taken from villages, confiscation of one-third of all land held by "friendly" hacendados, and full confiscation of land owned by persons opposed to the Plan of Ayala. Zapata, who was killed in an ambush in 1919, is still lauded by the peasants of southern Mexico as their true hero. Using Zapata as a symbol of revolutionary righteousness, the Zapatista movement continues to wage an armed struggle for land rights in the Chiapas region. This group, called the **Zapatista National Liberation Army (ELZN)**, appeared violently on the world scene in 1994, when it fomented an armed uprising against the Mexican government, to protest the distribution of land in the region. This movement better fits the definition of a guerrilla group than a subversive terror organization. The group uses many different terror tactics to achieve notoriety and influence political aims.

As we have seen in so many other conflicts, land was the primary issue that influenced the uprising. Mexicans who farmed and eked out their living had long been granted land for their families. This ended with NAFTA, when the Mexican government stopped its Land Distribution Program. Angry and well-armed men from Chiapas then came out of the hills and attacked the cities. The Mexican government responded by sending in the military. Chiapas became a region controlled by the Mexican army. Many of Mexico's problems revolved around the failing economy in 1994 and the slow rate of recovery. The erosion of the ruling Institutional Revolutionary Party's (PRI) power has not helped and continues to contribute to the unrest. In 1995, 30,000 Mexican soldiers, intent on the destruction of the ELZN guerrillas, invaded the Chiapas region. The exercise was an abject failure, and ELZN simply disappeared into the hills of Chiapas, much like the Viet Cong did in Vietnam. The soldiers continued to surround Realidad, believed to be the center of Zapatista operations. To appeal for the farmers' rights to the land and a cessation of the violence, Bishop Samuel Louis Garcia acted as a mediator for the ELZN, the people of Chiapas, and Mexican authorities. Chiapas remains a region of ongoing conflict and one of the main reasons for the fall of the long-ruling PRI in Mexico. The PRI lost both the presidency and the governorship in the province of Chiapas in 2000. Vincente Fox began his term with the intention of bringing an end to the ELZN rebellion in that region. The talks between Fox and the ELZN foundered, and the zones controlled by the Zapatista rebels, although much quieter now, continue to remain off-limits to government control.[3]

The Zapatistas, relying on the classic tactic of surprise attacks, and with considerable communications skills, initiated a public relations extravaganza. As the premier online guerilla group, it carefully disseminated many of its official documents and communiqués to a global online audience. While the group enjoyed some crucial successes, it has also been saddled with considerable political and military limitations. This predicament stands in sharp contrast to the context of the group's famous hero, Emilo Zapata, who also marched to the rhythm of global politics and, subsequently, achieved broad revolutionary goals.

The Chiapas regional conflict gets little press, but the issues of land grabs and unchecked violent attacks continue. Massacres of farm workers are not uncommon and the police do little to prevent such actions.

Right-Wing Violence

An extreme right-wing movement called "Peace and Justice" has been carrying out attacks against the ELZN and its supporters. This group pledges its support to the Institutional Revolutionary Party and operates as a death squad in the Chiapas region. The viciousness of the attacks seems to have the support of the military, as well as the local police authorities, and this has led to beatings, murders, and the mass evacuation of entire villages. Active units, pledging support for the government and finding support from the police, appear to have the same goals seen in state-sponsored terrorism: "the systemic and purposeful creation, by a political regime, of fear by violent means, and/or by the threat of such violence." The purpose of the systematic exercise of such publicly visible violence is to maintain, legitimize, or strengthen the social and administrative control of the state. The activities of the Peace and Justice Group seem destined to be part of the fabric of Mexican society for this region. By generating significant fear, this right-wing group is able to influence the predominantly Mayan Indian population of Chiapas.

Popular Revolutionary Army

The Popular Revolutionary Army (EPR) ranks second in strength to the Zapatista movement. With its base and origins in the southern states of Oaxaca and Guerrero, it gains support from the poverty-stricken villages of those regions. The topography of the regions … forested mountains and rugged terrain…makes an ideal home base for a guerrilla force. The EPR is a left-wing group, considered by the Mexicans to actually be several different movements operating under a single banner. EPR attacks have been sporadic and often without defining a clearly understood objective. Ambushes of federal police and military convoys are EPR's primary tactics. Their strength and size have yet to be determined, but the group claims to have over 20,000 guerrillas operating in the southern states. Support for the group has also come from an unknown outside source that may well be responsible for arming it with modern, Russian-made weaponry. In response to the logistics and training it has received from Peru's Marxist-oriented Shining Path, the EPR set up a Mexican support committee for the popular war in Peru. Sustained operations have been difficult, and it is questionable if the group has the ability to employ any effective tactics to disrupt or alter government policy. Some EPR attacks on the outskirts of Mexico City have occurred and communiqués have been issued to its members to target the "fat cat" capitalist businesses located there.

Other movements are surfacing in the poorer regions of Mexico as a result of the country's economic woes and the perception that the poor are getting poorer and the rich are getting richer. Such groups as the Revolutionary Army of Popular Insurgence and the Armed Front for the Liberation of the Marginalized People of Guerrero may be following the Zapatista uprising as a means for gaining concessions from the government. It is unclear whether the Mexican military can contain more than one guerrilla army at a time. Currently, it is fully occupied with the Chiapas region and it would seem incapable of handling yet another battlefront.

Mexico in the Twenty-First Century

As Mexico entered the New Millennium, the growing discontent and trouble from insurgent groups, especially in the poorer regions of the country, cannot be discounted. Unrest has begun to reach the cities where the abuses of paramilitary police produce the same results as those the Zapatistas have seen in the rural areas. Mexico currently does not have an effective means to deal with violence and corruption within the ranks of its police force. Situated conveniently between Colombia and the United States, Mexico is rife with a healthy drug trade, and associated with that comes the inevitable violence with cartels settling scores among them. Much of the killings tend to be within the cartels, but bribery of police and judiciary is also commonplace. New challenges confronting Mexico include the emergence of even more powerful drug cartels. These cartels operate at will and target police, journalists, and the judiciary with assassination. The most dangerous of these cartels were involved not so much in marijuana or heroin (traditional products of Mexico) but in transshipment of cocaine from Colombia. With an estimated over $7 billion in annual profits, these groups could easily spend as much as $500 million per year on bribery alone—more than twice the total budget of the Mexican attorney general's office! By the mid- to the late 1990s, Mexico had about a dozen drug organizations of truly international scope in Tijuana, Sinaloa, Ciudad Juarez, Guadalajara, and in the state of Tamaliupas (where traffickers operated a flourishing cocaine pipeline along the Gulf of Mexico). Drug cartels were implicated in a wave of violence that swept through Mexico, including the assassination of a Roman Catholic Cardinal in 1993. Former prosecutor, Eduardo Valle Espinosa, proclaimed that the country had fallen under the heel of drug traffickers and, like Colombia, could actually become a "narco-democracy."

Mexico elected Felipe Calderon to the office of president in December 2006; he took over the office from Vicente Fox, also a conservative politician.

GUATEMALA

Outside Communist influences in Guatemala during the last fifty years have done much to further human rights violations through the dictatorships and juntas that have to come to power. During the Cold War years, this influence was particularly strong. The United States assisted in the military overthrow of Guatemala's Communist regime in 1954, but the series of extreme right-wing military governments that followed did nothing to initiate reforms. Rather, they focused on campaigns against Communist infiltration. With so much oppression in the country, the peasantry began to retaliate by establishing the **Rebel Armed Forces (FAR)**, which began to take shape in the early 1960s and was the precursor to the Guatemalan National Unity (URNG), established in 1982. The military had little success in repressing such movements and, with the arrival of URNG, embarked on a campaign of state-sponsored terror.

The military was unleashed and clandestine death squads formed, while military and security police openly committed murder and torture. The resulting exodus from the region gradually gained international attention. Military leaders in Guatemala, however, were becoming desperate to remain in power, so they increased the tactics of state-sponsored terror and murder against their people. A "scorched earth" policy was employed in many instances and whole villages, as well as lands and crops, were destroyed. Torture of suspected Communists was commonplace, and the methods of torture were grotesque and usually fatal. Human rights in Guatemala, and past U.S. support for the regime, are issues to ponder, as are questions regarding the level of involvement of the U.S. government in political murders, torture, and human rights abuses.

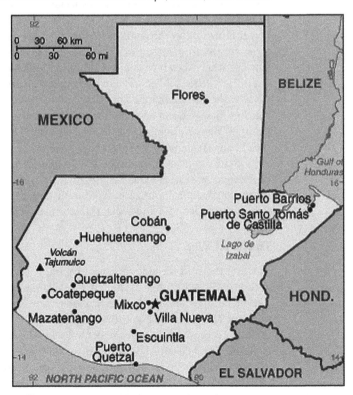

FIGURE 13-2 Map of Guatemala (Central Intelligence Agency, *The World Factbook, 2008*).

The Bishop of Guatemala—Monsignor Juan Gerardi Condera

Guatemala and its rebels signed a peace deal in 1996, which did little to eradicate the violence that permeated the country. In April 1998, Condera released his report "Guatemala Never Again," concerning human rights abuses and violations mainly perpetrated by the Guatemalan Army, and two days later was beaten to death as he returned to his home. Condera was the coordinator of the Archbishop's Human Rights Office (ODHA) and was the driving force behind the project for the Recovery of Historical Memory (REMHI), which had been created to shed light on the war's human rights violations. It seemed likely that his death was the work of a Guatemalan death squad. Death squads had killed with impunity during the thirty-six-year conflict.[4]

Impunity

The abuses and atrocities perpetrated by the Guatemalan state had relied on a system of impunity defined as "freedom from accountability for criminal wrongdoing, or freedom from other legal sanctions." The impunity system in Guatemala was conducted by several simple mechanisms. First, the state denies any state-sponsored violence, and second, those who would have made claims of torture and rights abuse had simply "disappeared." Such disappearances made it difficult to bring any judicial action against Guatemala. In the sixteen years leading up to 1990, it is estimated that over 100,000 Guatemalans were killed, and possibly another 40,000 disappeared without a trace! The government has a very thin veneer of democracy, and its ability to control the powerful military is doubtful, especially when it comes to human rights abuses. The peace accord, finalized in 1996, brought an end to thirty-six years of internal fighting, and Guatemalans began returning to their villages from neighboring countries. One such village that will likely never recover from atrocities committed by the military is the remote mountain hamlet of Plan de Sanchez where the army slaughtered more than 200 people, mostly Mayan women and children. On July 18, 1982, soldiers on anti-insurgency duties overran the hamlet, then raped and tortured villagers, herded them into a building and blew it up. No one has been prosecuted for the Plan de Sanchez massacre and few have faced justice for other rights abuses. In 2005, the Inter-American Court of Human Rights in Costa Rica awarded 317 family members close to $25,000 each to be paid by the Guatemalan government.[5]

State-sponsored terrorism in Guatemala has fostered a populace with a shared set of experiences of systemic human rights violations. It is a populace not only cynical of the formal, institutional applications of justice but also one that has experienced extralegal "justice" in the fight for social control and social transformation of Guatemalan society.[6]

The Civil War

The first thorn in the side of successive oppressive military governments was the Rebel Armed Forces (FAR), which began limited guerrilla operations as far back as 1962. Over the years, the movement grew among the indigenous groups and expanded to include the Guerrilla Army of the Poor (EGP) in 1972 and the Organization of People in Arms (OPRA). With the merging of these three guerrilla movements, all with the same causes and complaints, the Guatemalan National Unity Group (URNG) was formed. The military conducted operations in which they destroyed villages and killed entire populations. In some of these operations, their actions, which were collectively called "pacification," typified those used in the Vietnam War. They employed a scorched earth policy. By targeting the civilian population in the countryside, the military assumed it would stop support of the guerrilla army.

Since the 1996 Peace Accords, there have been many attempts to bring justice to Guatemala. Amnesty International has been prominent in detailing human rights abuses believed to be perpetrated by the military and the death squads. This has led to attacks against prominent Catholic Church leaders in Guatemala to try to silence their criticism.

By the end of 1998, climatic changes in the region prompted the government to suspend parts of its Constitution. Following the distinctive impact of Hurricane Mitch, which decimated several Central American countries, including Guatemala, the government of Alvaro Arzu suspended two articles of the country's Constitution: Articles Six and Twenty-Six. This is believed to be a direct result of the looting and violence in the cities following the hurricane and the government's fear of a resurgence of terrorism.[7] Article Six protects Guatemalans from detention or imprisonment without cause or in the absence of a court order, while Article Twenty-Six guarantees the right of freedom of travel. Such severe measures threaten to return Guatemala to a repressive government.

HONDURAS

Honduras has undergone the least turmoil of all the Central American republics. Rivalries between the Liberal and Conservative parties persisted to the mid-twentieth century, popular agitation has been minimal, and power has rested in the hands of a triangular alliance—landowners, foreign investors (mainly United Fruit), and the military. Because of its economic and political weakness, Honduras has been especially vulnerable to outside influence. Honduran history reveals a fundamental fact of Central American political life—the emergence of the military as an autonomous caste and as a supreme arbiter in national affairs. A career in the Honduran Armed Forces offers chances of upward mobility to middle-class young men. The aristocracy controls land, universities are restrictive, and there is hardly any industrial development. An ambitious person of middling origin has almost no alternative. As a result, recruits and cadets take immense pride in the honor and dignity of the military as an institution, and officers tend to look down on politicians and civilians.

Strife with neighboring countries has played an important part in Honduran history. During the 1960s, tensions with El Salvador mounted steadily. There have been long-standing, although minor, territorial disputes. El Salvador is a densely populated country; Honduras is just the opposite. Consequently, people from El Salvador looking for jobs in Honduras create

FIGURE 13-3 Map of Honduras (Central Intelligence Agency, *The World Factbook, 2008*).

resentment. A 1963 law prohibited companies from employing more than 10 percent foreigners (read Salvadorans), and a 1968 decree prevented Salvadorans from gaining title to Honduran land.

As has been evidenced throughout most of Central America, the paranoia that gripped the United States during the Cold War years was played out in its support of countries ripe for Communist influence. Honduras has benefited from decades of military support from the United States and was involved, throughout the 1980s, in fighting the invading Sandinistas and in hunting down rebel Contra bases. Geography made it inevitable that Honduras would be drawn into the U.S.-sponsored war against the Sandinistas. The United States rapidly transformed Honduras into a launching pad for Contra attacks against neighboring Nicaragua. Thousands of regular U.S. military and National Guard units rotated duty in Honduras, inundating the economy with hundreds of millions of U.S. dollars. All of these activities just reinforced the power of the Honduran military.

Morazanist Patriotic Front

The Morazanist Patriotic Front (FPM) is a small, extreme left-wing terror group that was violently opposed to U.S. intervention and support of the right-wing political government in Honduras. It first appeared in the late 1980s, and its attacks were aimed mostly at U.S. military personnel. It carried out bomb attacks on military buses carrying U.S. service personnel and, in 1989, claimed responsibility for just such an incident, in which three U.S. servicemen were wounded. Since then, FPM attacks have been sporadic and ineffectively executed.[8] Currently, there have been no known incidents arising from this organization and in the past had ties to the government of both Cuba and Nicaragua.

FIGURE 13-4   Map of El Salvador (Central Intelligence Agency, *The World Factbook, 2008*).

EL SALVADOR

As in Mexico, Salvadorians have been engaged in an ongoing demand for land reform and rights, dating back nearly seventy years. Much of El Salvador's economy was based on its coffee production and export, which was controlled by an influential group of families. The first protests date back to the first quarter of the twentieth century and to a campaigner from the Central American Communist Party, Augustin Farabundo Marti. His goal, like that of the Chiapas of Mexico, was not the overthrow of the government, but the redistribution of wealth from the land on an equitable basis. By 1930, the country was under military control of General Martinez, who sided with the society elite and coffee growers. Augustin Farabundo Marti Martinez was arrested in a military crackdown on his movement and was subsequently executed by a firing squad. The peasants were not organized in sufficient numbers to mount any sort of insurgent response. The military sought to purge the country of peasant "subversives" and went on a killing spree, accounting for more than 30,000 deaths. In 1981 alone, there were 12,501 murders reported in El Salvador.

In the late 1960s and 1970s, El Salvador provided further example of extreme right-wing terror used as a governmental tool to eradicate opposition. Again, death squads were utilized and two specific groups were formed, one covert and the other overt, to protect wealthy landowners and to spread fear among the peasants. In 1968, the commander of the El Salvador National Guard[9] formed the ORDEN. This was an intelligence-gathering organization that went beyond information gathering, and included kidnapping and murdering peasants. In attempting to analyze and define terrorism, some scholars believe that the actions of death squads are not terroristic in nature. However, the subversive actions of a terrorist or guerrilla organization spread fear, disorder, and uncertainty within the ruling government and the country as a whole. Repression by death squads or paramilitary groups has the identical impact. Periods of relative peace were interrupted by violence perpetrated by the death squads both clandestinely and openly. The violence ended in 1992 with a peace agreement. Liberal views made anyone a target for death squads, including priests and nuns who were murdered. Also targeted were outspoken labor leaders and politicians. Throughout the 1980s, fear was pervasive throughout El Salvador.

NICARAGUA

This small Central American country of 4.5 million has been embroiled in what can best be described as a struggle between superpowers. Nicaragua has had a leadership that boasts close ties to the United States and its military training institutions. Nicaragua has been supported by the United States since the mid-1930s, and its repressive National Guard was built and modeled on the U.S. National Guard and that is as close as the comparison can be. In power since 1937, the National Guard was separate from the military and operated as a private army and bodyguard for the Somoza family. It was allowed and encouraged to infiltrate and control all state operations and big business and ensured the Somoza family were fabulously wealthy. A very young but aggressive Anastasio Somoza García took over control of the National Guard when responsibility was turned over by U.S. marines in 1934. In the following years, Somoza consolidated his control over the Guard, purging any opposition from within, to his power base. On February 21, 1934, he ordered and approved the capture

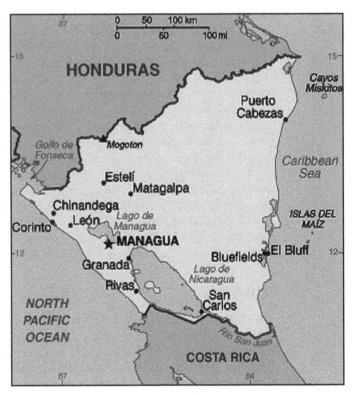

FIGURE 13-5 Map of Nicaragua (Central Intelligence Agency, *The World Factbook, 2008*).

and murder of Augusto César Sandino. Sandino's execution was followed by the persecution and execution of hundreds of men, women, and children living in the semiautonomous region previously set aside for the former guerrillas. Sandino had led a peasant revolt against the U.S. presence in Nicaragua and its support for the regime through the 1920s and 1930s. He was at the point of making a deal with the government when he was assassinated. By 1937, Somoza had enough control to overthrow the president and have himself installed in office. He remained in power until his assassination in 1956, but by then, he had secured the country for his family to rule with impunity and support from the United States. He was succeeded by his son Luis Somoza.

SANDINISTA NATIONAL LIBERATION FRONT (FSLN)

The Sandinista National Liberation Front was formally organized in Nicaragua in 1961. Founded by José Carlos Fonseca Amador, Silvio Mayorga, and Tomás Borge Martínez, the FSLN began in the late 1950s as a group of student activists at the National Autonomous University of Nicaragua in Managua. Many of the early members were imprisoned. Borge spent several years in jail, and Fonseca spent several years in exile in Mexico, Cuba, and Costa Rica. Beginning with approximately twenty members in the early 1960s, the FSLN continued to struggle and grow in numbers. By the early 1970s, the group had gained enough support from peasants and students groups to launch limited military initiatives.

On December 27, 1974, a group of FSLN guerrillas seized the home of a former government official and took as hostages a handful of leading Nicaraguan officials, many of whom were Somoza relatives. With the mediation of Archbishop Obando y Bravo, the government and the guerrillas reached an agreement on December 30 that humiliated and further debilitated the Somoza regime. The guerrillas received US$1 million ransom, had a government declaration read over the radio and printed in *La Prensa*, and succeeded in getting fourteen Sandinista prisoners released from jail and flown to Cuba along with the kidnappers. The guerrilla movement's prestige soared because of this successful operation. The act also established the FSLN strategy of revolution as an effective alternative to a policy of promoting change peacefully. The Somoza government responded to the increased opposition with further censorship, intimidation, torture, and murder.

That the Somoza regime was continually propped up by successive U.S. governments is no surprise. Nicaragua was an outspoken opponent of the Cuban revolution and provided support for the Bay of Pigs in 1961. The Cold War was not a distant memory for the United States, and military assistance was provided to the Anastasio government to fight the Sandinistas. Anastasio Somoza had succeeded his dead brother through rigged elections in 1967 and continued in the family tradition—he was president of the country and also in personal charge of the National Guard so exercised total military and political power over the country. By now both middle class and peasants alike flocked to the Sandinista National Liberation Front.

CONTRAS

The United States was willing to work with the FSLN, but by 1981, and with the arrival of President Ronald Reagan, the United States believed that the Sandinistas that were now the official government of Nicaragua were being actively supported by both the Soviet Union and Cuba and were arming the rebels in El Salvador. All support for Nicaragua was suspended, and the United States began providing support to Nicaraguan groups willing to overthrow the Sandinista government. The Contras is the name given to these groups, which included members of the now-defunct National Guard only too eager to return to the Somoza style of extreme right-wing government. The Contra leadership was represented mostly by former members of the National Guard; this fact made the movement highly unpopular among most Nicaraguans.

The Contras established operational bases in Honduras from which they launched hit-and-run raids throughout northern Nicaragua. The charismatic Edén Pastora abandoned the Sandinista revolution in July 1981 and formed his own guerrilla group, which operated in the southern part of Nicaragua from bases in Costa Rica. The United Nicaraguan Opposition operated in the northwest, the Opposition Block of the South operated in the southeast, and the Nicaraguan Coast Indian Unity operated in the northwest. Although the Sandinista army was larger and better equipped than the Contras, the antigovernment campaign became a serious threat to the FLSN government, largely through damage to the economy.

As the Contra war intensified, the Sandinistas' tolerance of political pluralism waned. The Sandinistas imposed emergency laws to ban criticism and organization of political opposition. Most social programs suffered as a result of the war because the Sandinista regime was forced to increase military spending until half of its budget went for defence. Agricultural production also declined sharply as refugees fled areas of conflict.[10]

For the United States, a far more significant political bombshell was about to detonate at the Pentagon. Questions arose concerning the level of U.S. involvement in drug trafficking in exchange for weapons to the Contras. There have been many sensational journalistic pieces that pointed a finger at the CIA and the Reagan administration. The 1995 Kerry Committee Report holds some interesting facts in its findings. The subcommittee found that the Contra drug links included the following:

- Involvement in narcotics trafficking by individuals associated with the Contra movement.
- Participation of narcotics traffickers in Contra supply operations through business relationships with Contra organizations.
- Provision of assistance to the Contras by narcotics traffickers, including cash, weapons, planes, pilots, air supply services, and other materials, on a voluntary basis.
- Payment to drug traffickers with U.S. Department of State funds authorized by the Congress for humanitarian assistance to the Contras, in some cases after the traffickers had been indicted by federal law enforcement agencies on drug charges, in others while traffickers were under active investigation by these same agencies.[11]

There is no doubt that those involved in these drug schemes on the U.S. side hoped to expunge any pending legal indictments in return for assistance to the rebel Contras. The level of exploitation by the drug traffickers was purely self-serving and certainly not ideologically driven.

When examining the infrastructure that was in place in the 1970s for the movement of illegal narcotics through Central America to the United States, it was a simple shift of purpose to include weapons into this mix. This was a method the Sandinistas used to bring Cuban weapons into Nicaragua. Supply and staging areas abounded along the Nicaraguan border with Costa Rica, and most of the neighboring governments, which supported the actions of the Sandinistas, offered them safe haven and the opportunity to transfer drugs and weapons for their cause. When the Sandinistas finally gained power, the gunrunning did not cease. In fact, all that changed was the end user. The suppliers now had El Salvadoran rebels as customers, and not the Sandinistas.

One name has become synonymous with the Contras in the 1980s: U.S. Lieutenant Colonel Oliver North, who at the time "managed" Contra operations on the southern front. Evidence in the Kerry findings relates also to a U.S. national living in Costa Rica, John Hull, an Indiana farmer who moved to Costa Rica and bought up large tracts of land. The area, known as Hull's Ranch, happened to include six airstrips, ideal for drugs and weapons smuggling. Hull helped the CIA with military shipments to the Contras and was also heavily involved in transshipment of drugs from Colombia. Added to this was the fact that the U.S. State Department was actively signing contracts with companies and their principals—companies that were either under investigation or had been indicted on narcotics-smuggling charges. These companies were used to make military hardware drops to the Contra rebels.

PANAMA

Formerly under Spanish rule, this tiny strip of land between the Pacific and the Atlantic first became a province of Colombia, before gaining its independence in 1903. Famous for the Panama Canal, which was under the control of the United States until the late 1970s, Panama has been a largely rural nation. The country has seen many varied forms of military governments over the past century or so, but the most notorious was that of General Manuel Noriega, who became president in 1983. From the time he came to power, he ran a corrupt government, made millions of dollars from drug trafficking to the United States and from diverting aid funds. Noriega controlled the public with strong-arm tactics and death squads. In 1988, a Florida grand jury indicted him on charges of racketeering and drug running. Up until 1989, Noriega continued to act with impunity. However, after the death of a U.S. Marine officer and Noriega's overturning the results of a democratic election, former president George H. Bush gave the almost unprecedented order for U.S. troops to invade Panama and restore the elected president. The marines seized Noriega and handed him over to U.S. marshals. He then stood trial and was sentenced to forty years in federal prison, he was granted conditional release in September 2011 and in December 2011 was extradited to Panama to serve a 20 year prison term. Some think the effort to restore democracy in Panama was more about trying to stem the endless flow of drugs into the United States than to bring Noriega to trial for his drug trafficking.

CENTRAL AMERICAN GANG PROBLEMS

Today, gangs are Central America's number one crime problem. Violent young men experienced in gunplay and in evading law enforcement efforts are being sent back to countries they haven't seen since they were children. Some are dropouts; many can barely speak Spanish. Gangs enlist teenagers who are abandoned, unemployed, and devoid of hope and teach them what they know best, that is, robbing, stealing cars, selling drugs, and killing. In the mid-1990s, the United States stepped up deportations of Central American criminals; many of them gang members from the 18th Street, or Mara 18, and its chief rival, Mara Salvatrucha 13 (MS-13).

     An estimated 150,000 gang members, or Mareros, control the streets of Central America, at times outgunning local police in El Salvador, Honduras, and Guatemala. Salvadoran officials say gangs are responsible for 80 percent of the homicides in that country. According to regional leaders, gangs are becoming the most destabilizing threat since the civil wars in Central America ended, over a decade ago. Some have been involved in extortion and mass murder, others linked to organized crime. As a whole, they threaten not only their rivals and public safety in general, but they even threaten the success of the Central American Free Trade Agreement (CAFTA). It is a fact that better economic and political conditions did not deter the explosion in the number of gangs throughout the 1990s. Across the board, Central America experienced economic growth after decades of internal conflicts. Yet, gangs grew in number, in part because of U.S. deportation policies that returned to the region thousands of gang members convicted of crimes, but primarily because of inaction or impotence of regional governments. In December 1994, leaders of the thirty-four democracies, meeting in Miami during the first Summit of the Americas, recognized

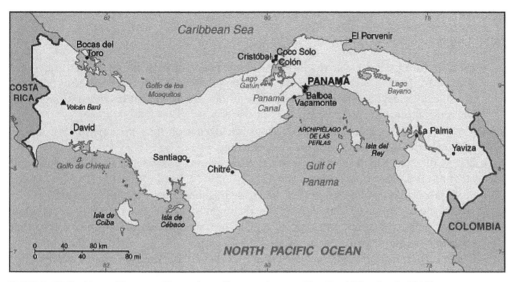

FIGURE 13-6   Map of Panama (Central Intelligence Agency, *The World Factbook, 2008*).

the threat of youth marginalization and the need to take practical steps to counter it. As yet, however, no unified regional strategy has been adopted.

Former U.S. secretary of defense Donald Rumsfeld warned of an "antisocial combination" of terrorists, drug traffickers, and gangs that is increasingly seeking "to destabilize civil societies" in the region. When it comes down to figuring out who in the U.S. government will take the lead to address this security threat, however, most security officials seem averse to even recognize that they are discussing it. Perhaps the reason for this is obvious. All security threats, and gang violence in particular, cannot be met by force alone. Addressing this issue will require a mix of law enforcement, prevention, rehabilitation, parental involvement, and after-school programs—a whole web of social initiatives that developing countries generally lack. Helping Central America get a grip on its gang problem would require a significant investment of time and resources from different agencies in the U.S. government. The Department of Justice and the U.S. Agency for International Development would have much larger roles than would the Pentagon or other security agencies.

U.S. officials failed to anticipate how other countries would be affected by the deportation of unwanted gang members: "The world is too global to export a problem and not expect it to come back," said David Brotherton, a professor at the John Jay College of Criminal Justice in New York, who has written two books on gangs. "In El Salvador, Guatemala, Honduras, and Mexico, there's a whole new inner-city youth subculture that originated in the First World. We've created an insoluble problem, and these countries just can't respond. There's no social work infrastructure. There's no rehabilitation. There's no money. They have enough trouble just providing basics for their own people." The U.S. Immigration and Customs Enforcement (ICE) launched a nationwide gang enforcement program in 2005 and began Operation Community Shield, a national law enforcement initiative that targets violent transnational street gangs through the use of ICE's broad law enforcement powers, including the unique and powerful authority to remove (deport) criminal aliens, including illegal aliens and legal permanent resident aliens.

In May 2005, it expanded Operation Community Shield to include all transnational criminal street gangs and prison gangs.

Results

Under Operation Community Shield, ICE:

- Partners with federal, state, and local law enforcement agencies, in the United States and abroad, to develop a comprehensive and integrated approach in conducting criminal investigations and other law enforcement operations against violent street gangs and others who pose a threat to public safety.
- Identifies violent street gangs and develops intelligence on their membership, associates, criminal activities, and international movements.
- Deters, disrupts, and dismantles gang operations by tracing and seizing cash, weapons, and other assets derived from criminal activities.
- Seeks prosecution and/or removal of alien gang members from the United States.
- Works closely with our attaché offices throughout Latin America and foreign law enforcement counterparts in gathering intelligence, sharing information, and conducting coordinated enforcement operations.
- Conducts outreach efforts to increase public awareness about the fight against violent street gangs.[12]

Central American governments are searching for strategies to combat gangs. The Honduran Congress unanimously passed one of the hemisphere's toughest antigang laws in 2003, setting a maximum twelve-year prison sentence for gang members. El Salvador followed with its own version of what has become known as the *mano dura*, or firm hand, which locks up any young man who bears gang tattoos. In May 2004, Mexico's southernmost state of Chiapas approved five-year prison sentences for anyone who simply belongs to a gang. Human rights activists complain that gang members are being hunted down and killed by police, but the crackdowns continue, especially against the Mara 18 and Mara Salvatrucha 13, which are Central America's largest and most violent gangs. The gangs have proven to be resilient. Every time they're uprooted, they resurface in another neighborhood, another city, and another country. They move with the assurance that no matter where they go, fellow gang members will feed them, house them, orient them, and provide them with weapons. The MS-13 gang had its origins in the 1980s in the United States and is a national and international criminal organization whose members conduct gang activities in the United States and Central America. According to the indictment, the term "Mara" is used in El Salvador for gang, while the phrase "Salvatrucha" is a combination of the words "Salva"—an abbreviation for Salvadoran—and "trucha," which is a slang term for the warning "fear us," "look out," or "heads up." Male gang members are required to complete an initiation process, often referred to as "jumped in," where the new member is beaten by other members until the count of 13. Female gang members are initiated by either being "jumped in" or submitting to sexual activity with gang members. MS-13 gang members often display their membership through tattoos reading "MS" or "MS-13" in gothic lettering and/or by wearing the gang's colors—blue and white—or clothing bearing the number "13" or numbers when added together total 13. MS-13 members pay dues that are used for the benefit of and provided to MS-13 members who are imprisoned in the United States, El Salvador, and Panama as well as to buy firearms to be used to conduct the enterprise's illegal activities.[13]

Drug- and gang-related violence in Mexico and particularly near the U.S. border has escalated since Mexican President Felipe Calderón took office in 2006 and vowed to fight corruption and drug cartels. Mexican drug cartels ship $17 billion and $38.3 billion in annual sales from Colombian-produced cocaine and Mexican heroin, methamphetamine and marijuana, according to the National Drug Intelligence Center.

A variety of U.S. reports from federal agencies estimated gang membership at 10,500 in El Salvador, 36,000 in Honduras, and 14,000 in Guatemala, while criminal organizations were becoming increasingly active in neighboring Belize, Costa Rica, and Panama. Central American gangs are increasingly transnational, noting that Salvadoran-based Mara Salvatrucha 13 is believed to have 10,000–20,000 active members operating in thirty-eight U.S. states and with between 80–100,000 international members. The violence in Mexico has reached epic proportions with several thousands of people killed, including journalists, police, lawyers, and judges as well as tourists caught in the middle of shootouts.[14] The southern border with Guatemala also poses significant risks for locals as a result of Mexican drug gangs infiltrating inaccessible areas such as the Petén region. The Mexican Zetas, an organized crime syndicate, use this area for drug smuggling activities and as a transshipment point for northerly routes. In May 2011, twenty-seven farmworkers were massacred and of those twenty-six had been decapitated; this method of execution is increasingly popular to demonstrate to locals the need for complete compliance with the drug gangs.[15]

COLOMBIA

Colombia's geography has had a significant effect on its history and on the evolution and development of what is often described as a fragmented and divided society. Colombia is bordered on the northwest by Panama, on the east by Venezuela and Brazil, and on the southwest by Peru and Ecuador. The eastern half is a low, jungle-covered plain, drained by spurs of the Amazon and Orinoco rivers and inhabited mostly by isolated, tropical forest Indian tribes. The fertile plateau and valley of the eastern range are the most densely populated parts of the country. Historically, the most populated areas have been divided by its three mountain ranges. The dispersion of much of the population into isolated mountain pockets has long delayed the development of transportation, adequate means of communication, and the formation of integrated national markets. Due to these geographic and spatial limitations, Colombia has developed local and regional cultures. Politically, this dispersion has created regional antagonism and local rivalries that were expressed in the nineteenth century in civil war and in the latter part of the twentieth century in intercommunity violence.

Over the last two centuries, Colombia has suffered through virtually continuous warfare. Colombia has been characterized by a pronounced fractured dispersion of power, further manifested by extreme levels of localism and regionalism. It is not surprising that all of this

FIGURE 13-7 Map of Colombia (Central Intelligence Agency, *The World Factbook, 2008*).

contributes to disproportionately high levels of violence in Colombia. One of the most severe challenges to U.S. policy toward Colombia derives from issues involving human rights. Political and extrajudicial actions involving government security forces, paramilitary groups, and members of the guerilla forces result in the deaths of thousands of civilians. Paramilitary forces are responsible for the great majority of these deaths. Many others are displaced by rampant and uncontrolled violence. The homicide rate is considered to be one of the highest per capita in the world. Government security forces are frequently involved in many of the abuses, including extrajudicial killings, and they sometimes collaborate directly and indirectly with paramilitary forces. And, although the government has worked to strengthen its human rights policy, the measures adopted to punish officials accused of committing violations, and to prevent paramilitary attacks, are insufficient. In the meantime, paramilitary forces have increased their social and political support among the civilian population in many parts of the country.

The U.S. Department of State has characterized the country as one of the most dangerous in the world to visit. Marijuana, cocaine, and kidnappings have been products of Colombia for more than forty years, but the market for drugs did not take off until the wealthy and middle classes in the United States began abusing them.

Cocaine became the drug of choice, and the opportunity for expansion into a North American market was huge. Drugs in Colombia are controlled in two regions of the country: Medellin and Cali. The Medellin and **Cali cartels** control nearly 80 percent of Colombia's distribution of drugs. Terrorist groups in Colombia have been fully involved in the sale and supply of narcotics for financial support in their bitter fight against successive Colombian governments. Terrorism has become a by-product of the drug trade and a means of control and power. Extortion, kidnapping, and murder are all hallmarks of the drug cartels. In a country where economics are dictated by drug barons, anarchy is never too far away. It is difficult to appreciate the enormous wealth that comes from the machinations of the drug trade. Drug barons are known to have utilized outside "sources" to assist their own internal security services. Colombia also has to contend with an insurgent group of left-wing rebels/revolutionaries/terrorists that have plagued the state for the last four decades.

A fifty-year insurgent campaign to overthrow the Colombian government escalated during the 1990s, fueled in part by funds from the drug trade. Although the violence is deadly and large swaths of the countryside are under guerrilla influence, the movement lacks the military strength and popular support necessary to overthrow the government. An anti-insurgent army of paramilitaries has grown to over several thousand strong in recent years, challenging the insurgents for control of territory and illicit industries such as the drug trade and the government's ability to exert its dominion over rural areas. While Bogotá steps up efforts to reassert government control throughout the country, neighboring countries worry about the violence spilling over their borders. In August 2000, the U.S. government approved "Plan Colombia," pledging $1.3 billion to fight drug trafficking. President Andres Pastrana, elected in 1988, used the plan to undercut drug production and prevent guerrilla groups from benefiting from drug sales. In August 2001, Pastrana signed "war legislation," which expanded the rights of the military in dealing with rebels. Alvaro Uribe of the Liberal Party won the presidential election in May 2002 and took office in August, pledging to get tough on the rebels and drug traffickers by increasing military spending and U.S. military cooperation. An upsurge in violence accompanied his inauguration, and Uribe declared a state of emergency within a week. In his first year, Uribe beefed up Colombia's security forces, with help from U.S. Special Forces, launched an aggressive campaign against the drug trade, and passed several economic reform bills.

In May 2004, the United Nations announced that Colombia's thirty-nine-year-long drug war had created the worst humanitarian crisis in the Western Hemisphere. More than

2 million people had been forced to leave their homes, and several Indian tribes are now close to extinction. Colombia now has the third-largest displaced population in the world, with only Sudan and the Congo having more. Uribe has produced some impressive results in fixing his country's ills, however. According to his defense minister, during 2003, more than 16,000 suspected leftist guerrillas and right-wing paramilitary vigilantes had surrendered, were apprehended, or were killed. The U.S. Office of National Drug Control Policy has announced that coca production has declined by 30 percent, but Colombia still continues to produce 75 percent of the world's cocaine.

Terrorism in Colombia

Colombia's democracy and its forty-plus million inhabitants have been under assault since the early 1960s and 1970s by three Marxist "narco-terrorist" groups: the **Revolutionary Armed Forces of Colombia (FARC)**, the National Liberation Army (ELN), and the **United Self-Defense Forces of Colombia (AUC)**. These three groups were capable of providing over 25,000 well-trained combatants. FARC and AUC have had a pronounced involvement at all levels of the drug trade and derive a considerable income from it—some estimates run as high as $300 million annually. In 2001, the AUC killed two Colombian legislators and FARC kidnapped six; and the three groups accounted for the assassinations of twelve mayors.[16]

FARC is a Marxist terrorist group that was established in 1964 by the Communist Party of Colombia to defend what was at that time communist-controlled autonomous regions. By any standards FARC is on record as being one of the best-equipped and best-funded terrorist organizations in Latin America. FARC has militia groups in the cities and special forces units that operate where "most needed;" the group also has a "vast support network full of logistical experts in bombing, transportation, kidnapping, arms trafficking, food storage, FARC's current structure is the same as the structure established in 1982, and the group's structure is centralized to an "extremely high" degree and described as follows:

Its basic military unit is the column, composed of 20 to 40 fighters; it is an operational unit in charge of the control of a certain territory, of collecting taxes and rackets and of military actions. A plurality of columns makes up a Front. The Fronts sometimes congregate in Blocks. Front and Block commanders respond directly, both militarily and financially, to the secretariat, which operationally is the supreme direction of the group.[17] FARC gains drug revenues from the production, manufacture, sale, and distribution of narcotics. The numbers of kidnappings according to the Colombian government dropped dramatically from the peak year in 2000 when 3,500 people were taken, down to 521 in 2007. As part of the U.S. government's Plan Colombia, which was focused on reduction of the flow of cocaine, the United States has provided some $5 billion worth of aid and a fraction of that amount has gone toward the Antiterrorism Assistance (ATA) program. The Colombian government gives credit to a little-known program, run by the U.S. State Department's Bureau of Diplomatic Security, which has trained more than 600 GAULA members. (GAULA is the Spanish acronym for Unified Action Groups for Personal Liberty.) The DS training, offered under its Anti-Terrorism Assistance program, has focused in particular on rescuing hostages.[18]

An extreme left-wing, Communist-inspired movement, FARC aspires to the overthrow of the Colombian government, and little else. In a country where kidnapping is commonplace, the FARC targets the government, military, locally elected municipal mayors, police, and civilians. Much of FARC's income is derived from not only drug trafficking but also robbery, kidnapping, and extortion. FARC is rabidly anti-United States and its campaign resembles that of Cuban-style revolution. FARC's membership of active terrorists was believed to number around 16,000 at its peak in the 1990s, which dwindled down to approximately 9,000 in 2008, but still managed to gain some support in rural areas from the indigenous population.

Most observers do not consider FARC's central demands as realistic, that is, their demands for the ending of privatization and reduction of the 20 percent unemployment rate and other reforms seem hopelessly futile. On the political front, the Colombian government of President Andreas Pastrana had made slow headway in negotiating a peace deal with FARC. In 2001, the year leading up to the elections, negotiations became bogged down and the Pastrana government threatened to end the deal that had created a demilitarized zone (DMZ) in southern Colombia, an area approximately the size of Switzerland, which had long been occupied by FARC. Since the events of 9-11, the Colombian government has been fortified with U.S. aid and military hardware for the express purpose of combating the drug trade in Colombia. This aid has given significant impetus to the Colombian military to go on the offensive against FARC, something of a novelty for Colombia's military, which has traditionally fought in defensive mode against FARC. Operation "Black Cat" commenced in February 2002. This military offensive was directed against FARC with the use of aircraft and helicopters. At the same time, Pastrana annulled the FARC's political status and issued arrest warrants for its leaders. In the February 2002 campaign, the Colombian military struck so far into FARC territory that the group was taken totally by surprise. The area attacked was the town of Barrancomina in eastern Colombia, an area where the sixteenth Front of FARC had been able to operate with complete impunity. The significance of the attack showed that the Colombian military had the skill and the intelligence support, as well as the military know-how, to attack FARC. In future campaigns, this will no doubt be a deciding factor in peace talks, if they ever resume. FARC's resilience has never really been in question and the organization has been a proven survivor. FARC cannot be called a truly Communist-inspired movement, even though committed Communists are included in its membership. FARC is also involved in the drug trade; although it cannot be considered a drug cartel, it is definitely involved in narco-terrorism. Because FARC flourishes in the deep rural and jungle regions of the state, it could be considered a peasant army. In some respects, this may be true but, because of its wide-ranging terror attacks, it cannot be termed as the vanguard of the peasant populace. FARC's appeal to the peasantry could be rationalized, as it offers a level of employment when there is no prospect elsewhere. The failures of the group's participation in government representation may spawn an organization that will feed off the lucrative trade in drugs, kidnappings, and extortion. However in the spring of 2011 FARC released a number of kidnapped military personnel who they had held for over 10 years. At the same time they renounced the further use of kidnapping.

FARC will likely continue to become even more marginalized as it sees itself up against the U.S.-backed Colombian military and an ever-growing number of paramilitary forces. In this context, it is expected that now that it has been hit systemically in areas where it once operated with complete freedom, it will have to reconsider its actions and adapt to survive in this new environment.

FARC's ability to strike against both the local political apparatus and the civilian population is well documented, and this is exactly what has happened since February 2002. With the arrival of the new president, Alvaro Uribe, who has committed himself to destroying FARC during his term of office, there is little doubt that further attacks will continue. Uribe also has some unfinished business with the rebels, who have tried on at least fifteen occasions to assassinate him. But more than that, the FARC killed his father in a botched kidnapping in 1983. Uribe hails from the Antioquia Province where he was the governor from 1995 to 1997. During his term, he promoted the "self-defense" groups, some of which evolved into paramilitary groups that, like the rebels they battle, are blamed for numerous civilian massacres. Juan Manuel Santos was elected to the Presidency in 2010. The Former Defence Minister had been responsible for curbing FARC activities which had seen the Colombian military engage in a large number of reported extra judicial killings.

NATIONAL LIBERATION ARMY (ELN)

The National Liberation Army, formed in 1963, is a smaller and less organized operation than FARC and has carried on a long-term campaign against the Colombian government. It is predominately a Marxist-inspired group and has a membership of about 3,000 fighters. Similar to FARC, the ELN is anti-United States and frequently engages in the profitable tactic of kidnapping. The target is usually a businessman from a foreign company working in Colombia. In addition, ELN targets U.S. and foreign installations for bomb attacks. ELN's operations are focused on Colombia's northwestern border with Venezuela—regions that produce cannabis and poppy opium. ELN and FARC have both systematically targeted Colombia's oil facilities and, in 2001, the government suffered nearly $500 million in lost revenues. To this end, the United States has supplied $6 million in foreign military funds (FMF) to train Colombian military units to protect the Cano Limon pipeline, which has been repeatedly bombed by both groups. ELN continues the practice of kidnappings for ransom.

Peace Talks

Peace talks between successive Colombian Governments, FARC and ELN have been a part of the political/insurgent process since the 1980s. FARC previously had little external support for its insurgent activities, and in 2006, FARC announced its conditions for agreeing to any bi lateral peace accord hostage/prisoner exchange. Since then, little has developed, and FARC continues to hold approximately 700 hostages. However, with the presence of the ubiquitous Hugo Chavez in neighboring Venezuela, who it is alleged has supplied millions of dollars of aid to FARC, will certainly complicate Colombia's peace overtures. Experts estimate that FARC takes in $200 to $300 million annually, at least half of its income, from the illegal drug trade. The FARC also profits from kidnappings, extortion schemes, and an unofficial "tax" it levies in the countryside for "protection" and social services. About sixty-five of the FARC's 110 operational units are involved in some aspect of the drug trade, according to a 2005 International Crisis Group report, but evidence from that period indicates they primarily managed local production.[19]

RIGHT-WING DEATH SQUADS

The right-wing death squads, which rose to prominence in Colombia, appear to have had the tacit support of both the government and the military. Many of these defense groups sprang up in the 1960s and 1970s in response to FARC's terrorist activities against wealthy landowners. Over the years, the groups, which tended to operate in select areas, moved from defensive to offensive strategies. They began to attack suspected members of FARC and intimidated peasant villagers believed to be helping the FARC.[20]

In central Magdalena, drug cartels began buying up rich tracts of land and were directly responsible for transforming the self-defense units into right-wing death squads.[21]

For the Colombian drug lords, the end justifies the means. This is the real issue in the rise of death squads and the necessity for terrorist actions in this country. In a country so heavily dependent on the production and export of drugs, the methods used to terrorize the populace are not intended as means to overthrow or replace a political system. These efforts are aimed at maintaining the status quo and fear, for the groups' own benefit, and for dissuading police, judges, and politicians from strict legal approaches in dealing with drug cartels. The rise of the right-wing death squads and paramilitaries dates back over thirty years, when rich landowners, farmers, and the drug cartels adopted their own small and very private protection forces. These have grown into a sort of loose coalition known as the United Self-Defense Forces of Colombia

(AUC). AUC and FARC have been responsible for more than 5,000 kidnappings and the deaths of more than 4,000 Colombians. AUC has publicly stated that it gains most of its support and income from the lucrative drug trade. Allegations of human rights abuses by the AUC abound. It has been linked on more than one occasion to senior members of Colombia's military elite. The AUC's methods of intimidation have resulted in more than 340,000 Colombians being forcibly evicted from their homes, bringing the total number of displaced persons to more than 2 million in just the last decade.

Alvaro Uribe, who swept to a landslide victory in the 2002 elections, was unable to exert much control outside the large urban centers. Uribe had ongoing talks with AUC, which was formed in 1997, but the group continued to indiscriminately slaughter leftist guerrillas, politicians, activists, union leaders, as well as civilians until 2003. Information from the Colombian National Police states that between January and October 2000, the AUC carried out 804 assassinations, 203 kidnappings, and 75 massacres in which 507 people died. Uribe's decommissioning of AUC began in earnest in 2003, and the number of attacks and assassinations dropped considerably and allowed the Uribe government to continue pursuing FARC and ELN. One of the major problems facing the Colombian government is AUC's deepening involvement with drugs. Since 2003, some 30,000 paramilitaries have been disbanded; however, this does not mean that they have been arrested but have more likely become involved in the lucrative drugs trade.

As for international links, one of bin Laden's close associates, Mohammed Abed Abel, a member of Egypt's largest militant group, Jamaat al-Islamiyya, was arrested in Bogotá, Colombia, in early November 1998. He was subsequently released by the Colombian authorities and deported back to Ecuador, his country of origin. Why would such a high-ranking and high-profile terrorist be in Latin America? It may be assumed that he was either studying the U.S. Embassy as a potential target or negotiating meetings with FARC or ELN to set up trade deals involving drugs for weapons. FARC and its connections to Irish paramilitary groups came dramatically to a head when the Colombian authorities arrested several senior IRA members in 2001. Prior to their arrest, Colombian authorities revealed that the IRA men had been involved in training members of FARC in military tactics, the use of explosives, and the manufacture of arms. General Tapias, chairman of the joint chiefs of staff for the Armed Forces of Colombia, made these claims in testimony before the U.S. House of Representatives International Relations Committee in April 2002. The types of attacks the FARC mounted in 2002 showed a higher level of sophistication than had previously been the case. The attacks' level of sophistication was similar to those of the IRA. The reason and background for IRA involvement is not yet clear but, of course, there is plenty of speculation from the various security organizations. In Britain, the suggestion is that the FARC paid the IRA $2 million for the training in explosives, and, of course, the U.S. concern is that it may be a hint of a much broader coalition of international terror relationships, but there is no hard evidence for this. The official response to the arrests from the IRA came from Gerry Adams, the leader of Sinn Féin. While Adams refused to testify before the U.S. House International Relations Committee, he did respond in writing to the chairman of the committee, Henry Hyde. Adams wrote: "Let me state again that neither I, nor anyone else, in the Sinn Féin leadership were aware that the three men were traveling to Colombia."[22]

Of course, the careful wording in this statement cannot be construed that Sinn Féin was not aware of their involvement, no doubt a good enough reason not to testify. It seems highly probable that FARC was delving deeper into drug trafficking in exchange for military hardware and much-needed cash reserves for its continuing fight.

From Counter-Narcotics to Narco-Terrorism

During the past several years, U.S. foreign policy toward Colombia has undergone significant changes. The events of 9-11, combined with the definitive rupture of the Colombian government's peace process with the rebels in February 2002, have converted this country into the primary training theater for U.S. counterterrorism operations in the Western Hemisphere today. Washington's traditional counter-narcotics policies have been based on repressive, prohibitionist, and hard-line language. The manner in which Colombia has addressed the drug problem derives substantially from the U.S. approach, with most of Bogotá's measures to fight the drug trade the result of bilateral agreements or the unilateral imposition of specific strategies designed in Washington DC. It has been theorized that these approaches have produced countless negative consequences for Colombia, aggravating the armed conflicts that continue to escalate and forcing urgent national problems such as the strengthening of democracy, the defense of human rights, the reduction of poverty, and the preservation of the environment to become secondary to countering the drug trade.[23]

Between 1996 and 2001, U.S. aid to Colombia (in the form of military and other government assistance) increased approximately fifteenfold, from $67 million to over $1 billion.[24]

At conceptual and practical levels, it is difficult for the United States to separate the war on drugs from its counterinsurgency efforts. Given that the global War on Terror has targeted the links that exist among terrorism, arms, and drugs, a new term "narco-terrorism" has been coined to describe players such as the FARC, former AUC, al Qaeda, and others that fund terrorist-related activities with drug money.[25]

In 2003, President Bush asked the Congress for an additional $600 million for Colombia, with the majority being in the form of military aid to rebuild and train the stagnating Colombian military. The request included line items to train and equip two new Colombian army brigades to protect the Cano Limon-Covenas oil pipeline, in which the American firm, Occidental Petroleum, is a large shareholder. Dubbed "Plan Colombia," the infusion of millions of dollars aimed at destroying the coca crops that so easily produce the cocaine for the cartels and FARC. FARC's significant control of the drug industry in Colombia is how it derives most of its financial support—estimated to be $1.3 billion per year. FARC has also been implicated in providing training to the kidnappers of former Paraguayan President Raul Cuba's daughter, Cecilia, who was abducted in September 2004 and found dead in February 2005. FARC was also responsible for the kidnapping of Colombian presidential candidate Ingrid Betancourt who remained a captive from 2002 through 2008 when she was rescued along with three U.S. employees of Northrup Grumman by Colombian Special Forces. Betancourt had been kidnapped while campaigning in the Demilitarized Zone (DMZ).

The drug trade drives Colombian terrorism from both the left and the right, and there is little evidence to suggest that the price of cocaine or its demand in the United States has declined as a result of around $8 billion being spent on trying to eradicate the problem. The Colombian cocaine trade was estimated at $35 billion in 2000.

The assistance given to the Colombian military by the United States has been rewarded by the death of one of their most wanted—Raul Reyes had been, until his death, the one and only spokesman for the FARC.

Luis Edgar Devia Silva aka Raul Reyes (September 30, 1948—March 1, 2008)

Raul Reyes, the central figure and spokesman for the FARC in almost all communications was killed on March 1, 2008, when the Colombian Air Force launched a bombing raid on an FARC camp about 2 miles from the Colombian border just inside Ecuador. Reyes had been sentenced in absentia for the deaths of thirteen policemen and eighteen soldiers, eighteen kidnappings and the deaths of a judge, a physician, three judicial auxiliaries, the ex-minister of Culture Consuelo Araújo, congressman Diego Turbay and his mother, Catholic monsignor Isaías Duarte, governor of Antioquia Guillermo Gaviria, the Colombian ex-minister Gilberto Echeverri, eleven members of the Valle del Cauca Assembly, and at least four other persons. Most of these persons were kidnapped before their deaths.[26]

The success of the Colombian military has pushed the FARC to its limits, and the deaths of many of its key players has meant that its force of around 18,000 fighters is now likely less than 8,000. In May 2008, FARC was dealt another significant blow to its already-flagging morale when it was announced that Manuel Marulunda, who had led the FARC for four decades, had died of an apparent heart attack.

FARC had also sought support from Venezuela and reports after the death of Raul Reyes that the Colombian military had found a number of files on his computer indicating that the government of Hugo Chavez was prepared to back FARC did nothing for regional stability. The claims were swiftly denied by the Venezuelan leader. In a similar operation carried out in September 2010, Jorge Briceño, also known as "Mono Jojoy," a longtime fighter and FARC's most senior commander was killed in an airstrike on his camp near Bogotá. By mid 2011, FARC were still active in pockets, mainly in the Medellin and Cali areas.

PERU

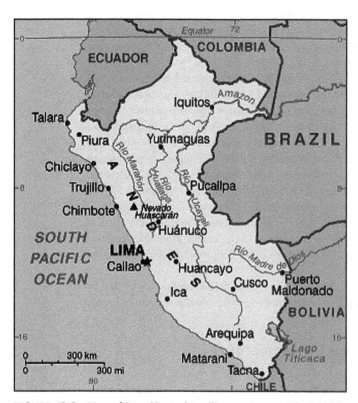

FIGURE 13-8 Map of Peru (Central Intelligence Agency, *The World Factbook, 2008*).

Peru is the second largest cocaine producing country in the world and a major exporter of cocaine and cocaine base to markets in South America, Mexico, the United States, and Europe. The U.S. Crime and Narcotics Center estimated that in 2008, 41,000 hectares of coca were under cultivation in Peru. In 2009, the Government of Peru manually eradicated 10,025 hectares of illicit coca. Eradication, linked closely to alternative development programs, has led to dramatic reductions of coca cultivation in the Upper Huallaga Valley where eradication efforts are focused; this is particularly evident in San Martin department. However, challenges remain in other parts of the country where State presence is limited, and where increased coca cultivation and trafficking have been reported, such as in the Apurimac and Ene River Valley. Peru is a key U.S. partner in the region, and the United States, is committed to working with the Peru to effectively address illicit coca cultivation, narcotics trafficking, and the related transnational criminal challenges that follow.[27] Peru is often remembered only for its fabulous Inca villages, Machu Picchu, and the high Andes Mountains. History informs us that an Inca chief, Tupac Amaru and his followers overcame their colonial Spanish masters in the latter half of the seventeenth century. The country has been under the control of military juntas throughout much of the twentieth century, but civilian rule returned to Peru in the 1980s. Peru suffers from two sources of indigenous terrorism: the Sendoro Luminoso (**The Shining Path**) and the Tupac Amaru Revolutionary Movement (MRTA).

Sendero Luminoso (The Shining Path)

Shining Path has its origins in the university city of Aucayacu, in the upper Huallaga region. Abimael Guzman, who received his indoctrination and training in China in 1965, at the start of the Chinese Cultural Revolution, created and led The Shining Path. His trips to, and training in, China, taught him to set up and organize clandestine political and terrorist activities against the democratic state. On his return he became the leader of the pro-Maoist faction of the Peruvian Communist Party. Guzman was working high in the Andes Mountains as a university lecturer studying the exploitation suffered by Peru's Indians. He had no trouble drawing parallels with the Chinese peasants who had fought for Mao Zedong three decades earlier. He recruited his students into the Maoist Party and sent them to agitate in the Indian villages.[28]

Students comprised the bulk of the organization, a reflection of the leadership's organizational strategy of tapping into the existing state-organized network of education to recruit Sendero devotees. His movement went underground in 1976 and began preparations for its campaign of terror and insurgency in 1980. Sendero derived much of its power by relying on ethnic factors and by resurrecting the feeling of historical greatness associated with the Inca civilization. A second and related story, from Peruvian history since the Spanish conquest in the early 1500s, concerned the effects of its subjugation, first to Spain, then to England, and most recently to the United States. It describes a legacy of exploitation, debt, and generally bad development that provided ready-made fuel for Sendero Luminoso to create and promote a radical and isolationist ideology.

Sendero burst onto the scene by assassinating any village leaders who resisted the group's call to smash authority and establish an egalitarian utopia. Many local police crumbled before the group, which issued no manifestos and maintained absolute silence about its structure and leadership. Mounting Sendero violence in the highlands forced the Peruvian government to authorize a military offensive, which left its own wake of repression. Peruvian military tactics failed to eliminate Sendero. On the contrary, the movement spread to other highland provinces and to Lima. More massacres in the Sierra and blackouts (from dynamited power lines) in greater Lima demonstrated growing Sendero strength. Sendero forced the government into greater reliance on the police and the military. Government forces killed indiscriminately, prompting the firing of numerous commanders for atrocities in the field and for the slaughter of numerous prisoners who had surrendered after a massive prison riot.

In 1976, while the Peruvian government was trying to restore the democratic processes and the economy of the country, Guzman and his Sendero Luminoso followers were training with automatic weapons. They were of the belief that Peruvian society had to be torn down, and a classless society designed to replace it. Guzman and his followers started out as the saviors of the poor of Peru. That was to quickly change as Guzman's Marxist style became similar, in his approach to the natives, to that of the Khmer Rouge in dealing with the Cambodians. In merging the extreme teachings of Chairman Mao with the philosophy of Che Guevara,[29] a dangerously violent hybrid emerged. Like the Khmer Rouge, Guzman and his guerrillas set about the destruction of the country by intimidating villagers into either joining the movement or die. Those who refused were promptly killed. The group quickly became a cult of mass murderers, feared for their savagery throughout Peru. Guzman's aim was to overthrow the Peruvian democratic government and replace it with a Marxist dictatorship, built in his own image. Over the next fourteen years, the group's reign of terror took the lives of 25,000 Peruvians and resulted in over $20 billion in damage to the country's infrastructure. Sendoro terrorists included a number of female operatives who have been known to use small children to deliver suicide bombs to public buildings and police stations. Guzman's philosophy and ideals spread farther than just Peru; he had goals of resurrecting the old Inca Empire; his terrorists threatened not only Peru but also Ecuador, Colombia, and Bolivia. Guzman's supporters believed him to be invincible, and they called him the "Fourth Sword of Marxism."[30]

Fortunately for Peru, this belief was to be rudely upset by his capture in September 1992. During the 1980s, terrorist activity had been so prevalent that villagers were fleeing to the urban slums of big cities, such as Lima, to escape the ravages of The Shining Path. International observers feared that the democratic government in Peru would not be able to deal with the onslaught from Guzman's Shining Path. After his capture in 1992, the movement staggered, lost direction, and began to disintegrate. President Fujimori was determined to overcome both narcotics trafficking and terrorism in Peru and seemed to have the overwhelming support of the people. Prior to Guzman's capture, several other key members of The Shining Path were behind bars. No doubt, information gathered during their interrogations assisted in Guzman's apprehension. Fujimori's democratic administration and revival of the country's economy had done much to defeat the terrorist threat, which, considering the meager level of counterinsurgency training available to the poorly equipped security police, is quite surprising. Following Guzman's capture, the void was temporarily filled by Oscar Durand, the group's strategist on military matters until he himself was captured by the Peruvian authorities in 1999.[31]

The Shining Path, in spite of the setbacks of the late 1990s, is still a credible and deadly force and a problem for Peruvian authorities. In the 2001 U.S. State Department *Patterns of Global Terrorism Report*, it indicates that in that year alone, the number of Shining Path terrorist acts in Peru was 130. Little has been heard of from Shining Path activities outside of Peru but the group is reemerging and continues sporadic attacks against police, military, and civilian informants. There is concern that the lack of coordination between the police and military on counter terrorism strategies as well as corruption within those forces is enabling Shining Path to continue to build and regroup into a very capable and threatening Maoist insurgency.

Tupac Amaru: Movimiento Revolucionario Tupac Amaru (MRTA)

The second of Peru's terrorist movements takes its name from the previously mentioned legendary Inca leader, Tupac Amaru II, a revered Indian rebel who led an uprising during the late eighteenth century against Spanish colonial arrangements. Movimiento Revolucionario Tupac Amaru (MRTA), considered in part a rival to Sendero, was actually less powerful, but still a very deadly Peruvian guerrilla organization during the late 1980s and early 1990s. The original rebellion by the Inca leader, Tupac Amaru II, was ultimately suppressed, but it remained a symbol of ethnic-political unity and hinted at prospects for more successful uprisings in the future. The greatness of the Inca Empire has remained alive in the hearts of many of Peru's indigenous population.

With the country heading toward elections in 1993, the levels of terrorism began to pick up and, by 1996, both MRTA and Sendero were resorting to campaigns of terror once again. Sendero was not able to deliver the same number of guerrillas to the campaign as it had previously, however, and the numbers of combatants were also significantly lower.

Victor Polay formed the Tupac Amaru in 1985. A traditional Marxist/Leninist movement, its goal was the overthrow of perceived imperialism in Peru. The group had no external support, and its membership was considerably less than that of Sendero. Polay was captured in 1992 and sentenced to life in prison. In a spectacular display of support and solidarity for Polay, Tupac Amaru stormed the Japanese ambassador's residence in Lima during a diplomatic Christmas celebration in December 1996. They took hundreds of guests, mainly diplomats, as hostages. In front of the world's press and television corps assembled outside, Tupac Amaru demanded the release of Polay. With the strong support of the Peruvian population, Fujimori stood his ground and did not give way to the threats from the terrorists. The assault on the ambassador's residence took place when about 400 guests were seated for a meal. The celebration was short lived, as more than a dozen heavily armed guerrillas stormed the grounds, firing weapons into the air. The attackers were calling themselves the Edgar Sanchez Special Forces, commanded by Comrade Edigirio Huerta. The assault began at about 8:00 P.M. on December 17, 1996. The situation was delicate, as a large number of foreign dignitaries and ambassadors were being held hostage, including the ambassadors of Austria, Brazil, Bulgaria, Cuba, Guatemala, Panama, Poland, Romania, South Korea, Spain, and Venezuela. The government of President Fujimori steadfastly refused to negotiate with the terrorists. Both political and economic implications would rest on the outcome.

The Tupac Amaru demands were as follows:

1. They would shoot hostages unless their demands were met.
2. Release of their imprisoned comrades, totaling up to 500.
3. Transfer of freed prisoners and hostages to a jungle hideout, with the last hostage to be released at the final destination.
4. Payment by the Peruvian government of a "war tax" of an unspecified amount.
5. An economic program to aid the Peruvian poor.[32]

The End of the Crisis

After dragging on for four months, the drama was eventually brought to its climax when Peruvian special security forces tunneled into the compound and rescued the hostages. Up until the middle of March, negotiations had been proceeding well, and the numbers of hostages had dwindled down to seventy-one, as concessions and counterconcessions were made. However, Fujimori would not budge on the terrorists' main demand, which was for the release of the imprisoned members of Tupac Amaru. At 3:20 P.M., April 22, 1997, the rescue began. The Peruvian government had authorized a rescue mission: tunneling, which had taken weeks, was now completed, allowing security forces to gain entry for a surprise strike. Explosions and gunfire were heard from inside the compound and plumes of smoke curled up from the residence windows. Within forty minutes, the 140-man rescue team had secured the residence, all fourteen Tupac Amaru guerrillas were dead, and twenty-five hostages were injured. Two members of the rescue team died in the operation. This incident brought worldwide congratulations to Fujimori for his stance against terrorism. But the attack was also a harsh reminder of the vulnerability of political leaders to terrorist attacks.[33]

In overall terms, the Peruvian authorities have seen some considerable success go their way in the war on domestic terrorism. In 2001, they had captured more than 259 suspected terrorists, and since the 9-11 attacks, Peru presented itself as a strong regional leader in the fight against terrorism and has participated in the U.S. State Department Antiterrorism Training Assistance program.

FIGURE 13-9   Map of Bolivia (Central Intelligence Agency, *The World Factbook, 2008*).

BOLIVIA

Bolivia, named after independence fighter Simon Bolivar, broke away from Spanish rule in 1825; much of its subsequent history has consisted of a series of nearly 200 coups and countercoups. It has been a land-locked country ever since the war of 1879–1884 when Chile seized the Port of Antofagasta and the surrounding area. As a result, Bolivia's relations with Chile have been troublesome throughout its history. Comparatively democratic civilian rule was established in 1982, but leaders have faced difficult problems of deep-seated poverty, social unrest, and drug production. During the last months of 2001, the country witnessed several corruption scandals involving government officials, growing crime rates, and evidence of a criminal network that had infiltrated national police authorities. Current goals include attracting foreign investment, strengthening the educational system, resolving disputes with coca growers over Bolivia's counter-drug efforts, and waging an anticorruption campaign. Bolivia is the world's third-largest cultivator of coca (after Colombia and Peru), with an estimated 8,450 hectares under cultivation in 2003, a 23 percent increase from 2002. Intermediate coca products and cocaine exports go mostly to or through Brazil, Argentina, and Chile to European and U.S. drug markets. Eradication and alternative crop programs have not been able to keep up the pace with farmers' attempts to increase cultivation. Money-laundering activities related to narcotics trade, especially along the borders with Brazil and Paraguay, have flourished.[34]

In August 1971, Colonel Hugo Banzer overthrew the leftist popular regime of Juan Jose Torres. The majority of the military, and the business class, supported the new regime. The Banzer administration could best be described as a return to an openly authoritarian state. He repressed all social groups opposed to his regime, especially workers and peasants. Between 1971 and 1978, around 19,140 Bolivians were exiled, including Juan Lechin, head of the Bolivian Workers Union and four ex-presidents.[35]

Thousands were detained at different times and were subjected to numerous kinds of torture. However, the number of persons actually killed by the state was relatively low. The universities were frequently closed and all union activity was forbidden. One particularly grisly event gained special notoriety: the so-called massacre in the Cochabamba Valley in January 1975. In protest against the prices fixed by the government, the peasants in that central region blocked the roads. In retaliation, the military harshly repressed them. Many died or disappeared.[36]

When a military coup toppled the Bolivian government in 1980, the usual array of journalists, opposition politicians, and trade unionists were detained by the secret police, the

Servicio Especial Seguridad (SES). However, most detainees were only held for a short period of time. Politically motivated assassinations have also been a hallmark of political unrest in the region. An outspoken member of the Socialist Workers Party was kidnapped in January 2002, and his tortured and bullet-riddled body was found two days later. Many of the violent gang activities are laid at the door of former groups involved in urban guerrilla activities in Chile. One of the main protagonists in Brazil's gang problems is Mauricio Norambuena, a leading figure in the Manual Rodriguez Patriotic Front (FPMR), which is now believed to have its base in Montevideo, Uruguay. The FPMR was as the armed wing of the Chilean Communist Party in 1983 and was named after Manual Rodriguez, hero of Chile's war of independence from Spain. FPMR splintered in the late 1980s, and one faction became a political party in 1991. The dissident wing FPMR/D is Chile's only remaining active terrorist group with less than thirty members.

BRAZIL

Brazil has become a seething hotbed for kidnappings and extortion. Although Brazil has a subversive and anti-Western group called the Tupac Katari Guerrilla Army (EGTK), the group's actions have been extremely limited. Brazil is famous in international terrorist circles for the pamphlet, *Mini-Manual of the Urban Guerrilla*, written by Carlos Marighella in 1969. On Tuesday, November 4, 1969, Carlos Marighella was assassinated in São Paulo. On that day, two missions were simultaneously interrupted. The first was the life of a man who, for nearly forty years, had been shaping theories in the struggle against the dominant system. The second was that of a determined urban guerrilla. Marighella was killed in an ambush as he was about to begin rural guerrilla warfare, the next step in his liberation cycle. He had the unique position of having made valuable contributions to the revolutionary cause in both theory and practice. During the last year of his life, as a parallel to the action he undertook, he wrote intensively to support his theories about the liberation of Brazil.

The *Mini-Manual of the Urban Guerrilla* has special importance. The work examines the conditions, characteristics, necessities, and methods of guerrilla warfare by the urban guerrilla, and demonstrates Marighella's sense of detail, organization, and mental clarity. It also shows, in passing, that Marighella was endowed with inexhaustible confidence and a youthfulness that belied his fifty-eight years. The manual became one of the principal books for every man

FIGURE 13-10   Map of Brazil (Central Intelligence Agency, *The World Factbook, 2008*).

who, in the inevitable battle against the bourgeoisie and imperialism, takes the road of armed rebellion.[37]

The Mini-Manual of the Urban Guerrilla

The chronic structural crisis characteristic of Brazil today, and its resultant political instability, is what has brought about the upsurge of revolutionary war in the country. The urban guerrilla is a man who fights the military dictatorship with arms, using unconventional methods. A political revolutionary and an ardent patriot, he is a fighter for his country's liberation, a friend of the people and of freedom. The guerrilla areas of operation are in the large Brazilian cities. There are also bandits, commonly known as outlaws, who work in the big cities. Many times, assaults by outlaws are taken as actions by urban guerrillas. The urban guerrilla, however, differs radically from the outlaw. The outlaw benefits personally from the action, and attacks indiscriminately without distinguishing between the exploited and the exploiters, which is why there are so many ordinary men and women among his victims. The urban guerrilla follows a political goal and only attacks the government, the big capitalists, and the foreign imperialists, particularly North Americans.

Another element just as prejudicial as the outlaw and also operating in the urban area is the right-wing counterrevolutionary who creates confusion, assaults banks, hurls bombs, kidnaps, assassinates, and commits crimes against urban guerrillas, revolutionary priests, students, and citizens who oppose fascism and seek democracy. The urban guerrilla is an implacable enemy of the government and systematically inflicts damage on the authorities that exercise power. The principal task of the urban guerrilla is to distract, to wear out, to demoralize the militarists, the military dictatorship and its repressive forces, and also to attack and destroy the wealth and property of the North Americans, and the Brazilian upper class.

The urban guerrilla is not afraid of dismantling and destroying the present Brazilian economic, political, and social system, for his aim is to help the rural guerrilla and to collaborate in the creation of a totally new and revolutionary social and political structure, with the armed people in power. He must have a certain minimal political understanding, and to gain that, he must read certain printed or mimeographed works such as follows:

- *Guerrilla Warfare by Che Guevara*
- *Memories of a Terrorist*
- *Some Questions about the Brazilian*
- *Guerrilla Operations and Tactics on Strategic Problems and Principles*
- *Certain Tactical Principles for Comrades Undertaking Guerrilla Operations*
- *Organizational Questions*
- *O Guerrilheiro, newspaper of the Brazilian revolutionary groups*

Personal Qualities of the Urban Guerrilla

His bravery and decisive nature characterize the urban guerrilla. He must be a good tactician and a good shot. The urban guerrilla must be a "person of great astuteness to compensate for the fact that he is not sufficiently strong in arms, ammunition, and equipment." The career militarists or the government police have modern arms and transport, and can go about anywhere freely, using the force of their power. The urban guerrilla does not have such resources at his disposal and leads a clandestine existence. Sometimes he is a convicted person or is out on parole and is obliged to use false documents.

Nevertheless, the urban guerrilla has a certain advantage over the conventional military or the police. It is that, while the military and the police act on behalf of the enemy, whom the people hate, the urban guerrilla defends a just cause, which is the people's cause.

The urban guerrilla's arms are inferior to the enemy's, but from a moral point of view, the urban guerrilla has an undeniable superiority. This moral superiority is what sustains the urban guerrilla. Thanks to it, the urban guerrilla can accomplish his principal duty, which is to attack and to survive. The urban guerrilla has to capture or divert arms from the enemy to be able to fight. Because his arms are not uniform, since what he has are expropriated or have fallen into hands in different ways, the urban guerrilla faces the problem of a variety of arms and a shortage of ammunition. Moreover, he has no place to practice shooting and marksmanship. These difficulties have to be surmounted, forcing the urban guerrilla to be imaginative and creative, qualities without which it would be impossible for him to carry out his role as a revolutionary.

The urban guerrilla must possess initiative, mobility, and flexibility, as well as versatility and a command of any situation. Initiative, especially, is an indispensable quality. It is not always possible to foresee everything. And the urban guerrilla cannot let himself become confused, or wait for orders. His duty is to act, to find adequate solutions for each problem he faces, and not to retreat. It is better to err acting than to do nothing for fear of erring. Without initiative there is no urban guerrilla warfare.[38]

URUGUAY AND PARAGUAY

In comparison to other Latin American states, Uruguay seemed to have an advantage with a prosperous economy built upon its sugar crop and its large export market. However, as has been evidenced in other regions of the world, the onset of severe economic downturns has led to the rise of worker parties, student revolts, and general unrest. This was the scenario in Uruguay when its economy crashed in the late 1950s. With the collapse came unrest, high unemployment, and inflation. The sugar workers had already organized labor unions, and by the end of the 1950s, the union was being led and influenced by extreme elements demanding social reforms and justice. Confrontation was the ultimate result.

National Liberation Movement (MLN): The Tupamaros

The Tupamaros movement grew out of the disillusionment of unionists, who marched on Montevideo, Uruguay's capital, in 1962. The name for the group is

FIGURE 13-11   Map of Uruguay (Central Intelligence Agency, *The World Factbook, 2008*).

FIGURE 13-12   Map of Paraguay (Central Intelligence Agency, *The World Factbook, 2008*).

taken from Tupac Amaru II, the leader of an eighteenth-century revolt over Spanish rule in Peru. The confrontations with police ended in numerous arrests. The government, unsympathetic to union demands, and rather than listen to its claims, portrayed the unionists as insurgents and guerrillas. Raul Sendic, a law student arrested during the clashes, rose to form the MLN in 1963. Sendic emerged from a brief spell in prison, bitter and determined to fight back. The government imposed more restrictions on rights and freedoms, which forged the beginnings of terrorism in Uruguay. Largely an agricultural country, to mount an effective campaign, the group decided that its base and battleground would be the streets of Montevideo. The aim of the MLN was not to replace the government, but to force issues and change policy for the redistribution of wealth. Although the MLN espoused Marxist theories, it did not engage in rhetoric at the expense of public support. By the end of the 1960s, the Tupamaros had grown significantly and were believed to number more than 2,000. The combatants had no doubt studied the *Mini-Manual of the Urban Guerrilla* as their activities and tactics mirrored Marighella's teachings. They used bank robberies and kidnapping to fund their operations. Their methods became an example for other terror groups operating in urban centers of the world. The police in Uruguay were unable to stop the growing surge of the Tupamaros. With the democratic fabric in tatters, the police resorted to torture to extract information and to deter would-be Tupamaros. Many suspected members of the MLN ended up in the country's top-security prison, the Penal de Libertad, under the control of the country's secret police, the *Organismo Coordinador de Actividades Anti-Subversivas*.[39]

Methods of torture were cruel, inhuman, but effective and included rapes, sensory deprivation beatings, burning, electrical shocks, and sleep deprivation.

The end for the Tupamaros came about unexpectedly. The chaos they had brought to the cities forced the government into a more vigorous application of repressive measures. In classic fashion, the Tupamaro's brand of terror forced the government to respond with its own brand of terror. However, they sought respectability and began to align with left-wing political movements to replace the government at the polling booth. This was a disaster, as left-wing constituents did not favor terrorism, and the bid for a socialist ticket failed. As socialists, they should have expected support from the working classes, but MLN was made up mainly of middle-class Uruguayans. With the failure of the political movement, a strong right-wing military government came into power. The populace endorsed its draconian measures in curbing the Tupamaros. The result was mass arrests and the end of MLN. The kidnapping of the British

Ambassador, Sir Geoffrey Jackson, in Montevideo in 1972 ultimately shattered the myth that the Tupamaros were invincible. Shortly after Jackson's release from captivity, a general election was held, and the *Frente Amplio* (Broad Front), a strong political supporter of the Tupamaros, was decimated at the polls. The government was returned to office with a clear mandate to try to end terrorism.

The Tupamaros serve as an example of how to organize an effective strike force of terrorists in an urban environment, using the city for cover and following the advice of the *Mini-Manual of the Urban Guerrilla*. Other terror groups have profited from this example in Northern Ireland and in West Germany. The tactics employed by these middle-class terrorists, as saviors of the poor of Montevideo, did not translate into popular support for the movement. To some extent, this organization was built on small independent units and a cell-like structure, also a hallmark of the Irish Republican Army.

Internationally, South American countries could become havens for Middle East and North African terrorist groups: not just a sanctuary but also a fertile recruiting, logistical, and financing region. Uruguay does not figure on the world map of terrorism but is an outspoken supporter of antiterrorism conventions in the region. Al-Said Hassan Mokhles, a suspected Armed Islamic Group (GIA) member, was discovered in Uruguay, and his presence immediately brought a request for extradition to Egypt where he was wanted on terrorist offences. GIA does have links with al Qaeda, and many Algerians have migrated to North America, in particular Canada, over the last two decades. Uruguay has also become a home base for the Chilean Urban Marxist Guerrilla movement, the Manuel Rodriguez Patriotic Front.

The terrorist organization Hezbollah has been active in the tri-border region where Argentina, Paraguay, and Brazil converge. Little has been done about Hezbollah's presence particularly in Brazil as that country does not recognize any issues with Hezbollah and appears unwilling or unable to confront the problem. The main issue here is that the Hezbollah are actively raising funds for terrorism activity elsewhere. Tracking terrorist fund-raising and financing is not a finite art, and Brazil has not had any success in this area. In addition, most South American countries with the exception of Argentina have not suffered from any Middle Eastern-influenced violence and are thus not motivated enough to go after Hezbollah. Hezbollah would certainly like to gain a foothold in Latin America and get closer to the United States to conduct intelligence operations. How extensive and well supported they are is still not known. Open support for Iran is continually being offered up by Venezuela's Hugo Chavez, and the specter of Hezbollah will be nearby!

ARGENTINA

Argentina has suffered through systematic human rights violations under strict military juntas since the mid-1970s. To escape those domestic problems, the military government called up their historic claims to the Falkland Islands in the South Atlantic. Argentina had claimed title to the islands, which are populated by British families. Before the battle for the Falklands (1982), Argentine's military had attempted to "remove" all political opponents to its regime. This was achieved by clandestine arrests, which were followed by the disappearance of those arrested. Brutalized and tortured bodies, dumped in the ocean, were pulled up in fishing nets.

Before World War II, Argentina had close ties to Germany. However, in 1945 the government of General Farrell severed its links and joined the allies in the defeat of Germany. Two of the most celebrated names associated with South American politics are Colonel Juan Domingo Peron and his equally famous wife, Eva. Peron was certainly responsible for initiating the use of what is

FIGURE 13-13 Map of Argentina (Central Intelligence Agency, *The World Factbook, 2008*).

now termed "death squads." His vision on coming to power as president in 1946 was to industrialize at the expense of the agricultural industry, which had been Argentina's economic mainstay for most of the century. With industrialization and heavy government spending came staggering inflation never before seen in Argentina. Left-wing political opposition to Peron's activities mounted, and as the 1950s dawned, Argentina was sliding down a dangerous slope, where food shortages and protests were the order of the day. In response, Peron nationalized the press and took total control over what was printed in the media. In 1949, he had created his own secret police force known as the CERT. CERT and its later version, the Division de Informacion Politicas Antidemocratic (DIPA), hid within its ranks a group designed for torture and repression called the Triple A, or the Argentine Anti-Communist Alliance. Peron was deposed in 1955, three years after the death of his wife, Eva.

The Triple A (AAA)

The AAA was an extreme right-wing death squad that functioned clandestinely at the beginning of the 1970s and consisted of members of the Argentine military and police. Many people suspected of being left-wing sympathizers were abducted, usually in the very early hours of the morning. The captors would explain that they were government agents. Death camps were set up apart from the normal prison structures of the country, making it almost impossible for relatives to locate those taken, let alone establish what kind of agency had detained them. There were forty-seven of these secret camps, which were similar to the concentration camps built by the Nazis, in World War II.[40]

As the years of unceasing military repression grew, so did the pressure from the Red Cross and Amnesty International who accused the military junta as accountable for those missing. In a remarkable piece of legislation passed by the Argentine government in 1979, those who were missing were presumed to be "legally dead" unless it could be proven otherwise!

International Terrorism in the Tri-Border Area (TBA)

The relatively lawless TBA region, the area where the borders of Paraguay, Brazil, and Argentina meet has been an area that has seen the development of international terrorist activity and which first came to notice with two bombings in Buenos Aires by Hezbollah in the early 1990s, the first

TERRORIST ATTACK BRIEF

Terrorist Group: Islamic Jihad

Case Facts: Five are killed and 106 wounded when a bomb destroys the Israeli Embassy building in Buenos Aires.

Investigation: Responsibility was claimed by Middle East terror group Islamic Jihad. The investigation was slow to proceed, and in 1994, a second bomb went off at a Jewish Community Center, also in Buenos Aires. The Argentine government did little to progress any investigation, and in 1998, evidence of Iranian government involvement was uncovered. The Argentine government expelled several diplomats, but since then no individual has been charged with any crime in relation to the embassy attack.

FIGURE 13-14 Bombing—Israeli Embassy—Buenos Aires—March 17, 1992. *Source*: Israeli Ministry of Foreign Affairs.

attack was a bombing of the Israeli Embassy which killed twenty-nine people, and this attack it is believed was aided by Iranian diplomats. The second attack was on a Jewish Community Center where eighty-five people were killed. In both instances, the finger is clearly pointed at Hezbollah who may well have been acting on behalf of Iran.

Fund-raising and recruitment for terrorist activities has gone relatively unchecked in the TBA and has for years drawn attention as a center for contraband smuggling, drug trafficking, and large-scale money laundering, in part because all of the countries whose borders are involved profit from the illicit trade. It is also an easy place to hide and move money. Estimates of the amount of drug money alone laundered through the two main urban centers in the TBA, Foz do Iguacu and Ciudad del Este, range as high as $12 billion a year. Hezbollah is not the only extreme Islamist group believed to operate in the Central American region as Intelligence Services have documented the presence of Hamas and al Qaeda.[41] Despite the presence of Islamists in the region, there have been no specific attacks in the last decade from them. It is likely that this area is used as a source of fund-raising for the various Islamists organization planning and coordination for operations elsewhere.

Montoneros

One of the military junta's main targets were the Montoneros (Movimiento Peronista Montonero) and its supporters. Set up as a left-wing Peronista movement after the death of Juan Peron, this group was active from 1975 to 1979. The Montoneros were violently opposed to the military takeover of the Argentine government. They attempted to organize the union movement as a cohort in their activities, but a brutal crackdown by the junta prevented any effective action in the cities, and the group had to settle for actions in the countryside. Their tactics were hit-and-run, using bombings and shootings. By 1979, the group had been totally destroyed.[42]

This is yet another example of how an extreme right-wing military government resorted to terrorism of its own to remain in control … by using torture, murder, and widespread intimidation.

CHILE

Chile had minor problems with terrorism from the Manual Rodriguez Patriotic Front, which was formed in 1983. As the armed wing of the Chilean Communist Party, it split into a faction, calling itself the Lautaro Youth Movement, which was a mixed bag of leftist elements and criminals that

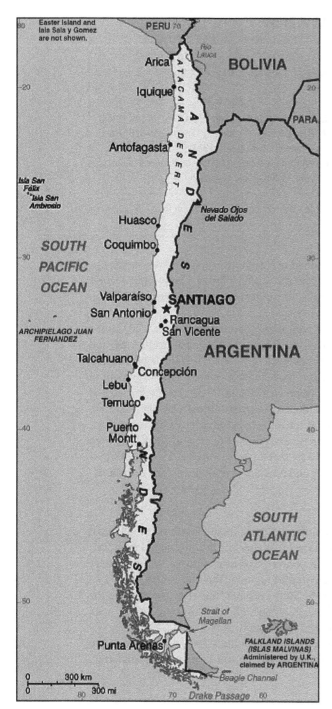

FIGURE 13-15   Map of Chile (Central Intelligence Agency, *The World Factbook, 2008*).

remained active through the early 1990s with the unlikely goal of overthrowing the government. The group targeted police and government officials and carried out bank robberies to fund its operations.

MILITARY DICTATORSHIP

General Augusto Pinochet, a military dictator of strong Fascist principles was one of the most significant influences in Chile over the past twenty-five years. He is considered by many as Chile's elder statesman. Few dictators ever successfully reach happy retirement, but Pinochet is an example of one who has "gone the distance," despite the appalling acts during his rule. Pinochet swept to power in 1973 during a bloody military coup that removed the Marxist regime responsible for the mismanagement of the country and its economy over a three-year period.

The Marxist leader Salvador Allende was the first democratically elected Marxist president to head any nation in the Western Hemisphere. Allende came to power in 1970 on a ticket promising social programs for Chileans. His government took immediate control of the country's copper mines and banking system. His huge increase in the minimum wage structure and attempts to keep the cost of consumer products at a low level fueled runaway inflation. Between 1971 and 1973, inflation rose by nearly 400 percent! The government was besieged on all sides. Violent protests began in the streets of Santiago. The military, assisted by the CIA, overthrew the Allende government on September 11, 1973. Allende was arrested and died in custody. Reports on the circumstances of his death vary from torture, execution, to suicide.

The Pinochet Years

The military coup, followed by yet another junta, was not widely popular. Fighting broke out between right-wing supporters of Pinochet and the extreme-left Communist elements. The junta cracked down hard on opposition by dissolving congress, restricting the freedom of the press, and privatizing nationalized industries. Pinochet banned all political opposition parties and ran the country as a dictatorship. The trigger point for the attempted coup was not a momentary aberration on the part of Pinochet; in fact, many of the high-ranking military generals actually served in the Allende cabinet. What caused the problems for the military was the inclusion of left-wing extremism into the fabric of Chile's society. Allende had placed Communist reactionaries in the armed forces to incite rebellion, and over 14,000 foreign agitators moved into Chile. These included Cuban DGI agents, who were in Chile to reorganize internal security for Allende, as well as Soviet, Czech, and North Korean military instructors and arms suppliers, and hard-line Spanish Communist Party members. Their intent was to organize revolutionary brigades to take on the established military. The 1970s were a decade of change for Central and South America, and insurgent terror groups and guerrilla movements were on the move from Montevideo to Managua.[43]

To stem the left-wing subversives, the Pinochet junta carried out mass arrests and used torture to gain both information and confessions. They arrested not only Chileans but also foreign subversive elements. These are the actions for which the international community wanted Pinochet held accountable. Executions were commonplace in Chile, and the targets were leftist politicians, trade unionists, and other activists. Many simply disappeared, never to be heard from again. The junta engaged semiofficial death squad organizations to do some of its dirty work. The Avengers of the Martyrs was a fascist paramilitary movement comprised mainly of military and police/security personnel. To ensure the security and paramilitary groups could conduct business in an unfettered manner, the military passed a decree to effectively denude the legal process and protection of the public. The Decree Law on Amnesty gave security forces total immunity from prosecution.

The Pinochet regime laid the foundation for a vibrant South American economy and passed it on to a democratic government that followed. Pinochet had turned Chile from a second-rate, Third World country into a strong market economy. Military dictators usually leave in the same violent manner by which they arrived in power, but Pinochet is considered by many in Chile to be a hero of the people, and to a great many others, a murderer.

In 1998, on a visit to Britain for back surgery, General Pinochet was arrested in his hospital bed and there were requests for his extradition. The highest court in Britain dealt a stunning blow to Pinochet, and in a stand for international law and justice, the British have hammered a nail into a portion of his coffin. Pinochet and the democratic government of Chile claimed he had diplomatic immunity as a former head of state and was therefore not subject to arrest and extradition. In the majority decision handed down in November 1998, Britain's Lord Nicholls commented: "The Vienna Convention on diplomatic relations may confer immunity in respect of acts performed in the exercise of functions, which international law recognizes as functions of a head of state, irrespective of the terms of his domestic constitution." Lord Nicholls further commented: "It hardly needs saying that the torture of his own subjects, or of aliens, would not be regarded by international law as a function of a head of state."[44]

Santiago's reactions to the decision led to waves of protest, as well as outpourings of relief. Pinochet subsequently returned to Chile and stood trial in what was termed the "Caravan of Death." Pinochet orchestrated political killings soon after he swept into power in 1973 and unleashed death squads to systematically execute political prisoners and subversives throughout the country. A ruling came down in March 2001, which was then appealed to the Chilean Supreme Court, which, in July 2002, accepted the earlier ruling that the former dictator was mentally unfit to stand trial. To many, his death on December 10, 2006, was a fitting end to his regime's horrendous abuse of civil liberties. On the international terror front, Chile experienced two terror-related incidents. In the wake of the 9-11 attacks, the U.S. embassy received a functional letter bomb, and an anthrax-laced letter was sent to a doctor's office. However, the composition of the anthrax did not match with those strains used in the U.S. attacks. In a wider investigation, the government of Chile began to take a serious interest in the activities of Lebanese businessman Assad Ahmed Mohamed Barakat. It is suspected that Barakat was involved in financial holdings and money transfers for the Lebanese Hezbollah terror group.

VENEZUELA

Venezuela was once considered a democratic oasis in a desert of military dictatorship, but not anymore. Unlike much of Latin America, Venezuela has had a history of democratic government since 1958, with lessening interference by the military. Venezuela suffers incursions by Colombian terrorists in the border villages and towns. Kidnapping and extortion are the main activities of both the National Liberation Army (ELN) and the Colombian People's Liberation Army (EPL).

Since the independence movement led by Venezuela's favorite son, Simon Bolivar, in the early 1800s, the country had been the home to a succession of military dictators. Venezuela began to prosper with the discovery of oil, becoming its main source of revenue. Mismanagement and corruption ended the military dictatorship of General Gomez in 1935, when the democratic movement, supported by the army, overthrew him and established a democratic government. The country has been ruled by two parties since 1958: the Accion Democratica (AD) and the Christian Democratic Party (COPIE). Each has had its share of periods in office. However, economic downturns have stalled government action on behalf of the many poverty-stricken Venezuelans. Although there is no active terror movement in the country, there are definite signs that reforms will be needed if democracy is to endure. The government has utilized severe measures to control the country in tough economic times. Hugo Chavez, president since 1999, seeks to implement his "21st Century Socialism," which purports to alleviate social ills while at the same time attacking capitalist globalization and existing democratic institutions. Current concerns include a weakening of democratic institutions, political polarization, a politicized military, drug-related violence along the Colombian border, overdependence on the petroleum industry with its price fluctuations, and irresponsible mining operations that are endangering the rain forest and indigenous peoples.[45]

There are also problems associated with cross-border incursions from Colombia and the probability that the

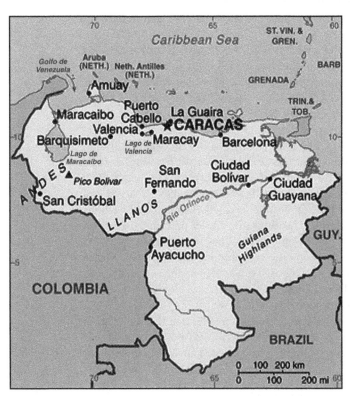

FIGURE 13-16   Map of Venezuela (Central Intelligence Agency, *The World Factbook, 2008*).

Venezuelan government has been turning a blind eye to such actions. For the landowners and ranchers in the border regions, this has meant reliance on vigilante squads and support from AUC in Colombia to combat the FARC incursions into Venezuela. Hugo Chavez had to contend with a coup attempt in April 2002, which briefly saw him ousted from power. A general strike in November 2002 shut down Venezuela's oil industry. Noticeably, the U.S. television news coverage had failed to note that this strike was not being led by the working-class masses but by the middle-class management population! In its attempt to unseat Chavez, the opposition party had attempted to illicit support for a coup from the United States; however, the Bush government was more concerned with global issues involving Iraq and North Korea and paid little attention to Venezuela. Chavez became rabidly anti-American with every speech he made. Before 2006, Chavez was little known to the U.S. public, but in his outburst at the UN General Assembly in September 2006, speaking the day after former president George W. Bush, he stated, "Yesterday the devil came here. Right here and it smells of sulfur still today." He made many odorous comments and called the U.S. president a drunkard and a terrorist and Condoleezza Rice (Secretary of State), a sexually frustrated and illiterate female; his goals were a direct challenge to the United States. Chavez sought alliances with most of the world's more extreme leaders, that is, Mahmoud Ahmadinejad of Iran, Bashar al-Assad of Syria, and Kim Jong-II of North Korea. Iranian factories are being constructed in Venezuela, and there are direct flights between Caracas and Tehran. He has been outspoken for his support of Hezbollah and been openly hostile to Israel for its Lebanon attacks in 2006. Clearly, he thinks he is a force to be reckoned with. Venezuela is oil rich and the current climb in oil prices has no doubt emboldened him, as his government reaps the riches from the soaring price of a barrel of oil. He has often threatened to cut off the supply of oil to the United States; however, this may not be a reality in the short term as Venezuela exports approximately 50 percent of its oil to the United States.

Chavez has also been involved in indirect talks with the FARC in an effort to have some of the numerous hostages released. In February 2008, the FARC released three hostages who had been held for more than six years. President Chavez caused considerable displeasure to the Colombian government by speaking directly with FARC, an action not sanctioned by the Colombians.

ECUADOR

Ecuador is not a region well known for terrorism and insurgency. In the past decade, it has remained relatively calm with the exception of the October 12, 2000, kidnapping of eight oil rig workers by armed men that lasted into early 2001.

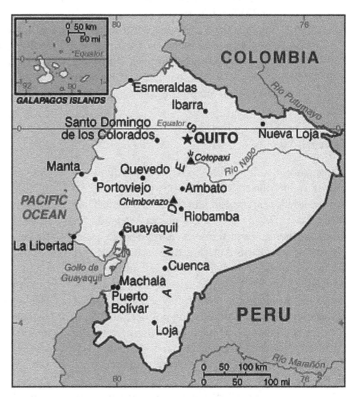

FIGURE 13-17 Map of Ecuador (Central Intelligence Agency, *The World Factbook, 2008*).

The hostage takers executed Ron Sander, one of the U.S. hostages. A little-known group calling itself the Revolutionary Armed Forces of Ecuador has taken credit for two bombs that exploded in the coastal city of Guayaquil. The FARE could be a front for the Revolutionary Armed Forces of Colombia (FARC) or a stand-alone group. Either way, its emergence suggests that the Colombian conflict soon will affect U.S. personnel and assets outside Colombia. In August 2002, a bomb attack on a McDonald's restaurant was claimed to be the work of an unknown terror group calling itself the FARE. FARE states that it is a prodigy of the Revolutionary Armed Forces of Colombia (FARC), and it threatened more violence and assassination. At this juncture, very little is known about the group, its makeup, or its aims. However, there is a probability that it could actually be a breakaway faction of the FARC and could be setting up in Ecuador to make the politicians wary of being aligned with the U.S. war on narcotics in the region. Elections held in October 2002, were a focal point for the FARE in its wish to influence any political outcome. Authorities have previously reported the presence of FARE, but no terror attacks have been previously attributed to the group, which authorities say may number several hundred members from both Ecuador and Colombia. The FARE does not appear to be linked to drug trafficking; however, if it is actually FARC by another name, narcotics trafficking may soon be on its agenda. The leftist governments of both Venezuela and Ecuador continue to lash out at their neighbor Colombia mainly for its pro-U.S. stance. In March 2008, Colombian aircraft crossed into Ecuador and killed Raul Reyes, raising the possibility of a military confrontation between the three. Ecuador has been tolerant of the presence of FARC rebels residing inside its territory and the March 2008 raid was roundly condemned by the main leftist governments in South America and this has fuelled Latin America's ideological divisions. Colombian President Alvaro Uribe had received vast sums for his campaign against the drug trade and FARC terrorists, and what was originally hailed as a major victory for the Uribe government became the focus of open hostility from Ecuador and Venezuela. Both countries view Colombia as a pawn of the United States. On the other hand, the Colombian military claimed to have discovered evidence that FARC was attempting to obtain materials to build a dirty bomb.

Summary

Central and South America have been mostly under strong right-wing military rule for many decades of the twentieth century, and into the twenty-first. They have also suffered the ravages of death squads. In studying the causes of terrorism and guerrilla activity throughout Latin America, there are trends that become apparent. In Mexico, El Salvador, Chile, and Uruguay, much of the activity was related to land claims, where the few wealthy landowners had immense influence on the ruling political and military governments. In protecting those interests, the extreme-right death squads operated with impunity. Violations of human rights and the prosecution of those responsible continue to the present. Argentina is recovering from the stringent rule of the military juntas of the 1980s and crushing humiliation and defeat in the Falkland Islands at the hands of the British. The loss of loved ones to death squads will continue to plague the citizens of new democracies as they strive to move forward. After four decades, Colombian terrorism seems likely to continue with an upsurge in attacks by FARC. The possibility that they would seek to use, and even build, a dirty bomb will give much cause for concern, as will the Hezbollah presence in the tri-border regions. South American countries still lead the way in kidnappings and extortion. The presence of Lebanese Hezbollah and Hamas members as well as the GIA will prompt U.S. power brokers to keep close watch on developments to ensure that international terrorism, with aims of attacking the United States and its interests, is not played out in the region.

Review Questions

1. What are the central issues in the long-running dispute in Colombia between FARC and the government?
2. What methods are used by FARC and others to exert influence over both the local populous and the government?
3. Describe how Mexican terrorism came about and why it has been easily sustained.
4. Why have military dictatorships been viewed as acceptable forms of government?
5. Describe some of the reasons why there has been little popular support in Peru for the Shining Path organization.
6. Which regions of South America are likely to be used by Islamic extremists as recruiting areas and regions for fund-raising?

Websites

1. **The Council on Foreign Relations**—*http://www.cfr. org/region/242/mexicol*
2. **Amnesty International**—*http://www.amnesty.org/en/ region/south-america*
3. **FBI Columbia Joint Terrorism Task Force**—*http:// Columbia.fbi.gov*
4. **Plan Columbia and Beyond**—*www.csmonitor. com/2006/0928/p01s03-woam.html*
5. **U.S. Department of Defense – CIA Che Guevara**— *http://www.paperlessarchives.com/guevara_.html*
6. **The Transnational Institute**—*http://www.tni.org*

End Notes

1. U.S. Census Bureau. http://www.census.gov/main/ www/popclock.html.
2. "Mexico, Post Rebellion Pains." *The Economist* (January 12, 2002, p. 35).
3. *Reuters News Service.* http://www.reuters.com/.
4. Piet van Lier: *War called Peace, Death of a Bishop* (1997). http:zena.securforum.com/znet/LAM/zGuatemala.html.
5. Mica Rosenberg, (February 9, 2006), www.Boston. com/news.
6. Frank M. Afflitto. Abstract from a paper presented at the Conference of the American Society of Criminology (San Diego, CA, November 20, 1997).
7. Global Intelligence Update. http://www.stratfor. com/standard/analysis.
8. "Patterns of Global Terrorism." *U.S. Department of State, Publication* 10321 (2008), http://www. strafor.com.
9. Jonathan R. White. *Terrorism: An Introduction* (Belmont, CA: Brooks Cole Publishing, August 2002, p. 157).
10. "Federal Research Division:Library of Congress Country Reports." *Nicaragua* (1996), http://countrystudies.us/nicaragua/.
11. The Kerry Committee Report (April 19, 1995).
12. *U.S. Immigration and Customs Service.* www.ice. gov/pi//investigations/comshield/index.htm.
13. "Anti-Gang Effort Leads to Indictment of MS-13 Gang Members," US Attorney's Office: Southern District of Texas (August 11, 2011), http://www. justice.gov.
14. *Mexican Drug Wars.* www.global security.org.
15. "Guatemalan Massacre Leaves 27 Dead." *Jane's Intelligence Review Country Risk Watch*, vol. 23, no. 6 (Coulsdon Surrey: IHS Jane's Sentinel House, June 2011, p. 5).
16. U.S. State Department International Information Programs. "Grossman Outlines Terrorist Threat to Colombia." Testimony by Ambassador Marc Grossman, Undersecretary of State for Political Affairs before the Senate Committee on Foreign Relations Sub-Committee for Western Hemisphere Affairs (April 24, 2003), http:///usinfo.state.gov/ topical/pol/terror.htm.
17. Immigration and Refugee Board of Canada, *Colombia: Revolutionary Armed Forces of Colombia (Fuerzas Armadas Revolucionarias de Colombia, FARC), including information on criminal activities, such as drug trafficking and kidnapping; state response to criminal activity (2009-February 2011)*, COL103709.E

(April 5, 2011), http://www.unhcr.org/refworld/docid/4dbfcc952.html, extracted April 6, 2012.

18. Kevin Whitelaw. The State Department is helping train elite police units to go after kidnappers and rescue hostages (February 27, 2008), www.USNews.com Inside Colombia's War on Kidnapping.

19. Stephanie Hanson. "Council on Foreign Relations." *FARC, ELN: Colombia's Left-Wing Guerrillas* (August 19, 2009), http://www.cfr.org/publication/9272/.

20. Stan Yarbo. *The Christian Science Monitor* (November 18, 1998).

21. Ibid.

22. U.S. Department of State International Information Programs. "U.S., Colombia Investigate Expansion of Terrorist Alliances." Charlene Porter Washington, File Staff Writer (April 25, 2002), http://usinfo.state.gov/topical/pol/terror02042500.htm.

23. Colombia Basic Information. http://www.infoplease.com/ipa/A0107419.html.

24. Noam Chomsky. "On the War on Drugs." Interviewed by Week Online *DRCNet* (February 8, 2002), http://www.chomsky.info/interviews/20020208.htm.

25. Mike Gray. *Drugs & Terrorism* (2001), http://www.narcoterror.org/mike_oped.htm.

26. U.S. Department of State Briefing Note (2008).

27. "Bureau for International Narcotics and Law Enforcement Affairs Program and Budget Guide." *Fiscal Year 2011* (US State Department, 2011).

28. Sam Dillon. "As Peru Votes, Insurgents Mystique Casts Shadow." *Miami Herald* (June 10, 1990, pp. A1, A26).

29. White. *Terrorism: An Introduction*, p. 82.

30. "The Shining Path Comes Back." *The Economist* (August 17, 1996, p. 35).

31. *Armed Conflict Reports* (Peru, 1980), http://www.ploughshares.ca/libraries/ACRText/ACR-Peru.html.

32. Gabriel Escobar. "Peruvian Guerrillas Hold Hundreds Hostage." *Washington Post*, Foreign Service (December 19, 1996).

33. CNN Interactive World News. "One Hostage Killed in Daring Peru Rescue." *CNN* (April 22, 1997), http://www.cnn.com/world19704/22/peru.update.late.

34. *CIA World Factbook*. Country Reports (2008), http://www.cia.gov/cia/publications/factbook/geos/bl.html.

35. San Jose State University, Economics Department. http://www2.sjsu.edu/faculty/watkiins/bolivia.htm.

36. "La Massacre del Valle de Cochabamba." *La Paz Cadernos* "Justicia Y Paz," (1975).

37. N. A. Keck. CPP. ASIS Presentation Paper (May 16, 1996).

38. Carlos Marighella. *Mini-Manual of the Urban Guerrilla* (Pamphlet, 1969, pp. 1–2).

39. Bruce Quarrie. *The World's Secret Police* (London: Octobus Books Ltd., 1986, p. 48).

40. Quarrie. *The World's Secret Police*.

41. Douglas Farah. "Hezbollah's External Support Network in West Africa and Latin America." (International Assessment and Strategy Center, August 4, 2006). www.strategycenter.net/research/pubID.118/pub_detail.asp.

42. White. *Terrorism: An Introduction*, pp. 48, 49.

43. Arnaud de Borchgrave. "Demonized for Killing a Left-Wing Plot." *The Washington Times* (October 1998, p. A15).

44. International News, *The Globe and Mail* (Canada, November 26, 1998).

45. "Country Reports Venezuela." *CIA World Factbook*. https://www.cia.gov/library/publications/the-world-factbook/geos/ve.html#top.

PART THREE

The War on Terror

14

Countering Terrorism

Who Dares Wins

—Motto, British Special Air Service Regiment

LEARNING OBJECTIVES

After studying this chapter, the student should be able to:

1. Discuss the evolving role of counterterrorism units and their original formation.

2. Understand the aspects of WMD and the threats they pose.

3. Discuss why intelligence sharing is such a key ingredient in the fight against terrorism.

4. Review and understand the various international conventions promulgated to combat acts of terrorism.

KEY WORDS TO NOTE

Emergency Provisions—Northern Ireland (Emergency Provisions) Act 1973—Established the Diplock Courts in which terrorist offences could be tried by a judge without a jury

General Staff Reconnaissance Unit Number 69—Formed in 1957; also known as Sayeret Mat'kal, the leading unit in Israel's counterterrorism arsenal

Grenzschutzgruppe 9 (GSG-9)—German Police unit formed as a direct result of the Munich Olympic Games massacre

Groupment d'intervention de la Gendarmerie Nationale (GIGN)—France's national police antiterror strike force

Interpol—International Criminal Police Organization created in 1923, it facilitates cross-border police cooperation and supports and assists all organizations, authorities, and services whose mission is to prevent or combat international crime

Joint Task Force 2 (JTF-2)—Canadian Forces special operations unit

Major Criminal Hijack (MCHJ)—International Maritime Organization definition as major transnational organized crimes at sea

Nerve Agents—A class of phosphorous containing organic chemicals

Radiological Dispersal Device (RDD)—A weapon designed to spread radiological materials

Special Air Service (SAS) Regiment—Elite British military unit formed in North Africa during World War II

Special Boat Squadron (SBS)—Waterborne counterpart to the SAS

Vesicants—Blistering agent used in chemical weapons

OVERVIEW

Since September 11, 2001, the world has had to take stock of the way it counters what has evolved into a global threat. The threats emanate not only from al Qaeda but also from religiously motivated Islamists, while al Qaeda has transformed itself into something akin to a very virulent cult following for extremist, ideological Islamists. During the last four decades of the twentieth century, the emphasis for countering terrorist attacks was focused upon the specific terrorist groups, targeting specific areas within many defined regions or countries. Urban terrorism, particularly in Western democracies, was unfamiliar to the security forces of most countries until the 1970s. Terrorist attacks such as the 1972 Munich Olympic Games massacre of Israeli athletes showed the world how unprepared security/police forces were at handling such situations. Individual countries had thus established elite counterterror units for both domestic and foreign deployment. Not a day passes without mention of terrorism or an insurgent atrocity or bombing in some area of the world. The United States has enacted legislation that is considered draconian in application and also, some would say, attacks U.S. civil liberties—laws that are barely raising a whimper from the public. The structure of U.S. security has been radically transformed, as a result of the attacks on September 11, 2001. The emphasis now is on protecting vital areas of national infrastructure, food sources, the material supply chain, roads, railways, aviation, bridges, dams, and computer systems. The government and its intelligence services are looking to the future on how to hopefully protect, prevent, deter, and detect the next major terror event.

This chapter looks at the unconventional forces that have been established to counter terror and discusses what may have changed since 9-11, particularly in the United States and Europe. We discuss attitudes aimed toward countering the scourge of terrorism. We will review the most effective and recognized response units for countering terrorism from around the world, some well known, and others less so.

Aviation still continues to present itself as a target of choice for terrorists, so we will look at the protection of aviation to both facilities and aircraft in flight. Should we develop and implement new efforts and systems to prevent hand-held missile attacks against civilian airliners? How do we propose to prevent and respond to chemical and biological threats? How will countries handle the threat of medically implanted explosives in the bodies of suicide terrorists?

If the primary objective of countering terrorism is the protection of democratic institutions, how far can we go in reaching that objective? Can we solve the issue of political violence, if governments and dictatorships are prepared to sacrifice all considerations of basic humanity and then totally ignore constitutional and judicial rights?[1]

THE ROLES FOR COUNTERTERRORISM

Are the actions of subversive groups, insurgents, and terrorists considered criminal behavior? Throughout this text the issue continues to surface, whether the issue of terrorism is in the Far East, Near East, Middle East, Europe, or North America and how best to legislate against those bent on terrorism. In many countries, legislation has been enacted not only to ban membership in terror organizations but also to sometimes allow for certain suspensions of civil rights to facilitate law enforcement and intelligence activities. To implement successfully in a democratic society requires that the government ensure that such legislation requires review and renewal on a regular basis. In the United Kingdom, the legislation restricting the Irish Republican Army and other terrorist groups required the government to regularly justify its need for such drastic powers because, without such justification, it would automatically lapse.

The terrorist tactics that strike fear in the public for political gain are well documented. Terror and insurgent groups operating in Iraq used a new tactic in 2004 and 2005, the Internet, and that continues with Jihadist website more popular than can be imagined. At the touch of a computer mouse, millions were witness to the grizzly decapitation of Western hostages. The political gain the terrorists seek, in this instance, is to place enormous pressure on government to respond in a specific manner—to either act or react in a determined manner. This has been clearly shown in the United Kingdom, where the Provisional IRA has waged a campaign of indiscriminate violence against authorities and innocent civilians. One of the earliest terror incidents in Great Britain was an attack on the Parachute Regiment Officers' Mess in Aldershot, southern England, which is located about 50 miles southwest of London. The bomb attack took place on February 22, 1972, and killed five female kitchen attendants and a padre and injured nineteen others. The public viewed the attack as reprisal for the "Bloody Sunday" massacre by British paratroopers in Northern Ireland that had claimed the lives of thirteen civilians three weeks prior to the Aldershot bombing.

The reaction depicted in local and national press coverage was complete outrage at such a senseless act. Immediately after the bombing, there were sporadic incidents against local Irish families, who were intimidated and even assaulted. The same reaction occurred after Irish republican terrorists struck at public houses in Guildford and Birmingham, killing and injuring indiscriminately. Calls for restraint from both sides of the British political and religious spectrum went out and diffused a major outpouring of hatred against the several million Irish citizens who have coexisted peacefully alongside their British counterparts.

In the same manner, the events of 9-11 allowed a frantic American public to then think that every Muslim or Arab was a terrorist in waiting. The way we regarded our ethnically and religiously different neighbors suddenly changed. It would be incorrect to cast a suspicious eye at every "Muslim-looking" person. Government intelligence and security forces have been criticized for "racially profiling" specific ethnic and religious groups. On 9-11, the attackers were of Middle East and North African origin, but does the color of the skin determine a person's political and ideological status in society? Intelligence, of course, is not the sole domain of their governments; in nearly all instances, the planning for any major assault, or a terrorist attack, has involvement in the gathering of intelligence by the terrorist group, individual, or organization. In the case of 9-11, there was ample time and opportunity for the terrorist groups to openly view and study the methods used at security checkpoints of the targeted airports, and, no doubt, they conducted dummy runs. In the theater of Northern Ireland, the Provisional Irish Republican Army (PIRA) has always used intelligence gathering successfully to execute operations and has used tactics designed to strike at security forces as they respond to a bomb attack. We have seen insurgents in Iraq and Afghanistan using this same tactic as they detonate one car bomb, and then a second when rescue workers and security personnel arrive on scene.

In the same way, we cannot characterize any group purely by their religious beliefs. Not every Catholic is, by any stretch of the imagination, a supporter of the Provisional Irish Republican Army and neither must one now make the mistake that every swarthy skinned person is therefore an Islamic extremist. Immigration must come under specific scrutiny in both the United States and Canada, as well as review method and process by which students and visitors visas are issued and how checks are made.

The problem for Americans, if, in fact it is considered a problem, is that they enjoy a free and open democracy and value their freedom of speech, their freedom of association, and an ability to travel without undue hindrance. This concept is in stark contrast to many countries, where such liberties are not accepted. The events of 9-11 were perpetrated by people who took advantage of those freedoms and liberties, and they will continue to attempt to destroy those values and freedoms wherever they can.

Maintaining Order

The past examples of the "Irish Troubles" have been remarkable in many respects. In Britain and Northern Ireland, the role of the policeman had always been very public, and the typical British "Bobby" was always on hand to assist. During the terrorist bombing campaigns of mainland Britain, from the late 1960 to 2000, the police had not resorted to a system of rigid rules and control. As has been evidenced in many Latin American countries, terrorist threats and very harsh intimidation have too often been met by even harsher measures inflicted by military and paramilitary police. For the British, terror against the public, in general, reached epidemic proportions in the 1970s. But order and calm prevailed, and public outrage was contained. Rather than form vigilante groups to hunt down suspected terrorists, the British public and media were fully supportive of police actions. TV news showed the police as the front-line troops, always the first on the scene of whatever new atrocity the PIRA or others had perpetrated. In the 1970s, London became a virtual battleground, but sound police tactics and investigative techniques did far more to bring the terrorists to justice than the suspension of any civil liberties might have done.

In many countries, armed and aggressive police forces are a reality. That was not the case in Great Britain, where police were predominately unarmed throughout the PIRA crisis. The police adhered to their role of identifying, tracking down, and apprehending the terrorists, just as they would any criminal. Police investigations are all about the necessity to gather information, intelligence, and, ultimately, solid evidence. Britain's Special Branch, which deals with terrorists, took the lead in gathering intelligence on subversive Irish groups operating in Northern Ireland and Great Britain. Success for such efforts, however, must be as a result of cooperation among police, the public, and the media. As evident in the United States, such cooperation among agencies can often be strained. Some police agencies jealously guard not only sources but information as well. The public is usually the last to know the true story. There is no simple right or wrong answers with the tactics in combating terrorism. There are, however, many examples of (how and how not) to deal with terrorist situations.

The most open display of police weaponry up until the terrorist attacks in 2005 was at London's Heathrow Airport, which has been the site of numerous false alarms, as well as actual terrorist bombings and mortar attacks carried out by Irish terrorists. The message is clearly sent that the police are ready to respond with overwhelming force. Sadly, since the London subway attack, the sight of armed police in the capital is now as common as it is in the United States.

Racial Profiling

In a world where we not only have to be seen to be politically correct but also to actually apply that correctness to such issues as national security is a considerable challenge. Clearly, the overall reliance on race as the predetermining factor when there are many other avenues or tools for law enforcement to use is incorrect. However, the mere mention of the word "profiling" gets politicians and rights groups in an uproar. The ultimate solution, one that would most effectively strike a balance between the preservation of civil liberties and the need for heightened security, has been elusive. Increased polarization about the effectiveness of racial profiling and its application by law enforcement toward terrorism will continue to be hotly debated. There are two kinds of glaring mistakes we could potentially make in regard to terrorism: One is failing to identify terrorists because we don't want to offend anyone, and two, investigating someone who resembles the profile of a terrorist and therefore upsetting them as a result if the person is not a terrorist.[2] An extreme example of what can go wrong relates to the London Underground bombing threat in 2005 where police had a suspect under surveillance at an apartment block in the capital. A male, who was seen leaving the premises, was challenged by police but did not stop. The police had a new "shoot to kill" policy if they "suspected" a suicide bomber. The unfortunate man was wearing a backpack and ran down into the Stockwell underground station, at which point he was shot five times in the head at point blank range. It turned out that Jean Charles de Menezes, twenty-seven, was not involved in terrorism but was a migrant worker possibly working illegally in the country.

Repression

To determine whether a state's repressive actions against terror are effective, one only has to examine the Soviet Union—before the fall of the Communist regime. Very few, if any, kinds of terrorist attacks were either recorded or reported in the former Soviet Union, which had a thriving community of secret police and thousands of informers permeating both business and society. This made it almost impossible for subversive ideas to become reality. The KGB would almost always snuff out such plots before they could be executed. With the breakup of the Soviet Union, we have witnessed a significant increase in both criminal and terrorist activities. The fall of the Soviet Union was so sudden and the Russian Federation of States underwent such rapid change that it eventually brought about the collapse of the state and of the well-structured and supported police service. In a vast empire that had relied on the state police for all forms of investigations and tactics, both overt and covert, there was now only chaos and a vacuum. The vacuum was filled by criminal and subversive elements that filled the void vacated by established authority.

The drastic reduction in the need for nuclear weapons capability created a ready illegal market in which radical, rogue governments could acquire nuclear technology and even create devices, especially if they could afford to bid at the highest prices. While no terror group has actually used a nuclear device so far, there is an obvious concern that the ingredients to make a "dirty bomb" could well come out of the former Soviet states where controls are weak and the tracking of such materials is suspect.

Great Britain, since the 1990s, is a very different battleground altogether. With ever-increasing demands on civilian police forces, they have adopted a significant "Big Brother" approach to their duties, maintaining a watchful eye on the communities they serve. Closed-circuit television cameras that monitor the heart of the major cities, as well as the network of the major motorway systems, have aided in the search for serious criminals and terrorists. Civil libertarians and the extreme left-wing agitators may argue that it is an invasion of privacy, but the London Metropolitan Police have had indisputable success in tracking down terrorists who abandon vehicles packed with explosives.

To observers, it would have been an acceptable solution in the wake of the PIRA bombing campaign to unleash the army against what were perceived to be vicious and callous terrorists. One must keep in mind that an army's main role is that of national defense, not policing. In Northern Ireland, when the Royal Ulster Constabulary was unable to protect Catholics from Protestant violence, the army was called in to "assist." That assistance to the Catholic community became the rallying call for the under-equipped Irish Republican Army of the day. As matters further deteriorated at the end of the 1960s, the army was brought into a policing role that involved searches of houses for weapons. At the very least, the army's actions were heavy handed and the soldiers became the objects of hatred and scorn for the local Catholics they were attempting to protect.

Military responses to terror events have also been graphically emphasized by the Israeli use of heavy armor, helicopters, and fighter aircraft to attack elements of Hamas in the West Bank and Gaza regions. Winning the war in Iraq is a point in question; winning the peace has been something else altogether. While military tactics have been used in attempts to "pacify" large areas of Iraq, little consideration was given to the ethnic, religious, clan, and social structures that fuel the counterinsurgency campaigns. Israel mounted a campaign in 2002 to identify locations where suspected terrorist leaders were and then hit them with extreme force. The problem was that Israel was actually targeting areas where civilians lived. Collateral damage can always occur where terrorists are concerned; however, firing rockets into densely packed apartment buildings with the express intent to kill one suspected terrorist will invariably result in the deaths of innocent civilians. We see and hear daily how many American soldiers are killed and injured in Iraq or Afghanistan but little or no figures are available on the significant casualty figures for the Iraqi or Afghan population when troops target a civilian area where insurgents are hiding. The international community questions Israel's actions but has not done so of the United States in regard to Iraq. Of note here is that Israel's military actions have not been successful in curtailing the never-ending cycle of violence in Israeli cities and in the Palestinian areas of the West Bank and Gaza Strip, nor has U.S. policy in Iraq or Afghanistan quelled the insurgency there. From Israel's perspective, its intelligence network has become so efficient in targeting suspected terror elements that it will continue targeting civilian areas as a means of routing out terrorists.

NORTHERN IRELAND

Without imposing martial law in Northern Ireland, the British government used a statutory instrument to control the lawlessness of the terror groups operating against security forces in the province. Special powers to deal with "The Troubles" came into effect in 1973. The Northern Ireland (**Emergency Provisions**) Act empowered the military to have a greater impact in dealing with the terrorists. "No go" areas sprang up in Belfast and Londonderry during the Troubles, allowing terrorists to remain in their "safe houses" within the communities they were fighting to protect. The emergency provisions gave sweeping powers to the military to search houses at any time without the necessity of search warrants. The security forces could detain and question anyone for up to four hours. These methods allowed the military to build up a significant database of information about the people of Northern Ireland. From 1972 to 1976, the army searched nearly 250,000 houses and uncovered 5,800 weapons and 661,000 rounds of ammunition. Added to these powers was the internment of active members of terrorist organizations. Hundreds of Irishmen were interned in the 1970s and, in hindsight, brought the Provisional IRA to the brink of defeat. Nearly all its executive and operations groups were either serving prison sentences or interned.[3] The IRA's call for a Christmas truce in 1974 was made from a position of extreme weakness. After all, there was no way IRA demands for the swift total withdrawal of the British from Northern Ireland and general amnesty for all convicted terrorists would be met. It would be another twenty-four years before the IRA terrorists would walk out of prison as part of the Good Friday Agreement of 1998.

Legislation

Many operational methods and legislated practices can be put into place, but it must ensure that civil liberties are not abrogated to such an extent that the public is duly affected by their restrictive nature. Over the past forty years, there have been significant pieces of legislation and internationally recognized conventions aimed at curbing and countering terrorist activities. The first major terror attacks that attracted global attention involved PLO hijackings of commercial airliners. Those hijackings coupled with the ineptitude of most governments in handling such crises, prompted international antihijacking legislation to be drafted. It also prompted a more fundamental approach by one of the target states, Israel.

Israel was one of the first states to provide trained and armed "sky marshals" on all of its aircraft. For all El Al flights, specially trained staff conducts stringent physical and profile security checks on every passenger. So effective was the El Al approach that the terrorists had to find a "soft underbelly" to attack. This, in several instances, was a ground-level attack at airport check-in counters and attempts to shoot down aircraft by means of RPG-7 rockets, as was the case with the failed attack by Black September terrorists at Orly Airport in France. The RPG-7 is a reloadable, shoulder-fired, muzzle-loaded, recoilless antitank and antipersonnel rocket-propelled grenade launcher that launches fin-stabilized, oversized rocket-assisted HEAT grenade from a smoothbore 40 mm tube. The launcher with optical sights weighs 15.9 pounds and has a maximum, effective range of 300 meters against moving point targets and 500 meters against stationary point targets and therefore ideal for use in and around airports and airfields.

The fundamental principle of international legislative instruments, such as the Chicago Convention and, in particular, Annex 17, was that they required member states to safeguard global air transportation from acts of unlawful interference. The convention applied a common set of standards for the security of international civil aviation.

TERRORISM AND AVIATION

Attacks against airliners has long been a choice target for terrorists dating back to the 1970s, and remains so today; however, 9-11 laid bare the blatant incompetence of airport security that Americans had become used to prior to that fateful date. The inadequacies of the airline security program to protect passengers flying out of international airports in the United States was totally exposed. Although aviation security was thrust to the forefront in 2001, the problem of lax airport security had been around for decades. In 1968, there were twenty-seven hijackings and attempts to hijack commercial airliners to Cuba. In 1969, Palestinian terrorists were responsible for a large majority of the eighty-two hijackings worldwide as they attempted to publicize their cause and to put pressure on the Israeli government to release Palestinian prisoners. It would be grossly unfair to be critical of only U.S. aviation when the problem is systemic across all countries, with the possible exception of Israel. The Federal Aviation Administration (FAA) has the responsibility for the safety of U.S. civil aviation. Although it has an excellent staff with immense expertise, it was severely hampered in its ability to implement the changes needed to protect civil aviation from terror attacks inside the United States. This was, in part, because the FAA lacked the funding for research and development of new technology. Also, a powerful aviation lobby had been successful in blocking some of the necessary changes. There are international conventions that cover protocols for dealing with hijackings, aside from the criminal statutes that nation-states have promulgated to deal with individual criminal acts. The enacting of international treaties covers the issue of international terrorism and the hijacking of aircraft. Twelve significant conventions, developed over the last sixty years and related to terrorism, are as follows:

1. Convention on Offenses and Certain Other Acts Committed on Board Aircraft ("Tokyo Convention," 1963—safety of aviation):
   - Applies to acts affecting in-flight safety;
   - Authorizes the aircraft commander to impose reasonable measures, including restraint, on any person he or she has reason to believe has committed or is about to commit such an act, when necessary to protect the safety of the aircraft;
   - Requires contracting states to take custody of offenders and to return control of the aircraft to the lawful commander.
2. Convention for the Suppression of Unlawful Seizure of Aircraft ("Hague Convention," 1970—aircraft hijackings):
   - Makes it an offense for any person on board an aircraft in flight [to] "unlawfully, by force or threat thereof, or any other form of intimidation, [to] seize or exercise control of that aircraft" or to attempt to do so;
   - Requires parties to the convention to make hijackings punishable by "severe penalties";
   - Requires parties that have custody of offenders to either extradite the offender or submit the case for prosecution;
   - Requires parties to assist each other in connection with criminal proceedings brought under the convention.
3. Convention for the Suppression of Unlawful Acts against the Safety of Civil Aviation ("Montreal Convention," 1971—applies to acts of aviation sabotage such as bombings aboard aircraft in flight):
   - Makes it an offense for any person unlawfully and intentionally to perform an act of violence against a person on board an aircraft in flight, if that act is likely to endanger the safety of that aircraft; to place an explosive device on an aircraft; and to attempt such acts or be an accomplice of a person who performs or attempts to perform such acts;
   - Requires parties to the convention to make offenses punishable by "severe penalties";
   - Requires parties that have custody of offenders to either extradite the offender or submit the case for prosecution.
4. Convention on the Prevention and Punishment of Crimes against Internationally Protected Persons (1973—outlaws attacks on senior government officials and diplomats):
   - Defines internationally protected person as a Head of State, a Minister for Foreign Affairs, a representative or official of a state or of an international organization who is entitled to special protection from attack under international law;

- Requires each party to criminalize and make punishable "by appropriate penalties which take into account their grave nature," the intentional murder, kidnapping, or other attack upon the person or liberty of an internationally protected person, a violent attack upon the official premises, the private accommodations, or the means of transport of such person; a threat or attempt to commit such an attack; and an act "constituting participation as an accomplice."

5. International Convention against the Taking of Hostages ("Hostages Convention," 1979):
   - Provides that "any person who seizes or detains and threatens to kill, to injure, or to continue to detain another person in order to compel a third party, namely, a State, an international intergovernmental organization, a natural or juridical person, or a group of persons, to do or abstain from doing any act as an explicit or implicit condition for the release of the hostage commits the offense of taking of hostage within the meaning of this Convention."

6. Convention on the Physical Protection of Nuclear Material ("Nuclear Materials Convention," 1980—combats unlawful taking and use of nuclear material):
   - Criminalizes the unlawful possession, use, transfer, etc., of nuclear material, the theft of nuclear material, and threats to use nuclear material to cause death or serious injury to any person or substantial property damage.

7. Protocol for the Suppression of Unlawful Acts of Violence at Airports Serving International Civil Aviation, supplementary to the Convention for the Suppression of Unlawful Acts against the Safety of Civil Aviation (extends and supplements the Montreal Convention on Air Safety, 1988):
   - Extends the provisions of the Montreal Convention (see No. 3) to encompass terrorist acts at airports serving international civil aviation.

8. Convention for the Suppression of Unlawful Acts against the Safety of Maritime Navigation (1988—applies to terrorist activities on ships):
   - Establishes a legal regime applicable to acts against international maritime navigation that is similar to the regimes established against international aviation;
   - Makes it an offense for a person unlawfully and intentionally to seize or exercise control over a ship by force, threat, or intimidation; to perform an act of violence against a person on board a ship if that act is likely to endanger the safe navigation of the ship; to place a destructive device or substance aboard a ship; and other acts against the safety of ships.

9. Protocol for the Suppression of Unlawful Acts against the Safety of Fixed Platforms Located on the Continental Shelf (1988—applies to the terrorist activities on fixed offshore platforms):
   - Establishes a legal regime applicable to acts against fixed platforms on the continental shelf that is similar to the regimes established against international aviation.

10. Convention on the Marking of Plastic Explosives for the Purpose of Detection (1991—provides for chemical marking to facilitate detection of plastic explosives [e.g., to combat aircraft sabotage]):
    - Designed to control and limit the use of unmarked and undetectable plastic explosives (negotiated in the aftermath of the 1988 Pan Am 103 bombing);
    - Parties are obligated in their respective territories to ensure effective control over "unmarked" plastic explosive (i.e., those that do not contain one of the detection agents described in the Technical Annex to the treaty);

- Generally speaking, each party must, among other things: take necessary and effective measures to prohibit and prevent the manufacture of unmarked plastic explosives; prevent the movement of unmarked plastic explosives into or out of its territory; exercise strict and effective control over possession and transfer of unmarked explosives made or imported prior to the entry-into-force of the convention; ensure that all stocks of such unmarked explosives not held by the military or police are destroyed or consumed, marked, or rendered permanently ineffective within three years; take necessary measures to ensure that unmarked plastic explosives held by the military or police, are destroyed or consumed, marked, or then rendered permanently ineffective within fifteen years; and, ensure the destruction, as soon as possible, of any unmarked explosives manufactured after the date-of-entry into force of the convention for that state.

11. International Convention for the Suppression of Terrorist Bombing (1997, UN General Assembly Resolution):
  - Creates a regime of universal jurisdiction over the unlawful and intentional use of explosives and other lethal devices in, into, or against various defined public places with intent to kill or cause serious bodily injury, or with intent to cause extensive destruction of the public place.

12. International Convention for the Suppression of the Financing of Terrorism (1999):
  - Requires parties to take steps to prevent and counteract the financing of terrorists, whether direct or indirect, though groups claiming to have charitable, social or cultural goals or which also engage in such illicit activities as drug trafficking or gun running;
  - Commits states to hold those who finance terrorism criminally, civilly or administratively liable for such acts;
  - Provides for the identification, freezing, and seizure of funds allocated for terrorist activities, as well as for the sharing of the forfeited funds with other states on a case-by-case basis. Bank secrecy will no longer be justification for refusing to cooperate.[4]

The application of an acceptable level of aviation security is well documented and was graphically detailed in a statement before the House of Representatives, Government Activities and Transportation Subcommittee in September 1989 by Homer Boynton, one year after the Pan Am disaster over Lockerbie, Scotland. Homer Boynton, security director of American Airlines, stated to the subcommittee that "In 1988, ICAO estimated that worldwide, 1.1 billion passengers flew on board 1,100 commercial aircraft, on 38,000–40,000 flight segments. During this period one explosive device caused the awful aviation disaster over Lockerbie, Scotland. If one looks at these statistics in their totality, security personnel were seeking one explosive device carried by one passenger among 1.1 billion passengers."[5]

Taking Boynton's comments in the context of the 9-11 events seems to underscore the point that even though security agents are on the job, they are not necessarily going to find everything. Unfortunately, the U.S. system had been so deplorable for the previous two decades; it is surprising that such an event had not happened earlier. Boynton's comments would seem to point the finger at security screeners missing a bomb in baggage, when, in fact, that was not the specific case in Pan Am 103; there were more factors to the inherent risk that passengers were taking by flying Pan Am in 1988. The President's Commission on Aviation and Terrorism concluded in 1990 that Pan Am was basically an accident waiting to happen and the Lockerbie disaster was preventable.

What are the undisputed facts in this case? A terrorist was able to place a bomb in a suitcase that went on board Pan Am 103. The bomb detonated at 31,000 feet, killing 259 persons on the aircraft and 11 on the ground. If this was preventable, perhaps it is important to understand how easy it was in 1988 for human elements to come into play. After the FAA inspected Pan Am's operation at Frankfurt, West Germany, it was concerned with the airline's lack of a verifiable tracking system for interline bags (i.e., bags transferring from other airlines) and the confused state of its passenger screening process. The FAA inspector wrote, "The system, trying to control approximately 4,500 passengers and 28 flights per day, is being held together only by a very labor-intensive operation and the tenuous threads of luck." The inspector went on to condone the actions by adding: "It appears the minimum FAA requirements are being met." Luck, however, was not on the side of passengers of Pan Am 103 in 1988. Among the many questions being asked after the Lockerbie bombing was, "How did the interline bag get onto the flight?" The answer to that is "with ease," given the vagaries of the systems at that time. Reconciliation of passengers with their baggage is a central issue—the requirement being that an aircraft on an international flight will only carry bags for the passengers it has checked in for the flight. Having stated that, there is obviously a weak link that is ready to be exposed by the current Islamic extremist terrorists prepared to die for their beliefs. The strategy for 9-11 was to identify the weaknesses of aviation security and exploit them in order to carry out the suicide mission. Purely ensuring that passengers fly with their baggage will not prevent a suicide attack.

Looking ahead, the old ways of doing things are gone forever. The U.S. Department of Homeland Security is implementing next-generation technology to identify many multifaceted threats, not only to aviation but also to a whole gambit of possible targets, in the fields of mass transit, ports, airports, and railways. Looking back at Pan American Airlines in 1988, one of the main problems was that the screening process for interline bags was by X-ray detection. Even with the X-ray technology in place, the system was incapable of detecting the trace elements of the Semtex explosive used in the Lockerbie explosion. What could have been detected were the sources used to detonate the explosive. As is so often the case, human error played a part in the bombings, as well as a lack of sufficient technology to detect the specific explosive. In Pan Am's defense, it informed the President's Commission that the FAA director of Aviation had given the airline verbal approval to X-ray interline bags rather than searching or reconciling them with passengers, which, not surprisingly, the FAA denied.

There are some eerie similarities between the intelligence failings in 1988 and what went wrong, thirteen years later, on 9-11. Prior to the bombing of Pan Am 103, the intelligence community had received warnings that trouble was brewing in Europe. A total of nine security bulletins that could have had relevance to the Pan Am tragedy were issued between June and December 1988. One bulletin described how a Toshiba radio cassette player, containing a fully primed bomb with a barometric trigger, was found by the West German police in a vehicle belonging to a member of the PFLP-GC. The FAA cautioned airlines that the device found by the West German authorities "would be very difficult to detect via normal X-ray" and informed U.S. airlines that passenger/baggage reconciliation procedures "should be rigorously applied." That specific threat was received by the U.S. Embassy in Helsinki on December 5, 1988, detailing a threat that a woman would carry a bomb on board a Pan Am flight from Frankfurt in the following two weeks, was released by the FAA and then redistributed by the U.S. State Department to U.S. embassies around the globe. The U.S. embassy in Moscow made the information public to the country's 2,000-member community of U.S. citizens, including alerting Moscow news media.[6]

It seems surprising that Pan Am management and security were then not paying specific attention to baggage reconciliation at this juncture. In view of the FAA's threat assessment, there were significant lapses in adherence to the careful application of the reconciliation process at Frankfurt on that fateful day in 1988. It is also important to appreciate just how impotent the FAA was in dealing with Pan Am's security problems. Even after the Lockerbie disaster, the FAA found numerous security discrepancies with Pan Am, at both Frankfurt Airport and London's Heathrow Airport. Only six months after Lockerbie, an FAA inspector's report on June 9, 1989, stated, "The posture of Pan Am is considered unsafe; all passengers flying out of Frankfurt on Pan Am are at great risk."[7]

Concerning the attacks on the World Trade Center and the Pentagon, an awakened and anxious public is now fully aware the plot to attack aviation was brought to the attention of the FBI from flight-training academies inside the United States and from reports from its own agents. The clear failure of any resource to follow up on such intelligence is but one issue that led to the tragic destruction on 9-11.

Security improvements in the 1990s, particularly in the light of the aforementioned President's Commission, fell woefully short. The viewpoint of the FAA was basically that "it won't happen here." Hijacking aircraft was not yet a North American problem as it was seen by U.S. authorities to be a European and Eastern European issue. After all is said and done, no one had been injured by an act of terrorism against airliners flying within or from the United States. Admiral Cathal Flynn stated that in the decade since (Pan Am 103) amid attacks on other carriers, no U.S. aircraft had been successfully attacked and not one person harmed on U.S. flag flights anywhere in the world, despite terrorist's determined efforts. He also said, "This owes a great deal to strengthened intelligence and law enforcement efforts and to international coopera-tion in fighting terrorism, both airport and carrier programs have been key factors."[8] Since these comments were made, it was clear that the intelligence process had failed and both airport and air carrier programs were shown to be completely inadequate to protect the traveling public and aviation facilities from terrorist attacks.

Passenger Screening at Airports

There are many issues surrounding passenger screening, and the related training of the security operatives. In the United States and Canada, in the decades leading to 9-11, aviation regulations had made the airlines responsible for security of passengers and baggage screening. In many other regions of the world, governments have made the airports responsible. As was shown after 9-11, passengers were able to board aircraft with small-bladed knives that were used to grue-some effect to disable pilots and eventually crash aircraft into the World Trade Center and the Pentagon. The need to apply screening processes developed as a result of hijackings by Middle East and European terror groups in the late 1960s and early 1970s. At that time, the threat posed was from gun and explosive-toting terrorists who were gaining access to aircraft. Their intent was not specifically to kill, but to use hostages as bargaining chips for the release of prisoners held in jails, in Israel and Europe. By 2001, the training and equipment for passenger screening had not changed that much since those early days. The message was clear to terrorists in the past and still is today: As long as aviation security measures are not in place, aviation is a lucrative, media-grabbing, and sensational target.

Tombstone Technology

When the body count becomes too much for an administration to bear, the cost of fixing most existing problems gets the necessary funding it should have had in the first place. We like to refer to this a, "tombstone technology." The fact remains that 9-11 could have been—and most

Blue "Trolley Bag"

FIGURE 14-1 Trolley bag bomb intended to blow up on an El Al flight at London's Heathrow Airport in 1986. The explosive device was hidden in the false bottom of the carryon bag (Jeremey Spindlove).

probably should have been—detected in advance and therefore prevented. This may be a very bold assertion, but it is an assertion we are definitely not alone in making. In North America, all the airlines were tasked (up until 2002) with the security of passengers. Costs are always an issue for airlines, and, in the United States, security companies were required to bid on security-screening contracts. The successful bid was almost always given to the lowest bidder. Our security was entrusted to low-paid, low-skilled, often untrained, poorly motivated individuals and, in many instances, new immigrants. Not only were they poorly paid, but a proportion of them were, in fact, illegal immigrants. This was the case in the United States in the last two decades of the twentieth century. The level of training and the types of test items that the staff used for training were totally out of context with the types of weapons and cutting devices available on the market. So, there were significant holes in the screening process, both in the United States and elsewhere. Inconsistency is also another issue. Different items attract attention at one airport, but perhaps not at another, and this problem continues.

A major flaw in the process, and one most noticeable in the United States, had been that passengers and the general public could go through security screening, but all this did was raise the obvious prospect of breaches and banned items getting through the security screening process. The security screeners, working at minimum wage and having been poorly trained, had only about seven seconds to determine what they were viewing on the X-ray monitor. Added to this, most passengers (before 9-11) took the view that security was a hindrance. The abuse suffered by low-paid screeners from irate passengers and airline staff is legend. In many cases, the decision on whether a passenger could take a specific item on board was referred to an airline supervisor for a decision. Most of the decisions were made in favor of the fare-paying passenger. This did little for the morale of the screeners and even less for security. The problem is underscored in such documents as the 1994 U.S. Government Accountability report to Congressional Committees on Aviation Security. In that report, which disseminated the President's Commission Report, the commission raised concerns about screeners' efficiency, mail and cargo, and the coordination of security between law enforcement and airport personnel. Little changed in the intervening years; "shutting the barn door after the horse has bolted" adequately describes what has taken place since 9-11. Responsibility for airport security was passed to the Department of Homeland Security's Transportation Security Administration (TSA). Now all airport security screeners are federalized, creating a long-awaited, consistent level of training, for all those employees. Added to this is the requirement to screen all hold baggage. The 100 percent screening of hold baggage has been a reality in the United Kingdom since 1998, but North America and some European countries were far behind. Since 9-11, funds have been budgeted and are being provided to support the security functions at U.S. airports and seaports; however, this may be too little, too late. Prior to 9-11, the opportunity existed for terrorists to openly observe the screening processes at U.S. airports, to assess where the weakest points were, to see how the screeners searched and what items they took from passengers. It is not improbable to suggest that they had done dummy runs with similar objects, and even if they had been detected, the outcome would not have brought them to the attention of the authorities.

An early attempt at a proxy suicide bombing involves the case of Nazer Hindawi, a Jordanian Palestinian who with the support of Syria had spent a considerable amount of time in Ireland and befriended a young Irish girl whom he managed to get pregnant. On August 17, 1986, he sent her back to the Middle East to meet his family and the route he chose for her was via an Israeli Airlines flight from London's Heathrow Airport. By the spring of 1986, the world was well accustomed to airport delays caused by security checks, with Heathrow being no exception. The traveling public was subjected to waiting in monotonous lines for hand luggage to be searched, blissfully ignorant that the suicide or mule bomber even existed. There had, at this juncture, been no recorded attempts to destroy an aircraft by suicide bombing. This was to change on that April day. Terminal One at Heathrow International was the hub for British Airways European and domestic arrivals and departures. However, on several days of the week, it was also the terminal used by Israel's El Al Airlines for its Boeing 747 flight to Tel Aviv, Israel. At mid-morning, with the El Al 747 at departure Gate 23, passengers for that flight began to come through the pre-boarding security checks. All passengers leaving the United Kingdom in 1986, and specifically those with checked baggage, were asked a series of questions:

- Is this your baggage?
- Did you pack it yourself and are you taking any packages for somebody else?
- Have you left your baggage unattended at any time?

After answering the questions, the passengers would proceed to an immigration desk for passport inspection, not far from the watching eye of Metropolitan Police Special Branch officers.

On this day, the young woman from the Republic of Ireland answered all the questions. Her passport was checked and her hand luggage and hold baggage were screened by X-ray. The girl proceeded to the El Al boarding gate with her single piece of carry-on baggage. The bag was of nylon construction with an expanding compartment at the base, a type of bag used by millions of travelers. El Al prides itself on being one of the most secure airlines in the world (with good reason); it always conducts its own secondary security check and questioning of every passenger. The pregnant girl was going to visit her boyfriend's family in the Middle East; he, however, was not traveling. The El Al security staff thought this was an unusual story, and while doing the physical check on the bag, noticed that even when empty it seemed overly heavy for its construction. At that point, a police explosive search dog reacted to the bag. Further inspection revealed several sheets of plastic explosive wired to a calculator and battery. The bomb was in a false bottom of the bag. The boyfriend, Nazer Hindawi, had befriended the young woman, gotten her pregnant, and was sending her to her death. He had gone to remarkable lengths and considerable planning to pull this attack off. He was sentenced to forty-five years in prison. The plan was for the bomb to detonate approximately two hours after departure. After the failed bombing, Hindawi sought refuge at the residence of a Syrian diplomat in the United Kingdom.

The Global Threat to Civil Aviation

The 1970s and 1980s were the decades of hijackings—preferred mode of attack for terrorists at that time. As effective security was moved against that threat, the terrorists shifted their attention to other areas of aviation they considered to be weak. Pan Am 103 is one example. The attacks against civil aviation tend to get lost in the mists of time. Few remember the specific threats and attacks, particularly when they occur in far-away countries. We list here some specific examples where the threat is from explosive devices, either placed in the hold or as cabin baggage. A Pan Am 747 had a bomb explode on board on a flight from Tokyo to Honolulu in August 1982, and also the same year an improvised explosive device (IED) was discovered on a Pan Am 747 at Rio de Janeiro airport. In December of the same year, a piece of checked luggage was removed from an Alitalia (Italian Airlines) flight when the passenger who checked the luggage did not board the aircraft. The passenger was checking the bag through to a Pan Am flight to New York. Police discovered a bomb inside the bag.[9]

The terrorist hijackings by Palestinian groups in the late 1960s and 1970s changed the face of aviation for the next thirty years. For the terrorists, a hijacked aircraft became a way to attract the worldwide media coverage that the group craved, allowing them to present an agenda or message about their cause instantly and universally. For respective governments and the public, the horror became too much to deal with. Measures to counteract these depredations were hastily drawn up and passenger screening for hand-carried baggage was born. Security is, in many ways, a reactive function, and this has been clearly demonstrated in the aviation industry.

Six years prior to 9-11, al Qaeda planned an attack targeting U.S. flights from Manila in the Philippines. Operation Bojinka was planned in 1995 and was uncovered by Philippine authorities—they stumbled by accident on a bomb making factory in an apartment block that had caught fire and discovered sulfuric acid, nitric acid, sodium trichlorate, ammonia, silver nitrates, and nitrobenzoyl and a document written in Arabic that detailed how to construct liquid bombs. They also found twelve forged Norwegian, Saudi, and Afghan passports. The apartment was rented by Ramzi Yousef, and details of the Bojinka plot were found on the hard drive of his laptop detailing flight schedules and detonation information. Yousef is currently serving 240 years in prison for the 1993 World Trade Center bombing.

Five years after 9-11, in 2006, a group of British Muslims allegedly planned suicide missions on at least seven international flights from London's Heathrow to North America. On this occasion, intelligence work was able to prevent the attacks being carried out. The attacks were to use items that could be legally carried on board an aircraft, hidden inside containers of liquid. The result being that the carriage of liquids and aerosol quantities is currently restricted. These items were never detected in the passenger screening process, but their intention was to get items that could be assembled into improvised explosive devices onto an aircraft for a suicide mission.

Airports are busy and often cramped locations designed and built in the decades before security of passengers and aircraft became such a significant issue. Even newly built facilities in the United States over the last five years of the twentieth century failed to factor in hardening of the facility for security purposes, especially the screening areas, or incorporating sophisticated detection devices into the baggage sorting/conveyor systems. A demand had now added an additional layer of baggage security to an already overburdened system. The problem facing the airlines was, "Who is going to pay for all this added security?" In the long run, it would, of course, be the traveling public, as it always is. After the bombing of Pan Am 103 in 1988, it was important to develop effective explosive detection equipment that could handle the heavy volume of baggage. Throughput was also part of the immediate challenge for airports and aviation security experts. Screening hold baggage had not been a priority for North America in spite of the President's Commission Report in 1990. Since 9-11 and the advent of the Transportation Security Administration in the United States, 100 percent screening of checked baggage at long last became a reality. As we move forward, the government (TSA) intends to continue research into more effective ways to scan baggage for explosive substances and devices by funding programs to efficiently inculcate the airport/airlines' baggage systems with state-of-the-art technology to screen checked baggage. The remaining gap in screening now reverts to the cargo hold and the amount of unchecked mail and freight. So as governments continue to find ever more sophisticated methods to prevent the next unthinkable attack, the very sobering message we now get from the terrorists is that they want nothing from us except our destruction! Hussein Mussawi, former Hezbollah leader, stated, "We are not fighting so that the enemy may offer us something. We are fighting to wipe out the enemy."

Airport Facilities

Airports are, by their very nature, open and public places. As a result, the opportunity for terrorists to leave bombs in such public places is always present. Only awareness, vigilance, and response by the public and police can help to avert disasters. What about security in the other sectors of the aviation industry? What about mail and airfreight carriers? How secure are they? Airlines move millions of tons of freight throughout the world and a large percentage travels without any serious screening in the holds of passenger aircraft. At the present time, this area of airline operation is open to attack. Furthermore, access to the aircraft by catering facilities, airport workers, and so on must receive serious attention if the sterility of the aircraft is to be maintained. It is of little benefit to any operation if the passengers are fully screened for weapons, but airport workers are allowed almost unrestricted access without checks. Without stating the obvious, the opportunity exists for airport workers to secrete weapons or even bombs on an aircraft. A comprehensive system must be employed to assure the integrity of all those persons who have access to restricted areas of the airport and also the bags and items that they carry in with them. Although measures are in place to verify freight by known shipper, this is a far cry from a totally secure cargo hold Inserting heavy duty screening equipment and bomb detection dogs into this mix will delay freight operations, but will it deter a would-be terrorist? In 2010, we saw terrorists in Yemen placing explosives in printer cartridges and having them shipped through Europe to the United States. In the 2010 incident, the cargo flights and the packages were subsequently intercepted in Dubai and at Britain's East Midlands Airport, but the door is still open. Our global economy is hugely dependent on air cargo, which ships billions of tons each year, and the fact that it has not been secure makes it a soft target for al Qaeda-inspired or -sponsored groups to attack.

PASSENGER TERMINAL ATTACKS

As already evidenced in Europe, threats also extend to passengers waiting at check-in counters. For airports and security, these areas require consideration and attention. Attacks can occur even at times of heightened security, and the United States most certainly was on guard on Independence Day in 2002, when a man of Middle East origin opened fire at the El Al check-in desks at Los Angeles International airport. The June 2007 vehicular attack on Scotland's Glasgow airport by two men driving a bomb-laden vehicle are prime examples of how easy it is for the determined terrorist in these cases to launch an attack. In January 2011, a suicide bomber attacked passengers in the arrivals area at Moscow's Domodedovo Airport, killing thirty-five. What do we learn from such events? El Al, the Israeli national airline, is a model for all other airlines. El Al prides itself on its stringent security systems and passenger profiling. El Al does not restrict its security activities solely to the airport and the perimeter areas of airport facilities but also includes hotels where its crews stay on international flights. The June 2008 information that was being gathered by a group from Hezbollah in Toronto, Canada, was specific to the location where the El Al crew was staying. El Al immediately changed its security procedures as a result, fearing an imminent attack against its personnel and operations.

Attacks on airports have been relatively few but have always taken authorities by surprise. The attacks on Heathrow Airport in 1994, the Scottish attack in 2007, and the attack in Moscow in 2011 are good examples of the lengths to which a group of committed individuals will go to in order to cause death and destruction.

Heathrow Airport Attacked by Irish Terrorists

FIRST ATTACK: On Wednesday March 9, 1994, between 5:00 P.M. and 5:30 P.M., using a recognized code word, telephone calls were received by various news organizations warning of the following:

- Bombs at Heathrow and
- In terminals and runways in one hour.

Just before 6:00 P.M., there was an explosion in a car in the parking lot of the Excelsior Hotel, on the north side of the airport. Several cars were engulfed in flames, and four mortars were found near the northern runway.

- None had exploded on impact.
- No damage or injury occurred.
- The hotel parking lot had in the past been utilized as an evacuation point.

SECOND ATTACK: On the following day between 5:30 P.M. and 9:45 P.M., a number of similar calls were received. At midnight, four more bombs were fired from wasteland beyond the perimeter on the southern side of the airport near Terminal Four. Again there was no explosion, damage, or injury. The launcher was a freestanding, purposely built apparatus, placed in undergrowth and concealed with plastic sheeting and branches.

THIRD ATTACK: Three days later on Sunday, March 13, 1994, there were again a series of similar calls between 6:00 A.M. and 6:40 A.M. Flights were diverted from the southern runway, and just after 8.00 A.M., rockets were again fired toward Terminal Four, from the opposite direction. One landed on the terminal without causing damage.

FOURTH ATTACK: Between 6:45 P.M. and 7:30 P.M. the same day, coded calls were received, giving the same unspecific information, stating that bombs had been placed at Heathrow and Gatwick. Contingency plans were implemented at both airports, but this was found to be a hoax. It is properly described as an attack because the disruptive effect was equal to that at earlier incidents.[10]

While the type of device used by the PIRA in this attack was crude and unsophisticated had they had the opportunity to use Man-Portable Air Defense Systems (MANPADS), they would surely have hit targets that they chose. There are an estimated 500,000 MANPADS currently in existence. Some of the simpler systems are available for as little as $1,000 on the open market. The MANPADS used thus far in terrorist attacks, such as the Russian-made SA-7, suggest that terrorist groups currently do not have access to more sophisticated systems, although general small-arms proliferation trends suggest that it is only a matter of time before they acquire more advanced systems. Many MANPADS are unaccounted for, including at least forty Stinger missile systems missing after the 1991 Gulf War, as well as hundreds of U.S.-made MANPADS shipped to foreign nations and then left untracked, with thousands of systems built by France, China, and Russia.[11]

In the Heathrow Airport attack, this was the first time police and intelligence had to not only be concerned with the airport facility and its protection but also evaluate the threat from areas surrounding the airport. The better use of closed-circuit television systems (CCTV) and better intelligence on who owns the lands and buildings in close proximity to airport facilities now had to be viewed in the overall risk assessment for an airport. Following 9-11, there was considerable concern about the use of and the availability of Stinger missiles against U.S. and UN targets. While there is no evidence to suggest that any Stinger missiles are in the United States, it is important to note that a U.S. military fact sheet details the Stinger in this manner: "The missiles' complexity can be accommodated by almost any potential user nation or group."

The "Stinger missile" is 5 feet long and weighs 34 pounds. It was and is manufactured by Raytheon and can be fired from a distance of five miles and has a vertical range of 10,000 feet. A Stinger would be a lethal weapon when used against a conventional civilian airliner. Stingers were originally sent to Afghanistan as part of the campaign to arm the local mujahedeen against the Soviet invasion. At the time of the transfer, there were advocates against such a move, with the outright fear that the Islamic fundamentalist who dominated the Afghan mujahedeen had about as much love of the West as they did for the Soviets. The opportunity for some to be traded to terrorist organizations was a genuine and highly conceivable proposition. Other countries that have Stinger missiles include Somalia, Iraq, United Arab Emirates, Qatar, Zambia, and North Korea.[12] Attacks by shoulder-fired missiles have been an ongoing concern since the November 2002 attack in Kenya against an El Al flight taking off from Mombasa. There are earlier recorded attacks, but the underlying worry is the existence of these systems in such large numbers.

In June 2007, a full frontal attack using a vehicle as a means to deliver an incendiary bomb took place at Glasgow International Airport in Scotland when two men of Middle East appearance drove a Range Rover SUV loaded with propane tanks and soaked in gasoline at the main doors of the terminal. The attack was thwarted by the reinforced doors to the building to prevent such attacks; the vehicle and its two occupants caught fire and both were arrested by members of the public and airport police. This is an example of the vulnerability of public locations to this type of uncoordinated but nevertheless deadly style of attack. Had they succeeded in breaching the doors the resulting mayhem and death would have been considerable.

A People Issue

Prior to the events of 9-11, a problem in U.S. and European airports had been the vast number of people having access to the restricted areas of airports. What measures can be taken to ensure that airport workers, baggage loaders, refuelers, aircraft cleaners, and the like have undergone sufficient background checks to assure authorities of their integrity? News reports out of the United Kingdom in early September 2002 indicated that at least fifteen illegal aliens were employed cleaning aircraft at London's Heathrow Airport.

The FAA studied weapon detection rates at the twenty-five largest airports in the United States and found that the lowest rates were at Boston's Logan International; Newark, New Jersey; and Dulles Airport in Washington DC. After the loss of TWA 800 off Long Island, New York, in 1996, the Gore Commission made many recommendations in regard to airport security, including positive bag matching for passengers on domestic flights. The airlines insisted that the resulting cost in delays was unacceptable and came up with a proposal to use Computer-Assisted Passenger Profiling. This would permit the airlines to identify from a set of parameters those passengers who might pose a threat. The four hijackings of 9-11 showed how devoid of any value that system turned out to be. Since 9-11, we have been led down a path; Americans falsely believe that the TSA has tightened airline security by federalizing all security screeners. However, as we approached the one-year anniversary of 9-11 in 2002, the new TSA reported that all was not well. It revealed that screeners at thirty-two of the largest U.S. airports failed to detect weapons and explosive devices in approximately 25 percent of the tests it carried out in June 2002. Granted tests are designed to show weakness in the system; however, 25 percent is higher than expected, and in airports such as Cincinnati, Jacksonville, and Las Vegas, the newly monitored screeners failed to detect at least half of the tests, and at Los Angeles International, the failure rate was 41 percent.[13]

The following Statistical Information was Provided by the U.S. Transportation Security Administration:
During 2006,

- TSA screened 708,400,522. The average wait time was 3.79 minutes and the average peak wait time was 11.76 minutes.
- TSA screened 535,020,271 individual pieces of checked luggage. Opened 16 percent of these checked bags (85,571,710 bags) searching for prohibited items.
- TSA intercepted 13,709,211 prohibited items at our security checkpoints. Of this, 11,616,249 were lighters and 1,607,100 were knives.[14]

A Transportation Security Administration report revealed that screeners at Los Angeles and Chicago O'Hare airports failed to find fake bombs in more than 60 percent of tests run in 2007. Rich Roth, an aviation security expert with CTI Consulting in Bethesda, Md., stated that screeners failed to detect fake dynamite hidden in bathroom kits and bomb residue on shoelaces. He notes, though, that the problems the tests revealed have since been addressed. Besides, the undercover agents had an advantage over would-be terrorists. They did not fear arrest while sneaking the fake bombs through security. A "bad guy" would likely be much more nervous, which might tip off screeners, Roth says. The report also tested private screeners, and unlike their federal counterparts, only 20 percent of the fake bombs made it through security. Roth says this might be because the private screeners are accustomed to being tested.[15] Inadequacies and failures in the security at airports will continue; there is no 100 percent security—security screeners like anyone else can and do make mistakes—the challenge for the terrorists is to find the loophole in the security system and exploit the errors or mistakes.

Passenger Profiling

Most civil liberty groups have denounced the practice of "profiling" airline passengers. The concept behind profiling is to utilize skilled practitioners to identify passengers who warrant more in-depth security screening before they board an aircraft. The screeners are trained in security-related issues and human behavior. El Al uses profiling and, of course, its safety and security record is second to none.

In November 2004, the U.S. Transportation Security Administration began testing a new form of passenger prescreening called "Secure Flight." This program was intended to replace the now-defunct Computer-Assisted Passenger Prescreening System (CAPPS II). CAPPS II was a very controversial and expensive U.S. government experiment that had been slow to get off the ground.

Under Secure Flight, TSA receives information for each passenger (from the airline). TSA then determines any matches of information with government watch lists and transmit matching results back to aircraft operators. To this end, the TSA has issued the *Secure Flight Notice of Proposed Rule Making* (NPRM), which lays out the Department of Homeland Security's plans to assume watch list matching.

Secure Flight, the Transportation Security Administration's behind-the-scenes watch list matching program, fulfills a key recommendation of the 9-11 Commission by assuming responsibility of watch list matching from individual airlines. By establishing a consistent watch list matching system, Secure Flight enhances aviation security and more effectively facilitates air travel for passengers. Secure Flight requires airlines to collect a passenger's full name (as it appears on government-issued ID), date of birth, gender, and Redress Number (if applicable). By providing complete information, passengers can significantly decrease the likelihood of watch list misidentification. Secure Flight watch list matching takes a matter of seconds to complete, and providing these data enables passengers to print their boarding passes at home or at an airline kiosk. Secure Flight does not conduct watch list matching or approve the issuance of a boarding pass by an airline if complete passenger data are not submitted.[16]

Secure Flight matches limited passenger information against government watch lists to do the following:

- Identify known and suspected terrorists.
- Prevent individuals on the No-Fly list from boarding an aircraft.
- Identify individuals on the Selectee list for enhanced screening.
- Facilitate passenger air travel by providing fair, equitable, and consistent matching process across all aircraft operators.
- Protect individuals' privacy.

Secure Flight compares passenger records to expanded "selectee" and "no-fly" lists already in use. Passengers whose records match names on the lists will be subject to commercial background checks to verify their identities.[17]

FIGURE 14-2   Secure flight process (U.S. Department of Homeland Security).

The TSA began Secure Flight by compiling a "Terrorist No-Fly Watch List." The entire program became fully operational in late 2010 for all flights operating to, from, and within the United States.

One problem with the program is the number of people who have been falsely identified as "terrorists" because their name matches, or closely resembles, names on the No-Fly list. Once a name is on the list, it is impossible to remove it and then some "innocent" travelers are detained every time they fly and they can't do anything to get their name off the list.

Screening Passengers by Observation Technique (SPOT)

The Israel's El Al has been profiling passengers for its flights for the past thirty-plus years with considerable success. Passengers and the public are monitored for behavior traits as they enter the airport and the observations extend to the airport perimeters and parking areas. In Canada in February 2008, the Chair of the International Pilots Association called for the Canadian authorities to adopt SPOT, claiming that it was already in use by the TSA in the United States. Under the U.S. SPOT program, TSA stopped 70,000 passengers between January and December 2006 for questioning, and although no terrorists were arrested, they did arrest more than 700 individuals. But that 1 in 100 hit rate involved alleged money laundering, drugs, and weapons possession to immigration violations to outstanding warrants. Following the Glasgow airport attack in 2007, the British have installed the technology version of the same process by funneling images from CCTV cameras to a computer system that will detect 10,000 separate facial "micro expressions," including signs of fear and deception and, reportedly, even an individual's skin temperature.

The TSA and DHS use layers of security to ensure the security of the traveling public and the Nation's transportation system. TSA checkpoints constitute only one security layer of the many in place to protect aviation. Others include intelligence gathering and analysis, checking passenger manifests against watch lists, random canine team searches at airports, federal air marshals, federal flight deck officers, and more security measures both visible and invisible to the public.

Each one of these layers alone is capable of stopping a terrorist attack. In combination, their security value is multiplied, creating a much stronger, formidable system. A terrorist who has to overcome multiple security layers in order to carry out an attack is more likely to be pre-empted, deterred, or to fail during the attempt.

European Civil Aviation Conference (ECAC)

Nations are responsible for implementing effective aviation security systems for flights leaving their country. Terrorism is an international issue as modern air travel allows terrorists to strike anywhere within hours. Therefore, it is necessary to have an international body to work with

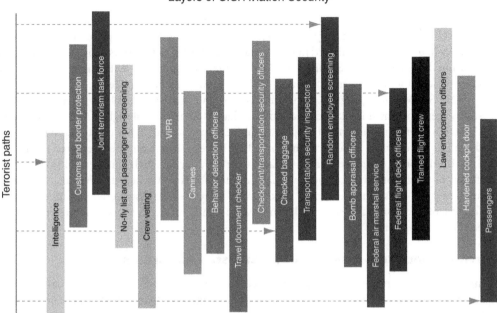

FIGURE 14-3 Layers of U.S. aviation security (U.S. Department of Homeland Security).

governments to develop measures, standards, and recommended practices...that body is the European Civil Aviation Conference (ECAC). The ECAC operates with the active support of the International Civil Aviation Organization (ICAO). ECAC, formed more than twenty years ago, has the following three principles in the area of aviation security:

1. The threat of unlawful interference with civil aviation in its many forms of violence is likely to persist.
2. The ICAO Standards and Recommended Practices in aviation security have to take into account the widely varying provisions available for their implementation in more than 180 contracting states of ICAO.
3. Mutual understanding and close and constant cooperation between all state authorities concerned are necessary to achieve and maintain a high standard of aviation security.[18]

COMBATING TERRORISTS

One of the first considerations any would-be hijacker would have looked for during the last two decades of the twentieth century was the amount of mass media publicity he or she could hope to achieve for the "cause." Hijacking an aircraft and demanding it be flown to JFK Airport in New York, or to London's Heathrow Airport, would gain worldwide media attention. Because of the size and complexity of these airports, the ensuing chaos and disruption to the traveling public would be horrendous. In combating a hijacking, it is imperative that authorities have the option to "direct" the hijacked aircraft to an airport of their choice. Authorities must be able to handle the incident without disrupting the major airports and airline systems of the world.

U.S. Sky Marshals (Federal Air Marshal Service—FAM)

In response to the hijacking of TWA Flight 847 in 1985, President Ronald Reagan directed the secretary of transportation, in cooperation with the secretary of state, to explore expansion of the armed Sky Marshal program aboard international flights for U.S. air carriers. Congress responded by passing the International Security and Development Cooperation Act (Public Law 99–83), which provided the statutes that supported the Federal Air Marshal Service.

The "Sky Marshal" program has in fact been around since the late 1960s, when armed U.S. customs agents operated in plain clothes on U.S.-flagged international flights. At the time of the 9-11 attacks, there were around fifty operational U.S. Sky Marshals. That was to rapidly change, and the U.S. government announced an immediate increase in the numbers required to protect U.S. civil aviation from future terrorist attack. Currently, air marshals staff several positions at different organizations such as the National Counterterrorism Center, the National Targeting Center, and the FBI's Joint Terrorism Task Forces. They are also distributed among other law enforcement and homeland security liaison assignments during times of heightened alert or special national events.

Aircraft Hijack Response Location—Stansted Airport, UK

London's third airport is little known to the international traveler, who will normally arrive at the gateway airports of Heathrow, on the outskirts of London, or Gatwick, about one hour south of London. Stansted, located to the east of London, has become the venue of choice for authorities in dealing with a hijacked aircraft. This supposes, of course, that they are able to hoodwink the terrorist into believing the plane is actually landing at Heathrow. The airport was first used to receive a hijacked aircraft in 1975, when a BAC1–11 was hijacked on a domestic flight between Manchester in the north of England and London. The hijacking took place as the aircraft was approaching Heathrow. The pilot managed to divert, without the hijackers' knowledge, to Stansted. The hijacker then demanded money and to be flown to France. By the time the pilot had flown around and landed at Stansted, the hijacker was convinced he was in France. Few police were available in those days to cover Stansted airport and, as a result of inadequate police power, some valuable lessons were learned. These lessons were incorporated into the training of the **Special Air Service (SAS) Regiment** for dealing with terrorist hijackings in the future. Security operations were lacking in the following:

- Numbers of police on hand to deal with an emergency of this magnitude.
- Designated emergency rendezvous points for emergency services.
- Communications between pilot and ground.
- A designated command post for the operation.

The requirement to train and maintain a level of response became of great importance. A second hijacking, originating in central Africa in 1982, ended up with an Air Tanzania Boeing 727 landing, after a circuitous route around Europe, at Stansted. On this occasion, the response was a combined police and military operation with the elite SAS in attendance to mount a hostage rescue if police negotiations failed. While police negotiated, a team of SAS members embarked on similarly configured British Airways 737 and flew directly from Heathrow to Stansted. As a result of protracted negotiations involving the Tanzanian high commissioner, the siege was brought to a peaceful conclusion some twenty-four hours later. Also apparent in this incident was the media's role and their release of sensational and news-breaking pictures. Images of armed police lying in wait near the aircraft could have been a considerable problem for the negotiators had the pictures reached the hijackers. In any democratic society, the value of the press and its principal focus of newsgathering must be weighed against the impact on the situation at hand. Close cooperation between the media and authorities is an issue that must be addressed in terror and hijacking incidents.

In August 1996, a Sudan Airways A310 Airbus, originating in Khartoum, was hijacked by an Iraqi group demanding that the plane be flown to Italy. Because of insufficient fuel, the aircraft landed in Cyprus, refueled, and then took off for London. Stansted, as a result of the valuable lessons of the last twenty years, was ready and waiting to receive the aircraft. This particular hijacking was to end peacefully. Stansted remains the airport of choice for receiving terrorist-controlled flights into the United Kingdom.[19] On February 7, 2000, an Afghan Airlines Boeing 727 was hijacked during a flight to the Afghan city of Mazar-i-Sharif and was then flown to the Uzbek capital of Tashkent. It eventually landed at Stansted. It has been the scene of international hijacking dramas three times in the past thirty years—all of which ended in the surrender of the hijackers without loss of life.

The Media Angle

Interfering with the media's "right to know" is, of course, frowned upon by journalists. However, there must be limits placed on the release of pictures and information while an incident is ongoing. As preservers of order in the fabric of democracy, the police and military are bound to come into conflict with the media about the control and dissemination of information. One example of such a conflict occurred during the Falklands War, when the media were given briefings by the government and the content of news was tightly censored so as not to give critical information to the enemy. During the Gulf War, the commander himself, General Norman Schwarzkopf, conducted press briefings. These briefings contained the diluted information that the military chiefs allowed for media release. The press was not allowed on the field of battle during the invasion's operations. In a terror incident taking place in a city, it is impossible to control media coverage in the first phase of the action. The bombing of the Federal Building in Oklahoma City brought the television crews to the scene at almost the same time rescue and police services were arriving, some even quicker. The graphic television coverage of the heroic deeds of firefighters and police officers goes a long way toward winning the public's acceptance of the methods they may subsequently use to catch terrorists. Police are seen as the front line against terrorism; they are part of the community and are, therefore, better appreciated.

Media coverage can also have negative effects in combating terror, even when government censors have neutralized the information. A disastrous media mistake involved a hijacked American airliner at Beirut International Airport in 1985. A rescue unit of Delta Force commandos was dispatched to the region, only to be thwarted by news coverage of their imminent arrival. This allowed the hijackers time to hide and move their captives throughout Beirut. Many analysts have discussed and reviewed the effects of media coverage on terrorist actions and many conclusions both for and against media coverage can surely be reached. The media, however, must understand that they should remain at "arms' length" so as not to become a tool of the terrorist.

Much media coverage is aimed at showing the horrors of the unfolding situation. The motivational drives of the terrorists are seldom considered, and the dramatic effects of the horror become the main coverage. Without intention, the media begins presenting the terrorists' side of the issues. When that happens, the media inadvertently serve the purposes of the terrorists, giving them precisely the attention they seek.

After all, terrorist actions are all about sending a message. Their preferred method of sending the message is via the broadest media coverage possible. No doubt, studies might conclude that sensational pictures of terrorist events do nothing to get "the message" out to the public but in fact, fuel public anger. Consider the insurgent/terrorist actions in Iraq in 2004 and 2005. Insurgents kidnapped Westerners, recorded their subsequent execution by grisly beheadings, and then broadcast the atrocity on the Internet. Although the broadcasts severely aggravated the sensitivities of those who viewed them, in the long run, they had no effect on the resolve of the majority of governments to acquiesce to any demands. Conversely, the terrorist attacks on trains in Madrid certainly had serious political implications for Spain and resulted in the pullout of Spanish troops from Iraq and a change in the democratically elected government of the day.

In a free society, the media and the government will invariably clash on what gets coverage and what should not. Much of what is reported will generally be acquired through government sources, which may appear to be manipulating the media. No one has suggested that the media were manipulated on 9-11, unless of course, you listen to the meanderings of the Iranian leadership who openly espoused that it was all a conspiracy theory! So back to reality; we believe that the media coverage awoke a nation to the true and cowardly nature of terrorists and their despicable acts. The live news footage of the World Trade Center attack as the second plane crashed into the second of the twin towers was more vivid than any Hollywood portrayal. The cataclysmic events of 9-11 were also viewed and broadcast in Middle Eastern countries. The following day, news articles and television coverage showed joyful Palestinians dancing in the streets. To most people, that was abhorrent, but it needed to be shown. In the same vein, Americans gathered and cheered outside the White House at the news of the death of Osama bin Laden. Censorship of the press and restrictions placed on it is undoubtedly a common practice in many countries, especially where military dictatorships and totalitarian governments are in power. A good example is the tactics and laws imposed by the Robert Mugabe government in Zimbabwe, which makes it a criminal offense to criticize the government and its ministers.

Arabic news media, Al Jazeera, is the largest and most controversial Arabic news channel in the Middle East. It offers news coverage twenty-four hours a day from around the world, focusing on the hottest regions of conflict. Al Jazeera could be termed the Arabic version of Atlanta's CNN. Programming also includes a wide selection of high-pitch political talk shows, documentaries, emotional debates, and sensational arguments covering events of the moment. Founded in 1996, and based in Qatar, the Al Jazeera news network is the fastest-growing and most controversial network among Arab communities and Arabic-speaking people around the world. The station has earned the loyalty of a large audience and the enmity of various critics who argue that Al Jazeera is overly sensational. Critics claim the network tends to show bloody footage from various war zones and gives disproportionate coverage to various fundamentalist and extremist groups. Criticism from various governments has helped the channel increase its credibility with an audience that is familiar with censorship and biased coverage from official government outlets. Al Jazeera is not likely to criticize its own benefactors, the Emir of Qatar and the government of Qatar.

Al Jazeera's programs are available worldwide through various satellite and cable systems. In the United States, it is available through satellite.[20] During 2004, U.S. commanders in Iraq were openly critical of the coverage they received from Al Jazeera, particularly during the battle for Fallujah. The news network claimed that U.S. forces were killing hundreds of innocent women and children—a claim the military hotly denied.

Policy

Western governments reacted to terrorist activity by responding to them swiftly and effectively. The use of military and spy satellites to track down terrorists has enhanced this effort. Is the problem of defining and dealing with terrorism a police or a military problem? Certainly, the bombing of U.S. embassies in Nairobi and Dar es Salaam in the summer of 1998 was very difficult for the local police to deal with. In trying to come to terms with an enemy not residing within its own borders, the United States responded with a preemptive military strike at the bases of suspected terrorists in both Sudan and Pakistan. Was the United States violating sovereign territory of these two countries? The primary target was Osama bin Laden and his al Qaeda network, who were suspected of being behind the two bombings, as well as the subsequent attacks against the USS *Cole* in Yemen. As a result of the two bombings, and the U.S. retaliatory strikes, we wondered who would fire the next shot in anger. We now know the next shot was from the Islamic extremists of bin Laden's al Qaeda on September 11, 2001.

International cooperation in dealing with global terrorism was addressed at the Lyon Summit Conference in 1996. Ministers responsible for state security agreed on a framework of some twenty-five measures. The agreement focused on the following main points:

1. Adopt internal measures to prevent terrorism by improving counterterrorism cooperation and capabilities. By adopting this strategy, governments could focus on training of counterterrorism personnel to prevent all kinds of terrorism actions including the use of chemical, biological, and toxic substance attacks.
2. Accelerate the research and development of methods to detect explosives and other harmful substances that cause death or injury and also to develop standards for marking explosives in order to identify their origin in postblast investigations.
3. In respect to prosecution and deterrence, the agreement noted that where sufficient justification existed according to national laws, that states must investigate organizations, groups, and associations, including those with charitable social or cultural goals, used by terrorists as a cover for their operations. (An example of such a group would be the Irish Northern Aid Committee or NORAID, which supports and collects funds for the IRA in the United States.)
4. Adopt laws for the restriction and control of weapons and explosives including export controls, to prevent their use by terrorist organizations.
5. Review and amend all current antiterror legislation.
6. In dealing with political asylum issues, states must ensure that the rights and freedoms of a country are not taken advantage of by terrorists who seek to fund, plan, and then commit terrorist acts.
7. Facilitate the exchange of information through central authorities to provide speedy coordination of requests. Direct exchange of information between competent agencies should be encouraged.
8. The exchange of information should specifically identify the following:

   - The actions and movement of persons or groups suspected of belonging to or being connected with terrorist networks.
   - Travel documents suspected of being forgeries.
   - Trafficking in arms, explosives, or sensitive materials.
   - The use of communications technologies by terrorist groups.
   - The threat of new types of terrorist activities including those using chemical, biological, or nuclear materials and toxic substances.[21]

UN SECURITY COUNCIL RESOLUTION 1373

After 9-11, the General Assembly of the United Nations, by consensus of the 189 member states, called for international cooperation to prevent and eradicate acts of terrorism. The United Nations also held accountable the perpetrators and those states that harbor and support them. UN Security Council Resolution 1373 was unanimously adopted on September 28, 2001, under Chapter VII of the UN Charter. Resolution 1373 is a legally binding resolution on all member states. It defined the new international campaign to deal with terrorism. It required, among other things, that all member states prevent the financing of terrorism and deny safe haven for terrorists. Resolution 1373 makes it imperative for all states to review and strengthen their border security operations, banking practices, customs and immigration procedures, law enforcement and intelligence cooperation, and share pertinent information with respect to these efforts. The full implementation of 1373 will require each member state to take specific measures to combat terrorism; most will have to make changes to laws, regulations, and practices.

The United States took the following steps:

- **September 23, 2001**—Executive Order 13224 froze all the assets of twenty-seven foreign individuals, groups, and entities linked to terrorist acts or supporting terrorism and authorized the freezing of assets of those who commit or pose a significant threat of committing acts of terrorism.
- **September 28, 2001**—The United States sponsored the UN Security Council Resolution 1373, calling on all UN members to criminalize the provision of funds to all terrorists, effectively denying terrorists' safe financial haven anywhere.
- **October 5, 2001**—The U.S. attorney general redesignated twenty-five terrorist organizations, to include al Qaeda, as foreign terrorist organizations pursuant to the Antiterrorism and Effective Death Penalty Act 1996. Giving material support or resources to any of these foreign organizations is a felony under U.S. law.
- **October 12, 2001**—Under Executive Order 13224, thirty-nine names were added to the list of individuals and organizations linked to terrorism or terrorist financing.
- **October 26, 2001**—The United States enacted the USA Patriot Act, which significantly expanded the capability of U.S. law enforcement to investigate and prosecute persons who engage in terrorist acts.
- **October 29, 2001**—The Foreign Terrorist Tracking Task Force was created and aimed at denying entry into the United States of persons suspected of being terrorists and locating, detaining, prosecuting, and deporting terrorists already in the United States.
- **November 2, 2001**—The United States designated twenty-two terrorist organizations located throughout the world under Executive Order 13224, thus highlighting the need to focus on terrorist organizations worldwide.
- **November 7, 2001**—The United States added sixty-two new organizations and individuals, all of whom were either linked to the Al Barakaat conglomerate or to the Al Taqwa Bank, which have been identified as supplying funds to terrorists.
- **December 4, 2001**—The United States froze the assets of the Holy Land Foundation in Richardson, Texas, whose funds are used to support the Hamas terrorist organization, and two other entities, bringing the total to 153.
- **December 5, 2001**—The secretary of state designated thirty-nine groups as terrorist organizations under the Immigration and Nationality Act, as amended by the USA Patriot Act.[22]

THE PATRIOT ACT

This hastily formed act was the congressional response to the events of 9-11; however, like other timed legislations, the Bush administration sought to have this act reinvigorated and the provisions in it made permanent. The act has allowed for expanded surveillance of terrorist suspects and increased the use of material witness warrants, which allow suspects to be held incommunicado. The act also authorized secret proceedings in immigration cases. Many of the provisions are due to expire. While Congress attempts to rework the act, it has been criticized from both Republicans and Democrats as a law that severely limits the rights and freedoms of individuals and infringes on the rights of law-abiding American citizens.[23]

U.S. NAVAL STATION—GUANTÁNAMOBAY—CUBA

U.S. Naval Station Guantanamo Bay is the oldest U.S. base overseas and the only one in a Communist country. Located in the Oriente province on the southeast corner of Cuba, the base is about 400 miles from Miami. The United States leased the 45-square-mile parcel of land in 1903 to use as a coaling station. The U.S. Department of Defense has been holding "detainees" at GITMO since the invasion of Afghanistan in 2002. The base is under a strict military rule and the majority of "detainees" are suspected Islamist militants who have been handed over to the Department of Defense (DOD) by both military and CIA.

The Joint Task Force is tasked with observing, interviewing, and interrogating the detainees. No doubt a certain amount of intelligence has been gathered in regard to bomb making activities and many have been identified as having studied at U.S. universities before embarking on their jihad with Osama bin Laden's al Qaeda movement. Unclassified reports from the DOD in 2005 indicate that one detainee identified eleven fellow detainees as Osama bin Laden's bodyguards, who all received their terrorist training at al Farouq, a known terrorist training camp. Another detainee, the probable twentieth 9-11 hijacker, confirmed more than twenty detainees as bin Laden bodyguards. The detainees in many cases when captured were wearing a type of watch that has been linked to al Qaeda and radical Islamist IEDs. The particular watch is favored by al Qaeda bomb makers because it allows alarm settings and therefore detonations more than twenty-four hours in advance.

Methods of interrogation have been surfacing and one of the more popular claims from released detainees and detainee lawyers is that some have been subjected to a form of torture termed "water boarding," an interrogation technique in which the detainee is put in fear of drowning. The use of this practice has been denied at GITMO; however, the CIA admitted to using the technique on al Qaeda detainee Khalid Sheik Mohammed (KSM). Under the Obama presidency, there has been significant pressure to close secret prisons, Guantánamo Bay in Cuba in particular; the president issued an Executive Order to that effect in January 2009:

> EXECUTIVE ORDER—REVIEW AND DISPOSITION OF INDIVIDUALS DETAINED AT THE GUANTÁNAMO BAY NAVAL BASE AND CLOSURE OF DETENTION FACILITIES
>
> Over the past 7 years, approximately 800 individuals whom the Department of Defense has ever determined to be, or treated as, enemy combatants have been detained at Guantánamo. The Federal Government has moved more than 500 such detainees from Guantánamo, either by returning them to their home country or by releasing or transferring them to a third country. The Department of Defense has determined that a number of the individuals currently detained at Guantánamo are eligible for such transfer or release...The individuals

currently detained at Guantánamo have the constitutional privilege of the writ of habeas corpus. Most of those individuals have filed petitions for a writ of habeas corpus in Federal court challenging the lawfulness of their detention…It is in the interests of the United States that the executive branch undertake a prompt and thorough review of the factual and legal bases for the continued detention of all individuals currently held at Guantánamo, and of whether their continued detention is in the national security and foreign policy interests of the United States and in the interests of justice. The unusual circumstances associated with detentions at Guantánamo require a comprehensive interagency review…The detention facilities at Guantánamo for individuals covered by this order shall be closed as soon as practicable, and no later than 1 year from the date of this order. If any individuals covered by this order remain in detention at Guantánamo at the time of closure of those detention facilities, they shall be returned to their home country, released, transferred to a third country, or transferred to another United States detention facility in a manner consistent with law and the national security and foreign policy interests of the United States.[24]

The detention of prisoners despite this order from 2009 continues and for the current administration how to deal with the remaining 200 prisoners (2011) is the central issue, so reviewing each individual currently being detained has to be completed and then a determination as to what to do with each one. Many have previously been sent to other countries and have either been released or remain in custody in those foreign countries.

Military Commissions (Tribunals)

Military tribunals are not a new concept and have historically been used to prosecute enemy combatants who violate the laws of war. The last time they were used by the U.S. military was during World War II. The concept and goal of the commission is to provide the accused with a full and fair trial and at the same time provide protection for classified and sensitive information and the protection and safety of all personnel participating in the process and that would include the accused.

The tribunals came in to force with the 2006 Military Commissions Act to try "unlawful enemy combatants" and sought to limit the ability of detainees to challenge their detention via habeas corpus petitions (a ruling later overturned) and allow hearsay evidence into trial. It was also intended to keep the death penalty as an option. President Obama amended this law with the Military Commissions Act of 2009, which placed greater restrictions on the use of hearsay and "coerced" evidence, and afforded detainees greater due process.[25] Under the George W. Bush government, it was necessary to establish the following in order to proceed with a military tribunal and determine that a detainee

- Is or was an al Qaeda member.
- Has engaged in, aided or abetted, or conspired to commit acts of international terrorism against the United States; or
- Knowingly harbored one or more of the individuals described above; and
- It is in the interest of the United States that such individual be subject to this order.

Once charges had been determined and laid by the chief prosecutor, a Military Commission Panel is appointed, and this panel will consist of a presiding officer who must be a judge advocate and at least three other military officers as members. Questions of law are ruled on by the presiding officer. Unlike a civil court, the panel members vote and, if necessary, on a sentence; however, the presiding officer does not have a vote in this process. The accused is entitled to hire a civilian defense counsel at no cost to the government as long as that counsel is a U.S. citizen and is admitted to practice in a U.S. jurisdiction, has not been sanctioned to disciplinary action, is eligible for and can obtain SECRET clearance, and will agree to follow the rules of the commission. In the modern era, these commissions have come in for a considerable amount of press and civil liberty scrutiny. Military tribunals continue but with the long-term goal of the Obama administration to have the case tried in civilian court.

INTERNATIONAL POLICING

International police cooperation has existed for several decades through the **International Criminal Police Organization (Interpol)**. Interpol considers terrorism to be "a crime, characterized by violence or intimidation, usually against innocent victims in order to obtain a political or social objective." Interpol distinguishes between terrorism and organized crime: Organized crime has a profit motive, whereas terrorism's goals are not primarily for financial but rather for ideological gains. Interpol considers terrorism to be its number-one focus. The international organization supports the 182 member countries with a multipronged approach in providing intelligence on terrorist groups and identifying terrorist suspects. Due to its European location, Interpol has lent support to the member states for training assistance in building counterterrorism capability. Interpol also fashions itself as the authority that is ready, able, and willing to facilitate liaisons among the agencies of law enforcement, immigration, and customs as well as military intelligence organizations.

INTELLIGENCE GATHERING

Intelligence gathering for terrorist offenses is primarily the domain of police forces, many of which grudgingly share information. When IRA attacks occurred in London in the early 1990s, the intelligence-gathering operations were transferred from the police to the arm of British intelligence known as MI5. MI5's analysis encompassed not only IRA terrorists, but all groups that could pose a threat. In March 1996, the British government published a report by the Parliamentary Committee on Security and Intelligence, which detailed that about 39 percent of the government's resources went toward compiling data on terror group membership, infrastructure, and methods. When cases of terrorism are brought to trial on evidence painstakingly gathered by both police and MI5, it would be counterproductive for a spy to appear on the witness stand to give testimony. Cooperation between these agencies is essential, and there has been successful cooperation between the British police and the intelligence community.

In the United States following 9-11, much was made of intelligence failings on the part of the U.S. intelligence community. It is, of course, easy to be critical after the event has taken place. However, there were indicators that were missed and relevant reports that were not followed up on. In order to determine the problems, we should first make an analysis of the current and historic state of the U.S. intelligence services. It has been said that the United States has the greatest intelligence gathering apparatus in the world. However, if the right people do not listen and react to the information, it just becomes another secret file to be uncovered in future decades. Many U.S. intelligence agencies have been focused on preventing large-scale conflicts. And there is a serious need for such intelligence; however, the risk from modern terrorism and unconventional attacks appears to warrant the same level of resources. The Cold War era of intelligence, by comparison, is viewed as a simpler mode. It was easier to train covert operators to operate in the former Soviet Union than it is to train operatives to go native and assimilate into Arabic cultures and communities, mainly due to the constraints of culture, religion, and self-identification.

Budget constraints on human intelligence (HUMINT) can be traced back to the 1970s, when the United States began spending huge sums on improving the eyes and ears of the intelligence community with modern technology and satellite programs. On the other hand, the field operative has the capability to make judgments that are specific to a designated target country or culture that an analyst located thousands of miles distant would be unable to achieve. A very good example of such a failing in a military context was the inability of the U.S. administration to have adequate intelligence about what Iraq's intentions were prior to its invasion of Kuwait. Similarly, it may also have been important to have intelligence targeting the activities of the Pakistan Inter Service Intelligence (ISI) agency and its support of the Taliban and Osama bin Laden's mujahedeen.

In addition to the lack of HUMINT resources, there is a balance in signals intelligence (SIGINT), in developing new systems and technologies to penetrate more sophisticated communications without forgetting how to decode the old systems of encryption. Since 9-11, the fear of "sleeper cells" has become a threat to the nation's security and this becomes a challenge for the forces charged with protecting domestic security. Quite obviously, any Islamic extremist elements would likely conceal themselves in regions where other members of the same religious ethnicity reside. The ability of the sleeper to elude possible detection relates to the likely communications gap among the U.S. State Department, which controls and issues visas; the Immigration and Naturalization Service (INS), which has responsibility for investigating and deporting illegal immigrants; and the Federal Bureau of Investigation (FBI), the organization tasked with domestic counterintelligence. The bureaucracies that have developed have also been the impeding factor in creating an effective means of performing counterterrorism operations and investigations within the United States. Harry S. Truman, for this very reason, combined the country's intelligence efforts under the Central Intelligence Group, the forerunner to the CIA, more than fifty years ago. However, with the speed in the development of technology and the vying for political influence and budgetary constraints, the notion of a synergistic approach to the development of intelligence has been overlooked.[26] The Department of Homeland Security, which was designed to be the all-encompassing body that would meld the intelligence communities together, runs the serious risk of continuing to be a bureaucratic behemoth that will fail. With control and oversight in so many areas of enforcement, it is natural to think that with its huge budget and vast array of departments; it is set up to fail. Although it is easy to be critical, we believe that protecting the homeland is the priority, but whether the amalgamation of so many diverse operations will be a long-term success story is yet to be established.

As the planning for terrorist attacks often spans countries and regions, fighting terrorism requires the same level of effort and cooperation among nations. Spearheading the International Police agency's (INTERPOL) antiterrorism efforts is the Fusion Task Force (FTF), created in September 2002 in the wake of the alarming rise in the scale and sophistication of international terrorist attacks.

FTF's primary objectives are to

- Identify active terrorist groups and their membership.
- Solicit, collect, and share information and intelligence.
- Provide analytical support.
- Enhance the capacity of member countries to address the threats from terrorism and organized crime.

As terrorist organizations' far-reaching activities are inextricably linked, the task force investigates not only attacks but also organizational hierarchies, training, financing, methods, and motives. INTERPOL has identified public safety and terrorism as a priority crime area, and countries can benefit from INTERPOL's unique position in the international law enforcement community in the fight against terrorism. The INTERPOL officials involved with the FTF are all terrorism specialists seconded from their home countries.

Regional and Global Efforts

Six regional task forces have been created in regions considered to be particularly susceptible to terrorist activity: Project Pacific (Southeast Asia), Project Kalkan (Central Asia), Project Amazon (South America), Project Baobab (Africa), Project Europe, and Project Middle East. An immediate goal is to increase the number of officers from the above regions to develop region-specific initiatives and enhance the effectiveness of the task force in these areas. In January 2008, 119 member states were contributing to terrorism-related matters.

Fusion Task Force in Action

INTERPOL works closely with organizations such as the United Nations al Qaeda and Taliban monitoring teams and the International Criminal Tribunal for the former Yugoslavia to maintain its lists of suspected terrorists. FTF also maintains a secure website for member countries, which includes all information on the Fusion Task Working Group Meetings, including presentations and analytical reports; photo boards of suspected terrorists; and notices and diffusion lists. In January 2008, 545 users were accessing the FTF-restricted website.[27]

INTELLIGENCE SERVICES

MI5 (Secret Intelligence Service)—United Kingdom

The origins of the British Secret Intelligence Service (SIS) are to be found in the foreign section of the Secret Service Bureau, established by the Committee of Imperial Defense in October 1909. The Secret Service Bureau was soon abbreviated to "Secret Service," "SS Bureau," or even "SS." The first head of the foreign section, Captain Sir Mansfield Cumming RN, signed himself "MC" or "C" in green ink. Thus began the long tradition of the head of the Service adopting the initial "C" as his symbol.

Cumming sought to ensure that the foreign section of the Secret Service Bureau maintained a degree of autonomy, but the War Office managed to exercise extensive control over his actions. The outbreak of the World War I in 1914 brought a need for even closer cooperation with military intelligence organizations within the War Office. The most significant manifestation of this was the virtual integration of the foreign section within the military intelligence directorate. Thus, for much of the war, Cumming's organization was known as MI1(c). The debate over the future structure of British intelligence continued at length post–World War I, but Cumming managed to engineer the return of the service to foreign office control. It was known in Whitehall by a variety of titles, including the "Foreign Intelligence Service," the "Secret Service," "MI1(c)," the "Special Intelligence Service," and even "C's organization." Around 1920, it began to be referred to as the Secret Intelligence Service (SIS), a title that it has continued to use and which was enshrined in statute in the Intelligence Services Act 1994.

"MI6" has become an almost interchangeable title for SIS, at least in the minds of those outside the service. The origins of the use of this other title are to be found in the late 1930s when it was adopted as a flag of convenience for SIS. It was used extensively during the World War II, especially if an organizational link needed to be made with MI5 (the Security Service). Although "MI6" fell into official disuse years ago, many writers and journalists continue to use it to describe SIS.[28]

Joint Terrorism Analysis Centre (JTAC)—United Kingdom

The Joint Terrorism Analysis Centre, or JTAC, was created as the United Kingdom's center for the analysis and assessment of international terrorism. It has been in existence since June 2003 and is based in Thames House. Although the head of JTAC is responsible to the director general of the Security Service, JTAC operates as a self-standing organization comprising representatives from eleven government departments and agencies. JTAC analyzes and assesses all intelligence relating to international terrorism, at home in the United Kingdom and overseas, and produces assessments of threats and other terrorist-related subjects for customers from a wide range of government departments and agencies. Within the Security Service, JTAC works especially closely with the International Counter Terrorism branch, which manages investigations into terrorist activity in the United Kingdom, in order to assess the nature and extent of the threat there. JTAC is also the agency that sets threat levels pertaining to threats from international terrorism.

U.S. National Strategy For Counter Terrorism (2011)

Disrupting, dismantling, and eventually defeating al Qaeda and its affiliates and adherents is at the center of the current U.S. strategy on counterterrorism.

The Threat We Face—The principal focus of the National Strategy for Counterterrorism is the collection of groups and individuals who comprise al Qaeda and its affiliates and adherents. The preeminent security threat to the United States continues to be from al Qaeda and its affiliates and adherents. A decade after the September 11, 2001, terrorist attacks, the United States remains at war with al Qaeda Although the United States did not seek this conflict, we remain committed, in conjunction with our partners worldwide, to disrupt, dismantle, and eventually defeat al Qaeda and its affiliates and adherents to ensure the security of our citizens and interests. The death of Osama bin Laden marked the most important strategic milestone in our effort to defeat al Qaeda It removed al Qaeda's founder and leader and most influential advocate for attacking the United States and its interests abroad. But, as the president has made clear, Osama bin Laden's demise does not mark the end of our effort, nor does it mark the end of al Qaeda, which will remain focused on striking the United States and our interests abroad. Since 2001, the United States has worked with its partners around the globe to put relentless pressure on al Qaeda—disrupting terrorist plots, measurably reducing the financial support available to the group, and inflicting significant leadership losses. Despite our many successes, al Qaeda continues to pose a direct and significant threat to the United States. In addition to plotting and carrying out specific attacks, al Qaeda seeks to inspire a broader conflict against the United States and many of our allies and partners. To rally individuals and groups to its cause, al Qaeda preys on local grievances and propagates a self-serving historical and political account. It draws on a distorted interpretation of Islam to justify the murder of Muslim and non-Muslim innocents. Countering this ideology—which has been rejected repeatedly and unequivocally by people of all faiths around the world—is an essential element of our strategy. Although its brutal tactics and mass murder of Muslims have undermined its appeal, al Qaeda has had some success in rallying individuals and other militant groups to its cause. Where its ideology does resonate, the United States faces an evolving threat from groups and individuals that accept al Qaeda's agenda, whether through formal alliance, loose affiliation, or mere inspiration. Affiliated movements have taken root far beyond al Qaeda's core leadership in Afghanistan and Pakistan, including in the Middle East, East Africa, the Maghreb and Sahel regions of northwest Africa, Central Asia, and Southeast Asia. Although each group is unique, all aspire to advance al Qaeda's regional and global agenda—by destabilizing the countries in which they train and operate, attacking U.S. and other Western interests in the region, and in some cases plotting to strike the U.S. Homeland. Adherence to al Qaeda's ideology may not require allegiance to al Qaeda, the organization. Individuals who sympathize with or actively support al Qaeda may be inspired to violence and can pose an ongoing threat, even if they have little or no formal contact with al Qaeda. Global communications and connectivity place al Qaeda's calls for violence and instructions for carrying it out within easy reach of millions. Precisely because its leadership is under such pressure in Afghanistan and Pakistan, al Qaeda has increasingly sought to inspire others to commit attacks in its name. Those who in the past have attempted attacks in the United States have come from a wide range of backgrounds and origins, including U.S. citizens and individuals with varying degrees of overseas connections and affinities. Beyond al Qaeda, other foreign terrorist organizations threaten U.S. national security interests. These groups seek to undermine the security and stability of allied and partner governments, foment regional conflicts, traffic in narcotics, or otherwise pursue agendas that are inimical to U.S. interests. Whether these are groups that operate globally, as Hezbollah or HAMAS do, or are terrorist organizations located and focused domestically, we are committed to working vigorously and aggressively to counter their efforts and activities even as we avoid conflating them and al Qaeda into a single enemy.[29]

CIA and FBI

Following the 9-11 attacks, two major pieces of U.S. legislation, the U.S. Patriot Act and the Intelligence Reform and Prevention of Terrorism Act, were designed to provide a cohesive level of coordination for intelligence and information sharing between the CIA and FBI. Prior to 9-11, each agency jealously guarded the information it gathered. The FBI intelligence program was built on the following core principles:

- Independent Requirements and Collection Management: While intelligence collection, operations, analysis, and reporting are integrated at headquarters divisions and in the field, the Office of Intelligence manages the requirements and collection management process. This ensures that the FBI focuses intelligence collection and production on priority intelligence requirements and on filling key gaps in its knowledge.
- Centralized Management and Distributed Execution: The power of the FBI intelligence capability is in its 56 field offices, 400 resident agencies, and 56 legal attaché offices around the world. The Office of Intelligence must provide those entities with sufficient guidance to drive intelligence production effectively and efficiently, but not micromanage field intelligence operations.
- Focused Strategic Analysis: The Office of Intelligence sets strategic analysis priorities and ensures they are carried out both at headquarters and in the field.
- Integration of Analysis with Operations: Intelligence analysis is best when collectors and analysts work side by side in integrated operations.

Concepts of operations (CONOPs) guide FBI intelligence processes and detailed implementation plans drive specific actions to implement them. CONOPs describe the Intelligence Requirements and Collection Management system and are supported by lower-level collection and collection support processes and procedures defined in the FBI's *Intelligence Requirements and Collection Management Handbook*. These concepts and processes complement FBI operations and are enhanced by the commission's recommendations.[30]

COUNTERTERRORISM UNITS

Great Britain

In the world of counterterrorism operations, few are as effective as the British SAS. Terrorism in the twentieth century has taken place primarily in the fifty-year period after World War II; therefore, counterterror and counterinsurgency units have also developed since the war. An eccentric Scot, David Stirling, formed the SAS during World War II. A commando officer, Captain Robert Laycock, ably assisted him. During the war, conventional army theoreticians frowned upon the activities being proposed by the unconventional Stirling. At 6'5", he was an impressive figure, and he believed passionately that there was an important role for "special operations" behind enemy lines. In Egypt, Stirling teamed up with a Welsh Guardsman and an Australian named Jock Lewes and formed the Special Air Service. Protocol was the order of the day, and for Second Lieutenant Stirling to communicate his ideas to the general commanding Middle East operations would require going through a long chain of command. Stirling thought the war would be over before his ideas reached the general. By fortuitous accident, he met with the deputy commander, General Ritchie, who was so impressed with the lieutenant's ideas that they were soon put into practice for operations behind German lines in North Africa. This first unit was named "L' Detachment, Special Air Service Brigade," and the SAS was born.

The SAS of the 1990s is a far cry from that of the war years and has developed into what is arguably one of the best counterterror units in the world. Many counterterrorism organizations around the world have been modeled after the SAS. The regiment is headquartered in Hereford in the west of England, but with government spending cuts, it was destined for a new home at Royal Air Force base at Creedenhill. The SAS is made up of a Special Projects Team, and it is from this team that the Counter Revolutionary Warfare Squadron was formed to handle both foreign and domestic terrorism issues. Training for the SAS is constant, with one squadron always on standby to leave at a moment's notice to deal with a terrorist situation. An Operations Research Unit supports all SAS projects and has developed weaponry specific to the needs of the Regiment. This unit developed the stun grenade, which is widely used by counterterrorism units around the world. The unit also developed night-vision goggles and special ladders for aircraft and train assaults.

As a peacetime unit, the SAS has been primarily involved in dealing with Irish terrorists. The Provisional IRA referred to the British application of the SAS in Northern Ireland as death squads sent to terminate Irishmen. Unfortunately, for the Provisional IRA, the SAS was extremely effective in the urban warfare of Northern Ireland. The speed and efficiency with which the unit carried out operations stunned the Irish terrorist community.

SAS activity is not restricted to the United Kingdom, however, and it is believed that the regiment has been involved in operations against Libya. Adding to their mystique is the anonymity of its members. A plethora of news cameras from around the world covered the hostage drama at the Iranian Embassy in London (April 30, 1980) and captured live the dramatic rescue by armed men dressed in black fatigues. The success of that raid, which led to the death of all but one of the terrorists, placed Britain firmly in the spotlight as a country that did not deal lightly with terrorists and was prepared to use whatever force was necessary to end a crisis. This operation had been under the control of the civil police authorities until the Home Secretary William Whitelaw gave the authority for the military (SAS) to advance an assault on the embassy. This was the first time the public saw the SAS in action, and although there was an outpouring of indignation from extremists, the vast majority of Britons supported the actions of the SAS team.

Their success has to be coupled with a highly competent intelligence network and through a variety of ways the security services in Northern Ireland became adept at infiltrating as well as coercing information from informants. In 1987, the SAS carried out one of its most successful operations in Northern Ireland when it ambushed a team of PIRA terrorists about to attack a police station in Loughgall. Their intelligence was so precise that they knew all the details of the attack right down to the equipment to be used and the exact time date and location for the attack.

Several RUC and SAS men stayed in the police station acting as decoys. Outside, the SAS set up ambush positions, alongside the road past Loughgall Police Station. Apart from the main ambush force, several cutoff groups were put in place to cover possible escape routes.

The attack began at 7 P.M., a stolen blue Toyota van was seen driving past the police station, presumably scouting the area ahead of the main attack group. A few minutes later, it returned, followed by a stolen JCB (digger), with three hooded men in its cab, and a large oil drum in its front bucket. The JCB crashed through the wire fence around the police station. The SAS watched as the three hooded men jumped from the cab, one of them lighting the fuse on the oil drum. As the three IRA men ran from the JCB, five armed men leaped out of the Toyota van and started firing at the station. The SAS immediately opened fire and within seconds all eight PIRA men were dead.

It had been the most significant firefight between the SAS and the PIRA and had a decidedly one-sided result. The incident seemed, at least temporarily, to rattle the PIRA, who were troubled by the breach of security that led to the ambush.[31]

The SAS has also been used effectively against the PIRA in Europe. In 1988, the SAS followed a PIRA unit to Gibraltar, where intelligence sources indicated the terrorists would detonate a bomb during a military parade. The SAS team attacked the three PIRA members and, according to witness reports, gunned them down in cold blood. The subsequent outcry over claims of the government's "shoot-to-kill" policy seemed too much for a democracy to handle. The PIRA now had its "martyrs" and an opportunity to haul the British government before the European Court of Justice, which condemned the assault. The resulting court decision showed that caution was required, lest the counterterrorist forces go too far. For the PIRA, it meant the group had the right to not only shoot first but to kill as well!

The SAS is on good terms with numerous countries and has actively assisted training many counterterror units. It is believed that the SAS is present, either officially or unofficially, at every terror incident to view how it was handled and to determine what went well and what went wrong. Thorough debriefs are held, and every minute detail of the operation is analyzed. The SAS was present and provided assistance to the Peruvian government when terrorists took control of the Japanese Ambassador's residence in Lima in 1996.

The British Royal Navy has its own counterterrorism unit to rival the SAS: the **Special Boat Squadron (SBS)**. This unit is highly trained to respond to maritime acts of terrorism, though it has not been widely used. Most notably, the unit responded with the SAS to the bomb threat on the ocean liner, Queen Elizabeth II, in the North Atlantic. Specifically designed for naval operations, the unit was deployed prior to the arrival of the Naval Task Force off the Falkland Islands in 1982 at the outbreak of war between Great Britain and Argentina.

SAS associates: Because of the proven effectiveness of the SAS regiment and its legendary exploits since World War II, other Commonwealth countries have modeled their counterterrorism units on the SAS. The Australian SAS and the New Zealand SAS have adopted the same name.

On the international stage, special forces units teamed up in Iraq. The year 2006 was one of the bloodiest years for suicide and car bombings, particularly in Baghdad. The environment would be uniquely suited to the expertise of the British SAS and the U.S. Delta Force. It is not by coincidence that the number of daily bomb attacks had all but dried up in Baghdad in 2007 and 2008, and this was not from a lack of will on the part of groups like al Qaeda in Iraq who have been responsible for a vast majority of the suicide and car bombings. British military sources indicated in late 2008 that over 3,000 terrorists had been either killed or captured by Special Operations units and this had reduced the number of attacks down from over 150 a month to around 3 or 4.

Australia

The Tactical Assault Group (TAG) and the Special Air Service Regiment (SASR) were originally formed in 1957 and comprise Australia's response to any outbreak of domestic terror. The Australian SAS was originally a single company. By 1964, two additional companies had been added and the unit was renamed the Special Air Service Regiment (SASR). The regiment saw military action in Borneo, and with the outbreak of the Vietnam War, was instrumental in training the Australian army for its role in Southeast Asia. By the time the Vietnam War ended, the SASR had achieved some impressive results in the area of "special operations." Since the Vietnam War, Australia has not seen terrorist activity at home and the unit has been scaled down. Like its British counterpart, SASR engages in training and assists other units in the West. SASR has staff based at Fort Bragg and Little Creek in the United States. A specialist unit, the Offshore Installations Assault Group (OAG), is also available for seaborne counterterror response. Since its creation, the SASR has lost a total of seventeen men: Six were killed on active duty in Vietnam, three in operations in Borneo, and eight during a training exercise near Townsville in 1996.

Rhodesian SAS

The Rhodesian SAS is part of the original regiment that was disbanded at the end of World War II. Rhodesians have a long and proud history of engagements on foreign soil. One World War II Rhodesian, Mike Sadler, served with the SAS in North Africa and was considered to be the best navigator in the Western Desert.[32] When the war was over, members of the SAS were returned to their respective countries. The regiment was almost disbanded, but survived as a territorial unit.

After World War II, the next problem facing the allied powers was the rise of Communism in the Far East. It was the Malayan crisis of 1951 that established the reasons for retaining a Rhodesian SAS regiment for actions at home and abroad. The Commonwealth countries were asked to supply volunteers for a force in Malaya to handle the entrenched Communist terrorists. It was commanded by Major "Mad Mike" Calvert, who had been given the go-ahead to form a self-sustaining warfare unit, trained in jungle conditions to operate for long periods of time. Its mission was to continually harass and disrupt Communist terrorist activity. Major Calvert flew to Rhodesia to meet with the contingent of 100 men and briefed them on the Malayan operation. The unit from Rhodesia would become C Squadron 22 SAS (Malayan Scouts).[33]

The Malayan emergency was to last until the end of that decade, and the Rhodesian SAS remained on station for two years. On returning to Africa, the unit was disbanded and the men returned to their civilian lives. The lessons learned in that Far East operation were of value in the country's development as it struggled for its identity and independence in the 1960s. Rhodesia's army was in need of specialized expansion and development. Following an assessment, it was decided that the Special Air Service Squadron would be established as a branch of the Rhodesian army. Training would be conducted under the auspices of the British SAS at Sterling Lines in Hereford, England. The Rhodesian military had a long and successful history of graduates at the Sandhurst Military Academy in England. Among those selected to join the newly formed Rhodesian SAS were remnants of the old Malayan task force of C Squadron.[34]

The Rhodesian SAS was exceptionally well trained and schooled in jungle warfare and were accomplished paratroopers. The squadron assisted the 22 SAS Regiment in operations with the British army in the Crater District of Aden (now Yemen) during that crisis. The 1960s were a time of rationalization and decolonization. The breakup of parts of Rhodesia began: The northern part became Zambia, and Nyasaland became independent Malawi. In 1964, Ian Smith, a Rhodesian-born former World War II fighter pilot, became prime minister of the country, determined to take Rhodesia to full independence from Britain. Politics would play a major role in the gradual demise of the SAS in Rhodesia. When Ian Smith was unable to convince the British government to grant independence to Rhodesia, he declared a Unilateral Declaration of Independence (UDI). This resulted in sanctions by Britain and a full trade embargo by the United Nations. The following fourteen years of turmoil in the region would end with a black nationalist government in power and the dissolution of the SAS. On December 31, 1980, the Rhodesian SAS disbanded and its members fled south to South Africa, taking with them the memorial to their war dead.

Republic of Ireland

The Army Ranger Wing (ARW) is classified as an elite counterterror force and Ireland's front line against terrorism. Not as well known as its British counterparts, the SAS, the ARW has an impeccable reputation. The unit is made up of approximately 100 members and is subordinate to the chief of staff of the army. Like the SAS it has some of the same basic responsibilities, including the following:

- Hostage rescue in extreme situations such as hijackings, both maritime and aircraft.
- Search and rescue operations.
- Close protection security to VIPs and selected government officials.
- Ongoing maintenance of contingency planning for terrorist attacks.

Although there are no current details of actions undertaken by the group, the unit has maintained close ties with European counterterrorism units, including the French GIGN and the German GSG-9. ARW has been involved in peacekeeping operations through the United Nations in Somalia, Bosnia, and Lebanon.

Spain

Grupo Especial De Operaciones (GEO) Spain, which has had problems with the ETA terrorist group, and also GRAPO, was late in establishing an effective counterterrorism unit. In 1978, following the successes of the German GSG-9, Spain sought help from Germany in setting up GEO. One of Spain's difficulties was finding fiscal and political resources with which to staff the unit. Spain has both left-wing and right-wing terrorist problems, so there was a desperate need for apolitical members of any elite unit for this type of activity. Spain's GEO is not well-known outside that country, but is a highly trained and effective force. Although Spain has a thriving munitions industry of its own, the GEO uses the same assault weapons as their counterparts in GSG-9, favoring the Heckler and Koch MP5. As secretive as their comrades in the SAS and GSG-9, GEO has had some unsung successes in dealing with terrorists. In May 1981, twenty-four right-wing terrorists occupied the Central Bank of Barcelona, taking over 200 hostages. GEO stormed the bank, killing one terrorist, freeing all hostages and capturing ten terrorists.[35]

Guarda Civil: Spain's second unit, the Unidad Especial de Intervencion (UEI), handles hostage taking and terrorist activity and operates within the structure of the Guarda Civil (National Police). UEI is responsible to the ministries of the interior and defense and forms part of Spain's national police force. Like the GEO, it is deployed across the country and has had notable successes in rescuing kidnapping and hostage victims from both ETA and GRAPO.

The Persian Gulf

Cobras (Sultan of Oman Special Forces, SSF): Britain continued its tradition of providing training and logistical support for friendly Middle East countries with close ties to the Royal Military Academy at Sandhurst. The Sultanate of Oman has seen very little terrorist activity but, when the region started to destabilize with pro-Communist guerrillas under the Popular Front for the Liberation of Oman (PFLO), the sultan requested assistance from Britain. The Oman rebellion lasted thirteen years between 1962 and 1975. During that time, the British SAS was actively involved in counterterrorism operations with the sultan's army. However, the sultan was not prepared for the kind of terror and insurgent tactics the guerrillas would use. The SAS assisted and was instrumental in bringing down the opposition forces. When the fighting was over, Sultan Qaboos decided that his country would never again be without a response unit for insurgency and terrorism.

The British SAS provided training and guidance in setting up the Sultan's Special Forces (SSF), the Cobras. Based in Dhofar and Muscat, they are considered the most elite force in the Persian Gulf region. Cobra teams are set up along the same military lines as the SAS and are on constant, fifteen-minute standby. From their bases in Dhofar and Muscat, they have provided assistance to neighboring Kuwait. The Cobras are seconded to the Omani police, who are less well equipped and trained and retain jurisdictional control of incidents. Jealousy and interservice rivalry have not helped efforts to maintain this effective force in the Gulf.

France

Groupment d'intervention de la Gendarmerie Nationale (GIGN): Unlike the SAS, the GIGN was formed following the terrorist attacks at the Munich Olympic Games and the takeover of the Saudi Embassy in Paris. The GIGN is a police unit, not military, and recruits to this unit come from the ranks of the paramilitary police service, the Gendarmerie Nationale (National Police). All members undergo eight months of rigorous training similar to that of the SAS, to include parachute qualification. On successful completion, they are based at the Maison Alfort near Paris. As a police unit, the GIGN is called on to deal with criminal incidents as well as terrorist attacks. The unit is heavily armed with Heckler and Koch MP5 submachine guns, as well as an assortment of sophisticated handguns. The GIGN is also trained in negotiating skills and recognizing psychological weaknesses and changes in the state of mind of the terrorist. Like the SAS, GIGN shuns publicity. It has had remarkable success in rescuing kidnapping victims. GIGN's most spectacular action was the 1994 storming of an Air France airbus at Marseilles, which resulted in the death of all thirteen hijackers, members of the Armed Islamic Group (GIA) from Algiers.

The Research, Assistance, Intervention, and Dissuasion (RAID) unit is currently the lead counterterror unit in France and has been leading the fight against radical Islamists in France. This special tactical unit was the result of the rapid rise in terror attacks in France during the 1970s and 1980s at a time when the French National Police were unable to handle rising numbers of terror attacks. Headquartered outside Paris in Bievres and consisting of around 100 members, this elite organization reports to the director general of French Police. It gathers and selects its members from the French National Police, and like other Western-style elite units, its organizational structure includes sections for intervention, negotiation, and tactical support units that flex to the threat being dealt with. RAID was first seen in action during a hostage standoff in Nantes in 1985—the same year it was officially launched. RAID was developed by Robert Broussard, a police/special operations expert who had been given the task of tackling rising criminal networks and terrorism.

Netherlands

Bijondere Bijstands Eenheid (BBE): "Qua Patet Orbis" (The Whole World Over) is the motto of the Netherlands Marine Corps. "Send in the marines" has always been an option for Western governments and is an often-used phrase. In the case of the Netherlands, that is exactly what takes place in response to hostage-taking and terrorist actions. The Netherlands has one of the oldest military organizations in the world (the Dutch Marine Corps), which was founded on December 10, 1665. Today's Royal Netherlands Marine Corps numbers about 2,800. The corps is split into two separate areas for operational purposes: one group in the Netherlands for NATO duties and the other stationed in Aruba in the Dutch Antilles. The Marines represent a strike force that can respond to any terrorist situation. A section of the Marine Corps handles counterterrorism operations and is called the BBE. Translated, this has the literal meaning "different circumstances unit." The Dutch government states that it does not negotiate with terrorists, although the country is not beset with severe terrorist problems. One incident that resulted in conflict relates to Dutch colonialism in Indonesia. In 1975, a group from South Molucca hijacked a train hoping to bring pressure to the Dutch government. The hijackers were members of the Free South Moluccans Youth Organization (VZJ) demanding an independent homeland.

The Netherlands' response was to send in the Marines (BBE). On this occasion, as with others involving the South Moluccans, the siege was ended by force, resulting in the death of the terrorists and minor injuries to the rescuers and the rescued. Each attack unit of the BBE consists of two, thirty-three-man platoons, each comprising four assault teams. They are further broken down into five-man units. The unit's functions are similar to those of the British SAS and are assisted with maritime operations from the 7th Special Boat Squadron, another elite unit made up of four, six-man intervention teams.

Norway

Forsvarets Spesialkommando (FSK, Special Defense Commando): Norway's elite military response unit was formed in 1982, primarily as a defensive unit to deal with terrorist attacks against its many North Sea oil rigs. It is also responsible for the close protection of the Norwegian Royal Family, the national assembly, and other government officials. The FSK is a branch unit of the Norwegian Army Jegercommand. This is another unit that has used the example of the SAS, and the start-up of the unit involved five years of close involvement between the two. FSK and SAS have maintained close ties and often train together on exercises. The close nature of the two units brought the FSK some unwanted publicity when it was reported in the Norwegian press that it had been involved in SAS operations against the IRA in Northern Ireland in 1994, a report that both governments strenuously denied. FSK has also seen service overseas when it was dispatched to Kashmir to help locate a Norwegian being held captive by Al-Faran guerrillas.

Germany

Grenzschutzgruppe 9 (GSG-9) is considered one of the elite terrorist response units of modern time. It was formed following the disaster at the 1972 Munich Olympic Games. After the horrendous events, the Germans were not prepared to allow such atrocities to happen again. In the case of the Olympics, it was the soft target with worldwide media coverage that the Black September movement was after. In the two decades after the end of World War II, Germany had taken pains not to produce any elitist forces for any purpose. GSG-9 was formed and was fully operational by April 1973, six months after the Munich massacre. Unlike the SAS, GSG-9 would form part of the Federal Border Police service and not part of the German military. Each member must be a volunteer and a member of the Border Police. The iconic leader and founding leader of GSG-9 was Colonel Ulrich Wegener who joined Germany's Federal Border Police in 1958. His training with both the FBI and the Israeli Secret Service gave him expert knowledge on terrorism and was the logical choice to lead the group. He is believed to have been involved with the Israeli raid at Entebbe in 1976. Wegener's orders had been to create a small and highly flexible antiterrorist unit that could be used and deployed at a moment's notice. Following his success at Mogadishu, he was promoted to brigadier and given ultimate control over the whole of the Federal Border Police.[36]

The group is split into three definable units, each with fifty members: GSG-9/1 is responsible for counterterrorism; GSG-9/2 handles maritime counterterrorism; and GSG-9/3 deals with airborne issues. The federal government supplies GSG-9 with the best and most advanced equipment available. The group operates in five-man units and is outfitted with two sets of combat gear: one for day and the other for nighttime operations.

Israel

SAYERET MAT'KAL: Sayeret Mat'kal is also known as the **General Staff Reconnaissance Unit #69** and was founded in 1957. This unit has been in the forefront of every Israeli anti- and counterterrorism strategy since its inception. It is the unit that is also dedicated to handling hostage-taking incidents. In wartime, this unit takes on the role of intelligence gathering. The Sayeret Mat'kal actively does the bidding of the Israeli government and has hunted down and executed known terrorists. After the Munich massacre, it was mandated to track down and kill those involved. Operation Spring Youth was an offensive strike carried out by the Sayeret Mat'kal in 1973. It has carried out actions that for nearly every other Western power would be unacceptable; however, to the embattled Israelis, the group's actions are accepted as a requirement in the protection of the state. On April 9 and 10, 1973, Sayeret infiltrated Beirut, which had to be considered extremely hostile territory, and assassinated the leaders of the Black September organization. This action was carried out successfully at three separate locations in West Beirut.

Czech Republic

Utvar Rychleho Nasazeni (URNA) is the Czech Republic's rapid response counterterrorist police and crime-busting force. URNA is modeled to be similar to its elite counterparts in the German GSG-9 and the French GIGN. It has specific responsibilities and as such is tasked directly from the ministry of the interior to protect foreign heads of state, secure major sporting events against sabotage, and assist the police in drugs and serious crime interdiction. By far, its most important role is its intervention in extreme terrorist situations, including hostage taking and hijackings. Although not as well known as other Western European counterterror units, URNA is considered one of the elite reaction units and is held in very high regard.

Indonesia

After the 2002 Bali bombings, Indonesia recognized that the main threat to national security came from regional terrorist networks whose leaders returned to Indonesia after Suharto fell from power in 1998. An elite counterterrorism unit, Densus 88 (Detasemen Khusus 88, or Special Detachment 88), was Indonesia's answer to the terrorists who exploited the country's weakened security environment. Among the terrorists were many former Afghan jihadis as well as Abu Bakr Ba'asyir and the late Abdullah Sungkar—the duo that founded Jemaah Islamiyah (JI) while in exile in Malaysia between 1985 and 1998.[37] Detachment 88 was formed within the Indonesian Police Service and is based outside Jakarta and has been funded by the U.S. government with training from the CIA and FBI as well as the U.S. Secret Service. The unit has over 400 members and became operational in 2005 and like many other antiterror units mirrors those already operating successfully in Western Europe.

HOSTAGE RESCUE UNITS (HRUs)

Most countries designate, train, and equip teams to deal with hostage-taking crises and the protection of VIPs and government officials. These units in the Philippines are called the Aviation Security Commando (AVESCOM) Unit. In Thailand, HRU functions are the responsibility of the Royal Thai Air Force. In India, the highly trained Special Counterterrorist Unit (SCU) is considered to be the best in Asia. Malaysia uses the Special Strike Unit of the Royal Malay Police, and Sri Lanka has the Army Commando Squadron. In the Middle East, Bahrain and Saudi Arabia have units trained by the British SAS and the French GIGN, respectively. The Hashemite Kingdom of Jordan maintains the 101st Special Forces Battalion, which also provides sky marshals for Alia, Jordan's national airline. Egypt has had a colorful history of failures in hostage rescue in recent decades. Both of the incidents occurred in the Mediterranean. Egypt uses the Saiqa unit for counterterrorism operations, as well as Force 777, created in 1978. The countries of Latin and South America use sections of the military and federal police services for HRU functions in most cases.

The United States of America

Hostage rescue, kidnapping, and their negotiations have long been the province of the Federal Bureau of Investigations (FBI), assisted by special police squads that are formed in almost every jurisdiction in the United States. These units are termed "Special Weapons and Tactical (SWAT) units." The FBI is the U.S. federal agency responsible for information and intelligence gathering at home, which is not, as many believe, the domain of the Central Intelligence Agency. The CIA is mandated for intelligence and field operations outside the United States and for protecting U.S. interests. With varying gun laws throughout the United States, weapons offenses are a daily diet for the state police, with SWAT teams regularly called upon to deal with many criminal activities, particularly bank holdups. With the hostage crisis in Tehran in the 1970s, the need arose to have dedicated and well-trained tactical teams to deal with subversive activities both at home and abroad.

Hostage rescue is a risky business, and usually when rescues go wrong they go wrong very quickly and often with disastrous results. In 1985, Egypt Air 648 was hijacked to the island of Malta in the Mediterranean. The Egyptian government dispatched its counterterrorism strike force, Force 777, to the island to assist with the hostage rescue operations. The Maltese government gave the go-ahead for Force 777 to take action against the terrorists. The assault began at about 8:00 P.M., lasting for more than a minute and a half, which is nearly four times longer than most antiterror groups will take to storm aircraft and release hostages. The series of mistakes, miscalculations, lack of intelligence, and planning resulted in the death of the passengers, some of whom were shot by snipers, who mistook escaping passengers for terrorists and gunned some of them down.[38]

"Delta Force" was the 1970s' brainchild of Charles Beckwith. Beckwith realized that the United States did not have the same capability for hostage rescue and counterterrorism response as the Europeans and proposed establishing an elite unit from the ranks of the U.S. Special Forces. Selection began, using the same disciplined methods as used by the SAS, which Beckwith himself had experienced with the SAS in the 1960s. After the seizure of the U.S. embassy in Tehran, in November 1979, the Delta Force was placed on standby to handle the rescue and evacuation of the hostages. Considerable intelligence gathering and logistical planning went into the plans to rescue the hostages, and the Delta team was front and center. The mission was to fail due to dust storms. One of the mission's helicopters crashed into a C-130 that was carrying munitions, resulting in the deaths of eight members of the U.S. Marine Corps.

The members of Delta Force managed to escape injury and returned to the United States without completing their mission. After the abortive mission to Iran, a Special Operations Group was initiated, and from that came the creation of SEAL Team Six in 1980. SEAL Team Six is the Navy's equivalent to the Delta Force and is responsible for handling counterterrorism in any maritime environment. Its beginnings relate directly to the failure of the Tehran operation, which had been designated by the code words, "Eagle Claw." The name SEAL Team Six was chosen as a ploy to confuse the Soviets as to exactly how many SEAL units the United States then had available at that time. All of the SEAL platoons were trained in counterterrorism. SEAL Team Six went through an extensive training regimen that involved training overseas with members of the SAS, GSG-9, GIGN, and other counterterrorism organizations. SEAL Team Six would undergo further changes to its structure, including a name change due to its poor reputation within the Navy. SEAL Team Six was embarrassed by its founding member, Commander Richard Marcinko, who was charged with an assortment of offenses, ranging from fraud to bribery, and was sentenced to a brief term of imprisonment. Following this fiasco, the unit designation was changed to the Naval Special Warfare Development Group (NSWDG). Structured on the same lines as the SAS and numbering approximately 200 men, the NSWDG covers a wide spectrum of abilities, much the same as the SAS and the SBS. Unlike their European counterparts, they have not had the opportunity to prove themselves, as the SAS had at Prince's Gate or the GSG-9 had at Mogadishu, although they have been in both covert and overt operations since the 1980s.

In 1985, NSWDG was on standby in the Mediterranean during the *Achille Lauro* hijacking, which claimed the life of Leon Klinghoffer, but it was not called into action. In the same year, the unit was used during the U.S. invasion of Grenada to rescue the governor of the island, Sir Paul Scoon. During that operation, four SEALs drowned during the helicopter insertion offshore. The SEALs were used for the initial landings in Somalia in 1992, when they came ashore in scuba gear to a media throng with video cameras and floodlights who broadcast their invasion, live, around the world. This was a prime example of poor understanding between operational forces and the media. The SEALs have their place in history with their most notable action, the attack on Osama bin Laden's Pakistan compound, the seizure of masses of intelligence, and the death of the U.S. Most Wanted Terrorist himself in May 2011.

In domestic situations, the United States uses the Alcohol Tobacco and Firearms (ATF) unit for dealing with criminals who are stockpiling illegal weapons. For weeks, the news media covered a major ATF operation in Waco, Texas. The ATF went to execute a warrant against the Branch Davidians, led by David Koresh. An ensuing gun battle and a long standoff later resulted in an ATF assault. A fire erupted and all inside the compound were incinerated. It was discovered after the event, however, that many had been killed or committed suicide before flames overtook the buildings.

CANADA

Joint Task Force Two (JTF-2)

From 1993 onward, responsibility for counterterror operations in Canada changed from a Royal Canadian Mounted Police (RCMP) role to a military function. A rather secretive military force known as **Joint Task Force 2 (JTF-2)** functions much in the same way as its SAS British counterparts. The unit is known to have operated in Eastern Europe, particularly in Bosnia and in regions of Afghanistan in pursuit of al Qaeda leader Osama bin Laden. JTF-2 arrived in Afghanistan in December 2001 and joined other Special Ops forces from the United States, Britain, and Australia, based at the former Taliban stronghold of Kandahar. The Canadians were assigned to Task Force K-Bar, a multinational special operations group led by U.S. Navy SEAL Captain Robert Harward.

K-Bar consisted of some 2,800 personnel, including support and air staff, and under Harward's command were Special Forces units from the U.S. Navy, Army, and Air Force, as well as forces from Denmark, Germany, Norway, Australia, Canada, New Zealand, and Turkey. U.S. Marine helicopters provided air transport.[39]

PIRACY

The Oxford English Dictionary defines "piracy" as "Robbery, kidnapping, or violence committed at sea or from the sea without lawful authority, especially by one vessel against another." The International Maritime Bureau Piracy Center provides a more recent definition of piracy: "The act of boarding any vessel with the intent to commit theft or other crime and with the capability to use force in the furtherance of the act." Article 101 of the United Nations Convention of the Law of the Sea defines piracy as follows:

> Piracy consists of any of the following acts:
>
> **a.** Any illegal acts of violence or detention, or any act of depredation, committed for private ends by the crew or the passengers of a private ship or a private aircraft and directed
>> **i.** On the high seas, against another ship or aircraft, or against persons or property on board such ship or aircraft;
>> **ii.** Against a ship, aircraft, persons or property in a place outside the jurisdiction of any State.
> **b.** Any act of voluntary participation in the operation of a ship or of an aircraft with knowledge of facts making it a pirate ship or aircraft;
> **c.** Any act of inciting or of intentionally facilitating an act described in subparagraph a or b.

Although sea piracy has been in existence for centuries and, to many, it will conjure up an almost romantic or exotic event, the truth is far different. Sea piracy remains a major economic and security threat. Areas of the globe most affected by sea piracy are located in the waters of the Horn of Africa, the Far East, the South China Sea, and the waters surrounding Indonesia and the Philippines. Frequent attacks on shipping go virtually unnoticed in the news media; however, crew deaths are not an uncommon result of piracy. In earlier days, almost all trade around the globe went via ships, and the lucrative routes between the Middle East and the Far East were the hunting grounds for myriads of pirates. The well-known, sixteenth-century English sea Captain Sir Francis Drake could also be likened to a pirate. His ships' targets were invariably those belonging to Spain. Britain had been on and off at war with Spain and the seizing of Spain's ships was not considered to be piracy, at least not by the British. Drake was deemed to be a "privateer," and his many countrymen operated under the same royal protection. However, the Spanish government considered Drake and Walter Raleigh to be dyed-in-the-wool pirates. Piracy on the high seas has developed and become more sophisticated with the passage of time and with obviously higher risks and greater rewards for the pirates. The International Maritime Organization has defined three types and levels of piracy:

1. An attack on a ship operating close to shore, often an opportunist attack, by pirates in small, high-speed, seagoing craft, with the intent to steal cash and personal valuables from the crew and the ship's safe. This is defined as a Low-Level Armed Robbery (LLAR).
2. Medium-Level Armed Robbery and Assault (MLAAR). This level of attack is invariably a deadly assault on the ship's crew and/or passengers, often by well-armed and equipped pirates. This type of attack has often been coordinated with the aid of a mother ship, enabling the attack to take place in international waters.
3. The most serious level defined by the organization, **Major Criminal Hijack (MCHJ)**, invariably involves international criminals who are well-equipped and trained. These groups will either take total control of the vessel, stealing the vessel's entire cargo and off loading it to another ship, or casting the crew adrift and re-naming the ship.

What makes piracy so lucrative and accomplishable in the twenty-first century? A large number of states have depleted their navies, thus leaving them unable to have a presence to deter pirate attacks on ships, both in international and territorial waters. Add to this a dimension of high technology in which many vessels are now dependent on much smaller operating crews, creating an opportunity for pirates to operate unhindered. Shipping in international waters is protected by the "flag" of the country in which it is registered. Many countries adopt a "flag of convenience" for their vessel, which means that a vessel owned in one country (such as the United States or Great Britain) can be registered in another country (Panama, Liberia, or Cyprus, for example), thus avoiding international safety and taxation regulations. Nearly 90 percent of ocean-going cargo ships entering U.S. ports are operating under foreign flags. Many of these ships, such as Greek-flagged and flag-of-convenience ships (officially called "open-registry ships"), operating out of Piraeus employ low-wage seamen from the developing countries of Pakistan and the Philippines. Flag-of-convenience countries are often unwilling to take any significant diplomatic action against countries from which pirates are operating. The International Maritime Bureau has a piracy center located in Kuala Lumpur, Malaysia, that has responsibility to provide information around the clock on piracy activities in all the regions of the globe.

As an example during the first three months of 2012 the International Chamber of Commerce's International Maritime Bureau (IMB) Web page provides startling numbers for attacks on shipping.

Worldwide Incidents:

Total Attacks Worldwide: 87

Total Hijackings Worldwide: 9

Incidents Reported for Somalia:

Total Incidents: 36

Total Hijackings:7

Total Hostages: 92

Current vessels held by Somali pirates: 13

Hostages: 197

By comparison, 2011 had been no better as Somali pirates took 361 sailors hostage and kidnapped 13 in the first six months of 2011. Worldwide, 495 seafarers were taken hostage. Pirates killed 7 people and injured 39. Ninety-nine vessels were boarded, seventy-six fired upon and sixty-two thwarted attacks were reported.[40]

The legal aspects of piracy are somewhat convoluted, if not complex. The international community recognizes that an act of piracy can only be committed in international waters and must therefore be dealt with under international law. Should the commission of a seaborne attack on a maritime vessel occur inside territorial waters, the responsibility for pursuing and prosecuting the incident as robbery falls to the state that claims the territorial right over that region. International law requires any warship or government vessel to "repress piracy on the high seas" and to come to the aid of any vessel under attack. The rules of engagement for sea piracy, as it affects government vessels, are that force should only be used as a means of self-defense against piracy. There are, in fact, no listed rules of engagement for sea piracy. The action of individual member state's navies is governed, therefore, by each state.

Historical data on piracy do not go farther back than 1980. In the early 1980s, private groups targeted ships at anchor and waiting to berth in the Nigerian ports of Lagos and Bonny. They would attack after dark and break into containers on board. The eventual outcome was a concerted crackdown by Nigerian police and customs to root out the pirates and their bases of operation. Piracy has also been highly prevalent in the Far East in the Straits of Malacca, one of the busiest shipping lanes in the world. In efforts to contain and minimize the attacks against commercial and other shipping, the International Maritime Organization established a working group to study the problem and come up with a methodology and recommendations. The results of the study were that the underreporting of acts of piracy should be discouraged and that masters should immediately report acts and attempted acts of piracy. Probably the most significant effort was the assistance of technology through the International Telecommunications Union and the International Mobile Satellite Organization (Inmarsat). This technology enabled the inclusion of "piracy/armed robbery attack" as a category of distress message that ships are now able to transmit through Digital Selective Calling (DSC) or by using Inmarsat.[41] The message will be received automatically by ships and shore stations in the area. Maritime piracy continues in many regions of the world and particularly in areas where it is easy for pirates to escape without detection. The vastness of the South China Sea is testament to that, and there are attacks on fishing vessels around the many islands of the Philippines. In these attacks, pirates take the fish and any other valuables on board or take the entire vessel.

The Piracy Reporting Center in Kuala Lumpur operates around the clock providing daily bulletins on pirate activity. The center is supported by voluntary contributions from shipping lines and insurance companies. Technology such as global positioning and tracking systems allows shipping companies to adopt such innovations as the SHIPLOC system, an inexpensive method of using satellite technology and the Internet to track individual ships. Irrespective of technology piracy is likely to continue as the pirates become more sophisticated in their modus

The USCG has a three-tiered system of MARSEC levels to reflect the prevailing threat environment to the maritime elements of the national transportation system. MARSEC levels are designed to provide a means to easily communicate pre-planned scalable responses to increased terrorist threats levels.

Level 1 indicates the level for which minimum appropriate security measures shall be maintained at all times and generally corresponds to DHS Homeland Security Advisory System (HSAS) Threat condition Green, Blue, or Yellow. Level 2 indicates the level for which appropriate additional protective security measures shall be maintained for a period of time as a result of a heightened risk of a TSI and generally corresponds to HSAS Threat Condition Orange. Level 3 indicates the level for which specific protective security measures shall be maintained for a limited period of time when TSI is probable, imminent or has occurred, although it may not be possible to identify the specific target and generally corresponds to HSAS Threat Condition Red. The Commandant of the USCG sets MARSEC levels, but because of the unique nature of the maritime industry, MARSEC levels will align closely with HSAS Threat Conditions but will not directly correlate. The international community also uses a three-tiered advisory system specified by the International Ship and Port Facility Security (ISPS) Code. MARSEC levels are consistent with the international three-tiered advisory system.

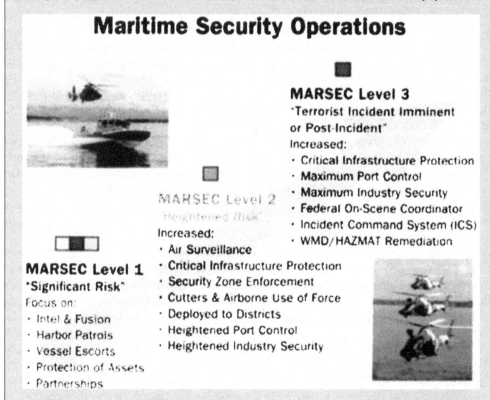

FIGURE 14-4   Maritime security levels (U.S. Department of Homeland Security).   *Source:*–DHS 2010 Transportation systems Sector-Specific Paln.

operandi. Whether a ship will be used in a terrorist attack, such as the destruction of a passenger cruise liner, with massive loss of life, is no doubt on the list of scenarios being looked at by the security and intelligence communities. As of July 2004, ships above 500 tons had to be equipped with alarm systems that silently transmit security alerts containing tracking information in case of emergency. Vessels were required to emboss their International Maritime Organization (IMO) number on their hulls. Since 2003, ship owners have been able to install high-voltage electric fencing to discourage intruders, although ships carrying highly volatile cargo (including oil) cannot use such fencing.[42]

The UN Convention of the Law of the Sea, Article 105

The seizure of a pirate ship or aircraft: On the high seas, or in any other place outside the jurisdiction of any state, every state may seize a pirate ship or aircraft, or a ship or aircraft taken by piracy and under the control of pirates, and arrest the persons and seize the property on board. The courts of the state that carried out the seizure may decide on the penalties to be imposed and may also determine the action to be taken with regard to the ships, aircraft, or property, subject to the rights of the third parties acting in good faith.[43]

Countering the Threats from the Sea

Terrorist groups such as Hezbollah, Jemaah Islamiyah, the Popular Front for the Liberation of Palestine-General Command, and Sri Lanka's Tamil Tigers have all at one time sought to develop a maritime capability. Intelligence agencies estimate that al Qaeda affiliates now operate dozens of phantom ships—pirated, repainted, renamed, and operating under false documentation, manned by crews with fake passports and forged competency certificates. Security experts have long warned that terrorists might try to ram a ship loaded with explosive cargo, perhaps even a dirty bomb, into a major port or terminal. Such an attack could bring international trade to a halt, inflicting multibillion-dollar damage on the world economy.[44] In 2004, Panama and Liberia agreed to allow countries that formed part of the Proliferation Security Initiative (PSI) to board ships sailing under both Liberian and Panamanian flags. The obvious value of this agreement was that any ships owned and operated by al Qaeda would likely be registered and flagged as either Panamanian or Liberian. More than half the ships that traverse the globe are covered by the so-called flags of convenience. Intelligence gathered on al Qaeda suggests that the group has had the opportunity to operate more than 300 vessels of varying sizes, posing a serious threat to ports, particularly in the United States and Europe. To complement the ability of the major navies of the world to board "suspect" ships on the high seas, additional measures have been established to protect the integrity of cargo—not just at the port of final destination but also at the port of export. Stringent global strategies came into force on June 1, 2004, including the International Code for the Security of Ships and Port Facilities (ISPS) and amendments to the International Convention for the Safety of Life at Sea (SOLAS). The new ISPS code and the amendments to SOLAS adopted by the 162-member International Maritime Organization (IMO) require all companies operating ships of more than 500 tons on international voyages to designate security officers, prepare contingency plans, and be fitted with new security alert systems.

There is one act of piracy/hijacking in the last quarter of a century that stands out not just for its boldness but for the callous actions of the terrorists involved. In 1985, the Italian cruise ship *Achille Lauro* was taken over by the Palestine Liberation Front terrorists at the exact same time as Palestinian/Jordanian talks were being conducted in London. The PLF demanded the release of fifty Palestinians held in Israeli prisons in exchange for the safe return of the cruise ship. Among the passengers were American Jews, and one an elderly U.S. citizen Leon Klinghoffer, who was confined to a wheelchair, was tossed overboard and drowned.

The hijackers eventually surrendered to Egyptian authorities, including the leader of the PLF Abu Abbas. As they began their flight from Tunis to Egypt, the aircraft was intercepted by U.S. Navy fighters and forced to fly to a NATO base in Sicily. Italian police arrested the hijackers, but not before diplomatic wrangling between the United States and Italy was eventually resolved with the intervention of President Reagan. It is believed the intended target was not the cruise liner, and in fact, the terrorists were planning a raid in Egypt when they were discovered on the *Achille Lauro* with weapons and explosives. While piracy is an ongoing problem for shipping in the South China Sea and Horn of Africa, particularly Somalia, the concern is also generated by the vast numbers of containers and container ships that circumnavigate the oceans. The potential that just one of these containers could contain a nuclear, chemical, or biological weapon for detonation at a U.S. port is of obvious concern. Prior to 9-11, the numbers of containers being screened entering the United States amounted to less than half of 1 percent of all container traffic. Reporting requirements are now placed on shipping lines prior to a ship's arrival; security officers are required on board ships; and stringent security protocols are in place at originating ports. The threat to the food chain and controls on imports of foods is the domain of the U.S. Food and Drug Administration (FDA), an agency not under the umbrella of Homeland Security. The FDA has oversight in areas of bio-defense when it comes to contamination of foods. The FDA is responsible for about 80 percent of the U.S. food supply and its oversight includes safe production, processing, storage, and holding of domestic imported food. Past concerns related to food safety have revolved around individual attempts to contaminate a specific food or food service location. In 2002, a restaurant owner in China added chemicals to a competitor's food, killing dozens and sending several hundred to hospitals. A more serious threat emanated from the United Kingdom in January 2003, when police arrested a group attempting to place "Ricin" into the food supply of a British military base. The FDA has formulated four major regulations under the authority of the Public Health Security and Bioterrorism Preparedness and Response Act of 2002. Owners and operators of foreign or domestic food facilities that manufacture, process, pack, or hold food products for human or animal consumption in the United States must submit information to the agency about their facility and emergency contact information.

Container Security Initiative

In January 2002, the U.S. Customs and Border Patrol (CBP) announced the introduction of the Container Security Initiative. This measure is intended to ensure that maritime containers posing a risk for terrorism are identified and examined at foreign ports before they are shipped to the United States. The initiative is founded on four core principles:

1. Using intelligence and automated information to identify and target containers that pose a risk for terrorism.
2. Prescreening those containers that pose a risk at the port of departure before they arrive at U.S. ports.
3. Using detection technology to quickly prescreen containers that pose a risk.
4. Using smarter, tamper-evident containers.

The CSI focused on the twenty foreign ports that ship approximately two-thirds of the volume of containers to the United States. Governments from these twenty foreign ports have agreed to implement the CSI. Since 2002, the program has expanded to include more ports based on volume, location, and strategic concerns. CSI is a reciprocal program that offers participant countries the opportunity to send their customs officers to major U.S. ports to target ocean-going, containerized cargo destined for their countries.

The following is an up-to-date list of those ports currently operating under this initiative:

Europe:

- Rotterdam, the Netherlands
- Bremerhaven and Hamburg, Germany
- Antwerp and Zeebrugge, Belgium
- Le Havre and Marseilles, France
- Gothenburg, Sweden
- La Spezia, Genoa, Naples, Gioia Tauro, and Livorno, Italy
- Felixstowe, Liverpool, Thamesport, Tilbury, and Southampton, United Kingdom
- Piraeus, Greece
- Algeciras, Spain

North America:

- Montreal, Halifax, and Vancouver, Canada

East Asia and the Pacific:

- Singapore, China
- Yokohama, Tokyo, Nagoya, and Kobe, Japan
- Hong Kong, China
- Pusan, South Korea
- Port Klang and Tanjung Pelepas, Malaysia
- Laem Chabang, Thailand

Threats to infrastructure have long been a concern and not least of oil and gas installations—many are remote by their very nature but that in itself may make the target more attractive. The risk profile (see Figure 14-5) developed by the U.S. Department of Homeland Security is an excellent example of both risk and threat.

Pipelines and aviation may pose a significant risk but so also does rail freight transportation systems, and while hardening around passenger rail is ongoing, the Department of Homeland Security is addressing rail freight as well within its National Strategy.

CHEMICAL AND BIOLOGICAL WEAPONS

Understanding Chemical, Biological, and Nuclear U.S. Food and Drug Administration Strategies

Prior Notification of Food Shipments: This regulation became effective in December 2003 and requires the FDA to receive prior notice of imported food shipments before the food arrives at a U.S. port. This would amount to more than 25,000 notifications about incoming shipments every day.

Establishment and Maintenance of Records: Manufacturers, processors and packers, importers, and others are required to keep records that identify the source from which they receive food and where they send it.

Administrative Detention: The FDA has authority to detain any food for up to thirty hours for which there is credible evidence that the food poses a threat to humans or animals.

The pipeline system is a vital part of the U.S. transportation and energy supply, with connections to other critical infrastructure such as airports and power plants. Since the attacks of September 11, 2001, numerous federal warnings have been issued specifically mentioning pipelines as terrorist targets. Many pipelines carry volatile and flammable materials that have the potential to cause serious injury to the public and the environment. The pipeline system is uniquely vulnerable to terrorist attacks because of the products transported, and because pipeline networks are widely dispersed across both remote and urban portions of the country. A pipeline facility could be vandalized or attacked with explosive devices, resulting in flow disruption or the release of its contents.

Pipelines are also susceptible to cyber attacks on their computer control systems. Cyber threats could result from the acts of a terrorist hacker, or a rogue employee with computer access. The latter threat requires that specific attention be given to personnel security credentials and access protocols, as well as general cyber security protocols. Additionally, attacks on other infrastructure such as regional electricity grids and communication networks could cause a serious disruption in pipeline operations, posing risks for all sectors serviced by pipelines, including the military and major commercial installations.

American transportation and manufacturing could be halted, homes could go cold for lack of natural gas or heating oil, and energy for vital defense use may begin to limit American defense capabilities.

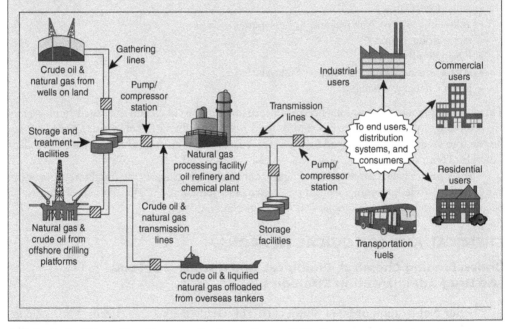

FIGURE 14-5 Risk profile—Threat to Pipelines. *Source*: DHS—Transportation Systems Sector-Specific Plan.

Combating the Proliferation of Weapons of Mass Destruction

The threat from WMD may be overstated or, depending on your viewpoint, the threat may be understated. Since the end of the Cold War, the world is awash with nuclear products, waste, and material. There has been debate about nuclear stockpiles and their accessibility in the former Soviet republics, and accounting for those stockpiles has not been an exact science. At a Global Threat

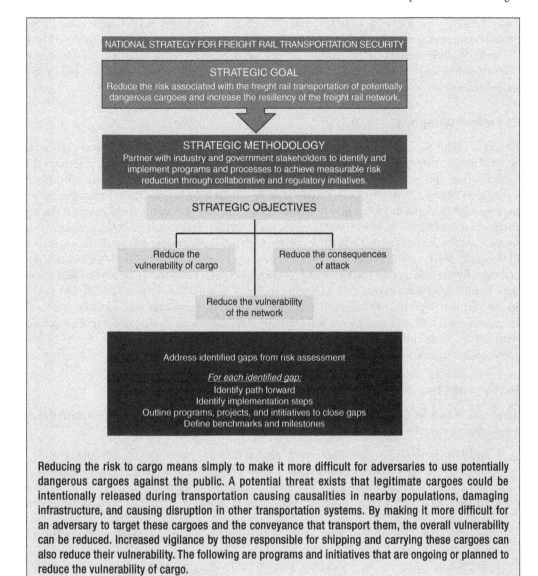

FIGURE 14-6 National strategy for rail freight transportation security (U.S. Department of Homeland Security). *Source*: DHS Transportation Systems Sector-Specific Plan.

Reduction Initiative conference in Vienna in 2004, the head of the UN Atomic Energy Agency (AEA) stated that there are about 350 sites in 58 countries that possess highly enriched uranium (HEU) and approximately two dozen of them have enough material to build a nuclear weapon. The director general believed it was just a matter of time before terrorists deployed a nuclear device. There are tens of thousands of unprotected, suitable radioactive sources available to terrorists, even in wealthy and well-ordered societies. There were fifty cases of illicit traffic in radioactive materials in 2003, and the smugglers often target materials used in the medical and science industries.[45] A 1991 official report by the UN Special Commission to Iraq (UNSCOM) stated that inspectors had found 46,000 chemical munitions in Iraq. From that, 20,000 were 120-mm CS-filled bombs; 14,000 contained mustard gas; and a further 11,000 were filled with the nerve agent Sarin. UNSCOM later discovered hidden stockpiles of 200 anthrax bombs and 80 Scud rockets at Salah Ad Din near Tikrit. The invasion of Iraq was predicated on the existence of Iraq's nuclear weapons capability and to date that appears to be somewhat of a fallacy.

Chemical Weapons

Chemical agents used in warfare dates back to World War I, with the first known use of a chemical agent. The German army began dispersing chlorine gas against British and allied troops on the battlefields of Europe in 1915. Mustard gas was first used during the trench wars of World War I two years later. Records show the Italians also used mustard gas against the Ethiopians when they invaded Ethiopia in 1935, and the Japanese used mustard gas and also chlorine gas during their invasion of China in 1930. The Germans made further developments in the production of nerve agents in the late 1930s. Both the Germans and the allied armies had significant stockpiles of chemical weapons but neither side used them during World War II (1939–1945). Mustard gas was used by the Soviets and the Egyptians in Yemen between 1963 and 1967. The United States used chemical defoliant agents such as Agent Orange, Agent Blue, and Agents Purple and White in the Vietnam War. Agent Orange, a herbicide made of two common weed killers, was used frequently—over 50 million pounds were dropped over Vietnam during the war. The Soviets used nerve agents and mustard gas against the mujahedeen in Afghanistan between 1977 and 1989. Both Iran and Iraq used mustard gas in their war from 1979 to 1989.

History of Chemical Terrorism

There has been a long history of terrorists and criminals using poisons and toxins for political assassination and other crimes with political motivation:

- **In 1976**, the Arab Revolutionary Army injected mercury into citrus food products.
- **In 1979**, the West German police raided a safe house of the Red Army Brigade and seized 400 kilograms of chemical precursors used to make nerve agents.
- **In 1985**, an Israeli military base discovered that its supply of coffee had been contaminated with a nerve agent.
- **In 1984**, several people died from arsenic poisoning after the drug Tylenol was contaminated with arsenic poison.
- **In 1994**, in Tokyo, the Aum Shinrikyo sect released Sarin gas into the subway system, killing twelve people and injuring more than 5,000.
- **In September 2004**, in the Ukraine, Viktor Yushchenko, president of Ukraine, was poisoned by dioxin, probably orally administered, and some suggest it may have been "Yellow Rain," a chemical agent used by the Soviets in the Afghan War.

There are a large number of chemical agents in existence today that could cause serious disruption if released into a general population:

- **Nerve agents:**
  GA—Tabun
  GB—Sarin
  GD—Soman
  VX—V agents

- **Vesicants or blistering agents:**
  H—mustard
  HD—distilled mustard
  HN—nitrogen mustard
  CX—phosgene oxime
  L—lewisite
- **Blood agents:**
  AC—hydrogen cyanide
  CK—cyanogen chloride
- **Choking agents:**
  Chlorine
  Phosgene
  Chloropicrin
- **Irritating agents:**
  CN—standard tear gas
  CS—stronger tear gas; induces vomiting
  DM—adamsite vomiting agent

Nerve Agents

These chemicals are designed to attack the body's nervous system in such a way as to cause convulsions or death. **Nerve agents** are liquid at ambient temperatures and are some of the most dangerous of all the chemical agents. Looking at Aum's attack on the Tokyo subway, all the symptoms of a nerve gas attack were prevalent: pinpoint pupils, blurred vision, eyes aggravated by light, excessive sweating, runny nose and nasal congestion, coughing and difficulty with breathing, nausea and vomiting, anxiety, and giddiness.

Some of the outward warning signs that could indicate a nerve agent attack include the following:

- Explosions that dispense gas, mists, or liquids
- Unscheduled or unusual spraying activities
- Localized explosion that destroys only a package or parcel
- Abandoned spray equipment
- Presence of large numbers of dead fish or animals and bird life
- Mass casualties without obvious trauma
- Definite pattern of casualties and symptom commonality
- Casualties located in possible obvious target locations, such as government and military establishment buildings, mass-transport systems, and so on

Vesicants

These chemicals are blistering agents. They were first produced for use in World War I. The vesicant used in the war was called mustard gas because it smells like mustard. These agents cause severe skin burns and damage to the eyes and respiratory system, if inhaled. If a large area of skin is exposed to the gas, absorption into the blood stream is usually inevitable. **Vesicants** are heavy, oily liquids and, in pure state, are almost colorless and odorless. They have a high propensity for penetration into layers of clothing and quickly absorb into the skin. They are extremely powerful but are far less lethal than nerve agents. A few drops of mustard gas on the skin can cause severe injury and three grams absorbed through the skin will likely be fatal.

Symptoms of vesicant poisoning include reddening of the eyes; congestion, tearing, a burning, gritty feeling in the eyes, followed by pain and spasm of the eyelids. The skin will blister depending on the level of exposure and initial itching and redness, followed by pain and tenderness. Blisters will appear and likely be fluid filled and are most common in warm, moist areas of the body, such as in the groin area and under the armpits. There will also be a burning sensation in the nose and throat, coughing, and shortness of breath.

Blood Agents

Most blood agents are derivatives of cyanide compounds and, therefore, packages of cyanide salt and acid precursors may be present in any attack scenario. Blood agents produce casualties by interfering with the blood's ability to transfer oxygen to the cells, which can lead to death by asphyxiation. These agents are common industrial chemicals and information is publicly available on them. The outward warning signs include large numbers of casualties displaying common symptoms; the strong smell of peaches or bitter almonds is also a good indicator of blood agents.

Choking Agents

These chemical agents attack the respiratory system and cause acute distress. They also produce copious amounts of fluid, which can result in death by asphyxiation which resembles drowning. The most common symptoms are choking and coughing. Outward signs are the obvious chemical odor, such as the strong smell of chlorine, while phosgene has the odor of freshly cut hay.

Irritating Agents

These are the most common agents and are found in products such as tear gas, designed to cause respiratory distress and copious tearing. They have the irritating smell of pepper but are generally nonlethal. Chemical agents are relatively easy to manufacture and just as easy to disperse. They are easier to control than a biological agent and, although not contagious, may contaminate by persistence. Chemical agents can be mass produced and are easier to hide and disguise, rather than a conventional weapon. The mere mention of the words "chemical weapons" will spread terror.

BIOLOGICAL WEAPONS

Biological weapons are, by their very nature, indiscriminate and difficult to contain and control. The delivery system for such a "weapon" continues to pose significant problems for a terrorist group. While a chemical attack would be the simpler attack to mount, the bio-attack weapon remains an ultimate weapon for the twenty-first-century terrorist.

History of Biological Weapons

- In 1346, the Tartar Army, led by Khan Janiberg, attacked the city of Kaffa and catapulted plague-infested bodies of their own men over the city walls.
- In the fifteenth century, the Spanish conquistador Pizarro gave clothing contaminated with smallpox to natives in South America.
- In 1940, the Japanese dropped "plague" on China.

- **In 1972**, 103 countries signed the Biological Weapons Convention, which prohibited the development of both biological and chemical weapons, as well as their use.
- **In 1980**, the German Red Army Faction was found in a Paris safe house making Botulin toxin.
- **In 1984**, Cuba reportedly was stockpiling toxins.
- **In 1991**, the Iraqi government admitted research in the use of anthrax, Botulinum, and Clostridium toxins.
- **In 1994**, the Aum Shinrikyo sect in Japan attempted an aerial drop of anthrax over Tokyo.
- **In 1995**, an Aryan nation's member was arrested in Ohio with a container of plague.
- **In October 2001**, envelopes containing spores of anthrax were sent to U.S. news media and government offices, causing nationwide panic.[46]

Soon after 9-11, letters laced with anthrax began appearing in the U.S. mail. Five Americans were killed and seventeen were sickened in what became the worst biological attacks in U.S. history.[47] In August 2008, Department of Justice and FBI officials announced a breakthrough in the case and released documents and information showing that charges were about to be brought against Dr. Bruce Ivins, who took his own life before those charges could be filed. On February 19, 2010, the Justice Department, the FBI, and the U.S. Postal Inspection Service formally concluded the investigation into the 2001 anthrax attacks and issued an Investigative Summary. The case involved the issuance of more than 5,750 grand jury subpoenas and the collection of 5,730 environmental samples from sixty site locations. In addition, new scientific methods were developed that ultimately led to the break in the case—methods that could have a far-reaching impact on future investigations.[48] This involved the anthrax bacterium, which produces shell-like spores that allow the bacterium to live in a dormant state in the soil. However, when anthrax is used as a weapon, the spores can become airborne and enter the lungs, where they become active. If enough of the spores are inhaled, the results can often be fatal. Anthrax is a serious infectious disease caused by the bacterium *Bacillus anthracis*. Anthrax is a disease that is common in cows, sheep, horses, and goats. The occasions of human contamination have been as a result of infection by persons coming into close contact with an infected animal.

Inhalational Anthrax

This is the most dangerous form of anthrax. It results when a person inhales anthrax spores into the lungs. Symptoms do not appear immediately, but usually within two to six days after being infected. It is possible that symptoms will occur as late as sixty days after initial infection. Symptoms included headache, fever, coughing, and difficulty in breathing, chills, weakness, and chest pain. This disease can be controlled by antibiotics if diagnosed promptly. Inhalation anthrax is not contagious and does not spread from person to person.

Cutaneous Anthrax

This form of anthrax occurs when the anthrax spores come into direct contact with a cut or break in the skin. Evidence of infection will become apparent within one to seven days of contamination with an itchy bump reminiscent of a small insect bite. The bump will develop blisters and then turn to a painless sore with a black center. Lymph glands in the area or near the affected area may begin to swell. This form is not as dangerous as the inhaled anthrax, but if not treated, this anthrax has a 20 percent mortality rate. This form is also not contagious and responds well to antibiotics.

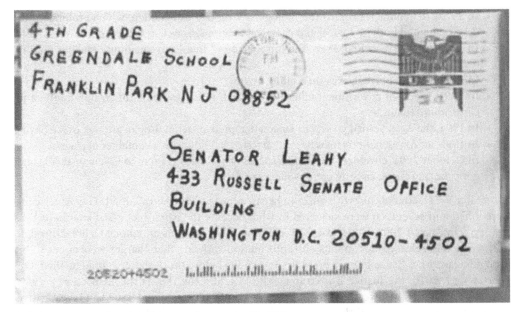

FIGURE 14-7   Anthrax letter sent to Senator Leahy (FBI).

Intestinal Anthrax

This form of anthrax occurs when a person eats meat from an infected animal that has died from anthrax, or drinks water or other liquids contaminated with anthrax spores. This form will cause vomiting, fever, pain in the abdomen, and diarrhea. Symptoms appear within seven days of infection. If left untreated, the form has a 60 percent mortality rate and, like the two previous forms, is also noncontagious.

Smallpox

This is a highly infectious, viral disease. The last recorded naturally occurring cases of smallpox were prior to 1977, when it was eradicated following a worldwide vaccination campaign. Smallpox comes with influenza-type symptoms and a rash spreading over the body. Pus-filled blisters develop and serious complications can result in blindness, pneumonia, and kidney damage. Infected persons who have not been vaccinated have a 30 percent mortality rate.

Toxins

The poisonous by-products of microorganisms, plants, and animals are called toxins. They tend to be stable because they are not living; however, toxins such as ricin and botulin have the advantage of being relatively simple to manufacture and are extremely lethal. Toxins can cause almost immediate paralysis of the cardio respiratory system in humans. Ricin is probably the deadliest known plant toxin and is a protein extracted from the castor bean seed. Ricin poisoning will result in nausea, muscle spasms, convulsions, and vomiting. There is no antitoxin or vaccine currently available and death from ricin poisoning can occur in three days.

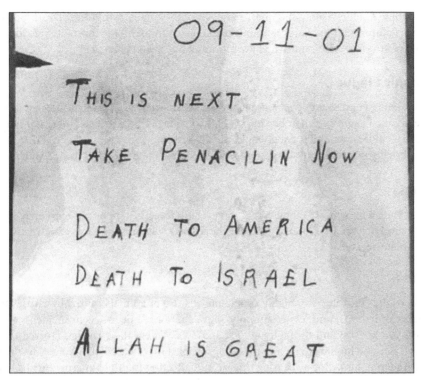

FIGURE 14-8 Letter contained anthrax and threatening note (FBI).

TERROIST ATTACK BRIEF

Terrorist Group: Unknown

Case Facts: A series of letters posted to senators and the New York Times contained Anthrax. This resulted in the deaths of five people, including letter carriers, and over thirty others were infected.

Investigation: These incidents coming so soon after the attacks of 9-11 were bound to initially focus on foreign terror organizations. By 2007, investigators conclusively determined that a single spore batch created and maintained by Dr. Bruce E. Ivins at the United States Army Medical Research Institute of Infectious Diseases ("USAMRIID") was the parent material for the letter spores. An intensive investigation of individuals with access to that material ensued. Evidence developed from that investigation established that Dr. Ivins, alone, mailed the anthrax letters. Ultimately, no one was prosecuted, and the FBI formally closed the case in 2010. At that time they were preparing to prepare charges against Dr. Bruce Ivins who committed suicide before charges could be laid.

FIGURE 14-9 Biological attack—Letters containing anthrax sent to U.S. Senators—October 2001. *Source*: FBI Amerithrax/Antrax Case.

Botulism

This neurotoxin is released by the bacterium *Clostridium botulinum* and is associated with rotting food. It is a very poisonous substance. If a person ingests or breathes in the toxin, symptoms of nerve disruption will occur. Cold and flulike symptoms, with a trace of numbness in the lips and fingertips, double vision, and chest paralysis are its many symptoms. Death occurs from respiratory failure. With the quick administration of an antitoxin, the mortality rate for botulism is 25 percent; however, if left untreated the mortality rate is 100 percent.

Pneumonic Plague

This condition is a rare result of *bubonic* plague and is caused by bites from an infected flea. It turns into pneumonic plague and then becomes a highly contagious and virulent form of pneumonia. Symptoms include fever, chills, coughing, difficulty breathing, and rapid shock. There is a 50–90 percent mortality rate if left untreated and 15 percent when diagnosed and treated with antibiotics.

Tularemia

Tularemia is also known as "rabbit fever" or "deer fly fever." Tularemia is extremely infectious. Relatively few bacteria are required to cause the disease, which is why it is an attractive weapon for use in bioterrorism.[49]

Avian Flu

Avian flu, or the "bird flu," is a highly contagious disease of animals caused by viruses that normally infect only birds, and less commonly, pigs. There have been recent incidents starting in Southeast Asia in 2003 and throughout 2004 and 2005, where the virus has crossed the species barrier and infected humans. The highly pathogenic bird flu is extremely virulent. It spreads very rapidly through poultry flocks, causing disease and affecting multiple internal organs, and has a mortality that can approach 100 percent, often within forty-eight hours. The causative agent, the H5N1 virus, has proved to be especially tenacious. Despite the death or destruction of an estimated 150 million birds, the virus is now considered endemic in many parts of Indonesia and Vietnam and in some parts of Cambodia, China, Thailand, and possibly also the Lao People's Democratic Republic. Control of the disease in poultry is expected to take several years. The widespread persistence of H5N1 in poultry populations poses risks for human health. Of the few avian influenza viruses that have crossed the species barrier to infect humans, H5N1 has caused the largest number of cases of severe disease and death in humans. Unlike normal seasonal influenza, where infection causes only mild respiratory symptoms in most people, the disease caused by H5N1 follows an unusually aggressive clinical course, with rapid deterioration and high fatality.

Of greater concern is that the virus, if given enough opportunities, will change into a form that is highly infectious for humans and spreads easily from person to person. Such a change could mark the start of a global outbreak (a pandemic). A pandemic can start when three conditions have been met: a new influenza virus subtype emerges; it infects humans, causing serious illness; and it spreads easily and sustainably among humans. The H5N1 virus amply meets the first two conditions: It is a new virus for humans and has infected more than 100 humans, killing over half of them. No one will have immunity should an H5N1-like pandemic virus emerge. All prerequisites for the start of a pandemic have therefore been met save one: the establishment of efficient and sustained human-to-human transmission of the virus. The risk that the H5N1 virus will acquire this ability will persist as long as opportunities for human infections occur. These opportunities, in turn, will persist as long as the virus continues to circulate in birds, and this situation could endure for some years to come.[50]

Contingency planning to meet and counter the threat of WMD since 9-11 has taken on monumental proportions. The U.S. government is spending in excess of $2 billion per annum to counter these threats.

Developing an effective response plan is critical not only to community and governments but also in the private business sector. While the likelihood of a terrorist attack having a sudden and direct impact on a particular business is relatively low, there is always the need to act prudently and prepare Business Resumption and Interruption Plans, as well as Disaster Planning and Critical Incident Command procedures. Although these plans are more likely to have been part of the planning process for national and state governments, there is every reason for individual companies to consider plans for disaster events, which should include flood, tornado, earthquake, major fire, chemical accident, and terror attack. Although the terror attack is the one significant incident that comes to most people's attention, the likelihood of the preceding five events occurring is much higher. It has been suggested that up to 70 percent of small- to medium-size businesses fail to recover from a disaster. For a national- or state-level plan to be implemented, it should include the following components:

- Information-gathering system
- Threat awareness—be able to determine what threats the organization must be aware of
- An effective communications plan and early-warning system coupled with evacuation procedures
- Particularly in the United States, interagency agreements on command and control in disaster situations
- Detailed procedures on how to identify the release of chemical or bio agents and equipment needed to respond to such a threat or incident
- An appropriate disposal capability
- Procedures for setting up and deploying decontamination stations and personnel to man them

Practical training either in a real-life setting, or a "table top" setting, should be conducted on a regular basis to determine the capability of responders to a specific incident involving mass casualties. This will involve having all the significant players represented at a "table-top" exercise to ensure that each group or organization is fully conversant with the role it has to play. The attacks of 9-11 were an example of the flaws in the emergency communications coordination, which seriously contributed to the high number of emergency responder losses on that fateful day.

DIRTY BOMBS

To better inform the public on what a dirty bomb is, and what terrorists might intend to try to accomplish in setting off such a weapon, the following information from the U.S. Regulatory Commission is provided.

Given the scores of exercises—federal, state, and local—being staged to assure that all emergency response organizations are properly equipped, trained, and exercised to respond to a terrorist chemical, biological, or radiological attack, we believe members of the public, as well as news organizations, will benefit from receiving concise, straightforward information.

Basically, the principal type of dirty bomb, or **radiological dispersal device (RDD)**, combines a conventional explosive, such as dynamite, with radioactive material. In most instances, the conventional explosive itself would have more immediate lethality than the radioactive material. At the levels created by most probable sources, not enough radiation would be present in a dirty bomb to kill people or cause severe illness. For example, most radioactive material employed in hospitals for diagnosis or treatment of cancer is sufficiently benign that about 100,000 patients a day are released with this material in their bodies.

However, certain other radioactive materials, dispersed in the air, could contaminate up to several city blocks, creating fear and possibly panic and requiring potentially costly cleanup. Prompt, accurate, nonemotional public information might prevent the panic sought by terrorists.

A second type of RDD might involve a powerful radioactive source hidden in a public place, such as a trash receptacle in a busy train or subway station, where people passing close to the source might get a significant dose of radiation. A dirty bomb is in no way similar to a nuclear weapon. The presumed purpose of its use would be, therefore, not as a weapon of mass destruction, but rather as a weapon of mass disruption.

Impact of a Dirty Bomb

The extent of local contamination would depend on a number of factors, including the size of the explosive, the amount and type of radioactive material used, and weather conditions. Prompt detection of the kind of radioactive material employed would greatly assist local authorities in advising the community on protective measures, such as quickly leaving the immediate area, or going inside until being further advised. Subsequent decontamination of the affected area could involve considerable time and expense.

Sources of Radioactive Material

Radioactive materials are widely used at hospitals, research facilities, and industrial and construction sites. Radioactive materials are used for diagnosing and treating illnesses, sterilizing equipment, and inspecting welding seams. The Nuclear Regulatory Commission, together with thirty-two states, which regulate radioactive material, has over 21,000 organizations licensed to use such materials. The vast majority of these sources are not useful for constructing an RDD.

Control of Radioactive Material

NRC and state regulations require licensees to secure radioactive material from theft and unauthorized access. These measures have been stiffened since the attacks of September 11, 2001. Licensees must promptly report lost or stolen material. Local authorities make a determined effort to find and retrieve such sources. Most reports of lost or stolen material involve small or short-lived radioactive sources not useful for an RDD. Past experience suggests there has not been a pattern of collecting such sources for the purpose of assembling a dirty bomb. Only one high-risk radioactive source has not been recovered in the last five years in the United States. However, this source (Iridium-192) would no longer be considered a high-risk source because much of the radioactivity would have decayed away since it was reported stolen in 1999. In fact, the combined total of all unrecovered sources over a five-year time span would barely reach the threshold for one high-risk radioactive source. Unfortunately, the same cannot be said worldwide. The U.S. government is working to strengthen controls on high-risk radioactive sources both at home and abroad.

What People Should Do Following an Explosion?

Move away from the immediate area—at least several blocks from the explosion—and go inside. This will reduce exposure to any radioactive airborne dust.

- Turn on local radio or TV channels for advisories from emergency response and health authorities.

- If facilities are available, remove clothes and place them in a sealed, plastic bag. Saving contaminated clothing will allow testing for radiation exposure.
- Take a shower to wash off dust and dirt. This will reduce total radiation exposure, if the explosive device contained radioactive material.
- If radioactive material was released, local news broadcasts will advise people where to report for radiation monitoring, blood and other tests to determine whether they were, in fact, exposed and what steps need taken to protect their health.

Risk of Cancer

Just because a person is near a radioactive source for a short time, or gets a small amount of radioactive dust on himself or herself, does not mean he or she will get cancer. The additional risk will likely be very small. Doctors will be able to assess the risks and suggest mitigating measures, once the radioactive source and exposure level have been determined. It should be noted that potassium iodide (KI) would not be protective except in the very unlikely event that the dirty bomb contained radioactive iodine isotopes in large quantities. Radioactive iodine isotopes are not particularly attractive for use in an RDD for a variety of technical reasons. KI only protects the thyroid from radioactive iodine, but offers no protection to other parts of the body or against other radioactive isotopes. A number of federal agencies have responsibilities for dealing with possible detonations of dirty bombs.[51]

Summary

The terrorist attacks on September 11, 2001, the Madrid train station bombings, the London subway bombings, and the Bali nightclub bombings, are a reminder that terrorism is a global issue. Not a day goes by without some form of atrocity in the name of terrorism perpetrated on an unsuspecting public. Protecting the public at large has been the main consideration of the United States and many Western governments. U.S. efforts have been centered on protecting the homeland and the rapid rejuvenation of its intelligence services and apparatus. While the tragic events of 9-11 recede somewhat from our memories, new terror events are taking shape daily such as the ongoing insurgency in Iraq and the threat to Western interests in Indonesia and the Persian Gulf. We continue to wonder what will happen next. Will we see an attack using chemical, biological, or radiological weapons against cities in the West? While governments attempt to make national security a front-line topic, how far do we go in this respect? How vulnerable are we to attack against our infrastructure? The Internet is a tool we have all come to rely on, so will

the hacking of systems and the insertion of worms and viruses become serious enough as to affect our daily lives? We are at war against an unknown and unseen enemy who wants nothing less than the seeming destruction of democratic societies. Where is the middle ground? How do we get to the point where negotiation can take place? With who and what do we negotiate for? Wars have a beginning and an end, although we see no end to global terrorism.

Specialized counterterrorism units have been used as a response mechanism and may be viewed as a well-advertised deterrent by governments unwilling to deal with terrorists. As can be seen with Northern Ireland, both police and specialized units have been deployed in the common cause of fighting terrorism. Special military powers to restrict, control, search, and intern suspected members of illegal or proscribed organizations have also been instituted. In democracy, specialist units like the SAS, GIGN, and GSG-9 can operate effectively and have the support of the government and the public they serve. It is also necessary and prudent to have strict guidelines and controls for the use of such counterterrorism units. In Northern Ireland, the accusations of a "shoot-to-kill" policy and "death squads" were hurled by the IRA in a desperate attempt by that subversive group to halt the activities of a response mechanism that was too effective for their purposes. Piracy on the seas shows that there are

regions of the globe susceptible to this type of rabid activity and the dangers it poses to the international community. Many ships containing extremely hazardous cargoes circumnavigate the globe, and the risks to nation-states and the opportunity for terrorists to take advantage must not be discounted.

Review Questions

1. How have governments used both military and police tactics to respond to terrorist hijackings?
2. Describe the methods employed by the United States to prevent contaminated cargo/freight entering the country.
3. Describe the vulnerabilities that exist at airports and how a terrorist can exploit those vulnerabilities—use examples from other chapters for this response.

4. Discuss the use of profiling as a security screening tool.
5. Discuss how you think intelligence gathering and sharing of information can be improved. Does the current system allow a significant opportunity only after an event to "connect the dots"?
6. Describe how terrorist attacks against Western targets have changed since 9-11 and some of the effective strategies used by terrorists.

Websites

1. **The Security Council Counter Terrorism Committee**—*http://www.un.org/en/sc/ctc/*
2. **America's Response to Terrorism**—*The Brookings Institute*—*http://www.brookings.edu/events/2001/0928terrorism.aspx*

3. **US Government Accountability Office**—*http://www.gao.gov/docsearch/featured/terrorism.html*
4. **International Institute for Counter Terrorism**—*http://www.ict.org.il/*

End Notes

1. Paul Wilkinson. *Terrorism and the Liberal State* (New York: New York University Press, 1979, p. 121).
2. "Is racial Profiling a Non Issue in the Age of Terrorism?" (2008), http://www.racerealtions.about.com
3. Paul Wilkinson. *Terrorism and the Liberal State*, p. 155.
4. United Nations Conventions Against Terrorism. (2011), http://www.un.org/terrorism/
5. *Terrorism*, vol. 13, no. 4–5 (July–October 1990); Aviation Terrorism Air Carrier Security Programs: Statement before the U.S. House of Representatives, vol. 13, pp. 353–357; Homer Boynton. Government Activities and Transportation Subcommittee (Taylor Francis, 1990).
6. Report to the President's Commission on Aviation Security and Terrorism (1990), www.frac.com.
7. Ibid.
8. Cathal Flynn. "Aviation Security Is Tight." *USA Today* (March 19, 1999, p. A14).
9. Billie Vincent. "Aviation Security and Terrorism." *Terrorism: An International Journal*, vol. 13, no.6 (December 1990, p. 404).
10. Commander David Tucker. London Metropolitan Police, Avsec World 94 Proceedings Chicago (October 23–26, 1994).
11. "Protect Airliners from Missiles." *The Post and Courier*, Charleston, SC (December 31, 2002, p. A10).
12. Alan J. Kuperman. "Stinger Missiles and US Intervention in Afghanistan." *Political Science Quarterly* vol 114, no. 2 (1999) http://www.jstor.org.
13. Ed. Stephen Ulph. *Jane's Terrorism and Security Monitor* (London: Jane's Information Group, 2002).

14. Transportation Security Agency. (2009), http://www.tsa.gov/research/screening_statistics.shtm.

15. NPR. www.npr.org/templates/story/story.php?storyId=15445779.

16. TSA Secure Flight Program Overview.http://www.tsa.gov/what_we_do/layers/secureflight/index.shtm

17. Electronic Privacy Information Center. www.epic.org/privacy/airtravel/profiling.html.

18. Alan Pangborn. "How Far Has Europe Come Since Pan Am 103?" *Intersec* vol. 6 (Three Bridges Publishing, May 5, 1996, p. 195).

19. Gerry Edwards. "Hijackers' Gateway." *Intersec*, vol. 8, no. 14 (Three Bridges Publishing, April 1998, p. 168).

20. Allied Media Corporation. http://www.allied-media.com/aljazeera.com.

21. Summary of the Ministerial Conference on Terrorism, Paris (July 30, 1996), www.efc.ca/pages/doc/g7.html.

22. Report to the United Nations Security Council Counterterrorism Committee (December 19, 2001), www.fas.org/irp/threat/unsc.html.

23. Deb Reichmann. "Bush Campaigns for Patriot Act Renewal." Associated Press, *Writer*, Yahoo News (June 10, 2005).

24. "Closure of Guantanamo Detention Facilities."—*The White House* (January 22, 2009), http://www.whitehouse.gov/the_press_office/ClosureOfGuantanamoDetentionFacilities/

25. Jonathan Masters, Closing Guantanamo—The Council on Foreign Relations http://www.cfr.org/terrorism-and-the-law/closing-guantanamo/p18525.

26. Sean Hill. "The Complexity of Intelligence Gathering." *Sam Houston University Crime and Justice International*, vol. 17, no. 56 (October/November 2001, p. 5).

27. —"Fusion Task Force, Operational Support." *Interpol* www.interpol.int/Public.

28. Mi5. https://www.mi5.gov.uk/output/Page57.html.

29. US National Strategy for Counter Terrorism.—"Homeland Security Digital Library."—https://www.hsdl.org/hslog/?q=node/6237.

30. "Creating a National Intelligence Director." Statement of John S. Pistole, Executive Assistant Director, Counterterrorism/Counterintelligence, Federal Bureau of Investigation, before the House Judiciary Committee Subcommittee on Crime, Terrorism and Homeland Security (August 23, 2004).

31. Elite Forces. http://www.eliteukforces.info/special-air-service/sas-operations/loughgall/.

32. Barbara Cole. *The Elite: The Story of the Rhodesian Special Air Service* (Transkei: Three Knights Publishing, 1984, p. 6.

33. Ibid.

34. Ibid., p. 15.

35. Leroy Thompson. *The Rescue* (Bolder, CO: Paladin Press, 1986, p. 84).

36. Ibid, p. 64.

37. Jacob Zenn "Indonesia's 'Ghost Birds' Tackle Islamist Terrorists: A Profile of Densus 88." *Terrorism Monitor*,—vol. 9, no. 32 (Janes Terrorism Monitor, August 2011).

38. Ibid, p. 20.

39. David Pugliese is author of Shadow Wars: Special Forces in the New Battle Against Terrorism as well as Canada's Secret Commandos: The Unauthorized Story of Joint Task Force Two.

40. ICC Commercial Crime Services. (2011), http://www.icc-ccs.org/news/450-pirate-attacks-at-sea-getting-bigger-and-bolder-says-imb-report.

41. "The Maritime Safety Division, International Maritime Organization." www.imo.org/home.asp.

42. Gal Luft and Anne Korin. "Terrorism Goes to Sea." *Foreign Affairs*, vol. 83, no. 6 (November/December 2004), http://www.iags.org/fa2004.html.

43. United Nations. http://www.un.org/Depts/Cos/Conventies.agreements.htm.

44. Luft and Korin, "Terrorism Goes to Sea".

45. Anthony A. Lukin, Ph.D. "Understanding Nuclear, Biological and Chemical Weapons." a presentation at the Justice Institute of British Columbia Provincial Emergency Program Academy (April 7–8, 1997).

46. Centers for Disease Control (CDC). (2011), www.cdc.org.

47. "The FBI Famous Cases and Criminals."(February 2011),http://www.fbi.gov/about-us/history/famous-cases/anthrax-amerithrax/amerithrax-investigation

48. Ibid.

49. Basic Information about Sars. "Centers for Disease Control and Prevention." http://www.cdc.gov/ncidod/sars/factsheet.htm.

50. UN Nuclear Regulatory Commission. "Fact sheet on Dirty Bombs." (August 2010), http://www.nrc.gov/reading-rm/doc-collections/fact-sheets/fs-dirty-bombs.html.

51. Ibid.

15

The Future—What Next for Terrorism?

To kill the Americans and their allies, civilian and military,
is an individual duty for every Muslim who can do it,
in any country in which it is possible to be done.

—OSAMA BIN LADEN (1957–2011)

THE PAST AND THE FUTURE

Now that we have entered the second decade of the new millennium, it's instructive to ask ourselves what terrorism might look like in the future. Certainly the decade following the terrorist attacks of 9-11 has significantly changed the way we view security, the Muslim world, Islam, multiculturalism, the economy, torture, assassinations, suicide bombers, and the use of response mechanisms to terror. How Americans view their Constitutional rights can be judged from discussions on Guantanamo Bay and detention of militant combatants, and on aerial drones attacking terror targets in Iraq, Afghanistan, and Pakistan. At the start of the twenty-first century, unmanned aerial drones were of little interest or value to us. Now over a decade later, the United States along with its counterterror arms mainly associated with the CIA uses thousands of unmanned drones to circle the globe to track down and gather intelligence on suspects and also to rain down missiles on targets. So if the past is a window to the future, then the next ten years will be equally challenging.

THE PAST

Possibly the very first aircraft hijacking dates back to Peru in 1931, and then again between 1948 and 1958, there was approximately one hijacking per year—of course air travel was in those decades for the rich almost exclusively. With the advances made in air travel, the decade of the 1960s saw a huge surge in attacks on aviation. In 1968 alone there were thirty-eight hijackings surpassed the following year with eighty-two. Airport security and passenger screening were aimed at preventing a hijacking primarily, and airline crews were taught how to respond to terrorists by following their instructions.

Until 2001 the understanding was that the terrorist did not want to die. Fast forward that ingrained thought to September 11, 2001, and we see the ease with which determined suicide hijackers were able to complete their missions. While the airline industry remains a constant target for terrorists, it has become extremely difficult to get explosives onto an aircraft. Modern technology and better training have made it almost impossible to get the items on board an airliner. To assemble the needed elements from household liquids would be almost impossible to manage. After 9-11, there have been two unsuccessful attempts at downing an airliner with a homemade bomb, Richard Reid the shoe bomber in December 2001 and the attempt to down Northwest 253 over Detroit on Christmas Day 2009. In both instances, there was a very small amount of TATP involved; however, the use of and acquiring and mixing the correct quantities while maintaining a very cool environment (otherwise the TATP significantly degrades) may lead to the handler blowing himself up even before he reaches the airport! No doubt the unskilled terrorists are trying methods to conceal, mix, blend, and hide the ingredients before attempting further attacks.

THE FUTURE

So how do we conclude by looking forward? It seems that all we can do now is make some modest comments as to the warning signs for the future. Many of these statements are extensions of what we have covered elsewhere in previous chapters. Europe has become a melting pot of immigrants, no doubt the vast majority seeking a better life, but this has also spawned ghettolike regions in major cities where the awful specter of radical Islam is present. From these migrants we have witnessed suicide bombers in Western cities. How and why have radical Islamists been able to recruit and corrupt intelligent young men to wage jihad against their adopted countries? In London, for example, there are regions that are virtually no-go areas for non-Muslims, with locals demanding the imposition of Sharia Law in areas such as Tower Hamlets. Remember, these fanatical Islamists seek to overturn and destroy Western culture and supplant it with an Islamic Caliphate, by causing mayhem, fear, and panic. Defeating terrorism will have to be about treating the underlying, deeply rooted causes that tempt and pull in young and intelligent minds. Is it despair at how they view the world? Or is it possibly how their religion is viewed by the West that turns them against their adopted country? Many have speculated that perhaps the London suicide bombings in 2005 could have been averted had the British government withdrawn its troops in Iraq. The failure of that argument is that this breed of Islamic terrorism was around long before the United States and its coalition, including the British, invaded Iraq. Iraq was invaded in 2003; New York and Washington DC were attacked in September 2001, and, prior to that, the U.S. embassies in Kenya and Tanzania, and before them, the suicide attacks on the USS *Cole* in Yemen. The year 2011 witnessed another startling phenomenon, "Arab Spring," when in the last weeks of December 2010 a Tunisian street vendor set himself on fire as a direct and very public protest against the government. This led to an uprising and the resignation of the country's president. This was quickly followed by similar but more deadly uprisings in Egypt, Libya, Yemen, and Syria, and no doubt this will have a significant effect on the foreign policies of Western governments when addressing the Middle East. Much of the information about these events was posted and spread on social media outlets such as Facebook. But what of the terrorists in these regions— strangely al Qaeda and its affiliates were somewhat muted and probably just as taken aback by the swiftness of events unfolding.

A STABLE MIDDLE EAST

The Arab Spring of 2011 has seen a demand for democracy in the Middle East in countries that have never known democracy. This does not bode well for the future for many reasons. There remains a significant power struggle between Shiite and Sunni Muslims in the Middle East, namely in Saudi Arabia (Sunni) and Iran (Shiite); the leaders of both countries have a lot to gain and lose. As Europe and the United States watched the unrest spreading through the Middle East, it eventually reached the oil patch of Bahrain, a very close neighbor of Saudi Arabia. The uprising in Bahrain by the majority Shiites was crushed with significant help from the Al Khalifa rulers of Saudi Arabia. A dominant Shiite government in neighboring Bahrain would have meant the immediate presence of Iran on its borders. So-called democracy was ushered into Iran by the student riots of 1979 that deposed the Shah, and the democracy that followed was dominated by a government of ultraconservative clerics—a government certainly not welcomed by Saudi Arabia. In Yemen, the ruling family is at best at odds with each other and the presence of al Qaeda and the rise of the Muslim Brotherhood would be a further problem for the oil-rich Saudi kingdom. With uprisings all around the Gulf, Saudi Arabia must maintain its control and influence in the region—if not, the rest of the world will need to find energy sources from other areas—for as long as Saudi Arabia continues to produce over 16 million barrels of oil every day for export, the rest of the world can rest easy; however, if regime change takes place that affects that export, the world economy will be severely damaged.

In Libya, we saw a rush by European countries led by France and the United Kingdom to save the people from the despot Qaddafi, and, in doing so, they supported the rebel cause. What was at first believed to be a quick opportunity for regime change very quickly became a quagmire for Britain and France in particular. There was waning European support for military actions continuing in Libya. Fortunately for the Europeans, an airstrike near Sirte targeted Qaddafi's escape column on October 20, 2011, which led to his capture by Libyan rebels the following day and his summary execution. The destabilizing effect of the revolution that swept Egypt in the spring of 2011 left a major problem in the Sinai region with its close proximity to Israel. The presence of al Qaeda–sympathetic groups including The Youth of Islam (al-Shabaab al-Islam) in the region will be problematic both for Egypt and prospects of terrorist incursions into Israel. These jihadist groups are demanding the tearing up of the long-standing treaties between Israel and Egypt and to follow that up with Egyptian military support for the Palestinians in the Gaza Strip. Much of the Egyptian security forces including the local police fled the region in early 2011 leaving the Sinai region to fester. In an effort to confront both the regime in Cairo and Israel these jihadist groups have attacked a natural gas pipeline to Israel. These attacks and the 2011 storming of a police station by armed militants in the regional capital of al-Arish have alarmed Cairo. The long-standing alienation of the Sinai Bedouin from the rest of Egypt and the growth of a radical Salafist movement influenced by like-minded groups in Gaza have combined to pose a serious challenge to a regime that is handcuffed in its response. Egypt's movement away from a police state and subsequent political reforms have made it difficult to maintain domestic security and keep militants under control particularly in the Sinai Peninsula. The current trends in this region are allowing a range of different Islamist actors to take stage in Egypt, the Muslim Brotherhood being one of the most prominent, Sufists, and Salafists; each group has some form of political agenda for the new government to be formed in Egypt—what this will do to undermine former Israeli-Egyptian peace initiatives is not yet certain. However, expect to see Hamas working with like-minded groups in Sinai to undermine not just Egypt but also any peace accord.

TERRORISM LARGER STAGE

Osama bin Laden is believed to have controlled a personal fortune estimated at over $300 million and spent it freely on his war against the United States and Western democracies. He combined financial muscle with religious extremism—a deadly cocktail! Terrorists exploit our weaknesses. For example, Canada is known for its liberal views, with a large and ethnically diverse population, including many Muslims residing in the large urban centers of Toronto and in other parts of that vast nation. Bin Laden and a coalition of Islamic extremist groups issued a fatwa (similar to that issued against Salman Rushdie in Iran) and named Canada specifically as being a "legitimate target." Its wording was chilling: "To kill the Americans and their allies, civilian and military, is an individual duty for every Muslim who can do it, in any country in which it is possible to be done." In spite of his death, we expect his jihad to continue on a global scale. One fear is that the next attack could involve weapons of mass destruction (WMD). The use of chemical or biological weapons is an obvious concern for intelligence analysts and national security organizations.

Prior to 9-11, our fears were focused on terrorism committed in other countries like Tanzania and Kenya—of course we are referring to the bin Laden-sponsored attacks on the two U.S. embassies in Africa. The U.S. response to such terror attacks was defined and targeted, limited to bombing attacks on bases in the Sudan and Afghanistan. Predicting the future is difficult and analyzing the past is obviously a lot easier. The al Qaeda as we now know is probably more predictable than we might have imagined. Over the last decade, it has responded to every U.S. operation mounted against it. The passage of time between attacks by extreme Islamic groups purporting to represent al Qaeda seems due, in part, to the planning that goes into each mission/assault. They plan their attacks carefully and leave little to chance. If the attack plan is put at risk, the perpetrators retreat until the timing is correct. Intelligence sources indicate that on 9-11 there were other terrorists in the air who could not or did not follow through with their missions. More recently, the attacks on the London subway system were well planned and coordinated. In Spain, the Madrid train station bombings went off during the morning rush hour; 9-11 also took place in the morning; and both the Madrid and London attacks occurred on a Thursday. As time and events unfold, it is this kind of information that will be used to identify trends and bring the full weight of the intelligence and counterterrorism apparatus to bear. London's attack on July 7, 2005, came on the opening day of the G8's Economic Summit in Scotland. The media and British security were focused primarily on this event. A distracting bonus for the terrorists, in this case, was that on the previous evening, Londoners were celebrating the city's selection as host of the 2012 Olympic Games and were in celebratory mood.

It is over a decade since the 9-11 attacks and the world is just as dangerous today, perhaps more so, than in the last years of the twentieth century. The threat is real—as real as it was in 2001. In fact, it is a permanent condition to which we all must adapt.

We already know what the terrorists want to do to us. We have it from their late leader, Osama bin Laden, in his own words, from a December 2001 videotape broadcast by the Arabic television news station Al Jazeera:

- "Our terrorism is against America. Our terrorism is a blessed terrorism…"
- "It is very important to hit the U.S. economy with every available means…[It] is the base of its military power."
- "If their economy ends, they will busy themselves away from the enslavement of oppressed people… it is important to concentrate on the destruction of the American economy."

To his second point, in 2010, we saw the economies of European nations collapsing and the crisis with the trillions of dollars of debt facing the United States in 2011. No doubt, bin Laden, if he were still alive, would like to lay claim to bringing the United States to its "financial knees," but as we know there were a multitude of financial failings that had nothing to do with the War on Terror.

WEAPONS OF MASS DESTRUCTION (WMD)

The United States is making alliances around the world, not just to track down the al Qaeda networks but also to identify those countries that are trying to acquire the materials to develop and construct such weapons of mass destruction.

A US Government Accountability Office (GAO) report to the Senate Intelligence Committee in February 2002 reports then CIA Director George Tenet's comments in a detailed briefing on national security threats. Tenet outlined the key dangers:

1. The al Qaeda is working on "multiple-attack plans" and putting cells in place to carry them out.
2. Iran continues to support terrorist groups and has sent arms to Palestinian terrorists and the group Hezbollah. Tenet said: "Tehran also has failed to move decisively against al Qaeda members who have relocated to Iran from Afghanistan."
3. Terrorists could attack U.S. nuclear plants or chemical industry sites using conventional means "to cause panic and widespread toxic or radiological damage."
4. Al Qaeda cells in major European and Middle Eastern cities could launch attacks, and al Qaeda is connected with groups in Somalia, Yemen, Indonesia, and the Philippines.
5. There are fears that al Qaeda and other terrorists will attack using nuclear, chemical, or biological weapons. Director Tenet said, "Terrorist groups worldwide have ready access to information on chemical, biological, and even nuclear weapons via the Internet, and we know that al Qaeda was working to acquire some of the most dangerous chemical agents and toxins."
6. Tensions between India and Pakistan continue to remain high over a December 13, 2001, terrorist attack on the Indian parliament, and the two nations could resort to nuclear weapons. Tenet said: "We are deeply concerned that a conventional war, once begun, could escalate into a nuclear confrontation."
7. Terrorists could attempt to attack the United States by conducting cyber-strikes designed to cripple U.S. electronic-based infrastructures. Countering the terrorist threat and determining the response will present the biggest challenge for the coming months, and for years to come.

This 2002 report may seem somewhat dated however it's valuable to look back and comment on the past as we predict the future.

Al Qaeda has spread into a global movement and multiple attack plans have been launched and fortunately not many with success, and we have seen the presence of trained fighters engaged in the Iraq insurgency, supported by Iran. Item number 3 in the above-mentioned list has not taken place; item number 4—we have observed the presence of more al Qaeda-affiliated factions across Europe and North Africa as al Qaeda reorganizes, reinvents, and rejuvenates itself; item number 5—we have seen in the United Kingdom incidents of potential attacks using ricin being disrupted by police as well as planned attacks of similar nature in Italy and Germany; item number 6—India remains the fastest-growing economy, but there are considerable tensions between Muslims and Hindus that could erupt in violence at any time. The brink of war with neighboring Pakistan has been averted but not helped by the bombings and killings in Mumbai in 2008.

Even more dated is the following extract from a 1997 Congressional Record on WMD and nuclear materials:

> At its peak in 1992, the Soviet Union possessed approximately 45,000 nuclear warheads and weapons grade nuclear material to fabricate thousands more. The Soviet Union also produced an unknown amount of highly enriched uranium for reactors and for their nuclear navy. That material is also weapons usable.
>
> While we will never know for certain how much of this material exists, the number 1,200 metric tons of weapons-usable material is frequently used.
>
> If one considers that a simple nuclear weapon requires 15 kilograms of highly enriched uranium and 4 kilograms of plutonium, there is enough weapons usable nuclear material in Russia to build more than 63,000 nuclear weapons, each of which could fit in a briefcase.
>
> Even when the material is in dedicated storage facilities it represents a threat. At Chelyabinsk-65, bulk plutonium is stored in a warehouse with glass windows and a padlock on the door. Inside the facility are over 10,000 ingots of separated plutonium stored in thermos-sized containers—perfect for picking up and walking out.
>
> If the terrorists who tried to blow up the World Trade Center had used a nuclear weapon made of that weapons usable nuclear material, Manhattan—all the way up to Gramercy Park, would have disappeared. If such a device had been set off in Oklahoma City, most of Oklahoma City would have disappeared.
>
> The examples I have given are using a simple weapon design that is available over the Internet. If a rogue nation were to hire a Russian weapons designer and have access to the necessary material, that designer could build a sophisticated, multiple-stage weapon many times more powerful.[1]

FIRST GULF WAR AND BEYOND

In the ten years following the end of the first Gulf War, former Iraqi president Saddam Hussein stated that he had always considered himself at war with America, and during that time, the United States had always considered him a threat. While America's military had unleashed its might against the Taliban and al Qaeda, President G. W. Bush and powerful forces in Washington considered attacking a much bigger target. The 9-11 attacks reenergized Saddam's strongest opponents in Washington. The weekend following 9-11 President Bush met at Camp David with his top advisers to formulate an attack strategy for Iraq.

Then U.S. Secretary of State Colin Powell stated that the Bush administration was examining a full range of options on Iraq in dealing with Iraqi president Saddam Hussein's refusal to permit UN international weapons inspections to resume. President Bush was "leaving no stone unturned as to what we might do," Powell stated. Secretary of Defense Donald Rumsfeld asserted that "previous weapons inspections inside Iraq were often ineffective and relied upon defectors." "Any new inspections program," he added, "must be much stronger and more intrusive to end Saddam Hussein's efforts to build weapons of mass destruction." Speaking on the CBS-TV program "Face the Nation" on February 24, 2002, Rumsfeld said, "The Iraqis have had more time to go underground. They've had lots of dual-use technologies that have come in. They've had lots of illicit things that have come in. They have advanced their weapons of mass destruction programs." As a result, Rumsfeld pointed out, "If you try to use the old regime, it wouldn't work. You would have to have a much more intrusive regime and many more inspectors and the Iraqis with no control as to when they could come in, where they could go, what they could do." President George Bush declared a "War on Terror" after 9-11, and singled out Iraq as part of an "axis of evil." Any evidence of Iraqi involvement in the 9-11 attacks is somewhat tenuous and relates to information that an Iraqi intelligence agent had met one of the 9-11 hijackers in Czechoslovakia. This was followed by a series of actions to begin the offensive in Iraq.

History will no doubt determine the long-term merits and failings of prosecuting a war in Iraq and the subsequent destabilization of the region. Many have commented that the British and the United States were unprepared for a long campaign such as this in Iraq. The intelligence on the threat of WMD was not only incorrect, but no threat appeared to exist! Linking Saddam Hussein to the War on Terror has also come in for much debate as to what links, if any, the Iraqi leader had with Osama bin Laden. Strong evidence has linked Iraq to supporting the Abu Nidal group and providing $25,000 rewards to the families of Palestinian suicide bombers. Other terrorists received sanctuary from the Ba'ath Party regime after escaping Italian police in October 1985 following the *Achille Lauro* hijacking. Thanks to Abu Abbas's Iraqi diplomatic passport, he finally ended up in Baghdad in 1994, where he lived until his capture by U.S. troops in April 2003. He died on March 9, 2004, in American custody, of natural causes.

AL QAEDA—THE FUTURE

Al Qaeda, little known before the September 11, 2001, attacks, became linked to almost every terrorist atrocity around the globe—rightly or wrongly. This is the most dangerous movement of the late twentieth and early twenty-first century that will shape our lives for the immediate future. Al Qaeda continues as the movement that rallies and influences jihad throughout the world. There is no indication from the al Qaeda leadership that there will be any let up in its plans to intensify attacks against the West. The goalposts appear to be in the same spot but the name of the game will evolve. While we see no calls for moderation from al Qaeda, what we do see is the continued decentralization of the pan Islamic jihadist movement, which makes it much more resilient. We believe that the glorification in mass casualty attacks is part and parcel of its grassroots movement and is typified in the low-cost suicide attacks that have taken place in Iraq, North Africa, Afghanistan, and Pakistan. The more determined attacks, which require a higher level of planning and sophistication to target more hardened targets such as airports, oil production, and military bases, will continue to be a focus of the core of al Qaeda and its professional jihadists. We have seen the spread of al Qaeda into the Islamic regions of North Africa, and in particular the movement has been noticeably backing Algerian jihadists who have rebranded as the al Qaeda in the Islamic Maghreb (AQIM). If we then consider the proximity of Pakistan to Afghanistan, the natural spread across the borders through the inhospitable North West Frontier region, al Qaeda's ascendency in Pakistan is assured and there is little that the security forces in the West can do about its spread.

That al Qaeda continues to grow with an ability to inspire and influence globally is a major problem. Muslims in many Western countries are being drawn into jihad movements inspired by al Qaeda affiliates, and while getting into countries such as the United States is not as simple as it used to be, one must consider that those inspired to jihad may already be residing in the United States and have been living the "American dream" for several decades as sleepers or have become radicalized over the Internet.

Terrorism expert Bruce Hoffman offered the following points in relation to the future and al Qaeda. The success of the 9-11 attacks was based on three capabilities that al Qaeda likely still retains:

1. The ability to identify vulnerabilities of the enemy (i.e., the West) that could mercilessly be exploited.
2. The effective use of deception (e.g., the passengers on board the hijacked airliners were lulled into believing that if they cooperated they would not be harmed).
3. The use of a suicide mission to ensure success.

We should maybe theorize that al Qaeda may be on the verge of collapse, thanks to the pressure from CIA drone strikes and the killing of Osama bin Laden. In July 2011, Defense Secretary Leon Panetta stated that the United States is close to strategically defeating al Qaeda. We would presume that strategically defeated means that the al Qaeda no longer has the capacity to carry out a major attack on the United States. This may be a short-sighted opinion as al Qaeda affiliates have the ability to mount attacks. Al Qaeda in the Arabian Peninsula (AQAP) is now seen as being a greater threat than al Qaeda. The ideology of al Qaeda is by no means dead and it will remain for some time a rallying point to jihadists globally as they regroup and strategize following bin Laden's death.

As counterterrorism continues to improve, al Qaeda and its affiliates will be challenged to adapt to new untried strategies or to work on established strategies used in other theaters such as Israel and the Indian subcontinent. Transportation and infrastructure, particularly civil aviation, will continue to be targets of choice to jihadists. The use of portable weapon systems such as SAM-7 missiles and suicide attacks on lightly protected mass transit systems, Major hotels, and convention centers and during events such as sporting venues will be areas where jihadists will concentrate their intelligence efforts for the future.

IRAN—AL QAEDA SPONSOR?

What role do we see Iran playing in the future of terrorism? Iran continues to push for nuclear dominance in the region and plays a role in destabilizing Iraq—but does it work with al Qaeda as well? An announcement from U.S. president Obama in 2011 that Iran is actively facilitating the financial aspects of al Qaeda, which needs significant funds to operate globally, is of concern but probably not a surprise. In al Qaeda's evolving strategy, targeting is not contingent on a state's political orientation or on the assistance it receives from governments such as Iran. Al Qaeda will have no qualms about biting the hand that feeds it, whether the patron is Pakistan, Saudi Arabia, Syria, or Iran. The Arab Spring has not yet reached Iran, but no doubt the regime is watching events unfolding in Syria with a very keen eye.

THE FUTURE THREATS FROM WMD

There is broad discussion about the countries that have the desire and capacity to build components for WMD. In fact, there are more than twenty-eight countries with the ability to build chemical agents, and some of them are not considered "friendly states." The United Nations Special Commission to Iraq found over 46,000 munitions filled with chemical agents; of these, 20,000 were 120-mm CS-filled bombs, 14,000 contained mustard gas, and 11,000 contained Sarin. Later discoveries were made near Saddam Hussein's Tikrit base, including 200 anthrax bombs. The fears for the future are real. UN inspectors were kept out of Iraq for years, and there is little doubt that development and production of chemical agents continued in secret, unabated. The key question is whether the Iraqi regime passed on any of its deadly technology or hardware to Islamic extremists with desires to continue attacks against the West—the United States in particular.

North Korea, according to a 1996 U.S. DOD report, "has the ability to produce limited quantities of traditional infectious biological-weapon agents or toxins." A 1988 comment by Iran's parliamentary speaker Hashemi Rafsanjani stated, "Chemical and biological weapons are a poor mans' atomic bombs and can easily be produced. We should at least consider them for our national defense." Syria is also considered to have one of the largest chemical warfare capabilities in the Middle East. So, is the threat of an attack by chemical or biological agents a credible threat? In the context of the 9-11 attacks, the future scenario seems just right for such an attack. If the aim of terror groups like al Qaeda is mass destruction, it behooves all of us to be cognizant of the risk of such an attack in the future.

Nuclear Threats

The threat of a terrorist attack with nuclear weapons may be the least likely, although there has been international concern about security of facilities in the former Soviet states and the rumors of accessibility of materials for arming nuclear weapons. Preparing and constructing a nuclear device is no small feat—it is hard to achieve and requires massive investment and considerable technical expertise. Osama bin Laden certainly had the wealth to achieve that goal, but his next problem would have been the method of delivery. The main constituent of a nuclear weapon is highly enriched uranium (HEU) or plutonium. The quantities of HEU estimated around the globe amount to around 2,000 tons, plus an additional 300 tons of plutonium. Building a nuclear warhead can be achieved with as little as 25 pounds of HEU. Without the sophisticated machine tools, electronic circuitry, and triggering devices needed to make a proper nuclear weapon, merely blowing up a lump of plutonium or HEU with conventional high explosives could still cause widespread and deadly radioactive pollution.[2]

Chemical and Biological Threats

In 1972, 103 countries signed the "Biological Weapons Convention," which prohibited the development of biological and chemical weapons and their use. We now know that the risks of biological and chemical attacks are very real. The anthrax attacks against U.S. public officials and their offices after 9-11 showed how easy it was for a relatively insignificant amount of "white powder" to stampede a public into mass panic and hysteria—presumably one of the aims of that specific act. The anthrax attacks of 2001 made whole governments sit up and take notice of the threat and also made governments realize how unprepared they were to respond.

Biological weapons are created in naturally occurring organisms that cause diseases. Two of the most common examples are the bacterium *Bacillus anthracis*, which produces a toxin, and smallpox, a viral disease that is highly infectious. Chemical weapons are poisons, such as the nerve gas sarin used in Japan's subways and mustard gas, which was used in trench warfare in World War I. Smallpox, on the other hand, was virtually eradicated worldwide by the end of the 1970s after an aggressive two-decadelong, worldwide vaccination campaign. This highly infectious viral disease could now be used against a generation that has not been so vaccinated, and the unvaccinated death rate would likely be about 30 percent. The only known remaining smallpox cultures being kept under tight security are in Kosovo, Russia, and Atlanta. Starting up a biological weapons laboratory merely requires a person with full knowledge of microbiology and a few thousand dollars' worth of equipment. Development may be one issue, but maintaining control over the culture could pose a very significant problem for the would-be terrorist. Probably one of the most significant reasons why we have not witnessed broad attempts at biological terror is the issue of containing the culture. Bacteria and viruses do not discriminate between terrorist and target and the person who releases the bioweapon can easily suffer its effects.

On the chemical front, sarin gas, which was used by the Japanese Aum Shinrikyo terror group to attack a Tokyo subway, has a devastating effect. The gas is odorless, colorless, and attacks the central nervous system. Death can occur within two to fifteen minutes. Cyanide, a more commonly known chemical agent, is a gas that can be produced in massive quantities with apparent ease. Cyanide acts almost instantly and the target that ingests it usually die within seconds. Tabun is a nerve agent that has been around since the 1930s and has been used as a pesticide in many regions of the world. Like many other nerve agents, it is absorbed via the skin. Tabun is resistant to heat and can be delivered in aerosol format, which would make it capable of delivery by artillery shell.[3]

A 1991 audit by the U.S. General Accounting Office indicated that nine chemical sites in the United States were potentially vulnerable to aerial attack, and that four of these sites may be susceptible and vulnerable to ground attack. Since 9-11, Homeland Security has focused resources on many of such sites in the United States. The use of chemical and biological agents may be restricted to those organizations bent purely on destroying democracy, rather than those that are using terrorism as a "bargaining chip" for their own styles of democracy.

HOLY TERROR

Terrorism motivated by religious imperatives is growing rapidly. So great is this change, according to Bruce Hoffman, we may have to consider revising our notions of the stereotypical terrorist organization. Hoffman explained that traditional terrorist groups could be characterized as those that engage in conspiracy as a full-time avocation, living underground and constantly planning and plotting terrorist attacks, perhaps even under the direct control or at the behest of a foreign government. What we viewed as an amateurish attack on the World Trade Center in 1993 reveals to us the kind of individual/terrorist groups that we must contend with in the future. From that investigation, it became evident that the Islamic extremists had not fully completed the attack. It was, however, completed eight years later by their brothers-in-arms in the suicide attacks of 9-11.

"Holy terror" and the purely so-called secular terror have radically different value systems, mechanisms for justifying their acts, and concepts of morality. For the religious terrorist, violence is a divine duty and divine writ. Secular terrorists generally regard indiscriminate violence as immoral and counterproductive; on the other hand, religious terrorists view such violence as both morally justified and necessary. Also, whereas secular terrorists will attempt to appeal to a constituency composed of sympathizers and the aggrieved people they claim to speak for, religious terrorists act for no audience but themselves and their faith. This absence of a constituency, combined with an extreme sense of alienation, means that such "holy" terrorists can justify almost limitless violence against virtually any target or group of people that are not considered adherents to their religious beliefs.

Religious or ethnic extremism could more easily allow terrorists to overcome the psychological barriers to committing mass murder than a radical political agenda has provided in the past. Many white supremacists actually welcome the prospect of a nuclear war or all kinds of terrorism. They see it as an opportunity to eliminate their avowed "enemies" and permit the fulfillment of their objectives—to create a "new world order" peopled exclusively by the white race. Any doubts about the seriousness of such hate groups were dispelled when police and federal agents raided a white supremacist compound in rural Arkansas in April 1984 and discovered a stockpile of some thirty gallons of cyanide to be used to poison municipal water supplies. The targets and tactics of "holy terror" operations that have occurred or been attempted during the past decade clearly lead to a conclusion that a possibility exists for far more destructive acts. Ominous examples already abound:

- Poisoning of water supplies of major urban centers—not only American white supremacists but also terrorists in India are alleged to have made such plans.
- Dispersal of toxic chemicals through internal building ventilation systems, which has been attempted by white supremacist "skinheads" in Arizona.
- Indiscriminate, wanton attacks on busy urban centers' transportation systems, as in Madrid, Spain, and London.
- Attacks on power grids to disrupt electrical service to large population areas, conducted by a black Muslim sect in Colorado.
- Poisoning of food, undertaken in Oregon by followers of the Bhagwan Rajneesh to influence a local election.

As the new millennium approached, the somewhat superstitious fears of a nation became real, when Ahmed Ressam was intercepted entering the United States from Canada with a bomb planned for use on the Los Angeles International airport. Ressam was convicted in July 2005 and sentenced to twenty-two years in prison. While our attention is now fully averted toward terrorist cells at large, we should not discount other threats that could still pose a significant danger. If we simply ignore the right-wing militias and the network they have stitched together across the nation, we will do so at our own peril. It is clear that militia movements are continuing to grow rapidly. We need only type in the word "militia" on any Internet browser and we will find dozens of examples.

SUICIDE AND RELIGIOUS TERRORISM

Suicide as a means to attack an enemy is not a new tactic; it dates back in the modern era to 1881, when a group of Nihilists wielding homemade bombs assassinated Tsar Alexander II in St. Petersburg, Russia, as he rode in his armored carriage near the Winter Palace. During World War II, the Japanese used Kamikaze pilots to dive bomb into the United States and allied shipping with devastating results. First used intentionally during the October 1944 Battle of Leyte Gulf, the kamikaze attackers succeeded in damaging allied warships, most notably the USS *St. Lo*, USS *Intrepid*, USS *Franklin*, USS *Bunker Hill*, and the Australian HMAS *Australia*. In addition, the Japanese developed weapons designed to carry out suicide attacks, including the Kaiten-manned torpedo, the Ki-115 purpose-built kamikaze plane, and the Ohka rocket-powered kamikaze plane.

U.S. Air Force intelligence has reported that the use of suicide bombers has spread worldwide since 1990. Between 1980 and 1990, suicide bombings occurred in three countries: Lebanon, Sri Lanka, and Kuwait. From 1991 to 2002, however, the tactic had spread to fifteen countries, from Algeria and Chechnya to Argentina and Croatia and to the United States,[4] and of course in 2005 it spread to the United Kingdom as well.

Terrorism associated with suicide attacks had for the most part been the signature style of the Palestinian bombers in Israel and the occupied territories and of the Tamil Tigers in Sri

Lanka. In the Iraq insurgency and in Afghanistan, suicide attacks have been regular occurrences. Suicide had been an alien form of attack in the West until the terrorist suicides and hijackings on 9-11 and the suicide bombing attacks in London. Britain was prepared and had consistently warned of an attack by Islamic militants. The British alert level had been high during the run-up to the spring 2005 general election, which returned Tony Blair to his post as prime minister. The security posture was somewhat heightened when the world leaders attended the G8 Economic Summit in Edinburgh, Scotland, with opening ceremonies slated for July 7, 2005. The attack on the London Underground transport system for all its planning and audaciousness shook British politicians and the public to the core—this was not the work of external groups but second-generation immigrants born, raised, and educated in England to mainly middle-class families!

In 2004–2005, there were over 400 suicide attacks, mostly in Iraq, and 2007 saw a total of 658 globally with 543 being in the Iraq/Afghanistan theater. The bombings have spread to dozens of countries on five continents, killed more than 21,350 people and injured some 50,000 since 1983, when a suicide attack blew up the U.S. embassy in Beirut. In addressing the root causes of terrorism, we believe that comments presented by the former British Prime Minister Tony Blair in the days after the London attack were overstated and not germane. He stated to a BBC interviewer that the underlying causes of these attacks were lack of democracy, the Middle East conflict, and poverty. Blair's belief that these are the root causes of terrorism is fundamentally flawed; if he believes that by creating democracy or removing poverty, terrorism will be eliminated, he is incorrect. The poorest nations of the world are not the ones producing the terrorist phenomenon. In discussing democracy, it is certainly not clear-cut that this is an important goal for the terrorists' agenda. With respect to the Middle East conflict, there is no evidence to support whether or not that conflict is a lightning rod for terrorism anywhere other than in that geopolitical region. The terrorists who perpetrated the 9-11 attacks, the Madrid train bombings, the London Underground attacks, and the attack on Glasgow airport in 2007 have been described as foot soldiers who had little frontline involvement in terrorist activities prior to the attacks. In all of these attacks, none of the perpetrators lived in abject poverty—in fact, the British attackers could be described as middle class and reasonably well educated, and in the Glasgow attacks the perpetrators were medical doctors. We need to focus on the root cause of international terrorism. The terrorist ideology supports a system of beliefs that allows for the devaluation of the lives of innocent victims, in most cases civilian victims of so-called targeted enemy societies; and encourages and promotes extreme violence, including suicide, as a method of responding to grievances. Why do extreme promoters of the Islamic faith use such an ideology to make use of poverty, repression, and conflict to aid in recruitment? Terrorist organizations are fundamentally organizations or businesses. While they may have been founded as a response to some grievance either real or perceived, they soon become focused on their own continuity and perpetuation; otherwise they sooner or later would just disappear. A successful terror organization does what is necessary for its own survival. To that end, it requires resources and recruits, so it produces ideology, propaganda, and terror attacks to compete for these inputs. We clearly need to understand that terrorism is an industry and terrorist organizations are not about to go out of business because of any social or political improvements we can bring about. We need to attack these organizations directly, reducing their ability to motivate, raise funds, recruit, and organize attacks.[5]

Because suicide attacks are dramatic and often effective for a relatively small economic cost, suicide bombings will continue to increase. There are approximately 1.6 million Muslims in Britain, according to the British Home Office. A 2004 report by the Home Office detailed that 13 percent of British Muslims believed that suicide attacks against Western targets were justified. Respondents linked this attitude to anger over foreign policies and the presence of British and

U.S. troops in the Middle East. In the United States, a 2009 Pew Report showed a total of almost 2.5 million Muslims residing there. If radicalization of even 1 percent were to take place, that would pose a significant problem for Homeland Security.

Children as Suicide Bombers

As ghastly as the heading may appear, this will be a reality in certain areas of the globe. That suicide bombers were traditionally young males has also changed as now we see more female and elderly suicide attackers and in Iraq we have witnessed the use of the mentally challenged to deliver suicide bombs. As for child bombers we have already seen photographs of Palestinian children in combat fatigues and mock suicide belts in training for missions. In 2005, we saw a mixed gender suicide attack on the Jordanian capital—although the target of the 2005 attack was not unusual, the make up of the suicide bombers was. Both were from al Qaeda in Iraq and were a married couple. In 2004, an Israeli soldier manning a checkpoint near the city of Nablus discovered a 13-pound explosive device in the backpack of a twelve-year-old Palestinian boy. The schoolboy had been tricked into carrying the bag by members of a Palestinian terrorist group. The soldier was alerted by the cell phone ring tone in the backpack. In 2006, a Palestinian mother of nine and grandmother of twenty-six was killed by Israeli security as she attempted to detonate a suicide vest. Currently, this lady is the oldest suicide bomber recorded to have successfully carried out a mission. In 2011, we saw jihadist websites showing children training in jihadist training camps using weapons and explosives. For the future we will need to be wary of attempts by terrorist groups, particularly al Qaeda attempting to get body bombs onto aircraft. Full body scan technology is not yet worldwide, and in Europe there is far less of these scanners than in the United States. Terrorists will attempt to conceal a bomb in a body cavity or as breast implants to detonate on board an airliner.

TECHNO TERRORISM

As the Internet user reaches the unnerving conclusion that terrorism, like the Internet, recognizes no national boundaries, law enforcement officials will seek more ways to ferret it out and take preventive actions. In the past, investigators have wielded telephone wiretaps against terrorists, but the Clinton administration pointed to the use of encrypted files by child pornographers, militia members, and spies to avoid discovery. Grave crimes, such as a plot to shoot down several airliners over Chicago, have been foiled by the use of wiretaps. Had the FBI been unable to read those transmissions, a major tragedy might have occurred. Strong language calls for regulation of the Internet's content, such as the Clinton administration's ill-fated attempt to curb child pornography via the Communications Decency Act.

Senator Dianne Feinstein (D-California) introduced a bill that would make it illegal to distribute explosives making information "by any means," including online, if the distributor intends or knows the information would be used in committing a crime. Encryption that is difficult to decipher should not be distributed to anyone. It's almost the same argument as that for gun control. The good citizen doesn't need a background check, but how can you tell that person from a bank robber without one? The use of the Internet has been dramatic for legitimate businesses, as well as for the business of terrorism and organized crime. The Internet has been used as a tool to frighten and export fear in "real-time," with almost instantaneous video footage of terrorist attacks. This has been a powerful tool and has likely been used not only for the value it gains from fear but also for recruiting and training.

INTERNET JIHAD

The threat from Cyber Terrorism

We live in a world of fast-paced media driven by online forums, Twitter, Facebook, and other social media outlets—all of which are available and used by terrorist groups and sponsors to spread information and to communicate with cells around the globe. The wealth of information spread through social media about bombs and bomb making materials should not be a surprise, and in so many cases intelligence organizations are often only able to respond after an event has taken place. An extreme right-wing Norwegian, who carried out the Oslo attacks in 2011, had actually posted his manifesto online, but many others online post similar diatribes and never carry their actions through. For many Western Islamists their only opportunity to connect with like-minded individuals to become indoctrinated and radicalized is through online forums and chat rooms—the Internet is an important tool to help radicalize and inspire jihad. Many of the young Western jihadists are likely self-radicalized and self-recruited without ever having contact with al Qaeda or its affiliates. The Internet has become the virtual world for training jihadists, and although it is no substitute for hands-on training at a training camp in Pakistan or Afghanistan, the risks of being detected on the Internet are considerably lower. The publishing of material on the Internet has influenced operational terrorist activity and will continue to do so. The Global Islamic Media Front published an article in the year prior to the Madrid Train station attacks in 2004, which according to the Spanish investigating judge was what had inspired the perpetrators of the attack. Certainly the Internet is helping geographically dispersed groups and individuals who enthusiastically want to join the jihad. It also encourages individual actions by small groups or individuals, which may be why events such as the airport attack in Glasgow Scotland in 2007 was relatively unsophisticated and crude in its execution.

JIHADIST WEBSITES

Far from hiding from view Jihadist websites are abundant and many are posted in English language and are easy to visit. The SITE monitoring service in the United States tracks and monitors a vast array of Jihadist websites—these sites are all about spreading the message of jihad, recruiting and inciting prospective jihadists. A quick look at the SITE page gives us a clear picture of just how much use the Jihadist make of the Internet and social media. The following are examples taken from SITE on August 17, 2011:

- A Yemeni jihadist gave news about recent incidents in Abyan and al-Jawf provinces of Yemen and remarked on what he called the "stupidity" of the Saudi government in Yemen in two messages posted on jihadist forums on August 14 and August 17, 2011.
- The Shabaab al-Mujahideen Movement reported that its fighters launched attacks in the Somali capital, Mogadishu, and managed to capture a Somali soldier during one of its operations.
- A jihadist called upon Muslims in America to assassinate television talk show host David Letterman, explaining that his mockery of Ilyas Kashmiri is deserving of death.
- Afghan Taliban claims suicide raids in Kandahar, Parwan
- German IMU member possibly injured
- A jihadist recalled his relationship with a fellow forum member who carried out a suicide bombing under the banner of the al-Qaeda-affiliated Islamic State of Iraq (ISI), in a message posted on the Shumukh al-Islam forum

- Jihadist reports death of forum member in Waziristan
- Husainan provides daily prayer program for Muslim women
- Shabaab reports increase in AMISOM casualties in Mogadishu
- Ansar al-Islam focuses on taking captives, celebrates slain commander[6]

TERRORISTS FOR SALE OR EXCHANGE

In an ideal world, governments would deal with any terrorists they apprehended. Alternately, if requested to do so, they would hand them over to the government of the country where the crimes were committed, for the purpose of trial. And, countries should fully expect reciprocal and similar treatment. Unfortunately, this seldom happens because one man's "terrorist" is another man's "freedom fighter" and suspicious governments seldom give away something for nothing. All want to retain a few bargaining terrorist chips, just in case—a terrorist in hand often has value. Years ago, the expression "he has a price on his head" was clearly understood: It meant that a person was "wanted" by justice authorities for either escaping from legal custody or being on the run for having allegedly committed a crime. A cash reward was invariably offered for the criminal's apprehension and conviction, especially in the days before modern police forces, to induce the public to bring him or her to justice. Cash rewards for these purposes brought about bounty hunting, a practice that lingers on in some countries. Nowadays, the expression that "every government has its price" might be more appropriate, particularly when dealing with the extradition of terrorists.

Extradition has always been a delicate subject, touching as it does on national sovereignty, seeming at times to be regarded more as a personal favor to the government asking for it than a routine, international transaction. Many suspect that there must be secret exchange channels, as all such transactions are carried out with the utmost discretion and are publicly denied.

Cash Value of Terrorists

In August 1994, the French government "purchased" the notorious terrorist "Carlos the Jackal" from the Sudanese government for a reputed US$2 million. The French admitted only that he had been arrested "outside the usual legal framework." Carlos (Ilyich Ramirez Sanchez) was a star terrorist captive, wanted for killing eighty-three people in a series of terrorist attacks, several in France. In December 1975, he had led the terrorist team that kidnapped eleven OPEC oil ministers in Vienna.

Carlos had long been sheltered in Middle Eastern states, courtesy of the KGB, but with the end of the Cold War, he had become an embarrassment. He was subsequently ejected from Syria, refused entry by Yemen and Libya, and forced to accept asylum in Sudan. Carlos still resides in a French prison, having been convicted in the killing of two gendarmes. The French government thought it made a good bargain, perhaps so too did the Sudanese government.

The Carlos incident established the fact that terrorists have a monetary value. The U.S. government has consistently offered monetary rewards for terrorists and in 2012 posted a reward of $10 million for the capture of the suspect in the 2008 Mumbai terrorist attacks. As the suspect Hafiz Mohammad Saeed, the founder of Lashkar-e-Taiba (LeT), is living relatively openly in Pakistan, it remains to be seen whether any assistance in his capture would come from Pakistan, given the level of political discord between the two nations since the killing of Osama bin Laden. This bounty is unlikely to be picked up by anyone in Pakistan. Saeed is intrinsically linked to the Pakistani ISI and therefore well protected as well as connected.

If a government happens to be sheltering a high-value terrorist, and it needs a cash infusion, it would certainly be tempting to bring him or her to trial for a price. Such show trials provide a major boost to the morale of national security services. Lower-profile terrorists could be obtained for lower prices—a process that might have been in operation for some time for all we know, as secrecy surrounds the process. Either the media were well ahead of the diplomats in the Carlos case, or the French government deliberately sought publicity.

The Western hostage crisis in Lebanon (1984–1992) saw most of them being ransomed eventually. Often, wealthy international concerns pay huge sums of money for the release of employees since it is against most governments' policy to deal directly with terrorists. In 1992, the last two German hostages, Kemptner and Strubig who were kidnapped in Beirut, were released after three years in captivity when the two Hamadi brothers, who were convicted of hijacking a TWA airliner in 1985, were released in a hostage for prisoner exchange. In June 1995, the German government paid a reputed $1 million to the poverty-stricken Yemeni government for the extradition of Johannes Weinrich, a colleague of Carlos in his heyday. He was wanted for murder and explosions in Berlin and, after twenty years on the run, is now in prison in Germany.

When the United States began its assault on Baghdad in 2003, it created a pack of playing cards, with each card displaying the face and name of a wanted Iraqi—the higher the card in the deck, the higher the monetary reward.

In October 1985, the Italian cruise ship *Achille Lauro* was hijacked in the Mediterranean, and one U.S. citizen was killed. The situation was resolved with the help of the Egyptian government, which provided an aircraft to the terrorists. Under President Reagan's "you can run, but you can't hide" policy, U.S. aircraft forced the plane down in Italy. There, the leader, Abu Abbas, a Palestinian terrorist mastermind, was allowed to escape to Yugoslavia. The other terrorists involved stood trial and were convicted in Italy. One, Magied al-Mulkil, was sentenced to thirty years' imprisonment and later jumped his parole, whereupon the U.S. government immediately offered a $2 million reward for his recapture.

After the terrorist massacre at Luxor (Egypt) in November 1996, the Egyptian government condemned the British government for harboring the Islamic fundamentalist terrorist leaders thought to be responsible. Britain through the 1980s and 1990s had long been a refuge for those wanting to escape harsh regimes in Africa and the Middle East, giving its capital city the unenviable nick name of "Londonistan." The United States offered a reward of $2 million for the apprehension of Ramzi Ahmad Yousef, the mastermind behind the conspiracy to blow up the World Trade Center in New York and other buildings and bridges. The CIA believed that Yousef was in Pakistan. Pakistani men smoke a lot, so the CIA issued thousands of small, green (a favorite Islamic color) matchboxes with Yousef's likeness on one side and details of how to obtain the reward on the other. This did the trick. Yousef was subsequently captured and is currently in a U.S. prison.

The Exchange Market

During the Cold War, we came to accept that spies were exchanged, so why not "terrorists" too? In the Middle East, terrorists have sometimes been selectively exchanged under cover of Red Cross prisoner-of-war transfers. Exchanging hostages is an ancient military custom, revived during the Lebanese civil war (1975–1992), when warring factions had their own private prisons where hostages were held as security insurance, for vengeance and for exchange actions.

Israel, on occasion, indulged in kidnapping raids to seize terrorist leaders, including Sheikh Abdul Rahman Obeid and Mustafa Dirani. According to the Israeli press, the Israeli government offered to release forty-seven Palestinians, including certain political prisoners loosely referred to as terrorists, for the freeing of one captured Israeli soldier. There have been other instances when "Arab guerrillas," meaning terrorists, have been released in exchange for Israeli prisoners.

In 1997, Jordanian authorities captured two Mossad agents after their failed attempt to assassinate Khaled Mishal, a Hamas leader, in Amman (Jordan), and four others, all with forged Canadian passports, took refuge in the Israeli Embassy in Amman. In exchange for the safe return of the Mossad agents, Israel agreed to exchange Sheikh Ahmad Yassin, imprisoned spiritual leader of Hamas. Israelis have made a few selective key terrorist exchanges over the years, with censorship invariably concealing precise details.

Hostages: A Sliding Scale

High prices have been demanded and obtained for the release of certain terrorist-held hostages, but the success of these extortion plans depended on someone's (usually not a government) ability to pay large sums of money. Wealthy commercial concerns might be prepared to meet a terrorist's demands for the release of one of their employees but would hesitate to embark upon such an illegal and secretive process. However, a few have done so, as indirectly as possible. Not all were wealthy, but many were able to raise lesser sums of money, so it is probable that there was a terrorists' sliding scale of ransom demands—a sort of actuary's table, understood only by terrorist masterminds and their intermediaries.

Comparatively few hostages are killed, as lucrative prospects seem to outweigh political scruples and vengeance. This does happen sometimes, particularly when terrorists quarrel among themselves over possession of the hostage and what to do with him or her. Occasionally, hostages have been sold or bartered between groups. One example is that of Ron Arad, an Israeli air force navigator shot down over Lebanon in 1986 and taken hostage by Islamic fundamentalist Amal militia and subsequently sold into the custody of the Iranian Revolutionary Guards, and has not been seen since. Led by Mustafa Dirani, the group, according to some intelligence sources, held Arad for two years before selling him for $300,000. His fate has never been fully determined, but it is believed he died in captivity in Lebanon possibly in the mid-1990s.

Terrorists with Shelf Life Expired

In 1999, when the Lebanese army was reasserting its control over parts of the lawless Beka'a Valley, it cleaned out a nest of miscellaneous international terrorists, including five members of the Japanese Red Army. They were all former prisoners of the Israelis who had been freed in a mass Red Cross-organized Arab/Israeli exchange. One was Kozo Okamoto, the surviving terrorist of the May 1972 massacre at Lod Airport, in which over twenty people had been killed and more than eighty injured. Another was Kazuo Tohira, the group's master passport forger. The JRA members had disappeared from public view and notice. Japan showed no interest in them at all, as their shelf life had expired and Japanese authorities were reluctant to resurrect the emotions of past terrorist dramas. In July 1999, the Lebanese government was reduced to charging the five JRA terrorists with illegal entry into Lebanon, and they were sentenced to three years' imprisonment, after which they were deported.

As we look to the future, we continue to look back over our shoulders at what has taken place. If 9-11 was a watershed for the West, what effect is it having on the aspirations of the Islamic extremist movements? We continue to believe that the Islamic terror threat emanates from al Qaeda and al Qaeda-affiliated groups. Al Qaeda has not made inroads into any political organizations around the world. In countries like Sudan, Egypt, Kashmir, Nigeria, Somalia, and Indonesia, we have witnessed attempts by Islamic groups to organize and destabilize the political roadmap. In each, we have witnessed both success and failure, and in each there have been somewhat spectacular acts of violence. If bin Laden expected a popular uprising from the millions of Muslims around the world, it has not happened. After the coalition invasion of Afghanistan, there were no calls from Muslim clerics to declare a holy war against an infidel West. Not only has there been silence, but there have even been calls from other extreme agents of Islam against the actions of al Qaeda. Following the London attacks in July 2005, the British Muslim community roundly condemned the actions of the minority that sought this destruction and brought shame on their religion. In Egypt, the imprisoned leader of al-Gama'a al-Islamiya issued a public declaration distancing his organization from the extreme activities of bin Laden and al Qaeda—hardly a recommendation for a worldwide holy war!

TECHNOLOGY AND SURVEILLANCE

Technology will continue to play a role in effectively preempting a terror strike. While some will advocate that advancements in technological protection and detection of terrorists has resulted in a far greater intrusion into peoples privacy many seem not to mind such intrusion. Technological advances in protecting the public in areas such as public transport, airports, and railroads where smart cameras are deployed to identify people by their mannerism, gait, and facial expressions are now deployed. Human intelligence coupled with technology will help detect and prevent an attack. Sensors have been developed to identify the minutest trace of explosives or deadly microbes in a water system.

Shipping and shipping containers are the lifeblood of the U.S. economy, and vast numbers of ships loaded with containers cross and crisscross the world's Oceans. The use of technology and globally agreed practices to screen products and identify shipments will go a significant distance to deter and delay the terrorists. However, the farther we get away from the target date of September 11, 2001, the more likely we are to forget those events and let down our guard; the terrorists only need to get lucky once—security forces need far more than luck on their side. As we have said previously, the terrorists of the twenty-first century still regard aviation as a target of choice and protecting against attacks both at airports and elsewhere continues to occupy the minds of security officials. Looking into the future we worry about the nature of the next major attack and where it is likely to be carried out. We try to determine if it will be chemical, biological, nuclear, or more conventional means. Can the current trends in suicide attacks in the Middle East, Asia, the United Kingdom, United States, and Indonesia be a window to future attacks against the United States and its interests both at home and abroad? Rogue states such as Iran that continues to build toward completion of a nuclear weapons program pose a futuristic threat to global security. A nuclear attack from space would wreak havoc far in excess of the damage done by the atomic bomb on Hiroshima in 1945. A nuclear device(s) detonated up to 500 miles above the earth would generate a massive electronic pulse, crippling satellites, radar, power stations, and hydroelectric power plants. Although the probability of a high-altitude attack by a rogue state or a terror group is currently assumed to be low, the possibility still remains, and governments should be preparing for such a futuristic threat.

As the United States and its allies continue to fight terrorism, it is time to take stock of where we are. Our world has changed since 9-11, but have our attitudes changed as well? Are we becoming too complacent? Do we honestly believe that all the legislation in place to fight terrorism and the increases in budget spending will prevent the next catastrophic event from taking place? How do we address global terrorism that seemingly will not go away? Perhaps it is time to take a long hard look at how we handle the scourge of terrorism. This has never been solely an American problem. There is a need to educate schoolchildren, college students, and blue-collar and white-collar workers on the causes, sources, and history of terrorism. From the way police and intelligence agencies recruit, to the skills they demand, to the relationships they build with one another, the whole approach must change. Extensive role-playing of the way terrorists might operate in both urban and rural settings, using a government-wide cross-section of expertise, is essential. Partnerships and exchange of ideas must become a critical element in the future fight against terrorism. It is apparent the United States cannot go this way on its own and must foster more solid global relations and use ideas and innovations from elsewhere. The ultimate goal must be to outwit and outthink the terrorists and expose to the whole world an unflinching resolve and determination supported by a strong coalition of governments by conveying a message of what the United States stands for and the exposing of terrorist hypocrisy.

Summary

Prior to 9-11, the United States never anticipated it would be at war with terrorism and, most certainly, not in the dimensions to which we are now witnessing. The risks, the dangers, and the threats from groups or individual cells—all hell-bent on the destruction of Western democracies—are now at hand. Could they create another 9-11? Are the London bombings a wake-up call? As should be abundantly clear, your authors have only been able to present the "tip of the iceberg." Events often move faster than we can get them down on paper! In this chapter, we have touched on just a few of the issues facing our terror-struck world as it stumbles forward deeper into the twenty-first century among all the probable threats for the future. It appears that it will be up to the next generation to try to find effective ways to eliminate bigotry and the conditions that separate people financially, ethnically, religiously, racially, tribally, politically, and traditionally. We know that, worldwide, we have failed to gather all the available intelligence and accurately analyze and spot the signs to interpret it. This will change, and the wheel will turn. We hope that this book has opened a window through which the reader will view the evening news from a far different perspective and with serious skepticism. If we have whetted your appetite for knowledge about how violence and terrorism came about, we are pleased and will feel that all this effort in writing it for you has been worth it.

As we attempt to look toward the future and what may lie ahead in the world of terrorist acts, we anticipate that terror networks and affiliates that attack in the guise of Islam will concentrate on spectacular events, but likely not on the dramatic scale of 9-11, which required a considerable amount of planning and training. The suicide bomber is able to strike at will and without warning and cause a large number of casualties. There is currently an almost unending supply of young fanatics willing to become suicide operatives in what might best be described as the poor man's smart bomb. In terms of modern-day terrorism, military occupation of Muslim lands by foreign armies is a contributing factor in the creation of a suicide bomber. From a broad perspective, suicide bombers are usually from outside the country they are attacking. The U.S. military notes that a significant number of attacks by suicide bombers in Afghanistan are carried out by foreign Arabs, while the suicide attacks in London were carried out by young British men of Pakistani and Jamaican descent. The ideology of al Qaeda has not become extinct through the War on Terror—rather, it has become entrenched at the grassroots level. There is no doubt that suicide attacks will continue in the foreseeable future as will low cost "lone wolf"–style attacks.

Websites

1. **The Future of Terrorism**—*http://www.terrorism-research.com/future/*
2. **World Future Society**—*www.wfs.org*
3. **American Society for Industrial Security**—*www.asisonline.org*
4. **International Center for Political Violence and Terrorism Research**—*http://www.pvtr.org/*

End Notes

1. US Congressional Record. *National Defense Authorization Act for Fiscal Year 1997* (1997).
2. Paul Cornish. "Sabotage by Sarin." *Intersec: The Journal of International Security*, vol. 7, no. 9 (Surrey, UK: Three Bridges Publishing, September 1997).
3. www.milnet.com.
4. Strategic Forecasting Inc.(2011), http://www.stratfor.com/.
5. Dan Radlauer. "The London Bombings and the Root Causes of Terrorism." Paper to the International Policy Institute for Counterterrorism (July 10, 2005).
6. SITE Intelligence Group. https://www.siteintel-group.com/ extracted August 17 2011.

GLOSSARY

Abdel Basset al-Megrahi—Libyan Intelligence officer convicted and subsequently released for the bombing of Pan Am flight over Lockerbie Scotland on December 21, 1988. Died of cancer in Libya May 2012.

Abu Hamza al Masri—Former imam of London's Finsbury Park Mosque.

Abu Musab al-Zarqawi—Jordanian militant who ran terror training camps in Iraq and formed al Qaeda in Iraq—was killed by US forces in 2006.

Abu Sayyaf Group (ASG)—A Philippine Islamic terror group that seeks an independent Islamic state along the Sulu archipelago.

Accion Nacional Espanila (ANE)—Spanish National Action, right-wing terror movement that targets Basque separatists.

Active service unit (ASU)—A term used by the Provisional IRA to describe one of its active terror units or cells.

Aden Protectorate—An area of southern Arabia that, by treaty, was under British Protectorate rule during the early to mid-twentieth century; now part of the Republic of Yemen.

Adherents—Individuals who have formed collaborative relationships with, act on behalf of, or are otherwise inspired to take action in furtherance of the goals of al Qaeda—the organization and the ideology—including by engaging in violence regardless of whether such violence is targeted at the United States, its citizens, or its interests.

Affiliates—Groups that have aligned with al Qaeda.

African National Congress (ANC)—Center left political party dates back to the early twentieth century. In 1944, the ANC youth wing was formed by Oliver Tembo and Nelson Mandela. Established to defend the rights of the black majority in South Africa and has been in power in South Africa since 1994.

Afrikaner Weerstandsbeweging (AWB)—The Afrikaner Resistance Movement; an extreme left-wing group comprising white South Africans.

Al-Fatah—A left-wing nationalist Palestinian political party and largest member of the PLO. It has supported a wide variety of European terrorist groups through the 1960s and 1970s.

Algerian Salafist Group for Preaching and Combat (GSPC)—An Islamic terrorist organization that has gained much support from disenfranchised Muslim youth in Europe and has emerged as a major source of recruiting and support for al Qaeda operations. A splinter faction of the Algerian Armed Islamic Group (GIA), the GSPC, is engaged in efforts to overthrow the secular government of Algeria and to organize high-profile attacks against Western interests.

Ai Hassan al-Majid—"Chemical Ali," first cousin to Saddam Hussein; the head of the Iraqi chemical weapons program through the 1980s and 1990s.

Al Jazeera—Qatar-based Arabic TV station; since the 9-11 attacks, it has aired many video messages from Osama bin Laden. Literal translation from Arabic means "an island."

Al Qaeda—An international terrorist movement first heard of in the late 1980s. Founded by Mohammad Atef and Osama bin Laden. Based in Afghanistan and supported by the Taliban government throughout the 1990s. Its aims are the destruction of non-Islamic governments. It is now spread throughout the world with many fighters in the mountains of Pakistan.

Al-Sabah Dynasty—Succession of rulers in Kuwait; Sabah al-Ahmad al-Jabir al-Sabah is the current prime minister of Kuwait and was appointed to this position by his brother, the emir of Kuwait, Jabir al-Sabah in 2003.

Al Shabaab—Islamic militant group based in Somalia seeking to create an Islamic caliphate in the region.

Anti-Fascist Resistance Group of October First (GRAPO)—Formed in 1975 as the armed wing of the illegal Communist Party of Spain during the Franco era. GRAPO advocates the overthrow of the Spanish government and its replacement with a Marxist-Leninist regime. The group is anti-United States and seeks the removal of all U.S. military forces from Spanish territory. The group issued a communiqué following the attacks of September 11 in the United States, expressing its satisfaction that "symbols of imperialist power" were decimated and affirming that "the war" has only just begun.

Antiterrorism and Effective Death Penalty Act of 1996—Laws enacted by the United States to combat terrorism and provide justice for victims of terrorism.

Anti-Terrorism Crime and Security Act 2001 (ATCSA)—Counterterrorism bill introduced into law by the government of the United Kingdom.

Anwar al-Awlaki—a dual citizen (US and Yemen)—believed to be in Yemen and has acted as a planner and trainer for al Qaeda and affiliates.

Apartheid—Policy of segregation along racial lines; prominently practiced in South Africa.

Ariel Sharon—Joined the Haganah in 1942, became Israel's prime minister in 2001. Suffered a massive stroke in March 2006.

Armata Corsa—An underground separatist movement established in 1999 opposing the links between nationalists and the Corsican Mafia.

Armed Islamic Group (GIA)—Islamic terrorist group operating in Algeria.

Armed Proletarian Nuclei (NAP)—Left-wing movement originating in the Italian prison system.

Armee Republicaine Bretonne (ARB)—Breton Liberation Army; a small nationalist antiglobalization movement with its roots in the Breton region of France.

Armenian Secret Army for the Liberation of Armenia (ASALA)—Marxist-Leninist Armenian terrorist group formed in 1975 with stated intention to compel the Turkish government to acknowledge publicly its alleged responsibility for the deaths of 1.5 million Armenians in 1915; led by Hagop Hagopian until he was assassinated in Athens in April 1988.

Army of God—U.S. domestic terror group that engages in violence; targets abortion clinics and medical practitioners.

Army Ranger Wing (ARW)—Republic of Ireland's elite counterterror unit.

Assassination—Targeted killing of an important person for political or ideological reasons.

Aum Shinrikyo—Japanese terror group known for the sarin gas attack on the Tokyo subway in 1995.

Autodeterminaziorako Bilgunea (AuB)—Formed in February 13, 2003. Comprises prominent representatives from the Basque left-wing pro-independence movement, as well as those from other political backgrounds. Political agenda to demand the right of the Basque people to make decisions regarding their future and supporting a democratic solution to the Basque political conflict.

Aviation Security Commando (AVESCOM)—Philippines hostage rescue unit.

Ayatollah Khomeini—Iranian Grand Ayatollah, leader of the Iranian revolution against the Shah of Iran in 1979.

Ba'athist regime—Pan-Arabic socialist party that was prominent in Iraq and continues in Syria; party of Saddam Hussein.

Babbar Khalsa International (BKI)—A Sikh terrorist group sponsored by expatriate Indian Sikhs demanding an independent Sikh state called Khalistan (Land of the Pure) from Indian territory.

Bahraini Hezbollah—Organization believed to be supported by Iran; seeks to overthrow the Bahrain government and replace it with a fundamentalist Islamic regime.

Bakassi Boys—A violent vigilante group that operates with almost impunity as supposed anticrime vigilantes.

Balfour Declaration—Lord Balfour's 1917 declaration pledging British support to a Jewish homeland in Palestine.

Basque Region—Area in northern Spain and southwest France (Pyrenees); the Basque people (approximately 2 million) inhabit the region.

Basque Socialist Coalition—Known as the Herri Batasuna (People's Unity) Party; led by Arnoldo Ortiz.

Batasuna, Herri—The People's Unity Party; Spanish organization led by Arnoldo Ortiz; officially denies any links or involvement with the ETA terrorist organization; also known as The Basque Socialist Coalition.

Black and Tans—British paramilitary force recruited to assist the Royal Irish Constabulary; members wore black and tan uniforms.

Black September—Palestinian fighters who attempted to seize power in Jordan; subsequently, the Jordanian military expelled thousands of Palestinians from Jordan in September 1970. Black September gained notoriety for the killing of eleven Israeli athletes at the Munich Olympic Games in 1972.

Boevaya Oranisatsia (BO)—Terror suborganization within the Social Revolutionary Party; given autonomy under the party (means "the fighting organization").

Boko Haram—Nigeria-based Islamist terror group demanding imposition of Islamic Law throughout the region.

Bolshevik—Extreme left-wing radicals, who favored revolution; led by Lenin.

Bureau of State Security (BOSS)—The South African state security service.

Cali cartel—A powerful drug cartel operating in Colombia.

Canadian Security Intelligence Service (CSIS)—A relatively young organization that tracks threats to national security within Canada.

Carlos the Jackal—Illich Ramirez Sanchez, an infamous terrorist in Western Europe in the 1960s; currently in a French prison.

Cheka—Communist secret police organization established during the Russian Revolution in 1917.

Chiapas—A state in southeast Mexico where a peasant uprising led by the Zapatista National Liberation Army continues to press for greater autonomy.

Cobras—Sultanate of Oman elite Special Forces unit.

Communist Combatant Cells (CCC)—A Belgian terror group.

Contras—Terrorist organization and armed opponents of Nicaragua's Sandinista Junta of National Reconstruction following the July 1979 overthrow of Anastasio Somoza Debayle and the ending of the Somoza family's forty-three-year rule.

CSI—U.S. Container Security Initiative—global security initiative established by U.S. Customs and Border Protection in 2002 to target and screen container traffic.

Customs and Border Patrol (CBP)—The U.S. Border Patrol; the mobile uniformed law enforcement arm of the Department of Homeland Security (DHS). Originally established on May 28, 1924, by an act of Congress passed in response to increasing illegal immigration.

Dada, Idi Amin—Self-declared president for life of Uganda who came to power following a coup in 1971; he purged the military and the country of most of his opponents and exiled 70,000 Ugandan Asians with British passports. He died in exile in Saudi Arabia in 2003.

Dal Khalsa—Sikh terrorist organization supported by ex-patriot Sikhs; their aim is to establish the independent Sikh state of Khalistan.

Decommissioning—Provision in the Northern Ireland Peace Agreement that puts weapons beyond the use of Irish terror organizations.

Democratic Front for the Liberation of Palestine (DFLP)—Marxist-Leninist organization founded in 1969 when it split from the Popular Front for the Liberation of Palestine (PFLP). The

DFLP believes Palestinian national goals can be achieved only through revolution. Joined other rejectionist groups to oppose the Declaration of Principles signed in 1993. In the 1970s, the DFLP conducted numerous small bombings and minor assaults and some more spectacular operations in Israel and the occupied territories, concentrating on Israeli targets. They have only been involved in border raids since 1988, but they continue to oppose the Israel-PLO peace agreement.

Democratic People's Republic of Korea (DPRK)—A communist state dominated by a one-man dictatorship. North Korea's long-range missile development and research into nuclear, chemical, and biological weapons and massive conventional armed forces are of major concern to the international community. The current ruler of North Korea is Kim Jong-un.

Democratic Progressive Party (DPP)—Taiwanese opposition party.

Department of Homeland Security (DHS)—U.S. government agency created after the attacks of 9-11.

Dev Sol—A left-wing Marxist group that has its origins in the Turkish People's Liberation Army.

Diplock Commission—Commission set up in 1972 to consider legal measures against terrorism in Northern Ireland, which led to the establishment of courts without jury; named after Kenneth Diplock.

Directorate of Inter-Services Intelligence (ISI)—Pakistani intelligence organization; founded in 1948 and has more than 10,000 members; it collects foreign and domestic intelligence and coordinates intelligence functions of the three military services.

Doc, Papa—The long-time dictator of Haiti, aided by the Ton-Ton Marquette terrorists.

Domestic terrorist acts—Terrorist actions conducted by Americans.

Emergency Provisions—Powers given to the military by the Northern Ireland Emergency Provisions to combat urban terror in Northern Ireland.

ETA-Military—Military branch of the Basque terrorist organization.

Ethnic cleansing—A term originally used to describe the Serbs' attack on Muslims in Bosnia during the breakup of Yugoslavia; a softer term than "genocide."

ETIM—East Turkestan Islamic Movement—a separatist group demanding independence from China

European Civil Aviation Conference (ECAC)—European organization responsible for developing policies and standards for civil aviation.

Euzkadi Ta Azkatasuna (ETA)—The Basques formed ETA (Basque Fatherland and Freedom) in 1959, and it has dedicated itself to promoting Basque independence and has become one of Europe's oldest terrorist organizations.

Executive Order 13224—An **executive order** signed into law by U.S. President George W. Bush on September 23, 2001, in response to the September 11, 2001, attacks.

Extraordinary rendition—The extrajudicial transfer of a person from one country to another—a practice of the U.S. government to transfer suspected terrorists to countries known to practice torture.

Falun Gong—Spiritual movement that came to prominence in the People's Republic of China and is widely repressed in that country.

Fatwa—An Islamic pronouncement or ruling—considered a scholarly opinion on Islamic law.

Fedayeen—Arab commando unit.

Federal Air Marshal Service (FAMS)—Federal Sky Marshall program designed to place armed guards on U.S. aircraft in flight.

Ferdinand, Archduke Franz—His assassination in Sarajevo in 1914 triggered the start of World War I.

Fiahs—Indonesian term for terrorist cellular structures; for fundraising, religious work, security, and operations.

Frankincense—Aromatic resin widely used in religious rites.

Freedom of Access to Clinic Entrances (FACE) Act—Activities by pro-life activists in the United States attempted to block free access to abortion clinics by surrounding clinics with picketers attempting to shut them down. This activity was prohibited by the FACE Act.

Frente Revolucionario Anti-Fascista Y Patriotico (FRAP)—Left-wing Maoist group.

Front de la Liberation Nationale de la Corse (FLNC)—A group of Corsican separatists.

Front de Liberation du Quebec (FLQ)—Canadian extreme separatist movement active in the 1960s and 1970s.

Front for the Liberation of Angola (FNLA)—The FNLA was founded in 1954 as the Union of Peoples of Northern Angola to advance the interests of the Bakongo rather than to promote independence.

Front for the Liberation of Mozambique (FRELIMO)—Movement against Portuguese rule; originated in early 1960s.

G8—A group of eight countries—the United States, Canada, Great Britain, Russia, France, Germany, Italy, and Japan—that meet as a world economic forum.

GAO—United Sates Government Accountability Office.

Gastarbeiter Program—Program that brought Turkish workers to Germany to help rebuild the country after World War II.

General Staff Reconnaissance Unit Number 69—Formed in 1957; also known as Sayeret Mat'kal, the leading unit in Israel's counterterrorism arsenal.

Genocide—The systematic and planned extermination of an ethnic, religious, political, or national group.

Good Friday Agreement—Plan for devolved government in Northern Ireland signed on April 10, 1998; includes terms of early release of prisoners and decommissioning of weapons.

Great Trek—1835–1843 journey by Afrikaner farmers from Cape colony of South Africa to escape British domination.

Grenzschutzgruppe 9 (GSG-9)—German counterterrorist group founded after the Munich Olympic Games attack by Palestinian terrorists.

Groupment d'intervention de la Gendarmerie Nationale (GIGN)—A French counterterror unit with a ninety-men-strong unit designed to antiterrorism and police operations similar to U.S. police

SWATs. It is organized in four 15-men groups. The GIGN have conducted counterterror actions outside France in Djibouti, Lebanon, and the Comoros Islands.

Grupo Especial De Operaciones (GEO)—Belgium's Para-commando Regiment contains two small units that are special operations capable. The first, ESR (Equips Speciales de Reconnaisance Compagnie) dates back to 1960, when it was formed to give the I Belgium Corps a long-range reconnaissance capacity. This unit is company sized and uses the standard weapons of the Belgium Army. Two similar units exist within the reserve structure. The second unit is a small frogman section. It is a highly secretive unit, but is known to be about platoon sized and is similar to the British Special Boat Squadron (SBS).

Guantanamo Bay—U.S. military base in Cuba where "detainees" and suspected Islamic militants from Iraq and Afghanistan are being held.

Guevara, Che—Dr. Ernesto Rafael Guevara de la Serna, Argentine-born Marxist revolutionary and Cuban guerrilla leader.

Gulags—Forced labor camps set up by the Soviet internal police for dissidents and politicians.

Gulf Cooperation Council (GCC)—Council comprising Qatar, Oman, the UAE, Saudi Arabia, Kuwait, and Bahrain; set up in 1981 to address common economic and social issues within the region.

Hague Conventions—International treaties first negotiated at The Hague in the Netherlands pronouncing formal statements on the laws of war.

Hajj—Muslim pilgrimage to the Holy City of Mecca.

Hamas—An offshoot of the Islamic Brotherhood and an acronym for the Islamic Resistance Movement.

Harakat-ul-Ansar (HUA)—Pakistani Islamic militant group that operates primarily in Kashmir.

Hashemite Kingdom—The official name for the Middle East kingdom of Jordan.

Hashisheater—Origin of the word "assassin" in ancient times.

HEU—Highly enriched uranium.

Hezbollah—Radical Arabic organization that established itself following the Israeli invasion of Lebanon; the group is often linked with terror attacks in the Middle East.

Hizb ut-Tahir—A global Islamic political party whose goal is to unite all Muslim countries to unify as an Islamic Caliphate.

Holocaust—Mass extermination of mainly European Jews during World War II by Nazi Germany.

Home Rule—The principle of self-government.

Human Intelligence (HUMINT)—An intelligence gathering by tracking suspects, interviews, and interrogations; primarily under the domain CIA in the United States.

IED—An improvised explosive device or homemade bomb sometimes using military munitions.

IICD—Independent International Commission to oversee the decommissioning of paramilitary weapons under the provisions of the Northern Ireland Peace Accord.

Immigration and Customs Enforcement (ICE)—Is the largest investigative arm of the Department of Homeland Security. As part of its homeland security mission, ICE seeks to maintain the integrity of the immigration system through effective enforcement of U.S. immigration laws.

IMU—Islamic Movement of Uzbekistan—militant Islamist group formed in 1991.

Indian National Congress—Created in 1885, the Indian party that led the drive for an independent India from British rule; its iconic leader after World War I was Mahatma Gandhi.

Information Analysis and Infrastructure Protection (IAFP)—The Department of Homeland Security would merge under one roof the capability to identify and assess current and future threats to the homeland, map those threats against current vulnerabilities, inform the president, issue timely warnings, and immediately take or effect appropriate preventive and protective action.

International Atomic Energy Agency (IAEA)—Formed in 1957 to promote the peaceful use of nuclear energy and to inhibit its use for military purposes.

International Criminal Tribunal for the Former Yugoslavia (ICTY)—United Nations court of law handling war crimes.

Internment—Confinement, often used in wartime; in this case, used in Northern Ireland during the 1980s.

Interpol—International Criminal Police Organization created in 1923 to assist with international police cooperation; headquartered in Lyons, France; has 184 member countries making it second in size to the United Nations.

Iranian Revolutionary Guard Crops (IRGC)—The Persian name for the Guards is Sepah and translated means Pasdaran. Formed in 1979 as a loyal force for the Ayatollah Khomeini, it is a military organization that functions to protect the revolution. The Guards fought alongside the military during the Iran–Iraq war.

Irgun—Hebrew term for the National Military Organization, a Zionist group that operated between 1931 and 1948 in British-mandated Palestine.

Irish Free State—Established by treaty with Great Britain as a dominion within the Commonwealth of Nations in 1922 and become a sovereign state in 1937 (Eire).

Irish National Liberation Army (INLA)—Irish Republican paramilitary organization was founded in 1974. Its terrorist activities have spread to mainland Britain, and it was responsible for the assassination of Airey Neave, a close political friend of British Prime Minister Margaret Thatcher.

Irish Republican Army (IRA)—A Catholic paramilitary organization.

Islamic Jihad—An umbrella organization of Palestinian terrorist groups operating from the Middle East; many terrorist groups add the word "jihad" to their title.

Islamic Sharia—Islamic law that influences legal process and codes in most Muslim countries.

Islamism—Islamic ideology demanding total adherence to Islamic laws.

Jaish-e-Mohammed (JEM)—The Army of Mohammed; an Islamic extremist group based in Pakistan formed by Masood Azhar upon his release from prison in India.

Jamaat al-Fuqra—Islamic sect that seeks to purify Islam through violence. Its leader is Pakistani cleric Sheikh Mubarik Ali Gilani, who established the organization in the early 1980s. Gilani now resides in Pakistan, but most Fuqra cells are located in North America and the Caribbean.

Janjaweed—Armed militia group operating in Darfur, western Sudan.

Japanese Red Army (JRA)—Marxist revolutionary terror group active in Europe during the 1970s.

Jemaah Islamiyaah (JI)—Shadowy Islamic terror group that has spread throughout southern Asia.

Jihad—Islamic term used to describe a holy war against religious or political oppression.

Joint Task Force-2 (JTF-2)—Canadian Special Forces unit established in 1993 when the Canadian armed forces took responsibility for counterterrorism operations within Canada; very secretive unit about which little is known.

Joint Terrorism Analysis Center (JTAC)—Organization that analyzes and assesses international terrorism in the United Kingdom; established in 2003.

JTTF—Joint Terrorism Task Force established in July 2002 to serve as a coordinating mechanism with the FBI's partners. Some 40 agencies are now represented in the National JTTF, a focal point for information sharing.

Justice and Equality Movement (JEM)—Organization in Darfur challenging the administration in Khartoum.

Jyllands-Posten—Danish morning newspaper that published cartoons of the Prophet Mohammed.

Keiretsu—Japanese term used to describe a close-knit group of manufacturers, suppliers, and distributors.

KGB—The Committee for State Security; Soviet secret police, founded by Felix Edmundovich Dzerzhinsky in 1954; lasted until the collapse of the Soviet Union and was dissolved in 1991.

Khalistan—Country formed on October 7, 1987, where the Sikh nation declared its independence from India.

Khmer Rouge—The Communist Party of Cambodia; during its reign of power from 1975 to 1979, it was responsible for the execution of several million Cambodians.

Khmer Royal Armed Forces (KRAF)—The 1993 merger of the Cambodian People's Armed Forces and the two non-Communist resistance armies; also known as the Royal Cambodian Armed Forces, or RCAF.

Killer College—A major training facility for terrorists in Russia.

Killer instinct—Predilection to kill, not in anger, not in the heat of the moment, but in cold blood.

KINTEX—Bulgarian weapons producing company.

Kirov, Sergei—Bolshevik who took part in the 1905 Russian Revolution and the Russian Civil War of 1920. He was a popular and loyal supporter of Josef Stalin and was assassinated in December 1934.

Kosovo Liberation Army (KLA)—A Kosovar Albanian group that sought to break away from the Federal Republic of Yugoslavia in the 1990s.

Kurdistan—Region of the Middle East inhabited by Kurds and covering areas of Turkey, Iraq, Syria, and Armenia. The region is not recognized demographically; however, it accounts for approximately 25 million Kurds.

Kurdistan Freedom and Democracy Congress (KADEK)—Also known as Kurdistan Workers' Party; was established in 1974; is a Marxist-Leninist insurgent group, which aims to create a democratic Kurdish state.

Kurdistan Workers' Party (PKK)—Marxist-Leninist insurgent group made up of Turkish Kurds; founded in 1978. The group's goal has been to establish an independent, democratic Kurdish state in the Middle East.

Lashkar i Jhangvi (LJ)—Extreme Sunni Muslim group that has its roots in a sectarian movement calling itself Sipah-i-Sahaba Pakistan; its main targets for attack are from the Shia religious sect. The group had ties to the Taliban in Afghanistan.

Laws—Rules established for the orderly operation of a society.

LeT/—Lashkar-e-Taiba; meaning Army of the Righteous—one of the largest Islamist terror organizations in Southern Asia—attacks both civilian and military targets.

Letter bomb—Small, improvised explosive device hidden inside an envelope or a package mailed to a targeted person or organization.

Liberation Tigers of Tamil Eelam (LTTE)—Sri Lankan terrorist movement seeking an autonomous homeland.

Lockerbie—Small village in southern Scotland where Pan Am 103 crashed, destroying many homes and taking the lives of all on board as well as many on the ground.

Lynch Law—The process of condemning and punishing a person by mob rule without any trial—dates back to the eighteenth century, when William Lynch self-instituted tribunals.

MI5—British intelligence organization.

Macheteros—Armed Forces of Puerto Rican National Liberation, also known as the Popular Boricua Army (Ejercito Popular Boricua), commonly known as the Macheteros, claimed responsibility for numerous bombings and robberies, causing a reign of terror in Puerto Rico. The goals of the Macheteros were complete autonomy and sovereignty for Puerto Rico.

Madrassa—an Islamic religious school that teaches and preaches strict adherence to Islamic codes-found widely in Pakistan.

Mahdi Army—formed in 2003 the Mahdi Army is an armed group loyal to Muqtada al-Sadr, a Shia leader from a family line of revered clerics persecuted under Saddam Hussein.

Major Criminal Hijack (MCHJ)—International Maritime Organization definition as major transnational organized crimes at sea.

Mancino Law—Italian law aimed at hate crimes.

Mandela United Football Club—Name given to the bodyguards of Winnie Madikizela-Mandela, wife of former president of South Africa, Nelson Mandela.

Mandela, Nelson Rolihlahla—The first black president of South Africa.

Man-Portable Air Defense System (MANPADS)—Systems as the Russian (SA-7 and SA-14, Igla SA-16 and SA-18) and the U.S.-manufactured FIM-92 Stinger; easy to use and readily available on the black market; pose an acute threat to military aircraft and civilian airliners.

Mau Mau—Insurgent movement in Kenya that attacked Europeans in the 1950s; comprising mainly Kikuyu tribesmen.

McVeigh, Timothy James—American who was convicted for the bombing of the Federal Building in Oklahoma City on April 19, 1995, killing 167 people; he was executed on June 11, 2001.

Mehmet Ali Agca—Turkish nationalist who attempted the assassination of Pope John Paul II in St. Peter's Square, Rome, on May 13, 1981.

MEND—Movement for the Emancipation of the Niger Delta-a militant group operating in the Niger Delta and claim to be fighting corrupt government practices.

Middle East—A region of the world comprising Israel, Lebanon, Syria, Jordan, the Gulf states, and Saudi Arabia.

Milli Görüs—Largest Muslim organization in Germany with over 27,000 members; its influence is felt within the tight-knit Muslim communities particularly in the Turkish Muslim areas; also known as National Vision.

Militia—A militia is a group of citizens organized to provide paramilitary service.

Monsignor Juan Gerardi Condera—Bishop of Guatemala was beaten to death two days after releasing a human rights report on April 26, 1998.

Montoneros (Movimiento Peronista Montonero)—Argentinean leftist guerrilla group active during the 1970s. *Montonero* was a local name for nineteenth-century guerrillas. The group formed around 1970 from the socialist supporters of Juan Domingo Perón.

Morazanist Patriotic Front (FPM)—A radical, leftist Honduran terrorist group that first appeared in the late 1980s; its attacks were in protest of U.S. intervention in Honduran economic and political affairs.

Mores—Accepted behaviors and customs within a social group.

Moro Islamic Liberation Front (MILF)—An Islamic terrorist group fighting for an independent Islamic state in the southern Philippines.

Mossad—Institute for Intelligence and Special Assignments; Israeli intelligence organization, founded in 1949 by David Ben Gurion.

Movimiento Revolucionario Tupac Amaru (MRTA)—Peruvian guerrilla organization during the late 1980s and early 1990s; smaller than The Shining Path but equally as dangerous and ruthless.

Movimento Politico Occidentale (MPO)—(Political Movement of the West)—Italian Skinhead organization.

Mujahedin-e Khalq (MEK)—Formed in the 1960s, the organization was expelled from Iran after the Islamic Revolution in 1979, its primary support came from the former Iraqi regime of Saddam Hussein starting in the late 1980s. They conducted anti-Western attacks prior to the Islamic Revolution. Since then, it has conducted terrorist attacks against the interests of the clerical regime in Iran and abroad. The MEK advocates the overthrow of the Iranian regime and its replacement with the group's own leadership.

Mujahideen—Muslim fighters engaged in jihad.

Mullah Omar—Leader of the Afghan Taliban and leader of the Afghan Government 1996–2001.

Muslim Council of Britain—Established in 1997 with membership from more than 250 Muslim organizations in Great Britain—its first secretary general was Iqbal Sacranie who received Knighthood from Queen Elizabeth II in 2006.

Multiculturalism—Official Canadian government policy since its introduction in the 1970s on the social importance of immigrants and their integration.

Myanmar—Originally Burma; the country was renamed in 1989.

Narodnaya Volya (NV)—A nineteenth-century Russian terrorist organization; translation means "The People's Will."

National Liberation Army—A terminology often adapted by a terrorist group in a fight against legitimate authority.

National Organization of Cypriot Combatants (EOKA)—Was a Greek Cypriot military resistance organization that fought for self-determination and for union with Greece in the mid- to late 1950s.

National Targeting Center (NTC)—Part of the U.S. Department of Homeland Security; provides tactical targeting and analytical research in support of customs antiterrorism efforts.

National Union for the Total Independence of Angola (UNITA)—Formed in 1966 by Jonas Savimbi, its charismatic leader. The group was formed from the politicized split in the Angolan independence movement. Until 2002, the group was largely a military force and had been fighting a civil war since 1975. Jonas Savimbi headed the group from its formation until his death in 2002.

Nerve agents—Chemical agents used to attack and disable the human central nervous system.

New People's Army (NPA)—Maoist group formed in December 1969 with the aim of overthrowing the Philippine government through protracted guerrilla warfare; the military wing of the Communist Party of the Philippines (CPP).

New World Order—Term used to describe what some extreme believers think the U.S. government is determined to create; often referenced by U.S. militia organizations.

Nidal, Abu—Born in 1937 Sabri al Banna; prior to Osama bin Laden, Nidal was considered one of the most dangerous terrorists. He spent many years in Syria, Libya, and Iraq, where he died under mysterious circumstances in 2002.

NORAID—Irish republican organization that (Irish Northern Aid Committee) actively collected funds in the United States to support republican activities in Northern Ireland.

North Atlantic Treaty Organization (NATO)—Alliance of twenty-six countries from North America and Europe committed to fulfilling the goals of the North Atlantic Treaty signed in April 4, 1949.

November 17—Greek terrorist revolutionary organization; is Marxist-Leninist, anti-imperialist, anti-United States, anti-Europe, and anti-NATO.

Ocalan, Abdullah—Imprisoned leader of the Kurdish Workers' Party in Turkey.

Ogaden National Liberation Front (ONLF)—Separatist group fighting for an independent state in the Ogaden region

Oklahoma City Federal Building—Building destroyed by a truck bomb placed by Timothy McVeigh.

Omar Khadr—A Canadian of Pakistani origin captured in Afghanistan and detained in Guantanamo; tried, convicted, and sentenced under U.S. Military Commissions Act 2009 after pleading guilty to killing U.S. serviceman Christopher Speer.

Operation Crevice—U.K. Police operation in 2004 to uncover Islamist terror cells operating in England.

Operation Desert Storm—The first Gulf War of 1991; led by the United States and a coalition of countries to remove Iraqi forces from Kuwait.

Orange Order—Originating in the seventeenth century, this is the largest Protestant organization in Northern Ireland and regards itself as defending civil and religious liberties of Protestants and seeks to uphold the rule and ascendancy of a Protestant monarch in the United Kingdom.

Organization of Petroleum Exporting Countries (OPEC)—Headquartered in Vienna, Austria, the principal aim of the organization is the determination of petroleum policies of its member countries and the determination of the best means for safeguarding their interests, individually and collectively. The member states are Algeria, Iran, Indonesia, Kuwait, Iraq, Libya, Nigeria, Qatar, Saudi Arabia, Venezuela, and the United Arab Emirates.

Palestine—Region of the eastern Mediterranean coast from the Red Sea to the Jordan valley and from the southern Negev desert to the Galilee Lake region in the north. The word itself derives from "Plesheth," a name that appears frequently in the Bible and translated to English is "Philistine."

Palestine Liberation Front (PLF)—Small breakaway group from the PFLP based in the West Bank and Lebanon.

Palestine Liberation Organization (PLO)—Established in 1964 as a political body representing the Palestinian people. It is also a paramilitary organization that has dedicated itself to the establishment of a Palestinian state in former Palestine. Yasser Arafat became chairman of the PLO in 1969 until his death in 2004.

Palestinian Islamic Jihad (PIJ)—Formed by militant Palestinians in the Gaza Strip during the 1970s; committed to the creation of an Islamic Palestinian state and the destruction of Israel.

Palestinian National Liberation Movement (Fatah)—Founded in 1959 by Yasser Arafat—Fatah joined the PLO in 1967 and Arafat took over as leader.

Pan Am Flight 103—Pan Am Boeing 747 destroyed by a terrorist bomb over Lockerbie, Scotland.

Papa Doc—Francois Papa Doc Duvalier—notorious ruler of Haiti throughout the 1960s.

Partisans—An irregular army evading and attacking an invading or occupying force.

People's Consultative Assembly—Indonesian legislative body largely appointed by the president himself; reelected Suharto to a seventh term.

People's Republic of China (PRC)—Often referred to as Red China, a Communist country in Asia with a population of 1.3 billion.

PETN—Explosive pentaerythritol tetranitrate—difficult to detect—explosive used by Richard Reid the Shoe Bomber.

Police Service of Northern Ireland (PSNI)—Predominantly Protestant police force formally known as the Royal Ulster Constabulary; name changed under the terms of the Northern Ireland Peace Agreement.

Pol Pot—Leader of Communist regime in Cambodia, which he renamed Kampuchea; in 1976, he unveiled a "4-Year Plan" that detailed the collectivization of agriculture, the nationalization of industry, and the financing of the economy through increased agricultural exports. Thousands starved to death as a result.

Popular Front for the Liberation of Palestine (PFLP)—Terrorist group under the umbrella of the PLO.

Popular Revolutionary Army (EPR)—Left-wing Mexican group; ranks second in strength to the Zapatista movement based in the southern states of Oaxaca and Guerrero; considered by Mexicans to actually be several different movements operating under one banner.

Prescribe—To establish rules, laws, and direction.

Proscribe—To outlaw and ban terror organizations.

Provisional Irish Republican Army (PIRA)—A splinter from the original IRA movement that has waged a terror campaign in the United Kingdom and Northern Ireland.

Pushkin Square—Locality in the center of Moscow; renamed after Alexander Pushkin in 1937.

Qods Force—Part of the Iranian Revolutionary Guard Corps (IRGC) responsible for extraterritorial operations, including terrorist operations. A primary focus is training Islamic fundamentalist terrorist groups.

Racial Profiling—The inclusion of race as a specific indicator as to whether that person is likely to commit a crime—used widely in the United States and challenged by human rights organizations as racism at worst.

Radiological Dispersal Device (RDD)—A weapon designed to spread radiological materials.

Rebel Armed Forces (FAR)—Leftist Guatemalan terror group. Formed in 1962 by junior officers of the Guatemalan military who had previously led an unsuccessful coup attempt against the conservative Guatemalan government; the officers created the FAR to continue their antigovernment attacks. The FAR allied with several leftist terrorist organizations in 1982 to form the Guatemalan National Revolutionary Unity (URNG).

Red Army Faction (RAF)—Western Germany's most active left-wing terrorist organization post–World War II. Also known as Baader-Meinhof Group (in German: Rote Armee Fraktion); operated during 1970–1998.

Reign of Terror—The period between 1793 and 1794 during the French Revolution when thousands were executed.

Revolutionary Armed Forces of Colombia (FARC)—Established in 1964 as the military wing of the Colombian Communist Party, FARC is Latin America's oldest and best-equipped insurgency of Marxist origin.

Revolutionary People's Struggle (ELA)—A Greek, violent Marxist-Leninist organization.

Robben (Island) University—Prison situated off the coast of South Africa prison for members of the previously banned ANC; where many prisoners learned the art of political debate.

Rogue states—Term applied to countries or states deemed as a threat to global security and/or supporters or sponsors of terrorism.

Royal Ulster Constabulary (RUC)—Paramilitary police force of Northern Ireland; the removal of the word "Royal" came about during the Northern Ireland Peace Agreement. The force is now the Police Service of Northern Ireland.

Russian Federation—The current government structure of the former USSR.

Sandinista National Liberation Front—(*Frente Sandinista de Liberación Nacional* FSLN),a socialist political party in Nicaragua, named after Augusto César Sandino leader the Nicaraguan resistance against the U.S. occupation of Nicaragua in the 1930s. Party members are called **Sandinistas** in both English and Spanish.

Sarin toxin—Deadly airborne poison used in the subways in Tokyo.

Satanic Verses—Novel written by British author Salman Rushdie in 1989, contained some unflattering references to Islamic history, which resulted in Iran's Ayotollah Khomeini calling for Rushdie's death.

SAVAK—Ministry of State Security during the reign of the Shah of Iran.

Sayeret Mat'kal—Also known as General Staff Reconnaissance Unit Number 69—is the Israeli elite counterterrorist organization.

Scheduled Offenses—Offenses such as terrorism tried in "Special Courts."

Sayyid Qutb—Egyptian and member of the Muslim Brotherhood.

Sectarian—Strict or rigid adherence to a particular religion; where two or more religions come into conflict, extreme actions and violence often occur, as seen in Northern Ireland.

Selassie, Emperor Haile—Born in July 23, 1892; was emperor of Ethiopia from 1930 to 1936 and 1941 to 1974. He was an Ethiopian Orthodox Christian his entire life. He was removed from power in 1974 and died in suspicious circumstances under house arrest in 1975.

Sharia—Arabic term for Islamic law, most often stemming from the Quran.

Shining Path (Sendero Luminoso)—Peruvian radical, Marxist group that grew out of the Communist movement in the 1960s. Its radical Marxist ideology was shaped by its founder, Abimael Guzmán Reynoso. Guzmán, a former university professor, was able to use his position within academia to gain credibility and entice students to

his fledgling Communist movement. He was captured in 1991 and remains in prison.

Shiromani Gurudwara Prabandhak Committee (SGPC)—Is the major Sikh terrorist organization in India.

Shumukh al-Islam—A jihadist forum that posts information related to jihadist ideology.

Signals Intelligence (SIGINT)—The discipline of intelligence gathering through electronic intercepts of messages by varied means.

Sinn Féin—Led by Gerry Adams—left-wing Irish republican political party that seeks an end to British rule in Northern Ireland.

Sithole, Ndabaningi—Leader of the Ndonga faction of Zimbabwe African Union (ZANU).

Special Air Service (SAS) Regiment—The elite British military unit used for counterrevolutionary warfare operations—established in North Africa during World War II and based in the west of England.

Special Boat Squadron (SBS)—British special forces unit; waterborne counterpart of the Special Air Service Regiment; employed in waterborne special ops for the British Royal Navy.

Special Category Status—A de facto prisoner-of-war status for Irish prisoners convicted during the Troubles.

Special Immigration Appeal Commission (SIAC)—U.K. Act established in 1997 providing a method of appeal for immigrants ordered to deport from the United Kingdom.

SPOT—A method employed to screen passengers by observation techniques.

Stalin, Joseph—Russian leader from 1928 to 1953; summarily executed millions of his opponents. "Stalin" means "Man of Steel."

Stansted Airport—A U.K. airport situated to the east of the capital and used as a hijack response location for aircraft hijackings.

Stammheim Prison—Prison where members of Germany's Baader-Meinhof Gang were imprisoned.

State Law and Order Restoration Council (SLORC)—Burmese military junta that controlled the region in 1988.

State Peace and Development Council (SPDC)—Burmese military renaming itself from SLORC in 1997.

State-Sponsored Terrorism—Term to describe governments that support terrorist groups either by ideology or through material support and training.

Sudan Liberation Movement (SLA)—Group originating in the region of Darfur to challenge the administration in Khartoum.

Sunni—The largest division of Islam; Sunni Muslims range from Indonesia through the Middle East and Africa.

SWAT—U.S. Special Weapons and Tactical units—established as hostage rescue units by most U.S. police forces.

Symbionese Liberation Army (SLA)—U.S. group made prominent by the kidnapping of Patty Hearst in 1974.

Sympathizers—Someone or a group that share and understand the same common goals.

Talwinder Singh Parmar—Considered part of the plot group that bombed Air India Flight 182 in 1985, killing over 300—also leader of the Babbar Khalsa terrorist organization. Killed by Indian police while in custody in 1992.

Tabun—used as a nerve gas in chemical warfare.

Task Force on Violence against Abortion Providers (TFVAAP)—An investigative arm of the Department of Justice, the Civil Rights Division of the Department of Justice. The TFVAAP investigates any instance in which customers or providers of reproductive health services are criminally threatened, obstructed, or injured while seeking or providing services.

TATP—Acetone peroxide or commonly called TATP is an organic peroxide and acts as a high explosive. It is highly susceptible to heat, friction, and shock. For its instability, it has been called the "Mother of Satan".

Terrorist incident—An attack or threat of an attack carried out by terrorists.

Terrorist No-Fly Watch List—A compilation of suspicious names gathered from airline passenger manifests.

Theo Van Gough—Dutch filmmaker murdered on the street in Amsterdam.

Transportation Security Agency (TSA)—U.S. agency created after 9-11 to replace low-paid, poorly trained airport screeners.

Troubles—Generally describes the period of conflict (Catholic vs. Protestant) in Northern Ireland between 1968 and the Belfast Agreement of 1998.

Turkish Revenge Brigade—A little-known, ultranationalist, extreme right-wing group operating in Turkey.

UN Security Council Resolution 1373—Resolution that called for international cooperation to prevent and eradicate acts of terrorism worldwide; unanimously adopted on September 28, 2001, under Chapter VII of the UN General Assembly by consensus of the 189 member states.

Unilateral Declaration of Independence (UDI)—Declared on November 11, 1965, by Ian Smith of Rhodesia.

Union of Islamic Communities and Organizations in Italy (UCOII)—The largest Muslim group in Italy. UCOII has a network of more than fifty mosques throughout the country. It has a network throughout Europe and supports an International Muslim Brotherhood.

UNRA—Utvar Rychleho Nasazeni (URNA) is the Czech Republic's rapid response counterterrorist police and crime-busting force.

United Self-Defense Forces of Colombia (AUC)—Group formed to combat the leftist terrorist organizations operating in Colombia, primarily the FARC and ELN. The AUC grew out of the paramilitary and self-defense groups formed in the 1980s.

U.S. Patriot Act—Law passed in 2001 following the 9-11 attacks in the United States; Uniting and Strengthening America by Providing Appropriate Tools Required to Intercept and Obstruct Terrorism Act came into force.

Uighur—Separatist movement in Turkistan.

VBIED—Term used to identify a vehicle-borne improvised explosive device.

Vesicants—Blistering agent developed for use in chemical warfare. A chemical weapon used in World War I and by Saddam Hussein against the Kurds.

Waco Massacre—Armed raid by members of the FBI and ATF on the Branch Davidian base in Waco, Texas.

Wahhabism—Islamic religious movement within Islam founded by Muhammad ibn Abd al-Wahhab (1703–1992).

War on Terror—Phrase established after the attacks on the World Trade Center and the Pentagon in September 2001 to detail the coming "war" against terrorism on worldwide scale led primarily by the United States.

World Trade Center—Group of buildings in New York City destroyed on September 11, 2001, by two hijacked aircraft that were flown into two of the towers.

Yasser Arafat—(August 24, 1929–November 11, 2004) Awarded the Nobel Peace Prize in 1994. Symbolically portrayed as the leader of the Palestinian struggle for an independent Palestinian state; often viewed by outsiders as a corrupt politician and a stumbling block to peace in the Middle East; considered a terrorist by Israel.

Zapatista National Liberation Army (ELZN)—Violent Mexican organization that opposes NAPTA.

Zimbabwe African National Union (ZANU)—Robert Mugabe's ruling political party.

Zimbabwe African People's Union (ZANPU)—Opposition group opposed to ZANU.

Zimbabwe People's Revolutionary Army (ZIPRA)—Opposition group opposed to ZANU.

INDEX